The Bahamas

written and researched by

**Gaylord Dold, Natalie Folster
and Adam Vaitilingam**

**ROUGH
GUIDES**

www.roughguides.com

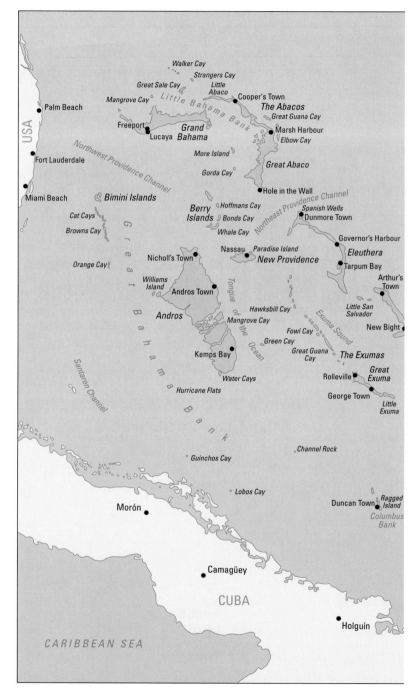

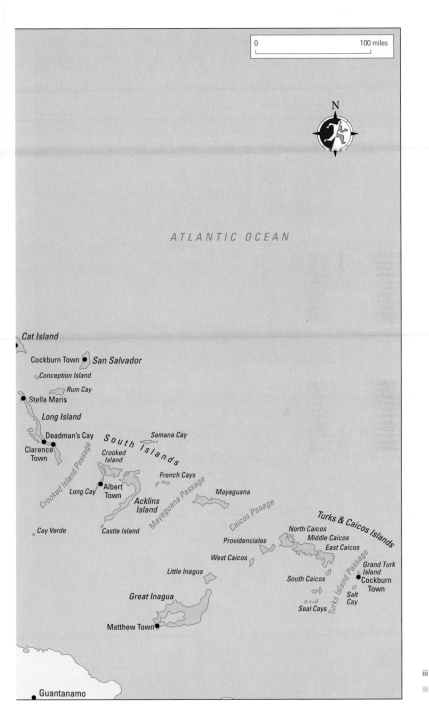

0 100 miles

N

ATLANTIC OCEAN

Cat Island

Cockburn Town ● San Salvador

Conception Island

Rum Cay

Stella Maris

Long Island

Deadman's Cay   Samana Cay

South Islands

Clarence Town   Crooked Island

Crooked Island Passage

Long Cay   Albert Town   French Cays

Cay Verde   Castle Island   Mayaguana Passage   Mayaguana

Acklins Island   Caicos Pasage

Turks & Caicos Islands

North Caicos

Providenciales   Middle Caicos

West Caicos   East Caicos

Little Inagua   Grand Turk Island
                                          Cockburn Town

South Caicos

Great Inagua   Seal Cays   Salt Cay

Matthew Town ●

Turks Island Passage

Guantanamo ●

Introduction to

The
Bahamas

Graced with beautiful beaches, evocative windswept panoramas and countless opportunities for diving, snorkelling and fishing, the Bahamas are well established as one of the world's top draws for both intrepid explorers and casual vacationers. An archipelago beginning a mere 55 miles east of Miami, the Bahamas include around seven hundred islands, no more than forty of which are inhabited, as well as scores of smaller cays (pronounced "keys"). Unlike some of its Caribbean neighbours, the impressive arc of islands offers an array of accommodation that ranges from exclusive high-end resorts to rustic lodges, appealing to travellers of all tastes and budgets. Indeed, more than three million people visit the country yearly, the majority here for outdoor sports and sun worship.

Though visiting each of the major islands on the Bahamian archipelago in one trip is unfeasible, it is well worth soaking up more of the region's culture by exploring several islands. The quickest way to island hop is by plane, though if time permits a trip on a government mail-boat or chartered yacht is both more relaxing and memorable. Most trips entail spending time in either New Providence or Grand Bahama, the two most cosmopolitan of the islands and the target of innumerable package

Fact file

• The name Bahamas comes from the Spanish *baja-mar*, meaning "shallow sea".

• The population of the Bahamas is approximately 300,000, of whom more than two-thirds live on the island of New Providence. Eighty-five percent of the populace is black, about twelve percent is white and the remainder is largely Asian or Hispanic.

• While the Bahamas achieved independence from Britain on July 10, 1973, the head of state is Queen Elizabeth II, who is represented in Nassau by a governor general. The Bahamas are governed by a prime minister, and the legislature is a bicameral body that is constituted by a sixteen-member Senate and a forty-member House of Assembly.

• The average per capita income in the Bahamas is a relatively high $11,940; tourism accounts for around seventy percent of the national income.

• The Yellow Elder is the national flower of the Bahamas, and the national tree is the lignum vitae, or tree of life.

• With a population of less than 20,000, the Turks and Caicos form a collective land mass that is only two and a half times the size of Washington, DC.

holidays. However, forays into the Out Islands – or even as far afield as the Turks and Caicos, in look and feel cut from the same cloth as the Bahamas – reward visitors with a slice of authentic fishing-village culture and a glimpse of Bahamian life outside of the pre-packaged tour circuit.

Wherever you happen to land, it is impossible not to immerse yourself in the Bahamas' intriguing mix of colonial and African traditions. This fusion is perhaps most apparent during Nassau's annual Junkanoo celebrations, when the exuberant street party propelled by African drumming and outlandish costumes marches past the capital's impressive colonial edifices. Other islands come to life for numerous sailing regattas, featuring beachside fish fries and the sounds of rake 'n' scrape, a distinctly Bahamian style of music.

The ocean, though, is still the main draw. Although deeper oceanic troughs surround some of the islands, most are encircled by shallow, crystalline water that reflects a light turquoise hue during the day and glows with purple luminescence at night. This combination of shallow and deep water makes for superb diving and snorkelling, with numerous reefs, wrecks and blue holes waiting to be explored just beyond the islands' shores.

These waters also boast some of the best fishing in the Caribbean. Schools of silvery bonefish swim just offshore and anglers of all levels stand waist-deep in the warm water awaiting the chance to pounce on and pull in these elusive fish. Those who prefer sport fishing can ride the waves stalking sailfish, tuna, marlin and even sharks in the improbably deep Tongue of the Ocean. Of course, if you are in search of a less taxing activity, there are always the beaches to while away your time on.

Where to go

The islands' most popular destination is **New Providence** – site of the bustling capital **Nassau**. With its resort areas in **Cable Beach** and **Paradise Island**, the island offers glamorous accommodations, enticing nightlife and casinos, fine restaurants and shopping and, of course, great beaches; Nassau Harbour is also a fixture on the Caribbean cruise circuit. Nearly everyone who visits the Bahamas will pass through the capital, the hub of intra-island travel, and those killing time before journeying on to

Diving in the Bahamas

The waters surrounding the Bahamas and Turks and Caicos afford the visitor a variety of world-class diving opportunities, from snorkelling just offshore to overnight scuba-diving trips. The Tongue of the Ocean, a cavernous channel that passes between Andros, the Exumas and New Providence, is abutted by walls, or cliffs, down which experienced divers can enjoy the exhilarating slide into the water. Andros is further celebrated for its majestic coral reef as well as its collection of blue holes (see p.173), underwater entrances to large circular limestone pits that range from around thirty to several hundred feet deep. The islands' history as a pirate haven and wrecking centre have left a legacy of numerous wrecks, particularly in the waters off Grand Bahama (see p.106). One of the most memorable experiences of any visit, though, is diving among dolphins and sharks – indeed, the Bahamas are one of the few countries that allows forays among the latter – which can be arranged in New Providence, Long Island or Grand Bahama. On some tours, you can even watch sharks being fed by a diver in a protective coat of chain mail.

another island will enjoy a jitney ride through **Old Nassau** and its stirring British colonial architecture, or even a tour of the **Atlantis** resort's 34-acre waterscape on Paradise Island.

Almost as popular as New Providence, **Grand Bahama** has been drawing tourists since the 1950s, when the resort town of **Freeport/Lucaya** sprung up expressly for that purpose. While the town of Freeport itself is of little interest, its seaside suburb Lucaya features several beaches and some of the most elaborate all-inclusive resort hotels in the country.

Many travellers prefer the quiet, remote charms of the **Out Islands** – essentially all of the Bahamian isles save for New Providence and Grand Bahama. Here the accommodation is often more rustic, the beaches and reefs virtually deserted and the vibe more laid-back. **Andros**, the largest island in the Bahamas, is fringed by the **Androsian barrier reef**, which presents wonderful snorkelling opportunities. Besides the reef – the third longest in the world – the island is celebrated for its **blue holes** and abundance of **bonefish**. Those who enjoy **sport fishing** will prefer the deep waters off the even calmer **Bimini and Berry islands** located due north, whose fishing was immortalized by Ernest Hemingway.

While there is certainly no shortage of **beaches** on the Bahamas, **Eleuthera** contains some of the very sandiest and most unspoilt of the lot, including the fabled Pink Sands Beach. The most populous of the Out Islands, Eleuthera is relatively untouched by tourism, though **Dunmore Town**, on Harbour Island just off its northern tip, boasts some of the Out Islands' more cosmopolitan restaurants and finer hotels.

Bahamian seafood

With the Bahamas' reputation as a fishermen's paradise, the wide array of seafood available is unsurprising. Ubiquitous on menus throughout the islands and a firm local favourite, conch (pronounced "konk") is a snail-like mollusc that can be broiled, grilled, steamed, stewed, served raw or presented "cracked" with its tenderized meat deep-fried in batter. Deep-fat-fried balls called conch fritters are a top side dish, while one of the islands' culinary delights is conch chowder; we've included a recipe below, though it undoubtedly tastes best when eaten beachside. The grouper, a light, fleshy white fish, is another staple of the Bahamian diet and, like much Bahamian fish, is most often served deep-fried in batter. Bahamian lobster can be eaten freshly grilled or broiled, steamed and curried, while crab is generally baked and served in the shell.

Perhaps the freshest – and certainly the cheapest – places to sample these dishes are the seafood shacks that are pervasive on all islands. From Arawak Cay (see p.75) in busy Nassau Harbour to those in rustic Out Island fishing hamlets, these low-key restaurants and grills should not be missed, both for the freshness of the food and the congenial atmosphere.

Conch chowder Bahamian-style

3 or 4 ground conch	1 bay leaf
2 medium diced onions	1/2 cup sugar
1 cup chopped celery	1 teaspoon oregano
1 medium green pepper, chopped	2 teaspoons lime juice
1/2 teaspoon thyme	1 large can of tomatoes
1 clove garlic	

Fry the onions, green pepper, celery, garlic and all the spices in a small amount of fat. When onions are transparent, add tomatoes and simmer for thirty minutes. Add conch and simmer for another thirty to forty-five minutes. Add lime juice and some sherry to taste after cooking and serve piping hot. If you'd like to eat it as the locals do, liberally add hot pepper sauce from time to time while the chowder is cooking.

Exploring the **Abaco** and the **Exuma** island chains is comparatively more difficult yet repays the effort with their peaceful fishing hamlets and quiet, untrammelled cays. The clapboard houses, neat lawns and picket fences on the **Loyalist Cays** attest to the immigration to the Abacos after the American Revolution of those still loyal to the Crown, while bird-watchers will relish **Abaco National Park** and its population of endangered Bahama parrots. The Exumas consist of some 365 cays and islets, fifteen of which comprise the **Exuma Land and Sea Park**, whose sea kayaking in the cobalt-blue Exuma Sound and the Great Bahama Bank is unparalleled.

The rest of the Out Islands feel light years away from New Providence and Grand Bahama. Much of isolated **Cat Island** and **San Salvador**'s interior is dense and impenetrable, though the latter – believed by many to be the site of Columbus's first landfall in the New World – offers great **birdwatching** if you can brave the mosquitoes. **Long Island** affords vis-

Rake 'n' scrape music

Throughout the islands, rake 'n' scrape music resounds in nightclubs and during most local celebrations. The most popular authentic Bahamian music form, it harks back to the days before most of the islands had electricity and makes use of a variety of handmade instruments, notably a saw, which is played by bending it and scraping it with a screwdriver to produce a rhythmic sound. The saw is generally joined by accordions, guitars, drums or maracas, devised from the pods of poinciana trees. Often the music is in three-four time, evocative of the waltzes and polkas from which rake 'n' scrape is derived.

Most islands are encircled by shallow, crystalline water that reflects a light turquoise hue during the day and glows with purple luminescence at night

itors the luxury of a few resorts in the midst of its rustic fishing settlements and untrammelled beaches, while **Great Inagua** is home to the 127-square-mile **Inagua National Park** and the West Indian flamingos it was established to conserve.

Independent of the Bahamas though of the same archipelago, the **Turks and Caicos Islands** have only become a tourist destination in the last twenty years. Since then, the majority of vacationers here have flocked to the resorts of **Providenciales**, most of which take advantage of majestic Grace Bay and its six-mile-long beach. The island is also the perfect springboard for day-trips to the beaches of the largely uninhabited **Caicos Cays** or more demanding jaunts to **North Caicos** or **Grand Turk**.

When to go

The southern Atlantic high-pressure system and constant trade winds make Bahamian **weather** consistent throughout the year, with temperatures in the mid-70s°F during the dry winter season from December to May, and 5–8 degrees warmer in the summer rainy

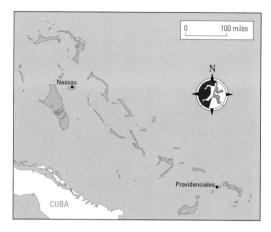

season. Just as a steady cooling breeze moderates the hottest hours of the day, nights in the Bahamas are temperate and, in the northern islands, even cool. Late summer and fall comprise **hurricane season**, delivering the occasional menacing tempest as well as less destructive tropical storms. Luckily, the Bahamas are rarely in the direct paths of hurricanes, which usually bypass the islands to the south before hitting mainland North America directly.

Predictably, **winter travel** is a major draw, with December-to-May prices as much as 25 percent higher than during the rest of the year. **Late spring** and **early summer travel** are popular with bargain hunters, divers, and anglers and sailors drawn by the summer round of fishing tournaments and regattas. Travelling during the Christmas **holiday season** can be bustling and wearisome, with tourists thick on the ground and many locals taking trips to the North American mainland. Likewise, college students often crowd the major resorts during Spring Break in February and March, while other travellers escape to the Bahamas during **late summer** and **autumn** to enjoy a respite in that relatively tranquil period, the odd hurricane notwithstanding.

Average monthly temperatures and rainfall

	Jan	Feb	Mar	Apr	May	Jun	Jul	Aug	Sep	Oct	Nov	Dec
Nassau												
max. temp. (°F)	87	87	89	90	90	90	93	95	93	90	89	87
max. temp. (°C)	30	30	32	33	33	33	34	35	34	33	32	30
min. temp. (°F)	65	66	66	71	76	78	79	79	78	73	71	66
min. temp. (°C)	18	19	19	22	24	25	26	26	25	23	22	19
rainfall (inches)	1.8	1.7	1.6	2.7	5.2	7.0	6.0	6.6	7.1	6.6	2.8	1.7
rainfall (mm)	46	44	40	70	130	178	152	170	180	170	73	44
Providenciales												
max. temp. (°F)	78	79	79	80	82	82	84	87	87	84	80	79
max. temp. (°C)	25	26	26	27	28	28	29	30	30	29	27	26
min. temp. (°F)	71	71	73	76	76	78	79	79	79	78	76	73
min. temp. (°C)	22	22	23	24	24	25	26	26	26	25	24	23
rainfall (inches)	1.6	1.4	1.0	1.6	1.4	2.1	1.4	1.8	2.5	3.0	3.8	3.5
rainfall (mm)	41	36	26	41	36	53	36	46	64	76	97	89

things not to miss

It's not possible to see everything that the Bahamas and the Turks and Caicos have to offer in one trip – and we don't suggest you try. What follows is a selective and subjective taste of the countries highlights: from their lush blue waters to their quaint colonial towns. They're arranged in five colour-coded categories to help you find the very best things to see, do, eat and experience. All highlights have a page reference to take you straight into the guide, where you can find out more.

01 Grace Bay Page **322** • The spectacular turquoise sea along six miles of magnificent Grace Bay beach in Providenciales offers some of the most pleasurable sailing and watersports in the Turks and Caicos.

02 Diving in the Biminis Page **197** • In the shallow waters surrounding the reefs and cays off the Bimini Islands, there's an amazing abundance of reef fish, along with squadrons of barracuda.

03 Straw Market Page **70** • Visit the Bahamas' most famous straw market in Old Nassau, featuring everything from straw baskets to carved mahogany dolphins to Voodoo charms.

04 Caicos Conch Farm Page **327** • Handle a queen conch – a giant sea snail, famous for its gorgeous pink shells – at the only conch farm in the world.

05 **Marine Park at Atlantis** Page **90** • The highlight here at the world's largest open-air aquarium is the shark-infested Predator Lagoon, viewed via an ingenious underwater walkway on Paradise Island.

06 **Out Island bar life** Page **32** • In the small hamlets and settlements of the Out Islands, tourists and locals congregate to enjoy cocktails like the Goombay Smash.

07 **Mount Alvernia Hermitage** Page **281** • The panoramic views of the Atlantic from the Hermitage atop 206ft Mount Alvernia on central Cat Island – the highest point in the Bahamas – are among the most spectacular on the islands.

08 **Lucaya National Park** Page **124** • A worthy escape from Freeport/Lucaya's tourist gridlock, this forty-acre park on Grand Bahama offers a maze of mangrove creeks tailor-made for sea kayaking.

09 Androsia Batik Factory Page **179** • Visit the Androsia Batik Factory in Fresh Creek on Andros and watch artisans create the vibrant batik fabrics that are sold throughout the islands.

10 Island hopping Page **25** • The best way to get around the islands is by boat, whether you travel by mailboat or are lucky enough to sail by private yacht.

11 Morton Salt Works Page **311** • All that's missing from this 34,000-acre salt plant on Great Inagua, the second largest in North America, is a giant margarita glass.

12 Eleuthera's beaches Page **214** • The beaches of Eleuthera, from Pink Sand Beach on Harbour Island to Club Med Beach outside of Governor's Harbour, may be the most idyllic.

13 **Uncle Ralph's Aura Corner** Page **230** • No visit to Dunmore Town in Eleuthera is complete without a visit to Uncle Ralph, whose trove of licence plates and painted signs affords a compendium of homespun wisdom.

14 **Swimming with dolphins** Page **107** • The best place in the Bahamas to swim, feed and frolic among dolphins is at Sanctuary Bay in Grand Bahama.

15 Thunderball Grotto Page **264** • Snorkel past stalactites and stalagmites in this undersea cavern, in the Exuma Cays, and see the colourful corals and fish – just as 007 did in *Thunderball*.

16 Old Nassau Page **69** • Whether on foot or on a horse-drawn surrey, a half-day tour of Old Nassau reveals fine Georgian architecture and a glimpse of Bahamian urban life.

17 Abaco National Park Page **163** • Glimpses of the rare and endangered Bahamian parrot can be had on a day-tour of lovely Abaco National Park in Great Abaco.

18 Seafood shacks

Page **76** • Some of the freshest and tastiest seafood throughout the islands can be found in waterfront shacks, such as those in Arawak Cay.

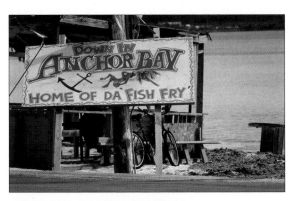

19 Nassau's Junkanoo festival

Page **69** • Nassau becomes a human maelstrom on Boxing Day (December 26) and New Year's Day, when marching bands, dancers and a swirl of spectators join the capital's biggest street celebration.

20 Out Island Regatta

Page **251** • Boaters from all over the Bahamas converge on George Town in the Exumas every April to race in this regatta, enlivened by musicians and revellers who party night and day.

21 Bonefishing Page **172** • Anglers come from all over the world for the bonefishing on Andros.

22 Hope Town Page **143** • The Elbow Cay Lighthouse towers over picturesque Hope Town, home to a charming array of New England-style architecture.

23 Pompey Museum Page **72** • An informative history of slavery in the Bahamas is revealed in this Nassau museum, located on the site of a former slave-auction house.

24 Our Lucaya Resort Page 112 • Love it or hate it, Our Lucaya in Grand Bahama is the epitome of a world-class all-inclusive resort, with three large hotels, eight acres of beachfront and over a dozen restaurants and bars.

25 The Caicos Cays Page 326 • The rock iguanas of Little Water Cay are one of the high points of the Caicos Cays, only a short boat trip from Providenciales in the Caicos Islands.

Contents

Using the Rough Guide

We've tried to make this Rough Guide a good read and easy to use. The book is divided into five main sections, and you should be able to find whatever you want in one of them.

colour section

The front colour section offers a quick tour of the Bahamas and the Turks and Caicos. The **introduction** aims to give you a feel for the place, with suggestions on where to go. We also tell you what the weather is like and include a basic country fact file. Next, our authors round up their favourite aspects of the Bahamas in the **things not to miss** section – whether it's great food, amazing sights or a special hotel. Right after this comes a full **contents** list.

basics

The Basics section covers all the **pre-departure** nitty-gritty to help you plan your trip. This is where to find out which airlines fly to your destination, what paperwork you'll need, what to do about money and insurance, about Internet access, food, security, public transport, car rental – in fact just about every piece of **general practical information** you might need.

guide

This is the heart of the Rough Guide, divided into user-friendly chapters, each of which covers a specific region. Every chapter starts with a list of **highlights** and an **introduction** that helps you to decide where to go, depending on your time and budget. Likewise, introductions to the various towns and smaller regions within each chapter should help you plan your itinerary. We start most town accounts with information on arrival and accommodation, followed by a tour of the sights, and finally reviews of places to eat and drink, and details of nightlife. Longer accounts also have a directory of practical listings. Each chapter concludes with **public transport** details for that region.

contexts

Read Contexts to get a deeper understanding of what makes the Bahamas tick. We include a brief history, articles about **society and culture** and **flora and fauna**, and a detailed further reading section that reviews dozens of **books** relating to the country.

index + small print

Apart from a **full index**, which includes maps as well as places, this section covers publishing information, credits and acknowledgements, and also has our contact details in case you want to send in updates and corrections to the book – or suggestions as to how we might improve it.

Map and chapter list

3

contents

map symbols

maps are listed in the full index using coloured text

------	Chapter division boundary	⚑	Golf course
═════	Paved road (regional maps)	⚘	Gardens
───────	Unpaved road (regional maps)	⛽	Petrol station
═══	Road (town maps)	✈	Airport
- - - - -	Footpath	✈	Airfield
— — —	Ferry route	★	Public transport stop
═════	Waterway	◉	Accommodation
▲	Mountain peak	ⓘ	Information office
⌒	Cave	✉	Post office
∴	Ruins	⊞	Hospital
♟	Fortress	▮	Building
♙	Castle	⊣	Church
Ⱳ	Spring	▨	Park
⚲	Lighthouse	▧	Beach
⊙	Statue	⊡	Salt lake
⤳	Diving site		

Basics

Basics

Getting there

The Bahamas are well connected to the outside world, with daily flights to and from numerous American cities and several flights per week to and from Canada and the UK. Unsurprisingly, the archipelago is also easily accessible by sea, with cruise ships calling in at Nassau and Freeport/Lucaya every week, and there are hundreds of marinas sprinkled throughout the islands suitable for private yachts.

When travelling to the Bahamas, it's almost invariably cheaper to buy a **package deal** covering transportation and accommodation from a tour operator or travel agent than it is to buy your own ticket and accommodation separately. Package holidays, though, are typically only worthwhile if you're planning on visiting the larger, busier resorts in Nassau/Paradise Island, Freeport/Lucaya or going to a few isolated resorts in the Out Islands. If you're looking to live by your own schedule and head off the beaten track some, you're best off booking your own way.

Airfares always depend on the season. Although the Bahamas are blessed with beautiful sunny weather and relatively constant temperatures year-round, **high season** for travel runs from mid-December to mid-April, when folks in the northern hemisphere are most eager to escape chilly temperatures. Fares drop during the "shoulder" season – May through September – and you'll get the best prices during the **low season**, from October to mid-December. Note also that flying on weekends ordinarily adds a few dollars to the round-trip fare.

Besides package deals, you can often cut costs by going through a **specialist flight agent** – either a consolidator, who buys up blocks of tickets from the airlines and sells them at a discount, or a **discount agent**, who in addition to dealing with discounted flights may also offer student fares and other travel-related services such as car rentals and tours. Some agents specialize in **charter flights**, which may be cheaper than

any available scheduled flight, but as with package deals departure dates are often fixed and withdrawal penalties can be high.

In addition to the sun and sand beach holidays offered by the tour operators listed below, several companies specialize in diving and kayaking expeditions and eco-tours in the Bahamas. See "Ocean activities and outdoor pursuits" on pp.37–41 for information on these niche operators.

Booking flights online

Many airlines and discount travel websites offer you the opportunity to book your tickets **online**, cutting out the costs of agents and middlemen. Good deals can often be found through discount or auction sites, as well as through the airlines' own websites.

Online booking agents and general travel sites

Ⓦ www.cheapflights.com Bookings from the UK and Ireland only. Flight deals, travel agents, plus links to other travel sites.

Ⓦ www.cheaptickets.com Discount flight specialists.

Ⓦ www.etn.nl/discount A hub of consolidator and discount agent web links, maintained by the nonprofit European Travel Network.

Ⓦ www.expedia.com Discount airfares, all-airline search engine and daily deals.

Ⓦ www.flyaow.com Online air travel info and reservations site.

Ⓦ www.gaytravel.com Gay online travel agent, concentrating mostly on accommodation.

Ⓦ www.geocities.com/Thavery2000/ Has an extensive list of airline toll-free numbers and websites.

Ⓦ www.hotwire.com Bookings from the US only. Last-minute savings of up to 40 percent on regular

For information on getting to the **Turks and Caicos**, see pp.320–321.

published fares. Travellers must be at least 18 and there are no refunds, transfers or changes allowed. Log-in required.

ⓦ **www.lastminute.com** Bookings from the UK only. Offers good last-minute holiday package and flight-only deals.

ⓦ **www.priceline.com** Name-your-own-price website that has deals at around 40 percent off standard fares. You cannot specify flight times (although you do specify dates) and the tickets are non-refundable, non-transferable and non-changeable.

ⓦ **www.skyauction.com** Auctions tickets and travel packages using a "second bid" scheme. The best strategy is to bid the maximum you're willing to pay, since if you win you'll pay just enough to beat the runner-up regardless of your maximum bid. Bookings from the US only.

ⓦ **www.smilinjack.com/airlines** Lists an up-to-date compilation of airline website addresses.

ⓦ **http://travel.yahoo.com** Incorporates a lot of Rough Guide material in its coverage of destination countries and cities across the world, with information about places to eat, sleep, etc.

ⓦ **www.travelocity.com** Destination guides, hot web fares and best deals for car rental, accommodation and lodging as well as fares. Provides access to the travel agent system SABRE, the most comprehensive central reservations system in the US.

ⓦ **www.travelshop.com.au** Australian website offering discounted flights, packages, insurance and online bookings.

Flights from the US and Canada

One of the greatest attractions of the Bahamas for North American sunseekers is the ease of access. With direct flights from several **American** and **Canadian** cities, you can leave New York or Toronto on a dark snowy morning and be on the beach with a margarita in hand in time for lunch. In high season, a non-stop flight from New York to Nassau costs in the range of US$350–600, with flights to Freeport starting from around US$300. Flights from Fort Lauderdale or Miami to Nassau or Freeport should cost US$180–250. Direct flights from Toronto or Montreal in high season can be had for around CAN$400, provided you book far enough in advance. The best deals generally require 21 days advance booking, but note that discounted seats can sell out several

months in advance. Nassau and Freeport are the major ports of entry for international flights, though a number of airlines fly directly from Florida to the Abacos, Bimini, Cat Island, Eleuthera and the Exumas, as listed below.

The Bahamas is a major destination for **package holidays**, and there is a wide selection of operators and vacations to choose from. The operators below offer mainly beach-based holidays ranging in price between US$500 and US$2000 a week, including transportation, accommodation of various grades and the option to purchase a meal plan. Most often these packages must be purchased through a travel agent.

Airlines

Air Canada ☏1-888/247-2262,
ⓦwww.aircanada.ca. Flies directly to Nassau from Toronto and Montreal once or twice a week (depending on the season), with connecting flights from other Canadian cities.
Air Tran Airways ☏1-800/Air Tran from the US or ☏770/994-8258 from Canada,
ⓦwww.airtran.com. Offers direct service from Atlanta and Chicago to Freeport.
American Airlines ☏1-800/433-7300,
ⓦwww.aa.com. Has direct service from New York and Newark and several flights a day from Fort Lauderdale, Miami and Orlando to Nassau and Freeport on the American Eagle connector service, with daily flights from Miami to George Town, Marsh Harbour and Governor's Harbour.
Bahamasair ☏305/593-1910 or 1-800/222-4262, ⓦwww.bahamasair.com. Has daily flights from Fort Lauderdale, Miami and Orlando to Nassau, Freeport and Marsh Harbour in the Abacos.
Chalk's Ocean Airways ☏305/363-1687 or 1-800/424-2557, ⓦwww.chalksoceanairways.com. Offers daily flights on a seaplane from Fort Lauderdale and Miami to Nassau, Paradise Island, Bimini and Walker's Cay.
Continental Airlines ☏1-800/231-0856,
ⓦwww.continental.com. Has daily service from Miami, Fort Lauderdale and West Palm Beach to Nassau, Freeport, Marsh Harbour, North Eleuthera and Treasure Cay.
Delta Air Lines ☏1-800/241-4141,
ⓦwww.delta.com. Features direct service to Nassau from New York/La Guardia, Boston and Atlanta several times a day.
Lynx Air ☏954/772-9808 or 1-888/LYNX-AIR,

www.lynxair.com. Flies several times a week from Fort Lauderdale and Miami to Cat Island; George Town, Exumas; Governor's Harbour, Eleuthera; and Marsh Harbour, Abacos.

Twin Air ☎ 954/359-8266, ⨌ 954/359-8271, ⓦ www.flytwinair.com. Offers regular flights from Fort Lauderdale to North Eleuthera; Governor's Harbour, and Rock Sound on Eleuthera; and Treasure Cay and Marsh Harbour in the Abacos.

US Airways ☎ 1-800/622-1015, ⓦ www.usairways.com. Has direct service to Nassau and Freeport from Charlotte, Philadelphia and New York. They also have a connecting service from Miami to Treasure Cay, Marsh Harbour, North Eleuthera and Governor's Harbour.

Discount travel companies

Air Brokers International ☎ 1-800/883-3273, ⓦ www.airbrokers.com. Consolidator and specialist in round-the-world tickets.

Airtech ☎ 212/219-7000 or 1-877/247-8324, ⓦ www.airtech.com. Standby seat broker; also deals in consolidator fares and courier flights.

Council Travel ☎ 1-800/226-8624, ⨌ 617/528-2091, ⓦ www.counciltravel.com. Nationwide organization that mostly, but by no means exclusively, specializes in student/budget travel. Flights from the US only.

Educational Travel Center ☎ 1-800/747-5551, ⓦ www.edtrav.com. Student/youth discount agent.

High Adventure Travel ☎ 415/912-5600 or 1-800/350-0612, ⓦ www.airtreks.com. Round-the-world tickets. The website features an interactive database that lets you build and price your own round-the-world itinerary.

Skylink US ☎ 212/573-8980 or 1-800/247-6659, Canada ☎ 1-800/759-5465, ⓦ www.skylinkus.com. Consolidator.

STA Travel ☎ 1-800/777-0112 or 781-4040, ⓦ www.sta-travel.com. Worldwide specialists in independent travel; also student IDs, travel insurance, car rental, rail passes, etc.

TFI Tours International ☎ 212/736-1140 or 1-800/745-8000, ⓦ www.lowestairprice.com. Consolidator.

Travac ☎ 1-800/872-8800, ⓦ www.thetravelsite.com. Consolidator and charter broker with offices in New York City and Orlando.

Travel Avenue ☎ 1-800/333-3335, ⓦ www.travelavenue.com. Full-service travel agent that offers discounts in the form of rebates.

Travel Cuts Canada ☎ 1-800/667-2887, US ☎ 1-866/246-9762, ⓦ www.travelcuts.com. Canadian student-travel organization.

Travelers Advantage ☎ 1-877/259-2691, ⓦ www.travelersadvantage.com. Discount travel club; annual membership fee required (currently US$1 for three months' trial).

Worldtek Travel ☎ 1-800/243-1723, ⓦ www.worldtek.com. Discount travel agency for worldwide travel.

Tour operators

Ambiance Vacations ☎ 1-800/861-1109, ⓦ www.ambiancevacations.com. Good-value operator with several options in and around Nassau and Freeport/Lucaya.

American Express Vacations ☎ 1-800/241-1700, ⓦ www.americanexpress.com/travel. Luxury vacations.

Caribbean Journey ☎ 602/820-7119 or 1-888/343-2101, ⓦ www.caribbeanjourney.com. Personalized tours throughout the country, including private island vacations.

Delta Certified Vacations ☎ 1-800/654-6559, ⓦ www.deltavacations.com. Vacations from most major US cities.

Grand Bahama Vacations ☎ 1-800/545-1300, ⓦ www.gbvac.com. Offers package holidays to Freeport/Lucaya from Baltimore/Washington, Charlotte, Cincinnati, Cleveland, Fort Lauderdale, Memphis, Nashville, Pittsburgh, Hartford, Raleigh/Durham and Richmond.

Leisure Time Travel ☎ 352/795-3474 or 1-800/771-2202, ⓦ www.leisuretimetravel.com. Tour operator specializing in fly fishing and light tackle vacations.

Maupintour ☎ 1-800/255-4266, ⓦ www.maupintour.com. Luxury tours including independent golf packages.

Flights from the UK and Ireland

The best bet for Bahamas-bound travellers from the **UK** is British Airways, who fly direct to Nassau several times a week. Expect to pay anywhere between £350 and £800. You can also fly from the UK to the US or Canada and then to the Bahamas on one of the North American carriers that fly to the islands. There are also a number of British **tour operators** that offer charter flights and package holidays in the Bahamas, as listed below.

Airlines

American Airlines UK ☎ 0845/7789 789 or

020/8572 5555, Republic of Ireland ☎01/602 0550, ⓦwww.aa.com.
British Airways UK ☎0845/77 333 77, Republic of Ireland ☎1800/626 747, ⓦwww.britishairways.com.
Continental UK ☎0800/776 464, Republic of Ireland ☎1890/925 252, ⓦwww.flycontinental.com.
Delta UK ☎0800/414 767, Republic of Ireland ☎01/407 3165, ⓦwww.delta.com.

Flight and travel agents

In the UK

Bridge the World ☎020/7911 0900, ⓦwww.bridgetheworld.com. Specializing in round-the-world tickets, with good deals aimed at the backpacker market.
Co-op Travel Care Belfast ☎028/9047 1717, ⓦwww.travelcareonline.com. Flights and holidays around the world.
Destination Group ☎020/7400 7045, ⓦwww.destination-group.com. Good discount airfares.
Flightbookers ☎0870/010 7000, ⓦwww.ebookers.com. Low fares on an extensive selection of scheduled flights.
Flynow ☎0870/444 0045, ⓦwww.flynow.com. Large range of discounted tickets.
North South Travel ☎ & ⓕ01245/608 291, ⓦwww.northsouthtravel.co.uk. Friendly, competitive travel agency, offering discounted fares worldwide – profits are used to support projects in the developing world, especially the promotion of sustainable tourism.
Premier Travel Derry ☎028/7126 3333, ⓦwww.premiertravel.uk.com. Discount flight specialists.
Rosetta Travel Belfast ☎028/9064 4996, ⓦwww.rosettatravel.com. Flight and holiday agent.
STA Travel ☎0870/1600 599, ⓦwww.statravel.co.uk. Worldwide specialists in low-cost flights and tours for students and under-26s, though other customers welcome.
Top Deck ☎020/7370 4555, ⓦwww.topdecktravel.co.uk. Long-established agent dealing in discount flights.
Trailfinders ☎020/7628 7628, ⓦwww.trailfinders.com. One of the best-informed and most efficient agents for independent travellers; produce a very useful quarterly magazine worth scrutinizing for international routes.
Travel Cuts ☎020/7255 2082, ⓦwww.travelcuts.co.uk. Canadian company

specializing in budget, student and youth travel and round-the-world tickets.

In Ireland

Aran Travel International Galway ☎091/562 595, ⓦireland.iol.ie/~arantvl/aranmain. Good-value flights to all parts of the world.
CIE Tours International Dublin ☎01/703 1888, ⓦwww.cietours.ie. General flight and tour agent.
Go Holidays Dublin ☎01/874 4126, ⓦwww.goholidays.ie. Package tour specialists.
Joe Walsh Tours Dublin ☎01/676 0991, ⓦwww.joewalshtours.ie. General budget fares agent.
Lee Travel Cork ☎021/277 111, ⓦwww.leetravel.ie. Flights and holidays worldwide.
McCarthy's Travel Cork ☎021/427 0127, ⓦwww.mccarthystravel.ie. General flight agent.
Trailfinders Dublin ☎01/677 7888, ⓦwww.trailfinders.ie. One of the best-informed and most efficient agents for independent travellers; they produce a very useful quarterly magazine worth using for international routes.

Tour operators

British Airways Holidays ☎0870/242 4245, ⓦwww.baholidays.co.uk. Using British Airways and other quality international airlines, offers an exhaustive range of package and tailor-made holidays around the world.
Caribtours ☎020/7751 0660, ⓦwww.caribtours.co.uk. Long-established operator offering tailor-made breaks – including trips designed for families, spa-seekers, island hoppers and honeymooners.
Complete Caribbean ☎01423/531031, ⓦwww.completecaribbean.co.uk. Tailor-made holidays mainly in and around Nassau for families, couples, adventurer-seekers, with accommodation in villas and hotels.
Discover the World ☎01737/218 803, ⓦwww.discover-the-bahamas.co.uk. Well-established operator specializing in the Bahamas.
Hayes & Jarvis ☎0870/898 9890, ⓦwww.hayes-jarvis.com, ⓔres@hayesandjarvis.co.uk. Particularly good on diving destinations. Exotic weddings organized.
JMC Holidays ☎0870/7580 2003, ⓦwww.jmc.com. A British tour operator, sells vacation packages to the Bahamas with weekly departures from Gatwick.
Kuoni Travel ☎01306/742 888, ⓦwww.kuoni.co.uk. Flexible package holidays with extensive presence in the Caribbean. Good family

offers and dive packages.

Thomas Cook ☎ 0870/5666 222,
🌐 www.thomascook.co.uk. Long-established one-stop 24-hour travel agency for package holidays or scheduled flights, with bureau de change issuing Thomas Cook travellers' cheques, travel insurance and car rental.

Thomas Cook Holidays ☎ 01733/563 200,
🌐 www.thomascook.com. Range of flight and board deals and tours worldwide.

Flights from Australia and New Zealand

There are no direct flights from **Australia** or **New Zealand** to the Bahamas, meaning travellers first have to fly to North America and connect with a flight to the Bahamas on one of the North American carriers listed below.

Airlines

Air Canada Australia ☎ 1300/655 767 or 02/9286 8900, New Zealand ☎ 09/379 3371,
🌐 www.aircanada.ca.

American Airlines Australia ☎ 1300/650 747,
🌐 www.aa.com.

British Airways Australia ☎ 02/8904 8800, New Zealand ☎ 0800/274 847,
🌐 www.britishairways.com.

Continental Airlines Australia ☎ 02/9244 2242, New Zealand ☎ 09/308 3350,
🌐 www.flycontinental.com.

Delta Air Lines Australia ☎ 02/9251 3211, New Zealand ☎ 09/379 3370, 🌐 www.delta-air.com.

Qantas Australia ☎ 13 13 13, New Zealand ☎ 09/661 901, 🌐 www.qantas.com.au. Can get you as far as Europe or North America.

United Airlines Australia ☎ 13 17 77, New Zealand ☎ 09/379 3800 or 0800/508 648,
🌐 www.ual.com.

Virgin Atlantic Airways Australia ☎ 02/9244 2747, New Zealand ☎ 09/308 3377,
🌐 www.virgin-atlantic.com. Flies to London and the US.

Travel agents

Budget Travel New Zealand ☎ 09/366 0061 or 0800/808 040, 🌐 www.budgettravel.co.nz.

Destinations Unlimited New Zealand ☎ 09/373 4033.

Flight Centres Australia ☎ 13 31 33 or 02/9235 3522, New Zealand ☎ 09/358 4310,
🌐 www.flightcentre.com.au.

Northern Gateway Australia ☎ 08/8941 1394,
🌐 www.northerngateway.com.au.

STA Travel Australia ☎ 1300/733 035,
🌐 www.statravel.com.au, New Zealand
☎ 0508/782 872, 🌐 www.statravel.co.nz.

Student Uni Travel Australia ☎ 02/9232 8444,
📧 australia@backpackers.net.

Trailfinders Australia ☎ 02/9247 7666,
🌐 www.trailfinders.com.au.

Tour operators

Adventure World Australia ☎ 02/8913 0755,
🌐 www.adventureworld.com.au, New Zealand
☎ 09/524 5118, 🌐 www.adventureworld.co.nz. Agents for a vast array of international adventure travel companies that operate trips to every continent.

Birding Worldwide Australia ☎ 03/9899 9303,
🌐 www.birdingworldwide.com.au. Organizes group trips for those wanting to glimpse typical, unique and rare species.

Caribbean Destinations Australia ☎ 03/9614 7144 or 1800/354 104,
🌐 www.caribbeanislands.com.au. A wide array of packages including culinary tours, cruises, cricket outings and more.

Flight Centre Australia ☎ 13 31 13,
🌐 www.flightcentre.com.au, New Zealand
☎ 0800/24 35 44, 🌐 www.flightcentre.co.nz. Specializes in discount international airfares and holiday packages.

Silke's Travel Australia ☎ 1800/807 860 or 02/8347 2000, 🌐 www.silkes.com.au. Gay and lesbian specialist travel agent.

Viatour Australia ☎ 02/8219 5400,
🌐 www.viator.com. Bookings for hundreds of travel suppliers worldwide.

Wiltrans Australia ☎ 02/9255 0899 or 1800/251 174. Luxury cruise and tour specialist.

Flights from other islands in the Caribbean

One of the joys of **Caribbean travel** is the ease with which travellers can journey between countries, taking in two or three different cultures in one trip. The Bahamas are well connected by local and international airlines, and the bigger airlines offer airpasses costing from US$300 for three stopovers to US$600 for unlimited Caribbean travel within an airline's range.

Air Jamaica US ☎ 1-800/523-5585, Canada ☎ 416/229-6024, 🌐 www.airjamaica.com. Flies between Montego Bay and Nassau.

Bahamasair ☎377-5505 or 1-800/222-4262, ☎011 44 129 359 6638 in Europe, ⓦwww.bahamasair.com. Flies to the Turks and Caicos several times a week.

British Airways ☎1-800/247-9297, ⓦwww.british-airways.com. Flies from Nassau to Grand Cayman and Providenciales in the Turks and Caicos.

Cubana Airlines ☎416/967-2822, ⓦwww.cubana.cu. Flies between Havana and Nassau.

Getting there by boat

Several **cruise ships** call at Nassau or Freeport offering tours through the Bahamas and the Caribbean lasting from three days to several weeks. Most of these cruise ships spend a day or two in port, with the opportunity to take a sight-seeing tour, do some snorkelling or log some beach time. Some of the large cruise lines own private beaches or entire small islands in the Bahamas, where they deposit their passengers for a day at the beach. These places are usually isolated from any settlement and are set up with handicraft kiosks, beach toys and snack bars.

The internet is a good place to start your research. **Websites** such as ⓦwww.cruise.com and ⓦwww.cruisereviews.com are helpful resources for deciding which cruise is best for you, taking into account price range, size of boat and length of trip. Travelocity.com (ⓦwww.travelocity.com) also provide useful reviews of the major cruise companies. While some companies offer cruises only, there are still many others that negotiate rates with major airlines allowing for fly/cruise options from most major airports in the US and the rest of the world.

You can also reach the Bahamas by **sea ferry** from Fort Lauderdale. The MSV *Discovery Sun* (☎305/597-0336 or 1-800/866-8687, ⓦwww.discoverycruiseline.com), a quadruple-decker passenger ferry/cruise ship sails daily between Fort Lauderdale and Freeport. It departs Florida at 8am, arriving in Freeport/Lucaya at 1pm, making the return journey at 4.45pm. The ticket office in Freeport/Lucaya is located at the Tanja Maritime Centre (☎352-2328), near the Port Facility. A same-day return special costs around US$140 with three meals included;

round-trip tickets cost you about US$180.

The Bahamas are also popular cruising grounds for private yachts, and listings of **marinas** are found throughout the guide. More detailed information for sailors and nautical charts for the Bahamas are found in several cruising guides to the Bahamas, as listed in the Books section beginning on p.368.

If you want to explore the islands by boat but don't have your own, several companies based in Florida **charter sailboats or motorized yachts** for use in the Bahamas, either with crew or bareboat. The cost ranges US$5000–25,000 a week for a crewed sailboat sleeping six passengers, depending on how much polished wood, brass and other touches of luxury you want.

Cruise lines

The fares quoted are for single person/double occupancy "inside" (no ocean views) cabins, outside of the high season (when prices can jump by US$300–500) and are exclusive of port charges, which add an extra US$200 or so.

Carnival Cruiselines ☎1-888/CARNIVAL, ⓦwww.carnival.com. A youthful cruise line with a big emphasis on fun, offering seven nights from Miami, Orlando or Fort Lauderdale from US$599.

Disney Cruise Line ☎1-800/951-3532, ⓦwww.disneycruise.disney.go.com/. Seven nights from Key West from US$829, including a trip to Disney's own Bahamian island.

Holland America ☎1-877/932-4259, ⓦwww.hollandamerica.com. Family cruise line, with hefty scheduled entertainment for both adults and kids. Week-long cruises from Fort Lauderdale from around US$700.

Princess Cruises & Royal Caribbean ☎1-800/PRINCESS, ⓦwww.princesscruises.com. Seven-day luxury cruises (including spas and scuba diving) from Florida for upwards of US$649.

Radisson Seven Seas ☎1-877/505-5370, ⓦwww.rssc.com. Fifteen-day cruises from Florida to LA via the Caribbean and South America, starting at US$5500 for two people.

Regal Cruises ☎1-800/270-7245, ⓦwww.regalcruises.com. A rare opportunity to cruise straight from New York to the Bahamas for upwards of US$669.

Silversea ☎1-800/722-9955, ⓦwww.silversea.com. Top-notch cruises and fly/cruise options from all over the world – all-inclusive packages start at around US$4100.

Cruise travel agents

Accent on Cruising ☎972/661-5151 or 1-800/317-3157, ⓦwww.accentoncruising.com. Agents for Radisson, Royal Caribbean, Celebrity, Princess and Silversea.

Adventure Travels ☎1-800/327-8967, ⓦwww.preferr.com. Agents for Carnival, Celebrity, Holland America, Princess, Radisson, Windstar, Royal Caribbean and Silversea.

Cruise Discounters ☎1-800/268-0854, ⓦwww.cruisediscounters.com. Discount agent for most major cruise lines.

Boat charters and booking agents

Atlantic Yacht Company ☎1-888/496-3287, ⓦwww.yachtworld.com.

Bareboat.com ☎1-800/227-3262, ⓦwww.bareboat.com.

Cruzan Yacht Charters ☎305/858-2822 or 1-800/628-0785, ⓕ305/854-0887, ⓦwww.cruzan.com.

Florida Yacht Charters ☎305/532-8600 or 1-800/537-0050, ⓕ305/535-3175, ⓦwww.floridayacht.com.

Moorings ☎727/535-1446 or 1-888/952-8420, ⓦwww.moorings.com.

Sailboat Charters of Miami ☎305/772-4221 or 1-800/328-8838, ⓔcaptaindavid@sailboat-charters.com.

Sailing Paradise ☎631/665-6777 or 1-800/864-7245, ⓕ631/969-1175, ⓦwww.sailingparadise.com.

Swift Yacht Charters ☎508/647-1554 or 1-800/866-8340, ⓕ508/647-1556, ⓦwww.swiftyachts.com.

Red tape and visas

US, UK and Commonwealth citizens do not need visas to enter the Bahamas. US citizens may enter the Bahamas for stays up to eight months without a passport provided they show proof of citizenship in the form of a birth certificate with a raised seal, or a certified copy, plus a photo ID of some sort, usually a driver's license. While citizens of the Commonwealth may enter the Bahamas for up to three weeks without showing a passport, they must have one for stays between three weeks and eight months, and should have onward/return tickets as well. In most cases, you'll be asked to show a passport upon returning home, so it's best to travel with one regardless of your length of stay.

Visitors to the Bahamas are required to fill out standard immigration cards upon disembarkation that should be kept with other travel documents. The immigration card must be surrendered to Bahamian immigration authorities upon departure. Travel within the Bahamas is unrestricted, and no travel permits are required.

All travellers should **photocopy** their documents, including passports, photo IDs, onward/return tickets and driver's licence. One copy of these documents should be left at home, and other copies should be carried separately when travelling. If you should lose your travel documents, contact the police as well as your embassy or consulate. In lieu of that, contact the Bahamian Ministry of Foreign Affairs, E Hill St, Nassau (☎322-7624). Specific questions about immigration and travel policy can be addressed to the **Bahamas Immigration Department** (☎377-7032 or 377-6337).

For information on red tape and visas in the **Turks and Caicos**, see p.321.

Customs

You may **enter** the Bahamas with up to US$10,000 in cash, one pound of loose tobacco, 200 cigarettes and fifty cigars. Computers, CD players, video games and

15

other expensive electronic gear are sometimes examined to prevent resale without import duty in the Bahamas, so be certain to back up your claims that the items being imported are for purely personal use. Firearms, illegal drugs, and plants and food items are prohibited from importation.

US citizens may take home US$600 worth of goods during stays of 72 hours or more. For stays of less than 72 hours, the exemption is US$200. In addition, US citizens may leave with 200 cigarettes, 100 non-Cuban cigars and one litre of spirits or wine. If you are contemplating bringing back antiques and the like, you should contact the US Customs Service (☎202/927-6724) and request booklets on the preference system.

Canadians may return home with goods up to CAN$200 if they've been outside the country more than 48 hours. Canadians outside the country for seven days or more may bring home CAN$500 worth of duty-free goods. They may also bring with them 200 cigarettes, fifty cigars, 2.2 pounds of loose tobacco and forty imperial ounces of spirits. In addition, Canadian citizens may mail home gifts to the tune of CAN$60 per day so long as the gifts are unsolicited and don't include alcohol or tobacco. Canadians should declare their valuables before leaving home on form Y-38, including the serial numbers of cameras and electronic gear.

UK citizens may bring back goods worth up to £145 along with 200 cigarettes, fifty cigars, 250g of loose tobacco and two litres of still table wine and one litre of spirits. Specific rules for UK citizens can be obtained from HM Customs and Excise (☎0181/910 3744) or on the web at ⊛www.open.gov.uk.

In addition to surrendering your immigration card when leaving, you will also be subject to a **departure tax** of US$15 (US$18 if you are leaving from Freeport). Immigration authorities will ask about your onward/return travel plans, and you should be prepared to show your airline tickets.

Bahamian embassies abroad

Canada High Commission for the Commonwealth of the Bahamas, 50 O'Connor St, Suite 1313, Ottawa, ON K1P 6L2 ☎613/232-1724, ℱ613/232-0097, ℯottawa-mission@bahighco.com.
UK and Ireland Bahamas High Commission, 10 Chesterfield St, London W1X 8AH ☎020/7408 4488.
US The Embassy of the Commonwealth of the Bahamas, 2220 Massachusetts Ave NW, Washington DC 20008 ☎202/319-2660, ℱ202/319-2668.

Embassies and consulates in the Bahamas

Canada Canadian Consulate, Shirley St Plaza, Nassau ☎393-2123.
UK and Ireland British Consulate, East St, Nassau ☎325-7471.
US US Embassy, Queen St, Nassau ☎322-1181.

 # Insurance

It is prudent to take out an insurance policy before travelling to cover against theft, loss, illness or injury. Before paying for a new policy, however, it's worth checking whether you are already covered: some all-risks home insurance policies may cover your possessions when overseas, and many private medical schemes include cover when abroad.

If your existing policy does not cover your possessions and medical treatment while you are abroad, you might want to contact a specialist travel insurance company, or consider the travel insurance deal we offer (see box opposite). A typical travel insurance policy

Rough Guides travel insurance

Rough Guides offers its own travel insurance, customized for our readers by a leading UK broker and backed by a Lloyd's underwriter. It's available for anyone, of any nationality and any age, travelling anywhere in the world.

There are two main Rough Guide insurance plans: **Essential**, for basic, no-frills cover; and **Premier** – with more generous and extensive benefits. Alternatively, you can take out **annual multi-trip insurance**, which covers you for any number of trips throughout the year (with a maximum of 60 days for any one trip). Unlike many policies, the Rough Guides schemes are calculated by the day, so if you're travelling for 27 days rather than a month, that's all you pay for. If you intend to be away for the whole year, the Adventurer policy will cover you for 365 days. Each plan can be supplemented with a "Hazardous Activities Premium" if you plan to indulge in sports considered dangerous, such as skiing, scuba diving or trekking.

For a policy quote, call the Rough Guide Insurance Line on US toll-free ☎1-866/220-5588; UK freefone ☎0800/015 0906; or, if you're calling from elsewhere, ☎+44 1243/621 046. Alternatively, get an online quote or buy online at ⒲www.roughguidesinsurance.com.

usually provides cover for the loss of baggage, tickets and – up to a certain limit – cash or cheques, as well as cancellation or curtailment of your journey. Most of them exclude so-called dangerous sports unless an extra premium is paid: in the Bahamas this can mean scuba diving and windsurfing, though probably not kayaking or jeep safaris. Many policies can be chopped and changed to exclude coverage you don't need – for example, sickness and accident benefits can often be excluded or included at will. If you do take medical coverage, ascertain whether benefits will be paid as treatment proceeds or only after return home, and whether there is a 24-hour medical emergency number. When securing baggage cover, make sure that the per-article limit – typically under US$1000 – will cover your most valuable possession. If you need to make a claim, you should keep receipts for medicines and medical treatment, and in the event you have anything stolen, you must obtain an official statement from the police confirming this.

✚ Health

The Bahamas present few major health issues for visitors. The quality of healthcare facilities is on par with those in the US, Canada and UK, and there are several private and government-funded hospitals and clinics in Nassau and Freeport. There are also government-run health clinics in the major settlements on each of the Out Islands, which have the capacity to transport patients to hospitals in Nassau or Freeport by air ambulance in the event of an emergency. Medical treatment can be very expensive, and it is strongly advised that you purchase traveller's health insurance (see above).

General issues

There are **pharmacies** in Freeport, Nassau and in the larger settlements on the Out Islands, but it is recommended that you carry sufficient supplies of any prescription medication and contact lens cleaning solutions for the duration of your trip. Be sure to bring a spare set of eyeglasses or contact lenses if you wear them.

There are **no vaccinations required** to enter the Bahamas unless you are coming from an area infected with yellow fever, in which case you need to have an International Health Certificate indicating that you have had immunization against yellow fever sometime in the past ten years.

The most serious health concerns for visitors to the Bahamas are overexposure to the powerful rays of the sun, which can cause sunburn and/or heat stroke; and insect bites, which are less debilitating, but nevertheless irritating.

Heat stroke

Heat stroke is a serious and sometimes fatal condition that can result from long periods of exposure to high temperatures. The tropical sun is intense and can fry unprotected skin to a crisp in short order. The wisest approach is to use a sunscreen with a high SPF (35 or over), not forgetting your lips, ears, eyelids, feet and around your nostrils, which can suffer a nasty burn from light reflected off the water. Wearing a wide-brimmed hat, sunglasses and covering exposed flesh with a long-sleeve shirt if you are spending a lot of time outdoors is also recommended. Above all, the best prevention is stay out of the sun as much as possible, and drink lots of water and/or soft drinks.

Symptoms of heat stroke include nausea and general discomfort, fatigue, a high body temperature, severe headache, disorientation and/or little or no perspiration despite the heat. Eventually, the sufferer can become delirious and fall into convulsions, and rapid medical treatment is essential. First aid is to seek shade, remove the victim's clothing, wrap them in a cool, wet sheet or towels and fan the air around them.

Bites and stings

Insect bites from mosquitoes and sand fleas are not life-threatening – there is no malaria in the Bahamas – but can spoil an otherwise perfect night outside under the stars. Fortunately, they are easily dealt with by using insect repellent, covering up with light-coloured trousers and a long-sleeved shirt, and avoiding scented soaps, shampoos and perfumes, which bugs find very enticing. While they are generally not a problem in urban and resort areas, in less developed parts of the islands they are most vicious at dawn and dusk, so you might also just yield the battlefield to them at these times.

Though there are no poisonous snakes in the Bahamas, there are **scorpions** that can sting but are not life-threatening. If you go tramping around in the bush, you should also be wary of brushing against the **poisonwood tree**, the sap of which causes the skin to blister, swell and itch, much like poison ivy. It grows mainly in coastal areas, has shiny green leaves and a reddish, scaly bark, and is well known to local inhabitants, who can point it out to you.

Medical resources for travellers

Websites

ⓦ **http://health.yahoo.com** Information on specific diseases and conditions, drugs and herbal remedies, as well as advice from health experts.
ⓦ **www.tmvc.com.au** Contains a list of all Travellers Medical and Vaccination Centres throughout Australia, New Zealand and Southeast Asia, plus general information on travel health.
ⓦ **www.istm.org** The website of the International Society for Travel Medicine, with a full list of clinics specializing in international travel health.
ⓦ **www.tripprep.com** Travel Health Online provides an online-only comprehensive database of necessary vaccinations for most countries, as well as destination and medical service provider information.
ⓦ **www.fitfortravel.scot.nhs.uk** UK NHS website carrying information about travel-related diseases and how to avoid them.

Other sources of information and health services

Centers for Disease Control 1600 Clifton Rd NE, Atlanta, GA 30333 ☎404/639-3534 or 1-800/311-3435, ℱ1-888/232-3299, ⓦwww.cdc.gov. Publishes outbreak warnings, suggested inoculations, precautions and other background information for travellers. Useful website plus International Travellers Hotline on ☎1-877/FYI-TRIP.

International Association for Medical Assistance to Travellers (IAMAT) 417 Center St, Lewiston, NY 14092 ☎716/754-4883, ⓦwww.sentex.net/~iamat, and 40 Regal Rd, Guelph, ON N1K 1B5 ☎519/836-0102. A nonprofit organization supported by donations, it can provide a list of doctors in the Bahamas, climate charts and leaflets on various diseases and inoculations.

International SOS Assistance 8 Neshaminy Interplex Suite 207, Trevose, PA 19053-6956 ☎1-800/523-8930, ⓦwww.intsos.com. Members receive pre-trip medical referral info, as well as overseas emergency services designed to complement travel insurance coverage.
MEDJET Assistance ☎1-800/863-3538, ⓦwww.medjetassistance.com. Annual membership programme for travellers (US$175 for individuals, US$275 for families) that, in the event of illness or injury, will fly members home or to the hospital of their choice in a medically equipped and staffed jet.
Travel Medicine ☎1-800/872-8633, ℱ413/584-6656, ⓦwww.travmed.com. Sells first-aid kits, mosquito netting, water filters, reference books and other health-related travel products.

Information, websites and maps

Information on the Bahamas is readily available from the official Bahamas Tourist Offices (see box overleaf) and from one of many websites maintained by tourism officials. The tourist offices can provide maps, hotel directories, and slick colour brochures about the islands themselves. No tourist office acts as a reservation centre, though there is a Bahamas reservation office in North America (☎1-800/700-4752).

In addition to the Ministry of Tourism's information offices, the islands of New Providence and Grand Bahama have their own individual promotion boards, which offer island-specific travel information, hotel guides, shopping directories, and informal maps. For **New Providence** information, the Nassau/Paradise Island Promotion Board is located at Hotel's House, Dean's Lane, Nassau (☎322-8383 or 1-800/327-9019, ℱ305/931-3005, ⓦwww.nassauparadiseisland.com). **Grand Bahama** is represented by the Grand Bahama Island Promotion Board at the International Bazaar, PO Box F-40252, Freeport, Grand Bahama (☎352-8044 or 1-800/448-3386, ℱ352-2714, ⓦwww.grand-bahama.com).

Travellers interested in visiting the **Out Islands** should contact the Bahama Out Islands Promotion Board, which shares an office in the US with the tourism office in Miami (see overleaf). You can phone them at ☎1-800/688-4752 or 305/931-6612.

For exact locations and details on specific tourist information offices in the Bahamas, see the "Information" sections on specific islands.

Maps

The Bahamas Ministry of Tourism publishes several free maps. Among them, the general **Road Map to the Bahamas** is quite small, although it is serviceable for people wishing only an overview. The Out Islands

Bahamas Ministry of Tourism offices

US
Atlanta 2957 Clairmont Rd, NO. 150, Atlanta, GA 30345 ☏770/270-1500
Boston PO Box 1039, Boston, MA 02117 ☏617/485-0572
Charlotte 11133 Leaden Hall LN. Charlotte, NC 28213 ☏704/543-0091
Chicago 8600 W. Bryn Mawr Ave, Suite 820, Chicago, IL 60631 ☏773/693-1500
Dallas World Trade Center, 2050 Stemmons Freeway, Suite 116, Dallas, TX 75258
☏214/742-1886
Los Angeles 3450 Wilshire Blvd, Suite 208, Los Angeles, CA 90010 ☏1-800/439-6993
Miami 1 Turnberry Place, 19495 Biscayne Blvd 809, Aventura, FL, 33180
☏305/932-0051
New York 150 E 52nd St, NY 10022 ☏212/758-2777

Canada
Toronto 121 Bloor St E, Suite 1101, Toronto ON M4W 3M5 ☏416/968-2999

UK
England The Billings, Walnut Tree Close, Guildford, Surrey GU1 4UL
☏01483/448900

Promotion Board (see p.19) also publishes a series of wallet-size maps of Andros, Eleuthera, Exuma and the Abacos, but none for the southern islands, Cat Island or San Salvador as yet. Many of these islands, though, are tiny and have only one major road, so they are not difficult to navigate in any regard. The Out Islands Promotion Board can also supply the **Bahama Out Islands Travel and Map Guide**, a newspaper foldout format that has maps and hotel information for all the Out Islands. It can be ordered from Star Publishers (PO Box N-4855, Nassau, Bahamas; ☏322-3724, ⓔboipb@ix.netcom.com).

Most major bookstore chains carry the useful **International Travel Maps** of the Bahamas, published in a scale of 1:1,100,000. If you need greater detail, try a series of maps published by **Omni Resources** (PO Box 2096, Burlington, NC 27216; ☏910/227-8300 or 1-800/642-2677). In the series are a general 1:1,000,000 physical map of the Bahamas (US$14.95), 1:500,000 scale road maps of the northern and southern islands (US$7.95) and a Nassau city atlas (US$12.95). **Island Maps** (PO Box WK485, Warwick WKBX, Bermuda) publishes a 1:32,000 scale road map of New Providence which is available at some bookshops in Nassau. Slick four-colour *Trailblazer Maps*, which feature the streets of Nassau or Freeport, are available at hotels and tour agencies everywhere in those cities.

Ordnance survey maps are not particularly useful in the Bahamas, given the small size of the islands and their relative topographic sameness.

Map outlets

Many shops now specialize in maps, travel books, and accessories. Almost any of these shops will carry a suitable map of the Bahamas, and the larger ones either carry or can order more detailed maps.

In the US and Canada

Adventurous Traveler Bookstore 102 Lake St, Burlington, VT 05401 ☏1-800/282-3963, ⓦwww.adventuroustraveler.com.
Book Passage 51 Tamal Vista Blvd, Corte Madera, CA 94925 ☏1-800/999-7909, ⓦwww.bookpassage.com.
Distant Lands 56 S Raymond Ave, Pasadena, CA 91105 ☏1-800/310-3220, ⓦwww.distantlands.com.
Elliot Bay Book Company 101 S Main St, Seattle, WA 98104 ☏1-800/962-5311, ⓦwww.elliotbaybook.com.

Forsyth Travel Library 226 Westchester Ave, White Plains, NY 10604 ☎1-800/367-7984, ⓦwww.forsyth.com.
Globe Corner Bookstore 28 Church St, Cambridge, MA 02138 ☎1-800/358-6013, ⓦwww.globercorner.com.
GORP Travel ☎1-877/440-4677, ⓦwww.gorp.com/gorp/books/main.
Map Link 30 S La Patera Lane, Unit 5, Santa Barbara, CA 93117 ☎805/692-6777, ⓦwww.maplink.com.
Rand McNally ☎1-800/333-0136, ⓦwww.randmcnally.com. Around thirty stores across the US; dial ext 2111 or check the website for the nearest location.
The Travel Bug Bookstore 2667 W Broadway, Vancouver V6K 2G2 ☎604/737-1122, ⓦwww.swifty.com/tbug.
World of Maps 1235 Wellington St, Ottawa, ON K1Y 3A3 ☎1-800/214-8524, ⓦwww.worldofmaps.com.

In the UK and Ireland

Blackwell's Map and Travel Shop 50 Broad St, Oxford OX1 3BQ ☎01865/793 550, ⓦhttp://maps.blackwell.co.uk/index.
Easons Bookshop 40 O'Connell St, Dublin 1 ☎01/873 3811, ⓦwww.eason.ie.
Heffers Map and Travel 20 Trinity St, Cambridge CB2 1TJ ☎01223/333 536, ⓦwww.heffers.co.uk.
Hodges Figgis Bookshop 56–58 Dawson St, Dublin 2 ☎01/677 4754, ⓦwww.hodgesfiggis.com.
James Thin Booksellers 53–59 South Bridge, Edinburgh EH1 1YS ☎0131/622 8222, ⓦwww.jthin.co.uk.
The Map Shop 30a Belvoir St, Leicester LE1 6QH ☎0116/247 1400, ⓦwww.mapshopleicester.co.uk.
National Map Centre 22–24 Caxton St, London SW1H 0QU ☎020/7222 2466, ⓦwww.mapsnmc.co.uk, ⒺInfo@mapsnmc.co.uk.
Newcastle Map Centre 55 Grey St, Newcastle-upon-Tyne NE1 6EF ☎0191/261 5622.
Ordnance Survey Ireland Phoenix Park, Dublin 8 ☎01/8025 349, ⓦwww.irlgov.ie/osi, Ⓔosni@osni.gov.uk.
Ordnance Survey of Northern Ireland Colby House, Stranmillis Ct, Belfast BT9 5BJ ☎028/9025 5755, ⓦwww.osni.gov.uk.
Stanfords 12–14 Long Acre, London WC2E 9LP ☎020/7836 1321, ⓦwww.stanfords.co.uk, Ⓔsales@stanfords.co.uk. Maps available by mail, phone order, or email. Other branches within British Airways offices at 156 Regent St, London W1R 5TA ☎020/7434 4744, and 29 Corn St,

Bristol BS1 1HT ☎0117/929 9966.
The Travel Bookshop 13–15 Blenheim Crescent, London W11 2EE ☎020/7229 5260, ⓦwww.thetravelbookshop.co.uk.

In Australia and New Zealand

The Map Shop 6–10 Peel St, Adelaide, SA 5000 ☎08/8231 2033, ⓦwww.mapshop.net.au.
Mapland 372 Little Bourke St, Melbourne, VIC 3000, ☎03/9670 4383, ⓦwww.mapland.com.au.
MapWorld 173 Gloucester St, Christchurch, New Zealand ☎0800/627 967 or 03/374 5399, ⓦwww.mapworld.co.nz.
Perth Map Centre 1/884 Hay St, Perth, WA 6000, ☎08/9322 5733, ⓦwww.perthmap.com.au.
Specialty Maps 46 Albert St, Auckland 1001 ☎09/307 2217, ⓦwww.ubdonline.co.nz/maps.

Useful websites

An impressive array of **websites** can guide visitors through a welter of information about airfares, hotel, lodge, and bed and breakfast accommodations, museum visits, eco-tours, cultural events and excursions. The list below highlights a few of the best.

> Websites relating to sports and outdoor activities are listed on pp.38–41.

General

ⓦwww.abacos.com Basic site that evaluates places to stay on the Abacos as well as events and activities like fishing. The information included is bought and paid for, so keep in mind the commercial strings attached.
ⓦwww.bahamas.com The Bahamas Ministry of Tourism site, covering everything from travel info, watersports and accommodation to local cuisine.
ⓦwww.bahamasnet.com Comprehensive website with details on accommodation, activities and restaurants, and a calendar of events.
ⓦwww.bahamas-on-line.com Directory of restaurants, accommodations, dive shops and more.
ⓦwww.caribbeanaviation.com Very up-to-date and comprehensive website detailing charter and scheduled airlines serving the Caribbean.
ⓦwww.cruisecritic.com Detailed reviews of cruise ships serving the Caribbean.
ⓦwww.interknowledge.com/bahamas A site that includes a clickable map for virtual island hopping.

Ⓦ **www.roughguides.com** Post any of your pre-trip questions – or post-trip suggestions – in Travel Talk, our online forum for travellers.

Accommodation

Ⓦ **www.escapeartist.com/bahamas/bahamas** A practical guide for people interested in real estate and business – or for folks planning to build a home in the Bahamas.
Ⓦ **www.the-bahamas.com** A site highlighting hotels and properties including condos and vacation homes.

News and current events

Ⓦ **www.bbc.co.uk/caribbean** Audio news reports, including the week's highlights, plus arts, entertainment and sports coverage.
Ⓦ **www.thenassauguardian.com** Website of one of the two leading dailies, with the usual departments plus links to other local papers.

Costs, money and banks

The Bahamian dollar is on par with the US dollar, and both currencies are accepted throughout the country. Because all hotels and tourist facilities freely exchange both US and Bahamian currency, there is little need to formally change US dollars before travelling here. American dollars are accepted for any transaction, though most locals frown on accepting oft-counterfeited US notes in denominations of 50 and 100 dollars.

Currency

Bahamian **coins** come in denominations of 1, 5, 10, 25 and 50 cents, while **notes** are issued in denominations of 50 cents, 1, 3, 5, 10, 20, 50, 100 and 500 dollars. While any bank will change foreign currency into US or Bahamian dollars, visitors carrying Bahamian dollars should be advised that banks will only exchange amounts of $70 Bahamian or less at a time. Please see "Red tape and visas" for currency import limitations.

Average costs

Despite the relatively cheap air transportation to and from the islands themselves, the Bahamas are ultimately an expensive destination. Budget accommodation options are few and far between, and almost everything Bahamians use on a daily basis is imported, some of it subject to high duties and tariffs.

Travellers in the Bahamas should budget their money as though they were travelling to a major US city.

The average **room rate** for a decent tourist hotel in the Bahamas is around $100 per night double occupancy. Nassau and Freeport often have budget options that go for as little as $25–60 per night, but these properties are often small, noisy motel-style lodgings in the town centre. Many middle-of-the-road hotels that charge $75–100 per night are somewhat grim at best. Conditions are no different on the Out Islands, where there are typically a few budget-option motels, but where most hotels are rather expensive.

Other than seafood and some fruit, **foodstuffs** in the Bahamas are imported either from the US or UK. An average breakfast costs about $5, lunch $9, and dinner $15. Of course, you can find roadside food stalls and fruit stands, and there are budget take-away joints on almost every street corner, but the food in budget joints is almost always deep-fried and difficult to stomach

For information on currency in the **Turks and Caicos**, see p.321.

day after day. Modest local restaurants do exist everywhere, but even their costs are relatively high, a dinner costing about $10 exclusive of drinks and tip. Self-caterers in condos and vacation homes can save a little money by cooking for themselves. Nevertheless, groceries often stock expensive canned goods, dairy products, and sweets that have been imported from the US and UK.

Inter island travel varies in cost from budget ferries and mailboats that ply slow routes between islands on long and short hauls carrying both passengers and cargo, to expensive charter flights one-way to remote spots. Flights on Bahamasair can cost as little as $40 on the route from Andros to Nassau, or as much as $150 one-way to a remote Out Island during the holiday season. The cost of flying commercially in the Bahamas is increased because everybody flying between islands on Bahamasair must return to Nassau for the next leg. The best way to cut costs is to take a mailboat from Potter's Cay in Nassau. The journey can take anywhere from four to fifteen hours, but it can save you a tidy sum.

Cash and travellers' cheques

Cash and travellers' cheques denominated in US dollars are accepted throughout the Bahamas for any transaction. On some remote Out Islands, US denominated travellers' cheques may be refused, but this is rare. Travellers' cheques can be purchased at almost any bank, lending agency, or currency exchange in the world, with the major brands being American Express, Thomas Cook, and Barclay's Bank. On occasion, restaurants and hotels will charge a fee for cashing travellers' cheques, and all banks levy a small $1 charge for each cheque cashed.

The usual fee for travellers' cheque sales is one or two percent, though this fee may be waived if you buy the cheques through a bank where you have an account. It pays to get a selection of denominations. Make sure to keep the purchase agreement and a record of cheque serial numbers safe and separate from the cheques themselves. In the event that cheques are lost or stolen, the issuing company will expect you to report the loss forthwith to their office. The book of cheques you receive will always carry detailed instructions on how to report and replace lost or stolen cheques. Most companies claim to replace lost or stolen cheques within 24 hours.

Automated Teller Machines (ATMs) can be found in major tourist centres in the Bahamas, like Nassau, Paradise Island, and Freeport/Lucaya, yet they are scarce or even non-existent on the Out Islands. Most accept Visa, MasterCard and American Express via international networks like Cirrus and Visa Plus. Always check with your local bank on the hows of making ATM withdrawals in foreign countries. Usually it is as simple as keying in your personal identification number (PIN) after punching in the card. Your cash will be issued in Bahamian dollars and debited to your home account, less a fee.

Credit and debit cards

Major **credit cards** are accepted readily at most hotels, resorts, restaurants and shops on New Providence, Grand Bahama, the Abacos and Eleuthera. On some Out Islands, credit cards are not accepted, and you should check with your destination hotel for information on card use. The credit cards widely accepted in the Bahamas are MasterCard, Visa, American Express, Diners Club and Discover. Most hotels and resorts will ask for an imprint of your card before check-in. If you allow such an imprint to be made, do not sign a blank charge form. Sign the imprinted credit card form only upon checking out of the hotel, and after you've perused all the charges for accuracy and completeness. For travel in the Out Islands, it is best to have a supply of cash and travellers' cheques in reserve.

Credit cards are a handy backup source of funds, and can be used either in ATMs or over the counter. Remember that all cash advances are treated as loans, with interest accruing daily from the date of withdrawal; there may be a transaction fee on top of this. However, you may be able to make withdrawals from ATMs in the Bahamas using your debit card, which is not liable to interest payments, and the flat transaction fee is usually quite small – your bank will be able to advise you on this. Make sure you have a personal identification number (PIN) that's designed to work overseas.

Wiring money

Having **money wired from home** using one of the companies listed below is never convenient or cheap, and should be considered a last resort. It's also possible to have money wired directly from a bank in your home country to a bank in the Bahamas, although this is somewhat less reliable because it involves two separate institutions. If you go this route, your home bank will need the address of the branch bank where you want to pick up the money and the address and telex number of the Nassau head office, which will act as the clearing house; money

wired this way normally takes two working days to arrive, and costs around $40 per transaction.

Money-wiring companies

American Express Moneygram
US and Canada ☎1-800/926-9400,
Australia ☎1800/230 100, New Zealand ☎09/379 8243 or 0800/262 263, UK and Republic of Ireland ☎0800/6663 9472, ⓦwww.moneygram.com.
Thomas Cook US ☎1-800/287-7362, Canada ☎1-888/823-4732, UK ☎01733/318 922 (Northern Ireland ☎028/9055 0030) Republic of Ireland ☎01/677 1721, ⓦwww.us.thomascook.com.
Western Union US and Canada ☎1-800/325-6000, Australia ☎1800/649 565, New Zealand ☎09/270 0050, UK ☎0800/833 833, Republic of Ireland ☎1800/395 395,
ⓦwww.westernunion.com.

Getting around

The Bahamas archipelago is spread out over a great chunk of south Atlantic ocean. While the proximity of some islands to one another suggests inter-island travel would be quick and convenient, island hopping is actually quite difficult unless you are sailing your own vessel, flying your own plane or willing to spend considerable money chartering aircraft from local airports.

Whether travelling within the Bahamas by air or by sea, you'll invariably have to return to Nassau before setting out for your ultimate destination, even if it means heading in the wrong direction. "Getting around" sections for each island, with full details on public transportation, taxis, rental options and tours appear in the introductions to each chapter. For information on getting around in the **Turks and Caicos**, turn to p.321.

By air

The largest inter-island airline by far is **Bahamasair** (Nassau ☎377-5505; Freeport ☎352-8343; in North America ☎1-800/222-4262), which serves nineteen airports on twelve islands and offers a schedule of

almost bewildering variety. Its main arrival and departure areas at Nassau's International Airport are almost constantly under construction or repair, though its basic service with prop planes and small jets is good. On holidays, weekends and during winter tourist season, the check-in counters in Nassau are scenes of near-chaos, with long lines of passengers tugging huge piles of baggage and packages. Be patient, as flights are sometimes cancelled or take off hours late.

The best way to prepare for a flight on Bahamasair is to book early, make certain to double-check flight schedules by phone on the day of departure, and arrive at the airport early. If you are told a flight is sold out, simply continue standing in line. Often, flights are overbooked by Bahamians who catch other flights, having made two or three reservations.

Bahamasair does have an **airpass programme** that allows travellers to fly to a number of different islands from Miami or Orlando through Nassau. The cost of the airpasses is subject to perpetual change, no route changes are permitted and no refunds are allowed. All must be purchased from your home country before you depart and used within 21 days of issue.

Most of the Out Islands are served by **charter companies** that have adopted one or two islands as a home. Roughly speaking, charters can range from a low of $100 (Nassau to Andros) for one person up to around $600. Naturally, flying charters between islands saves enormous amounts of time and can sometimes save on hotels and meals when an overnight stay in Nassau is required for scheduled services. Charter services are sometimes provided by hotels and resorts. See the "Getting there" sections in each chapter for specific details.

Inter-island airlines

Bahamasair Nassau ☎377-5505; Freeport ☎352-8343; in North America ☎1-800/222-4262
Cat Island Air ☎377-3318
Cherokee Air ☎224/367-2089
Cleare Air ☎377-0341
Congo Air ☎377-5382
Falcon Air ☎377-1703
Island Express ☎954/359-0380
Long Island Wings ☎357-1013
Major's Air Services ☎352-5778
Seaplane Safaris ☎393-2522
Sky Unlimited ☎377-8993
Taino Air ☎352-5175
Trans-Island Air ☎327-5979

By mailboat and ferry

Bahamian **mailboats** are holdovers from a long tradition of maritime service going back to 1832. These days, mailboats carry passengers along with cargo, and the official headquarters of the mailboat service is the **Dockmaster's Office** (☎393-1064) under the Paradise Island Bridge on Potter's Cay in New Providence. Most mailboats sail from Potter's Cay, although a few depart from

Prince George Wharf a few miles away in downtown Nassau. There are 29 mailboats now in service, coming in varying sizes, states of repair and levels of comfort, and they serve all of the inhabited Bahamian islands on journeys that take anywhere from four to 24 hours. **First- and second-class tickets** are available, with first class costing $5 more and entitling you to a small bunk – if one is available. On average, tickets range from $25 to $60.

Beware that scheduled departures, especially on longer trips, are often delayed, and difficult weather or high seas can stretch a ten-hour journey into fifteen hours. Moreover, some passages are difficult anyway, especially those like the Crooked Island Passage, where crosscurrents toss the boat up and down. Only occasionally are snacks available on the boats.

If you take a mailboat you'll be riding a high-sided rusty cargo freighter with a couple of rows of bench seats down the port and starboard gunwales, and on longer journeys overnight, an inside cabin with a few bunk beds for first-class passengers. The deck may be piled with cases of liquor and soft drinks, mounds of coal or gravel, drums of industrial chemicals, even bunches of bananas. Nevertheless, for travellers with time, mailboats can be an enjoyable experience, a chance to rub elbows with Bahamians from many walks of life. It is also a much cheaper, more relaxing way to travel than by air, which can entail long waits in lines at Nassau's International Airport. See the "Getting there" sections in each chapter for more details.

In sharp contrast to the mailboat, privately operated **ferry services** are speedy and luxurious. The slick **Bahamas Fast Ferry** ($100 round-trip; ☎323-2166), operating out of Potter's Cay, connects Nassau to Harbour Island in North Eleuthera, then to Governor's Harbour in Central Eleuthera. A nicely appointed high-speed airboat catamaran with an enclosed cabin, upper observation deck and food service, it makes the trip in under two hours, and while the fare is higher than the mailboat it is no more than an airfare.

Another ferry service, the **Bahamas SeaRoad Link** (☎323-2166), carries passengers, cars and some cargo between

Nassau and Eleuthera three times a week, and between Nassau and points on Andros twice a week. The trip both ways takes about four hours for a fare of $40.

By car

Renting a car is a simple affair. For stays of three months or less, your homeland licence is valid and no other licence is needed. Beyond that, you'll need an international licence, available from either AAA in the US or AA in the UK. Keep in mind that public transportation, taxis, motor scooters, tours and bicycle rentals are available almost everywhere, especially in Nassau and Freeport, and that long-term rental of a vehicle is not necessary except in unusual cases.

On both New Providence and Grand Bahama, the major international car rental agencies are all represented, each them offering a wide selection of vehicles ranging from small compacts ($60 per day on average) to large four-wheel-drive SUVs (around $125 per day), with added fees for taxes and insurance. See pp.63 and 104 respectively for specific information.

On the Out Islands, conversely, most rental cars are offered by small agencies operated by locals who often rent out their personal cars – often clunkers at best – at more expensive rates. And with few rental cars available in Out Island settlements, they can be scarce as well.

Should you wish to rent a vehicle, try to do so in advance as you'll often save up to 25 percent. There are no seasonal adjustments for rental car rates, which are fairly high by world standards. Cars become scarce at Christmas and New Year's, and may become unavailable on the Out Islands during these seasons.

Driving on the islands is usually a snap, though North Americans should remember that one must **drive on the left**. Speed limits are usually 30mph in settlements and 50mph on the highway. **Gasoline** is readily available at Shell, Esso and Texaco stations, though it's expensive at $2.50–3.50 per gallon. Stations in most areas are open from 8am to 7pm, closed Sundays. Stations in Nassau and Freeport are open all the time, even on Sunday. Even the most remote Out Islands have gasoline stations.

Driving **conditions** on the islands are generally good, with the major highways paved and in decent condition. On New Providence, the main highways are in excellent shape, with only a few potholes making it dicey. Conditions in Nassau are different, with frequent traffic jams and slowdowns, and drivers sometimes becoming impatient or rude, as in any larger city. On the Out Islands, it is impossible to get lost, as there is almost always only one main road – usually called the King's or Queen's Highway. Side roads often lead inland through scrub brush where the going can get tough on muddy and rutted roads, yet Out Island side roads often lead toward isolated beaches. Those roads often become sandy, making driving a chore for anything other than 4WD.

Car rental agencies

A number of agencies have international offices where you can arrange a rental before your trip.

In North America

Avis US ☎1-800/331-1084, Canada ☎1-800/272-5871, ⓦwww.avis.com
Budget US ☎1-800/527-0700, ⓦwww.budgetrentacar.com
Hertz US ☎1-800/654-3001, Canada ☎1-800/263-0600, ⓦwww.hertz.com

In the UK

Avis ☎0870/606 0100, ⓦwww.avisworld.com
Budget ☎0800/181 181, ⓦwww.budget.co.uk
Hertz ☎0870/844 8844, ⓦwww.hertz.co.uk
National ☎0870/5365 365, ⓦwww.nationalcar.com

In Ireland

Avis Northern Ireland ☎028/9024 0404, Republic of Ireland ☎01/605 7500, ⓦwww.avis.co.uk
Budget Republic of Ireland ☎01/9032 7711, ⓦwww.budgetcarrental.ie or ⓦwww.budget-ireland.co.uk
Hertz Republic of Ireland ☎01/676 7476, ⓦwww.hertz.co.uk

In Australia

Avis ☎13 63 33, ⓦwww.avis.com
Budget ☎1300/362 848, ⓦwww.budget.com

Hertz ☏13 30 39, ⊛www.hertz.com
National ☏13 10 45, ⊛www.nationalcar.com.au

In New Zealand

Avis ☏0800/655 111 or 09/526 2847,
⊛www.avis.co.nz
Budget ☏0800/652 227 or 09/976 2222,
⊛www.budget.co.nz
Hertz ☏0800/654 321, ⊛www.hertz.co.nz
National ☏0800/800 115 or 03/366 5574,
⊛www.nationalcar.co.nz

Bicycles, motorcycles and motor scooters

Renting a **bicycle** can be a convenient and cheap way to see small areas surrounding a resort, or to ride to and from town for supplies. Most hotels and resorts rent bicycles for $7–20 per day, though you probably won't find fancy ten-speed bikes for rent, or mountain bikes either for that matter. Nassau and Freeport aren't particularly suited to touring by bike, but resort areas on the Out Islands, where traffic is light, roads flat and distances short, are perfect.

Another good option for getting around are **motorcycles** and **motor scooters**. Many local agencies rent motorcycles for $30–50 per day plus insurance and tax. Motor scooters cost $20–40 per day, though many agencies offer an hourly rate. You must wear a helmet when operating a motor scooter or motorcycle and a deposit is always required. Beware that in the Bahamas, storms can come up fast and obscure vision and wet the roads, loose gravel can challenge your balance and potholes abound in some places.

Taxis

Taxis are abundant in and around Nassau and Freeport, where they are licensed by the government and the fares are set by law. Metered rates in Nassau and Freeport are $2 for the first quarter-mile, 30 cents for succeeding quarter-miles, each additional person charged $2 extra, though extra charges are assessed for large amounts of baggage. From the airports in Nassau and Freeport, established rates – posted in the taxi – are in operation for trips to various hotels and resorts and should be agreed upon before setting out. Some hotels and resorts have taxi or limousine service to pick up guests at airports, a service that is usually included in the room price.

Most Out Island taxi drivers are locals who own their own cars and answer calls as needed. A few taxis meet incoming flights the majority of the time, and most Out Island resorts and hotels will make certain that guests are met by one. Phoning for a taxi on your own is an unreliable way to get service on the Out Islands, so if you need a taxi on an Out Island, make arrangements through your hotel, resort or lodge.

Taxis are authorized by the government to conduct **tours**, and while rates are supposedly set by regulation, most taxi drivers and travellers simply eyeball the situation and agree on a fee. Rates vary, but average about $150 per day, more for minivans and extra persons. Almost every Out Island taxi driver who meets a plane will also offer to conduct visitors on a tour of the island. Many are quite good at their job, and if you wish to see an island without the hassle of renting a car, it can be a bargain.

Tipping is not an established custom in the Bahamas, though feel free to do so if you feel the driver deserves it.

By bus

While there are excellent **bus** services on New Providence and Grand Bahama, there is no organized bus service at all on the other islands. Called "jitneys", Nassau buses are actually minivans or large Mitsubishi buses that run regular routes around the city and to the western and eastern suburbs. On Grand Bahama, buses are an excellent means of leaving Freeport/Lucaya for the eastern and western ends of the isle.

On a few Out Islands, enterprising individuals drive minivans on hypothetically pre-established routes, but they are few and far between.

Accommodation

Although there are relatively few inexpensive places to stay in the Bahamas, the islands do offer a wide variety of accommodation choices for travellers. Super-deluxe resorts, some all-inclusive properties, small budget motels, cozy inns and family-run guesthouses are available on most of the islands. Some resort and hotel properties are dedicated to diving, snorkelling and watersports, while others are geared to relaxation and fine dining. Many visitors, especially those with large families, those making extended stays or those with hefty budgets, choose time-share condos, vacation homes or island cottages where self-catering is an option.

While Out Island resorts tend to cater to yachters and sailors, in Nassau, Cable Beach, Paradise Island and Freeport/Lucaya, many hotels cater to package tourists, who come for the special weekly rates and casinos. Bear in mind that nothing is really cheap in the Bahamas, and that many "first class" properties may be run-down or have poor service.

Neither **camping** nor **youth hostels** exist in the Bahamas. Though some campers manage to pitch a few tents with permission of landowners, camping on the beach is absolutely prohibited. There is a single youth-hostel-style dormitory in Nassau, but elsewhere, neither youth hostels, student discount cards, or any form of discounts are in vogue.

Rates

Rates vary from $25 for a run-down mosqui-to-infested upstairs room in a hotel in down-town Nassau (with shared bath and no hot water) to $500 per night (and more) for a penthouse suite in a deluxe resort. During the **low season**, from mid-April through mid-December, rates are 25–40 percent less than during the corresponding **high season**, when many upscale resort hotels and all-inclusives are booked solid months in advance.

When booking a hotel, be certain to account for all the charges, taxes, tips and incidentals involved as the basic room rate is rarely the whole story. Some hotels and resorts quote rates as a **Continental Plan** (room and breakfast), a **Modified American Plan** (room plus breakfast and dinner), or an **American Plan** (room plus three meals). Check about local and national taxes as well. The Bahamas room tax is 8 percent (10 percent in Nassau and on Grand Bahama), and some hotels include an automatic 15 percent gratuity for staff. Some hotels and resorts add a housekeeping charge ($3–4 is typical). You will often be charged more for ocean-view rooms, or rooms around or near the pool. If you choose to stay at a hotel or inn on the windward side of an island, you can expect strong trade winds, access to

---

Accommodation price codes

All accommodation reviewed in this guide has been graded according to the following price codes in Bahamian dollars. Unless noted otherwise, the prices refer to the least expensive double or twin room in high season.

① Under $50
② $50–75
③ $75–100
④ $100–125
⑤ $125–150
⑥ $150–175
⑦ $175–200
⑧ over $200

Atlantic beaches, and cooler nights. Staying at a leeward resort expect shallow, snorkel-friendly waters, calm conditions, and warmer nights.

So-called **budget** accommodations are usually commercial-style motels that charge $60–80 per night, often for one-bed, slightly seedy rooms. Most resort hotels charge $95–125, while deluxe hotels and resorts charge $150 and more.

All-inclusives

All-inclusives are supposed to be the ideal cash-free, self-contained resort paradigm. In truth, some charge extra for alcoholic drinks, watersports and services like laundry and island excursions, yet some really do offer complete cash-free service. There are three major all-inclusive chains in the Bahamas – *Club Med*, *Sandals* and *Superclubs Breezes*. Their rates begin at about $225 per day per person, and include all three meals, entertainment, drinks, and many excursions and watersports. *Club Med* charges extra for alcoholic drinks. *Club Med* has properties on Paradise Island, San Salvador and Governor's Harbour, Eleuthera. *Sandals* operates the *Royal Bahamian* on Cable Beach for couples only, while *Superclubs Breezes* is also on Cable Beach. For information and contact numbers, see the "Accommodation" sections in the relevant chapters.

Villas, self-catering condos, vacation homes and cottages

The Bahamas offer a wide variety of houses, condos, villas and vacation mansions for rent. Some **villas** and small **self-catering condos** on Cable Beach in New Providence, for example, are modern two-bedroom split-level apartments with a full kitchen and two baths. These rental units are excellent for large families staying a week or more, or for friends who want to share expenses. Some have access to a swimming pool or tennis court, and a number of upscale resorts have villas scattered about their grounds. Rates for basic condo accommodation begin at $1000 per week and can run as high as $8000 per week for families of four.

Usually the property of absentee owners who let their premises out during certain months of the year, **vacation homes** run as high as $5000 per week for a four-bedroom house, while a luxury estate might run as high as $25,000. These homes usually have three or four bedrooms, several bathrooms, and large patios and kitchens. Many are on waterways or near the beach, and can be quite expensive. The Bahamas Tourist Office, various Promotion Boards, and Caribbean travel magazines often feature these types of luxury homes for rent. Luxury vacation homes are available on New Providence and Grand Bahama of course, but most are on the Out Islands, particularly Exuma, Eleuthera, the Abacos and Andros.

Many families rent **cottages**, which are particularly common on the Loyalist Cays. The closer you are to the beach, the higher the vacation rental. Cottages are almost always booked five to six months in advance for high-season vacations.

For a general **listings** of condos, villas, vacation homes and cottages in the Bahamas, try VHR Worldwide (☎1-800/843-4433, ⊛www.hideawaways.com), which also publishes the *Hideaways Guide* of home rentals throughout the world. Rent-a-Home International (☎1-800/488-7368, ⊛www.rentavilla.com) specializes in condos and villas.

Eating and drinking

The eating and drinking habits of Bahamians have been influenced first and foremost by being surrounded by one of the most abundant marine life realms in the world, an environment where seafood of nearly every type is readily available. For the Lucayans, who inhabited the Bahamas before Columbus's arrival, fish and lobster were the central sources of protein, and today, basic seafood and vegetables like the potato are the backbone of Bahamian cuisine.

The second basic influence on Bahamian cuisine is the **African**, the result of slaves and freed blacks bringing their own indigenous cooking and ingredients with them from their homelands, including flavourings like nutmeg, ginger and chili pepper. These days, dishes like grits, johnnycake, peas 'n' rice are the result of African modifications of Bahamian/English dishes.

Another influence is the **English colonial cuisine**, which affected virtually every nuance of Bahamian diet. Today, meat pies, stews and breads all show a distinctly English influence. At a Bahamian restaurant, you can order smothered grouper with a distinctly African-style sauce, or an old-fashioned English shepherd's pie with a side of macaroni and cheese or chips.

More and more, tourism demands have created an influx of **nouvelle cuisine**. Particularly in Nassau, Paradise Island and Freeport/Lucaya, restaurants abound that specialize in Continental, Asian and North American cuisine. Many fine chefs now make their homes at Bahamian resorts, blending cuisine from exotic cultures and faraway places with Bahamian seafood or vegetables. You can encounter blackened grouper, sweet-and-spicy mango sauces, and "Pacific Rim" chutney with lobster broil. A further influence of tourism is that Bahamians are eating more **fast-food** pizzas, burgers and fried chicken or doughnuts from corporate-owned franchise outlets, so while tourists are finding their choices expanding, the daily eating habits of Bahamians are being gradually homogenized.

Ultimately, the menus at most Bahamian-style restaurants look pretty much the same, with a heavy emphasis on grouper, peas and rice, potatoes and heavy English-style desserts.

Seafood

No single marine organism contributes more to the Bahamian diet than the **conch** (pronounced "konk"), a snail-like mollusc encased in a beautifully curled, pinkish-coloured shell. Bahamians love conch because it's cheap and plentiful; it reportedly also acts as an aphrodisiac. Bahamians hold conch-cracking contests on National Heroes Day, and locals demonstrate their dexterity by hitting the shell with a heavy implement at the correct spot, then "jewking" the meat by an appendage and pulling it from its shell.

The conch's delicate whitish meat forms the basis of myriad dishes: it can be eaten fried, broiled, grilled, steamed, stewed or raw in conch salad, the meat diced and mixed with chopped onion, tomato, cucumber, and celery, then sprinkled with lime juice. Because the conch meat itself is both rubbery and somewhat slimy, it must be liberally tenderized by pounding, then rinsed in salt water or lime juice, and often marinated before it is ready to eat. **Cracked conch** is tenderized meat deep-fried in batter and usually served with french fries. **Conch fritters** are deep-fat-fried balls of conch covered with corn batter that has bits of sweet peppers, onions and tomato included. Conch is also made into a light chowder (for a recipe, see p.ix).

Crawfish, locally referred to as a Bahamian lobster, is another popular seafood, and is caught fresh in the months between April and late August. Bahamian lobsters have no claws, and only the tail is eaten. They can be eaten freshly grilled or broiled, steamed and curried and are often served cold in salads with local ingredients including coconut and lime juice. The **land crab** is another mollusc that winds up on Bahamian tables, especially during summer's rainy season when they are plentiful near the beaches. The most common dish is the baked crab where the meat and eggs are combined with breadcrumbs and served in the shell.

The waters surrounding the Bahamas teem with grouper, shrimp, tuna, jack, snapper and whelk. A particular favourite, the **grouper**, a light fleshy white fish, is most often served baked with a red tomato sauce accompanied by the ubiquitous peas and rice and french fries. Grouper is just as often eaten deep-fried in batter, or cut into "fingers" and fried. On the Out Islands in particular, baked bonefish in a creole sauce is popular, and in many places, especially the Exumas, turtle is still eaten, despite its status as an endangered species.

A very common Bahamian dish is **boil fish**, sometimes referred to as stew fish. Boil fish, a stew of grouper, salt pork, onions, potatoes, celery, tomatoes and spices, can be served for any meal, and many Bahamians start their day with boil fish and coffee.

Meats and vegetables

Bahamians depend on simple staples like imported rice, potatoes, peas, red beans, pigeon peas and lima beans, all of which they serve with seafood or stew. A generous pile of grits (ground corn), cornmeal mush, or potatoes, often forms the basis of a meal in the typical Bahamian home. You're unlikely to escape **peas and rice**, but there are as many ways to prepare the dish as cooks in the islands.

Souse is also a vitally important dish in the Bahamas. Basically a combination of very inexpensive cuts of meat (sheep tongue, chicken wing, conch, pig ears) boiled with salted water and spices, souse is usually flavoured with lime juice and pepper, then eaten with freshly cooked bread. English-influenced dishes like meatloaf, pasties, macaroni and cheese, and broiled or fried chicken are also popular.

Fruit

During the nineteenth century, many types of edible exotic **fruit** were imported to the Bahamas, some becoming the basis of once-thriving industries, like the sweet Eleutheran pineapple and the Androsian orange. These days, only small quantities of fruit are commercially produced and sold, though fresh fruit and vegetables are available everywhere in groceries, markets and roadside fruit stands. Check the box and very often the fruit will be from Florida or Mexico.

Nevertheless, visitors to the Bahamas can enjoy the luxury of buying fresh, tree-ripened papayas and mangoes, and in some markets the deliciously sweet sugar loaf or Spanish scarlet variety of pineapple. Open-air markets and roadside food stands often feature fruit that are unknown in many parts of the world. The dark green **soursop** looks like a pinecone and weighs from one to five pounds. Its fibrous white pulp is both slightly sweet and tart at the same time, and although children eat it as a treat, it is mostly used in puddings, ice cream or drinks. The **sugar apple** is related to the soursop, though a lighter green, and is about the size of a tennis ball. You eat it by splitting open the fruit and spooning out the smooth white flesh. It is filled with black seeds, however, so you need patience to get a good mouthful. Oval and brown, the smallish **sapodilla** has a tan-coloured flesh that tastes something like pear. Other distinctly exotic fruit available in the Bahamas include the **jujube**, the yellow flesh of which is used to flavour the gumdrops of the same name, the leathery dark purple **star apple**, and the delicious **ugli fruit**, a roundish fruit with a green skin and a sweet, ready-to-eat pulp.

Bahamians often use their exotic fruit to flavour many kinds of jams, jellies, ice cream, pudding and punch. The **guava** is blended into puddings called "duffs", a favourite Bahamian dessert. A duff is essentially a boiled pudding filled with any kind of fruit. It has a cake-like consistency and is typically covered by a special sauce.

Drinking

While **tap water** throughout the Bahamas is drinkable, it's often highly saline due to its surface source, making it brackish at best. Anything made with tap water, including coffee and tea, is likely to take on a brackish flavour as well, so most people choose bottled water, which usually costs $1 per litre, though grocery stores and markets sell larger, bargain one-gallon containers. On some Out Islands, rainwater is a major source of drinking water and every house has a cistern to catch and store rainwater. It is never a good idea to drink cistern-stored rainwater, and bottled water in these areas is a must. Resorts tend to double-filter their water, and add extra chlorine.

Most North American soft drinks are available in the Bahamas, and locally produced soft drinks like the favourite **Goombay Punch** are very much sweeter than their North American counterparts. Fresh-fruit drinks tend to take the edge off hot days and many visitors enjoy lime coolers, orange juice and pineapple juice with shaved ice.

The alcoholic drink of choice in the Bahamas is the very fine **Kalik beer**, a lager brewed on New Providence. Its premium brand, Kalik Gold, is slightly stronger, with a deeper texture and colour. Many Bahamians drink locally brewed Heineken, or imported beers like Amstel Light, Guinness, or commonly available American and Canadian beers. Many pubs in Nassau offer English ales on tap.

Unlike many of their Caribbean neighbours, the Bahamas never had an active sugar plantation culture, and therefore never had a large-scale **rum** culture. Some rum is distilled in the Bahamas, and many poor Bahamians choose to drink stiff shots of high-octane white rum on hot days. Brands include Bacardi, Ron Matusalem and Todd Hunter. Many of the fancier rum drinks are concocted to serve to tourists at resort bars and restaurants. The famous **Bahama Mama** (rum, bitters, creme de cassis, grenadine, nutmeg, citrus juice), **Goombay Smash** (see p.155), and the **Yellow Bird** (rum, creme de banana, Galliano, apricot brandy, pineapple or orange juice) were all created strictly for the tourist trade. A very popular liqueur is the rum-based **Nassau Royale**, which comes in several flavours, including coconut, banana, and pineapple, and can be mixed in cocktails, or splashed over ice and drunk straight.

Wines were never particularly popular in the Bahamas because of importation costs and the ready availability of beer and rum. These days, many restaurants in better hotels have exhaustive wine lists to cater to international tastes.

A bottle of Kalik at most bars costs $1, though at fancier places the price will be at least twice that. Rum-based drinks usually go for $3–4, though in some discos and dance palaces in Nassau or Paradise Island that cater to a late-night crowd, the price of drinks skyrockets.

Communications

The last ten years have seen a revolution in Bahamian communications. While every settlement, city and town has long had a post office and regular mail service, on-time delivery has improved greatly, though it still has a ways to go before reaching acceptable world standards. The real revolution, though, has been in telephone service, cable TV, and email, all of which have come into their own in the Bahamas. You'll have little trouble staying in touch during your visit to the Bahamas.

Post

In general, **post offices** are open Monday–Friday 8.30am–5.30pm and Saturday 8.30am–12.30pm. Larger post offices are full-service operations that sometimes offer telegraph and fax. Service is generally friendly and efficient, though delivery can be somewhat slow. It is always a good idea to mail letters and parcels by airmail, for surface delivery is undependable and slow.

Postcards to the US, UK, Canada, Europe and Australia cost 50 cents, yet many visitors who send postcards home find that they arrive back before their postcards. In general, postcards take ten days to arrive in North America or Europe from Nassau, somewhat longer from Out Islands. Airmail letters cost 65 cents per half-ounce to those same destinations. All airmail parcels should be securely wrapped.

UPS, **DHL**, and **Federal Express** have offices in Nassau and Freeport. Each has some agents on larger Out Islands, and it seems only a matter of time before UPS and Federal Express come to the Out Islands in full force. UPS offers 24-hour delivery and customs clearance to North America on parcels sent from Nassau.

Stamps are available from many hotel desks and gift shops, as well as from bookstores. Many of these souvenir shops will mail your postcards as well, as will most hotels. Public **mailboxes** are very rare, and you should always hunt out the post office to mail your most important items. Bahamian postal rates for in-country service are 15 cents per half-ounce, 25 cents for each half-ounce thereafter. Remember that airmail packages and letters mailed from overseas to any Out Island probably go by airmail to Nassau, and then by boat to the specific destination, so mailing letters and parcels to Out Island destinations can be desperately slow.

Nassau's main post office on East Hill Street offers a **Post Restante** service. Letters may be addressed to you in Nassau in care of this general delivery service, and they will be held for three weeks. Letters should be marked "to be collected from the General Delivery desk". To receive a parcel in the Bahamas, you must collect it from Customs. Mail and telegrams can be received through American Express Travel Service in Nassau and Freeport by prior arrangement (☎1-800/221-7282).

Telephones

Communication by **telephone** in the Bahamas has grown by leaps and bounds in the last decade. In recent years, almost every hotel has installed a fax machine and email capability, and now direct dial long distance between North America and Nassau, Grand Bahama, the Abacos, Andros, Berry and Bimini Islands, Eleuthera, Harbour Island, Spanish Wells, Exumas, and Long Island is available. On the other hand, some of the more remote islands and cays still have limited phone service, often a single antiquated phone at the best hotel or lodge in the area. Much communication on these isolated cays is accomplished by radio.

Telephone services in the Bahamas are a monopoly of the government-owned **Bahamas Telecommunications Corporation** or BaTelCo (☎323-4911), with its national headquarters on John F. Kennedy Drive in Nassau. The centralized branch of BaTelCo is in downtown Nassau on East Street off Bay, and you'll find a local BaTelCo office in almost every town and settlement throughout the islands. **Local and inter-island** calls can be made from any hotel or BaTelCo office, as well as from a phone booth. There are many phone booths through the Bahamas, even in the most remote settlement on the Out Islands. Those phone booths that are operational – and there are many which aren't – often accept Bahamian 25 cent pieces to make local calls or to reach the international assistance operator. Old booths operate by first dialling the number and then, when a tone appears, putting in the coin. Many newer phone booths are geared to accept **calling cards** – purchased from any BaTelCo office – issued by BaTelCo in the denominations of $5,10, 20 and 50.

For **local calls**, simply dial the seven-digit phone number to be connected. For calls from one island to another, dial the **country-wide area code** plus 1 – ☎1-242 – and the seven-digit number. You'll need a BaTelCo calling card to make inter-island calls.

International calls may be made from many phone booths, from hotels, or from any BaTelCo office. Direct-dial international calls are offered by some phone booths, especially with calling cards (see below), and from some hotels. In general, calls to the US are $1 for the first minute, 80 cents thereafter. Calling Canada costs $1.25/1.15, while rates to Europe average $2.75/2. Costs to call Asia and Australia are considerably higher. Operator-assisted calls from hotels are expensive., and you can save a lot of money by calling home from abroad with a **telephone charge card** (see below for details). Also keep in mind that most toll-free 800 numbers cannot be accessed from the Bahamas. Numbers with 1-880 prefixes cost about $1 per minute to use.

Calling the Bahamas from overseas is easy. From the US or Canada, simply dial 1 plus the area code, ☎242, and the seven-digit local number. From all other countries, dial 001-242, plus the seven-digit number.

If you bring a **cell phone** into the Bahamas you may be charged a temporary customs fee, refunded on exit. However, your cell phone will not send or receive in the Bahamas without first registering it for use on a roaming cellular line through BaTelCo. You can get a roaming cell number in advance from Cable and Wireless Caribbean Cellular (☎1-800/262-8366 in the US; ☎1-800/567-8366 in Canada; ☎268/480-2628 elsewhere). Cable and Wireless also arranges for cellular service from yachts and other vessels. You can establish a system for billing your cellular service to your credit card.

Note that the ☎1-800 numbers listed throughout the guide can only be dialled from North America and not from the Bahamas themselves.

Calling cards

One of the most convenient ways of phoning home from abroad is via **telephone charge card** from your phone company

back home. Using a PIN number, you can make calls from most hotel, public and private phones that will be charged to your account. Since most major charge cards are free to obtain, it's certainly worth getting one at least for emergencies; enquire first, though, whether your destination is covered, and bear in mind that rates aren't necessarily cheaper than calling from a public phone.

In the **US** and **Canada**, AT&T, MCI, Sprint, Canada Direct and other North American long-distance companies all enable their customers to make credit-card calls while overseas, billed to your home number. Call your company's customer service line to find out if they provide service from Bahamas and, if so, what the toll-free access code is.

In **the UK** and **Ireland**, British Telecom (☎0800/345 144, ⓦwww.chargecard.bt .com) will issue free to all BT customers the BT Charge Card, which can be used in 116 countries. NTL (☎0500/100 505) issues its own Global Calling Card, which can be used in more than sixty countries abroad, though the fees cannot be charged to a normal phone bill.

To call **Australia** and **New Zealand** from overseas, phone charge cards such as Telstra Telecard or Optus Calling Card in Australia, and Telecom NZ's Calling Card can be used to make calls abroad, which are charged back to a domestic account or credit card. Apply to Telstra (☎1800/038 000), Optus (☎1300/300 937), or Telecom NZ (☎04/801 9000).

Useful Bahamian phone numbers

Operator, International Calls ☎0
Country-wide area code ☎242
Weather Hotline ☎915
Directory Assistance ☎916
Time ☎917
Emergencies/Police/Fire ☎919
(Nassau), ☎911 (Freeport/Lucaya)

Fax and email service

Fax service is available at most major hotels and resorts, from any BaTelCo office, and from many souvenir shops which sell stamps and postcards. Most hotels also have facilities for sending and receiving **email**, or for plugging in your laptop to an internet service. So far, there are very few internet cafés on the islands, though it's only a matter of time before they start popping up with greater frequency.

The media

The Bahamas have an independent if somewhat unsophisticated press that exercises its freedom to criticize the government without recrimination. You'll get most of your on-island information from just a few key sources.

Two daily **newspapers**, the *Nassau Guardian* and the *Tribune*, are available in New Providence, on Grand Bahama and in some of the larger settlements in the Out Islands, while Grand Bahama has its own daily, the *Freeport News*. All cover local, national and international news. The *Nassau Guardian* also publishes free monthly newspapers devoted to local news and events on several of the Out Islands. The *Bahamas Journal* is a national weekly published out of Nassau and available mainly in the larger centres. Foreign newspapers and magazines can be bought at newsstands in Freeport, Nassau and some of the more heavily touristed settlements in the Out Islands.

The government-owned Bahamas Broadcasting Corporation (BBC) is the major source of national news on **radio** and **television**. ZNS (for Zephyr Nassau Sunshine) Channel 13 broadcasts the national news on television at 7pm nightly. Most hotels have satellite or cable TV. The BBC ZNS-1, which broadcasts on AM 1540kHz and FM 107.1 MHz throughout the islands, is devoted to national and local news, talk shows focused on political issues and some music. There are also several commercial radio stations that play music of various genres.

To find all the world service frequencies around the world check out **BBC** (Ⓦwww.bbc.co.uk/worldservice), **Radio Canada** (Ⓦwww.rcinet.ca) or the **Voice of America** (Ⓦwww.voa.gov).

Opening hours, holidays and festivals

Regular business hours at government and private offices are Monday–Friday 9am–5pm. Regular banking hours are Monday–Thursday 9.30am–3pm and Friday 9.30am–5pm, although there are some exceptions to this rule in smaller branches on the Out Islands as noted throughout the guide. Shops are generally open from 9am or 10am to 5.30pm or 6pm Monday to Saturday. In most communities, at least one grocery store and gas station will open for business early Sunday morning – 7.30 or 8am to 10.30am – and then close for the rest of the day. Restaurants are generally open seven days a week, although some are closed one day a week and/or close for a couple of hours in the late afternoon.

Public holidays

The following are **public holidays** in the Bahamas, and government offices, banks, schools and shops are generally closed. Note that holidays that fall on a Saturday or Sunday are usually observed on the previous Friday or following Monday.
New Year's Day January 1
Good Friday the Friday before Easter

Easter Monday the Monday after Easter
Whit Monday seven weeks after Easter
Labour Day first Friday in June
Independence Day July 10
Emancipation Day first Monday in August
National Heroes Day (formerly Discovery Day) October 12
Christmas Day December 25
Boxing Day December 26

Special events

January
Junkanoo Parade, New Year's Day. Beginning at 1am in Nassau, with prizes for best floats awarded at 8am; see p.69 for more information. Several settlements throughout the Out Islands also hold Junkanoo festivities, notably in Staniel Cay in the Exumas.

February
Farmer's Cay Festival, first Friday of the month.
Combination Homecoming and regatta in the Exumas. Overnight boat excursions from Nassau are available. Contact Terry Bain (☏355-4006 or 2093) for details.

March
George Town Cruising Regatta, first Friday of the month.
A week-long party in the Exumas, drawing yachters from all over.

April
Out Island Regatta, late April. George Town's biggest regatta and the best in all the Out Islands; see p.251 for full details.

June
Goombay Summer Festival, month-long into August.
Rotating between Marsh Harbour and Treasure Cay in the Abacos, with concerts, food and dancing. Call ☏367-3067 for details.
Cat Island rake 'n' scrape Music Festival, late June.
New Bight comes alive for this annual event. Contact Eris Moncur (☏342-3030).

Pineapple Festival, early June. Three-day extravaganza in Gregory Town, Eleuthera, featuring pineapple -eating contest, music, games and a pineathelon – a combined swimming, running and bike race.

July
Goombay Festival, Fridays through July and August.
Festival throughout Andros featuring rake 'n' scrape bands, dances and lots of native cuisine. Contact Doris Adderley (☏368-2117) or Andros Tourism (☏368-2286) for details.

August
Rolleville Sailing Regatta, Emancipation Day weekend.
Great Exuma. Contact Kermit Rolle (☏345-0002).
Annual Cat Island Regatta, early August.
Every August this race draws hundreds of yachters to New Bight for Cat Island's biggest event of the year. Call Philip McPhee for details (☏368-2286).

December
Festivale Noelle, the first week of the month.
Freeport's Rand Nature Centre hosts this festival, featuring live music, wine tasting, arts and crafts. Call ☏352-5438.
Plymouth Historical Weekend, mid-December.
The Abacos' Green Turtle Cay hosts this event, a celebration of the settlement's Loyalist heritage with musical concerts, art exhibitions, drama and picnics.

Festivals

While the Bahamas are host to a variety of **special events** throughout the year (see box opposite), none is as big as Nassau's Junkanoo celebration, a city-wide carnival on Boxing Day (December 26) that is repeated on New Year's Day. Each year, the capital is engulfed in the music of this raucous street extravaganza, which is repeated on a smaller scale on several of the islands.

Few Bahamian festivities are as intimate as the annual **Homecoming** festivities on the Out Islands. These occur when prodigal sons and daughters return for a visit from Nassau and Freeport, where they are forced to seek their fortunes. Locals and visitors whoop it up for a few days with events that include street fairs, concerts, games, lots of food and often sailing races, and visitors are welcome to attend.

As a big-time sailing nation, with a long tradition in wooden boat building, the **annual regattas** held throughout the island chain are well worth attending. They are generally accompanied by music, food and other festivities on land. Some of the larger events are listed in the box opposite, while others are listed throughout the guide.

For detailed **information** on upcoming events, including regattas, Homecomings and special events, and for precise dates – which can change from year to year – contact the Ministry of Tourism (☎356-4231, ⓦwww.bahamas.com) or the Bahamas Out Islands Promotion Board (☎1-800/688-4752, ⓦwww.boipb.com). Detailed calendars of upcoming events are also found at ⓦwww.bahamas.com, ⓦwww.whatsonbahamas.com/calendar, ⓦwww.grand-bahama.com for events on Grand Bahama Island and ⓦwww.nassauparadiseisland.com for listings for Nassau and Paradise Island.

Ocean activities and outdoor pursuits

With great weather year-round, warm waters, miles of pristine beaches, and rich, teeming coral reefs surrounding the islands, the Bahamas offer endless amusement for outdoor enthusiasts, especially for divers and snorkellers.

Watersports

The Caribbean's vast, clear waters make the region a veritable playground for watersports. The quality of **diving** and **snorkelling** in many places is superb, thanks to the sheer abundance of marine life, and there are excellent opportunities for **sport fishing**, **water-skiing**, **windsurfing**, **parasailing**, **jet-skiing**, **kayaking**, **glass-bottomed boat trips** and **sailing**, most of which are usually offered by the major resorts for free. Resorts are also packed with operators offering dive trips and snorkelling excursions; the most reputable are listed throughout the guide.

Diving and snorkelling

The Bahamas are a **diving** and **snorkelling** idyll. The crystal-clear waters surrounding the islands are filled with luxurious multi-coloured coral reefs and spires, sea gardens, underwater mountainsides, canyons and valleys carpeted with sponges and corals, home to a multitude of tropical fish and other sea creatures. The Bahamas are also renowned for their blue-hole diving, especially in Andros or Long Island. In many places, notably Grand Bahama, dive operators offer several speciality excursions, including diving with dolphins or sharks, or around one of dozens of offshore wrecks. Most islands – with the exception of the undeveloped southernmost Bahamas – have at least one dive operator, and these are listed in the "Diving and watersports" sections of each chapter.

The most popular destinations for divers are Andros, the Exumas, Grand Bahama, Long Island and San Salvador. Operators charge around $70 for a two-tank dive and many offer all-inclusive packages in conjunction with a resort. Diving and snorkelling are great year-round in the Bahamas, but at their best in the summer months when the water is generally flat and still, although the heat topside can be intense.

If you wish to spend your entire time on or in the water, there are also a number of operators who offer **live aboard dive excursions**, on vessels ranging from purely functional but comfortable to luxury yachts serving gourmet meals. You live at sea for a few days, a week or more, travelling from dive site to dive site. These trips range $900–1600 per person for a week all-inclusive, and many can be chartered by a group.

If you have never dived before, the Bahamas make for a great location to learn and several dive operators offer complete PADI or NAUI **certification courses** for around $400 for three to five days of instruction, as noted in the chapters on each island. One of the most popular and well-established places to do this is at UNEXSO, the Underwater Explorers Society (☎373-1244, ☎1-800/992-3483 in the US or ☎954/351-9899, ℻373-1244, ⓦwww.unexso.com), on Grand Bahama. Note that if you want to do this, some operators, including UNEXSO, require you to complete some coursework at home using materials they will send to you in advance of your trip. If you just want a taste of the underwater world, you can take a resort course, which gives you some basic instruction and a shallow-water dive with an instructor for around $90. A number of dive operators also offer advanced certification courses for experienced divers.

Anybody can **snorkel**, and most dive operators rent snorkelling gear for $7–10 a day and offer guided excursions for around $30 for a half-day trip. It is amazing what you can see by just wading into the water

and floating over a promising dark clump of coral, let alone the magic that awaits in the magnificent reefs and sea gardens in the shallow waters surrounding the islands. Don't miss the chance.

Useful contacts for divers

Bahamas Diving Association
ⓦwww.bahamasdiving.com. This website contains listings of dive operators in the Bahamas, descriptions of some of the prime dive sites in the islands, including the wrecks that are certified for recreational use.

NAUI ☎813/628-6284 or 1-800/553-6284, ℻813/628-8253, ⓦwww.naui.org. The National Association of Underwater Instructors is geared mainly to professional divers, with information on courses and certification.

PADI ☎949/858-7234 or 1-800/729-7234, ℻949/858-7264, ⓦwww.padi.org. The Professional Association of Diving Instructors presents basic information on diving, courses, and certification as well as a dive-trip booking service. They also sell medical insurance for divers, who are often not covered under basic travel insurance policies.

Full-service diving trips

Blackbeard's Cruises ☎305/888-1226 or 1-800/327-9600, ℻305/884-4214, ⓦwww.blackbeard-cruises.com. Blackbeard's runs live-aboard scuba-diving trips on three 65ft sailboats with room for 22 passengers; on the sailboat *Cat Ppalu*, which sleeps twelve, and on the spanking new 102ft motorized catamaran the *AquaCat* with room for thirty. Details of dive sites, which include the Exuma Land and Sea Park are posted on the website. Seven-day/six-night all-inclusive trips departing Miami or Nassau cost US$874–1700 a week per person including tax, depending on the vessel. Longer and shorter expeditions and group charters available.

Bottom Time Adventures ☎1-800/234-8474, ℻954/920-5578, ⓦwww.bottomtime2.com. Features diving with wild dolphins and humpback whales, with accommodations aboard a luxury motorized catamaran sleeping fourteen divers. $1400 a week per person.

Nekton Diving Cruises ☎954/463-9324 or 1-800/899-6753, ⓦwww.nektoncruises.com. Offers dive trips on the *Nekton Pilot*, a catamaran like a small floating hotel, with en-suite cabins and a Jacuzzi on board. $1500–1600 a week.

Sea Dragon ☎954/522-0161, ⓦwww.seadragonbahamas.com. A 65ft research vessel that can accommodate eight in four double cabins. The *Sea Dragon* can be chartered for $10,200 a week meals included, or $1275 plus 4 percent tax per person on scheduled diving excursions.

Sea Fever ☏ 757/481-9116 or 1-800/443-3837, Ⓕ 757/481-2075, Ⓦ www.seafever.com. The *Sea Fever* offers dolphin encounter trips for $1400 a week, with trips to other dive sites throughout the Bahamas departing from Miami, Bimini, Nassau and Freeport for $1000 a week per person. The *Sea Fever* is a 90ft diesel-powered craft with seven staterooms. Group charters and individual bookings available.

Fishing

Fishing is a way of life as well as a pastime in the Bahamas, and the islands are a fabled destination for sport fishers, particularly for bonefishing on shallow sapphire and white sand flats, reef fishing for snapper and grouper and for deep-sea fishing for big-game fish. There are dedicated fishing lodges catering to serious fishers with guides, boats and equipment for hire in the Biminis, Exumas, Andros, Grand Bahama and Long Island. There are also fishing charter outfits on many islands, as listed throughout the guide. You must have a **permit** to fish in the Bahamas if on your own ($25 per trip, $150 yearly), obtainable at the Customs Office at your Port of Entry or from the Department of Fisheries, PO Box N-3028, Nassau (☏ 393-1777).

Sea kayaking

Sea kayaking is an increasingly popular way to explore the Bahamas, and outfitters offer day-trips and overnight paddling and camping excursions in the Abacos, on Grand Bahama and in the Exumas. These trips explore the coastline, mangrove-fringed tidal creeks or hop between sandy beaches on the cays that surround the larger islands. In addition, many seaside resorts have recreational – as opposed to excursion – kayaks for guests to paddle about for a few hours.

The prime destination for sea kayakers is the Exuma Cays, a forty-mile-long string of small, mainly uninhabited islands set in shallow turquoise waters. In the middle of this island chain is the serenely beautiful Exuma

Land and Sea Park (see p.265), a wilderness area encompassing 176 square miles of pristine water and twenty-odd islets rimmed with fine white sand for camping. Several outfitters offer guided kayaking excursions in the Exuma Cays, as listed below.

Kayaking outfitters

Abaco Outback Ⓦ www.abacooutback.com, VHF Ch 16 "Abaco Outback". Based in Marsh Harbour, this outfitter offers day-trips exploring tidal creeks in the Abacos.
Ecosummer Expeditions ☏ 1-800/465-8884, Ⓦ www.ecosummer.com. Offers one- and two-week guided sea-kayaking expeditions in the Exuma Cays, including the Exuma Land and Sea Park.
Ibis Tours PO Box 208, Pelham, NY 10803 ☏ 1-800/525 9411 in the US or 914/738 5334, Ⓔ info@ibistours.com. Runs guided expeditions through the Exuma Land and Sea Park.
Kayak Nature Tours ☏ 373-2485, Ⓦ www.bahamasvg.com/kayak. Runs paddling excursions on Grand Bahama, offers both day-trips and overnight camping expeditions.
North Carolina Outward Bound 2582 Riceville Rd, Asheville, NC 28805 ☏ 828/299-3366, Ⓕ 299-3928, Ⓦ www.ncobs.org. Offers an eight-day sea-kayaking course in the southern Exuma Cays.
Starfish The Exuma Activity Center in George Town ☏ 1-877/398-6222, Ⓕ 336-3033, VHF Ch 16 "Starfish", Ⓦ www.kayakbahamas.com. Starfish offers kayaking day-trips and multi-day camping and paddling expeditions through the southern Exuma Cays.

Sailing

Sailing is an integral part of Bahamian culture, and the annual calendar of sailing regattas in the islands is quite full (the more major annual regattas are listed under "Festivities", p.36). Everybody is welcome to come and watch and partake in the music, eating, drinking, and other festivities that accompany the races. Some race events are open to visiting yachts.

The Bahamas, especially the Abacos and the Exumas, are favoured destinations for yacht cruisers and the harbours and anchorages in the islands are filled with visiting pleasure craft throughout the winter season. If the idea appeals to you, but you don't have your own vessel or a clue how to pilot one if you had it, see 'Getting there' p.15 for a list of companies chartering yachts for excursions through the Bahamas.

Many of the larger resorts have small sailboats, sunfish or hobiecats available for guest use, and there are boat rental agencies in several communities, as listed in the chapters on each island.

Other outdoor activities

While the sea is definitely the star attraction in the Bahamas, there are plenty of activities on dry land to add some variety to your days.

The Bahamas attract serious **golfers** with nine championship-grade courses. There are three on New Providence and five on Grand Bahama, most of which have undergone major re-landscaping and upgrading in the last couple of years, plus one on Treasure Cay in the Abacos. Greens fees for eighteen holes range from $70 to $225 including cart and you can rent clubs for $20–50 a day. All of the Bahamas' major golf courses are part of resorts, which offer all-inclusive golfing packages; please see individual resort reviews for details.

Horseback riding is also available for an hour or two on Grand Bahama, New Providence and Harbour Island. Stables offering trail rides through forests and along the beach are listed in the "Outdoor activities" sections on these chapters.

The Bahamas are pretty flat and not known as a **hiking** destination, and Mount Alvernia on Cat Island, the tallest peak in the archipelago, is only 206ft high. Despite that, there are walking trails ranging from a few hundred yards to three or four miles in length on several of the islands as well as miles of empty beach to walk. Good destinations for day hikes are Warderick Wells Cay in the Exuma Land and Sea Park, where there are seven miles of walking trails crisscrossing the island; Abaco National Park with trails along the shore and through the forest; the Mount Alvernia Hermitage on Cat Island; and the short walking paths through Lucayan National Park on Grand Bahama.

Sunny weather and a generally flat topography make for easy **cycling** in the Bahamas. As spectacular as the ocean views are, however, island roads often cut through long, monotonous expanses of scrubby bush. If you want to do a lot of cycling, head for Long Island, where there is little traffic and particularly beautiful and varied scenery along the Queen's Highway. Many resorts have single-gear bicycles for guest use, but if you have serious peddling in mind, bring your own bike as well as a tyre patch kit and spare inner tubes.

Eco-tour vacations

The Bahamas offer several unique eco-tour style holidays, ranging from assisting marine biologists conducting scientific research to learning about Bahamian culture in its ancient or modern forms.

Deadman's Reef Archeological Dig ☎352-5438. Each summer, the Grand Bahama Branch of the Bahamas National Trust and Wake Forest University run a four-week dig at the site of a Lucayan settlement. Living expenses are covered for volunteers (16 and over), but transportation to the Bahamas is not. Call the BNT at the Rand Nature Centre for further information. See p.109 for details.

Dolphin Research ☎1-800/326-7491, ⓦwww.oceanic-society.org. Since 1984, the Oceanic Society, a nonprofit marine research organization based in San Francisco, California has sponsored field research on dolphin behaviour in the waters off Grand Bahama.

Earthwatch Institute 3 Clock Tower Place, Suite 100, Box 75, Maynard, MA ☎978/461-0081 or 44(0) 1865 318838 in the UK, ⓕ978/461-2332, ⓦwww.earthwatch.org. Earthwatch accepts volunteers to assist scientists on several ongoing research projects in the Bahamas. Current projects include the Bahamian Reef Survey which is examining the impact of coral bleaching in the waters around San Salvador Island; the coastal ecology of southern Eleuthera; and long-term research on dolphins and whales near Sandy Point in the Abacos. Trips are offered several times throughout the year and cost from $1350 for one week.

Exuma Land and Sea Park ☎359-1821, ⓔexumapark@aol.com, VHF Ch 16 "Exuma Park". In the remote Exuma Cays, the park runs a volunteer programme for those with an interest in environmental conservation. See p.265 for details.

Ocean Explorer ☎561/288-4262 or 1-800/338-9383, ⓦwww.oceanexplorerinc.com. The *Ocean Explorer* is a 55ft dive boat with room for up to four passengers to accompany researchers on expeditions to explore blue holes, wrecks and reefs as well as to observe and interact with wild dolphins;

$2000 per person per week. The dive boat is also available for charter.

People to People ☎ 356-0435. The Ministry of Tourism co-ordinates this programme, which connects visitors interested in learning more about life in the Bahamas with local volunteers on several islands for a meal or a community get-together.

! Crime and personal safety

The crime rate in the Bahamas as a whole is extremely low, and in resort areas as well as on the Out Islands, crime is rare. Nevertheless, when travelling in and around Nassau, Freeport, Cable Beach and Paradise Island, you should exercise the same caution you would in visiting any major tourist area. The only significant dangers in tourist areas are from petty crime like pickpocketing and theft, or from involvement in drugs.

During the 1980s and early 1990s, the Bahamas suffered a period of turmoil connected with the drug trade, particularly cocaine shipped from Colombia through the Out Islands. At the same time, gun violence became somewhat common in the suburban Over-the-Hill neighbourhoods of Nassau as rival gangs and drug dealers had showdowns over turf and money. By the early 1990s, however, the Bahamian government began co-operating with the American Drug Enforcement Agency to crackdown on drug smuggling, an operation that saw DEA agents swarm over places like Bimini. While drug smuggling is still a problem in the islands, with boats hauling loads of marijuana and cocaine to the coast of Florida and being chased and followed by Coast Guard planes and boats, the trade has diminished considerably. Gun violence in Nassau's neighbourhoods has taken a concomitant drop. Serious crime on the Out Islands is almost unknown.

Other than normal precautions against pickpockets and petty thieves in resort areas and on casino floors, you should take care to avoid Nassau's rougher neighbourhoods south of downtown, particularly after dark. Women travelling alone should avoid Nassau's nearly deserted streets after dark – though after 6pm, there is almost nothing to do in downtown Nassau anyway. If you wish to travel to a nightclub, pub or bar near downtown Nassau, take a taxi.

Always lock the doors of a rental car, and never leave valuables in plain view. If you must take valuables along, lock them in your trunk and never leave them in a hotel room. Most hotels provide a safety deposit box in their lobbies. Use it.

Drugs are an absolute no-no in the Bahamas. The penalties for possession and use of illegal drugs are severe. It will make no difference that you are a foreign citizen, and prison sentences can be long.

Harassment is not really a problem in the Bahamas, and for the most part there is no macho culture making life unpleasant for women travelling alone (see "Women travellers", p.45). You will not encounter panhandlers or beggars.

The Bahamian **police** are both professional and helpful. A police station is located in every settlement, usually near the commissioner's office or other government buildings. See the "Listings" section in each chapter for police station locations.

Shopping

Offering savings of 30–50 percent below international retail prices, duty-free shopping is a popular way to find bargains for luxury goods like jewellery, perfume, watches, china, crystal and liquor, with the tourist zones of Nassau and Freeport providing particularly good buying opportunities.

Nassau's Bay Street is famous for its **Straw Market**, offering a wide array of mats, baskets, hats, dresses, T-shirts, and handcrafted items at bargain prices. While many items at the market are cheap imports, others may be genuine, so a close inspection of the merchandise is usually worthwhile. There are also large straw markets in Freeport and Port Lucaya on Grand Bahama Island selling a mix of locally made straw work and cheap manufactured knockoffs. While straw market purchases are subject to negotiation, **bargaining** is not a typical Bahamian custom. In small shops in many settlements in the Out Islands, you can buy handmade straw work directly from local artisans.

The Bahamas are also known for their **Androsian batik** fabrics made by a small operation in Andros Town on Andros. Although the factory is fascinating to visit, **batik** items are available at many outlets in Nassau, Freeport, and major Out Islands like the Abacos and Eleuthera.

Cuban cigars and **local art** are often worthwhile purchases as well, with Bahamian painters, water-colourists, wood carvers and jewellers creating original works for sale in **galleries and giftshops** in Nassau and Freeport and throughout the Out Islands, as noted in the chapters on the various islands.

Travellers with disabilities

The Bahamas are gradually upgrading public facilities to meet international standards of access for people with physical disabilities, but travelling in the islands still poses some (not insurmountable) challenges for disabled visitors. Public transport is not adapted to accommodate wheelchairs, and broken pavement or nonexistent sidewalks can make getting around somewhat difficult. Few older multistorey buildings are wheelchair-accessible, though the newer resorts in Nassau and Freeport are equipped with ramps and elevators with braille signage and bells.

The organizations listed below can offer advice and information on the facilities of hotels and cruise lines in the Bahamas.

Contacts for travellers with disabilities

In the Bahamas

Bahamas Council for the Handicapped ☎ 322- 4260.

Bahamas Association for the Physically Disabled ☎ 322-2393, ℱ 322-7984. Provides a minibus service for disabled visitors and offers guided tours of Nassau and New Providence.

In the US and Canada

Access-Able ⓦ www.access-able.com. Online resource for travellers with disabilities.
Directions Unlimited 123 Green Lane, Bedford Hills, NY 10507 ☎ 914/241-1700 or 1-800/533-

5343. Tour operator specializing in custom tours for people with disabilities.

Mobility International USA 451 Broadway, Eugene, OR 97401, voice and TDD ☎541/343-1284, ✆www.miusa.org. Information and referral services, access guides, tours and exchange programmes. Annual membership $35 (includes quarterly newsletter).

Society for the Advancement of Travelers with Handicaps (SATH) 347 5th Ave, New York, NY 10016 ☎212/447-7284, ✆www.sath.org. Nonprofit educational organization that has actively represented travellers with disabilities since 1976.

Twin Peaks Press Box 129, Vancouver, WA 98661 ☎360/694-2462 or 1-800/637-2256, ✆www.twinpeak.virtualave.net. Publisher of the *Directory of Travel Agencies for the Disabled* (US$19.95), listing more than 370 agencies worldwide; *Travel for the Disabled* (US$19.95); the *Directory of Accessible Van Rentals* (US$12.95) and *Wheelchair Vagabond* (US$19.95), loaded with personal tips.

Wheels Up! ☎1-888/389-4335, ✆www.wheelsup.com. Provides discounted airfare, tour and cruise prices for disabled travellers; also publishes a free monthly newsletter and has a comprehensive website.

In the UK and Ireland

Irish Wheelchair Association Blackheath Drive, Clontarf, Dublin 3 ☎01/833 8241, ✆833 3873, ✆iwa@iol.ie. Useful information provided about travelling abroad with a wheelchair.

Tripscope Alexandra House, Albany Rd, Brentford, Middlesex TW8 0NE ☎0845/7585 641, ✆www.justmobility.co.uk/tripscope, ✆tripscope@cableinet.co.uk. This registered charity provides a national phone information service offering free advice on UK and international transport for those with a mobility problem.

In Australia and New Zealand

ACROD (Australian Council for Rehabilitation of the Disabled) PO Box 60, Curtin, ACT 2605 ☎02/6282 4333; Suite 103, 1st Floor, 1–5 Commercial Rd, Kings Grove 2208 ☎02/9554 3666. Provides lists of travel agencies and tour operators for people with disabilities.

Disabled Persons Assembly 4/173–175 Victoria St, Wellington, New Zealand ☎04/801 9100. Resource centre with lists of travel agencies and tour operators for people with disabilities.

Gay and lesbian travellers

Gay and lesbian travellers are unlikely to encounter overt discrimination in the Bahamas, where citizens generally subscribe to a "live and let live" philosophy of life. However, open displays of affection by same-sex couples are apt to draw attention and occasional hostility. On several occasions in recent years fundamentalist Christian preachers have led demonstrations against gay cruise ships visiting Nassau. The prime minister has made subsequent speeches denouncing homophobia in Bahamian society, although there remains no legal protection from discrimination in Bahamian law.

Sexual activity between consenting adults in private is beyond the purview of the state. However, sexual activity in a public place is an offence punishable by up to twenty years in prison.

Contacts for gay and lesbian travellers

In the Bahamas

Bahamas Gays and Lesbians Against

Discrimination (BGLAD) ☎327-1247, ✆bahamianglad@yahoo.com. A support and advocacy group with a phone hotline open 9am to midnight.

Hope TEA ☎328-1816. A support group and phone hotline 9pm–midnight. Mon (lesbians), Tues (transvestites/transsexuals) and Wed (gay men).

In the US and Canada

Damron Company PO Box 422458, San Francisco CA 94142 ☎415/255-0404 or 1-

800/462-6654 ⓦwww.damron.com. Publisher of the *Men's Travel Guide*, a pocket-sized yearbook full of listings of hotels, bars, clubs and resources for gay men; the *Women's Traveler*, which provides similar listings for lesbians; and *Damron Accommodations*, which provides detailed listings of over 1000 accommodations for gays and lesbians worldwide. All of these titles are offered at a discount on the website.

Gay Tours and Vacations ⓣ877/901-8687, ⓦwww.gaytoursandvacations.com. Offers all-inclusive holidays in the Bahamas and elsewhere.

International Gay & Lesbian Travel Association 4331 N Federal Hwy, Suite 304, Fort Lauderdale, FL 33308 ⓣ954/776-2626 or 1-800/448-8550, ⓦwww.iglta.org. Trade group that can provide a list of gay- and lesbian-owned or -friendly travel agents, accommodation and other travel businesses.

Pied Piper Travel and Cruises ⓣ212/239-2412 or 1-800/874-7312, ⓕ212/239-2275, ⓦwww.gaygroupcruises.com. Offers Caribbean cruises that call at Nassau for an exclusively gay/lesbian clientele.

Sailboat Charters of Miami ⓣ305/772-4221, ⓔcaptaindavid@sailboat-charters.com. A gay-friendly company offering day-trips, weekend or seven-day sailboat charters to the Bahamas including excursions for gay passengers only. US$125 a person per day to a maximum of six passengers for all-inclusive charters; bareboat with skipper also available at reduced rate if you want to cook for yourself.

In the UK

ⓦwww.gaytravel.co.uk Online gay and lesbian travel agent, offering good deals on all types of holiday. Also lists gay- and lesbian-friendly hotels around the world.

Dream Waves Redcot High St, Child Okeford, Blandford DT22 8ET ⓣ01258/861 149, ⓔdreamwaves@aol.com. Specializes in exclusively gay holidays, including summer sun packages.

Madison Travel 118 Western Rd, Hove, East Sussex BN3 1DB ⓣ01273/202 532, ⓦwww.madisontravel.co.uk. Established travel agents specializing in packages to gay- and lesbian-friendly mainstream destinations, and also to gay/lesbian destinations.

In Australia and New Zealand

Gay and Lesbian Travel ⓦwww.galta.com.au. Directory and links for gay and lesbian travel worldwide.

Gay Travel ⓦwww.gaytravel.com. The site for trip planning, bookings, and general information about international travel.

Parkside Travel 70 Glen Osmond Rd, Parkside, SA 5063 ⓣ08/8274 1222, ⓔparkside@herveyworld.com.au. Gay travel agent associated with local branch of Hervey World Travel; all aspects of gay and lesbian travel worldwide.

Silke's Travel 263 Oxford St, Darlinghurst, NSW 2010 ⓣ02/8347 2000 or 1800/807 860, ⓦwww.silkes.com.au. Long-established gay and lesbian specialist, with the emphasis on women's travel.

Tearaway Travel 52 Porter St, Prahan, VIC 3181 ⓣ03/9510 6644, ⓦwww.tearaway.com. Gay-specific business dealing with international and domestic travel.

Women travellers

A relatively safe and hassle-free destination for women travellers, incidents of sexual assault are comparatively rare in the Bahamas, while on the Out Islands crime rates in general are so low that few people even lock their cars or houses. It is nevertheless wise to stick to the common-sense rules of not walking alone at night or accepting rides from strangers, especially in the cities of Nassau and Freeport.

Bahamians in general treat each other and visitors with kindness and respect, and while a woman travelling alone may attract some unsolicited male attention, a polite "no thanks" is usually sufficient to reclaim your privacy. Other tourists, of course, come in all stripes and degrees of offensiveness. There is a Women's Crisis Centre (☎328-0922) located on Shirley Street in Nassau.

Directory

Airport departure tax Every traveller departing the Bahamas by plane must pay an airport departure tax of US$15 (US$18 if you are leaving from Freeport). You pay the tax at the departure desk of your airline.

Children While many people see the Bahamas as an adult-oriented, honeymoon and cruise-ship destination, an increasing number of resorts cater for children, offering kids' meals, activities and watersports. Be sure to check with your accommodation about bringing children as some hotels prefer couples-only. When children are catered for, however, facilities can range widely from the odd banana boat rides, evening disco, afternoon tennis match or tortoise race to comprehensive activity programmes involving nature walks, arts and crafts, pool games and even field trips.

Electricity Bahamian current is 120volt/60cycle, compatible with all US applicances. Electrical outlets are the common two- or three-pronged outlets common in the US and Canada.

Emergencies Police and firemen can be summoned anywhere in the Bahamas by dialling ☎919, or by dialling ☎911 in Freeport/Lucaya. An ambulance may be summoned in Nassau by dialling ☎322-2221; in Freeport/Lucaya the number is ☎352-2689. In the event of an emergency at sea, call the Bahamas Air-Sea Rescue Association at ☎322-3877, VHF Ch 16. The Nassau Marine Operator is at VHF Ch 27 or 2198 SSB.

Film Nassau, Freeport and Marsh Harbour are well stocked with camera stores that sell a limited range of cameras, lenses, filters and film.Film is expensive in the islands, and on some remote Out Islands, not available at all, so purchase your film in advance.

Hurricanes The hurricane season begins around June or July, lasts six months or so and is most threatening between August and October. If a hurricane watch is posted, it means hurricane conditions are possible within the next 36 hours; if a warning is posted, conditions are expected usually

45

within 24 hours. Advice about dealing with watches and warnings is usually posted in hotels and guesthouses, but should you be away from your accommodation, get indoors and stay away from windows. Be aware, too, that a tornado will often follow a hurricane.

Laundry Coin-operated laundromats are common in Nassau and in Freeport/Lucaya. Dry-cleaners are also common in Nassau, Freeport and in the major settlements of the Out Islands. Many hotels and resorts have coin-operated laundry facilities as a service to guests, or will do laundry and dry-cleaning for an added charge.In every small settlement, someone usually takes in laundry at their homes.

Measurements Bahamian measurements are made in the British imperial system, which uses inches, feet and miles, along with ounces, pounds and tons. Road maps show distances in miles and speed limits are denominated in miles per hour. All liquid measurements are in standard pints, quarts and gallons, which includes measurements at the gas pump and pub.

Public toilets Public toilets in the Bahamas are nearly unknown. Saunders Beach, the public beach in Nassau on West Bay Street, has a public toilet that is suitable for men and women to change into a bathing suit, but little else. Almost all hotels won't mind a visitor slipping into one of its toilets in an emergency.

Time The Bahamas is in North America's Eastern Standard Time Zone (the same as New York and Atlanta) and five hours behind Greenwich Mean Time (GMT).

Tipping Nearly all restaurants in the Bahamas add a 15 percent gratuity to the food bill as a tip for the servers. Some hotels also include a gratuity on the bill for their staff, though this is less common. In smaller Bahamian restaurants and bars, there is no commonly accepted tradition of tipping, but where a gratuity has not been added to your bill,and you have received good service from a single waiter or waitress, a tip is always good manners. Visitors who stay at condos, villas, or self-catering units should tip the grounds staff or others who look after the property.

Guide

Guide

New Providence and Paradise Island

CHAPTER 1 # Highlights

✳ **Horse-drawn tours of Old Nassau** Catch a surrey at Rawson Square and get a guided thirty-minute tour of Old Nassau's stately colonial architecture. See p.63

✳ **The Junkanoo Rush** Join the crowds in Nassau on Boxing Day (December 26) or New Year's Day and see the marching bands, dancers and the whole colourful pageant of Nassau's biggest celebration. See p.69

✳ **The Straw Market** The handcrafted baskets, carved mahogany dolphins and Voodoo charms at the busy Straw Market offer some of the best shopping in the islands. See p.70

✳ **Fort Fincastle** The short climb up Bennet's Hill to the fort and its adjoining

Water Tower repays visitors with breathtaking views of Nassau Harbour, Paradise Island and the Atlantic Ocean. See p.73

✳ **Arawak Cay** On weekends on this islet just west of downtown Nassau, you can listen to local music and enjoy a fresh conch salad, then hop over to nearby Crystal Cay Marine Park for the views of sunset from its 100ft observation towers. See p.75

✳ **Atlantis Hotel** The highlight of this garishly fun resort – seemingly shipped straight from Vegas – is the Predator Lagoon and Reef, a massive aquarium filled with sharks and reef fish that is visible through an underwater tunnel. See p.90

New Providence and Paradise Island

N EW PROVIDENCE ISLAND, and its smaller sister PARADISE, form the heart of the Bahamian archipelago. The larger island is home to over 200,000 (more than two-thirds of the nation's population), its capital Nassau and most of the country's banking, educational and tourist institutions. Tourism is a major industry here, and nearly two million people visit New Providence and Paradise Island annually.

Twenty-one miles from east to west and a mere seven miles north to south at its widest, the island can be covered easily by car, taxi or bus in day. Crowded, busy Nassau, which hugs the northeast shore of the island and spreads far inland, is centred on the shopping arcade of Bay Street. Old Nassau boasts some of the finest British colonial architecture in the Caribbean, the vibrant Straw Market and a wide range of restaurants, yet the resort life is never far. Indeed, just across the Nassau Harbour is Paradise Island, a glitzy tourist enclave that includes the mega-resort *Atlantis*, as well as a warren of hotels, shops and beaches connected by narrow motorways and paths.

Much of the eastern half of New Providence is covered by unattractive sprawl. To the west of Nassau, however, along beautiful stretches of beach, lies a strip of hotels called Cable Beach, home to exclusive resorts, private homes, condominiums and time-shares. The western shore, which stretches for twelve miles from Cable Beach to Clifton Point, contains the most secluded and peaceful sections of the island, though many of the beaches are private, including the one at super-exclusive Lyford Cay.

The under-visited south shore has few beaches of any note, and even fewer hotels. It does, however, boast Coral Harbour, which has become the centre for dive- and snorkel-related activity on New Providence, while the tiny village Adelaide is a refreshing change from urban Nassau. Much of the central interior of New Providence is marshy scrub that is largely unvisited except with a few local eco-tourism outfitters that operate combination biking-kayaking tours.

Some history

Years before the first package tour, the first foreign visitor to the island, William Sayle, sailed south from Bermuda in 1648 and gave it his own name

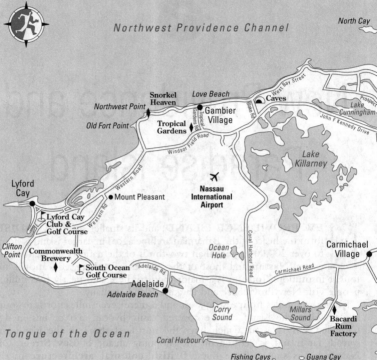

before moving on to Eleuthera to found a doomed colony. Sayle's Island possessed a harbour, protected on the north by Paradise Island and its surrounding reefs, on which **Charles Town**, modern-day Nassau, was established in 1666.

The winds of war that swept across Europe in the seventeenth and eighteenth centuries were keenly felt in Charles Town, which was simultaneously claimed by England and Spain. With England, Spain and France almost constantly at war with one another, the seas were open to pirates and privateers, who made the town a "stinking hole" of dirt streets, brothels and taverns. In 1684 Spaniards attacked Charles Town and plundered it in retribution for constant attacks launched by pirates against their shipping. The town, renamed in 1695 in honour of the Dutch prince of Orange-Nassau, who became King William III of England that year, was sacked again in 1703 by a combined French and Spanish fleet.

The first royal governor arrived in 1718 to find Nassau in shambles. **Governor Woodes-Rogers**, a tough English aristocrat set every available man to work cleaning up the place, draining mosquito-breeding swamps and reconstructing Nassau. Despite all Woodes-Rogers' work, Nassau remained a haven for pirates like Edward "Blackbeard" Teach and Henry Jennings of the 1720s, and **wrecking and salvaging** had become a central activity in Nassau as well (see box on p.54).

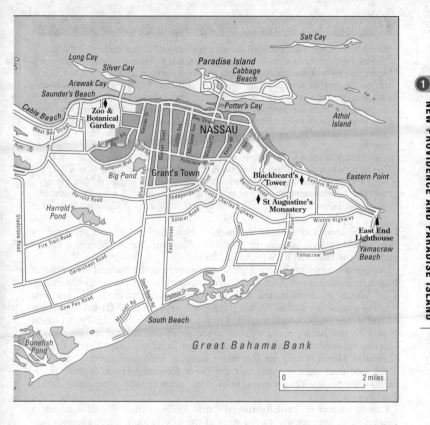

This rebellious period survived until the arrival in 1760 of **Governor William Shirley**, who laid out streets, drained the remaining swamps and organized plantations. The American Revolution further boosted the city's fortunes as former pirates and privateers turned to running the English blockade to trade with North America. At the same time, many **Loyalists** from America fled to Nassau, bringing with them new energy and a new architectural style. Additional streets were laid out, docks were built, a new jail and workhouse constructed, and a roofed market put up for trade.

Arriving with the Loyalists was the dissolute **Earl of Dunmore**, who in 1787 became royal governor and set up residence in Nassau. Dunmore surrounded himself in Nassau with thieves and hangers-on, and promptly went on a spending spree that nearly bankrupted the treasury. His legacy includes forts Fincastle and Charlotte, yet only the outbreak of the Napoleonic Wars saved him from an investigation that would have exposed his corrupt ways.

Nassau soon became a slow-paced town where Loyalist planters lived languid lives, amassed small fortunes and introduced **slavery**. While less an institution in Bahamian life than it was in the Caribbean's sugar islands because of poor soil, slavery soon became a part of Nassau's history, and at least 4000 slaves inhabited New Providence in the late eighteenth century. Most of them were brought over from sub-Saharan West Africa, particularly from modern Nigeria,

❶

Salvagers in New Providence

Since 1648, when the Eleutheran Adventurers (see p.213) first came to Bahamian shores, Bahamians have been **salvaging ships** and their cargoes wrecked on the rocks and reefs of the shallow seas that surround the islands. One of the first acts of the Eleutherans was to establish *Articles and Orders* governing the wrecking industry. As trade increased in the islands, and between North America and England, Nassau's wrecking industry took off, and, following 1815, many in town had wrecking as their second calling. At the call of "Wrack Ashore", farmers dropped their hoes, fishermen their nets and carpenters their hammers to board a wrecking vessel.

By 1856, 302 ships out of Nassau were licensed to engage in salvage, and nearly ten percent of the population held individual salvage licences. The bulk of salvage went through Nassau's Vendue House, with the proceeds at auction divided among the government, warehousemen, agents, wreckers and, finally, if lucky, the owners.

Dahomey, Togo and Ghana. In 1804, the last slave sales were recorded in Nassau, and in 1833 parliament passed the Abolition Statute. Slavery formally ended in the Bahamas in September 1834.

During the nineteenth century, Nassau's economic life danced to a tune of North American events. Construction in Nassau boomed during the American Civil War as residents traded with the rebellious American South. The first wealthy tourists arrived in Nassau during the heyday of the **Royal Victorian Hotel** in the 1870s, which was filled to capacity every winter. In 1900, tycoon Henry Flagler, having made millions in real estate and railroad construction in Florida, turned his attention to Nassau and built the magnificent **British Colonial Hotel**, which set the resort standard here until burning down in 1922. Less than eight months later, the **New Colonial Hotel** took its place, built, some say, with revenues from rum running and smuggling during Prohibition.

Thanks in part to **Prohibition**, the mid-1920s witnessed a land boom in Nassau, with large estates to the west of the city being built. Air service was established between Nassau and Florida in 1929 – just in time for the Great Depression, although World War II quickly revived Nassau's fortunes. In 1950, Englishman **Sir Stafford Sands** arrived with the task of expanding tourism, which the concomitant availability of air conditioning made viable. The stage was set for the construction of the first large post-war hotels, the **Emerald Beach** in 1954, the laying out of Nassau's **International Airport** in 1957 and, finally, the dredging of a deepwater harbour during the 1960s. Sands liked to predict that Nassau would host one million tourists by 1970, a number that was reached two years earlier. One wonders what Blackbeard would think of his ramshackle town now.

Arrival

Regardless of their final destination, a great percentage of visitors to the Bahamas fly into **Nassau International Airport** (☎377-7281), located a pleasant ten-mile ride from downtown Nassau in west-central New Providence, while most domestic travellers fly through it on their way from one place to another in the outer islands. The number of flights in and out of Nassau each day is staggering, with jets and turboprops arriving from Miami (not half an hour away), Fort Lauderdale, West Palm Beach and Orlando on a regular basis, as well as from New York, Montreal, Toronto and London among others. In the airport arrivals area, you will find rental car agencies (see p.63 for details), as well as a post office, a bank and Bahamasair's offices. Unless you've rented a car at the airport, **taxis**, lined just outside the arrival gate, are the only way into Nassau, Cable Beach or Paradise Island. The fare into downtown is $18 for one person, and should be agreed to in advance.

The **Paradise Island Airport** is a small jetport serving commuter aircraft, with short runways and limited facilities. Though renovations were under way at the time of writing, the airport will never serve large commercial aircraft, meaning most visitors fly into Nassau's much larger airport and shell out $26 for the taxi ride over, unless their hotel provides free transfers. Puddle-jumper services to Paradise Island Airport are run mainly by Paradise Island Express (℡1-800/7-BAHAMA), with flights from several cities in Florida as well as from Freeport, and Pan Am Air Bridge (℡1-800/424-2557), with a daily service from Miami.

Cruise ships arriving in Nassau dock at Prince George Wharf at the foot of Rawson Square, within walking distance of all the sights and shopping in Old Nassau.

Information

Tourist information is readily obtainable in Nassau, though none of the information centres is equipped to make bookings for accommodation or tours. The Ministry of Tourism operates an understaffed booth at the airport (daily 8am–midnight; ℡377-6833 or 377-8606), as well as two information centres within Nassau itself. The main information booth is located on the north side of Rawson Square (Mon–Fri 8.30am–5pm, Sat 8.30am–4pm, Sun 8.30am–2pm; ℡326-9781). It has a stock of maps and brochures and is manned by a friendly, but often overworked, tourism employee. The smaller information centre is centrally located adjacent to the Straw Market on Bay Street (Mon–Fri 9am–5pm; ℡356-7591) and is likewise a good spot to nab maps and brochures. If you're utterly confused upon arrival, try phoning the **Tourism Help Line** (Mon–Sat 9am–5.30pm, Sun & holidays 9am–11.30pm; ℡325-4161), only designed to answer brief, relatively simple inquiries.

There are no Ministry of Tourism booths on **Paradise Island**, as the island is self-contained and hardly confusing for visitors. The slick tourist magazine *Paradise Islander* is available all over the island, coming as standard equipment in every hotel room.

You can also look for the ubiquitous and free tabloids and handouts on such topics as *Where to Dine, Where to Shop*, and the best of the bunch, *What's On* and *Tourist News*, each of which contains maps, schedules of events and discount coupons.

Sports and outdoor activities

Surrounded on all sides by a lovely coral reef and splendid shallow turquoise ocean, New Providence and Paradise Island are a water-lover's heaven. Experienced **divers** gravitate to New Providence's South Beach area for its

Beaches on New Providence and Paradise Island

The **beaches** of New Providence and Paradise Island have gained a worldwide following of sunbathers and swimmers. The city beach for Nassau, the **Western Esplanade**, extends roughly from the *British Colonial Hotel* in the east all the way to *Crystal Cay* in the west. While sometimes roughed up with garbage and litter, the beach itself is pleasant enough, and provides hotel guests on nearby West Bay Street with a convenient opportunity to diverge from poolside lounging. There isn't any snorkelling to be had here, but the beach is conveniently stocked with food vendors and restrooms.

Just past the Western Esplanade is **Saunders Beach**, a local favourite that stretches for perhaps half a mile beneath casuarina trees, imported from Australia to provide an erosion barrier but which now pour needles down onto the sand. Saunders is a weekend hangout for locals, who set up barbecue rigs and drink beer, but is still less crowded than Cable Beach and those on Paradise Island.

Further west sits **Cable Beach**, perhaps the most famous of the New Providence beaches. The four-mile-long strip is fronted by massive resort hotels, chopped into zones of influence and spheres of operation, mostly on behalf of hotel operators and vendors. In the east, the water is rough and rocky, growing calmer the farther west you go. On most days, the beach is a hawker's nest.

About seven miles west of Nassau on West Bay lies small and secluded **Cave Beach**, right at Rock Point where the main road turns off to the airport. Cave Beach lies directly on the north shore and is relatively protected from waves by the points nearby and by the offshore reef. In truth, the reefs on all these beaches are too far out to safely swim to, but the sunbathing opportunities on its fine white sand are impeccable.

Just east of Northwest Point and just beyond the lodgings at Compass Point lies **Love Beach,** situated across from Sea Gardens, and just before Orange Hill. Love Beach along with **Orange Hill Beach**, which stretches for about half a mile to the *Traveller's Rest* restaurant, are two of the finest beaches on the island. With gentle slopes, white sand, an offshore reef, and no crowds, these two beaches are the favourites of folks with transportation and time for picnicking and sunbathing. Wind

deepwater and its walls, while **snorkellers** find plenty to do and see at any of the reefs fringing Nassau Harbour or on any of the smaller cays nearby. **Anglers** also have a wealth of options to choose from. Naturally, watersports are not the only outdoor diversion on New Providence, and other favourite activities run the gamut from **birdwatching** to **golf**. For a complete look at sports in the area, call the Bahamas Sports and Aviation Information Centre (☎305/932-0051 or 1-800/32-SPORT). The centre is primarily a clearing house for information on private flights to and from the islands, but also provides backgrounds on diving, snorkelling, boating, and other sporting activities. You can write them at 19495 Biscayne Blvd, Suite 809, Aventura, FL 33180.

Diving and snorkelling

Because many tourists flock to Nassau and Cable Beach for their hotels, restaurants and casinos, it is easy to forget that New Providence's south shore is one of the premier **dive** and **snorkel** destinations in the world. Scuba operators (see p.58) here are sometimes quite a distance from popular dive sites, which number in the hundreds but are mainly concentrated to the south and west of New Providence. Many of the best operators are on the south shore. Thus, staying at the south shore for divers is a plus that avoids long van shuttles during along this coast can be a problem, though, as can access. Love Beach, good for snorkelling, is sometimes accessed through private property. Most of the beach area beyond Orange Hill, all the way to **South Beach**, is owned by rich expats who've built residential and retirement homes nearby. South Beach is Nassau's beach of choice for the Over-the-Hill gang and is reached directly from that Nassau neighbourhood via Fox Hill Road. On weekends it is wall-to-wall with people, while on weekdays it is nearly deserted.

More isolated, the little-known **Old Fort Beach** lies fifteen minutes by car west of Nassau International Airport, very near the fashionable enclave of Lyford Cay. Though windy and cool in the winter, the beach is a paradise in summer. Even more remote is windy **Adelaide Beach**, which runs on both sides of Adelaide village on the south shore and offers good white sand to the few who venture in this direction.

Most tourists, however, do make it to two pink-sand beaches on Paradise Island. Washed by tall surf and steady trade winds from the north and west, these wide beaches are quite spectacular. At the far western edge of Paradise Island, **Paradise Beach** is accessible to guests of Nassau hotels or cruise ships, who can walk, drive, or take a boat ($4) to this beach from Prince George Wharf and make a day of it here. While Paradise Beach is backed by resort properties, many allow swimmers to use facilities for a small fee. More spectacular yet, and at three miles end to end one of the longest beaches in the Bahamas, **Cabbage Beach** is – under the right combination of sunshine and salt spray – as pink as a light-coloured rose. Stretching from *Atlantis'* manmade lagoon to Snorkeler's Cove, this public beach attracts many from the nearby resorts, a lot of whom come to parasail and windsurf.

Finally, **Blue Lagoon Island** deserves mention because of its fine isolated beach of white sand. About three miles offshore, Blue Lagoon Island can be reached by Calypso Getaway, a concession located under the Paradise Island Bridge (see *What's On* for schedules). It has seven beaches, and you'll surely find one that is secluded enough.

early-morning rush hours. Dive Dive Dive and Sunskiff have accommodation to rent, ranging from moderate to expensive. Snorkellers who wish for more adventure than simple near-shore reefs, may hook up with any of the day-excursion operators in town for trips to Rose Island Reefs, Southwest Reef, Razorback Reef or Booby Rock Reef (see p.64). Check *What's On* or *Tourist News* for particulars and coupons. In-shore snorkellers need not fear, for there is plenty to see and do. Love Beach is a particularly fine place to snorkel off. Besides the trips offered by several of the dive operators (see p.58), Barefoot Sailing (☎393-0820, ⓦwww.thebahamian.com/bsc) and Sea-Island Adventures (☎325-3910, ⓦwww.bahamasnet.com/seaisland) both offer half- to full-day excursions for $40–60 per person.

Blue Lagoon Island is the best snorkelling spot near Paradise Island. Nassau Cruises (☎1-800/338-4962, ⓦwww.nassaucruises.com) offer half-day trips for $20 with equipment, as well as six-hour ($35) and full-day ($45) snorkelling cruises. Snorkelling takes place in shallow calm water where a wide variety of reef fish as well as the occasional ray are clearly observable. Also located on Blue Lagoon Island is **Stingray City** (☎363-3577; $25), a manmade facility where you can snorkel among rays, even feeding them if you wish. Several other companies offer various cruises to snorkelling spots from Paradise Island, including Flying Cloud Catamaran (☎393-1957) and Out Island Voyages (☎394-0951), both of whom

Dolphin Encounters

With incredible beaches so near, most visitors to Paradise Island make snorkelling, swimming, sunbathing, windsurfing and parasailing their daily activity. However, one of the most popular and entertaining activities centred on the island is run by **Dolphin Encounters** (☏363-1653 or 363-1003), which provides trips to Blue Lagoon Island (Salt Cay), off the eastern tip of Paradise. Programmes run from 8am to 5.30pm, and the cost depends on the kind of day you want to have. Many enjoy a two-hour "close encounter", standing in waist-deep water while dolphins cruise about ($50), while others choose the self-explanatory "swim with the dolphins" option for $115. An all-day training session costs around $200. As these dolphin swims are incredibly popular, **reservations** are necessary.

operate out of a dock 200 yards west of the Paradise Island Bridge and charge $30 for half-day snorkelling trips. On the island itself, **Snorkeler's Cove Beach** is a paradise for snorkellers, especially younger ones, who can enjoy safe explorations in a shallow water environment.

New Providence and Paradise Island dive operators

Bahama Divers Coral Harbour ☏393-1466 or 5644. With 29 years in the business, this outfit operates custom dive boats that make two excursions a day each and take in all the famous Tongue of the Ocean and "Fish Hotel" sites, among others. Snorkellers may make the trips too. PADI certification courses offered. Rates are variable, but range from $27 for snorkelling to $70 introductory to scuba trips.

Custom Aquatics Coral Harbour ☏362-1492. A charter-only dive operator with two instructors and two boats. No PADI course given, but they do hit all the wrecks, reefs and blue holes. Rates are arranged in advance depending on the dive; ask about their three-tank specials when calling.

Dive Dive Dive, Ltd Coral Harbour ☏362-1143 or 362-1401. This operation has nine instructors, two boats, and offers all the specialty dives along with snorkel trips. PADI certification offered as an all-day four-tank special with lunch. Special shark dives too. Rates $25–110 a day.

Diver's Haven Paradise Island Ferry Terminal ☏363-3333. With five instructors, three boats, and PADI certification offered, this small operation offers competitive rates on dive packages. One-tank dives cost $35 while an intro to scuba course runs $65; snorkel trips begin at $25.

Nassau Scuba Centre Coral Harbour ☏362-1964 or 362-1379. Eleven instructors, two boats and PADI. Offers a special "shark suit adventure" and all major dives.

Stuart's Cove's Dive South Ocean Coral Harbour ☏362-4171 or 5227. This is the largest operator on the island, with nearly thirty guides and six boats. Their specialty is an all-day "wilderness trip", which goes to some of the more open ocean spots. They also offer all the major reef dives, plus a shark dive. Two-tank dives $65, PADI certification $350.

Sunskiff Divers Coral Harbour ☏362-1979. A small charter-only operator with a single boat and rates variable depending on the kind of custom dive. Kayak dives are also offered.

Sport fishing and sailing

For many, the lure of **sport fishing** off New Providence is irresistible. Its shallow waters attract grouper and snapper, while the deeper waters of the Tongue of the Ocean, just west of Nassau, provide a terrific habitat for blackfin tuna, bonito, blue marlin and more. However, the list of sport fish available offshore is seemingly endless, and visitors enjoy trolling for wahoo and dorado, casting shallows for snapper, grouper, amberjack and yellowtail, bottom fishing by anchor and even fly-fishing for bonefish here and there. The only drawback is that this kind of deep-sea angling is expensive. You have to consider the cost of the boat, lunch and sometimes dinner, gear, bait, rigging, tips, fuel and so forth. Parties of two to six can expect to pay $350–400 for half-day, $700 up for full-day charters. Almost all the big hotels make arrangements for guests to go fishing.

A reliable general **operator** in Nassau is the Charter Boat Association (☎363-2335), which offers a fleet of about ten vessels, all operating either out of (or near enough) the main wharf at Potter's Cay or by the Paradise Island Bridge landing. Chubasco Charters (☎324-FISH), operated by Mike Russell, runs four boats equipped with fish finders. Born Free Charters, run by Philip Pinder (☎363-2003 or 393-4144), is located at the dock on the Paradise Island side of the bridge and he offers a ten to fifteen percent discount on direct bookings. Similarly, Marine Adventure Company (☎363-2003), who also offer snorkelling trips aboard their *Three Queens* boat, give a fifteen percent discount on direct cash bookings. Other less organized boats operate off the dock at Paradise Island Bridge, from Hurricane Hole on Paradise Island, or from Nassau Yacht Haven.

Sailing is another comparatively expensive pastime in Nassau. Most people who have boats here either own their own and dock it in a local marina, or travel from nearby ports in Florida. Because two large bridges connect New Providence to Paradise Island, boats with masts larger than 72ft must enter the east approach to Nassau Harbour for marinas east of the bridges. It is possible to rent sailboats at most marinas and yacht harbours upon advance notice and proof of experience. Rates of dockage start at $1 per foot and go way up, along with charges for water and electricity. Rates for rented vessels vary widely as well, depending upon the size and type of vessel, and upon whether it is crewed or not. Marinas include Brown's Boat Basin (☎393-3331), East Bay Yacht Basin (☎394-1816), Lyford Cay (☎362-4131), Nassau Harbour Club (☎393-0771), Nassau Yacht Haven (☎393-8173) and Atlantis (☎363-3000).

Eco-tours, birdwatching and horseback riding

With its heavy emphasis on resort life Nassau has never been particularly eco-conscious, yet as more and more precious habitat (both marine and terrestrial) disappears beneath the contractor's shovel, nature and **eco-consciousness** are becoming increasingly popular. A number of outfits on New Providence can get visitors away from their hotels and casinos and closer to nature on New Providence. The relatively new Peddle and Paddle Adventures (☎362-2772 or 361-4075, ☎362-2044, ☎cwardle@batelnet.bs) offers a variety of trips, including birdwatching, nature walks, and kayak trips, that provide an alternative to heavily invested resort options. With both full- and half-day trips, the company targets its programmes to please all ages and walks of life.

Another good general alternative for nature tours is the Bahamas National Trust (☎393-1317 or Lynn Grape at BNAT Ornithology Group, ☎362-2772), which offers **guided walks** every month. They can also recommend guides for private **birdwatching** tours, a burgeoning island activity. Many birders find the Paradise Island Golf Course a good place to identify sea and shore birds. Birders so inclined must check in at the clubhouse before beginning their investigations. Birds that are particularly prominent include great blue herons, egrets, blue, green and yellow-crowned herons, ducks, moorhens, Caribbean coots, and varieties of ospreys and kingfishers. Migratory songbirds also make New Providence a home, including redstarts, warblers, black-throated blue warblers, Cape May warblers, palm warblers, and the smooth-billed ani. The Bahama woodstar is particularly common and beautiful. For any interested birdwatcher, the magnificent *A Birder's Guide to the Bahama Islands* (see Books p.372) is the beautifully complete local birding bible. For **horse** lovers, Coral Harbour's Happy Trails Stables (☎362-1820 or 323-5613) has horses for hire, and gives guided tours of wooded areas and beaches along the south coast. Happy Trails will send a bus for you at your hotel, and private tours are limited to ten persons. Also on the south coast is Cantalupa Riding School Carmichael Village (☎361-7101), with an array of offerings including lessons and ponies for kids.

Golf

Golf is an expensive pastime on New Providence and Paradise Island, partly because land is so expensive and scarce. Visitors to Nassau have three courses to choose from. Most highly regarded, the Cable Beach Golf Course (☎327-6000) is open to guests of the *Radisson* hotel at reduced rates. Non-guests pay $105 for eighteen holes, though there is a special nine-hole rate of $85 after 2.30pm; greens fees include cart. The second option, located on the island's south shore, is the *Clarion Resort*'s recently renovated South Ocean Golf Course (☎362-4931). Available for public play, the greens fees are $110 per person with shared cart. Finally, the Paradise Island Golf Club (☎363-3925) sits on the eastern end of the island near the airfield, and its many sand-traps include one billed as the world's largest. It is reserved for guests of *Atlantis* and the *Ocean Club* exclusively.

Nassau

Picturesque and compact, the easily negotiable city of **NASSAU** is a treat thanks in large part to its effervescent blend of British colonial architecture and modern convenience. Though its population of 170,000 – including suburban sprawl – seems to occupy most of the eastern half of the island, the Nassau most visitors see is at most a square mile of shops, government buildings, colonial offices, parks, restaurants and malls. This part of town, **Old Nassau,** extends for perhaps ten or twelve blocks along **Nassau Harbour** and out toward **Paradise Island Bridge** on East Bay Street, and five or six blocks south, or inland, toward **Fort Fincastle**. Taking **Rawson Square** or the celebrated **Straw Market** as starting points, several walking tours provide even the day tourist with an opportunity to dig into Nassau's bustling heart.

Nassau also affords the finest **shopping** opportunities in the Bahamas, ranging from jewellery and art to straw goods and liquor, along with the country's widest range of **restaurants**. These pursuits, however, can be hampered by the fact that, several times a week, as many as six huge cruise ships dock at the wharf – some carrying up to five thousand passengers – expelling droves of sun-and-fun seekers to descend on the city. For at least half of every week then, Nassau is jammed with bermuda-shorted passengers taking advantage of the town's limited facilities, meaning lines can form for everything from sitting down to eat to buying a postcard to even crossing the street.

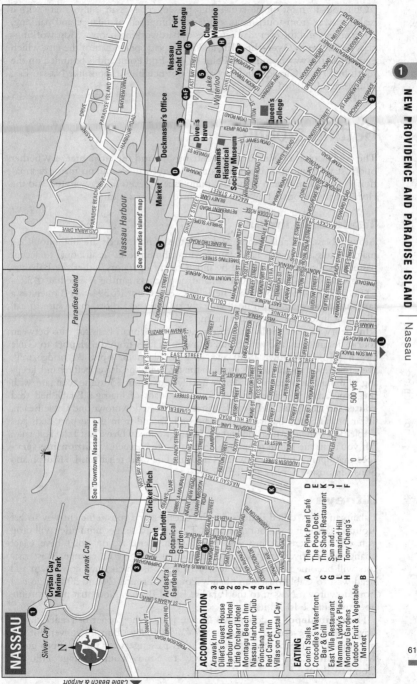

NASSAU

Cable Beach & Airport

Paradise Island

Nassau Harbour

See 'Paradise Island' map

See 'Downtown Nassau' map

Silver Cay

Crystal Cay
Marine Park

Arawak Cay

Ardastra
Gardens

Botanical
Garden

Fort
Charlotte

Cricket Pitch

Market

Dockmaster's Office

Dive's Haven

Bahamas Historical Society Museum

Queen's College

Nassau
Yacht Club

Fort
Montagu

Club
Waterloo

Lake
Waterloo

ACCOMMODATION

Arawak Inn	3
Dillet's Guest House	6
Harbour Moon Hotel	8
Little Orchard Hotel	7
Montagu Beach Inn	4
Nassau Harbour Club	9
Poinciana Inn	5
Red Carpet Inn	1
Villas on Crystal Cay	1

EATING

Conch Stalls	A
Crocodile's Waterfront Bar & Grill	C
East Villa Restaurant	G
Mamma Lyddy's Place	L
Montagu Gardens	H
Outdoor Fruit & Vegetable Market	B
The Pink Pearl Café	D
The Poop Deck	E
The Shoal Restaurant	K
Sun and....	J
Tamarind Hill	I
Tony Cheng's	F

Oblivious to most of the cruise-ship passengers, Nassau is also a city with a real life away from tourism, an existence composed of finance and banking, government and the everyday activities of hardworking people. Most working-class locals live in **Over-the-Hill**, and in the vast sprawl east of the city, which extends all the way from Dick's Point to East End Point and is bounded on the south by Prince Charles Highway, an area of neighbourhoods like Nassau East along Fox Hill Road.

Getting around

The compactness of Nassau makes **getting around** the city a breeze. Whether one is staying out at Cable Beach or in downtown Nassau, no major destination is more than fifteen or twenty minutes away, even in heavy traffic, and the city is easily negotiated by taxi, jitney, surrey or on a tour.

Taxis and limos

Around Nassau, Cable Beach, and near the airport, **taxis** are ubiquitous. All major hotels and resorts have stands, with cabmen ready at all hours to accept passengers. Taxicabs are owned by independent operators, either the Bahamas Transport or the Taxi Cab Union, and dispatchers can be reached at ☎ 323-5111, 312-5114 or 323-4555. The Jolly Green Giant (☎ 394-8294) operates a taxi service as well. If you need an early ride to the airport, make sure to call the night before for a morning pickup.

In theory, fares are set by the government on a "zonal" basis for trips between tourist destinations, and you should be aware of fares from the **airport** to Cable Beach ($12), downtown ($18) and Paradise Island ($20 plus $2 bridge toll). Regardless, you should always establish the fare with the driver beforehand, keeping in mind that a second passenger usually adds about $3 to the total fare, with the same amount being added for unusual loads of luggage. Established **taxi routes** run along East and West Bay Streets between downtown and Cable Beach, as far out as Sandy Point and often beyond. To and from the airport, taxis pass Cable Beach then turn inland and use John F. Kennedy Drive past Lake Killarney.

If you're in the mood to splurge, there are a few expensive **limousine services** that operate mile-long white Cadillacs. The most reliable is Lil Murph and Sons Limousine Service (☎ 325-3725).

Jitneys

Bahamian buses, called **jitneys**, are the cheapest and most efficient way to get around Nassau and surrounding areas. These 32-passenger minibuses will drop you off anywhere for just 75¢ (50¢ for children). If you don't have exact change, your driver will take a dollar bill, but will give no change. Most visitors will become familiar with routes 10 and 38, which leave downtown and head west to Cable Beach and Sandy Point, and routes 24 and 30 that go east from downtown Nassau to the Paradise Island Bridge. Note that no bus route goes to Paradise Island itself.

The **main depot** in downtown Nassau is near the corner of Frederick and Bay streets, cater-corner to the *British Colonial Hotel*. Equally convenient is a bus stop opposite the hotel, which accepts passengers for the #10 bus going west toward Cable Beach, all the way to Sandy Point, Orange Hill and Compass Point.

Rental cars, scooters and bikes

Narrow roads, heavy traffic, unusual driving rules (for North Americans at least) and expensive gasoline make **renting a car** in New Providence or Paradise Island a tricky luxury. Of the **international chains**, Avis has four locations: downtown Nassau (west of the *British Colonial Hotel*, ☎326-6380); Cable Beach (1 West Bay St, ☎322-2889); the airport (☎377-7121); and Paradise Island (Casino Drive between P.I. Bridge Exit and Comfort Suites, ☎363-2061). Budget, which also rents jeeps, has two locations: the airport (☎377-9000) and Hurricane Hole, Paradise Island (☎363-3095). Hertz (☎377-8684) and Dollar (☎377-7301) each have two locations, a main office at the airport and offices downtown, Dollar near the *British Colonial*, Hertz on East Bay Street, one block east of the original Paradise Island Bridge. And National (☎327-8231) has an office at the airport. Several **local agencies** have opened offices to compete with the big boys, and offer lower prices. Orange Creek Car Rentals, with the widest selection of vehicles, is centrally and conveniently located on West Bay Street (☎323-4967 or 1-800/891-7655), while Teglo Rental Cars is in Mt Pleasant Village (☎362-4361) near Cable Beach. The relatively new Lil Creek Rentals (☎326-2247 or 324-7309) offers Minis for as little as $39 per day, along with a selection of jeeps, Caravans and Corsicas.

Scooters and **bicycles** can be rented at a number of locations in and around Nassau and Cable Beach. The best-known is Knowles Scooter and Bike Rental, located just outside the west end of the *British Colonial Hotel* (☎356-0741), which offers scooters, insurance and helmets for about $50 per full day, $40 half-day. Smaller agencies are located up and down the south side of West Bay on Cable Beach. Many hotels also offer their own scooter rental, as well as bicycles to ride. However, streets and highways on New Providence have no shoulders and are pre-eminently unsuited for comfortable and safe biking. Bicycling in downtown Nassau is not recommended either because of heavy traffic, hills and narrow streets. Should you feel the need to bike, several eco-tour operators can oblige (see "Tours", p.59) with tours on the south and central parts of New Providence, where roads are much less congested.

Surrey and ferry

Almost every tourist who emerges from one of the cruise ships that dock along **Prince George Wharf** is tempted by a horse-drawn surrey master with a parked **surrey** near the gangway off Rawson Square. Tours wind uphill past the Houses of Parliament, then east along Bay Street onto Dowdeswell, to Devaux Street and onto Shirley Street, on the way passing some of the major sights in Nassau. Most days, traffic is abysmally heavy on these routes, so it might be best to pick a day for a surrey ride when cruise ships aren't in town. The cost is $10 per person and each tour lasts about 25 minutes.

For those wishing to go from downtown Nassau to Paradise Island and avoid the expense of a taxi, a number of gaily painted old tugboats known as the **Paradise Island Ferries** run daily from Prince George Wharf between 9am and 6pm. The fare is $2 per person. Every captain waits until his boat is filled, so if you see a ferry that has only one or two customers on board, you may as well sightsee for a while, coming back when the boat is almost full. Ferries deposit their passengers just near the Paradise Island Bridge, returning to Nassau from the same spot.

Guided tours

Aside from the Rawson Square surrey rides, perhaps the most enjoyable way to see Nassau from an expert's perspective is the **Goombay Guided Walking Tour** (☎326-9772; $12, under 12 $2). Arranged by the Ministry of Tourism, these tours leave from the information booth at Rawson Square daily at 10am, 11.30am, 1pm, 2.30pm and 3.45pm. Lasting 45 minutes, the tours take in some of Nassau's most historic buildings and are accompanied by an informative commentary on architecture and tradition.

Among the privately owned tour companies, **Majestic Tours** (☎322-2626) is likely your best bet. Among their many offerings are a two-hour tour of the city that takes in all the main sights, an extended city and country tour that includes Ardastra Gardens, and tours of Blue Lagoon and Rose islands, offshore cays that are a popular day-trip destination for snorkellers and swimmers. Smaller in scope is **Bahamas Experience Tours** (☎356-2981), which operates basic two-hour bus tours of the city for reasonable rates that vary by season.

Water tours

Boat excursions and **undersea tours** are a growing business in Nassau. The typical boat excursion leaves from the Paradise Island side of the causeway, to the west of Paradise Island Bridge, and includes all-day or half-day snorkelling and sunbathing trips to nearby cays and islands, like Rose or Blue Lagoon islands. Some offer drinks and lunch, and provide towels and snacks. The rowdy "booze-cruises" leave in the early evening and are excuses for passengers to watch a sunset and guzzle as much rum as possible. A few tours are undersea adventures, and come in various forms from semi-submarine adventures to walks through a reef environment made possible by covering your head with a helmet supplied with oxygen.

Although these companies come and go with surprising frequency (see *What's On* and *Tourist News* for a full list), there are a few firmly established operations to look out for. **Topsail Yacht Charters** (☎393-0820) operates three sailboats and offers full-day trips to Rose Island for snorkelling, lunch and a picnic (half-day $35; full day $50). Likewise celebrated for its cruises is **Booze and Cruise Ltd** (☎393-3772), which hosts a long four-hour tour of the harbour aboard the *Lucayan Queen* that departs from Nassau Yacht Haven on East Bay every day at 1.30pm ($30). They also offer an all-day cruise ($50), as well as sunset cruises. **Barefoot Sailing Cruises** (☎393-0820, ☻393-5871) also offers snorkelling cruises to outlying cays (half-day $35; full day $55), as well as a sunset cruise, while **Flying Cloud** (☎363-4430) operates half-day catamaran cruises at 9.30am and 2pm for $35. All of these companies can arrange private charters as well.

The rather unusual **Hartley's Undersea Walk**, leaving from Nassau Yacht Haven (☎393-8234 or 393-7569; $36), takes you on a short cruise on a 57-foot catamaran. After lunch, you can don a diving bell helmet to walk along a reef. Trips leave daily at 9.30am and 1.30pm, and last approximately four hours. From the docks on Devaux Street, **Seaworld Explorer** (☎356-2548; $20) operates ninety-minute tours in a semi-submerged vessel with windows below the water for views of such sights as Nassau Sea Gardens Marine Park. Also at the Devaux Street docks is the **Nautilus** (☎325-2876), a submarine-style vessel that offers semi-submerged trips around Nassau harbour. For those who don't mind high speeds and diesel fumes, **Powerboat Adventures** (☎327-5385, ☻328-5212) can take you to the northern Exuma cays (see p.270) aboard a 900hp cigarette boat that departs from the Devaux Street dock. Most

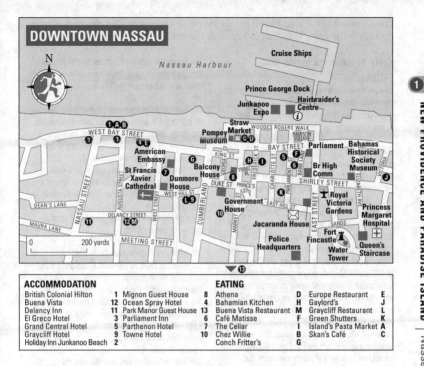

DOWNTOWN NASSAU

N

Nassau Harbour

Cruise Ships

Prince George Dock

Hairbraider's Centre

Junkanoo Expo

Straw Market

Pompey Museum

WEST BAY STREET

American Embassy

St Francis Xavier Cathedral

Dunmore House

Balcony House

WOODES ROGERS WALK

BAY STREET

Parliament

Bahamas Historical Society Museum

Br High Comm

SHIRLEY STREET

Government House

Royal Victoria Gardens

Princess Margaret Hospital

Jacaranda House

Police Headquarters

Fort Fincastle

Water Tower

Queen's Staircase

DEAN'S LANE

MAURA LANE

NASSAU STREET

AUGUSTA STREET

DELANCY STREET

MEETING STREET

CUMBERLAND

MARKET STREET

EAST STREET

ELIZABETH AVE

VICTORIA

SANDS

0   200 yards

ACCOMMODATION			
British Colonial Hilton	1	Mignon Guest House	8
Buena Vista	12	Ocean Spray Hotel	4
Delancy Inn	11	Park Manor Guest House	13
El Greco Hotel	3	Parliament Inn	6
Grand Central Hotel	5	Parthenon Hotel	7
Graycliff Hotel	9	Towne Hotel	10
Holiday Inn Junkanoo Beach	2		

EATING			
Athena	D	Europe Restaurant	E
Bahamian Kitchen	H	Gaylord's	J
Buena Vista Restaurant	M	Graycliff Restaurant	L
Café Matisse	F	Green Shutters	K
The Cellar	I	Island's Pasta Market	A
Chez Willie	B	Skan's Café	C
Conch Fritter's	G		

excursions, which average $90 per person, include shark feeding, lunch, and free rum drinks.

Accommodation

Lodging in Nassau can be expensive, yet there are more budget options here than anywhere else in the Bahamas, mostly buried in the heart of downtown or "Over-the-Hill". During high season, especially at Christmas and New Year's, hotels are often fully booked, making reservations hard to find; prices go down and availability up during the summer months, though places like *Atlantis* on Paradise Island are almost always full. Standards of comfort vary considerably, even in the poshest of resorts, and the constant heat, din of traffic, thin walls and surly service can make relaxation difficult and nights long. Many hoteliers in downtown Nassau ask guests to sign blank charge card forms and fill in the amounts upon check-out – resist this practice if at all possible and offer a charge card instead; sign the check only when everything has been reasonably settled.

Choosing to stay in or near **downtown Nassau** means putting up with a degree of urban clatter – though it also puts you near the action. Other options include staying well outside the city and taking a cheap jitney to town for fun and supplies; you can get around fairly quickly and easily, so it is feasible to bunk at places like Paradise Island (see p.89). For many, **Cable Beach** is a good accommodation option because it offers comparative quiet, a full range of beach and shopping options, and is an easy ten-minute bus or taxi ride away from town. Most Cable Beach hotels are more expensive than those in Nassau, though some offer breakfast along with the price of accommodation.

Old Nassau and the Hillside

British Colonial Hilton Nassau 1 Bay St ☎322-3311 or 1-800/742-4276, ℻323-8248, ⓦwww.nassau.hilton.com. Built in 1922, this grand dame is the poshest, most expensive hotel in Old Nassau. A huge pool dominates the courtyard, with two great restaurants inside on the ground floor alongside lounges and bars. The western end of the structure has been converted into condos and shops, and there is a private beach out back with snorkelling, windsurfing and charters for boating and fishing. Of the hotel's 305 rooms, the more expensive rooms are on higher floors and face the ocean. Rates begin at $300 per double in high season. ❽

Grand Central Hotel Parliament and Bay sts ☎322-8368. One of several basic, but perfectly serviceable commercial hotels in central Nassau. The plain rooms have TV and air conditioning and not much else, and there's no pool or restaurant on site. ❸

Graycliff West Hill St ☎322-2796, ℻326-6110, ⓦwww.graycliff.com. Perched on a hill above downtown Nassau and just across from the Government House, the *Graycliff* is a wonderful example of Georgian colonial architecture. The main house was built by John Howard Graysmith, a pirate who pillaged Spanish shipping as commander of the *Graywolf*, and inside are most of the inn's fourteen antique-filled accommodation options. There are, though, a few private cottages to choose from as well. Amenities include a large pool – in which The Beatles once swam – hot tub, health club and one of the finest restaurants in town (see p.82). Guests are met at the airport in a Mercedes. Rates range $220–300. ❽

Mignon Guest House 12 Market St ☎322-4771. One of the best budget choices in town. Run by a Greek family, there are six clean rooms on offer, and though bathrooms are shared each room comes with TV and air conditioning. Kitchen privileges are available, saving even more on the already rock-bottom year-round rates. ❶

Park Manor Guest House Market St ☎356-5471 ℻325-3554. A decent self-catering choice, the *Park Manor* offers an array of efficiencies and apartments for up to four people. There's a tiny pool, and all rooms have air conditioning. ❸

Parliament Hotel Parliament St near Shirley St ☎322-2386, ℻326-7196. This unassuming hotel has boxy rooms with the standard tropical prints

and rattan wickerwork furniture. Nothing special, though there are some triple rooms handy for those in small groups. No TVs or phones in rooms. ❷

Parthenon Hotel West Bay St ☎322-2643, ℻322-2644. A quiet option in downtown Nassau, the *Parthenon's* eighteen rooms are housed in a two-story L-shaped building overlooking a garden. Add $3 for Continental breakfast. ❷

The Towne Hotel 40 George St ☎322-8450, ℻322-1512, ⓦwww.townehotel.com. One of the oldest hotels in Nassau, *The Towne* has certainly seen better days. The 46 modest rooms of varying sizes all have TVs and overlook a small central courtyard and pool. ❸

West of downtown

Arawak Inn West Bay St near Chippingham St ☎322-2638, ℮arawakinn@iboxtv.com. About three miles west of downtown Nassau sits the *Arawak*, offering six rudimentary rooms with dated decor. The grounds are rather grungy, but there is a hot tub. Bus #10 goes right by, so transport isn't a problem. Noise might be, though, as West Bay is constantly busy. ❷

Astoria Hotel West Bay and Nassau sts ☎322-8666, ℻322-8660. Overlooking a swimming beach at the west end of Nassau's Bay Street, the slightly downtrodden though still clean 70-room *Astoria* has largish, bright rooms with double or king-size beds and cable TV. Located near Nassau Street, it's convenient to taxis and buses. ❹

Buena Vista Hotel Delancy St at Augusta St ☎322-2811, ℻322-5881. Housed in a venerable mansion that has seen better days, the *Buena Vista* has buckets of charm along with some rust. A highlight of the nineteenth-century interior is the unique winding staircase with Victorian-style hand-carved rails and balusters. Lots of flowers, big rooms and an eponymous restaurant (see p.82) that's one of the best in town keep things cheerful. No pool, but a public beach is half a mile away downhill from the hotel. ❸

Delancy Inn 4 Delancy St ☎325-2688. A budget choice with nine basic rooms with ceiling fans, shared baths and a claustrophobic feel. At only $25 for a night, the price is the only incentive. ❶

Dillet's Guest House Dunmore Ave at Strochan St ☎325-1133, ℻325-7183, ⓦwww.islandeaze.com. Run by a welcoming mother-daughter team, this B&B, located in the once-posh West Nassau neighbourhood of Chippingham, presents an imposing sight down a long walkway off the street. The guesthouse has seven rooms – either extra-large or extra-small – and all have private bath, air conditioning and cable TV. There's a daily afternoon tea in the lovely downstairs sitting room, and you can cool off in a small pool on the spacious grounds. Rooms on the northwest can be noisy, so try for the front or south side. ⑤

El Greco Hotel West Bay St at Augusta St ☏ 325-1121, ⓕ 325-1124, ⓦ www.bahamasnet.com/elgrecohotel. The 26-room *El Greco*'s two storeys crowd around a central courtyard complete with a pool and dense foliage, and Western Esplanade beach (see p.56) is just across the street. As West Bay Street is always noisy and diesel-fumed out front, ask to stay in back of the hotel if possible. You may be offered a poolside room, which sounds nice but can be noisy after swimmers knock back a few daiquiris. ④

Holiday Inn Junkanoo Beach Hotel West Bay St ☏ 356-0000, ⓕ 323-1408. A favourite with business travellers, this relatively new, five-storey *Holiday Inn* has 175 clean rooms, each decked out with modern furniture and bathrooms. There is access to the beach across the street along with a large pool in the courtyard out front. Some rooms have ocean views. ⑦

International Travellers Lodge 23 Delancy St ☏ 323-2904. Nassau's version of a youth hostel features fourteen basic rooms in a building wedged onto a narrow strip of land next to a beautiful, but crumbling Bahamian colonial gem. It is affiliated with the VIP Backpackers organization, and provides dormitory beds for guests and Continental breakfast next door in a house notable for its unusual collection of African masks, plants and prints. Credit cards are only accepted with advance approval. Doubles are $40, singles $26. ①

Ocean Spray Hotel West Bay St ☏ 322-8032, ⓦ www.oceansprayhotel.com. This concrete building just east of *El Greco*, and just across from Nassau's main public beach, makes for a decent beachside budget option. The fifty rooms have twin beds, plain motel furniture and small bathrooms. Bay Street is very noisy, so rooms at back are best. The bar-restaurant *Europe* is on the bottom floor. ③

Villas on Crystal Cay Silver Cay ☏ 328-1036, ⓕ 323-3202. Located two miles west of downtown, adjacent to Arawak Cay, these 21 private single-level villas are owned by the Marriott people of Cable Beach. Luxurious and expensive, the one- or two-bedroom villas have large couches and TVs,

Italian-tile bathrooms with oval tubs. Rates begin at $235 in high season. ⑧

East of downtown

Harbour Moon Hotel East Bay St at Devaux St ☏ 323-8120, ⓕ 328-0374, ⓦ www.harbourmoon.com. A run-down, fifty-room lodge whose front rooms abut busy Bay Street, while its rear rooms look over the wharf where boats unload commercial wares. The noise inside, then, varies from loud to very loud, but rooms have a TV and air conditioner, and the rates are low at around $50 for a single. ②

Little Orchard Hotel Village Rd ☏ 393-1297, ⓕ 394-3526, ⓦ www.orchardbahamas.com. Three miles east of downtown, the *Little Orchard* offers both rooms and cottages on two acres of garden-like grounds wrapped around a central swimming pool. The complex is in a residential area far from beaches with no restaurant, but patrons can take bus #17 to Bay Street in about five minutes, or walk to nearby restaurants and shops. Room ③, cottage ④

Montagu Beach Inn Village Rd at Shirley St ☏ 393-0475, ⓕ 393-6061. Just down the block from the *Little Orchard*, the *Montagu* has 33 relatively large rooms, a pool and a nightclub. Though plainly designed with motel-style furnishing, the rooms are clean and are within walking distance of Montagu Beach. Overall a good value. ③

Nassau Harbour Club East Bay St ☏ 393-0771, ⓕ 393-5393. A popular hangout for yachties, the *Harbour Club* rents out fifty air-conditioned rooms done up in blazing tropical colours. Built in the 1960s, the two-storey pink buildings are near busy Bay Street at the edge of a channel where yachts moor in the marina. It's loud at times, and the bar/restaurant *Passin Jacks* is a floor above the lobby. ④

Poinciana Inn Bernard Rd ☏ 393-1897. In the Fox Hill neighbourhood of east Nassau, this basic and cheap hotel with sterile rooms is popular with locals, who jam the bar and pool area. ②

Red Carpet Inn East Bay St ☏ 393-7981, ⓕ 393-9055. Even though this forty-room motel-style lodge is located on Nassau's busiest street, high wrap-around walls ensure a sense of tranquillity. Popular with divers due to its proximity to the harbour, the rooms here are clean and comfortable. Both the *Barn Bar* and the *El Rancho* restaurants on site serve reliable fare to boot. ③

Over-the-Hill

Olive's Guest House Blue Hill Rd ☏ 323-5298. An old, two-storey Over-the-Hill house with a few rooms to let at about $30 a night. Suitable only for those desperate to get a closer look at local life off the tourist trail. ❶

Cable Beach

Casuarinas of Cable Beach West Bay St ☎ 327-7921 or 1-800/327-3012, Ⓕ 3278152, Ⓦ www.casuarinashotel.com. A less expensive alternative to the large nearby resorts, this 78-room property spills across both sides of busy Bay Street. While somewhat run-down, the rooms are pleasant enough, though the small strip of beach is a bit of a letdown. There are, however, two pools, a bar, a lounge and a tennis court. Ask to see your room first before committing, as some are musty and dark. However, the local owner and staff are friendly and the on-site *Albion's* restaurant is enjoyable. ❺, two-bedroom suite ❼
Guanahani Village West Bay St ☎ 327-7962 or 327-7568, Ⓕ 327-5059, Ⓦ www.guanahanivillage .com. A 35-unit collection of time-shares designed for long stays by groups of four to eight. Ideally suited for those into self-catering, each unit has a kitchen, dishwashers and laundry room along with cable TV and patios. There's a shared pool that overlooks the ocean, though the beach is still a short walk away. Rates begin at $300 per night, $2100 per week. ❽
Nassau Beach Hotel West Bay St ☎ 327-7711 or 1-888/627-7278, Ⓕ 327-8829. Venerable hotel, built in the 1940s, with over 400 rooms, six restaurants, three bars, tennis courts and all the typical watersports offerings. Rooms range from elegant (ocean view) to serviceable, and the hotel is located across from an excellent golf course and next to a large casino. All-inclusive packages available. ❼
Nassau Marriott and Crystal Palace Casino West Bay St ☎ 327-6200 or 1-800/222-7466, Ⓕ 327-6308. This monster resort has nearly 750 rooms and 125 suites, and its garish neon lights make it look at night like a jukebox on steroids. Its five towers are home to oak-panelled rooms, many of which have wide-angle ocean views, and the top suites are fabulously expensive, going for as much as $1000 per night. There are five restaurants, five bars, complete watersports options, a large pool (complete with 100ft waterslide), plenty of beachfront and a massive casino. ❼
Radisson Cable Beach Resort West Bay St ☎ 327-6000 or 1-800/333-3333, Ⓕ 327-6987, Ⓦ www.radisson.com/nassaubs_cable. This recently renovated high-rise, featuring an Aztec facade and plenty of fountains, feels like a Vegas

import. The highlight for many of the 700-room resort's guests is either gambling or golf, though the hotel also boasts eighteen tennis courts, a health club, squash, racketball, three pools and plenty of watersports. The rooms are modern and comfortable, if uniform, and the hotel horseshoes around its beach property. All-inclusive packages available. ❺
Sandals Royal Bahamian Resort and Spa ☎ 327-6400 or 1-800/726-3257, Ⓕ 327-6961, Ⓦ www.sandals.com. This Roman spa-style resort, the most expensive on Cable Beach, sits behind high walls and iron fencing. With only 125 rooms and 280 suites, it's billed as an intimate couples spot, though it is restricted to heterosexual partners only. There are eight restaurants, including the elegant *Crystal Room* for Continental dining and *Kimono* for Japanese, seven bars, five swimming pools, and a complement of accoutrements including a dive shop and a spa catering to couples who want to enjoy massage therapy and other delights in unison. The rooms are deluxe, ranging from bedrooms at the *Manor House* to elegant suites. Rates are all-inclusive and are generally booked in seven-night blocks ranging from $2000 to $4000 during high season. ❽
Sun Fun Resorts West Bay St ☎ 327-8827, Ⓕ 327-8802, Ⓦ www.sunfunbahamas.com. A drab but serviceable alternative to the big boys lining the shore. There is a pool and restaurant, but the beach is a short walk away. ❹
Superclubs Breezes West Bay St ☎ 327-5356 or 1-800/859-7873, Ⓦ www.superclubs.com. This huge nearly 400-room hotel angles around five pools and has beachfront access, tennis courts, and just about every kind of organized and disorganized activity imaginable from volleyball to dancing and billiards. There is a good Italian restaurant on the bottom floor, and the rooms are pleasant enough, have cable TV, air conditioning and reasonably clean decor. Some, though, may find the cruise-ship atmosphere – think talent shows and bikini contests – unpleasant at best. All-inclusive (rates begin at $250 a night) and limited to guests 17 and older. ❽
West Wind I West Bay St ☎ 327-7211 or 7019, Ⓕ 327-7529, Ⓔ westwindl@batelnet.bs. These 54 time-share condo villas have two bedrooms, two baths and full kitchens, making them affordable for families or groups who can share costs. Swimming pools, a barbecue area and two tennis courts accent the grounds. Rates range $220–275 for four guests. ❽

Old Nassau

While **OLD NASSAU**'s narrow, bustling streets are hard on vehicular traffic, they are ideal for a brisk walk around the district, with appropriate pause for refreshment. The best place to begin a tour is **Rawson Square**, and you should allow at least half a day to take in all the sights.

Rawson Square and around

RAWSON SQUARE, the small cobblestone square formed by Bay and East streets just across the concrete gangway from Prince George Wharf, is the genuine crossroads of Old Nassau, a place where tourists, government personnel, hawkers and musicians congregate. Nothing, though, comes close to the mayhem that occurs here during the Junkanoo festivities (see box below) that take place between Christmas and New Year's, when bands and marchers converge here along with 30,000 onlookers.

Just off the waterfront, Rawson Square is lined on all sides by pastel-painted colonial-style government buildings, the majority built between 1785 and 1815. From the centre of the square, you get a fine view uphill along Parliament Street toward the capital's massive houses of government. Several public sculptures are scattered about Rawson Square, including one of **Sir Milo Butler**, first governor-general of the independent Bahamas. On the south side of Rawson Square is the unobtrusive **Churchill Building**, where the controversial Sir Lynden Pindling held sway as prime minister from 1967 until 1992, when he was ousted in a tempestuous political affray. The northern end of the square is bounded by the two-block-long **Woodes–Rogers Walk**, named for a governor of the colony whose political and economic troubles led to a stint in a London debtors' prison during the eighteenth century, though he eventually returned to Nassau in triumph with a royal appointment. On the

---

Junkanoo festival

The **Junkanoo festivities** which take place in Nassau, and on other islands like Grand Bahama and Eleuthera, are the most exuberant expression of Bahamian music and art. Reminiscent of New Orleans' Mardi Gras and Rio de Janeiro's Carnival, Nassau's Junkanoo parade takes place on Boxing Day (December 26) and again on New Year's Day (January 1) from midnight until eight in the morning, or later if the marchers and bands have energy to spare. Parade participants, arranged in groups of up to 1000, are organized around a particular theme, and spend much of the year preparing songs, choreographed dances, and music with which they hope to win a prize. The best vantage points for viewing the proceedings are from second-storey windows along the street, or from the sidewalk bleachers erected for the parade. Many, however, simply wander from spot to spot partaking of the many sights and sounds.

Some believe that the origin of the word Junkanoo is from "John Canoe", a mythical African chief who demanded the right to celebrate with his people even after he was brought to the West Indies as a slave. Others believe the name derives from the French *gens inconnus*, or unknown people, a term referring to those who wear masks and costumes. Whatever the derivation, Junkanoo began as a temporary celebration of freedom for slaves who were given three days off from hard physical labour during Christmas. Donning masks, they played homemade musical instruments like goatskin drums and cowbells, and cavorted freely.

harbourside, the walk is lined with stalls that feature shoddy crafts, along with conch, fish or locally grown vegetables. Skip the stands and walk along **Prince George Wharf**, which offers great views of the buzzing harbour, where water taxis, huge cruise vessels and tour boats all use the crowded blue water.

Back on the city side of Woodes-Rogers Walk is the **Junkanoo Expo** (daily 9am–5.30pm; $2; ☎356-2731), a museum being refurbished as part of the reconstruction of the entire wharf area. Unfortunately, the renovation is progressing at a snail's pace, and the exhibit was still closed at the time of writing. The Expo is set to feature a collection of handmade floats and authentic costumes used by revellers during Junkanoo at Christmas, as well as original instruments like goatskin drums, cowbells and brass. Once the overall area renovations are completed, the new wharf area is to include new shops, an information centre, and a walkway from the Straw Market (see below) to the wharf. For now, the first port of call for many cruise-ship visitors is the **Hairbraider's Centre** just east of the Expo, where Bahamian women will braid hair for around $1 a strand. Elaborate dos with twisting phantasmagorias of braids go for as much as $100.

Parliament Square

Across Bay Street, south of Rawson Square, stands **PARLIAMENT SQUARE**, the centre of Bahamian government that includes the Opposition Building to the east and the Senate facing north. To the west, the House of Assembly is the oldest legislative body continuously in session in the western hemisphere, dating from 1729. All three buildings of government are superb examples of the Georgian style of architecture that was so popular in the early 1800s at the height of the Napoleonic Wars, featuring smooth cream-coloured limestone facades, Neoclassical pillars and pilasters, and broad staircases. A statue of **Queen Victoria**, erected in 1905, looks down sternly from the Senate steps. Most of the government buildings, regularly patrolled by colourfully dressed members of the Bahamian Police Force, are not open to the public. However, free tickets are available to sessions of the House of Assembly from the clerk in the building's main floor, though the discussions held within are usually quite staid. Behind the Senate is the **Supreme Court**, a less imposing Georgian structure than the other government buildings, and its **Garden of Remembrance**, whose cenotaph recalls the Bahamian dead of the World Wars.

The Straw Market and around

Heading west along Bay Street will bring you to Nassau's celebrated **Straw Market**. Filling much of a square block, the market is a covered warren of upwards of 150 vendors who congregate each morning to peddle everything from cheap bric-a-brac to exquisitely beautiful artworks. While Santo Domingo's Mercado Modelo is larger, and Port-au-Prince's Iron Market more arcane, the Straw Market is a world-class open-air *souk* and one of the Caribbean's finest.

Near the information booth on Bay Street, you'll often find **carvers** at work, usually creating large mahogany dolphins or whales. T-shirts, handbags, dolls, beads, totes, baskets, slippers, wall hangings, sunglasses, carvings and the occasional oil painting are also prominent in the market. Among the more unusual items are shark-tooth necklaces, Voodoo-style charms and hexes, and batik fabrics from Andros (see p.179). Hand-carved wood and shell pieces tend to fetch the highest prices, yet bargain hunters will always find something to

△ Parliament Building, Nassau

please. While many visitors bargain with vendors, haggling is not a cultural rite with Bahamians, and many have already priced their goods quite low.

Due south of the Straw Market is **Balcony House**, Bay and Market streets (Mon, Wed & Fri 10am–1pm & 2–4pm; donations; ☎326-2566), a home once owned by an eighteenth-century merchant that now operates as a kind of funky local history museum. Inside and up a creaky flight of stairs there's a rather dark time capsule of colonial merchant life, including household goods, furnishings, and kitchenware. Beware that opening hours are erratic at best. Head further south along Market Street, then turn on Trinity Place and come to the modern **Central Bank of the Bahamas** (Mon–Fri 8.30am–6pm; free). Dedicated by Prince Charles in 1973 and officially opened by Queen Elizabeth in 1975, the bank itself is an unremarkable modern structure, yet its lobby does host **art exhibits** on a regular basis, a kind of free gallery of contemporary Bahamian work.

Just west of the Straw Market, on the corner of George and Bay streets, is the **Pompey Museum** (Mon–Fri 10am–4pm; $1), a slavery museum housed in a building dating back to 1769, making it one of the oldest in Nassau. Originally called the Vendue House, it was later renamed in honour of a slave who led an uprising and then hid out on the Exuma Cays during the 1830s (see p.243). Now in fabulous condition, the museum holds a collection of such artefacts as chains and restraints, as well as mouldy documents tracing the history of slavery in the Bahamas, an exercise particularly poignant as slave auctions were held on the site during the 1700s. Also featured are the works of local artists, including the widely praised Amos Ferguson, whose landscapes feature plenty of religious imagery.

Continue along Bay to Cumberland Street to a complex of buildings that include the sweeping and majestic **British Colonial Hotel**, which is worth a peek, particularly for its exclusive shops and restaurants. Next door, the **Royal Bank of Canada** and the **Masonic Temple** are excellent examples of Victorian construction technique.

The Hillside

South of Bay Street, Old Nassau gives way to the leafy **HILLSIDE**, roughly bounded by Elizabeth Avenue to the east and Cumberland Street to the west. A mostly residential neighbourhood filled with charming side streets, where the favoured bright Bahamian colours – blue, yellow and red – contrast with the deep green of shade trees. Not only do the crowds thin considerably here, but the Hillside is liberally sprinkled with small cafés good for a refreshing drink or a full-fledged lunch. In no small measure, Nassau's true character is revealed on the Hillside, much more than on busy Bay Street.

The Nassau Public Library and Museum and Royal Victoria Garden

One block south of Parliament Square, on Bank Lane, the **Nassau Public Library and Museum** (Mon–Thurs 10am–8pm, Fri 10am–5pm, Sat 10am–4pm; free) is housed in a former city jail built in 1797. This octagonal-shaped structure is cramped and rather mysterious, with piles of mouldering books lining what were once jail cells, and stacks of newspapers placed here and there in no apparent order. On the second floor, reachable by a rickety metal staircase, is a mouldering historical collection of artefacts, maps, photos and parchments. The staff are carefree and friendly, and somewhat oblivious to the books rotting away in the humid Bahamian climate.

Nearby, just south of Shirley Street, the **Royal Victoria Garden** occupies the site of the former *Royal Victoria Hotel*. Opened at the beginning of the American Civil War in 1861, the hotel played host to Confederate officers, gunrunners, spies and officials in town doing business with Nassau's smugglers and blockade runners. It burned down in 1971 and part of the site is now occupied by a public parking lot, though a corner was saved as a small government office building. The free and public garden that takes up the remaining area features 300 species of tropical plants like orchids and bromeliads, and is a great place to wander during the heat of the day.

Fort Fincastle, the Queen's Staircase and the Historical Society Museum

A steep half-mile hike up East Street leads to Sands Road, then Elizabeth Avenue where Bennet's Hill offers sweeping views from **Fort Fincastle** and the **Water Tower**. Shaped like a paddle-wheel steamer, the fort was built in 1793 by Lord Dunmore, the royal governor (Viscount Fincastle), as a lookout against pirates and marauders. During the middle of the nineteenth century, the fort was also used as a lighthouse. The adjacent 126-foot-high water tower – still used to store some of the city's water – has a four-person elevator (50¢) to the top, or you can brave the steep, rather narrow stairs; either way, the views up high are remarkable.

To the east of Bennet's Hill is Prospect Ridge, a shady residential area that houses Nassau's middle and working classes. Several yards away from the Water Tower, the **Queen's Staircase** leads down from Bennet's Hill and Prospect Ridge to Elizabeth Street and back into Old Nassau. A deep limestone gorge near where Elizabeth Street and East Street meet presented slaves in the 1790s with the "opportunity" of carving wide stairs leading up to a hillside where Nassau's rich resided. Renamed in honour of Queen Victoria's 65-year reign (the staircase has 65 steps), the stairs themselves are basically curiosities now, with gaggles of guides at each end ready to regale you with stories they've been rehashing for years. A mini-tropical garden has been planted to lend charm to the otherwise stark staircase.

At the bottom of the steps, on Shirley Street at Elizabeth Avenue, stands the **Bahamas Historical Society Museum** (Mon–Fri 10am–4pm, Sat 10am–noon; $1; ☎322-4231). With a modest but entertaining collection of anthropological materials and artefacts, this museum is devoted to life in the Bahamas before European settlement and during early colonial times. A chief attraction in the museum is its collection of prints and lithographs featuring high-seas adventures, colonial life, historical scenes and a structurally perfect model of the Spanish galleon *Santa Luceno*.

East Hill, Duke and West Hill streets

A half-mile southwest of the Bahamas Historical Society, **East Hill Street** clings to the edge of Prospect Ridge, furnishing a unique glimpse of Bahamian architecture at its best.

At the corner of East Hill and Glinton streets is the **Ministry of Foreign Affairs**. Though off limits to visitors, its exterior is worth a look for its Georgian-style architecture, with bold, cream-coloured stone walls, moulded cornices, fountains and formal grounds complete with cannon. Two blocks west, the private, two-storey **Jacaranda House** looks a little ramshackle today, its faded exterior complete with peaked roof and decorative scroll and spider-web-carved accoutrements. It was once owned by the murdered Sir Harry Oakes (see p.353) and later by the Duke of Windsor during his tenure as royal governor of the Bahamas during World War II.

East Hill continues towards Market Street, where the intersection is marked by **Gregory's Arch**. Named for John Gregory, royal governor from 1849 to 1854, this passage was built in 1850 for black Bahamians to go "over the hill" to **Grant's Town**, named for Governor Lewis Grant, who laid out the area for freed slaves. Early visitors to Nassau often treated Grant's Town as a pleasure dome, visiting pubs and bawdy houses. These days, the suburb is tamer, though there are still lively restaurants and taverns. Just north of East Hill, **St Andrew's Kirk** on Prince's Street was built in 1810 but altered over the years, and features stone constructions based on basic Norman designs that are much in evidence in English country churches. Home to the first non-Anglican worshippers in the Bahamas, it is now a Presbyterian church.

Duke Street, which connects East Hill to West Hill Street, is dominated by **Government House**, on the corner of George Street. Presided over by a statue of Christopher Columbus, this huge pink-tinged structure, with its graceful columns, broad driveways, quoins (cross-laid cornerstones) and louvred windows, is the quintessence of British-Bahamian colonial style. It was built in the mid-1730s by Royal Governor Fitzwilliam, extensively rebuilt in 1806 and then again in 1932 after a hurricane destroyed the old structure. Continuously operated by the colonial government and home to the governor general, the house is not open to visitors, though you can stroll the pleasant grounds to get a close-up as well as attend the **Changing of the Guards** every other Saturday morning at 10am, an event modelled upon the Buckingham Palace ceremony. The guards are headed by the Royal Bahamian Police Force, who wear red tunics, white pith helmets, and march to the beat of drummers dressed in leopard-skin.

Among the more prominent buildings on West Hill Street is **Graycliff**, built in 1720 and blessed with turrets, verandas and cornices galore. Perched on Prospect Ridge near Blue Hill Road, the fabulous Georgian-style hotel is technically not open to non-guests (see p.66 for a review), but one way to get a look around the property is to visit their new **Cigar Factory** (☎322-2796), which operates in a wing of the old Victorian pile. Overseen by Avalino Lara, the factory features fine hand-rolled cigars made from Cuban tobacco.

Further west, **Dunmore House**, a three-storey mansion on a steep slope, is the former residence of Lord Dunmore, who came to the Bahamas in 1787 and established a shady reputation for double-dealing before selling the house to the local government in 1801. These days Dunmore House is a remarkable sight, complete with wraparound verandas and hurricane shutters. Undergoing repairs, it may one day regain its status as a showplace if enough private funds are dedicated. At the end of West Hill Street is the **St Francis Roman Catholic Church**, the first Roman Catholic church in the Bahamas, constructed during 1885–86. The bell-tower of the church is something of a Hillside landmark, its light calmly piercing the tropical night.

Marlborough and King streets

Turn north from the cathedral up West Street, past the **Greek Orthodox Church** that serves a small but vibrant Orthodox community, and you will come to **Marlborough Street**, a lively thoroughfare known mainly for shopping. A short detour west along Marlborough leads to Virginia Street, where **St Mary's Church**, built in 1868, offers an almost perfect example of late Anglican stone-building techniques, giving the structure a resemblance to the old Norman stone churches that predominate in the north of England.

Retrace your steps back along Marlborough, where several fine colonial structures line the street as you head east, including **Devonshire House**, on Queen Street, as well as **Cumberland House** and **The Deanery**, both on Cumberland Street. At its eastern end, Marlborough Street turns into King Street, where you'll find the hard-to-miss **Pirates of Nassau**, on the corner of George Street (Mon–Fri 9am–5pm; $15, children $5; ℡356-3759), of interest mainly to those with children in tow. Hawkers outside beckon you inside this tourist trap, where visitors are treated to historical dramas, including a fight at sea on a simulated pirate ship, geared to recreate a "pirate experience". At the corner of George Street, **Christ Church Cathedral** (Mon–Fri 8.30am–6pm), built in 1837, has a small garden outside for quiet contemplation.

West of downtown

Two blocks past the *British Colonial Hotel* (see p.66), Marlborough Street becomes **West Bay Street**, a busy, shaded two-lane road that heads west past a couple of decent public beaches on its way to Cable Beach. Local Bahamians often park their cars on the sand to snooze, have lunch or drink a beer amid the rusting cannons along the beachside, which is most popular on Sundays and holidays. Narrow, shoulder-less and choked with traffic, West Bay is a trick to walk, and should be avoided by bicyclists altogether. The easiest way to get around the area is by hopping on a #10 bus in front of the *British Colonial*.

Clifford Park and Fort Charlotte

Half a mile down West Bay Street, on a hill overlooking a beach, lies **Clifford Park**, where the Bahamian Cricket Association holds games every Sunday around 1pm. The games can be watched for free, though they're best experienced from the association's pitch-side pub and restaurant, where basic Bahamian and American fare is served along with cold beer. A breezy balcony gives great views of the field and the ocean nearby.

Another half mile or so beyond the cricket pitch, slightly run-down **Fort Charlotte** (daily 9am–4.30pm; free) occupies a magnificent overlook between Nassau Street and Chippingham Road. Construction was begun in 1787 by Lord Dunmore, who managed to complete the building in 1790 – at an enormous cost to the English treasury – in the hope of protecting the colony from possible French invasion. Chiselled from solid limestone, the walls are buttressed by cedar, and there's a surrounding moat, a warren of dungeons and supply rooms, as well as a keep and cannonades. At the end of the regular fifteen-minute **tour**, be sure to give a donation to the guide – who may or may not be dressed in period costume – of $2–3 per person. Deep inside the fort is a wax museum of tortures consisting of racks, thumbscrews and stocks.

Arawak Cay and the Crystal Cay Marine Park

Directly opposite Fort Charlotte across West Bay Street is the manmade **Arawak Cay**, a popular hangout that shouldn't be missed by anyone interested in local culture. Built originally as a harbour entrepôt, the cay is now home to dozens of food shacks where cooks prepare cracked conch, conch salad, and fried conch, along with smothered grouper and other seafood treats at good prices. On weekends, the grounds are rocking with Bahamians who come to play loud music and drink gin and coconut milk.

Directly connected to Arawak Cay is Silver Cay, home to one of Nassau's most famous exhibits, **Crystal Cay Marine Park** (Mon–Fri 9am–4.30pm, Sat & Sun 9am–4pm; $16, $8 for guests of the *Nassau Marriott* and *Nassau Beach* hotels; ℡ 323-1036, ℻ 323-3202). Crystal Cay is meant to be a hands-on experience of marine life, and to some extent it succeeds, albeit in an artificial way. Looming up from stands of casuarina trees, the park has several silver domes that mark its boundaries and that can be seen from mainland Nassau, a spectacular sight especially on moonlit nights. Visitors tread paths to turtle pools, shark pools and stingray pools, while children can handle starfish and feed sharks and turtles in "encounter pools". A spectacular winding staircase descends to an underwater marine observatory, an enclosure 20ft below the surface of the harbour, which gives visitors a glimpse of natural habitats in full 360-degree splendour (visibility depends on weather conditions). The park's sixteen acres also include a 100-foot **observation tower**, from which one can see breathtaking panoramas of Paradise Island, Nassau Harbour, and most of Cable Beach, as well as snorkelling ($55 rental fee) trips into the nearby reefs. Most visitors to the park arrive by **shuttles** that run between Prince George Wharf and the park.

The Botanic Gardens and Ardastra Gardens and Zoo

For those seeking quiet, the **Nassau Botanic Gardens** on Chippingham Road (Mon–Fri 9am–4.30pm, Sat & Sun 9am–4pm; $1; ℡ 323-5975) are a godsend. Just uphill along the western boundary of the cricket pitch, the gardens occupy the site of an old limestone quarry, now planted with a riot of some 600 species of tropical vegetation, much of it native to the Bahamas. You can roam the 26 acres at will, walking through an almost preternaturally bizarre conch-shell-lined tunnel and visiting a model Lucayan village composed of several grass and wattle huts, all under huge poinciana trees that bloom into a brilliant burst of red in summer. Not all the plants, shrubs and trees are labelled, and the grounds themselves can be shabby, but the overall effect more than compensates.

Pink flamingos

The **West Indian flamingo** (*Phoenicopterus ruber*) is larger and more intensely pink than its Old World and South American relatives. Its docility and habit of feeding and breeding in dense colonies led to its easy destruction by human populations, and as early as the 1880s its demise was predicted by most ornithologists. By 1952, Bahamian flamingos appeared only in Inagua, and would likely have been destroyed there save for the establishment in 1952 of the Society for the Protection of the Flamingo, and the hiring of two game wardens. Ten years later, the Bahamas National Trust acquired 287 square miles of Inagua wilderness as a flamingo sanctuary (see p.310). Today, Inagua has the largest breeding colony of West Indian flamingos on earth, and the project has been so successful that a small colony was recently discovered on nearby Acklins Island, proof that flamingos are beginning to return to their former habitats.

On Columbus Avenue, just behind the Botanic Gardens, the six–acre **Ardastra Gardens and Zoo** (daily 9am–5pm; $10, children $5; ☎323-5806) houses about fifty species from around the world, including some from the African savannah. There are a few examples of rare Bahamian animals, like the nearly extinct agoutis and hutias, tiny rodent-like nocturnal mammals that are hunted out in the wild. A welter of pathways connected by bridges wind around the grounds, where one can spot caged parrots and a large boa constrictor that can be handled with permission from caretakers. Flamingos are grouped together for show three times a day at 9am, 1pm and 4pm, though not on Sunday; see the box opposite for more on these colourful birds.

Cable Beach and around

With its hotels, restaurants and sport facilities, easy-going **CABLE BEACH** offers tourists a functioning, rather affordable self-contained base. The six major hotels (see "Accommodation", p.68) here – which in terms of style and aesthetics very much resemble the ocean-going vessels that dock at Prince George Wharf – are well endowed with a variety of bars, pools, shops and water-side activities. The **beach** itself is four miles in length, its sand broader and cleaner than any of Nassau's public beaches. Non-guests of the seaside resorts can enjoy the sandy stretch, though some short portions are claimed as private, reserved for hotel guests. Although *Sandals* is open only to its all-inclusive guests, the facilities at *Breezes* are open to non-guests for free use and make for a good place to lunch or grab a drink.

Five miles west of downtown Nassau, Cable Beach is an easy taxi ride from either the city or the airport, and is also served by a steady stream of jitneys (route #10) and shuttles. On the Nassau side, along West Bay Street, lies **Saunders Beach**, very popular on weekends with locals. Whispering

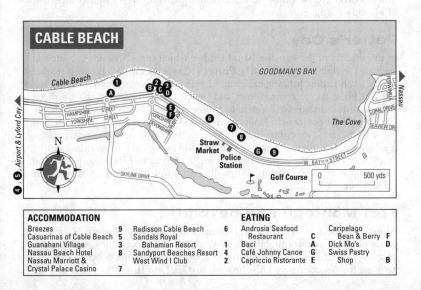

ACCOMMODATION			EATING			
Breezes	9	Radisson Cable Beach	Androsia Seafood		Caripelago	
Casuarinas of Cable Beach	5	Bahamian Resort 1	Restaurant C		Bean & Berry F	
Guanahani Village	3	Sandyport Beaches Resort 4	Baci A		Dick Mo's D	
Nassau Beach Hotel	8	West Wind I Club 2	Café Johnny Canoe G		Swiss Pastry	
Nassau Marriott &			Capriccio Ristorante E		Shop B	
Crystal Palace Casino	7					

casuarinas line the beach, opposite which stand the *Villas on Crystal Cay* and a small shopping strip. The area around Saunders Beach used to be a massive sissal grove developed by English interests, but is now the exclusive **Highland Park** residential area. Just west is a dangerous curve in the road that marks **Brown's Point**, a small isthmus that marks the leading or windward edge of **Goodman's Bay**, which swings down toward Cable Beach itself. Locals call the road turn "Go-Slow Bend", though many ignore the injunction at their peril. After about half a mile, the big hotels loom up out of the casuarinas, and for the next two miles or so the roadway divides into two avenues split by a wide central median used by walkers and joggers from the hotels.

Offshore here lie several cays, including **Balmoral Island**, leased by *Sandals*, but open to the public. Ferries run from *Sandals* or the pier at the *Radisson* and *Marriott* taking day-trippers to Balmoral, which has good swimming, a bar and restaurant, as well as several quiet areas to snorkel. Another all-inclusive, *Breezes*, now occupies the spot where the late Sir Harry Oakes built his house called Westbourne – and was mysteriously murdered there in 1943 (see "History", p.353).

Towards the west end of Cable Beach is **Delaporte Point**, which recently has been developed into a glamorous Venice-like development of condos, residences, shops and restaurants interspersed with manmade canals and landings. **Rock Point**, one mile further west, marks the official end of the Cable Beach district.

East of downtown

It is almost impossible to walk the length of **East Bay Street**. The majority of the strip is a jumble of commercial enterprises, fast-food joints, construction projects and smaller government buildings, along with hotels used mostly by Bahamian salesmen and Out Islanders here on short stays. One pleasant exception is **Potter's Cay**, a mile from Rawson Square but still a major component of Nassau's central core.

Potter's Cay

In the shadow of the Paradise Island Bridge, which spans Nassau Harbour and leads to Paradise Island (see p.87), **Potter's Cay** is home to a bustling market where locals peddle fish, vegetables and hardware. A slice of Out Island life, the cay is a place where fishing boats and sloops from all parts of the northern Bahamas haul in their fresh catch, including grouper, mackerel, snapper, turtle and the ubiquitous conch. Stalls open around 9am every morning, at which point fresh herbs, vegetables and fruit – especially paw-paw (papaya), pineapple, bananas, Eleutheran tomatoes and avocados – are sold. Keep in mind, too, that Potter's Cay is the departure point for the ferries to Eleuthera (p.211) and Andros (p.167), while Out Island mailboats also pick up and discharge their cargoes here.

Fort Montagu and beyond

Around a mile past Potter's Cay, the main road becomes Eastern Road and passes old **Fort Montagu**, built in 1741 and now an abandoned and neglected ruin. Though it was intended to protect the eastern approaches to Nassau's harbour, the Americans in 1776, Spanish in 1782, and British Loyalists in 1783 captured the fort without firing a shot by landing soldiers on the eastern edge of New Providence, then overrunning the fort at night. Due to these inadequacies, the fort saw little further action and was left to decay. What remains are a few crumbling walls which face a broad public beach that stretches for about a mile in front of the fort, and look out to Montagu Bay, where many yacht regattas and sloop races are held.

One mile south of the fort, down Village Road, is **The Retreat** (Mon–Fri 10am–4pm; $2; T 393-1317), an eleven-acre botanical garden nicely maintained by the Bahamas National Trust. It is mainly devoted to the palm, of which there are 200 species in evidence. Scattered among the palms are examples of many orchid species, ferns and hardwoods now rare on the islands due to over-harvesting. The gardens also have many arbours on which bougainvillea and orchids grow, stone arches which act as passageways and even a Buddha statue. Half-hour **tours** are conducted by a botany expert (Tues, Wed & Thurs 11.45am).

Two miles due south of Fort Montagu, along the major Yamacraw Road, is a ruin known locally as **Blackbeard's Tower**. A pile of tile-like stones that rises to a height of fifteen feet, the tower is free and open to the public. According to legend, it was built by the pirate Edward "Blackbeard" Teach as a lookout against officials hunting his fellow freebooters. In truth, the structure was built in the late 1700s, well after Teach died. Windswept and eerie, it offers fine views of the island, and the stretches of ocean off to the east. Finding the tower, though, can be a trick. To do so, head south on Fox Hill Road, a major road off Eastern Road, to a house called Tower Leigh on Yamacraw Road. The path to the tower is unmarked, but you'll see it in the distance. Continuing south on Fox Hill Road leads to the suburb of **FOX HILL**, established in the mid-1700s as a settlement for freed slaves. By far the best time to visit the suburban neighbourhood is during its **Emancipation Day celebrations**, held on the second Tuesday in August, when bands play all day and craft exhibits, especially quilts and straw work, and copious food stalls are in evidence. Call the Ministry of Tourism (T 322-7000) for more information. During the rest of the year, the neighbourhood's highlight is the Romanesque **St Augustine's Monastery** (T 364-1331), on Barnard Road, a working monastery and small college where Latin is still taught to the local boys who attend. Begun in 1946 under the guidance of Benedictine monk Father Jerome (see p.281), the structure of blocky sandstone stands on a nearby outcrop and is surrounded by neatly tended gardens. Call ahead and the friendly monks will conduct a tour of the place for a small donation.

Back up at the coastal Montagu Fort, Eastern Road continues east past **Montagu Foreshore**, an area of palatial homes perched on shaded cliffs above a beach. The road here is narrow and winding, and there is no access to the beach, though you can get down to the water at Montagu Ramp, a boat launch and market where locals bring conch to sell. Further along Eastern Road sits the **East End Lighthouse**, an automated signal not open to the public that constitutes the farthest eastern point on New Providence Island.

Over-the-Hill

True to its name, **OVER-THE-HILL** sits on the inland side of Nassau's Prospect Ridge, the largest hill in Nassau. It's a relatively poor residential area where descendants of former slaves built compact wooden houses and painted them in rainbow colours. Though there are some points of cultural interest here – shops selling local crafts and hardscrabble bars featuring rake 'n' scrape bands – it's not really a place to wander, and can be dangerous, especially at night.

Eating

In response to the heavy influx of tourists from all over the world, Nassau's **restaurants** have mastered seemingly every style of cooking, at prices ranging from moderate to ludicrously expensive. On top of the kaleidoscopic array of international cuisine, though, the city offers great opportunities to feast on strictly Bahamian fare and to grab a cheap but delicious bite at a bakery or café. There are also a number of **take-out** places in town useful for eating on the quick. Usually featuring variations on chicken-in-a-bag, barbecue, or tuna-johnnycakes, best of the bunch are *Imperial Take-Away*, across from the *British Colonial Hotel*, *Ro-Lay's Take Away* on Victoria Avenue just behind the Royal Bank of Canada, the *Souse Pot* on Bay Street and Christie, and the *Bistro Bahama* on East Bay. Don't forget also the food stalls at **Arawak Cay** (see p.75), a must-visit for local culture and deliciously fresh seafood.

On **Cable Beach**, one is never far from food or drink. Dining here, though, presents few budget options, with most prices ranging from moderate to very expensive. Some all-inclusives, including *Sandals*, are not an option for non-guests, though *Breezes* is one place where, for about $60 per person, non-guests can participate in both dining and leisure activities.

Cafés and bakeries

The Bonefish Beverage Emporium Charlotte St, just off Bay ☎ 323-1332. Advertising itself as an "eclectic bar and coffee house", this airy joint offers light jazz, acoustic music, and an array of coffees, sandwiches and drinks. Open until 2am most nights.

The Bread Shop Shirley St, east of Mackey St ☎ 393-7973. A simple yet popular family-run operation producing great pound and banana cake, as well as notable raisin bread and pineapple tarts.

Cafe Caribe Harbour Bay Shopping Centre, East Bay St ☎ 394-7040. Tucked into a small corner of the Logos Bookstore, this café makes for a pleasant spot to stop for sandwiches and coffee during an afternoon of shopping. Closes at 6pm.

Cafe del'Opera Marlborough St ☎ 356-6118. Unpretentious and pleasant Italian café specializing in filling pasta dishes for around $10.

Cafe Paradiso Bay St near Victoria ☎ 356-5282. A small coffeehouse, open evenings and popular with locals, doling out sandwiches and tasty desserts. Closed Sun.

Cappucino Cafe Royal Palm Mall, Mackey St ☎ 394-6332. Best for lunch – it closes by 6.30pm – including good tuna melts, Greek salads and mini-pizzas. The bread is fresh-baked, and save room for the great desserts.

Jitter's Coffee House Bay St near the Straw Market ☎ 356-9382. If you're lucky enough to nab a seat – it's typically jam-packed here – this upstairs coffeshop on Nassau's main drag makes for a great place to watch the crowds flow by.

Kelly's Bakery Market St just off Bay St ☎ 325-0616. A must-visit for their devastatingly great bread pudding and gingerbread, both only 50¢ a hunk. Even when the shelves look bare, you should be able to find these trusty items.

Model Bakery Dowdeswell St ☎ 322-2595. Though not worth the trip out, this bakery on the far eastern end of town is worth a stop when in the neighbourhood. The cinnamon twists and danish are tops.

Inexpensive restaurants

Cellar Restaurant 11 Charlotte St at Bay St ☎ 322-8877. Though in the heart of town, this is a quiet and cool escape for lunch (it doesn't serve dinner) with its breezy fans and wood tables. Menu items include quiche, smothered grouper and shepherd's pie. Closed Sun.

Conch Fritters Bar and Grill Marlborough St ☎ 323-8778. Many tourists wind up at this popular place, terrific for breakfasts that include fabulous French toast, johnnycakes and omelettes. Later in the day, the burgers and conch salad are worth-while, and most evenings you can relax to live music while watching folks buzz past the *British Colonial Hotel* right across the street.

Double Dragon Chinese Restaurant Mackey St at Bridge Plaza Commons ☎ 393-5718. Reliable chain that can be counted on for decent, not amazing, Chinese food. Delivery available.

Green Shutters Restaurant and Pub Parliament St ☎ 322-3701. A centrally located pub that's authentically English in atmosphere and tone, serving standards like shepherd's pie and bangers and mash along with some simple sandwiches and Bahamian dishes. English ales are on tap, and the 190-year-old house adds to the enjoyment as patrons are surrounded by true Victorian furnish-ings.

Skans West Bay St at Frederick St ☎ 322-2468. A classic Bahamian joint, catering both to tourists and locals who crowd inside for boiled fish and conch. Closed Sun night.

Moderate restaurants

Athena Restaurant Bay St at Charlotte St ☎ 322-1936. Upstairs and overlooking busy Bay, this Greek establishment is a fixture with the afternoon cruise crowd. The mains, such as moussaka, sou-vlaki and spanakopita, are all well prepared and fairly priced at $8–13. Closed Sun.

Bahamian Kitchen Trinity Place off Market St ☎ 325-0702. A down-home back-street restaurant that's one of the most authentic Bahamian places in downtown Nassau. It serves the big three – grouper, snapper and conch – at about $10 a plateful, and while its popularity makes for long waits, the tomato-smothered grouper and delicious peas and rice are worth it.

Cafe Matisse Bank Lane and Bay St, off Parliament Sq ☎ 356-7012. Not a café, but an upscale bistro featuring an eclectic menu of spe-cialty seafood items like duck-filled ravioli or seafood pizza. Jazz is sometimes played on Thurs or Sun nights, and there's a nice happy hour every evening from 5pm to 7pm. Favoured by local busi-ness types for lunch, dinner sees a pleasing mix-ture of tourists and locals sitting down to dig in. Closed Sun.

Chippie's Wall Street Cafe Colony Place Shopping Arcade, Bay St at George St ☎ 356-2087. Though rather cramped, this upstairs restaurant features a fabulous corn-banana soup for lunch, and fine seafood and chicken stews for dinner. Dessert – especially the cheesecake – is recommended.

Crocodile's Waterfront Bar and Grill East Bay St near Paradise Island Bridge ☎ 323-3341. For the most part, this loud restaurant serves average standardized Bahamian fare like grouper fingers and fritters, though you can also get a monstrous T-bone steak. It's a popular hangout nonetheless, and the deck, where food is served at tables under thatched parasols, has a buzzing, good atmos-phere, fuelled in part by the delicious Bahama Mama rum special.

Europe Restaurant and Bar *Ocean Spray Hotel*, West Bay St ☎ 322-8032. Located on the bottom floor of the *Ocean Spray* across from the beach, this dark Vienna-style pub serves wiener schnitzel and pork dishes along with some Bahamian spe-cialties. Worth visiting for the eclectic clientele and imported beer selection.

Island's Pasta Market Bahamas Stock Exchange Bldg, 1 Bay St ☎ 322-1188. Next door to the *British Colonial Hotel*, this relaxing establishment features good Italian food, including a seafood pizza fresh from the brick oven. Some tables over-look the harbour.

Mamma Lyddy's Place Market St at Cockburn St ☎ 328-6849. Open for breakfast, lunch and dinner, this Bahamian restaurant, located in an old house, has diners streaming in at all hours for boiled fish, conch, friend snapper, pork chops and fried chick-en. The tangerine colour scheme is set off by exposed wood and local Junkanoo art, and all plat-ters come with side-dishes in delicious profusion, including macaroni and cheese, cream corn, peas and rice, coleslaw and grits. Carry-out available. Closes Sat at 6pm.

Native's East Bay St at Maud St ☎ 394-8280. As one might expect when eating in a house painted in bright colours, this restaurant features strictly local Bahamian fare, including a not-too-greasy fried snapper. It is, in addition, a cultural stage where local bands sometimes play in the evening. Outdoor seating under poinciana trees available. Closed Mon.

The Poop Deck Nassau Yacht Haven, East Bay St ☎ 393-8175. The original *Poop Deck* is a popular seafood restaurant just east of the Paradise Island Bridge. A second has been opened at Sandyport Beach, west of Cable Beach. Both feature fine Bahamian grouper and snapper specials, an exten-sive wine list, and a justly famous guava duff, a light pudding, for dessert.

The Shoal Restaurant Nassau St ☎ 323-4400. This family restaurant, located between Meadow St and Poinciana Drive, features a traditional Bahamian breakfast of boil fish and johnnycake, which may not be to everyone's taste. For lunch, try the spiced mutton and okra soup. Locals pour in here on Saturday mornings. Open until 12.30am.

Tamarind Hill Restaurant Village Rd near Shirley St ☎ 394-1306. *Tamarind Hill* offer sandwiches and salads, as well as mango chicken and other exotic dishes at $8–15 in a circa-1920 Bahamian house with tropical furniture and outdoor tables.

Expensive restaurants

Buena Vista *Buena Vista Hotel*, Delancy St ☎ 322-2811. Located in a nineteenth-century manor house, this elegant and expensive Continental-style restaurant offers outstanding caesar salads, smoked salmon, duck pate, jumbo shrimp and a fabulous wine list. The cheapest entree is $30.

Chez Willie West Bay St ☎ 322-5364. Located just west of the *British Colonial Hotel*, this cordial French restaurant serves up excellent mussels in wine and a delicious steak tenderloin, which can be complemented by a choice from the exhaustive list. Entrees $30 and up.

East Villa Restaurant East Bay St ☎ 393-3377. Next to the Yacht Club, this combo Continental/Chinese place is relatively upscale and features both Szechuan and Cantonese, along with a scrumptious rack of lamb. The back-lit aquariums and faux classical statues throughout make for intriguing dinner conversations.

Gaylord's Dowdeswell St near Victoria St ☎ 356-3004. Located in a charmingly ornate 1870 mansion, this Indian restaurant, featuring plenty of draped silk and quiet music, offers succulent traditional entrees including well-prepared tandoori dishes. The menu features several vegetarian dishes as well. No lunch on weekends.

Graycliff *Graycliff Hotel*, West Hill St ☎ 322-2796/7. The *Graycliff's* flagship restaurant has four indoor dining rooms and a beautiful outdoor dining terrace. Surrounded by art and music, diners can choose from one of many three-course set meals. Stone crab, caviar, duckling with calvados and apples, and rack of lamb are all part of the amazing menu. The 300,000-bottle cellar is world-famous. For a less expensive meal, try lunch during weekdays. Reservations and jacket and tie required. Entrees $30–70.

Humidor Restaurant *Graycliff*, West Hill St ☎ 328-7050. A part of the hotel's newish Cigar Factory, this bistro serves memorable lunches and early dinners for slightly less than the hotel's larger restaurant. The menu features tuna *tartare*, lobster and lamb, and a brunch on Sundays (10am–3pm) includes oysters and French toast with champagne. No dinner Sun.

Montagu Gardens East Bay St at Waterloo, ☎ 394-6347. In an old mansion on the east edge of Bay St, this elegant and eclectic Continental restaurant sits near Waterloo Lake and boasts an elegant walled-courtyard and garden dining area. Seafood and steak are the specialties, with entrees ($20–40) like filet mignon, lobster and some special Bahamian dishes like minced crawfish. Closed Sun.

The Pink Pearl Cafe East Bay St, east of Paradise Island Bridge ☎ 394-6413. In a converted house near the water, this restaurant combines ambience, service and great food in surprising ways. Specialties range from grouper ragout to grilled beef and crab-stuffed coconut shrimp, but it's all delightfully different. For example, the chef uses a cream base for the conch chowder instead of tomato, and serves homemade breads in a calabash shell. Closed for lunch on weekends.

Sun and... Lakeview Rd and Shirley St ☎ 393-1205. Ultra-expensive, this dinner-only restaurant is worth it for the Belgian owner/chef's soufflés, specialty salmon dishes and veal. With gardens, rock pools, and a jacket-only policy, this is one of the Nassau establishments favoured by visiting superstars. Closed Mon and Aug–Sept.

Tony Cheng's Chinese and Seafood Restaurant Nassau Harbour Club, East Bay St ☎ 393-8669. An elegant and dimly lit upscale Chinese restaurant open for lunch and dinner. The menu features walnut chicken, steak kew and Cantonese lobster (all $15–20), among many other special choices.

The Wedgewood *British Colonial Hotel*, 1 Bay St ☎ 322-3301. Elegant hotel dining surrounded by textured wood, blue wallpaper and glass-enclosed booths. The subdued lighting and quiet tone are English to the bone, as is the food, with Dover sole, a special seafood pepper pot, and cock-a-leekie soup. Good selection of grilled meats and seafood, best paired with a bottle from the fine wine list.

Cable Beach

Androsia Steak and Seafood Restaurant Cable Beach Shoppers Haven (Henrea Carletta Bldg) ☎ 327-7805 or 6430. Upscale but not brutally so, *Androsia*'s house specialty is a very fine pepper-steak au Paris. Veal and local seafood round out the menu ($15–25), all served in a soothing nautical atmosphere with lanterns and striped curtains. Dinner only and reservations suggested.

Baci West Bay St at Skyline Drive ☎ 327-6936. A comfortable cubbyhole, this Italian restaurant doles out decent food at honest prices. Try the special antipasto plate followed by clams steamed in wine. Good selection of Italian wines. Dinner only.

Cafe Johnny Canoe *Nassau Beach Hotel* ☎ 327-3373. Awfully fun café, especially when sitting outside where people-watching is a delight. Great fried chicken, meat loaf, and fixings, including knockout macaroni and cheese. Forget the diet and dive into the desserts, including a great New York cheesecake. The bar's a good place to oil up an appetite too, with occasional live music.

Capriccio Ristorante West Bay St ☎ 327-8547. A good wine list and some basic Italian dishes are combined with spotty service. The minestrone, pesto and veal scallopini are much raved about by regulars, though, and you can bring your own bottle of wine if you wish, with no corking fee. Reservations are recommended. The outdoor terrace is on noisy Bay Street. Open dinners only on Sun.

Caripelago Bean and Berry Royal Palm Mall, West Bay St ☎ 327-4749. Across from *Sandal's*, this is a casual spot for fried chicken and Bahamian seafood, like the traditional grouper with mango sauce.

Dickie Mo's West Bay St ☎ 327-7854. This popular spot, where waitresses are decked out in sailor suits, serves all kinds of seafood and Bahamian specialties, including conch, stone crab, grouper and snapper. Most of the dining is outside, though there is a covered bar where soca and calypso are played 7–11pm. Daily 4pm–midnight.

Swiss Pastry Shop West Bay St, across from *Sandals* ☎ 327-5368. Divine cream shells and various kugels are the reason for dropping into this attractive bakery.

Drinking and nightlife

To a very large extent, Nassau's **nightlife** is tourist nightlife. All the large tourist hotels feature both small **bars** and lavish **nightclubs**, and many guests choose to attend these exclusively, never straying far from their temporary homes. There are, though, several bars and nightclubs worth seeking out in town, while Arawak Cay and Potter's Cay offer local hangouts that sometimes feature upstart bands.

Downtown Nassau is usually deserted by 6pm most evenings, and on Sunday night, it looks like a plague has struck. There are a number of local hangouts, favoured by Bahamians who like to sit and watch satellite TV, play dominoes and pool, and drink a quiet beer – if that's what you're looking for, try the *Pacific Bar* on Victoria Street or *Millie's Place* just off Devaux Street. Over the Hill is filled with these little places as well, including the *Silver Dollar* and *The Outback*, though it's best at night to visit this neighbourhood with a local as guide.

Almost all the Cable Beach hotels have their discos, similar in theme, including Sandal's Royal Bahamian at *Sandals* and Fanta-Z-Disco in the *Radisson Cable Beach* hotel. For the latest on disco, club and bar happenings, flip through the tourist tabloid *What's On*.

Gambling at the two large **casinos** on Cable Beach and Paradise Island as well as the *Nassau Marriott and Crystal Palace Casino* is strictly the product of tourism; Bahamians themselves have neither the time nor the money to devote to such pastimes.

Bahama Boom Beach Club Elizabeth Ave at Bay St ☎ 325-7733. One of the new dance clubs on the scene, *Bahama Boom* is located very near the wharf. The music is played by DJs at a high volume. Like most hotel discos, it features flashing lights and a suntanned touristy crowd.

Cafe Johnny Canoe West Bay St, Cable Beach ☎ 327-3373. A small calypso band plays here on weekends. The bar is pleasant enough with plenty of rum drinks to choose from, though it mainly caters to diners waiting for a table.

Club 601 East Bay St ☎ 322-3041. Exclusive and thoroughly chic club open Thurs–Sat (5pm until late) only. The dress code bars shorts and sneak-

ers, and the entertainment revolves around live bands – The Baha Men (of "Who Let the Dogs Out" fame) sometimes play here – and standard club tunes. Thursday is Ladies Night, when the ladies get in free before 11pm; otherwise, cover is $15–20.

Club Waterloo East Bay St, one mile east of Paradise Island Bridge ☎ 393-7324. This splashy, crowded disco features five bars and dancing until 4am, with a four-hour happy hour beginning at 4pm daily. It can be amazingly expensive, with a cover of $30 on weekends ($25 weekdays), though many hotels can hand out a "visitor pass" that entitles you to enter for $5. Free buffet on Friday.

Cocktails and Dreams West Bay St ☎ 328-3745. A small nightclub just west of the *British Colonial Hotel* with a postage-stamp-size dance floor, dartboards and daily drink specials.

Conch Fritter's Marlborough Street, next to *Dunkin Donuts* ☎ 323-8778. Though essentially an eatery, *Fritter's* features a live band Tues–Sun from 7pm to 11pm, and live Junkanoo Sat at 8pm. Grab a stool at the bar and try to avoid being sucked into the satellite TV, an overbearing staple of bar life in Nassau, that stares at you from five angles.

Culture Club Nassau St and West Bay St ☎ 356-6266. For a small cover that varies with the day of the week, one gets admission to a loft-style dance club with both DJs and live bands. The DJ plays a mix of rock, pop and funk, while the live music features mainly rock bands.

The Drop-Off Bay St between Charlotte St and Frederick St ☎ 322-3444. A lively pub with the advantage of being right on Bay Street where the ships offload. Pub food, eclectic music, a varied clientele and English ales on tap make this place a good choice. Large aquariums heighten the offbeat ambience. Open 11am–6am.

Hammerheads Bar and Grill East Bay St, just west of the Paradise Island Bridge ☎ 393-5625. A small, unpretentious beer bar with a few booths and a jukebox open 11am–1am daily, with a happy hour 4–7pm.

Last 1/4 East Bay St ☎ 323-3341. Located in a pink stucco building, this club is home to a maze of rooms, a pleasant patio and pool tables. One of the few quieter approaches to entertainment, with featured bands performing blues, funk and soft rock. Open Tues–Sat, $10 cover on Fri and Sat.

Rock and Roll Cafe West Bay St, next door to the *Nassau Beach Hotel* ☎ 327-7639. A *Hard Rock Café* rip-off, this bar features lots of rock memorabilia on the walls, big-screen TVs and loud music, most of it from DJs though a worthwhile band is occasionally featured.

Rumours Charlotte St ☎ 323-2925. Housed in an old colonial building, this quiet wine bar features soft background music, a few booths and tables and is a haven from the storm of tourism outside. Happy hour 5–8pm.

Silk Cotton Club Market St, one block up from the Straw Market ☎ 356-0955. A great jazz club, featuring performances by the musician owner and guest artists. There is a cover charge only when a special performer is scheduled. Open Wed–Sat 8pm–2am; food served.

Tequila Pepe's *Radisson Cable Beach* hotel, West Bay St ☎ 327-6000. This faux Mexican café and bar provides its primarily tourist diners with a fiesta spirit, fake cacti and good margaritas. Open Thurs–Tues 6–10.30pm for food, though later if the mood warrants. Check for a schedule of live bands and salsa contests.

The Zoo West Bay St, opposite Saunders Beach ☎ 322-7195. This converted warehouse, painted garish Rasta colours and operated by the owner of *Cafe Johnny Canoe*, is the loudest, most crowded, most expensive dance club on the island. The *Zoo* offers five themed bars, an upper and lower level, VIP area and a huge ground-floor dance area that's typically packed with a youngish crowd. Patrons of *Johnny Canoe* receive a coupon worth $5 toward entry. Also, look in the tourist mags for coupons on drinks and food. Open 8pm–4am; cover $20–30.

Theatre and floor shows

Many of the **performing arts** have taken their sweet time in reaching the Bahamas. While native revues featuring limbo and calypso seem quite dated, they continue to make regular appearances on the hotel scene, and there's really only one spot in town where serious **theatre** and other similar performances are held on a regular basis. *What's On* is your best bet for the latest, as it carries a topical selection of theatre offerings along with listings for the floor shows at various hotels around town.

Dundas Centre for the Performing Arts Mackey St ☎ 393-3728. This lovely white stucco theatre is the sole venue in Nassau to offer world-class as well as student drama, occasional dance and readings by both local and international artists. The Sunday Nassau newspaper carries listings of its performances, which are mostly during the winter season, or you can call the box office during the week.

Kings and Knights *Nassau Beach Hotel* ☎ 327-5321. This floor-show extravaganza is the largest and most elaborate on the island, featuring King Eric and his Knights who have been performing for many years. The show highlights steel-drum music, limbo, fire dancing and Junkanoo. There are two performances Tues–Sat at 8.30pm and 10.30pm, with a single Mon performance at

8.30pm. Admission is $20, which entitles you to a drink as well. Dinner is served separately at 7pm. **Palace Theater** Crystal Palace Casino, *Nassau Marriott Resort*, Cable Beach ☎ 327-6200. Every night of the week this big hotel theatre presents a Las Vegas-style show replete with bosomy dancers and show tunes. These spectaculars are presented at 8.45pm and 11pm, save for Sun and Thurs, when only the earlier show is put on. While the main shows are adult-only, a special "covered" show is presented on Tues and Sat at 8.45pm. Advance reservations are almost always necessary. Tickets for the show are $30, $59 with dinner.

Shopping and crafts

For many, duty-free **shopping** is the activity of choice during their stay in Nassau. On any day of the week save Sunday, Bay Street is likely to be jammed with shoppers perusing the aisles of a bewildering array of stores. As far as duty-free items are concerned, the best deals can be had on **jewellery** and **watches**, including great deals on Colombian emeralds, and **liquor** – a fine bottle of Bahamian or Haitian rum costs about $6. **Cigars** can also be a good buy, and are best found at either *Graycliff's* Cigar Factory (see p.74) or the Pipe of Peace, located on Charlotte and Bay streets (☎ 325-2022). Bay Street is also home to most of Nassau's **bookstores**, perhaps best for picking up a Bahamian cookbook or two. Despite heavy pressure to stay open, shops in Nassau **close** around 6pm, and are always closed on Sunday. Even with cruise ships in town, you will find Nassau nearly deserted on Sunday.

Nearly everybody who comes to Nassau winds up at the **Straw Market** (see p.70) on the western end of Bay Street, only a couple of blocks from Rawson Square and a good place to search out locally crafted items. Also worth noting is the Bahamian Ministry of Tourism's **Authentically Bahamian** programme, which includes a group of shop owners, artists and craftsmen who offer only Bahamian-made goods. Besides those listed below, you can locate participants of this programme by the programme's window sticker.

Serious shoppers should obtain a copy of the glossy tourist mag called *What to do: where to shop*, available at hotels and in all information booths.

Antiques and crafts

Art Mon Bay St ☎ 356-2470. This small shop offers a selection of prints, mostly from Bahamian artists, which feature pastels and watercolours of beach and ocean scenes.
Bahamacraft Centre Paradise Island Drive, near Hurricane Hole Plaza. A bright, tropically themed building in which craft vendors offer straw work, shell collages, beads and the like.
Bahamian Antiques and Gallery Bay St ☎ 323-7421. Mostly art prints, though there is a good selection of ceramics and other assorted hand-made crafts.
Balmain Antiques Bay St at Charlotte, 2nd Floor Mason Bldg. Up a long flight of stairs, this friendly old-time shop is a great place to roam. Items on sale include prints of old ships, maps, out-of-date guidebooks, photographs, and watercolours, all with a suitably worn appearance.
Doongalik Studios Village Rd ☎ 394-1886. An art studio located in a Bahamian house with gardens.

Basically a Junkanoo studio, with curios and furniture, masks and sculptures. The wire sculptures are particularly beautiful.
Kennedy Gallery Parliament St ☎ 325-7662. A serious art gallery featuring the best of Bahamian artists, including emerging talent.
Marlborough Antiques Marlborough St, across from the *British Colonial Hotel* ☎ 328-0502. Cluttered traditional antique store loaded with an expensive assortment of English Victoriana, glassware, prints, oddities. Worth a look, even if you're not buying.
Nassau Art Gallery East Bay Shopping Centre ☎ 393-1482. A no-nonsense gallery that displays local paintings and sculptures.
The Plait Lady Bay St at Victoria St ☎ 356-5884. Plaits, or straw weaves, are owner Clare Sands' specialty. She collects items from all the far-flung corners of the islands, and displays them in her colourful and friendly shop. Everything in the store is guaranteed handmade by a Bahamian.

Books and music

Anglo-American Bookstore Prince George Plaza, Bay St. This hole-in-the wall bookshop stocks used paperbacks perfect for the beach, some maps and a good selection of local and international newspapers, including the Sunday *New York Times*.

Cody's Record and Video Store East Bay St ☎325-8834. Slightly away from downtown Nassau, Cody's is the largest record store in town. Its stock – rather dusty and expensive – features a decent selection of Junkanoo, soca, calypso and Jamaican reggae.

The Island Shop and Island Bookstore Bay St ☎322-4183. A well-stocked second-floor bookstore features hardback and paperback best-sellers, and a good selection of serious books about history, geography and science, along with guidebooks and coffee-table pictorials. Many self-published Bahamian histories, as well as a stock of Bahamian secondary school materials, make for interesting browsing.

Logos Bookstore Harbour Bay Shopping Centre, East Bay St ☎394-7040. Located near the *Cafe Caribe*, this small shop features picture books and cookbooks, cards and gifts.

Pyfroms Bay St ☎322-2603. Cluttered store in downtown Nassau with an amazing blend of tourist junk and steel drums, along with a selection of CDs from the islands. A good place to buy snorkel gear, coconut carvings and some straw work.

Authentic Bahamian

Animal Crackers Prince George Plaza, Bay St. A small store in the plaza selling confections ranging from guava dips to tomato chutney, as well as some locally created stuffed animals.

Green Lizard Bay St ☎323-8076. For the most part this shop sells standard tourist gizmos, though there's also a selection of Bahamian concoctions like coconut confections and condiments, as well as hand-carved items and prints.

Island Treasures International Bazaar, Bay St ☎323-7568. Many people stop in here for cameras and film, or to buy a postcard. In back, however, is a nice selection of Bahamian-made handicrafts, including straw bags and hats, shell and bead jewellery, as well as prints and watercolours.

Taste of the Islands International Bazaar, Bay St ☎356-7632. Just as The Plait Lady is the place to go for Out Island straw ware, Taste of the Islands is the place to go for locally made spices, jams, jerks, sauces and seasonings. Everything in the shop is guaranteed Bahamian-made.

Listings

Banks/ATMs There are a cluster of banks on and around Bay Street, including Bank of Nova Scotia (☎356-1400), Royal Bank (☎326-CARD) and Novus Services (Discover Financial Services; ☎356-8500). Most are open Mon–Thurs 9.30am–3pm, Fri 9.30am–5pm. American Express has representation at Playtours, 303 Shirley St (☎322-2931). ATMs dispensing either US or Bahamian dollars are easily located throughout Nassau.

Consulates and embassies US Embassy Consular Section, Mosmar Bldg, Queen St (☎322-1181); Canadian Consulate, Shirley Street Shopping Plaza, Shirley Street (☎393-2123); British High Commission, Bitco Bldg, East and Shirley sts (☎325-7471).

Dockmaster Call Potter's Cay dockmaster (☎393-1064) for mailboat departures and arrivals, as well as information on departures and arrivals of the three-times-a-week service to Andros.

Emergencies Police and fire dial ☎911. There are police stations in every district of Nassau, painted green, with officers out front in most cases. The main department is off Parliament Square. Bahamas Air-Sea Rescue can be reached on ☎325-8864 or 322-3877.

Eyeglasses and optics The Optique Shoppe, 22 Parliament St (☎322-3910; Mon–Fri 9am–5pm, Sat 9am–noon) has special services for glasses repair, contact lenses, with one-hour service.

Gyms/spas Indoor fitness addicts can get their fix at several gyms and spas in the city. All are stocked with the standard workout equipment. The best include Gold's Gym, Bridge Plaza (☎394-4635), which has aerobic classes, a juice bar, and first-rate equipment; fees average about $8 a day. Another good choice is Windermere, East Bay Street (☎393-0033), which offers an upscale approach, with spa-style layout, facials and massages. It also has a steam and sauna unit and clean showers. Fees average $20 per day, with treatments in a variety of ranges from $35 to $70. The largest hotel gym is the Palace Spa in the Crystal Palace complex (☎327-6200). Near the *Radisson Cable Beach* hotel, it features a complete gym with bikes, sauna and various classes. Fees are $10 per day, $35 weekly, with discounts for guests of the *Nassau Marriott* and *Nassau Beach Hotel*.

Hospital Princess Margaret Hospital (☎322-2861) is a government-run facility with emergency care.

Laundry Superwash, Nassau Street and Boyd (☎323-4018), is open 24 hours daily. In the same building is Oriental Dry Cleaner (☎323-7249). Many hotels offer laundry and dry-cleaning service as well.

Libraries The main library is the Nassau Public Library on Shirley Street (☎322-4907; Mon–Thurs 10am–8pm, Fri 10am–5pm, Sat 10am–4pm).

Pharmacies People's Pharmacy, Elizabeth Street near Bay (☎356-9806), is most convenient for shoppers and cruise-ship passengers. Other options include branches of the Lowes Pharmacy

in the Harbour Bay Shopping Centre (☎393-4813) and Town Centre Mall (☎325-6482).

Post office The main post office is on East Hill Street at Parliament (☎322-3025; Mon–Thurs 8.30am–5.30pm, Fri 8.30am–12.30pm). There's also a Federal Express on Frederick Street (☎323-7611).

Telephones There's a BaTelCo storefront on East Street (☎323-6414; 7am–10pm daily), with booths for international calls.

Travel agents Bowtie Tours (☎325-8849); Happy Tours (☎323-5818); Leisure Travel Tours (☎393-1989); Majestic Tours (☎322-2606); Playatours Ltd (☎322-2931); Richard Moss Tours (☎393-1989).

Paradise Island

A monument to the reckless buildup of 1990s international tourism, **PARADISE ISLAND** consists of 686 acres of hard-pack coral and windblown sand just north of New Providence and conveniently connected by a purpose-built bridge.

Visitors on package tours come in droves for three- and four-day vacations at the resort hotels, and the place is overbuilt almost to the point of lunacy. Nevertheless, Paradise Island still has a marvellous north coast where pink sand meets mellow turquoise water, explaining why commercialism found the isle in the first place.

After its early settlement in the seventeenth century by wandering fishermen sent off by Eleutheran Adventurer William Sayle, Paradise Island was given over to the raising of pigs, giving the cay its once richly connotative name, Hog Island. Though essentially uninhabited, Nassauvians soon began rowing over to the cay to spend a leisurely day on its deserted beaches. During the late eighteenth century, an ornate Banquet House was built on the island and local Bahamians offered boat rides to the island, provided changing rooms for bathers, and began to sell fresh fruit, especially the succulent oranges that were cultivated there.

As Nassau built its early hotels catering to winter visitors and multimillionaires, so Hog Island too began to cater to the rich. It drew the attention of Swedish industrialist Axel Wenner-Gren, who arrived in Nassau in 1939, dredged a brackish sump-hole, renamed it Paradise Lake and constructed some canals linking it with Nassau Harbour. Wenner-Gren sold his estate to an even richer man, Huntington Hartford, who renamed the island **Paradise**, and was soon busy building the posh **Ocean Club**, a 59-room Georgian-style charmer.

In the late 1960s, the Mary Carter Paint Company organized the various holdings on the island into Resorts International. In 1967, Resorts built the

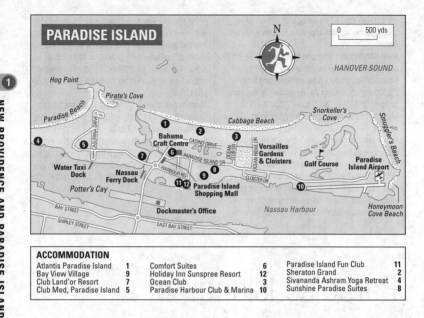

ACCOMMODATION

Atlantis Paradise Island	1	Comfort Suites	6	Paradise Island Fun Club	11
Bay View Village	9	Holiday Inn Sunspree Resort	12	Sheraton Grand	2
Club Land'or Resort	7	Ocean Club	3	Sivananda Ashram Yoga Retreat	4
Club Med, Paradise Island	5	Paradise Harbour Club & Marina	10	Sunshine Paradise Suites	8

arching **Paradise Island Bridge** linking the island with Nassau directly. After TV producer Merv Griffin bought Resorts, he added casino gambling, and brought a small airport to the eastern end of the island.

In 1994, Griffin and Resorts cashed out their considerable investment, paving the way for billionaire Sol Kerzner's Sun International, a mega-developer, which now owns seventy percent of the island, including the *Ocean Club* and *Paradise Paradise*. Sun International expanded the *Atlantis Resort and Casino* complex to include a Mayan temple, waterslide and the Dig, a simulated exploration of mythical Atlantis under the ocean. A second phase of spending added the huge casino and a $15-million marina that attracts yachts from around the world. In December 1998, a second bridge was completed spanning Nassau Harbour, assisting with traffic flow and increasing ties to New Providence.

Getting around

If you are staying on Paradise Island, don't bother **renting a car** unless you plan to tour New Providence; see p.63 for a list of recommended agents on the larger island. It's easy to **taxi** or **shuttle** your way anywhere on Paradise Island cheaply – a Casino Express shuttle, for example, makes the rounds of major hotels on the island for only $1. Those interested in walking around Paradise Island should keep in mind that distances are greater than they appear on the tourist maps, roads are often congested and much of the island property is private and protected by security.

Getting **to New Providence** from the smaller island is likewise easy. A **water taxi** service ($3 one-way) leaves the docks about every half-hour

8.30am–6pm. In addition, a larger ferry ($2 round-trip) leaves the docks just west of Paradise Island Bridge every half-hour between 9.30am and 4.15pm. For those in a hurry, taxis operate all over the island. A trip over to Nassau is about $8, including the $2 bridge toll. Water taxis also run to and from the west and middle of Paradise Island, serving *Club Med*, Pirate's Cove and **Paradise Beach**.

Accommodation

Almost nothing is cheap on Paradise Island, and much is downright expensive, so you'll have to work at trying to find good-value **accommodation**. Paradise Island does have, costs notwithstanding, some real treasures though, including a few small hotels or guesthouses that are great alternatives to massive tourist enclaves.

Hotels and resorts

Atlantis, Paradise Island Casino Drive ☎ 363-3000 or 1-800/321-3000, ☏ 363-3524, ⓦ www.atlantis.com. This Roman-epic hotel has two massive wings of rooms, a central tower topped by a huge dolphin statue surrounded by concentric rings, 2119 rooms and 230 suites. There are 21 places to eat (see p.91 for reviews of the best), seventeen bars of varying sizes, nine swimming pools, a huge outdoor snorkelling/aquarium area, watersports galore, casino, children's programmes and a comedy club. Each room, most done up in a wicker-rattan theme in pale hues, is upscale with balcony and cable TV. Rates average out at about $350 per double in winter, with summer rates much lower. ⓾

Bay View Village Bay View Drive ☎ 363-2555 or 1-800/757-1357, ☏ 3632370, ⓦ www.bayviewvillage.com. Relatively secluded in a residential area, this four-unit condo-style resort that includes a few villas. The condos (either one- or two-bedroom units) and three-bedroom villas are all spacious and immaculately clean. The property, a ten-minute walk from Cabbage Beach, also boasts three swimming pools. Condos ⓻; villas ⓾

Club Land'Or Resort Paradise Beach Drive ☎ 363-2400 or 1-800/446-3850, ☏ 363-3403, ⓦ www.clublandor.com. On Paradise Lake, this time-share condo outfit has 72 two-bedroom suites that can sleep up to four. Guests can use the facilities at *Atlantis*, and the on-site restaurant is terrific. ⓾

Club Med, Paradise Island Casuarina Drive ☎ 363-2640 or 1-800/258-2633, ☏ 363-3496, ⓦ www.clubmed.com. This all-inclusive *Club Med* stretches from the north shore to Nassau Harbour, and has just about everything on its grounds. A recent renovation has added some single rooms to its 320 doubles, and has improved the original look of the grounds by adding new landscaping and gardens dense with hibiscus and bougainvillea, along with an Olympic-size swimming pool. Preferred mainly by honeymooners and adult couples travelling alone, the 26-acre complex is also home to a pair of restaurants and bars, a nightclub, eighteen tennis courts and lots of watersports options. Privacy, though, is hard to come by as much of the dining and most of the activities are in large groups. Rates average $300 per double in winter, single rooms much higher. ⓾

Comfort Suites Casino Drive ☎ 363-2234 or 1-800/451-6078, ☏ 363-2588, ⓦ www.comfortsuites.com. A reasonable alternative to the high-rise luxury resorts that dominate the scene, this three-storey pink hotel is home to 320 junior suites, basically nicely furnished double rooms with king-size beds, sofa, cable TV and a big bathroom. There is a pool and hot tub, and Cabbage Beach is nearby. ⓺

Holiday Inn, Pirate's Cove Sunspree Resort Harbour Rd ☎ 363-2100, ☏ 363-2006. Besides its mouthful of a name, the 564 rooms here are pretty much what you'd expect from a *Holiday Inn*. The twist is a large pool with rocks and an elaborate waterfall. Overlooking Pirate's Cove. ⓺

Ocean Club Golf and Tennis Resort Casuarina Drive ☎ 242-2501 or 1-800/321-3000, ☏ 1-800/258-2633, ⓦ www.oceanclub.com. The island's original high-end resort, originally a private residence but now an exclusive getaway with only fifty rooms along with a few suites and villas. Located on quiet Cabbage Beach, the *Ocean Club* is home to the spectacular Versailles Gardens along with three restaurants and three bars, a pool, golf privileges and tennis courts galore. For the basic $550 per night, you get 35 acres of luxury and quiet. ⓾

Paradise Harbour Club and Marina Harbour Drive ☎ 363-2992 or 1-800/742-4276, ⓕ 363-2840, ⓦ www.phclub.com. A small collection of accommodations ranging from king-size hotel rooms to two-bedroom apartments with kitchens and views of the harbour. Most rooms are suitable for extended stays, and a water shuttle to Nassau is included in the rates. The worthwhile *Columbus Tavern Restaurant* is here too. ❻

Paradise Island Fun Club Harbour Road ☎ 363-2561 or 1-800/952-2426, ⓕ 363-3803. One of two all-inclusives on the island – *Club Med* is the other – this 250-unit has nice-sized rooms and unobtrusive, though far from memorable, decor. Pool, sundecks and watersports. ❻

Paradise Paradise Paradise Beach ☎ 363-3000 or 1-800/321-3000, ⓕ 363-2540. A Sun International property, the *Paradise Paradise* has 100 standard/superior rooms. Watersports and use of *Atlantis* facilities a plus. $125–140.

Sheraton Grand Resort Casino Drive ☎ 363-3500 or 1-800/325-3535, ⓕ 363-3900, ⓦ www.sheratongrand.com. Close by *Atlantis*, this high-rise was recently purchased by Sheraton and given a bigger lobby, fresh landscaping and an updating of its older accommodations. The 350-odd rooms are tropical in decor and feel and quite comfortable. A fabulous stretch of beach lies nearby as does its busy all-inclusive watersports centre, with tennis courts, exercise room, dive shop, snorkelling and much besides. Rates vary throughout the year, but count on around $280 for a double in winter. ❽

Sunshine Paradise Suites Paradise Island Drive ☎ 363-3955 or 1-800/813-6847, ⓕ 363-3840. The *Sunshine* offers sixteen simple one- and two-bedroom self-catering units that are popular with large groups. The hotel also has a small pool and a courtyard. ❼

Guest houses and retreats

Chaplin House West island ☎ 363-2918. A charming and isolated cluster of hardwood, whitewashed cottages in varying sizes and types, especially good for long stays, with self-catering kitchens and air conditioning. A winsome getaway accessible only by boat, the *Chaplin's* lush grounds are full of birds, and each cabin has a veranda. ❹

Howelton Rose House (The Pink House) Casuarina Drive ☎ 363-3363, ⓕ 377-3383. The only B&B on the island, this old Georgian-style home features four slightly dowdy and overused rooms. However, the overall charm of the place is winning, with full breakfasts served on the front porch. The Pink House, as it is better known, sits on its own plot of land right in the middle of *Club Med*, an ironic curiosity in itself. ❹

Sivananda Ashram Yoga Retreat West island ☎ 363-2902, ⓕ 363-3783, ⓦ www.sivananda.org. Located on four acres of private beach, accessible only by boat from Paradise Island's dock, this ashram is a place of great natural beauty and solitude. The purpose of the retreat is to join in twice-daily yoga sessions, meditation and to partake of a regular vegetarian diet. A teacher's training course is also offered, as is tenting on the grounds. There are basic but comfortable cabins (no air conditioning, just fans) including single rooms and dormitory-style accommodations. ❷

Exploring the island

Orienting yourself on Paradise Island is simple as there are only a few main roads, though side roads are a maze of interconnecting streets. The best place to get your bearings is from the one-way **Paradise Island Bridge**, which loops over the harbour from Nassau and lands you slightly west of a huge **roundabout** – the second Paradise Island Bridge, also one way, is used for exiting the island.

The northern route off the roundabout leads to **Atlantis**, undoubtedly the biggest tourist sight on the island. Comparable to a major Las Vegas casino hotel complex, the huge structure is something from Captain Nemo meets *Jurassic Park*. Its two wings rise dramatically from a central tower, and its overall pink tinge is garish fun. Open 24 hours a day, anyone can walk inside, though **guided tours** ($25; ☎ 363-3000) of the complex are given several times a day. To the east of the main hotel is a massive swimming and snorkelling lagoon replete with waterfalls and underwater walkways covering 34 acres, including a five-storey replicated Mayan temple and waterslides. The main sight here is the thirty-yard underwater tunnel running through the **Predator Lagoon and Reef**, home to sharks, spotted and eagle rays, and reef fish. A suspension bridge hangs over the lagoon for viewing the feeding, which occurs on alternate days; predators are fed at 3pm daily, remaining fish are fed at 4pm, though schedules frequently change. Nearly as popular as the aquarium is the resort's massive **Casino**, free to non-guests – assuming, of course, that they don't blow their money at the roulette tables.

North of *Atlantis* lies **Cabbage Beach** and its two miles of perfectly sculpted pink-toned sand. Just to the east, separated by a small anvil-shaped headland, **Snorkeler's Cove Beach** is an often deserted stretch of land that is perfect for snorkelling. East again is **Smuggler's Beach**, which takes up most of the eastern shore of the island and is good for swimming and picnicking.

Back at the roundabout, **Paradise Island Drive** heads east, ending at the Paradise Island Golf Course. Sights are limited in the extreme on this end of the island, which is mainly home to the airport, private residences and a few hotels, but the *Ocean Club* is home to the elaborate **Versailles Gardens.** Bisected by Paradise Island Drive, this forty-acre garden contains a massive sundial on a medieval pedestal, two fountains and sculptures of historic and mythic figures.

Again from the main roundabout, **Paradise Beach Drive** heads west. About a mile down the road lies *Club Med*, while just north on Casuarina Drive you'll find **Pirate's Cove Beach**, another secluded windswept path of sand. From Pirate's Cove Beach, **Paradise Beach** stretches two sugary miles west but the entire western end of Paradise Island, past *Club Med*'s property, is accessible only by boat, or by walking along Paradise Beach to Colonial Beach and the red-and-white striped Paradise Island Lighthouse.

Eating and drinking

On Paradise Island, you're pretty much committed to either taking a boat across to Nassau for **food** (see pp.80–83) or to dining in one of the big resort complexes. There are only a handful of independent restaurants not connected to hotels or resorts on the island, but luckily Paradise Island has some of the best hotel restaurants in the Bahamas. Unfortunately, these restaurants tend to be expensive.

In the *Atlantis*, there seems to be a place to eat around every corner. The hotel boasts perhaps the most elegant and expensive Italian restaurant on the island, *Villa d'Este* (entrees $25–50), where all the pasta is freshly made and house specialties include veal served in a variety of ways. Other notable *Atlantis* restaurants include: the *Atlas Bar and Grill*, featuring burgers, sandwiches and ribs; the *Clock Tower*, serving pizzas and cocktails on an outdoor terrace; *Five Twins*, specializing in exotic Asian cuisine, including sushi; *Seagrapes*, home to a worthwhile breakfast buffet along with elegant lunches and dinners; and *Mama Loos*, good for anyone craving Chinese cuisine. Like its large competitor, the *Sheraton Grand Resort* itself features a great Italian restaurant, *Julie's Ristorante Italiano*, as well as *The Rotisserie*, which features lobster, char-broiled steaks and fresh seafood, and the popular *Verandah*, where diners can enjoy huge breakfasts on a deck with breathtaking ocean views. Of the other hotel restaurants, the *Courtyard Terrace* at the *Ocean Club* is most notable, though perhaps not for its food as much as its understated elegance, with its flagstone courtyard, colonial veranda, palms and flowering shrubs and Wedgwood china. The expensive menu features mainly French classics like steak tartare, rack of lamb, and shrimp provençale. Diners at the *Columbus Tavern* at the *Paradise Harbour Club* can watch boats bobbing in Nassau Harbour while sampling lobster, steak and crème brûlée.

Inexpensive or moderately priced places to eat on Paradise Island are few and far between, save for bland snack bars found at the big hotels. *Anthony's Caribbean Grill*, on Paradise Drive in the Paradise Island Shopping Centre (☎363-3152), is one of the exceptions. Although it looks plastic and themed, this grill is pretty good, and the pizza, lobster or chicken entrees are fairly priced. About the only other down-to-earth restaurant on Paradise Island is *Island Restaurant,* just off Paradise Beach Drive (☎363-3153), which serves inexpensive breakfasts of boil fish, johnnycake, and grits for $3, or Bahamian lunches and dinners in the $8–10 range. Near the docks at Hurricane Hole Marina, just under the Paradise Island Bridge, two tiny carry-outs serve a good breakfast and lunch, mostly things like meatloaf, macaroni and cheese, or fried fish, for around $6.

Nightlife

Most of the hotels and resorts on Paradise Island have **bars** and **lounges**, some of which feature live music. Of particular note are the *Oasis Lounge* in the *Club Land'Or* and the *Club Pastiche* at *Atlantis*. Down on Hurricane Hole, the *Blue Marlin,* which has lunch and dinner specials in an outdoor setting, also features music on occasion, mostly Junkanoo, steel band, and limbo, all for an admission fee of about $10. The *Dragons Lounge and Dance Club* at *Atlantis* presents live entertainment against the backdrop of a huge "video wall", and you can boogie at *Le Paon* in the *Sheraton Grand Resort* (Thurs–Sun 9pm–2am), which features live music most nights.

Shopping

Just west from the roundabout on Paradise Beach Drive, then north on Casuarina Drive, is a local **Straw Market**, which has been gaining in popularity and prestige over the years. Island goods like hats, handbags, woven placemats and Androsian batik are brought here from many of the Family Islands to be sold. Also worth a look is the **Bahamian Craft Market**, featuring interesting folk art objects, and just across the street from the Hurricane Hole shopping mall.

The rest of New Providence

The **western** and **southern** portions of New Providence are undervisited and can be taken in with an island loop drive in a half-day or so. However, the quiet beaches, good diving and a reasonable choice of small restaurants make them a welcome option, and you might want to explore longer.

To the west of Nassau the beaches, particularly **Orange Hill Beach** and, just beyond it, **Love Beach**, are both pretty and quiet, offering swimmers and picnickers the perfect getaway from the crowds. To many, **Old Fort Beach**, a small patch of sand just north of **Lyford Cay** along Western Road, is the most perfectly shaped beach on the island, though its small size can be a drawback on weekends. Beyond Lyford Cay, where millionaires live in gated splendour, lies Clifton Point, a windy jut of land that overlooks an ocean bristling with dive and snorkel sites. **Adelaide Beach**, on the south shore, leads toward Coral Harbour, a retirement housing development that also sports the main dive operations on New Providence (see p.58). Just inland from the south shore, the quiet village of **Adelaide** represents a quieter type of small-town Bahamian life that looks as though time were frozen fifty years ago.

Getting around

The best way to see the western and southern portions of New Providence is by car, taking West Bay Street all way around to the south shore, returning by Adelaide and Carmichael Road into Nassau. Many visitors also rent **motorbikes** and make the run to Compass Point and on to the south as well. Nassau **taxis** can be seen as far west as Compass Point, but as the evening progresses they become fewer and fewer. The fare from central Nassau to Compass Point is $12 for one person, an extra $2 for each additional person.

By far the cheapest mode of transportation is the public **buses**. To go west out of Nassau toward Compass Point, simply catch a #10 anywhere downtown or in Cable Beach. For 75¢, these buses go only as far as Compass Point. **Western Transportation** buses make the trip from Nassau around the western rim of the island all the way to the *Clarion Resort*. The *McDonald's* parking lot across from the *British Colonial Hotel* in downtown Nassau is the informal depot for these buses, and you can obtain a schedule from any driver. The fare is $1.75 and buses run hourly from 7am until dark, including Sunday.

To go directly to the south shore from downtown Nassau catch a #6 bus which runs to Carmichael Road, then along Adelaide Road.

Accommodation

Compass Point West Bay St, Gambier Village ☎327-4500 or 1-800/688-7678, ℱ327-3299, Ⓔoutpost800@aol.com, ⓌWww.islandoutpost.com. Popular with honeymooners and jetsetters, *Compass Point* is the brainchild of reggae-promoter Chris Blackwell. Six miles east of Cable Beach, this upscale but not particularly pretentious resort has only eighteen units, some of which are independent apartment-style rooms, and others free-standing on stilts over a small sandy beach. Each is a kind of private hut, painted in rainbow hues, and several have full kitchens. Set on only two acres, it is a bit cramped by the side of the road, but the views are marvellous, and there is a small sandy cove for swimming. Rooms are comfortable and big and the *Compass Point Restaurant* is excellent (see p.96). Rates for a double begin around $215. ⑧

Coral Harbour Beach House Coral Harbour ☎362-6514, ℱ361-6514. Eight rooms in a two-storey hotel in a lonely spot along the beach. No restaurant, but there is a barbecue pit and hammocks. ❷

Corner Hotel Carmichael Rd, Carmichael Village ☎361-7445. The *Corner* is a bare-bones hotel made of concrete breeze-block. The rooms have fans and motel-style furniture, and there's a simple but decent restaurant on site. ❷

Gum Elemi Townhouses of Gambier West Bay St, Gambier Village ☎328-8472, ℱ325-7138, ⓌWww.islandeaze.com. Owned and operated by a charming mother-daughter team, the two *Gum Elemi* townhouses are a great alternative to hotel life, and not expensive if shared. Both are three-bedroom, two-bath places, with kitchens, laundry and a central open courtyard, a/c and TV. The pool in back is fabulous. The staff will take you to the airport for a small fee, and *Traveller's Rest* and *Compass Point* restaurants are just down the road. **⑥**

Orange Hill Beach Inn West Bay St at Blake ☎ 327-7157, ℱ 327-5186. This quiet, breezy and unassuming resort offers 32 rooms with basic furnishings along with apartments that have kitchens, most overlooking the beach. The pool is huge and gorgeous, though the grounds and lounges are not looked after properly. The small bar can be a fun time, and the lobby is a good place to hang out, with books, TV and free coffee in the morning. The #10 bus runs right along West Bay, so going into Nassau is a swift, cheap ride, and the resort is only five minutes away from the airport. The

restaurant serves, most nights, basic Bahamian dishes for under $20. **④**

South Ocean Golf and Beach Resort South Ocean Drive ☎ 362-4391 or 1-877/766-2326, ⓦ www.southoceanbahamas.com. With a relatively recent refurbishment and new ownership, this secluded resort is exquisite for the price. There are a total of 249 rooms, most in the main building, which is done up tropical-style, while others face the oceanfront and are more plantation-style. Every room has a balcony overlooking either pools and gardens, or the ocean. The golf course is superb and there are four lighted tennis courts. All-inclusive option available. **⑥**

West to Gambier Village

Six miles west of downtown Nassau, steadily narrowing West Bay Street becomes a tricky two-lane highway loaded with numerous curves and blind turnoffs. The views of the sea to the north are utterly magnificent, as are the colours at sunset, but keep in mind that much of the beach along here is private. Shortly after Rock Point comes **The Caves**, a naturally occurring depression resulting from wave after wave pounding against the limestone coast. In truth there is little to them save for a small inscribed plinth commemorating the arrival of Prince Albert, Duke of Edinburgh (the consort of Queen Victoria) on December 3, 1861, the first member of the royal family to visit the Bahamas. Opposite here is a large luxury condominium, which marks the turnoff of Blake Road leading to John F. Kennedy Drive, and Nassau International Airport. At this spot, marked by planted trees, US President Kennedy, Canadian Prime Minister Diefenbaker and British Prime Minister Harold Macmillan met in a Cold-War summit conference during 1962. Bahamians still call the spot **Conference Corner.**

Just beyond the corner stands the Orange Hill area, so called because of a huge orange grove that stood here as part of a large estate. Both the grove and estate are long gone, but the *Orange Hill Beach Inn* (see above) is here, while below, along the ocean, **Orange Hill Beach** runs for half a mile. The beach, excellent for bathing and picnics, is backed by sea grape and palms.

The increasingly rocky coastline approaches **GAMBIER VILLAGE** about a mile beyond Orange Hill. The village is a scattered settlement of wood-frame and concrete houses originally inhabited by liberated African slaves from a vessel captured on the seas by Britain's Royal Navy during and after 1807. Another group of residents came from the slave ship *Creole*, whose slaves revolted in 1840 near the Abacos.

Love Beach to Lyford Cay

Just beyond Gambier Village is the exclusive *Compass Point* resort (see p.93), hard to miss due to its kaleidoscopic colour scheme of pinks, blues and corals. Not far past it is **LOVE BEACH**, a small but nice stretch that's the home of

Snorkel Heaven (☎327-8676), a tiny shop that rents snorkel equipment for $20 used to explore the reef fifty yards offshore. The water is shallow, and the snorkelling good for reef fish, some grouper and rays, plus you'll often have the beach to yourself.

Another mile west is **Old Fort Beach**, a perfectly shaped half-moon with fine coral-coloured sand that's usually empty and which was once part of a large private estate called Charlotteville – there's still a deserted plantation house on the site. The road then juts inland slightly, joins Western Road and passes **LYFORD CAY** another two miles farther on, perhaps the toniest, most elegant and private housing development on New Providence. Named for the Loyalist William Lyford, the cay boasts huge homes and is protected by a rigid security apparatus, bounded all around by a high fence. Its residents, who live in walled-off splendour, include such celebrities as Sean Connery and many wealthy business types. Despite its exclusiveness, there is continued building going on, as young billionaires compete to buy homes priced in the millions, and offshore bank and trust companies occupy executive office suites. Just outside the gates is **Lyford Cay Centre**, a shopping centre with boutiques, dry-cleaners, gas station, a pharmacy, furniture shop and small art gallery. Nearby, Bahamians live in **Mount Pleasant**, a tract of modest homes with a few shops for locals, and commute to work in Lyford or elsewhere on the coast.

Clifton Point and Adelaide

Western Road soon reaches **CLIFTON POINT**, the westernmost point on New Providence. In the early 1800s, William Wylly ran a large plantation near the point, and his Great House lies there in ruins, as do the slave quarters. Clifton Point is now heavily industrialized, being the site of Bahamas Electricity Corporation's main plant, a gasoline storage depot – you can watch tankers offload – and the Commonwealth Brewery where Kalik is brewed.

As the road turns back east and south, it comes upon the newly refurbished *South Ocean Golf and Beach Resort* (see opposite), which boasts a terrific golf course, and has magnificent views of the ocean. Once the road passes the resort, it turns inland, losing its views of the beach.

By turning south and heading a couple miles, however, one reaches the unassuming village of **ADELAIDE** at Southwest Bay. The village was founded in 1831 when Governor Sir James Carmichael Smyth settled 157 Africans, liberated from a Portuguese slave ship named *Rosa*, on this south shore site, providing them with basic supplies and land. The Africans established a school and church, then commenced lives as fishermen and subsistence farmers, living for the most part in thatched huts, a few of which could be seen even into the 1960s. Today, some modern trappings have settled in – electricity, phones, good roads – though not enough to upset the laid-back, ramshackle character of the place.

Coral Harbour and north

Heading east on Adelaide Road will bring you to a roundabout, from which you can head south to **Coral Harbour**, a residential marina-style district with manmade canals and a yacht harbour. It's here that many of Nassau's dive operators have their centre of operations (see p.58). The main highway, Carmichael Road, leads to a turnoff for the **Bacardi** distillery (Mon–Thurs 9.30am–4pm, Fri 9.30am–3pm; free; ☎362-1412), where the famous rum is made. Bacardi moved much of its business to the Bahamas after the Cuban revolution in 1959, and visitors are welcome for free tours, best of course for the free samples of rum provided. Also in Coral Harbour is Happy Trails Stables (see p.60).

Carmichael Road winds gradually back into the southern sprawl of Nassau, passing by the old Carmichael Bible Church, a clapboard relic of bygone days, and a half-mile farther on the site of an abandoned village known as Headquarters, one of the earliest residences of liberated African slaves. All that is left are a few barely observable foundations. Near the end of Carmichael Road at Blue Hill, and just at Golden Gates Estates, is the popular **Nola's Bake Crabs**, which sells wonderfully spiced crab delicacies baked in the shell.

Eating and drinking

Though none of the following **eateries** is worth heading out of Nassau for in their its right, each makes a worthwhile pit stop when touring through this undervisited area of New Providence.

Avery's Restaurant and Bar Adelaide Village, off Carmichael Rd ☎362-1547. Simple and cheap Bahamian fare in a reasonably pleasant atmosphere. Weekends often see a live band play.

Compass Point Restaurant West Bay St, Love Beach ☎327-3299. Although the hotel is quite exclusive, one can dine in relative ease at this terrific restaurant. For such good food, the prices are quite reasonable. The menu is varied and delicious, with everything from Bahamian dishes to Pacific Rim cuisine, and the service is friendly and prompt.

Honeycomb Beach Club Adelaide Beach ☎362-1417. Visitors in the vicinity of Adelaide Beach should stop in at the tiny shoe-box-sized

Honeycomb Beach Club, which has a short bar, two pool tables, and a loud TV. On the concrete-floored patio out front cold beer goes well with great ocean views, and the cracked conch, pork chops and chicken fingers aren't bad.

Traveller's Rest West Bay St, Gambier Village ☎327-7633. This popular, very friendly restaurant, featuring music and a terrace for dining, is a favourite among Bahamian business people and folks who work at the airport. The food is strictly Bahamian, but with flair. The smothered grouper is swamped in peppers, onions and tomatoes, making for an out-of-this-world taste. Also good are the fried pork chops.

Grand Bahama

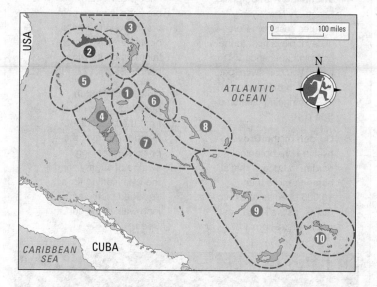

CHAPTER 2

Highlights

✳ **Kayaking** Paddling excursions to Lucayan National Park might include kayaking through a mangrove creek, a nature walk through the park and a picnic lunch on spectacular Gold Rock Beach. See p.108

✳ **Swimming with dolphins** Sanctuary Bay, twenty minutes east from Port Lucaya, plays host to the Dolphin Experience, where you can swim, pet, and watch the feeding of, these intriguing creatures. See p.107

✳ **Garden of the Groves** A twelve-acre botanical garden in Lucaya that's home to more than 10,000 species of exotic plants, as well as a host of parrots. See p.116

✳ **The Stoned Crab** An upscale seafood restaurant overlooking Taino Beach, known as much for its double-pyramid roof as its exquisite crab claws, lobster and fresh fish dishes. See p.120

✳ **Friday Night Jam** Every Friday, *Our Lucaya* resort presents this free celebration, centred on a bonfire and live entertainment on its wide beach. See p.122

✳ **Gold Rock Beach** Seemingly a world away from the beaches of Freeport/Lucaya, this pristine, sweeping swathe of sugary sand is the ideal setting for a secluded picnic and a long walk in the surf. See p.124

Grand Bahama

GRAND BAHAMA offers gorgeous sugary white beaches, aquamarine sea and a colourful, exotic profusion of lush coral reefs and sea
gardens lying beneath the water's surface, yet its greatest attraction is
probably its accessibility. Just 55 miles east of Miami – with daily ferry
service as well as direct flights from several major American cities – the 96-
mile-long island exists almost solely as a big offshore playground for North
Americans.

Most of the approximately half-million annual visitors who come to Grand
Bahama do not stray far beyond the urban conglomeration of **Freeport** – three
miles inland from the south coast – and its seaside suburb **Lucaya**, which, together, are home to most of the island's 47,000 residents. Long regarded as a cut-rate
package holiday destination passed over by more discerning travellers in favour
of Nassau and Paradise Island, Freeport/Lucaya sprang up almost overnight in the
1950s as a "destination" rather than as an organic Bahamian community.

Among Freeport/Lucaya's attractions are four championship golf courses,
two casinos, a good range of nice restaurants and several good beaches within
easy reach, especially the mile-long **Lucayan** strand and the less developed
Taino Beach. During the daytime hours there's an almost endless variety of
well-organized day-trips and outdoor activities, including world-class watersports, swimming with dolphins, boat excursions and duty-free shopping, while
nightly entertainment – manufactured solely for the pleasure of vacationers –
ranges from live music and dance clubs to bonfires on the beach and sunset
dinner cruises.

If the idea of miniature golf or the sight of other tourists grows distasteful,
though, it's possible to leave the tourist gridlock behind without actually leaving the island. To the **east of Freeport** are the unspoilt and empty sands of
Barbary, **High Rock** and **Gold Rock** beaches and the nature preserve of
Lucayan National Park, which encompasses walking trails, limestone caves
and mangrove creeks that can be explored by kayak. Also here, only an hour
out from Freeport, are two small fishing villages, **McLean's Town** and
Sweeting's Cay, offering a glimpse of what life on Grand Bahama was like
before the invention of *Club Med*.

There is less to see as you go **west of Freeport**. The best attraction hereabouts is **Deadman's Reef**, the site of several Lucayan archeological excava-
tions, around which are accessible snorkelling grounds. At the island's western
tip, the scruffy settlement of **West End** has a wildly romantic history of pirates,
sunken treasure and rum-runners. Though it isn't much to look at these days,
the expanding *Old Bahama Bay* luxury resort nearby may help turn things
around.

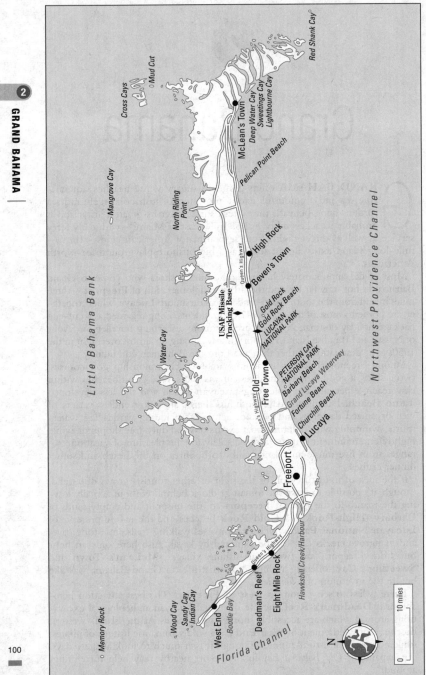

The mainly uninhabited north shore of Grand Bahama is dominated by a swash of mangroves littered with choice fishing grounds that draw **bonefishing** fanatics from around the globe. For those who really want to get off the beaten track, the tiny settlement on **Water Cay** off the north coast can be visited by powerboat or on a kayaking expedition.

Some history

Archeologists exploring the country have made some of their most exciting discoveries of Lucayan artefacts on Grand Bahama, particularly at Deadman's Reef in the west and in the caverns that are now part of Lucayan National Park to the east. Traces of Lucayan culture have still been few and far between in the Bahamas, thanks to Spanish Conquistadors, who had exterminated nearly all the natives by the end of the fifteenth century. Though Ponce de León stopped here briefly in 1513 to take on water on his quest for the Fountain of Youth, most subsequent vessels traversing the waters of the Bahamas over the next couple of centuries passed Grand Bahama by and the island remained virtually uninhabited.

Throughout the seventeenth and eighteenth centuries, about the only group who set foot here were the bands of pirates and privateers camped out around the West End, ambushing ships as they sailed through the Florida Channel headed for Europe and loaded with treasure. Many a Spanish galleon and British man-of-war wrecked on the reefs that encircle the island, and some of these wrecks have only recently been discovered. Although thousands of **Loyalists** – and their slaves – from the southern states flooded the Bahamas after the end of the American Revolution, none settled on Grand Bahama, most likely because of its poor soil and lack of a natural harbour. The island's first recorded settlement – also at West End – was not made until 1806, and it took the Emancipation of slaves in 1834 for any form of significant growth to occur.

The island experienced another spurt of growth during the **American Civil War**, when the West End became a staging ground for Confederate blockade runners smuggling guns and supplies into the southern states (much as it was to become a base for rum-runners during Prohibition in the 1920s). Despite this nefarious economic activity, there were still less than 700 people living on the island by 1888, the majority getting by through fishing, turtling, sponging and minimal cultivation.

Half a century later, American businessman **Wallace Groves** acquired the rights to harvest timber on Grand Bahama and, looking out over acres and acres of bush and swamp, envisioned a thriving new city and a winter playground for the rich and famous, and set about building it. The 1955 Hawksbill Agreement and subsequent amendments between the Bahamian government and Groves' company, **Grand Bahama Port Authority Ltd**, earned the company the rights to develop and administer 150,000 acres of land – where Freeport and Lucaya now stand – for a period of 99 years. Freeport/Lucaya was declared a tax-free zone, and the Port Authority was also granted control over immigration into the city and the licensing of businesses to operate there. Development of Lucaya as an oceanfront resort area began in the 1960s, and the Grand Lucayan Waterway, which bisects the island east of Freeport/Lucaya, and the other manmade channels and canals in Lucaya, were built to increase the value of real estate by creating more waterfront property.

In the 1970s and 1980s, the novelty of Freeport's casinos and hotels began to fade, leaving Freeport and Lucaya the target of continuous waves of Spring Break college students and cruise-ship day-trippers coming to play the slots and buy some duty-free. Over the last five years, though, Freeport/Lucaya – and

Grand Bahama as a whole – has enjoyed a dramatic economic rejuvenation fuelled by a number of large, five-star resort developments, which are helping the island shake off its image as Nassau's poorer, unsophisticated cousin.

Getting there

Containing the island's airport, dock and five of its six official **marinas** (see box below), Freeport/Lucaya is the island's obvious point of entry. The **Grand Bahama International Airport** (☎352-6020), located on the northern outskirts of the city, is only a half-hour flight from Florida, and a bit over two hours from New York, with direct flights from several other US cities.

Marinas

There are five full-service **marinas** in Freeport/Lucaya – three of which are official ports of entry to the Bahamas – and one located at *Old Bahama Bay* at the west end of the island, 25 miles from Freeport. Dockage rates range between 75¢ and $1.50 per foot/per day and all have electricity and freshwater hookups, as well as showers, bathrooms, and laundry facilities. All marinas monitor VHF Ch 16.

In Freeport/Lucaya

Lucayan Marina Village (☎373-7616, ℻373-7630, ⓦwww.lucayanmarinavillage.com) can accommodate vessels up to 150ft long in 125 deepwater slips. It is an official port of entry with 24-hour customs and immigration services, a fuelling dock, waste pumpout, and phone and cable TV hookups. A one-minute water shuttle departs every halfhour to Port Lucaya, where there are provisions stores, hotels, restaurants and other tourist amenities.

Ocean Reef Yacht Club (☎373-4661 or 373-4662, ℻373-8261, ⓦwww.oryc.com) lies on an inland waterway carved out just west of Silver Point Beach. The 55 slips here have a depth of 6ft at low tide and can accommodate boats up to 140ft, with phone and satellite TV hookups and hotel accommodations on site and a shuttle service to the shopping district of Lucaya. Not an official port of entry.

Port Lucaya Marina (☎373-9090, ⓦwww.portlucaya.com) is an official port of entry in the centre of Lucaya (entrance through Bell Channel) and can accommodate vessels up to 175ft in 106 slips, some in front of hotel rooms in the contiguous *Port Lucaya Resort and Yacht Club*. All amenities are close at hand, and guests have access to the facilities at *Our Lucaya Beach Resort* across the street.

Running Mon Marina (☎352-6834, ⓦwww.running-mon-bahamas.com) is located near Xanadu Beach about two miles south of Freeport centre and is an official port of entry with seventy slips and floating docks. The draw in the channel is 6.5ft at low tide, and the *Running Mon* resort is nearby.

Xanadu Beach and Marina Resort (☎352-6782, ⓦwww.xanadubeachhotel.com) is to the west of the Running Mon Marina with its entrance on a separate channel. It can accommodate 77 boats, and its office sells fuel and marine supplies. Not an official port of entry.

West of Freeport/Lucaya

The Marina at Old Bahama Bay (☎346-6500, ⓦwww.oldbahamabay.com) is the only official port of entry on Grand Bahama not in Freeport/Lucaya. Twenty-five miles outside of Freeport, the marina has 72 boat slips for vessels up to 120ft; the entrance channel is 13ft deep and the inner basin is 8ft deep. Customs and immigration is open 8am–5pm.

American Airlines, Continental Connection/Gulfstream, and US Airways run flights into Freeport every day, and Bahamasair flies several times a day from Nassau and Florida. Though there is no public transport available from the airport, many hotel packages include free transfers; if that's not an option, taxis cost $8–10 to Freeport and $13–15 to Lucaya; it's also possible to rent a car from here (see overleaf for a list of operators).

Cruise ships and **ferries** (mainly the MSV *Discovery Sun*; see "Getting there" p.14 for details) from Florida come ashore at Freeport Harbour, five miles west of Freeport proper. There is no public transport from the dock, but both taxis and tour buses can take you into town for around $0. The more plebeian government M/V *Marcella III* **mailboat** departs **Nassau** on Wednesdays at 4pm, arriving in Freeport twelve hours later, heading back to Nassau on Fridays at 5pm; tickets are $45 one-way (call the dockmaster's office in Nassau (☎393-1064) for details or Freeport Harbour (☎352-9651) to confirm departure). You will have to take a taxi ($10 to Freeport; $12 to Lucaya) to get between the mailboat dock and town.

Lastly, access to Grand Bahama is also available **from the Abacos** via a thirty-seater passenger ferry ($60 round-trip) that crosses between Crown Haven in Little Abaco (see p.159) and McLean's Town, sixty miles east of Freeport. It leaves Crown Haven daily at 7.30am and 2.30pm; and departs from McLean's Town wharf at 8am and 4.30pm. Buy your ticket on the dock upon departure.

Information and maps

The **Grand Bahama Island Tourism Board** (PO Box F 40251, Freeport, Grand Bahama Island, Bahamas; ☎1-800/448-3386 or 352-8044, ⒻF352-2714, Ⓦwww.grand-bahama.com) has information booths at the airport, the cruise-ship dock, in Port Lucaya Marketplace and a main office in Freeport's International Bazaar. They dispense maps and brochures and the knowledgeable officers can offer advice on things to do and see. They also co-ordinate the 'People to People' cultural exchange programme (see p.41). If your travelling plans incline more toward the natural world, check in with the Ecotourism Association of Grand Bahama (c/o Rand Nature Centre, PO Box F 43441, Freeport, Grand Bahama Island; ☎352-5438, ⒻF351-4192), a consortium of tour operators and conservation organizations committed to promoting the island's natural environment. A brochure of theirs outlining various eco-adventures on offer on Grand Bahama is available from the Tourism Board and in hotel lobbies throughout Freeport/Lucaya.

For current affairs and events, look out for the *Freeport News*, published daily except Sunday, or the free *Happenings Around Town* monthly community newspaper. More tourist-oriented publications include *What's On*, a self-explanatory free newspaper, and the gratis and pocketsize *Grand Bahama Island* magazine, containing good maps, a dining guide and suggested activities.

While free **maps** of Grand Bahama, Freeport and Lucaya can be picked up just about anywhere, the *Bahamas Trailblazer Map of Grand Bahama Island, Freeport and Lucaya* published by Etienne Dupuch (Ⓦwww.bahamasnet.com) is the most detailed of the bunch. Visitors seeking a map of island diving sites should purchase *A Grand Bahama Island Snorkelling Map* ($10), designed by local diving legend Ben Rose, on sale at the UNEXSO dive shop in Lucaya (see p.106).

Getting around

You can give the whole of Grand Bahama a quick once-over in a day or two, although **exploring** its many secluded beaches could easily absorb a week or more. Most visitors never feel the need to venture beyond Freeport/Lucaya, where the major attractions can easily be reached on foot, bicycle, motor scooter, or bus. Complimentary shuttle buses to beaches, restaurants and the town centres of Freeport and Lucaya are also offered by most hotels, and many of the restaurants located on the outskirts of town will pick you up for dinner and drive you home again. For those who want to roam further afield, a variety of modes of transport are available. With a sizeable urban conglomeration and the attendant petty crime that comes with it, hitchhiking on Grand Bahama, though, is not recommended.

Buses

Freeport/Lucaya and the communities to the east and west of the city are well connected by a fleet of privately owned **buses**, though note that most don't run on Sundays. To get from Freeport to Lucaya or vice versa catch a bus at the stop in front of the International Bazaar in Freeport or on the corner of Seahorse Road and Royal Palm Way in Lucaya. The buses leave when full and cost $1 anywhere within the city limits. Buses to settlements east and west of Freeport/Lucaya leave from the pink **main bus stand** in the parking lot of the Winn Dixie Plaza in downtown Freeport. The hourly #16 bus departs for West End ($4) on the hour between 6am and 6pm, while rides to the eastern end of the island are less frequent – the #10 bus to McLean's Town ($8) leaves from near the main bus stand at 11.30am and 2pm. A last bus departs from here at 5.30pm, going only as far as High Rock.

Car and beach buggy rentals

Car rentals on the island start from about $80 a day. Note that the major rental agencies prohibit the use of their cars on dirt roads, meaning if you want to explore the bush tracks and side roads that crisscross the island a jeep or truck is necessary. The following companies have desks at the airport – in a separate building across from the terminal – and will even deliver a car to your hotel. Avis (airport ☎352-7666; Port Lucaya (☎373-1102); Brad's (☎352-7930); Dollar-Rent-a-Car (☎352-9325); Hertz (☎352-3297); Thrifty (☎352-9308). If you like the idea of channelling the spirit of Malibu Beach Barbie or Ken for a day, try zipping around town and down to the beach in a life-size cotton-candy-coloured dune **buggy**. Be warned that these are not suitable for long road-trips – the noise from the motor is like a jackhammer and the fibreglass buggies come in varying degrees of sturdiness. Try Bahama Buggies ($50 a day plus optional $15 insurance;   ☎352-8750, ©buggies@batelnet.bs), who offer complimentary pickup and drop-offs.

Scooters and bicycles

Motor **scooters** are a fun way to explore the quiet (until you get there) residential streets of Lucaya and the beaches east of town. West of Freeport, however, the heavy truck traffic from the port and local cement plant make it a less attractive option. Scooters with a top speed of about 30mph can be rented for $50 a day in the parking lot across the street from *Reef Village* in Port Lucaya, at *Running Mon Resort and Marina* (☎352-6834) and at the *Island Palm Resort* (☎352-6648) in Freeport. Most hotels can also arrange rentals.

The flat terrain of Grand Bahama makes for easy **biking**, but the traffic in Freeport/Lucaya and the vast stretches of unbroken bush along the Queen's Highway beyond the city limits dampen the appeal. However, there are numerous (unmapped) dirt-logging roads through the tall pine forests of the island to be explored by the adventurous. Kayak Nature Tours (T373-2485, Wwww.bahamasvg.com/kayak) offers guided cycling day-trips ($69 including cycle rental) on quiet and scenic bush tracks along the south coast. Well-maintained beach cruisers with one gear can be rented by the hour, day or week in Lucaya at *Reef Village* (in the front parking lot; T373-1333), and at *Running Mon Resort and Marina* (T352-6834) for about $30 a day. If you are planning to put in some heavy mileage, bring your own bike.

Taxis

Taxis meet every arriving flight and cruise ship and any hotel will call one for you. Flat rates for frequently travelled routes are set by the government, and the fare from the airport to hotels in Freeport or Lucaya is around $8–10/$13–15 respectively. To order a taxi, try Freeport Taxi (T352-6666) or the Grand Bahama Taxi Union (T352-7101).

Bus and boat tours

If you'd rather let someone else do the driving, several companies on the island offer guided tours. On land, Executive Tours (daily 9am & 1pm; $30, children $18; T373-7863) offer three-hour **bus tours** of Freeport/Lucaya and the surrounding area taking in local attractions including the Garden of the Groves, Freeport's open-air fruit market and the International Bazaar for some shopping. They'll also pick you up from your hotel. Similar tours are given by H. Forbes Charter and Tours (morning and afternoon tours; $35, children $25 including transportation to and from your hotel; T352-9311, Ehforbes@grouper.batelnet.bs), including a three-hour Super Combination Tour that includes the highlights listed above as well as the port facility and the local distillery. Forbes also offers tours of Lucayan National Park ($50/35 per adult/child including lunch) and of Freeport/Lucaya and the West End of the island ($50/40 per adult/child).

A slightly more adventurous option is a **boat excursion**. From their booth at the *Port Lucaya Hotel*, Pat and Diane/Fantasia Tours (T373-8681) organize an array of boat cruises daily, including a four-hour trip to Peterson Cay National Park for some swimming, snorkelling and a picnic ($59, children $35). Reef Tours ($25, children $15; T373-5880) at Port Lucaya Marketplace offer daily hour-and-a-half tours aboard a glass-bottomed boat, the *Mermaid Kitty*, which allows you to view the colourful wonders of the sea without getting wet. They also offer two-hour "booze cruises" with music, snacks and tropical drinks Tuesday, Thursday and Saturday evenings for $30 per person, along with a more subdued wine and cheese sunset sailing cruise ($40 per person, space limited). And lastly, Smiling Pat's Adventures ($50–100; T373-6395, Epath@grouper.batelnet.bs) heads out on a different outing each day, including beach-hopping trips, spear-fishing expeditions, and all-day boat excursions to Abaco and to Peterson Cay National Park that include lunch and snorkelling.

A final and unique option is offered by East End Adventures ($110, children $55; T373-6662, Eeastendsafari@yahoo.com), who run an excellent all-day **cultural tour** to the unspoiled eastern tip of the island. Along the way, you visit peaceful fishing villages, bump along bush trails and sample wild fruits before zipping along by boat to Sweeting's Cay for a conch-cracking demonstration. Then it's on to the pristine powdery beaches of Lightbourne Cay for a picnic lunch, some lolling in the sun, followed by snorkelling. Group size is limited to eight people.

Ferries

A public passenger ferry runs between Port Lucaya and the *Ritz Bay Resort* on Taino Beach every hour between 8am and 11pm. It leaves the dock behind the *Flamingo Bay Hotel* at Taino Beach on the hour for the ten-minute trip ($3/5 one-way/round-trip), and returns from the dock at Port Lucaya next to the *Ferry House Restaurant* at quarter past the hour. Because the ferry is not licensed to carry luggage, only daypacks and handbags are permitted.

Diving and watersports

One of the most attractive features of a vacation on Grand Bahama is the huge array of organized **watersports** on offer in Freeport/Lucaya, including **snorkelling** and **diving**, **kayaking** and **fishing**, and even **swimming with dolphins**. Most tour operators will pick you up at your hotel in the morning and deposit you back there again in time for cocktails, and most hotels can also help make the bookings for you. The downside of this efficiency is that tour groups in many, though not all cases can be large, and the experiences on offer can seem manufactured solely for the entertainment of tourists.

If looking to partake in some less time-intensive watersports than those listed below, outfitters located by most of the beachfront hotels can help sort you out. If your dream of a Caribbean holiday includes parasailing, you can do this from Port Lucaya through Reef Tours (℡373-5880) for $40 a pop; they also offer banana boat rides and rent jet skis. On the beach at *Our Lucaya*, Ocean Motion Watersports (℡373-2139) can also set you up for a parasail, along with water-skiing, banana boat rides or a round on their water trampoline. They also rent jet skis, sailboats, kayaks and windsurfers. At Xanadu Beach, Paradise Watersports (℡352-2887 or 352-4233) offers much the same, while on Taino Beach you should look out for Lucayan Watersports (℡373-9744) by the *Ritz Beach Resort*.

Diving

As Grand Bahama is well known for both its underwater caves and shark dives, experienced divers won't want to pass up at least a day spent in the waters around the island. As home to the well-regarded UNEXSO organization, Freeport/Lucaya also makes for a great place to get certified.

Underwater Explorer's Society (UNEXSO) Port Lucaya ℡373-1244 or 1-800/992-3483, ℻373-1244, ℗www.unexso.com. This well-established operation offers a variety of daily dives. The most highly adventurous will want to look into either a long dive into Ben's Cave (see p.124) or a shark dive, during which a decoy dressed in chainmail feeds the sharks to keep them occupied while you observe them from a few feet away. A one-tank dive is $35, two-tank $70, shark dive $89, dolphin dive $169 and night dive $49 – all including equipment rental. UNEXSO also offers a range of courses for beginners and more experienced divers. A five-hour introductory "resort course" is $99. Full PADI/NAUI certification costs $449.

Xanadu Undersea Adventures Xanadu Beach ℡352-3811, ℻352-4731, ℗divexua@batelnet.bs. Dive shop offering a full range of guided excursions and certification courses, including shark, night, reef, wreck and cave dives, and day-long excursions to sites at the east and west ends of the island. One dive costs $37; a ten-dive package is $255. A night dive is $52, and a swim with the sharks at Shark Alley $72. Note that these rates do not include equipment rental, which is $20 per dive, $45 full day. A three-day resort course is $79. The advanced training courses range from PADI first aid to underwater navigation and photography.

Up close with the dolphins

Getting face to face with a highly sociable dolphin is one of the most popular tourist activities on Grand Bahama. Run by UNEXSO, **The Dolphin Experience** (☎373-1244 or 1-800/992-3483, ℻373-1244, ⓦwww.unexso.com) departs from their dock at Port Lucaya, heading out on a twenty-minute boat ride to Sanctuary Bay, where the dolphins live in a quiet cove donated by a local philanthropist. Three dolphin experiences are offered.

The Close Encounter As you sit with your feet dangling in the water, the dolphins swim around a small pool and perform synchronized tricks in response to their trainers. Stand waist-deep in the water, while an accommodating dolphin swims alongside to be petted. $39, free for children under 5.

Swim with the Dolphins After animal-care staff give you some guidelines for interacting with the dolphins, take to the water in Sanctuary Bay and swim with them. $99; under-16s must be accompanied by an adult (must be over 12).

Assistant Trainer Programme Spend the whole day observing the dolphins, participating in their feeding and training sessions in Sanctuary Bay and out on the open water. $179; must be over 16.

Dolphin research

For those who want a more in-depth educational encounter with dolphins, the Oceanic Society, a nonprofit marine research organization based in San Francisco (☎1-800/326-7491, ⓦwww.oceanic-society.org), sponsors **field research** on dolphin behaviour in the waters off Grand Bahama. Living aboard the 68-foot vessel *Hanky Panky* for a week at a time, participants can assist scientists in identifying individual animals and collecting data on their movements and behaviour. You must know how to swim and snorkel, but no specials skills or experience are required. Maximum group size: eight. Departures from Lucaya weekly from mid-July through mid-August. $1650 (in double-occupancy cabins with shared bath).

Snorkelling

While many hotels rent out **snorkelling** gear, a multitude of outfitters can offer guided snorkelling trips to the island's best locations, with gear included, for not much more.

East End Adventures ☎373-6662, ⓔeastendsafari@yahoo.com. A quality outfitter offering a seven-hour Blue Hole Snorkelling Safari – in groups limited to eight or less – that explores the vibrant profusion of marine life in a series of blue holes off the eastern end of Grand Bahama. The tour is followed by a barbecue lunch on a deserted cay. $85, children $35, including pickup at your hotel.

Nautical Adventures ☎373-7180. Affordable one-hour snorkelling cruises aboard the *Coral Princess* departing from the Port Lucaya Marketplace three times daily. $30, children and non-snorkellers $16.

Paradise Cove Deadman's Reef ☎349-2677. A great day twenty minutes out of town on a secluded beach, where you can snorkel from shore over a lush reef, float in a glass-bottomed kayak or simply relax on the sand. $30, children $23, including transportation to and from your hotel, lunch, and use of equipment.

Reef Tours Port Lucaya ☎373-5880 or 5891, ⓔreeftours@grandbahama.net. This large outfit offers a variety of snorkelling trips on both motorized and wind-powered catamarans – the ride out to the reef is half the fun. $30–45, half that for children; reservations required.

Superior Watersports ☎373-7863. Besides the more typical one-hour snorkelling trips along Treasure Reef, Superior offers a daily 5hr Robinson Crusoe Beach Party that includes 90min of snorkelling followed by a full buffet lunch on a deserted beach, volleyball and plenty of time to chill out. Free rum punches and soft drinks served all day. Includes pickup and return to your hotel. $59, children $39.

Fishing

Though not as fine a **fishing** destination as the Biminis and Berry islands to the south, Grand Bahama is still a popular retreat for anglers, home to some fine **bonefishing** at the eastern end of the island around McLean's Town in particular (see p.125). The following is just a small selection of angling outfitters in the Freeport/Lucaya area; if looking to make a full day of it, it's worth trolling the marinas to haggle for a charter – with a party of five, expect to pay around $400 for a half-day, twice that for a full one. Captains to call direct include John P. M. Roberts (☎352-7915) and Walter Kitchen (☎373-2222 or 1090).

Captain Phil and Mel's Bonefishing Guide Services McLean's Town ☎353-3023, ⓦwww.bahamasvg.com/p&mbonefishing. Based near the prime bonefishing flats at the eastern end of the island, Captains Phil and Mel offer guided excursions for $350 a day ($250 half-day). **Paradise Watersports** Xanadu Beach ☎352-2887, ⓦwww.bahamasvg.com/paradise.html.

Besides charter rentals, Paradise run four-hour morning and afternoon deep-sea sessions for $80 per person.
Reef Tours Port Lucaya ☎373-5880 or 5891. Offers half-day deep-sea and bottom-fishing excursions twice daily for $80 and $45 respectively. You can also charter a boat and crew for the whole day.

Kayaking

Kayak Nature Tours (☎373-2485, ⓦwww.bahamasvg.com/kayak) runs a variety of enjoyable and well-organized **paddling excursions** that explore the varied geography and ecology of Grand Bahama. The naturalist guides, who are well versed in local history, give six-hour excursions to Lucayan National Park that include a leisurely paddle through a mangrove creek, a nature walk through the park and a picnic lunch on spectacular Gold Rock Beach, twelve miles east of Freeport/Lucaya. They also offer a five-hour snorkelling tour to Peterson Cay National Park featuring a thirty-minute paddle to the cay followed by snorkelling and a picnic on its powder white beach. Both tours are offered daily for $69, and are suitable for children and beginners. Those seeking a more intense wilderness experience might enjoy the moderately strenuous day-trip ($110) to the tiny remote settlement of Water Cay (see p.126) or the three-day camping expedition on the same cay ($150 a day all-inclusive). Both trips include several hours of paddling, nature walks, birdwatching and fishing.

Other outdoor activities

Unlike the majority of other islands throughout the Bahamas, Grand Bahama offers up a good mix of inland outdoor activities to choose from. The most popular choice is undoubtedly **golf**. There are five courses on the island, with two more planned for the near future. The lush and challenging Emerald and Ruby courses at *Royal Oasis Golf Resort and Casino* (☎350-7000; $85) have been recently relandscaped and refurbished, while the championship Reef Course at *Our Lucaya* (☎373-2002; $60-120 depending on season) is known for its numerous water hazards. The links of the Lucayan course – also at *Our Lucaya* (☎373-1066; $65-120 depending on season) – host the Caribbean Open in December, and are home to the expensive Butch Harmon School of Golf (☎1-877/687-2474; day session from $299). The nine-hole course at Fortune Hills (☎373-4500; $48) is a lot less glamorous, but it provides some variety for insatiable golfers. The derelict Shannon course next to the Garden of the Groves is slated for a five-million-dollar renovation and rebirth as Raspberry Falls in the near future.

Another option is **horseback riding**. Pinetree Stables (☎373-3600, ⓔpinetree@batelnet.bs; closed Mon) offer a pleasant two-hour guided trail ride ($65) on well-cared-for horses through a tall sun-dappled pine forest, along the beach and finally into the surf à la *The Black Stallion*. No experience necessary, though the rider weight limit is 200lbs and the minimum age is 8.

Freeport/Lucaya

The only inland town in the Bahamas, **FREEPORT** is a commercial and industrial centre deliberately built in the interior of Grand Bahama to preserve the oceanfront property of **LUCAYA** for the development of tourism. The master plan for the city was drawn up by a group of urban planning students at Cornell University in 1960, hired on contract by the Grand Bahama Port Authority Ltd. Envisioning an urban centre with an eventual population of 200,000, the class laid out a broad grid of streets and roads, extending from Freeport Harbour on Hawksbill Creek west of the main commercial district, to the manmade Grand Lucayan Waterway, fifteen miles to the east.

Today, a map of Freeport/Lucaya, with its intricate web of dozens of avenues, drives and crescents, might give the impression of a large, densely populated metropolis. In reality, though, the city only has about 40,000 residents, and many of these roads lead nowhere, through undeveloped bush and grandly named but deserted subdivisions still waiting for the houses and people to come. Here and there throughout the grid are what Bahamians call "pocket houses" – husks of concrete in various stages of construction or disrepair. It is difficult for most Bahamians to get a mortgage, so many build their homes out of their own pocket bit by bit over several years.

A utilitarian town with no organic centre or street life – everyone lives in the suburbs – Freeport is not a city for strolling or sightseeing, though it is easy enough to get around on foot to do your shopping, go out to eat or to see a movie. Lucaya, which runs along the oceanfront three miles south of Freeport, has a more festive atmosphere, centred around the Port Lucaya Marketplace and the busy Port Lucaya Marina. Both Freeport and Lucaya, though, are dominated by a large resort, the *Royal Oasis Golf Resort and Casino* and *Our Lucaya Beach and Golf Resort* respectively, surrounded by several other smaller hotels, restaurants, and tour operators geared to vacationers. A steady influx of holidaymakers, including daily arrivals from several mammoth cruise ships and packs of Americans who hop over for the weekend, contributes to Freeport/Lucaya's party hearty atmosphere, but it is still remarkably easy to escape the crowds. Within the city limits is the **Rand Nature Centre**, a forest preserve offering a peaceful respite from the daily grind of lying on the **beach**. In regards to beaches, there are six in the immediate area, ranging from the typically bustling Lucayan and Xanadu beaches to the more secluded Taino and Fortune beaches.

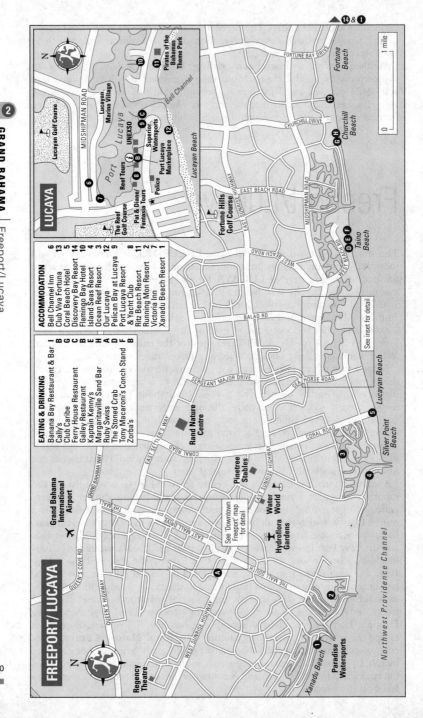

FREEPORT/LUCAYA

Grand Bahama International Airport ✈

Regency Theatre

Paradise Watersports

Xanadu Beach

Pinetree Stables

Water World

Hydroflora Gardens

Rand Nature Centre

See 'Downtown Freeport map for detail

See inset for detail

EATING & DRINKING

Banana Bay Restaurant & Bar	I
Cally's	B
Club Caribe	G
Ferry House Restaurant	C
Galley Restaurant	E
Kaptain Kenny's	H
Margaritaville Sand Bar	A
Ruby Swiss	D
The Stoned Crab	F
Tony Macaroni's Conch Stand	
Zorba's	B

ACCOMMODATION

Bell Channel Inn	6
Club Viva Fortuna	13
Coral Beach Hotel	5
Discovery Bay Resort	10
Flamingo Bay Hotel	4
Island Seas Resort	3
Ocean Reef Resort	12
Our Lucaya	9
Pelican Bay at Lucaya	8
Port Lucaya Resort & Yacht Club	11
Ritz Beach Resort	7
Running Mon Resort	2
Victoria Inn	
Xanadu Beach Resort	1

LUCAYA

Lucayan Golf Course

Lucayan Marina Village

Pirates of the Bahamas Theme Park

The Reef Golf Course

Reef Tours

Pat & Diane/ Fantasia Tours

Police

Port Lucaya Marketplace

Superior Watersports

UNEXSO

Fortune Hills Golf Course

Port Lucaya

Bell Channel

Lucayan Beach

Northwest Providence Channel

Silver Point Beach

Taino Beach

Churchill Beach

Fortune Beach

0   1 mile

Accommodation

Accommodation in Freeport/Lucaya ranges from the luxurious and secluded to no-frills mass-market-oriented motels. Though there is little available for the real budget traveller, you can often snag a discounted rate on a package deal by keeping a vigilant eye on resort and tour operator websites or by calling them direct. In almost all cases, you should be prepared to share the experience with at least a few hundred other holidaymakers.

Though inland and not especially attractive, the advantage of staying in Freeport is that the accommodation options – some of them quite nice – are generally more affordable than those in Lucaya. Perhaps the best resort here is the *Royal Oasis Golf Resort and Casino*, the island's oldest resort though it's undergone a major overhaul over the last couple of years. If you do stay in Freeport, frequent complimentary shuttle buses head to the beach at Xanadu or Lucaya (five- or ten-minute drives away, respectively). By far the largest resort on the island is Lucaya's *Our Lucaya Beach and Golf Resort* (see box overleaf), which encompasses 372 acres, including two championship golf courses – the Lucayan and the Reef – and seven acres of gorgeous white sandy beach.

Bear in mind that the price ranges quoted below are based on rack rates – the price you would pay if you walked in off the street – and you can almost invariably get a better deal by booking ahead of time. Note also that it seems as if most of the hoteliers in Freeport made a pact to confuse prospective travellers by using the words "royal", "palm" and/or "island" in naming their establishments – a curious fetish given that royal palms are not indigenous to the island. Hotels east and west of Freeport/Lucaya are covered within those sections later on in this chapter.

Freeport

Best Western Castaways Resort East Mall Drive ⊕352-6682 or 1-800/700-4752, ⑤352-5087, ⓔcastaway@batelnet.bs. With 139 attractively furnished rooms and suites overlooking the pool or the street, this refurbished resort is an excellent budget option. Within a few minutes' walk of several restaurants, movie theatres, the casino at *Royal Oasis* and the International Bazaar, its amenities include a pool, a bar and pleasant restaurant, laundry facilities, and a complimentary shuttle service to the beach. Like the *Island Palm* below, it is a comfortable place to lay your head at night after a day out and about, rather than a holiday destination in itself. ❸

Island Palm Resort East Mall Drive ⊕352-6648, ⑤352-6640, ⓔispalm@batelnet.bs. Another decent budget choice located several blocks north of the *Best Western Castaways*, but still within walking distance of the International Bazaar and other tourist amenities. Bright and cheerful, the comfortable air-conditioned, TV-equipped rooms surround a courtyard and a small pool. On site there's an outdoor bar, a dark restaurant that becomes a disco at night – you'll probably want to eat elsewhere or on the pool patio – and a complimentary shuttle bus several times a day to the pleasant beach at the *Island Seas Resort* in

Lucaya. Motor scooter rentals available as well. ❸

Royal Islander Hotel East Mall Drive ⊕351-6000, ⑤351-3546, ⓔroyalisland@hotmail.com. For about $30 more a night than the cheapest accommodations in town – the *Victoria* and *Bell Channel* inns in Lucaya – you can stay in this gem of a small hotel located in the midst of Freeport's tourist facilities. Its 100 rooms are done up in neutrals with floral accents and built on two levels around the central palm-shaded courtyard, where you could easily spend an enjoyable day poolside, dipping in the hot tub or sitting at the pool bar downing a light meal and drinks. The pleasant, airy restaurant serves three meals a day, and there is free transportation to Xanadu Beach. All-inclusive packages available. ❺

Royal Oasis Golf Resort and Casino Ranfurly Circus, next to the International Bazaar ⊕350-7000 or 1-800/545-1300, ⑤350-7002, ⓦwww.theroyaloasis.com. Built in the 1960s, this gaudy doyen of Freeport hotels was, at the time of writing, undergoing extensive renovations, including the removal of faux Moorish flourishes like the gold onion dome over its casino, the closing of the road that separates its two hotels – the *Holiday Inn Sunspree* and the *Crowne Plaza* – and the construction of a million-gallon freshwater, sandy-bottomed pool complete with a three-storey

Our Lucaya Resort

Opened in 2000 and easily the best resort on Grand Bahama, **Our Lucaya Beach and Golf Resort** (T373-1333, 1-877/OUR-LUCAYA (US), 1-800/848-3315 (Canada), F373-2396, Wwww.ourlucaya.com) matches anything on offer in Nassau or Paradise Island. It is also the island's biggest, with 1350 rooms in three hotel complexes and a high-season occupancy rate of 3000.

The three hotels – *Reef Village*, *Breaker's Cay* and *Lighthouse Pointe* – all face the sea, each just a few steps from the beach. The grounds, liberally dotted with lush flowering shrubs and palm trees, boast nine curving swimming pools, four tennis courts, a pair of golf courses and fourteen restaurants and bars (see "Eating" p.120 for a selection of the best). There's also a fitness centre and a spa offering a full range of health and beauty treatments, a high-end shopping arcade, and at the time of writing a casino was scheduled to open in 2003.

Accommodations range from $130 for a standard double to $5500 a night for the two-bedroom Lucaya Suite with private beach access and a butler. It is always worth checking the resort's website for specials and package deals. If you don't intend to stray far from the beach, it may be more economical to opt into the meal plan at the outset rather than to pay as you go. Plans including breakfast and dinner daily and soft drinks throughout the day range $49–69 per adult, $25–35 for a child aged 4–12, including gratuities. All rooms have TV, air conditioning, and dataports and about half have ocean views.

Breaker's Cay Rising ten stories high in the middle of the resort, *Breaker's Cay* affords spectacular floor-to-ceiling views of the serpentine pool, palm trees and the turquoise sea – ask for an ocean-side room, the higher the better. Its bright, airy feel is enhanced by light-wood furniture, warm neutrals on the walls and carpets, with crisp turquoise and blue accents. For about $10 extra a night, you can join the *Harbour Club* on the ninth and tenth floors, with morning coffee and pastries and evening cocktails with hors d'oeuvres served in the lounge or in your room. **⑦**

Lighthouse Pointe At the quiet end of the resort near the spa and an infinity pool, the hotel's rooms look either onto the Bell Channel or the ocean. Its two hundred rooms, contained in a three-storey structure built around narrow plant-filled courtyards, are favoured by those seeking more privacy. They have the same layout and pleasing decor as *Breaker's Cay*, but not its open, airy feel. **⑦**

Reef Village Catering to families and others on all-inclusive packages, the *Reef Village* is generally a hive of activity. The spacious, tastefully designed rooms are done up in bright tropical colours and warm natural-wood furniture in a low-rise building curving around the Sugar Mill Pool, each with its own balcony or patio. **⑤**

waterfall. The casino, two golf courses, seven restaurants and 965 guestrooms were also receiving makeovers to appeal more to families and the convention crowd. Of the two hotels, the ten-storey *Crowne Plaza* has the better rooms, slightly larger and decorated to the hilt in pleasing patterns of green, rose and magnolia with polished wood furniture. Other facilities on site include twelve tennis courts (six lit for night play), a golf-pro shop, babysitting service, fitness centre and two swimming pools. All-inclusive packages are available. *Holiday Inn Sunspree* **⑤**; *Crowne Plaza* **⑥**

Royal Palm Resort East Mall/Settler's Way T352-3462, F352-5759. Isolated at the far end

of East Mall Drive, the budget-priced *Royal Palm* has fallen on hard times. The 47 white-tiled rooms fronting a central courtyard are decent enough but somewhat worn – their kitchenette facilities have been removed, giving them a stripped-down atmosphere. There are tennis courts, a swimming pool and the nondescript *Red Snapper Restaurant* serving three meals a day. Free transportation to Xanadu Beach on request. **③**

Running Mon Marina and Resort Kelly Court T352-6834, F352-6835, Wwww.running-mon-bahamas.com. A bit off the beaten track a couple of miles south of Ranfurly Circus, but with complimentary transportation to downtown Freeport and Xanadu Beach and the advantage of quiet surroundings. Well maintained, with a bright orange exterior and 31 scrupulously clean rooms painted a fresh green and done up with floral linens, rattan furniture, and terracotta tiled floors. Amenities include a laundromat, children's play area, internet access, a pleasant bar and the very nice *Main Sail Restaurant* (see p.120), plus a full-service marina. Bicycle, motor scooter, and boat rentals available on site. All-inclusive packages available and discounts given for stays of a week or longer. ❺

Lucaya and the adjacent beaches

Bell Channel Inn King's Rd ☎ 373-1053, ℗ 373-2886, ⓦ www.bahamasvg.com/caribdiv. Located on the backside of the Port Lucaya Marina, with dated, carpeted rooms overlooking either a small dipping pool or dumpsters and the flotsam and jetsam floating the channel. Amenities include TV, a/c and a fridge in each room, a utilitarian bar and restaurant and an on-site dive operator. ❸

Club Viva Fortuna Fortune Beach ☎ 305/266-6465 or 1-800/898-9968, ℗ 305/266-6367, ⓦ www.vivaresorts.com. Bright yellow and green with a constantly jammed lobby and music blaring out of seemingly every door, this is an all-inclusive summer camp for adults and families, attracting a predominately Italian clientele. Located a couple of miles east of Lucaya on a stretch of Fortune Beach, the all-inclusive resort has nearly 300 rooms, spread across a complex of twenty-odd buildings on 26 acres of nicely landscaped grounds. Besides a large swimming pool next to the beach, amenities include two restaurants, two discos, tennis courts, a gym and children's day camp. Organized activities include diving and snorkelling, day-trips around the island, dance classes and live entertainment nightly. ❻

Coral Beach Hotel Royal Palm Way/Coral Rd ☎ 373-2468, ℗ 373-5140. At the opposite end of the noise and activity spectrum from *Club Viva* is this quiet, secluded high-rise condominium complex on Lucayan Beach, about a 15min walk from the Port Lucaya Marketplace. Most of the units are time-shares occupied by American retirees, but there are ten large guestrooms rented on a daily or weekly basis: four with kitchenettes, six with just a coffeepot and refrigerator. Clean and comfortable, with red carpets, white walls and floral bedspreads, the rooms do not face the ocean, but the private beach and swimming pool are only a few steps away. Not recommended for families with small children to entertain. ❹

Flamingo Bay Yacht Club and Marina Hotel Taino Beach ☎ 373-4677 or 1-800/824-6623, ℗ 373-4421, ⓔ taino@batelnet.bs. This property is part of the grandly named but rather tacky *Ritz Beach Resort* (see overleaf), which also includes the *Ritz Beach* and *Taino Beach* time-share condominium complexes and the Pirates of the Bahamas theme park. On the edge of the waterway connecting Taino Beach to Port Lucaya, the three-storey, 68-unit *Flamingo Bay* is a 3min walk across the parking lot and grounds to a fine white-sand beach. The pastel and white rooms are pleasant enough, and the small palm-shaded pool with its waterfall and grotto bar is a delightful flight of fancy, but the whole place suffers from poor management and a badly trained staff – you could wait hours to be served in the bare-bones dining room or the otherwise inviting beachside patio café. ❸

Island Seas Resort Silver Point Drive ☎ 373-1271, ℗ 373-1275. A small beachfront hotel with a pleasant, relaxed atmosphere. The one- and two-bedroom suites available come with fully equipped kitchens and living quarters furnished with rattan, floral fabrics, tiled floors, a/c and cable. The blocks of rooms are situated in a quadrangle around a large swimming pool with a rock garden and waterfall, a swim-up bar, and the attractive open-air *Coconuts Grog and Grub* bar (see p.121). On the pretty curve of soft golden sand in front of the hotel, *Zonk the Conch Man* cooks up the Bahamian delicacy eleven different ways, while thatched umbrellas provide shade for sunbathers. Watersports, bicycle rentals and a free shuttle bus to the International Bazaar are offered. A bit isolated – you would have to take a taxi to eat out or go sightseeing – but a pleasant place to be stranded. All-inclusive packages available. ❼

Ocean Reef Yacht Club and Resort Bahama Reef Blvd ☎ 373-4662 or 373-4661, ℗ 373-8261, ⓦ www.oryc.com. Built on a quiet canal in a residential area near Silver Point Beach west of Lucaya, this resort caters primarily to boaters. Captain or not, though, it's worth looking into as the grounds are well maintained and the suites nicely fitted out with the ubiquitous rattan furniture, floral print fabrics and polished tile floors, with boat slips in front of each unit. Amenities include two small swimming pools, an outdoor hot tub, two-person in-room whirlpools, laundry facilities and a cosy pool bar serving light meals. Complimentary shuttle service; larger apartments and weekly rates available. ❽

Pelican Bay at Lucaya Seahorse Rd ☎ 373-9550, ℗ 373-9551, ⓦ www.pelicanbayhotel.com. Across the street from *Our Lucaya*, this lovely hotel is built on a far more intimate scale around a quiet, landscaped courtyard with a swimming pool, hot tub and open-air bar serving light meals. The forecourt of the hotel is not very attractive – a big parking lot and a construction site that will presumably disappear at some point – but once inside, you enter a green oasis of calm. The comfortable rooms are done up in neutral colours and tile floors, each with TV, refrigerator and air conditioning and a deep balcony furnished with Adirondack chairs looking into the courtyard and the marina beyond. The recent addition of a few dozen luxury suites with kitchens provides an attractive self-catering option as well. Guests have access to the beach at *Our Lucaya*. All-inclusive packages available, with meals served at the *Ferry House Restaurant* (see p.120) next door. ❻; suites ❽

Port Lucaya Resort and Yacht Club Seahorse Rd, Freeport ☎ 373-6618, Ⓕ 373-6652, ⓌWwww.portlucaya.com/resort. Conveniently located next door to the Port Lucaya Marketplace and Marina, and across the street from Lucayan Beach, with boat slips just outside the rooms. The resort features a large swimming pool and hot tub set in a broad expanse of lawn devoid of shade and encircled by the multicoloured two-storey buildings housing over 150 guestrooms. The pleasant and spacious rooms have terracotta tile floors, bright floral print textiles and white rattan furniture, along with either a patio or balcony overlooking the marina or pool. The pleasant *Tradewinds Café* in the courtyard serves à la carte and buffet meals, and an activities co-ordinator will book outings for you. All-inclusive packages available. ❸

Ritz Beach Resort Taino Beach ☎ 373-4677 or 1-800/824-6623, Ⓕ 373-4421, Ⓔ taino@batelnet.bs. A time-share complex located on a lovely stretch of beach, some of the opulent gilt and marble condo suites here are rented by the night or week. The suites are Las Vegas-grade glitzy, with sunken tubs in the bedroom, lots of mirrors and glass, a kitchenette and a waterfall-fed hot tub on the private balconies overlooking the ocean. Guests share the swimming pool, tennis courts, watersports and other amenities with the *Flamingo Bay* condos (see p.113), but are also subjected to its unprofessional service. Particularly off-putting is the resort's time-share selling approach, which includes rounding people up on the streets of Lucaya with the promise of a free buffet breakfast and tour of the resort that turns out to be an aggressive hard-sell spiel and video presentation. Beware. ❼

Victoria Inn, King's Rd ☎ 373-3040, Ⓕ 373-3874. A dive with soiled carpets, mildewed shower curtains and grubby windows. Rates, though, are as low as it gets in town, rooms have TV and a/c and there's also a swimming pool. ❸

Xanadu Beach Resort and Marina Sunken Treasure Drive ☎ 352-6782, Ⓕ 352-6299, ⓌWww.xanadubeachhotel.com. Pity the poor newlyweds who get sucked in by the glossy brochure and find themselves spending their honeymoon at this desolate, shabby, peeling monument to 1980s kitsch, with its litter-strewn patch of beach. Notable only as the last binennial residence of reclusive billionaire Howard Hughes (see box on p.118), it is ridiculously overpriced and not recommended. ❺

Downtown Freeport and around

The main commercial district, **DOWNTOWN FREEPORT**, is centred along **The Mall**, the main thoroughfare that runs between Ranfurly Circus and Churchill Square, about ten blocks to the north. Just north of Ranfurly Circus, The Mall divides to surround the city centre, which is bound on one side by West Mall Drive, and on the other by **East Mall Drive**, where most of the hotels and restaurants are located. In truth, though, the twenty square blocks that make up downtown Freeport offer little in terms of worthwhile exploration, being home to little beyond banks, the main bus stand, a post office and large apartment complexes – colonial-style confections in pink, blue and yellow – separated by blocks of pine forest that threaten to swallow the city back up.

   Churchill Square itself is just a tiny patch of littered earth sandwiched between strip malls and parking lots surrounding **Winn Dixie Plaza**, where a small bust of Winston Churchill stands, the plaque missing. Tourist activity is focused at the other end of East Mall Drive, around **Ranfurly Circus** (named

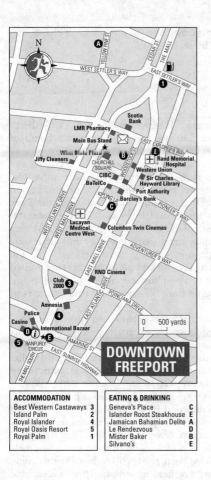

DOWNTOWN FREEPORT

0   500 yards

ACCOMMODATION	
Best Western Castaways	3
Island Palm	2
Royal Islander	4
Royal Oasis Resort	5
Royal Palm	1

EATING & DRINKING	
Geneva's Place	C
Islander Roost Steakhouse	E
Jamaican Bahamian Delite	A
Le Rendezvous	D
Mister Baker	B
Silvano's	E

for the British governor of the Bahamas who supported the development of Freeport in the 1950s). The **International Bazaar** here, marked by red Japanese-style gates, preserves a faded warren of tacky shops and cafés – and keeps intact the most horrifying aspects of the 1970s conception of leisure for the masses. The bazaar was created by a Hollywood set designer hired to build a tourist attraction with a cosmopolitan feel, and its roots show in the flimsy plaster archways and garish paintwork meant to mimic Chinese, Middle Eastern, South American and Parisian architecture. In addition to several serviceable but uninspired restaurants, a straw market and shoddy souvenir stands, there's a collection of average duty-free shops selling jewellery, perfume, Cuban cigars, rum, crystal and the like. However, the same type of shops are found at Port Lucaya Marketplace (see overleaf), which at least has a more lively atmosphere and fresher paint.

Northeast of the city centre, with its entrance on East Settler's Way just east of Coral Road about a mile east of Ranfurly Circus, is the more worthwhile **Rand Nature Centre** (Mon–Fri 9am–4pm, Sat 9am–1pm; $5, children $3; ☎352-5438, Ⓦwww.grand-bahama.com/rand). Named for its benefactor James Rand, the inventor of the telephone dialling system who lived in Freeport on his yacht in the 1960s, this peaceful wooded retreat covers a hundred acres. Besides an assortment of easy-going nature trails and a pond that's home to a small flock of West Indian flamingos amongst other native birds, exhibits here explore the natural history of the island, from marine life and bush medicine to Lucayan artefacts recovered at Deadman's Reef. The local office of the Bahamas National Trust is here as well, where you can find a good selection of books on the Bahamas.

While the Rand Nature Centre offers a natural slice of Grand Bahama's flora and fauna, the **Hydroflora Gardens** (Mon–Fri 9am–5pm, Sat 9am–4pm, closed daily for lunch 1–2pm; $5; ☎352-6052) present a carefully cultivated representation. Located a short distance south of Ranfurly Circus, on East Beach Drive off the East Sunrise Highway, the garden's three-acre plot is a riot of colour, laced with all manner of tropical and subtropical plants and fruit trees. When in season, the garden's fresh tropical fruits – including jackfruit,

akee, and starfruit – are available for tastings. Also on site is a small chapel surrounded by flora mentioned in the Bible.

Lucaya

Heading off Ranfurly Circus on Sunrise Highway then south on Seahorse
Road takes you two miles to **Port Lucaya** and the beachfront hotels of
LUCAYA. Unsurprisingly, this resort area has a more cheerful, holiday atmos-
phere than downtown Freeport, with carefully tended gardens and tidy, candy-
coloured shops and houses. Lucaya itself is dominated by the massive *Our
Lucaya Beach and Golf Resort* (see box on p.112), which leads on to Lucayan
Beach (detailed on p.118). Across the street from *Our Lucaya* stands the **Port
Lucaya Marketplace** (shops open Mon–Sat 10am–6pm), a busy, colourful
pedestrian-only outdoor market overlooking the boats at Port Lucaya Marina
on Bell Channel. Open-air stalls display straw work, jewellery and other souvenirs, and several lively restaurants and bars full of vacationers surround the
harbour-facing **Count Basie Square**, the market's performance space named
for the jazz musician who lived in Freeport for several years. There is live
entertainment here every night, ranging from fire-eaters and dance troupes to
calypso music or Sinatra standards.

The market area is flanked on both sides by canals and quiet residential
neighbourhoods where Lucaya's predominantly expatriate and seasonal population lives. If you'd like a glimpse of how the tax-fleeing upper crust lives, head
east on **Spanish Main Drive** to check out the palatial multimillion-dollar
beachfront properties that line the street. In the same direction, **Sanctuary
Bay**, an inland waterway east of the Lucayan and Taino beaches, is likewise surrounded by sumptuous winter villas. But it's also home to a pod of sixteen
semi-wild **dolphins**, donated by Hollywood producer Merv Griffin in 1987
to the Underwater Explorer's Society (UNEXSO), which moved the dolphins
several years ago from Port Lucaya because of water pollution. They have since
been joined by other dolphins, some of which came in from the sea of their
own accord, and others of which were born at Sanctuary Bay. Free to come
and go as they wish, the dolphins are not held in pens, but they are sociable
animals which seem to like human company. The Dolphin Experience, operated by UNEXSO from Port Lucaya, runs several tours out to Sanctuary Bay
daily; see p.106 for details.

Continue east from Sanctuary Bay on Midshipman Road and you come to
the **Garden of the Groves** (daily 9am–4pm, tours daily 11am; $10, children
$7; ☎373-5668, Ⓦwww.gardenofthegroves.com), on Magellan Drive about
100 yards north of Midshipman Road. A twelve-acre botanical garden containing more than 10,000 species of exotic and indigenous plants, it was built
in 1973 and dedicated to Freeport's founder Wallace Groves and his wife,
Georgette, and is now operated by Parrot Jungle theme parks of Florida. The
winding paths, footbridges over lily ponds and a little whitewashed chapel
make it a popular setting for weddings. The café and Grand Bahama Museum
formerly located here are now both closed, though, and only avid gardeners or
amateur botanists will find the gardens interesting. Kids will probably get a kick
out of the parrots that fly about, but little effort has been made to provide
information for the visitor about the multitude of plants here and the rooms
of the interpretative centre stand sadly empty.

△ Garden of the Groves, Lucaya

The beaches

Of the six public beaches within the city limits of Freeport/Lucaya, **Xanadu Beach**, just two miles south of Ranfurly Circus, is the closest to downtown Freeport. Unsurprisingly given such proximity, this charmless broad swath of coarse brown sand is heavily used and backed by faded souvenir kiosks. Truncated by a wire fence demarcating the boundary between the *Xanadu Hotel* (see box below) and the Princess Isles gated community, Xanadu Beach is where many of the hotels in Freeport deposit their guests for the day. About the only good reason to visit here is to sign up for diving or snorkelling tours run by Paradise Watersports or Xanadu Undersea Adventures (see p.106), both of whom have offices here.

About a mile to the east of Xanadu Beach, separated from it by two water channels, is a far prettier and more relaxing curve of golden sand in front of the *Island Seas Resort*. Thatched umbrellas are available for shade here, as are refreshments at the *Coconuts Grog and Grub* bar and grill (see p.121), as well as from *Zonk the Conch Man*'s kiosk in front of the bar. One manmade channel to the east is the little-used **Silver Point Beach** (accessible from the southern terminus of Coral Road or by walking west down the beach from *Our Lucaya*), a white sandy strand worth heading to during the not-infrequent times when the adjoining **Lucayan Beach** gets crowded. Justifiably popular, the Lucayan Beach runs for about a half-mile in front of *Our Lucaya Beach Resort*, with several beach bars and restaurants to choose from along with the Ocean Motion Watersports outfitter (see p.106), which offers up parasailing, water trampolines and the like. Both the Lucayan and Silver Point beaches are within walking distance of all of the hotels in Lucaya.

On the east side of Bell Channel and accessible by water taxi (see p.106), **Taino Beach**'s soft white sand fringed by palms and pines makes for a pleasant outing from Port Lucaya. The *Ritz Beach Resort* fronts the beach and offers the usual array of watersports, but you can usually find a secluded patch of sand to spread your blanket by walking east. Consider bringing your own lunch as the resort's snack bar is mediocre at best, though also look out for *Tony Macaroni's Conch Stand*, a mobile kiosk often found on the beach during high season – the proprietor serves island-famous grilled conch and conch salad.

A mile or so further east, on the far side of Sanctuary Bay, are two more equally pleasant and relatively empty beaches with cool drinks and snacks close at hand. **Churchill Beach** is pretty, but little used and perhaps for that reason, the patio furniture, oil cans and other marine refuse that washes up on shore

---

Howard Hughes and the Xanadu Hotel

For those with an interest in the weird and wonderful, the highlight of Freeport might well be the **Xanadu Beach Resort and Marina,** a pink and green tower on the edge of the ocean two miles south of the International Bazaar. Now just a peeling shadow of its former glamour, the *Xanadu* opened in 1969 with luminaries like Frank Sinatra and Sammy Davis Jr on hand. It is most famous, however, as the final residence of reclusive billionaire **Howard Hughes**, who arrived in December 1973 on his private jet, and ensconced himself on the twelfth and thirteenth floors of the hotel, which he subsequently bought. Intensely paranoid and agoraphobic, he stayed in his blacked-out rooms for more than two years, running his empire in pyjamas and partaking in such bizarre pursuits as collecting his toenail clippings and urine in jars. Hughes left the Xanadu just a few weeks before his death in 1976.

all over the Bahamas stay here a long time before they are removed by local volunteers. **Fortune Beach**, named for a treasure-loaded shipwreck found here by a group of scuba divers in 1965, adjoins Churchill to the east and is itself about five miles from Port Lucaya. The powdery stretch of sand here is lovely, long and often deserted, with the all-inclusive *Club Viva Fortuna* resort located in the middle.

Eating

Eating in Freeport/Lucaya tends to be expensive. As residents prefer take-out – either traditional dishes or fast food – to dining in, the most pleasant surroundings and the best food are generally found in **hotel restaurants**. With the opening of *Our Lucaya Beach and Golf Resort*, the options for diners took a giant leap forward – there are thirteen restaurants and cafés on its grounds, ranging from a couple of casual and inexpensive grills to formal, polished-wood and marble dining rooms. While not the place to seek out an authentic down-home Bahamian meal, the restaurants here are of uniformly high quality, and we've listed the most noteworthy below. On the beaches just east of Freeport/Lucaya are some cheerful and relaxed **beach bars and restaurants** that make a change of pace. Note that the restaurants on Taino Beach and Fortune Beach listed below are not within walking distance of the *Ritz Bay Resort* or the ferry dock – try calling ahead if you don't have a car as some establishments offer complimentary transportation.

Freeport

Geneva's Place East Mall Drive at Kipling Lane ☎352-5085. Popular and lively local restaurant dressed up with red-and-white checked table-cloths, serving Bahamian and American food at reasonable prices.

Islander's Roost Steakhouse *Pub on the Mall*, East Mall Drive ☎352-5110. Moderately priced surf and turf dishes are served here on two levels, with outdoor seating available upstairs. Appetizers include chicken wings, conch fritters and onion blossoms; for mains, try the sandwich platters served on Italian bread, filet mignon and lobster tail or the Bahamian steamed chicken stuffed with tomatoes, mushrooms and cheese. Dinner only; closed Sun.

Jamaican Bahamian Delite Yellow Pine St ☎352-7248. No-frills local eatery – take-away available – serving Jamaican and Bahamian dishes, including jerk chicken, curried goat or chicken and steamed oxtail. All meals served with typical Bahamian side-dishes – peas 'n' rice, macaroni and cheese or plantains. Breakfast and lunch only; closed Sun.

Le Rendezvous International Bazaar ☎352-9610. An inexpensive, pseudo-Parisian sidewalk café in the middle of the bazaar serving good sandwiches, salads and burgers.

Mister Baker East Mall Drive. Delicious fresh-baked muffins, cookies and pastries are the big draw here, with seating available in the vinyl and tile café.

Pier One Freeport Harbour ☎352-6674. Though the seafood served at the waterside *Pier One* is only middling, the restaurant manages to keep busy thanks to a prime location by the cruise-ship docks, a pleasing interior filled with nautical paraphernalia, and outdoor seating on timbered verandas. Evening feedings of the sharks circling below (7, 8 and 9pm) don't hurt either. Reservations essential.

The Ruby Swiss West Sunrise Highway and Atlantic Drive ☎352-8507. Popular with the Freeport business crowd during lunch and dinner hours, the *Ruby Swiss* really lights up late night when a younger clubbing crowd takes over. The satisfying if uninspired seafood-heavy menu contains an extensive selection of American and European dishes, including a $10 all-you-can-eat spaghetti buffet, served in a large, high-ceilinged dining room with attentive service.

Silvano's *Pub on the Mall*, East Mall Drive ☎352-5111. Good Italian cuisine served in an agreeable Mediterranean-styled environment, with a rough stone floor and sunny yellow walls. There are also three additional tables on a *terrazzo* outside, though traffic somewhat spoils the ambience. Be sure to save room for some *gelato* from *Silvano's Ice Cream Parlour* next door, which also serves breakfast, pastries and sandwiches all day.

Lucaya and the adjacent beaches

Banana Bay Beach Bar and Restaurant Fortune Beach ☎ 373-2960. A delightful spot for breakfast or lunch, either in the brightly painted café with its tropical fish tank and murals or on the broad wooden deck overlooking a lovely stretch of beach. Imaginatively presented lunch plates include conch burgers, cheese quesadillas, crab cakes and mouthwatering desserts. Caters primarily to day-trippers off cruise ships, but worth the short drive out from Freeport. Daily 9am–5pm.

Cally's Port Lucaya Marketplace ☎ 352-5932. *Cally's* serves tasty and inexpensive to moderately priced Greek and Bahamian dishes, including fresh Greek salad and a savoury grilled vegetable wrap. The overall atmosphere is cheerful and relaxed, and both indoor and outdoor seating on the wooden veranda is available.

China Beach Our Lucaya Resort ☎ 373-1333. On the water in front of *Breaker's Cay*, moderately priced *China Beach* is one of the few spots on the island that can satisfy an Asian cuisine fix. Decorated in rich red tones and black lacquered wood, it has a varied menu including Pad Thai chicken with grilled papaya, dim sum and even make-it-yourself sushi.

Churchill's Chophouse Our Lucaya Resort ☎ 373-1333. Located in the Manor House, this elegant and expensive dining room with attached piano bar is open for dinner only, serving steak, lobster and other seafood dishes as well as a selection of vintage wines. Long pants are required for gentlemen.

Club Caribe Churchill Beach, at Mather Town off Midshipman Rd ☎ 373-6866. Inexpensive and unpretentious, *Club Caribe's* umbrella-shaded picnic tables within view of the sea make for a near-perfect spot to down drinks or munch on simple pub-grub-style lunch or early dinner. Call ahead for transportation from Freeport or Lucaya. Closed Mon.

The Ferry House Port Lucaya waterfront ☎ 373-1595. One of the Grand Bahama's culinary highlights, the *Ferry House* offers imaginative dishes like grouper braised in Nassau Royale sauce and shrimp with ginger glacé. All dishes are created with flair by the two Scandinavian chefs and served in a relaxed and elegant dining room; sunny and inviting at breakfast, candlelit with a view of the harbour lights in the evening. Moderate to expensive.

Galley Restaurant at the Pub at Port Lucaya Port Lucaya Marketplace ☎ 373-8450. One of the better Marketplace choices, with a good view of

the marina and Count Basie Square from its busy, outdoor patio. Selections off the varied international menu include crab claws, lobster bisque, and several salads for starters, and entrees ($8–22) of seafood, lamb, chicken, ribs, and traditional English pot pies. This is also one of the few places on the island where vegetarian choices extend beyond grilled cheese and fries. Also worth a stop for the entertaining drinks menu, including such colourful selections as Nelson's Blood – named for Horatio Nelson. Legend has it that his body was returned to England in a cask of Pusser's Rum and that the sailors tapped into it on the way home, thereby drinking "Nelson's blood".

The Main Sail Running Mon Resort ☎ 352-6833. Home to a creative Austrian chef, the *Main Sail* offers a constantly changing menu featuring dishes like lobster bisque, salmon with dill, wiener schnitzel, and a vegetarian pasta dish. The circular dining room overlooking the marina is admirable, as is the wine list – reputedly the island's most extensive. Expect to pay $20–30 per entree.

Margaritaville Sand Bar Churchill Beach off Midshipman Rd ☎ 373-4525. The interior of this small candy-striped bar next to *Club Caribe* is cool and dark, with a sand floor and coloured lights. You can have burgers, sandwiches, conch fritters and occasionally wild boar at picnic tables under a thatch roof overlooking the beach – and then play some volleyball afterwards. Transportation from Freeport/Lucaya available; closed Mon.

Portobello's Our Lucaya Resort ☎ 373-1333. At *Lighthouse Pointe* overlooking the ocean, *Portobello's* is an upscale Italian dining room with stone floors, heavy wooden furniture and an outdoor terrace for alfresco dining. The expensive menu features fresh-baked breads and pastries, pasta, seafood dishes and pizza cooked in the wood-fired oven. Open for breakfast and dinner.

The Prop Club Our Lucaya Resort ☎ 373-1333. Located on the beach in front of *Breaker's Cay*, this casual restaurant and sports bar is decked out like a weather-beaten airplane hanger and is the place to head for dinner if on a tight budget but still looking for holiday atmosphere and a view of the ocean. The menu – made of airplane steel – features a flavourful and inexpensive margarita pizza, chicken, ribs and lots of fruity drinks dressed up with mini-umbrellas. There is a pool table, and music and dancing at night.

The Stoned Crab Taino Beach ☎ 373-1442. Notable for its distinctive double pyramid roof, this upscale seafood restaurant serves delicious crab claws, lobster and seafood platters, along with some meat and pasta dishes, in a relaxed, tastefully designed dining room overlooking the beach. **Willy Broadleaf** *Our Lucaya Resort* ☎373-1333. Overlooking the beach on the ground floor of *Breaker's Cay*, *Willy Broadleaf* offers heaping breakfast, lunch and dinner buffets. The relatively expensive menu is a delightful romp around the globe, featuring Middle Eastern and Indian dishes, Mexican favourites, fresh pasta, crepes prepared as you watch, and sweet delicacies like baklava and Bahamian guava duff. In different parts of the room, the decor evokes an African village, a Mediterranean villa, and a sultan's tent, all suffused by candlelight in the evening.

Zorba's Port Lucaya Marketplace ☎373-6137. *Zorba's* does a booming business in tasty and inexpensive Greek favourites like souvlaki, pita wraps and salads. Take-away is available or you can eat in a no-frills dining area.

Drinking and nightlife

For a daytime drink, you're best off hitting up any of the myriad poolside bars located in nearly every resort. In the evening hours, though, there are plenty of **bars** and **clubs** throughout Freeport/Lucaya – ranging from pseudo-English pubs to classy high-end lounges – where bathing suits are not *de rigueur*. On the whole, the most lively spots are either in the Port Lucaya Marketplace, patronized primarily by holidaymakers and yacht cruisers, or a few bars and dance clubs around Freeport's International Bazaar. For a less traditional night out, think about heading out on a **booze cruise** (see box on p.105) or if you prefer dry land, hitting up one of the various **bonfires** or **fish fries** held on the beach (see box overleaf). Another option is the **casinos** at the *Royal Oasis* and *Our Lucaya* resorts, big draws with cruise-ship passengers, package tourists and the occasional high roller.

For a more tame night out, there are two cinemas on Freeport's East Mall Drive – Columbus Theatre (☎352-7478) and RND Cinemas (☎351-3456) – each with several showings a day. Two local **amateur dramatic** societies, the Freeport Player's Guild (☎352-5533) and the Regency Theatre (same number), also put on plays throughout the year. Both are located in the same theatre on Regency Boulevard, just west of the Ruby Golf Course.

Freeport

Club 2000 East Mall Drive ☎352-8866. Locals and visitors mix it up at this large International Bazaar club. There's a large dancefloor inside, though the most popular place to hang out seems to be the large wrap-around veranda. Open Tues–Sun 10pm–3am.

Coconut Bar *Royal Oasis Resort and Casino* ☎352-6721. This sophisticated bar in the resort's *Tower* makes for a pleasant – and quiet – antidote to the more festive poolside bars that dominate the scene.

Prince of Wales Lounge *Pub on the Mall*, East Mall Drive ☎352-2700. This watering hole, located across the street from the International Bazaar, is one of Freeport's pseudo-English pubs, decorated with lots of polished dark wood and upholstered booths. Moderately priced seafood is also available. A sports bar, *Red Dog*, is located next door, as is *Silvano's* Italian restaurant (see p.119).

Lucaya and the adjacent beaches

Churchill Bar *Our Lucaya* ☎373-1333. A polished piano bar on the ground floor of the resort's *Manor House* featuring live jazz Thursdays through Sundays. Upstairs, the deep comfy chairs on the veranda are an ideal place to toast the sunset.

Coconuts Grog and Grub *Island Seas Resort* ☎373-1271. A relaxed atmosphere surrounds this poolside bar, which serves moderately priced American favourites stretching from bacon and eggs early in the day to burgers and fries or seafood specials later on, best chased with a frozen tropical cocktail. Live entertainment some nights.

Havana Cay Cigar Bar *Our Lucaya Resort* ☎373-1333. Connoisseurs of fine wines and cigars should pay this bar a visit, an elegant stop for a cocktail or a nightcap while puffing on a fine Cuban smoke. Open daily 6pm–2am.

Bonfires, fish fries and more

Though undoubtedly touristy, taking part in one of the many pre-packaged nights out organized (mainly) by local hotels and restaurants around Freeport/Lucaya can also be a great night out. What follows is just a sample of what's on offer; check the listings in the *Freeport News* and in *Happenings Around Town* for more options.

Monday: Smiling Pat's Adventures (℡373-6395) offers a four-hour bar-hopping safari ($45), starting at 7pm. Stops range from a locals' bar in William's Town to drunken limbo dancing at Port Lucaya's *Rum Runners*.

Tuesday: Fortune Beach's *Margueritaville Sand Bar* (℡373-4525) hosts a beach party with a bonfire, food and party games, and free transportation from area hotels.

Wednesday: Local residents host a fish fry at Smith's Point on Taino Beach.

Thursday: The Pirates of the Bahamas Theme Park (℡373-8456) manufactures some fun for tourists with a bonfire on Taino Beach, including live entertainment, party games and a buffet dinner ($46, children under 12 $30, including transportation).

Friday: *Our Lucaya* presents the free "Friday Night Jam" with a bonfire and live entertainment on the beach at *Reef Village*.

Saturday: The *Royal Oasis Golf Resort and Casino* presents the "Goombaya Show", a stylized performance of Bahamian music and dance with a buffet dinner ($39).

Sunday: The Pirates of the Bahamas Theme Park replay their Thursday night antics on Taino beach.

Rum Runner's Bar Count Basie Square ℡373-7233. A popular Port Lucaya Marketplace bar with views of the marina and the bandstand, where there is live entertainment – Caribbean rhythms, dancing, or fire-eating – every night. Don't leave without sampling one of their potent coconut and rum based concoctions.

Shenanigan's Irish Pub Port Lucaya Marketplace ℡373-4734. Friendly pub that's home to a selection of beers from around the world, including perhaps the finest draught pint of Guinness in the Bahamas. Open from 5pm until late.

Listings

Banking Banks are open Mon–Thurs 9.30am–3pm, Fri 9.30am–5pm. There are branches of the Bank of the Bahamas (℡352-7483), Barclays (℡352-8391), British American Bank (℡352-6676), CIBC (℡352-6651), Royal Bank of Canada (℡352-6631), and Scotiabank (℡352-6774) in Freeport and a Royal Bank of Canada (℡373-8628) at Port Lucaya Marketplace. Scotiabank ATMs dispensing American currency are located in the casino at *Royal Oasis Golf Resort and Casino* in Freeport and on the ground floor of *Reef Village* at *Our Lucaya*. There's a Western Union (℡352-6676; Mon–Fri 9am–4pm) office at the British American Bank on East Mall Drive.

Dentist Bain Dental Office, Pioneer's Way, Freeport (℡352-8492 or 351-2569).

Gas There are gas stations on the corner of East Sunrise Highway and Coral Road (nearest to Lucaya) and on the corner of East Settler's Way and East Mall Drive in Freeport, and a few more around town.

Groceries In Freeport, Winn Dixie supermarkets (Mon–Sat 7.30am–9pm, Sun 7–10am) are located at Lucayan Shopping Centre on Seahorse Road (℡373-5500) and in downtown Freeport at Winn Dixie Plaza (℡352-7901). They offer free delivery to visiting yachts on orders over $100. The open-air fruit and seafood wholesale market (closed Sun) across the street from Winn Dixie Plaza is open 7am–7pm. Butler's Specialty Foods (℡373-2050) in Port Lucaya Marketplace has a tantalizing selection of gourmet foods, deli meats and cheeses.

Internet access Head for the *.com Cybercafe*, in the Port Lucaya Marketplace (Mon–Sat 9am–10pm, Sun 11am–8pm).

Laundry Jiffy Cleaners and Laundromat (℡352-7079), corner of West Mall Drive and Pioneer's Way. Most hotels offer a laundry service or have a laundromat on site.

Library The Charles Hayward Public Library is on East Mall Drive near Pioneer's Way.

Medical services Rand Memorial Hospital (☎352-6735) is located on East Mall Drive near Pioneer's Way in Freeport. The Lucaya Medical Centre/West (☎352-7288) is on Adventurer's Way in Freeport. The Lucaya Medical Centre/East (☎373-7400) on East Sunrise Highway at Seahorse Road is the closest clinic to Lucaya. New Sunrise Medical Centre and Hospital (☎373-3333), also on East Sunrise Drive, has out-patient services 8.30am–5.30pm and a walk-in clinic 5.30–10.30pm. For an ambulance call ☎352-2689; in emergencies dial ☎911.

Pharmacy A pharmacist is on duty at LMR Drugs, 1 West Mall Drive (☎352-9075), Mon–Sun 8am–3pm. For non-prescription drugs and toiletries, LMR has shops at *Reef Village* in *Our Lucaya*, the *Tower* at *Royal Oasis* and *Seahorse Plaza*; or try Oasis pharmacies, located at Port Lucaya Marketplace, in the International Bazaar, and at the airport (☎352-5001).

Police There are police detachments at the International Bazaar in Freeport (☎352-4156) and on Seahorse Drive in Lucaya (☎373-1112). In emergencies dial ☎911.

Post office The main post office (☎352-9371) is located on Explorer's Way in the commercial district of Freeport and is open 9am–5.30pm weekdays. You can purchase stamps at the Oasis pharmacies and post mail at the reception desks of most hotels.

Telephone Payphones may be found in hotel lobbies and shopping centres. You can purchase prepaid BaTelCo debit cards at the phone company (☎352-9352) on Pioneer's Way in Freeport or at Oasis pharmacies and *Zorba's Restaurant* in Port Lucaya Marketplace. Cell phones from the US can be connected for local use for $75 at BaTelCo; calls cost 40/20¢ a minute during the day/night.

East of Freeport

Escape from Freeport/Lucaya's crowded resorts lies east of the city, and the Queen's Highway, which extends for sixty miles out to **McLean's Town**, can spirit you away. Leaving the city, the road cuts a straight flat line through tall pine forest with an understory of emerald-green thatch palm. Less than half an hour out, the road passes unspoilt **Barbary** and **Gold Rock beaches**, sharp contrasts to the crowded beaches of Lucaya, as well as **Lucayan National Park**, encompassing a varied landscape of blue holes, mangrove creeks, coastal forests and beach traversed by several hiking trails. McLean's Town itself is a small fishing village with little to see or do, but from which you can visit the handful of small **cays** that sit just a short distance offshore. If you are counting on public transport to **get around**, the #10 **bus** runs to and from Freeport and McLean's Town twice a day (see p.104).

Barbary Beach and Old Freetown

Fifteen miles east of Freeport, **Barbary Beach** is a long, empty stretch of white sand backed by casuarina trees. Initially, the students of Cornell who designed the master plan for Freeport in 1960 (see p.101) envisioned a university town here, but the founding fathers of Freeport didn't buy the idea, and it remains an undeveloped piece of coastline that you will likely have all to yourself. A mile offshore is tiny **Peterson Cay National Park**, a conservation area for sea-birds with an inviting beach and good snorkelling. Kayak Nature Tours offer day-trips to the cay – see p.108 for details.

A few miles further east, just off the main highway, are the ruins of **Old Freetown**, one of the first settlements of freed slaves on the island; there isn't much left to see except the remnants of a few stone foundations. As you continue further eastward, keep an eye out on the left-hand side of the highway for the huge **sound stage** in the woods, built by Bahamian favourite son Sidney Poitier and other investors in 1968 in hopes of sparking a local movie industry. Some scenes from various James Bond movies set in the Bahamas were filmed here, but the buzz fizzled shortly thereafter.

Lucayan National Park and Gold Rock Beach

Straddling the Queen's Highway less than thirty miles east of Freeport is **Lucayan National Park** (☎352-5438; daily 9am–4pm; $3; tickets available at the Rand Nature Centre in Freeport or at Smitty's One Stop gas station in Beven's Town. The park encompasses forty acres of mixed forest, limestone caverns and sinkholes, mangrove creeks, a spectacular beach and several nature trails all less than a mile long. One of these leads from the parking lot on the north side of the highway to Ben's Cave and the Burial Mound Cave, which are part of a six-mile-long **underwater cave system**, one of the world's longest. In one of nature's mysteries, a lens of fresh water rests atop the salt water that fills the underground caverns. Certified divers may explore the underwater stalactites and stalagmites of the tunnels with a permit obtainable from the park; or UNEXSO (see p.106) offers guided expeditions. The opening of Ben's Cave, accessible by a steep staircase, is home to a large colony of buffy flower bats and is closed to visitors in the summer months when they nurse their young. Nearby, in Burial Mound Cave, another limestone sinkhole, divers discovered the skeletons of four indigenous Lucayans.

Perhaps the Lucayans who lived hereabouts were attracted to the spot by the stunning vista of **Gold Rock Beach**, accessible by a trail on the south side of the highway across from the parking lot. At high tide, it's just another pretty strand of powdery white sand edged with feathery casuarina trees. But when the tide heads out to sea, it reveals a pristine, sweeping expanse of beautiful rippling patterns carved into the sand by the retreating waves – the ideal setting for a picnic and a long walk in the surf. Half a mile offshore lies Gold Rock, the minute cay that gives the beach its name, and behind it is the ocean outlet of the underwater cavern system that connects to Burial Mound Cave and Ben's Cave.

Continuing east a few miles on the Queen's Highway, beach lovers should make a beeline for **High Rock Beach**, a long ribbon of white sand with a gentle surf, accessible at the village of High Rock and extending for several miles in either direction. A further ten miles or so east, the highway runs alongside another pearly white beach fringed with coconut palms at the sleepy hamlet of **Pelican Point**.

Practicalities

The best **tours** of Lucayan National Park are run by Kayak Nature Tours (see p.108 for details), whose trips include plenty of paddling along with short hikes and lunch. Public buses also pass by three times a day (see p.104) if you're willing to visit alone. Note that as a national park, fishing and the removal of any material from the park are not permitted.

If thinking about **spending the night** in the area, *Bishop's Bonefishing Resort* in High Rock (☎353-4515, ☎353-4417; ⑤) offers half a dozen large and modern motel-style rooms steps from lengthy High Rock Beach. Guided fishing packages are available, and meals are served in a friendly, simple bar and dining room next door. A bit closer to Freeport but no less secluded is the all-inclusive *North Riding Point Club* (☎353-4250, ℉353-4059; ❸), a relaxed yet elegant hideaway catering exclusively to fishermen. The club offers accommodation for up to fourteen guests in charming wooden cottages, shaded by mature trees and fronting the beautiful, private white-sand beach. The rooms, each with two double beds, are simple but tastefully furnished and each cottage sports a deep, screened-in porch facing the water. The most affordable accommodation in the area is Pelican Point's beachfront *Pelican Beach Lodge* (☎353-6064; ❸), a low-slung building with a small two-bedroom unit, two twin rooms and a double, each with a kitchenette and air conditioning. It's pretty basic – the decor could best be described as garage-sale eclectic – but perfectly liveable for those who don't require many creature comforts.

Eating options in the area are also pretty basic. There are a couple of basic roadside bars along the Queen's Highway and Smitty's One Stop gas station (open 8am–8pm) at Beven's Town five miles east of the park has a convenience store and a small café serving home-cooked Bahamian staples like conch fritters and fried chicken. In Pelican Point village, *Breezes Bar and Restaurant* – overlooking the beach and open on weekends only – dishes out standard Bahamian cuisine. Off the highway at High Rock, *Bishop's Bar and Restaurant* (☎353-4515; signposted) serves similar basic but satisfying fare within sight of High Rock Beach.

McLean's Town and the east-end cays

Marking the eastern terminus of the Queen's Highway, **McLEAN'S TOWN**, a small fishing village of a dozen or so modern bungalows, was originally a base for harvesting sponges. There are no real sights to speak of in town, though if you're around on National Heroes Day (October 12), be sure to call in for the annual **conch-cracking contest**. There are several separate cracking and eating events – including a division for tourists who've never conked a conch before – along with a Junkanoo parade, three-legged races, greasy-pole climbing and music from the local police force band.

The rest of the year, the majority of visitors out to McLean's Town are here to catch the ferry to Crown Haven (see p.159) or to visit one of the nearby cays that curve off the frayed southeastern end of Grand Bahama. The bonefishing around them is superb, and anglers looking to head out should contact local captains Phil and Mel (see p.108 for details). The closest of the cays to town is **Deep Water Cay**, the site of an exclusive bonefishing club that no longer accepts paying guests. Three miles further south is the tiny fishing settlement on **Sweeting's Cay**, home to a few cottages, a primary school, and a huge pile of empty conch shells near the wharf. It is accessible only by boat and only recently got electricity, offering a delightful glimpse of Out Island life. Uninhabited **Lightbourne Cay**, separated from Sweeting's Cay by a narrow channel, boasts a long, broad swath of brilliant white sand lapped by shallow, clear waters frequented by graceful eagle rays and schools of bonefish.

Practicalities

The best **tours** around McLean's Town and the nearby cays are run by East End Adventures (see p.107 for details), who offer excellent snorkelling and sightseeing excursions that include visits to Sweeting's Cay and a picnic on Lightbourne Cay. Another good option is the local *Cardy's* restaurant (see below), who offer pickups from Freeport/Lucaya, and it's also possible to hire a water taxi on the wharf in McLean's Town to visit the cays, though be prepared to haggle for a fair fee.

As far as **accommodation** goes, your options are limited. The owners of the three-storey green and pink house on your left as you enter McLean's Town (☎ 353-3440; ❶) rent out very basic rooms, mainly to people arriving or departing on the ferry to Abaco. Out on Sweeting's Cay, *Twin Gables* (☎ 373-6662, ✉ eastendsafari@yahoo.com; ❻) is a large two-storey, three-bedroom cottage with satellite TV and air conditioning, sitting on the water's edge at a discreet distance from the village centre.

The hub of activity in town is *Cardy's* **restaurant** (☎ 353-3150), serving down-home Bahamian specialties like cracked conch and sheep's-tongue souse, as well as burgers, fries and sandwiches. The proprietors, Cardinal and Ginny Higgs, also organize a **fish fry** every afternoon at nearby Crabbing Bay Beach (noon–4pm; $55, children under 12 $27.50; ☎ 353-3150), an outing that includes transportation to and from your hotel in Freeport/Lucaya, a picnic lunch, conch-cracking demonstration and games. They also rent kayaks, paddle boats, snorkelling gear, and will take you fishing, sightseeing or snorkelling through the cays and blue holes off the east end. On Sweeting Cay, the *Seaside Fig Tree* is a pleasant lavender-painted restaurant with a veranda lapped by the turquoise water that's great for a cool drink or a meal. The restaurant serves basic Bahamian and deep-fried fare all day.

West of Freeport

Unless you're staying at the *Old Bahama Bay* luxury resort, there are really only two reasons to head **west of Freeport**. The first is the stunning, wild beach around the *Paradise Cove* resort – a picturesque strip of sand made even finer by **Deadman's Reef** just offshore. The second reason, and really one that's only attractive to history buffs, is the storied settlement of **West End**, a once bustling rum-running centre.

To get here without a car, take the #16 bus from downtown Freeport; it leaves several times a day (see p.104 for details).

Paradise Cove and Deadman's Reef

Leaving Freeport, the Queen's Highway skirts an industrial landscape surrounding Freeport Harbour, including the oil bunkering facility and the massive container port. It's ironic that while settlers and trading vessels over the centuries passed Grand Bahama by because of its lack of a natural harbour, Freeport has become one of the busiest ports in the Caribbean. Ten miles west of Freeport, the road enters **Eight Mile Rock**, a string of high-density, low-income settlements spread out along eight miles of rocky shore. If you are just looking for a quick bite to start your trip west, look for the *E and E Snack Shop* in Eight Mile Rock's Russell Town. A simple local hole in the wall (closed Sun), the restaurant features a "Praise the Lord" breakfast served every day, along with traditional Bahamian delicacies like steamed turtle, oxtail, fried fish and fresh-made bread.

A couple of miles further on, a sign on the left marks the turnoff to *Paradise Cove* (T 349-2677, F 352-5471, W www.deadmansreef.com; ❹–❼). The resort has two homely, well-maintained two-bedroom cottages right on the beach, as well as a one-bedroom apartment and a two-bedroom villa. The resort's beach is a beautiful stretch of white sand backed by tall grass and bush, and there is great snorkelling from the shore over a lush sea garden protected by the exposed dark coral hump of Deadman's Reef, which runs parallel to the beach about fifty yards offshore. The owners of the resort run a friendly and relaxed snack bar here, rent snorkelling gear and glass-bottomed kayaks, and offer day excursions to Paradise Cove from Freeport/Lucaya, which include a day of swimming, snorkelling and beaching as well as lunch at the snack bar.

Several hundred yards long, **Deadman's Reef** is the site of an important archeological find – the remains of a Lucayan settlement from the twelfth or thirteenth century, which was discovered in 1996. Since then, over 60,000 artefacts have been uncovered by researchers and volunteers, including shell beads and tools, pottery and animal bones. The site itself is on private land, so you can't just drop by, but each summer, the Grand Bahama Branch of the Bahamas National Trust (BNT) and Dr Perry Gnivecki and Dr Mary Jane Berman of Wake Forest University run a four-week dig at the site. Living expenses are covered for volunteers (16 and over), but transportation to the Bahamas is not. Call the BNT at the Rand Nature Centre for further information (T 352-5438).

The most notable **restaurant** near Deadman's Reef is the *Buccaneer's Club* (T 349-3794), an atmospheric seaside restaurant with a touch of Bavarian beer garden about it; the menu features mainly seafood and German dishes that are best enjoyed on the outdoor terrace. Courtesy pickups from Freeport/Lucaya are available.

West End and the Inn at Old Bahama Bay

A village of less than a hundred residents located a couple of miles west of Deadman's Reef, **WEST END** was the scene of much wild intrigue as a hideout for pirates in the days of Blackbeard as well as during Prohibition times when rum-running drew bootleggers and thrill-seekers here. Warehouses – some of which are still standing – bars, and flophouses sprang up along the waterfront, and up to thirty flights a day took off from the airstrip cut out of the bush where the *Inn at Old Bahama Bay* (see below) stands today. With Miami so close, dozens of boats a week left the wharves at West End loaded with contraband. Ingeniously, they often left towing their cargo in aluminum tubes that could hold up to 400 cases of liquor – if the Coast Guard appeared, the lines were cut and retrieved from the sea only after the Coast Guard left empty-handed. The fun and games and easy money ended with the repeal of Prohibition in 1933, and the town's been on a decline ever since.

The West End of days gone by was just the kind of place that would appeal to the macho Ernest Hemingway, who reputedly stayed at the now near-derelict **Star Hotel, Restaurant and Bar** (T 346-6207), built in 1946. The hotel is closed, and the closure in 1982 of the *Jack Tar Village*, another large all-inclusive resort built on the site where the new *Inn at Old Bahama Bay* stands today, put many locals out of work, an economic blow from which West End has never recovered. You can have a drink for old times' sake at the *Star*, whose friendly and knowledgeable proprietor Robert Grant can fill you in on local lore. The *Star* also hosts a street party every weekend, with music and fresh conch salad and other foods grilled on the waterfront; call for details. Another **dining** option in town is *The Village Tavern*, located in a tidy, bright-yellow building on a side street in West End; inside you can order Bahamian food like souse, fried chicken and boiled fish breakfasts.

Following the road out of West End about two miles leads you to the luxurious *Inn at Old Bahama Bay* (T 346-6500, F 346-6546, W www.oldbahamabay .com; ❽), a development that encompasses several hundred secluded wooded acres on the tip of the island, crisscrossed with peaceful walking and jogging trails. Major construction is under way on the water's edge, where lots are being sold for luxury vacation homes, and a full-service marina has recently opened (see p.102). The sumptuous guestrooms – done in soothing neutrals with dark-wood accents, rich fabrics and luxurious touches like feather duvets and leather steamer trunks – are housed in pastel gabled cottages with private verandas overlooking a palm-fringed curve of white sand. The point is surrounded by rich, teeming sea gardens and reefs, and seven different snorkelling trails have been mapped out, accessible either from the shore or by boat. A variety of watersports and fishing trips can been arranged, and a spa, tennis courts, and eighteen-hole golf course are all under construction. The inn also features the *Dockside Grill* (T 346-6500), a cheerful, relaxed **bistro** with open-air seating and a view of the marina.

The Abacos

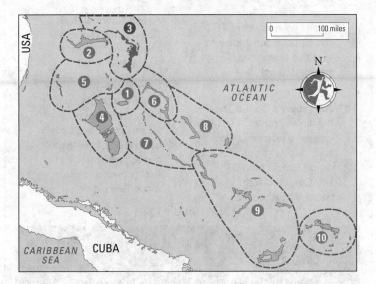

CHAPTER 3 # Highlights

✳ **Elbow Cay Lighthouse**
Climb the stairs at the
lighthouse in Hope Town
for an unforgettable 360-
degree view of the
Loyalist Cays and Sea of
Abaco. **See p.144**

✳ **Captain Jack's** After
wandering the quaint
streets of Hope Town,
refresh yourself with a
scrumptious conch burg-
er at this celebrated
local restaurant. **See
p.146**

✳ **Joe Albury's Studio** The
Bahamian craft of
wooden sailboat building
is on display at this studio on remote Man O'
War Cay, filled with
authentic sailboats as

well as wooden models.
See p148

✳ **Pelican Cays Land and
Sea Park** The spectacu-
lar snorkelling here fea-
tures coral tunnels, spires
and caves that make for
intriguing underwater vistas. **See p.161**

✳ **Abaco National Park**
Home to the rare and
endangered Bahamian
Parrot. **See p.163**

✳ **Hole-in-the-Wall**
Located along the cliff-
bound seashore of
South Abaco, sea birds
abound and trails lead
through lush stands of
wild orchids and sea
grass. **See p.164**

3

The Abacos

The northernmost of the Bahamian islands, the **ABACOS** – 200 miles east of Miami and 75 north of Nassau – are the most accessible of all the Bahamian Out Islands, and, consequently, the most developed, visited and affluent. Each year the Abacos, whose population hovers around 10,000, receive more than 120,000 visitors, a good portion of whom arrive on yachts and other sailing vessels, taking advantage of fine marina facilities and excellent shallow-water cruising amid the many cays and islands.

The Abacos' two main islands, **Little Abaco** and **Great Abaco**, form a boomerang running from northwest to southeast, and run parallel to a stunning chain of approximately 25 cays that constitute a 200-mile-long barrier and reef system off the Abacos' Atlantic coast. Two additional reef systems oceanward of the cays provide additional protection for the mainland against the waves and occasional storms of the cool Atlantic Ocean. **Marsh Harbour**, located on the northern tip of Great Abaco, is the administrative, accommodation and yachting centre of the Abacos. With a population of nearly 4000, the town attracts visitors in all seasons and serves as the gateway for activities in the **Loyalist Cays**, home to the enchanting towns of **New Plymouth** and **Hope Town** on Green Turtle and Elbow cays respectively. **Treasure Cay**, just north of Marsh Harbour and actually a peninsula not a cay, also has excellent marina facilities and year-round tourist accommodation.

Despite the influx of tourists, naturalists are well served on the Abacos. Because of the heavy forestation of Great Abaco, it is the best island for **birdwatching** in the Bahamas. Warblers, West Indian woodpeckers, yellowthroats, flycatchers, swallows and Cuban emeralds all call the Abacos home. And in southern Great Abacos' **Abaco National Park**, 2500 acres have been set aside as a reserve to protect the endangered **Bahamian parrot**, colourful birds referred to locally as "rainbows in the sky". Besides birds, everything from wild horses and boars to several varieties of bats inhabit the islands. It's along and in the water, though, that you'll want to do most of your explorations. Southeast of Marsh Harbour, the Abacos' only underwater park is 1200-acre **Pelican Cays Land and Sea Park**, which protects a large area of shallow reefs and mangroves. Harbouring a vast array of marine life, including the endangered green turtle, it is popular with snorkellers and divers alike. The western seaboard of northern Great Abaco, called the **Marls**, is one vast wetland, an important nursery for many reef fishes and invertebrate populations (see box overleaf).

The **climate** of the Abacos is markedly different from the other Bahamian islands due to its northern latitude and abundant rainfall. The climate falls between temperate and subtropical, with its average rainfall of 50–60in

The Marls and eco-tours on Great Abaco

Perhaps the least explored part of Great Abaco is the nearly uncharted **Marls** of the west coast, a great pattern of small cays, rocks and inlets. At high tide, water depth in creeks on the Marls' shoreward side might be only three feet, a perfect depth for kayaks which draw only six inches of water. Paddling in the Marls one can see red mangroves which pioneer the making of new land by rooting directly in the mud under shallow water, then sending out a system of stilt roots that catch creek silt, thus providing a home for reef fish, nurse sharks, and stingrays. Black mangroves are abundant in the Marls as well, though they have no stilts, sending up breathing tubes from their roots as sources of oxygen. The Marls, thick with marine life, are also loaded with birdlife like beautiful green-back herons, terns, turkey vultures, Great White Egrets, and Little Blue Herons. The rock islands throughout support pines, bromeliads and orchids and the quiet lagoons dotted here and there are good for snorkelling.

Eco-tourism is the specialty of **Abaco Outback**, based in Marsh Harbour (Ⓦwww.abacooutback.com), who run tours of the Marls as well as Abaco National Park. Call Erin Lowe or Ron Pagliaro at ☏447-5682, or email at Ⓔabacooutback@oii.net, or via regular mail at PO Box AB-21013, Marsh Harbour, Abaco, Bahamas.

per year, encouraging the many citrus farms on the island. Winter is a long, dry period here, when **forest fires** often flare, some started by farmers to clear land or drive away the endemic wild hogs. Fire-cleared land makes way for a blooming of pines, orchids, and the typical **fresh grass** (*Andropogon glomeratus*) of the Abacos. Soon after a fire, you can see tiny pine seedlings peeping up through the soil of Great Abaco, a pulse of green against the red-grey land.

Some history

Though the original Lucayans disappeared about fifty years after Columbus sailed through the Bahamas in 1492, the Spanish, who moved on once their slave raids had decimated the population, kept the Lucayan name, **Habacoa**, for the islands. No remains of an early French attempt at colonization in 1625 have been found, and the main wave of settlement here came in 1783, when immigrants from New York, the Carolinas and Florida came to stay at the end of the American Revolutionary War.

Most of the **original inhabitants** of the Abacos were these Loyalist settlers. Some of them were freed black slaves who arrived near present-day **Treasure Cay** aboard the *Nautilus* and *William*, founding the village of Carleton, naming it for Sir Guy Carleton, commander of British forces in North America. Most of the early Carleton Loyalists went their separate ways after disputes over lands that had been granted them by the Crown, with splinter groups settling on the **Loyalist Cays**.

The Loyalist settlers eventually dwindled from 2000 to about 400 hardy souls, most of whom made a living through fishing, trade and crafts, though a healthy minority also engaged in wrecking. From their American homes they brought with them a dour **Calvinist Protestantism**, much of which lives on today in the spiritual life of the Loyalist Cays. They also patterned their villages on the New England mould – clapboard houses with steeply pitched roofs, tiny lawns surrounded by picket fences and a narrow complex web of streets with the church at its centre of life. Unlike the New England model, though, the Abaco style features bright paint and a profusion of flowers like oleander, hibiscus and bougainvillea decorating each lawn.

Self-reliant, church-going and serious yet friendly, today's residents of the Abacos are among the most industrious in the Bahamas. Many still fish for conch and spiny Bahamian lobster, and continue to make money from boat building and maintenance, repair and storage, as well as charter businesses. People in the Abacos are increasingly employed in the tourist industry, while the islands have drawn large numbers of wealthy North Americans and a growing number of retirees, who have built luxury homes in and around Marsh Harbour.

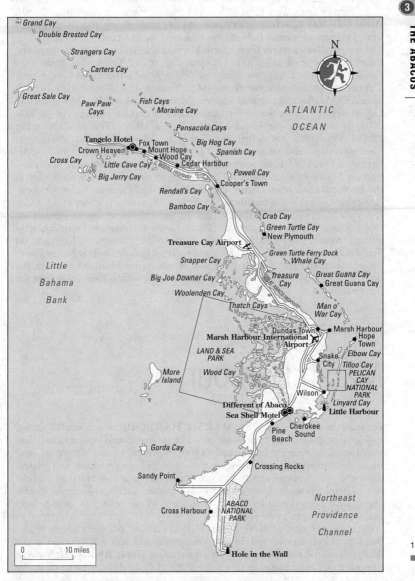

Getting there

The main entry point for visitors to the Abacos is **Marsh Harbour International Airport**, three miles southwest of Great Abaco's main settlement, though other airports are located at Treasure Cay (see p.156) and Walker's Cay (see p.160). As far as direct flights from the US are concerned, both Bahamasair (☎377-5505 or 1-800/222-4262) and American Eagle (☎954/367-2231 or 1-800/433-7300) fly into Marsh Harbour from Florida – the former from West Palm Beach and Miami, the latter from Miami only. Bahamasair also flies daily from Nassau to Marsh Harbour, and Tains Air flies from Freeport on Grand Bahama via Treasure Cay to Marsh Harbour.

Many **smaller carriers** serve Marsh Harbour and Treasure Cay. Air Sunshine (Marsh Harbour ☎367-2800; Treasure Cay ☎242-8900) flies from Fort Lauderdale, while US Airways Express (☎1-800/622-1015) and Continental Connection (Marsh Harbour ☎367-3415; Treasure Cay ☎365-8615) fly from several Florida locations. Island Express (Marsh Harbour ☎367-3597; Treasure Cay ☎365-8697) flies from Fort Lauderdale. For many, Cherokee Air (☎367-2089) is the choice for island hopping in the Abacos. The small Twin Air (☎954/359-8266) has scheduled flights to Marsh Harbour from Fort Lauderdale, and also runs charters. Visitors to Walker's Cay fly Pan-Am Air Bridge in Fort Lauderdale, seaplanes that depart from the north side of the airport on North Perimeter Road. Those going to the exclusive Spanish Cay in the far north most often charter flights or use Island Express charter services.

Another option is the **mailboat** M/V *Mia Dean*, which leaves Potter's Cay Dock in Nassau (see p.25) every Tuesday, and calls in at Green Turtle Cay, Hope Town, Marsh Harbour and Turtle Cay, returning on Thursday; trips average around twelve hours. Likewise, the M/V *Champion II* departs on Tuesday from the Potter's Cay Dock and makes scheduled calls at Sandy Point, More Island, and Bullock Harbour, also returning on Thursday. Consult the dockmaster (☎393-1064) in Nassau for the latest sailing times and fares for both mailboats.

Marsh Harbour

Founded by Loyalists in 1784, **MARSH HARBOUR** was a small logging, sponging, and wrecking town with only a single paved road until relatively late into twentieth century. In the early 1980s, however, a combination of drug money and tourism began changing the scene, and once yachters and retirees discovered the harbour and its charms, Marsh Harbour blossomed in pleasant ways. These days the harbour is lined with expensive yachts, as longtime British expats have been joined by North Americans, whose collection of expensive homes continues to grow yearly.

With a population of 4000, Marsh Harbour is now the third largest settlement in the Bahamas, and is the commercial and tourism centre for the Abacos. Located on a peninsula just off the main **Great Abaco Highway**, a smooth paved road that runs down the spine of Great Abaco, the town is also

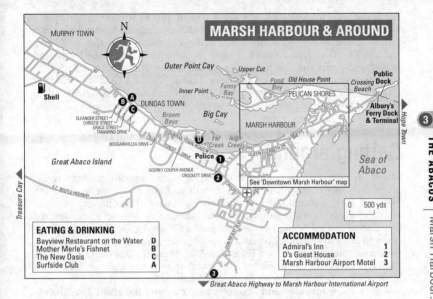

MURPHY TOWN

N

Outer Point Cay
Upper Cut

Fanny
Inner Point Bay

Pond
Bay Old House Point

Crossing
Beach

Public
Dock

PELICAN SHORES

Albury's
Ferry Dock
& Terminal

Shell

DUNDAS TOWN

Brown
Bays

Big Cay

MARSH HARBOUR

OLEANDER STREET
CHRISTIE STREET
GRACE STREET
TAMARIND DRIVE

BOUGAINVILLEA DRIVE

Far
Creek

High
Creek

QUEEN ELIZABETH DR

Great Abaco Island

Police

GODFREY COOPER AVENUE
CROCKETT DRIVE

S.C. BOOTLE HIGHWAY

Sea of
Abaco

See 'Downtown Marsh Harbour' map

Treasure Cay

Hope Town

THE ABACOS | Marsh Harbour: Arrival and information

3

0   500 yds

EATING & DRINKING

Bayview Restaurant on the Water	D
Mother Merle's Fishnet	B
The New Oasis	C
Surfside Club	A

ACCOMMODATION

Admiral's Inn	1
D's Guest House	2
Marsh Harbour Airport Motel	3

Great Abaco Highway to Marsh Harbour International Airport

the jumping-off point for travel to and from the Loyalist Cays and around both Little and Great Abaco. Though not the flashiest of places, it makes for a useful base for stocking up supplies and exploring the rest of the region, and it's more orderly than the average large Bahamian settlement. Here you'll find many of the services available in any small American town, from an excellent post office and telephone service to grocery stores, travel agencies, boutiques and laundries. Don't, though, come here looking for a party; nightlife – save around the harbourside resorts – is nearly nonexistent, and Sundays are downright anemic.

Arrival and information

Marsh Harbour lies three miles northeast of its eponymous international **airport** (see opposite), through which most visitors to the Abacos will pass. The airport itself does not have any car rental agencies, but there are plenty of **taxis** into Marsh Harbour. Fares from the airport to downtown or the marinas on Bay Street average $10, a few dollars more to Albury's Ferry Dock.

If arriving by boat, there are four main **marinas** in Marsh Harbour. All offer slips, hookups, groceries, laundry, electricity and water. Boat Harbour Marina (☎367-2736 or 1-800/468-4799) has 165 slips for yachts up to 150ft. The Conch Inn Marina (☎367-4000, ☎367-4004), also called The Moorings, has 75 slips, while Mangoes Marina (☎367-4255) has thirty slips. On the north side of the harbour, Marsh Harbour Marina (☎367-2700) has 56 slips.

The **Abaco Tourist Office** (Mon–Fri 10am–3pm; ☎367-3067), located near the heart of town in a small shopping centre on Queen Elizabeth Drive, stocks a small quantity of basic maps and hotel brochures. **The Out Islands Promotion Board** (☎305/931-6612 or 1-800/688-4752, ☎www.bahama-out-islands.com) offers complete information and maps of the island as well.

For more information, look out for a trio of **publications** that provide a wealth of information: the glossy *Abaco Life* ($2) runs regular history and events features along with community news, while *The Abaconian* is distributed free and the *The Abaco Journal* is sold cheaply on the streets. Follow the locals' lead as well and check out the hilarious and informative Radio Abaco (93.5 FM) for news, weather and music. **Yachters** use the *Cruising Guide to the Abacos* (Steve Dodge, White Sound Press; $9.95), which includes charts and tide tables among other features.

Getting around

Marsh Harbour is small enough that walking is the favourite mode of transportation. Only if you plan a journey north to Little Abaco, or south to the National Park, will renting a car become necessary. Regardless, there are a number of **car rental agencies** in town, though most have a very limited selection of cars and charge a rather expensive $70–100 a day. During high season, and especially during holiday and special events, agencies sell out, so book well in advance to guarantee a ride. A&P Auto Rentals (☎367-2655), on Don McKay Boulevard, has a decent collection of mid-size cars, as does H&L Rentals (☎367-2840 or 2854), at the Shell station downtown.

Many rely on **bicycles and scooters** to get around the island. R&L Rent-a-Ride (☎367-4289; closed Sat and evenings), located at the entrance to *Abaco Towns-by-the-Sea*, has bicycles and 80cc Yamaha cycles for rent on hourly, daily or weekly rates. Sea Horse Rentals (☎367-2513), at the *Abaco Beach Resort and Boat Harbour*, rents bicycles for $10/day and 35/week.

A wide variety of **boat rentals** are also available in Marsh Harbour, with and without crews, though almost all companies cater to experienced sailors only. D&E Boat Rentals (☎367-2182), between *Tiki Hut* and *Mangoes* on Bay Street, has 21ft Paramounts and a 24ft Thompson. Laysue Rentals (☎367-4414) has both 21ft and 25ft Sea Cat Catamarans with T-Tops and VHF radios. Florida Yacht Charters in Boat Marina Harbour (☎367-4853) offers Mainship trawlers, Hunter sailboats, cruising catamarans, on either bareboat or crewed charters. They also offer a weekly learn-to-sail class. And the Moorings (☎367-4000) at the *Conch Inn* has a selection of 35–40ft sailboats, and 37–42ft catamarans.

If heading to the Loyalist Cays (see p.140), your best bet is the reliable Albury's Ferry Service (☎365-6010 or 367-3147, 🖷365-6487, VHF Ch 16), located on East Bay Street, about half an hour's walk from the *Conch Inn* or a $4 taxi ride from downtown. See the individual cay accounts later on in this chapter for specific details.

Accommodation

Most yachties and tourists stay in **lodges** that surround the harbour itself. There are a number of less expensive options scattered around Marsh Harbour, but some of them leave you far from the action. Though not actually in town, *Different of Abaco*, an eco-resort featuring fishing for tarpon and bonefish located ed twenty miles south of town on an isolated stretch of beach, is one of the Abacos' most appealing resorts and therefore well worth looking into as well; see p.163 for more information.

Abaco Beach Resort and Boat Harbour Boat Harbour Marina ☏ 367-2158, ☏ 367-2819, ⓦ www.abacobeachresort.net. Resort featuring eighty oceanfront rooms, six two-bedroom cottages and a large marina with 180 slips. The grounds are lush, and there is a nice pool, swim-up bar, tennis, scuba and an elegant dining pavilion. Rooms all have satellite TV and kitchenettes. ⓻

Abaco Towns-by-the-Sea Boat Harbour Marina ☏ 367 2227, ☏ 367 0027 or 1 000/057 7757. Graced by tennis courts and a large pool, this seaside property has 64 villas with either garden or ocean views. All are two-bedroom and self-catering. ⓺

Admiral's Inn Admirals Yacht Haven, Dundas Town Rd ☏ 367-2022. On the fringes of Dundas Town near the water, this inn offers half a dozen modest motel-style rooms with a/c and TV. ⓶

Conch Inn and Marina East Bay St ☏ 367-4000, ☏ 367-4004 or 1-800/688-4752. Centrally located on Bay Street, this motel-style inn has nine pleasant rooms with private baths and a small veranda. The marina has 75 slips and all services and a

good dive shop; sailboat charters, kayaks and sailboard rentals are available. The on-site restaurant is one of the best in town for the money (see p.139) with good breakfasts and elegant outdoor dining. ⓷

D's Guest House Forrest Drive ☏ & ☏ 367-3983. Designed for couples, this is a quiet and pleasant four-room house, west towards the airport. There's no restaurant, but a grocery is next door and all rooms have fridges. ⓷

Island Breezes East Bay St ☏ 367-3776. Located on Bay Street, this simple nine-room motel-style lodge has neither pool nor restaurant, but its rooms are adequate, with a/c. ⓷

Lofty Fig Villas East Bay St ☏ 367-2681, ☏ 367-3385 or 1-800/688-4752, ⓔ loftyfig @mymailstation.com. Across from the *Conch Inn*, this small six-room resort is a nice choice for longer stays. It offers yellow cottages around a small central pool, the grounds are tenderly cared for and each cabin has a queen bed, small kitchen, screened porch and sofa. Guests can rent bicycles, scooters, cars or boats. Weekly rates available. ⓷

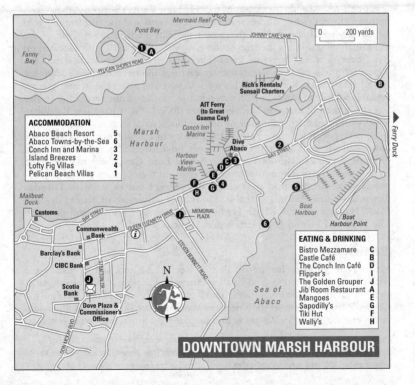

ACCOMMODATION

Abaco Beach Resort	5
Abaco Towns-by-the-Sea	6
Conch Inn and Marina	3
Island Breezes	2
Lofty Fig Villas	4
Pelican Beach Villas	1

EATING & DRINKING

Bistro Mezzamare	C
Castle Café	B
The Conch Inn Café	D
Flipper's	I
The Golden Grouper	J
Jib Room Restaurant	A
Mangoes	E
Sapodilly's	G
Tiki Hut	F
Wally's	H

DOWNTOWN MARSH HARBOUR

Marsh Harbour Airport Motel Don MacKay Blvd ☎ 367-4402, ⓕ 367-4401. This seven-room motel near the airport has large and clean rooms, but is a long way from the action at the harbour. Worth looking into only when the similarly priced options in town are full. ➌

Pelican Beach Villas Pelican Shores ☎ 367-3600

or 1-800/642-7268, ⓔ pelican@g-net.com. On an isolated peninsula off Pelican Shores Road, the six villas here each have two bedrooms, a kitchen, fan, TV and rattan furniture. The *Jib Room Restaurant* is here (see opposite), there's an on-site dive shop along with boat and bicycle rentals, and Mermaid Reef, good for snorkelling, is nearby. ➎

The town and around

From the airport, the Great Abaco Highway turns slightly east and becomes **Don McKay Boulevard** once in Marsh Harbour. At the town's only stoplight, the boulevard intersects **Queen Elizabeth Drive**, home to many shops and stores, before ending at **Bay Street**, which runs east along the harbour itself until it ends at the exclusive **Eastern Shores** housing development and the **Albury Ferry Dock**.

The only real sight in Marsh Harbour is the Moorish-looking yellow **Seaview Castle**, which overlooks the town from a lofty hill to the east, along the road towards the Albury Ferry Dock. This crenellated fantasy, now the *Castle Café* (see opposite), was the creation of Evans Cottman, an author and doctor who settled in Marsh Harbour in 1944. To reach the castle, it's about a twenty-minute walk east of the *Conch Inn* on East Bay Street, a pleasant but not particularly inspiring stroll.

Though you wouldn't seek out Marsh Harbour for its **shopping**, there are a number of worthwhile outlets featuring island crafts and the handcrafted gold items that have become something of a specialty item in town. One of the most intriguing shops is the tree-house-like A Touch of the Tropics, located on Bay Street next to Memorial Plaza. The store is owned by local artist Don Wood, who sells his own woodcarvings, earrings and necklaces, shell sculpture and metalwork. He'll explain all his work to you, and given the swamp of junk available for sale in most shops, his tree-house is an authentic treat. Also on Bay Street, Cultural Illusions, in Memorial Plaza (☎ 367-4648), has a few Bahamian straw works and a large number of dolls, quilts, stained glass and bags.

If you've got time, a bike ride or long walk east out of town to gawk at the substantial vacation and retirement homes on Eastern Shores is worth a go. From here, you can also look south to **Sugar Loaf Cay**, home to even more huge mansions rising from the scrub. For a look at the opposite side of the economic scale, head instead west along **Bay Street** out of town to **Dundas Town**, a flat area of shanties inhabited mostly by Bahamians of African descent. Many Haitians also call Marsh Harbour home, living in hovels and shacks in The Mud and Pigeon Pea quarters near Dundas Town.

Eating

Marsh Harbour **eateries** are divided between those attached to resorts and hotels mainly clustered around East Bay Street and those in town, mainly takeaways and local Bahamian cafés. During the early afternoon, George the Conch Salad Man sets up shop near the shore on East Bay Street and prepares fresh conch salad for $6. Watching him prepare your lunch from scratch is a joy.

Angler's Restaurant Abaco Beach Resort ☎ 367-2158. Specializing in seafood for dinner with entrees around $20, they serve special dishes like

lime grouper, papaya soup, lobster pate and curried conch. Their desserts, including a killer Key Lime pie, are homemade and well worth saving room for. Check out the Thursday buffet, which features fried chicken and ribs.

Bayview Restaurant on the Water Dundas Town Rd ☎367-3738. West of the main harbour area, this restaurant features prime rib, a Sunday champagne brunch and Bahamian seafood. Expect to pay $8–12 per entree.

Bistro Mezzamare East Bay St ☎367-4444. Next door to the *Conch Inn Café*, this sophisticated Italian bistro features such entrees as pasta with fresh scallops, lobster and conch served many ways in a marina setting for $10–20 a plate.

Castle Café ☎367-2315. On the hilltop overlooking the harbour, the *Castle* is open only for lunch and early dinners (closes at 5pm). The basic menu features large sandwiches (try the grilled grouper on French bread) and soups, which vary day to day but are homemade and delicious. Closed Sat & Sun, and all of Aug–Oct.

The Conch Inn Café Conch Inn Marina, East Bay St ☎367-2800. Good breakfasts and elegant dinners, either outside or in (evenings can be cool), are available at the *Inn*. The menu is delightful, with plenty of esoteric specialties like stuffed jalapeños and calypso grouper. Lunch consists of good burgers and sandwiches. Dinner entrees run $20–30.

Flippers Memorial Plaza ☎367-4657. This wonderful bistro features delicious chowders, soups and curries – owner Marcia Albury makes a stellar macaroni and cheese in a country known for the dish.

Jib Room Restaurant *Pelican Beach Villas* ☎367-2700. The *Jib Room* presents rather simple lunches, but dinners feature lobster, ribs, and steaks, along with a variety of seafood choices in the $15–30 range.

Lovely's Take-Away Queen Elizabeth Drive ☎367-2710. This carry-out serves decent chicken in a basket, conch, and fresh-baked bread. There are picnic tables nearby.

Mangoes Bay St ☎367-2366. This upscale restaurant is a favourite of the yacht crowd. Its cedar-top bar, vaulted ceilings and memorable dishes – including a good pork tenderloin in mango sauce, tasty grilled chicken with garlic and ginger and a fine veal *piccata* – make it the most popular of the expensive restaurants.

Mother Merle's Fishnet Dundas Town Rd ☎367-0770. About two miles north of the stoplight, the popular *Mother Merle's* in Dundas Town is family-run, simple and affordable, offering fish, chicken, and peas and rice. Open only for dinner every night but Wednesday.

Sapodilly's Harbour View Marina ☎367-3498. *Sapodilly's* offers a menu that ranges from cracked conch and superb blue cheese and mushroom burgers, to $20 entrees like grilled fresh catch-of-the-day. You can play pool amid picnic tables and shade trees.

Tiki Hut East Bay St ☎367-2575. This popular mixing spot for lunch and dinner is across from *Wally's* and the Harbour View Marina. It offers live music Thurs & Fri evenings, a good bar, Bahamian dishes, sandwiches and sunset views.

Wally's East Bay St ☎367-2074. Located in a beautiful Bahamian-colonial house near the marina, *Wally's* is a bit more informal than *Mangoes*, with a lively bar and live music on Wednesday and Saturday during dinner. Filled with Haitian art, it fairly blazes with light and colour during the evenings when great cracked conch, dolphin fish and grilled lamb chops are served along with such specialty drinks as the Bahama Mama and Goombay Smash. Lunch is $8–12; dinner $20–30. Closed Sun and Sept & Oct.

Drinking and nightlife

Nightlife in Marsh Harbour is basically limited to a handful of bars, where you'll find the occasional live entertainment and dancing, along with pool tables, TV and lots of relaxed camaraderie over the bar. **Waterfront bars** almost all offer open-air on all but the chilliest evenings. A few, like the *Tiki Hut* and *Conch Inn*, offer live music on weekends. Some, like *Wally's*, are known for their specialty drinks, usually rum-based concoctions. The *Sand Bar* at the *Abaco Beach Resort* is popular with yachties, while the *Ranch* on Don McKay Boulevard is a sports bar with satellite TV, darts, pool tables and cold drinks. There is dancing on Friday and Saturday nights. In Dundas Town, *The New Oasis* on Dundas Town Road offers reggae and soca for a $5 cover charge (ladies free) Wednesday to Sunday from 10pm–3am. Also in Dundas is the *Surfside Club*, next to the ballpark and open for dancing on Friday nights only.

Diving and watersports

While the **diving** along the Abacos' two outer reefs is not as spectacular as at Cat Island or San Salvador for example, a number of wrecks, caverns and towering coral formations keep things interesting, and three sites near Walker's Cay in the far north are known for shark sightings. Dives out of Marsh Harbour concentrate on sites north and west of town near Green Turtle Cay and Great Guana Cay, usually taking no more than half an hour to reach good spots on the outer reefs.

In and around the Marsh Harbour area are several professional **dive shops** that offer an array of services. The Abaco Beach Resort Dive Centre (T & F 367-4646, 1-800/327-8150, E danny@GreatAbaco.com) offers a wild variety of dives, including night dives, and can also conduct tours in English, German, French, Italian and Spanish. Dive Abaco (*Conch Inn and Marina*; T 367-2787, F 367-4779, E stm@mail.bahamas.net.bs) is a small but well-established operation offering many types of dive packages, including reef dives, wrecks, and cave dives, along with **snorkelling** trips and certification courses. For those with time and a naturalist bent, marine-life expert and dive master Skeet LaChance runs Immerse Yourself (T 367-2014), two-day educational snorkel trips for up to six people. On these trips snorkellers head to the shallower outer reefs and LaChance provides good background material on marine biology. Prices are negotiable.

Listings

Banks There are five banks in town, generally open Mon–Thurs 9am–3pm, Fri 9am–5pm. Bank of Nova Scotia (Scotia Bank) is located in Abaco Shopping Centre, while Barclays Bank is downtown near the stop-light. CIBC is located on Don McKay Blvd near the Shell station. Also downtown are the Commonwealth Bank and the Royal Bank of Canada.
Hospitals Abaco Medical Clinic, Marsh Harbour,

Don McKay Blvd (T 367-2510 or 4010).
Police The police station (T 367-2560 or 2594) is located on Dundas Town Road just west of downtown. Dial T 919 for emergency response.
Post office Drive Plaza, Don McKay Blvd (Mon–Fri 9am–5pm).
Travel agents A&W Travel, in the Abaco Shopping Centre (T 367-2806), or The Travel Spot in Memorial Plaza (T 367-2817).

The Loyalist Cays

A half-moon chain of teardrop islands, the **LOYALIST CAYS**, originally settled by fleeing Englishmen and their slaves after the American Revolution, run southeast to northwest of Marsh Harbour. There are four main cays in all: **Elbow Cay** in the southeast, followed northward by **Man O' War**, **Great Guana**, and finally, opposite Cooper's Town on northern Great Abaco, **Green Turtle Cay**. All the Loyalist Cays are reachable by ferry from Marsh Harbour, except Green Turtle Cay, which is accessed by water taxi from the Treasure Cay airport, or by ferry from the dock two miles south of the airport. Green Turtle Cay is the most popular Loyalist Cay because of picturesque **New Plymouth**, the tiny colonial-style town with New England-style clapboard houses and flower-strewn gardens. Elbow Cay, with its **Hope Town Lighthouse** and enchanting harbour, is popular as well.

Elbow Cay

Just six miles southeast of Marsh Harbour, **ELBOW CAY** is home to 600 residents, many of whom have family histories here going back centuries. Most live in **Hope Town**, the only real settlement and the arrival point of most visitors, which is located at the northern end of the isle. The five-mile-long cay – at its widest only 400yd across – is crossed by two narrow lanes called Back Street and Bay Street (also called "Up Along" and "Down Along" by locals). No cars are allowed in Hope Town, and most people get around the cay by golf cart, though these too are banned from Hope Town's narrow lanes.

Founded in 1785 by Loyalists from South Carolina, Elbow Cay had relatively humble beginnings, though boat building, wrecking and some pineapple agriculture did bring cash into the economy during the nineteenth century. During the 1920s, the town boomed with sponging and shipbuilding at its core – the harbour often home to as many as 200 schooners – and the cay thrived on the export of rare turtle shell, oranges and sisal. Hope Town builders created a famous style of wooden dinghy and sailboat building, carried on today by artisans who continue to build them by hand.

Arrival, information and getting around

East of Great Abaco's Marsh Harbour, Albury's Ferry Service has seven round-trips (Mon–Sat 7.15am, 9am, 10.30am, 12.15pm, 2pm, 4pm, and 5.30pm; $12, children $6; ☎367-3147) to Hope Town. The ride takes twenty minutes and the ferry lays over long enough to take on passengers before returning to Great Abaco. Other arrival options include the **water taxi** ($7 one-way) that runs from Man O' War Cay to Hope Town every morning at 7.30am, returning at 4.30pm, and the mailboat *Mia Dean*, which sails from Nassau on Tuesdays (see p.134).

Yachts can arrive at one of a number of good **marinas** on Elbow Cay, most located in Hope Town's harbour. Hope Town Marina (☎366-

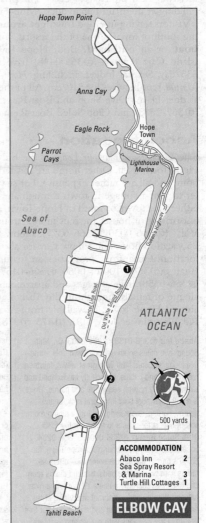

ACCOMMODATION

Abaco Inn	2
Sea Spray Resort & Marina	3
Turtle Hill Cottages	1

ELBOW CAY

0003) is located on the west side of the harbour and has dockage, water and ice and is also the site of the *Club Soleil* restaurant. At the harbour entrance, the Lighthouse Marina (☎366-0154) provides not only dockage but fuel as well, along with water, ice, rigged bait, repairs and caulking, with storage for boats up to 28ft. Across from Hope Town on the harbour, the Hope Town Hideaways Marina (☎366-0224) accommodates boats up to 70ft, specializing in visitors to its villas.

The **visitor's information bureau** is located in a turquoise municipal building at Hope Town's government dock, but don't expect anything beyond an unmanned booth with some pamphlets. Look for the nearby bulletin board where you'll find more information on local events, restaurant menus and the like. The **BaTelCo** office is at the south end of Hope Town just off the Queen's Highway near the *Harbour Lodge*. The **post office** is in the historic waterfront building at the main public dock (Mon–Fri 9am–1.30pm & 2.30–5pm).

Visitors staying in Hope Town **get around** by foot or bicycle. If you are staying south of town at one of the resorts, you may wish to rent a **golf cart**, **sailboat** or an **outboard.** Both Hope Town Cart Rentals (☎366-0064) and Island Cart Rentals (☎366-0448) have four-seater electric carts starting at $35/day. Several lodges, including *Hope Town Harbour Lodge* and *Sea Spray Marina*, rent bicycles for $10/day. All of the marinas rent boats of various kinds, as does Dave's Dive Shop and Boat Rentals (☎366-0029), Sea Horse Rentals (☎367-2513) and Club Soleil Boat Rentals (☎366-0003).

Accommodation

The *Hope Town Harbour Lodge* is the only **hotel** located inside the limits of Hope Town itself. Other hotels are located on White Sound, or across the harbour, and all are rather expensive. For stays longer than a few days, some prefer to rent a cottage in town through an agent. Others prefer a resort or villa, either near town, or south of Hope Town. Tanney Key (☎366-0140) has a wide assortment of houses for rent in and around Hope Town as does Hope Town Villas (☎366-0030, ℱ366-0377). Elbow Cay Properties (☎366-0035) offers 25 vacation homes on Elbow Cay for about $450/week and up depending on location. Oceanfront properties are naturally more expensive. Both Malone Estates (☎366-0100 or 0060, ℱ366-0157) and Russell Rentals (☎366-0046, ℱ366-0358) have cottages and apartments in Hope Town. Finally, a huge catalogue of rentals throughout the Abacos, including cottages and homes in and around Hope Town, is available from Abaco Vacation Rentals (40 Stone Hill Rd, Westminster, MA, USA 01473; ☎978/874-5995 or 1-800/633-9197).

Abaco Inn ☎366-0133, ℱ366-0133. On White Sound, two miles south of Hope Town, this attractive lodge sits on a bluff with great views, fourteen rustic villas and cabins, beautifully landscaped and surrounded by natural sea grape and palms. There is a saltwater pool built into coral rock, beach nearby, surfing, snorkelling, fishing, a dining room, and transport for guests to and from town. ❹

Club Soleil Resort ☎366-0003, ℱ366-0254. Located across the harbour from Hope Town, the *Soleil* – part of the marina complex – offers six rooms with twin double beds, bar and dining room and dockage. Each room has a TV, a/c and a nice balcony. With a good restaurant and views of the harbour, it offers a big pool and a pleasant bar that fills up in the evenings with sailors and yachters

taking advantage of the full-service marina. ❹

Hope Town Harbour Lodge ☎366-0095, ℱ366-0286 or 1-800/316-7844. At the upper road with both harbour and ocean views, the only in-town hotel has twenty rooms that overlook the harbour and cottages that tumble down toward the beach – all gorgeously furnished and decorated with twin or queen beds, private bath and a pool. *Hope Town* offers plenty of watersports, excellent breakfasts and dinners, and lively and friendly staff. There is an old comfortable house for rent on the grounds for $1000/week which sleeps six comfortably. ❹

Hope Town Hideaways ☎366-0224, ℱ366-0434 or 1-800/688-4752. On eleven beautiful acres near the lighthouse opposite Hope Town, the *Hideaways* offers four fabulously large two bedroom, two-bath luxury villas with fully equipped kitchens, outside veranda, all richly furnished with a/c, TV and VCR. Some eco-tours and watersports are also offered. **7**

Sea Spray Resort and Marina T 366-0065, F 366-0383 or 1-800/688-4752. At the southern tip of White Sound, *Sea Spray* lies three miles from Hope Town. On the six-acre property sit four one-bedroom and four two-bedroom villas with kitchens and patios. The dockside restaurant features Bahamian and American cuisine, and there is a pool and plenty of watersports, as well as bicycles

and a clubhouse with pool table and TV. Rates are weekly, averaging $700 for a one-bedroom villa, $750 for two-bedroom villas on the harbour. **4**

Turtle Hill Cottages T & F 366-0557 or 1-800/339-2124. Four luxury villas constitute the newest addition to Hope Town's arsenal of luxury accommodations. Although south of Hope Town, there is easy access to the Atlantic beaches and dockage for rented boats. The four two-bedroom a/c villas surround a swimming pool and sleep six at $225 a night. **8**

Hope Town

Hope Town, located on the eastern side of a nearly enclosed harbour of the same name, is hopelessly picturesque, its hundred or so clapboard houses

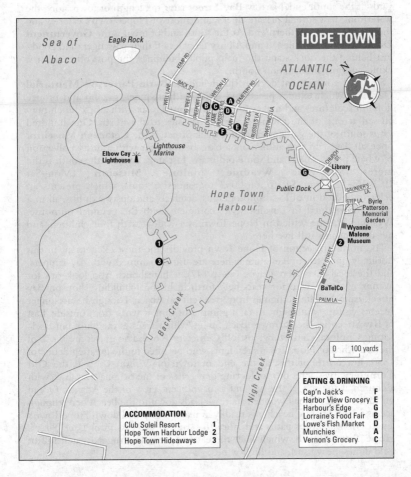

huddled together on dunes, each home surrounded by a picket fence and clusters of colourful orange, red and yellow hibiscus, purple bougainvillea, and pink oleander. The New England-style houses are mostly painted white with pastel trim, and these days many serve as rental cottages for the island's growing rank of visitors. Despite these crowds, the lack of motorized activity brings a refreshing naturalness to Hope Town, and the place exudes a real charm.

The town's tranquil harbour is usually jammed with sailboats anchored by the red-striped **Elbow Cay Lighthouse**, on the west shore directly opposite the town itself. Built in 1863, it's kerosene-powered and keepers still use a system of weights to wind it daily. At sunset, its mirrors magnify the mantle's beam and are brilliantly illuminated, and after dark the light is visible for twenty miles. If you can, hitch a ride on a local boat across the narrow harbour and climb the 100 steps for a spectacular 360-degree view of the outer cays.

The town itself lies north to south on a hook-shape of land that is around a thousand yards wide at its north end, narrowing to no more than one hundred yards at the south end. Narrow **Bay Street** runs the length of town along the waterfront, past several private docks, and most of Hope Town's eateries and shops towards its northern end. At the south end of town is the **Government Dock**, where the mailboats and Albury ferry let off their passengers and goods. Just behind the dock stand the main public buildings, the post office, library, clinic, and tiny information booth.

South of government dock is the delightful **Byrle Patterson Memorial Garden**, which exudes peace and quiet with its pines, gazebo and bronze dolphin sculptures and makes for a great spot to relax with a box lunch purchased at one of the town's groceries or cafés to the north. One hundred yards south of the gardens, on quiet Back Street, is the **Cetacean Museum**, open all day with free admission, a bare-bones affair with a dusty collection of whale bones, charts and some old maps. Just steps away to the south is the more worthwhile **Wyannie Malone Museum** (Mon–Sat 10.30am–12.30pm; $1; ☎366-0033 to request a tour), which presents an eclectic collection of local photographs, artefacts and dusty exhibits, all in a house maintained in Loyalist style, complete with the original outhouse. Wyannie Malone settled in Hope Town as a widow with four children, and her descendants still live here.

The northern section of Hope Town provides the most excitement in this distinctly quiet town. Restaurants here are usually jammed with day-trippers, and the local dive shop, Dave's (see p.147), is hereabouts. Also look out for **Winer Malone**, who for years held forth in his boat-building shop on Bay Street, hand-building dinghies from trees cut on Abaco. Though he no longer accepts visitors, you might catch a glimpse of him at work from outside. East of Bay Street lies the narrower Back Street, which accesses the glum but fascinating **Cholera Cemetery**, just off Cemetery Road. The graves are those of the one-third of Hope Town's residents who perished in the great epidemic of 1850. Just north of this, at the end of town off Wilson Lane, is the **Old Cemetery**, two acres of mouldering grave sites of the original Loyalists, with a church at the top of the hill and a magnificent view of the Atlantic Ocean off to the west. A small wooden staircase leads down to the beach here, though access to the Atlantic beaches is readily available all up and down Hope Town's length via numerous paths and lanes that run to the east from Back Street. **Hope Town Beach**, which lines the eastern shore, is a rugged patch full of wild dunes, heavy surf, and high winds.

△ The Elbow Cay Lighthouse, Hope Town

Around Hope Town

Outside of Hope Town, Elbow Cay is basically a big sand dune covered by windswept sea grape and palmetto scrub. To the north, the Queen's Highway soon becomes a dirt lane, running to Cook's Cove and ending at **Hope Town Point**. This northern end is especially good for **snorkelling**, with a reef loaded with fine stands of elkhorn, staghorn and brain coral close enough to swim to.

South of Hope Town, the Queen's Highway turns inland slightly and becomes Centre Line Road, which leads past a nude beach on the leeward side, and **Garbanzo Beach**, excellent for swimming and sunning, directly opposite White Sound about two miles south of Hope Town. Farther south, a dirt road leads to **Aunt Pat's Bay**, a pretty little curve of beach that fronts a wild Atlantic shore. At the farthest south part of Elbow Cay is the fantastic **Tahiti Beach**, backed by palm groves and home to many marine turtles. It is idyllic, but before coming to it you'll encounter what appears to be a private estate barring the way. The road is public, so proceed ahead ignoring all signs saying otherwise.

Eating, drinking and nightlife

If you looking for fancy dining, the resorts are undoubtedly your best bet, yet cheaper options in Hope Town can be quite good. Vernon's Grocery sells freshly baked bread, cakes and pies – including a tasty Key Lime – in the town centre. For an informal lunch, try the "Conch Lady" who sets up a stand in the sand near *Cap'n Jack's*. Elbow Cay has no tradition of active **nightlife**. About the best one can do is watch satellite TV at *Cap'n Jack's* or *Munchies* or listen to one of the few bands playing at either on Wednesday or Friday night.

Abaco Inn ☎ 366-0133. This inn serves all three meals; reservations suggested at dinner. Open-air terrace dining features blackened fish, lobster, and Bahamian-style seafood like smothered grouper.

Boat House Restaurant *Sea Spray Resort* ☎ 366-0065. Located 3.5 miles south of Hope Town on White Sound, this restaurant is open for breakfast, lunch and dinner. Breakfasts ($4) are substantial, lunches include a mixed green salad with fresh fish, and dinners cover the gamut from steaks to seafood ($17). Reservations are required for dinner.

Cap'n Jack's ☎ 366-0247. Anyone who wanders around Hope Town will find themselves at *Cap'n Jack's*, in the middle of town overlooking the harbour. Specialties include the superb conch burger for lunch, and grilled grouper with macaroni and cheese. *Jack's* has live music on Wednesday and Friday, and there's usually a crowd on the outdoor dance floor. Breakfast is $10, while lunches and dinner range as high as $40.

Club Soleil ☎ 366-0003. At the Hope Town Marina, *Club Soleil* will transport diners across the harbour for free. Reservations are required for the three dinner seatings at 6.30pm, 7.30pm and 8.30pm. Check out the Sunday champagne brunch, centred on a glorious seafood buffet. Other meals run the gamut from burgers and conch salad to expensive Continental-style cuisine.

Harbour's Edge ☎ 366-0087. The informal *Harbour's Edge*, located close to the main government dock and post office, offers crawfish salad, burgers and Saturday night pizza. The patio outside has covered seating with picnic tables, while there is air conditioning inside. Closed Tues.

Hope Town Harbour Lodge ☎ 366-0095. Very popular for breakfast on the veranda when huge omelettes and tasty French toast is featured. The *Lodge* serves lunch by the oceanfront pool, happy hour is 4–5pm, and dinner is served until 9pm.

Munchies ☎ 366-0423. Essentially a take-out, *Munchies*, in the town centre, is known for fried fish and Bahamian fast food like their special hot chicken wings and conch burgers.

Rudy's Place ☎ 366-0062. This two-room favourite tucked away about a mile outside town to the south is simple, good and relatively cheap. The salted crayfish is unmissable. Closed Sun and Sept & Oct.

Diving and watersports

Diving and snorkelling, as well as deep-sea, reef, and bonefishing, are all excellent around Elbow Cay. Dave's Dive Shop on Bay Street (☎366-0029) is a fully equipped operation renting out gear and leading various scuba and snorkelling trips, including trips out to some fabulous nearby wrecks (see box below). Also out of Hope Town, Froggies Out Island Adventures (☎366-0431) conducts half-day and full-day scuba and snorkelling trips, including trips to the **Pelican Cay Land and Sea Park**. The 2100 acres of the park are free to all, and present snorkellers with an unprecedented expanse of shallow reef riddled by gullies, canyons, caverns and mazes that play host to many reef fish and turtles, as well as spotted eagle rays. These cays are also a birdwatchers' paradise, with nesting terns in abundance. Nalu Charters (☎366-0224) offers snorkelling, island hopping, sunset cruises and picnics aboard a 50ft catamaran, and Sail Abaco (☎366-0172) will charter a catamaran for full- or half-day trips.

Deep-sea, reef and bonefishermen have a number of guides and services from which to choose, including Maitland Lowe (☎366-0234) and Wild Pigeon Charters (☎366-0461), both of whom conduct bonefishing trips, with Wild Pigeon also offering deep-sea and reef fishing as well. A final watersports option is **windsurfing**, one of the specialties of *Sea Spray Resort* (see p.143).

Exploring the Adirondack and Deborah K II wrecks

Thanks to countless miles of treacherous reefs, rocks and sandbars, the Bahamas is a great spot for exploring wrecks. No more than a thirty-minute boat ride away from Elbow Cay, are two wrecks of particular note. On the inner reef just off Man O' War Cay is the hulk of the wooden screw sloop **Adirondack**, launched in June 1862. A British gunship 207ft long and weighing 1240 tons, she ran aground en route from Port Royal to Nassau and quickly broke up in heavy surf before she could be salvaged. Now in 10–25ft of water, two of her larger cannons can be clearly seen, and plenty of reef fish like sergeant majors and damselfish make the wreck their home. On the outer reef between Fowl Cay and Man O'War Cay lies the wreck of the recently scuttled coastal freighter **Deborah K II**, once used to carry supplies around the Abacos; 165ft long, she sits upright and intact, covered by algae that attracts wrasse and damselfish.

Man O' War Cay

While Elbow Cay bustles with tourism, quiet **MAN O' WAR CAY,** slightly more than three miles north and a thirty-minute ferry ride from Marsh Harbour, is little touched by visitors. The island is prim, almost placid, and its residents maintain a strict code against the sale of alcohol on the island, although they don't mind if visitors bring their own, so long as they're reasonable about its use. The tiny main settlement is scattered along the east shore of North Harbour, almost smack in the middle of the cay itself. Most of the homes are modern breeze-block or stucco constructions, though there are a handful of gingerbread classics mixed in along with three churches, all faithfully attended, a one-room schoolhouse, and a small number of shops, groceries, bakeries and restaurants, none of which opens early, or at all on Sundays.

The cay is five miles long, at most six hundred yards wide near the settlement, and is home to no more than 300 residents, descendants of Loyalists who

The Alburys

On Man O' War Cay, the name **Albury** is ubiquitous. The original Albury family of Benjamin and Eleanor Albury – part of the Loyalist migration – had thirteen children, most of whom also had large families; in no time, Man O' War Cay was overrun with Alburys. These days the family is still involved in shipbuilding, the oldest traditional craft on the island, with Joe Albury's Studio and Emporium (☎365-6082) on the Lower Road displaying wooden models. Joe Albury's long-ago ancestor Billie Bo is renowned for building the first sailboat in the Abacos, and Lewis Albury created the distinctive hourglass shape for ships.

initially inhabited other cays, then migrated in the 1820s to farm its modestly productive soil and build handcrafted boats by traditional methods. In the village, you can see a veritable beehive of shipwright activity, with boats of all sizes and shapes bobbing in the narrow and protected harbour, set off from the Sea of Abaco by narrow Dickens Cay.

There are two main roads on the island, the **Lower Road**, or Sea Road, which runs north to south along the waterfront, and the island-long **Queen's Highway** that, in town, is also called the **Upper Road**, which holds the shops, churches, schoolhouse, post office and most of the homes. Follow the Queen's Highway from the centre of town south to the Church of God, take a left, and you'll find Man O' War's in-town **beach**, just as beautiful as Hope Town's. Man O' War's other beaches are along the Atlantic coast, accessible by footpath. North of the village, Upper Road becomes a dirt path winding through scrub, occasional pinewoods and mangrove, where secluded private homes are set behind gates and fences; it's a couple of hours there and back.

Practicalities

Albury's Ferry Service ($12 round-trip, children $6; ☎367-3147) at Crossing Beach has five scheduled crossings to Man O' War from Marsh Harbour each day except Sunday, the last one leaving at 3.15pm. A **water-taxi** service operates between Great Guana Cay and Man O' War at 7.30am and 3.30pm on Fridays, while another service operates between Elbow Cay and Man O' War at 7.30am and 4.30pm, also on Friday only. For those with their own boats, the full-service Man O' War Marina (☎365-6008, ☎365-6151, VHF Ch 16; ✉talbury@batelnet.bs) has sixty slips and a small dive shop. The Marina Dive Shop (☎365-6013) rents some equipment, including snorkelling gear for $8/day but does not offer dives.

Along the Upper Road in town is a **BaTelCo** (☎366-6001), located next to the post office and library. There are two **banks** as well: a CIBC (Thurs 10am–2pm; ☎365-6098) at the Man O' War Marina on Lower Road, and a Bank of Canada branch (Fri 10am–1pm; ☎365-6323).

Accommodation on Man O' War is limited to a few rental cottages and one resort. Abaco Vacation Rentals (see p.21) has a selection of houses and cottages, though you can also check the pole in the centre of town, where local restaurants also post their menus and locals post items for sale, for listings. At *Schooner's Landing Resort* (☎365-6072 or 1-800/633-9197, ☎365-6285, esawyer@batelnet.bs; ❻), the accommodations are in two-storey, two-bedroom townhouses decorated with white linen with TV, a/c, and VCR, along with a dining room and patio. The beaches are nearby in both directions, and the management assists with snorkelling, fishing and sailing, and yachties can use the private dock.

As with accommodations, choices for **eating** at Man O' War are slim, most not opening until late morning. Many people simply stock up at Albury's Bakery (☎365-6031) in a house on Upper Road, where you can get fabulous fresh conch fritters, homemade bread, buns and cookies. The local **groceries**, Albury's Harbour Store (Mon–Fri 8am–5.30pm, Sat 8am–9pm; ☎365-6004) at the north end of Lower Road and Man O' War Grocery (Mon–Fri 7.30am–5.30pm, Sat 8am–9pm; ☎365-6016) on Queen's Highway in the centre of town, are likewise good places to stock up on supplies. As far as eating out goes, *The Pavilion Restaurant* (Mon–Sat 10.30am–2pm & 5.30–8.30pm; ☎365-6187), at the marina, is the premier location with its barbecue on Friday and Saturday nights, burgers, peas and rice and homemade pie, along with Bahamian seafood served on a raised patio. *Ena's Place* (☎365-6187), straight up and to the left of the ferry office, features baked goods, burgers, sandwiches, and conch, along with fabulous coconut or pumpkin pie, served to guests on a covered patio. It is open until 9pm on Wednesday, Friday and Saturday, but closes at 6pm on other days. *Tamarind Take-Away* sits next to Joe's Studio on the Lower Road and serves simple fried carry-out meals. For a change of pace, try *Sheila's Deli* (☎365-6118), where Sheila herself serves delicious food out of her home for takeaway, or for dining on the patio, starting at 5.30pm. Most dinners are homely fare like fried grouper, pork chops or macaroni and cheese in huge portions.

Great Guana Cay

The least built-up of all the Loyalist Cays, **GREAT GUANA CAY** is nevertheless becoming increasingly developed as more and more vacation mansions are thrown up. The cay, which lies five miles northwest of Marsh Harbour, is the permanent home to no more than 150 residents, many of whom make their living by lobstering or subsistence farming. Some work in burgeoning construction and tourist trades on the Guana Harbour Settlement on the developed southern part of the seven-mile-long island. There are no automobiles allowed on the island, and most visitors walk in the village, which takes about ten minutes to circumnavigate on foot, though some prefer to rent golf carts or bicycles.

Great Guana Cay's singular gift is the fringing reef that circles it about fifty yards from shore, making the island ideal for **snorkelling** and **diving**. Most divers are day-trippers from Marsh Harbour, who come on organized trips out of the dive shops there (see p.140). Only a five-minute boat ride north and east on the first barrier reef from Guana Cay lies a superb cave dive known as **The Cathedral**, well suited to beginners as it's located in shallow water and has a roomy entrance and large chambers cut by sunlight. Thereabouts the reefhead is teeming with damselfish, red-lipped blennies, bluehead wrasse and striped parrotfish. The cavern itself is covered with fragile spiky coral forms, as well as white and cream sponges.

Back on the mainland, the **Guana Harbour Settlement** residents go about their business rather quietly, and some seem to resent intruders, though they make much of their income from cottage and cart rental or at the three nearby resorts. The settlement has a liquor store, grocery store, a variety store and several gift shops. Behind the two dozen houses in the village, and up a slight sandy rise, lies a graveyard dating from Loyalist times, an Anglican church, and a one-room schoolhouse that hosts no more than twenty students at a time.

South of the settlement, a new 215-acre real estate development is gaining steam, and looks set to become home to more and more rich North Americans. Even now, over fifty vacation homes are scattered throughout the island, most hidden behind high gates. Because of this isolation, which at times can be almost intimidating, many visitors make their way around the island by rented boat, exploring the ethereally beautiful **Atlantic beach**, a five-mile stretch of white sand, reachable by several dirt tracks, that makes up almost the entire windward coast of Guana. Some yachties make **Baker's Bay** in the north their permanent anchorage, or tie up at *Guana Beach Resort* in the south, which has a deepwater **marina** with protected dock facilities. The leeward coast is rugged, rocky, and beset with coves and shallow bays perfect for bonefishing, but accessible by boat only. In July, Great Guana is host to the **Regatta Week**, during which time the place is besieged with yachts.

Arrival, information and getting around

Visitors who don't **arrive** on Guana Cay by private boat take the thirty-minute Albury's Ferry (daily 10.15am, 1.15pm, 3.30pm and 5.30pm, with return trips at 8am, 11.30am, 2.30pm and 4.45pm; $8 one-way, children $4, $12 round-trip children $6; ☎367-3147) from Great Abaco's Marsh Harbour. An additional trip leaves early mornings at 6.45am every day except Saturdays, Sundays and holidays. Albury's also charters service for groups to Guana Cay beginning at $80 for up to six people, $12 per person for each extra person. **AIT** (☎365-6010, VHF Ch 16) also operates a scheduled **water taxi** service from Marsh Harbour's *Conch Inn and Marina* at 9am, noon, 4pm and 6pm, with a late ferry at 11pm on Wednesday night, for $6 per adult one-way. Because *Guana Seaside Village* is located up the coast from Guana Cay's only settlement, you should request to be let off there if that's your destination.

All of the resorts have telephone service, but there is a **BaTelCo** office next to the school in the centre of the settlement with the **post office** just next door. There is also a public payphone on the waterfront at Kidd's Cove, but there is no bank. The resorts rent bikes and golf carts, as does Donna's Golf Cart and Bike Rentals (☎365-5196). A golf cart rents for $35/day, $200/week.

Accommodation

Though Guana Cay has three fine resorts, perhaps the best way to experience the isle's isolation is to rent a small cottage or home near the settlement and enjoy the Atlantic beaches, only a short walk over the dunes. Abaco Vacation Rentals (see p.21) has a good selection. The main local agents are Donna Sands Cottages (☎365-5195, ℱ365-5196) or Pinder's Real Estate and Cottage Rentals (☎365-5046).

Dolphin Beach Resort ☎ & ℱ365-5137 or 1-800/222-2646, ℮relax@dolphinbeachresort.com. An upscale B&B-style fashioned from Abaco pine. The two-storey main building has four rooms painted in Junkanoo colours, while its three cottages are individually furnished, have room for at least six and include a kitchen. Breakfast and lunch are served around an outdoor pool; dinners are served in the pavilion next to the main building. The staff arrange for bonefishing, kayaking, snorkelling, bikes and island-hopping trips. The popular *Nipper's* restaurant is a five-minute walk away. ❻, cottages ❼

Guana Beach Resort and Marina ☎365-5133, ℱ365-5134 or 1-800/227-3366, ℮guanabeach @guanabeach.com. With eight hotel rooms and seven suites, the resort is set in a coconut palm grove just west of the settlement and offers dockage for boats up to 150ft, as well as bayside anchorage. Rates include snorkel gear, watersports

and a water-taxi trip from Marsh Harbour. **⑤**
Guana Seaside Village ☎365-5106, ⑤365-
5146, ✉guanaseaside@oii.net. Two miles north of
the settlement on an isolated beachfront, this new
resort features eight rooms, including two suites.

Try to get an oceanfront room. There is a small
restaurant, pool, bar, grill and a dock and bar for
boaters who drop in. The resort offers boat rentals,
bonefishing and lots of peace and quiet. **⑦**

Eating

Though **eating** on Guana is largely restricted to the resorts, the wildly colourful *Nipper's* (☎365-5143; open lunch till late), a wood-flame bar and grill on the
Atlantic side, features a menu that includes great conch burgers, salad and fried
chicken for $7 at lunch; the seafood dinner is $14. A pig is roasted on Sunday
afternoon, and you can partake of the pork for $15. In the settlement, the *Sand
Dollar Cafe* (Mon–Sat 10am–2pm; ☎365-5021) offers simple Bahamian fare,
while *Tom's Gift Store* on the waterfront is open for early coffee every day except
Sunday. Otherwise, *Guana Beach Resort's* restaurant serves lunch and dinner to
non-guests, with reservations suggested for dinner. Wednesday and Friday are
"special nights" at the *Guana Beach Resort*, with conch on Wednesday and barbecue on Friday. *Guana Seaside Village* serves dinner nightly, but you must call
ahead for reservations to make the trip up. **Groceries** are available at Guana
Harbour Grocery (Mon–Thurs 8am–5.30pm, Sat 8am–6.30pm; ☎365-5067,
VHF Ch 16), which is located on the waterfront near the public dock. The grocery also has some nonprescription drugs and sundries.

Green Turtle Cay

Eight miles due north of Treasure Cay and eighteen miles northwest of Marsh
Harbour, **GREEN TURTLE CAY**, with its bays, inlets, sounds and amazingly well-preserved New England-style village, **New Plymouth**, is the most
popular of all the Loyalist Cays. Not only does the cay have a varied leeward
shore – including three large enclosed sounds, an area of bluffs and cliffs on the
White Sound peninsula, and mangroves in the north – but its Atlantic coast is
replete with stunning beaches and rimmed by a close-in reef tailor-made for
snorkelling and diving. Because New Plymouth, on the southwest tip of the
island, is only a ten-minute ferry ride from the Treasure Cay Marina (see
p.157), the town often teems with day-trippers crowding its narrow streets and
winding windblown lanes.

Arrival and getting around

The Green Turtle Ferry ($6 one-way; ☎365-4166 or 4151 or 4128, VHF Ch
16 "Bolo") operates out of the Treasure Cay airport dock on the Abaco mainland. Eight trips a day are scheduled, commencing at 8am, with seven trips back
to the mainland. The trip takes about fifteen minutes, but can take longer as the
ferry may make intermittent stops around the island. AIT ($8 one-way; ☎365-
6010, VHF Ch 16) also operates a ferry to Green Turtle, but leaves from the
Green Turtle Dock, two miles south of Treasure Cay airport, at 2.30pm and
4pm. Both Green Turtle and AIT will operate charters with advance notice at
$25 minimum charge for the run to New Plymouth, with higher rates for
White and Black Sounds.

The major **marina** on Green Turtle is Black Sound Marina (☎365-4221,
⑤365-4046), a full-service facility. Black Sound is considered hurricane-safe.

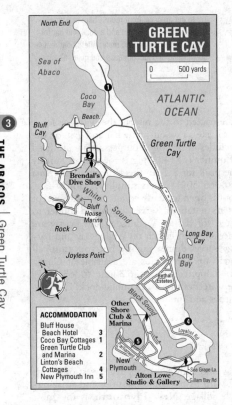

Green Turtle Club (☎365-4271, ℱ365-4272) on White Sound and Other Shore Club and Marina (☎365-4195) also offer dockage and fuel. Green Turtle Club also offers showers and all amenities, plus scooter rentals on the premises, along with a dive shop. Bluff House (☎365-4247, ℱ365-4248) on White Sound also has dockage and hookups. Many marine services are available on both White and Black Sounds, including the large Abaco Yacht Services (☎365-4033, ℱ365-4216) on Black Sound which offers dry storage, carpentry and mechanical services, parts and equipment and a full marine store.

The most popular modes of **transportation** on the island are the golf cart, scooter or bicycle, all of which can be rented at C&D Rentals in New Plymouth (☎365-4161), Curtis Hodgkins Bicycle Rentals on Green Turtle Ferry Dock (☎365-4128) and D&P Rentals, which has an office at the Green Turtle Club on White Sound. There are two **taxi** services operating on Green Turtle. Both Omri Taxis and McIntosh Taxis use the same phone number (☎365-4406), and a ride from New Plymouth to Coco Bay will cost about $8.

Accommodation

The major **resorts** on Green Turtle are located either around White Sound, or in a cluster from New Plymouth to Gilliam Bay. For those wishing to avoid resorts and hotels, Green Turtle has an astounding variety of **cottages**, **villas**, and **apartments** for rent, usually by the week. Besides those listed below, other small cottages are offered by Noel and Ivy Roberts (☎365-4089), Ocean Blue Properties (☎365-4234) and Roberts Cottages and Apartments (☎365-4105).

Apartments, cottages and villas

Coco Bay Cottages ☎365-4464, ℱ365-4301 or 1-800/752-0166. The most unusual offerings are the four two-bedroom cottages located on a five-acre orchard. The cottages are tastefully decorated and have full kitchens, decks, ceiling fans and phone. Most rent for $150/900 per day/week.

Linton's Beach and Harbour Cottages ☎365-4003 or 615/269-5682. On the Atlantic side at Long Bay Beach, just northeast of New Plymouth,

Linton's has two cottages with full kitchens amid 22 acres of grounds, each with two bedrooms, patio, ceiling fans and bicycles for guests. Rates average $150/1000 per night/week September to December, about 20 percent higher in winter.

Sand Dollar Apartments ☎365-4221, ℱ365-4046. Luxury second-floor accommodations above the Sand Dollar Shoppe are available here, each with a/c, private bath, kitchen and veranda view of the harbour.

Resorts and hotels

Bluff House Beach Hotel ☎ 365-4247, ℱ 367-4248. Sitting on a hill eighty feet above White Sound, this upscale resort has great views of the island and village. It is composed of hotel rooms, townhouse suites, and three-bedroom villas, including a "treehouse" with kitchenette and stove. There are two miles of beaches here, as well as a tennis court, boat rental, gift shop, bar lounge and a marina. ❺

Green Turtle Club and Marina ☎ 365-4271, ℱ 365-4272 or 1-800/688-4752, ✉ info@green-turtleclub.com. At the north end of White Sound, the *Green Turtle Club* has 32 poolside rooms and eight villas. The deluxe are decorated with period mahogany furniture and hardwood floors have rugs. The full-service marina has 35 slips and is the island's largest, accommodating yachts up to 150 ft. ❼, villas ❽

New Plymouth Inn Parliament St ☎ 365-4161, ℱ 365-4138. A restored 150-year-old building in the heart of the village, the inn once served as home to a sea captain's family. Now it is a garden of elegance with its two stories housing nine smallish rooms with ceiling fans, four-poster queen-size beds, all decorated in colonial style. There is a bar, dining room, enclosed porch, and saltwater pool. ❹

Treehouse by the Sea of Abaco ☎ 365-4259, ✉ treehouse@oii.net. You can sleep six comfortably in the three octagonal tree-houses perched on pedestals and fronting the ocean between White Sound and the Sea of Abaco. Each has two bedrooms, hand-painted linens, two baths, living room and kitchen. Tree-houses are from $200, depending on numbers of guests and season. ❽

New Plymouth

Compactly laid out on a peninsula formed by Black Sound and Settlement Creek, **NEW PLYMOUTH** is a joy, if rather a quiet one. Visitors come year-round to gawk at its gingerbread-trimmed houses painted in lively pastel colours, as well as its often noisy gospel churches or the picturesque school-

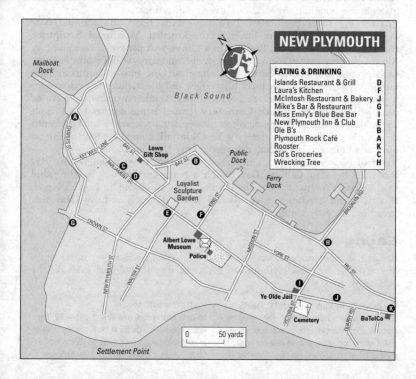

NEW PLYMOUTH

EATING & DRINKING

Islands Restaurant & Grill	D
Laura's Kitchen	F
McIntosh Restaurant & Bakery	J
Mike's Bar & Restaurant	G
Miss Emily's Blue Bee Bar	I
New Plymouth Inn & Club	E
Ole B's	B
Plymouth Rock Café	A
Rooster	K
Sid's Groceries	C
Wrecking Tree	H

house perched on a hill overlooking the settlement. For a good view of it all, head behind the village where a slight rise reveals clear vistas of the waterfront and harbour.

Like other cay settlements in the Abacos, New Plymouth began with Loyalists fleeing America in 1783, including 500 Irish New Yorkers, Protestants whose property was taken by American rebels, who soon established the town as one of the busiest in the islands. At one point in its history, New Plymouth was the second largest city in the Bahamas, and a centre for banking, smuggling, and even rum-running during Prohibition. Things are quieter now, and though you may notice a stiff reserve in some of the residents who aren't particularly fond of outsiders, tourism is the prime source of income for residents, though lobstering remains important as well.

To many, the highlight of New Plymouth's year is the annual **Junkanoo** festivities, which begin on Boxing Day, and are held again on New Year's Day. On each of those two nights, the streets are thronged with dancers and musicians, all decked out in colourful Junkanoo costumes. The most popular sight in New Plymouth the rest of the year is the **Albert Lowe Museum** on Parliament Street (Mon–Sat 9–11.45am & 1–4pm; $3; ☎ 365-4094), housed in a 200-year-old colonial house refurbished in 1976. The collection consists of old photos, model ships, paintings and memorabilia from the Abacos' past, and works by James Martin, a local sculptor. The museum is the work of Alton Lowe, whose father Albert was a much noted mariner, inventor, musician, artist and historian. **Schooner's Gallery** is located in the basement of the museum, and displays paintings by Alton himself. More of Lowe's paintings can be seen in the **Alton Lowe Studio** about half a mile outside New Plymouth in a handsome pastel house on a hill; any local can give you directions.

Across the street from New Plymouth's only hotel, the splendid *New Plymouth Inn* on Parliament Street, is the **Loyalist Memorial Sculpture Garden**, free to the public. Laid out in a Union Jack pattern as conceived by Alton Lowe, the garden memorializes Loyalists and slaves with 25 bronze busts, with plaques to detail their accomplishments. One plaque commemorates Jeanne I. Thompson, a Bahamian playwright and the nation's second woman lawyer, whose roots go back to Loyalist times. Another worthwhile place to stroll is the **New Plymouth Cemetery** located at the southeast end about 250yd down Parliament Street, whose graves date back to the late eighteenth century. Across from the cemetery is **Ye Olde Jail**, unused for several generations and housed in a building damaged by the 1936 hurricane.

East of New Plymouth, a ten-minute walk from town down Gilliam Bay Road, lies beautiful **Gilliam Bay Beach**, a gently curving slice of white sand that is perfect for swimming. The Atlantic coast, reachable by Loyalist Road, also has good beaches, particularly the secluded beach at **Long Bay** that stretches for nearly a mile.

Eating

Beside the resort **restaurants** – of which the *New Plymouth Inn*'s is the best – dining options in New Plymouth are represented by several small cafés and the odd bar or two.

The Green Turtle Club ☎ 365-4271. *The Green Turtle Club* accepts reservations – which must be made by 5pm – for dinner at its exclusive restaurant. Evening specialties include veal and huge slabs of prime rib, and you can have breakfast or lunch on the patio as well.

Islands Restaurant and Grill ☎ 365-4082. The hidden gem of the diners in town, the tiny *Islands* is located in Lowe's Food Store on Parliament Street, where it serves exquisite baby back ribs, jalapeño poppers and T-bone steaks, as well as wonderful desserts.

Laura's Kitchen ☎ 365-4287. This simple two-room Bahamian-style eatery on King Street serves a mean conch burger and will fetch you from your hotel if you call ahead.

McIntosh Restaurant and Bakery Across from the cemetery ☎ 365-4625. Specializing in breakfast and lunch, the *McIntosh* has especially wonderful baked bread, homemade ice cream, and doooot Bahamian dinners until 9pm every day but Sunday.

Mike's Bar and Restaurant ☎ 365-4219. On the waterfront of Black Sound, *Mike's Bar and Restaurant* serves good conch burgers, but is open for lunch only until 2pm.

New Plymouth Inn ☎ 365-4161. For fancy dining, this is the place to go in town. Breakfast is

served at 8–9am, lunch noon–2pm, and a single sitting for dinner at 7.30pm, for which you must reserve a seating early. The inn prepares three special dishes each night for dinner – fish, fowl and meat – along with a fine Sunday brunch.

Paradise Restaurant ☎ 365-4409. The *Paradise Restaurant* serves deli-style food like freshly-prepared sandwiches, macaroni salad and fresh conch salad, and also offers fresh produce.

Plymouth Rock Cafe Parliament St ☎ 365-4234. For simple conch burgers and sandwiches for lunch, try this café at the main government dock.

Wrecking Tree Bay St ☎ 365-4263. The *Wrecking Tree* is one of the best places for breakfast and lunch and serves dinner until 9.30pm. Its specialty is fried chicken. No lunch Sun.

Drinking and nightlife

When it comes to **drinking**, Green Turtle Cay is on the teetotal side, as are most of the Loyalist Cays, but there are a few places worth visiting. **Theatre** enthusiasts should check out the offerings at the Garden Theater on Black Sound, out by the Alton Lowe Studio; you can find flyers and playbills in town.

Bert Reckley's Sea Garden Club Victoria St. This little spot caters mainly to locals who listen to the jukebox, play cards and dominoes, and partake of concoctions like coconut rum and milk or Goombay Smashes. 6pm–2.30am.

Bluff House Beachside Bar White Sound ☎ 365-4247. A quiet bar overlooking the sound, and New Plymouth in the distance, that often plays host to live bands Thurs–Sat nights. The *Beachside* is also open for lunches of burgers, seafood platters and the like.

Miss Emily's Blue Bee Bar ☎ 365-4181. For sheer ambience and history, nothing on Green

Turtle Cay surpasses *Miss Emily's*. Founded by Miss Emily, the originator of the Goombay Smash, this bar is a wooden structure tattooed with business cards, with underwear on the ceiling and a rowdy mood. Open 9am until late, it gets quite raucous, especially on weekends.

Rooster's Rest ☎ 365-4066. On weekends, you'll find music over the hill by the schoolhouse at the *Rooster's Rest*, often authentic rake 'n' scrape by local musicians the Gulley Roosters.

Diving and watersports

The centre of **diving activity** on the island is Brendal's Dive Shop (☎ 365-4411) on White Sound. Operated in conjunction with the *Green Turtle Club and Marina*, Brendal's offers basic scuba instruction ($450 for the certification package), wreck, cavern and catacomb diving, and all-day scuba and snorkelling tours and picnics. Its other services include glass-bottom-boat trips and sailboat cruises and rentals. Brendal's offers a two-day four-tank package at $130 and snorkel trips are $30. Snorkellers usually ride along on dive trips to the fringing reef, about ten minutes by boat to the north and east of the cay.

The resorts at Green Turtle can arrange **sport-fishing** packages and advise about guides, boats and excursions. However, there are a number of individuals on Green Turtle who specialize in fishing expeditions as well. Ronnie Sawyer (☎ 365-4070) is the premier bonefishing guide on Green Turtle, though he's available only April through July. Ricky Sawyer (☎ 365-4261) specializes in drift fishing, reef and light-tackle fishing, as well as bonefishing, and Joe Sawyer (☎365-4173) has a well-equipped 28ft Uniflite for either reef or bottom fishing. For bigger trips, Lincoln Jones (☎365-4223) has a 26ft Mako and operates full day-trips for fishing, snorkelling and sightseeing to nearby cays, including a beach picnic day where he cooks up the catch, and serves it with conch salad and drinks. The highlight of the fishing season is the annual **billfish tournament** in May, hosted by the *Green Turtle Club*. Regatta Week is also a big deal on Green Turtle in July, when dozens of races and festivities are in swing.

Boat rentals and excursions are offered by a number of companies on Green Turtle. Donny's Boat Rentals (☎365-4119, VHF Ch 16) has 13–23ft boats with optional sun tops at daily and weekly rates. Dames Rentals (☎365-4247) at *Bluff House Beach Hotel* also has boats for rent.

North of Marsh Harbour

Back on the mainland and just south of Green Turtle Cay, the resort of **Treasure Cay** is the first major settlement north of Marsh Harbour. The thirty miles from Treasure Cay Airport to the tip of **Little Abaco** can be covered in less than an hour and will appeal most to those who feel like dropping nearly completely off the map. Otherwise, the main reason for passing this way is to access the unspoiled **Northern Cays**, which are known for their sport fishing.

The largest town en route is **Cooper's Town**, from where it's possible to head over to the high-end resort on **Spanish Cay** by ferry. Beyond Cooper's Town, the highway heads north and crosses a narrow causeway to Little Abaco. There isn't much to the island, and the settlements are small and poor, with most of the population making its living off fishing and lobstering. Well to the north of Little Abaco, due north of Grand Bahama, lie the Northern Cays.

Treasure Cay

Actually not a cay but a slender peninsula, **Treasure Cay** is a self-contained community that spills around a large 150-slip marina. Its beach, which stretches in a mild semi-circle for four miles along the Sea of Abaco, is not spectacular, but good for swimming and sunning; the water is shallow and rather tame most of the time. Between the beach and the outer island of **Whale Cay** are shallow banks that shimmer with turquoise and green colours, and are especially lovely during sunrises and sunsets.

Treasure Cay started life in 1783 as **Carleton Point**, a Loyalist settlement of about 600 who hoped to develop a major commercial and agricultural centre at the northern end of what was known then as Sand Banks Cay. Owing to civil strife, land disputes and a devastating hurricane, the settlers soon abandoned the town, and it wasn't until 1979 that the eighteenth-century site was located with the discovery of several artefacts like anchors and various glasswork – now preserved in the Albert Lowe Museum in New Plymouth (see p.154). For those hardy souls wishing to make the trek to the bronze historical **plaque** placed at Carleton Point near the original settlement in 1983, it is located two miles down the beach from the *Treasure Cay Beach Hotel*.

In the 1950s, the first tourist hotel on the Abacos was built here, ushering in a period of development, and Treasure Cay now supports a variety of villas, condos, time-share units, and fancy resorts – even Abaco's only **golf course**. North Americans currently make up the bulk of the cay's residents, maintaining more than 150 expensive vacation and retirement homes.

Arrival and getting around

Treasure Cay Airport is located fifteen miles north of the community, and a taxi from the airport costs $15. Bahamasair (☎365-8600) flies directly from Nassau daily, and offers flights from Miami and West Palm Beach as well. Other carriers include: Gulfstream International (☎365-8615 or 1-800/992-8532), which flies from several Florida cities, as well as Atlanta, Georgia, and Mobile, Alabama; and Island Express (☎365-8697 or 1-800/622-1015) and US Airways Express (☎367-2231 or 1-800/622-1015), both flying from Fort Lauderdale. Yachters arrive at the **Treasure Cay Marina** (☎365-8250 or 1-800/327-1584), where there is a full range of dock services, electricity and water, as well as watersports rentals, fishing guides and boat rentals.

Most visitors to Treasure Cay get around using golf carts, bicycles or scooters. C&C Rentals at the Treasure Cay Marina (☎365-8582) has scooters available on a daily and weekly basis, while Wendell's in the Shopping Plaza (☎365-8687) rents bicycles for $6/day. Chris Carts by the Harbour Shoppe (☎365-8053) and Resort Cart Rentals in the Mini Mart Building (☎365-8465) both rent carts for $35/189 daily/weekly. For those who want to rent a car for sightseeing down Great Abaco, Tripple J (☎367-2163) has a few late models for $75/day.

Accommodation

The centre of activity on Treasure Cay, and the chief **lodge**, is the *Treasure Cay Beach Hotel Resort and Marina* (☎365-8250 or 1-800/327-1584, ℱ954/525-1699, ⓔinfo@treasurecay.com; rooms ❸, villas ❽), which features a large array of hotel rooms, suites, condos and small family villas, plus golf, tennis and dive packages at special rates. The *Banyan Beach Club* (☎365-8111 or 1-888/625-3060, ℱ561/625-5301; ❾) is located on the beach at Treasure Cay, and offers condos with two or three bedrooms, high ceilings, tile floors, and private patios with ocean views. Each condo has TV, full kitchen and pine furnishings, and amenities include a pool and watersports rentals. Weekly rates range between $1500 and $2000. Several private agencies offer **villas and condos** for rent on Treasure Cay. Anne Albury (Four Winds Cottages, ☎365-8568) has weekly and monthly rentals, as does Newport International (☎365-8508), Mariner's Cove Condominiums (☎365-8017) and Royal Palm Condominiums (☎365-8507).

Eating and drinking

Food choices are limited and nightlife is sparse on Treasure Cay. North of the resort on the Queen's Highway is the best Bahamian **restaurant**, *Touch of Class* (☎365-8195), serving super grouper and delightful desserts. On Treasure Cay in the plaza not far from the marina office, *Cafe La Florence*

(☎ 367-2570) is essentially a bakery, but serves good quiche and cinnamon rolls; there is an ice cream parlour next door. *The Spinnaker* (☎ 365-8489), on the Treasure Cay dock, serves wonderful johnnycakes for breakfast, specializes in conch salad for lunch and catch-of-the-day for dinner, with an outside deck to enjoy them on.

Diving and watersports

The major **watersports** on Treasure Cay are diving, snorkelling, bonefishing and deep-sea fishing. Divers Down (☎ 365-8465) is the premier dive shop, and is associated with the *Treasure Cay Beach Hotel Resort and Marina*. It rents scuba equipment and offers a number of dive packages, along with certification classes. Dives cost $50/70 for one/two tanks, and snorkellers are welcome on boats for $35. The most popular sites for do-it-yourself snorkelling are around No Name Cay and Whale Cay, an area just offshore from Treasure Cay that is a watery home to the wreck of the *San Jacinto* and where you can find rays and moray eels. Most of the watersports action takes place near or on the *Treasure Cay Beach Hotel Resort and Marina*, where you can also take part in **windsurfing**.

A number of classy **fishing guides** are available for bonefishing in the Marls, as well as deep-sea fishing. Claude Burrows ("One Son" at VHF Ch 16) is a deep-sea specialist and does island hopping and snorkel trips, while Mark Carroll (☎ 365-8582) specializes in free-dive spear fishing, bottom fishing and boat tours. Orthnell Russell (☎ 365-0125) is known as the "bonefish king" hereabouts and Kingsley Murray ("Kingfish II", VHF Ch 16; Treasure Cay Marina) does deep-sea fishing aboard a 31ft Bertram.

For those interested in **sailing**, C&C Boat Rentals (☎ 365-8582, VHF Ch 16), located at the *Treasure Cay Beach Hotel Resort and Marina*, rents a host of watersports equipment, including 17–26ft boats at daily, three-day and weekly rates, along with sunfish, windsurfers, and hobiecats. They deliver boats to Great Guana Cay and Green Turtle Cay as well. Also at the marina, the smaller JIC Boat Rentals (☎ 365-8465) rents out 20–28ft boats. Sidney Hart Sightseeing (☎ 365-8582) takes small groups on shelling and snorkelling trips, and has some fishing and beach picnics.

North Great Abaco

Ever since the SC Bootle Highway was paved, more and more travellers have been heading north of Treasure Cay to see what's up in **north Great Abaco**. Smooth ride or not, the answer, really, is not too much. Essentially, this thirty-mile stretch between the airport and the tip of Little Abaco holds little more than some decent accommodations, a few restaurants, bars and nightclubs.

The scenery in north Great Abaco is much the same as the rest of the island – low ridgelands, rocky outcroppings and dense pine forests, while the few beaches here are bound by rocks and shallows, and are not particularly good for swimming. A number of beautiful islands lie off the coast, though, including **Powell Cay**, a favourite stopover spot for yachters on day-trips, and the exclusive Spanish Cay (see opposite). The largest village in north Great Abaco is **COOPER'S TOWN**, fifteen miles north of Treasure Cay, with a population of nearly 2000. A sleepy place, Cooper's Town does have grocery stores, clothing shops and boutiques, some bars, restaurants, and even small motels and hotels. The tiny **Albert Bootle Museum**, devoted mainly to fishing artefacts, is located in a restored building on the government dock at Cooper's Town, but you'll have to get the key from a caretaker who lives nearby. It offers rather musty exhibits of island life and local genealogy.

The best **accommodation** in Cooper's Town is *M&M Guest House* (☏365-0142; ❷), located at the south end of town, with simple single/double rooms with private bath. As for **eating** in Cooper's Town, try the guesthouse's *M&M Restaurant and Bar*, which specializes in lobster, chicken, big burgers and hearty breakfasts. You can dance there at nights on the weekends. *Conch Crawl* (☏365-0423) is a lively waterside bar and grill that stays open till midnight and features cracked conch, grouper and fries, as well as fried chicken. Its bar has fishnet decor with wood-beam floors and an open-air area consisting of a suspended water-porch. Murray's General Store (☏365-0242) has a complete stock of dry goods, while Wright Seaside Grocery and Bakery (☏365-0057) on the waterfront in Cooper's Town sells both fresh-baked bread and crawfish.

Spanish Cay

SPANISH CAY's well-heeled visitors are lured by the luxurious and expensive homes, suites and apartments that, together, constitute *The Inn at Spanish Cay*. A privately owned 200-acre island just three miles off the northern tip of Great Abaco and due north of Cooper's Town, Spanish Cay is named for galleons that sank off the coast during the seventeenth century. Uninhabited for many years, the island is rocky, windswept and nearly barren, and its five beaches and seven miles of shoreline are gorgeous. Like Walker's Cay far to the northwest, Spanish Cay was bought by Dallas Cowboy owner Clint Murchison in the early 1960s, who planted hundreds of palms that thrive in the sandy-coral soil; there are now more than 6000.

Most visitors **arrive** either by private plane at the 5000ft airstrip or come by yacht to the 75-slip state-of-the-art marina at the cay's resort, which also houses the island's PADI-certified dive shop. If staying overnight, the resort will arrange for a ferry for guests from Cooper's Town. **Accommodation** can be found at *The Inn at Spanish Cay* (☏365-0083, ☏365-0466 or 1-800/688-4752; ❼ and up), where guests reside in one- or two-bedroom apartments or villa suites, both with private garden, double beds, and refrigerator. The apartments have a full kitchen, living room, dining room and deck overlooking the marina. The resort also leases expensive private homes. Two waterfront **restaurants** at the resort, *Point House* and *Wrecker's Raw Bar,* serve Bahamian, Continental and American food, with fresh fish predominating at dinner.

Little Abaco

Shaded by pines and casuarinas, the SC Bootle Highway through **LITTLE ABACO** passes a number of quiet beaches, though there's very little in the way of notable sights on your way to the Northern Cays. **Cedar Harbour,** 22 miles from Treasure Cay, is the largest settlement on Little Abaco, where you'll find *Nettie's Snack Bar*, a pleasant place for conch and fried fish. In **Fox Town,** another seven miles down the road, local Gladys Saunders operates the *Tangelo Hotel* (☏365-2222; ❷), which has twelve plainly furnished and basic rooms with a/c, TV and both double or twin beds. Call ahead, and the owners will send a car for you. The small restaurant serves basic fish dishes for $8. The end of the line is tiny **Crown Haven**, a quiet tumbledown village with a wooden wharf and a struggling lobster business.

The Northern Cays

The exclusive **NORTHERN CAYS** are quite remote and fifty miles from the northern tip of Little Abaco. **Walker's Cay** and its little sisters **Grand Cay** and **Seal Cay** are worth considering only for their sport fishing or for getting off the beaten path indeed.

Walker's Cay

A small coral outcrop that forms the northernmost limit of the Little Bahamas Bank, **Walker's Cay** is a yachting and fishing resort, home to the renowned *Walker's Cay Hotel and Marina* and privately owned by Robert Abplanalp, who made his millions by inventing the aerosol valve. Ringed entirely by a fantastic shallow reef and surrounded by deep water outside the reef (the water drops off 1000ft at some points), the cay itself covers only 100 acres, most of it scrub and rock inhabited only by lizards and terns, who play among the ficus, cactus and palmetto. To the west and north of the private airstrip are two crescent-shaped sand beaches that can be hiked to by guests of the resort.

Sport fishing, diving, and yachting account for the island's lure: barracuda, bonefish, grouper, sailfish, as well as the great blue marlin are in abundance, and its **Bahamas Billfish Championship** (☎ 1-800/432-2092) in April attracts fishermen from miles around. Fish scraps from tournaments are frozen into big drums called "chumsickles", which are then used to attract black tip and reef sharks. In addition to diving the numerous wrecks, caves and coral gardens of the reef, visitors enjoy yachting to nearby cays like **Tom Brown's Cay**, **Seal Cay** and **Sit Down Cay** for an entire day of isolated snorkelling and swimming.

The diving north of Walker's Cay is punctuated by such alluring spots as **Spiral Cavern**, a spectacular shark dive, **Barracuda Alley**, where large 'cuds lurk amid the gullies and reef canyons, and **Pirate's Cathedral**, a coral canyon famous for its mazes of coral teeming with reef fish. These dives are all located fifteen to twenty minutes by boat north of Walker's Cay, and conditions on the surface are choppy.

Practicalities

The only **accommodation** on the island is the rather exclusive *Walker's Cay Hotel and Marina* (700 SW 34th St, Fort Lauderdale, FL 33315; ☎ 353-1252 or 1-800/925-5377; ⑤), which offers 62 rooms and three villas. The resort has two pools, along with two **restaurants**, *The Conch Pearl* and *The Lobster Trap*, which serve seafood and Bahamian/Continental dishes. The rooms are nicely decorated, but don't have TV or phone. More expensive suites, including two-bedroom varieties, are available, as are a number of octagonal-shaped villas above the ocean. The resort also rents a three-bedroom house on the marina.

The only way to visit Walker's Cay is by airplane or yacht, and the hotel will arrange for a ferry pickup of mainland Abaco visitors at Cooper's Town on northern Great Abaco. **Pan-Am Air Bridge** flies to Walker's Cay from Fort Lauderdale. Walker's Cay's **marina** has 75 slips, a bar, commissary, and general services. Dockage is $1.25 daily, with special room/dockage rates applying. At the marina, Sea Below (☎ 352-5252 or 1-800/327-8150, ⓔ NealWatson@aol.com) offers a complete line of equipment to rent, and offers PADI instruction for $300. Two dive trips are arranged each day averaging about $40/60 for one/two-tank dives, slightly more for night dives. Snorkellers are welcome on the boats at $20. **Sport fishing** and **bonefishing** trips can be booked at the marina as well. The marina fleet includes dirft fishing boats, flatboats and some 50ft sport fishermen. Most deep-sea trips cost $200/300 half/full day. Yachters must clear customs and immigration at the dock. Pilots must also clear customs and immigration at the airstrip.

Grand Cay

Most of the people who work on Walker's Cay live on **Grand Cay**, only a few miles east. For a quirky experience, visitors can head here, most likely by hitching a ride on a yacht from Walker's Cay ($10) and stay at the idyllic *Island Bay Restaurant and Motel* (T 353-1200; ❷), which has twenty basic rooms with TV and kitchenette. The motel also is home to a **marina** with fifteen slips. On the west side of Grand Cay is the fabulous **Well's Bay**, two miles of superb, supersecluded white beach. Several locals guide bonefishermen to the west coast of Grand Cay.

South of Marsh Harbour

Cool breezes caress the majestic Caribbean pines lining the well-paved **Great Abaco Highway**, leading south out of Marsh Harbour and making for an altogether delightful drive. While occasional paved or dirt roads head off toward the Atlantic coast, where limestone cliffs enclose tiny beaches, this part of the Abacos is not known for its swimming because of the predomination of cliffs, rocky shores and muddy creeks.

Abaco Farm Road, five miles south of the hamlet of Spring City, leads east to the Atlantic and **Pelican Cays Land and Sea Park**, though most people who visit the park do so as part of package tours, or on their own yachts and sailboats. Lying eight miles north of Cherokee Sound, and just south of Tilloo Cay, the park encloses 2100 acres of shallow reefs and tiny cays. The reefs are host to numerous marine species, including turtles and eagle rays, and are known for their maze-like canyons, gullies and byways. Here and there deep

---

Birding guides in South Abaco

The Abacos are blessed with an abundance of **birds**, and there's nowhere better on the island to go birding than southern Great Abaco. From its pine forests, which harbour such lovely species as the West Indian red-bellied woodpecker and the Bahama parrot, to the Sandy Point creeks, where you're likely to spot roseate spoonbills, grey kingbirds, and a host of shorebirds like terns and herons, this area is truly a birder's dream. To help facilitate your search, think about hiring a local **guide**. In Sandy Point try Patrick Roberts (T 366-4286), Paul Pinder (T 366-4061) or Lensworth Bain (T 366-4280). In Marsh Harbour contact Reggie Patterson (T 366-2749). Abaco Outback (see box on p.132) also run well-regarded birding tours of the area.

in the reef are caverns that divers explore. A clearly marked dirt road five miles south of Abaco Farm Road leads to **Cherokee Point**, a beautiful Loyalist fishing village that stands at the point of a peninsula that juts out from Great Abaco like an anchor. The northern spike of the anchor leads to **Little Harbour**, set on a semi-circular bay of great beauty and charm overlooked by an old lighthouse and lots of bougainvillea and hibiscus.

At **Abaco National Park**, further south along the highway, lives the endangered Bahamian parrot, sheltered amid casuarinas and Caribbean pines. Continuing south to the highway's end brings you to **Sandy Point**, a cozy fishing village that is home to an airstrip and mailboat dock, as well as a telephone station and clinic.

Getting around

Taxi tours of south Great Abaco out of Marsh Harbour are tremendously expensive: a simple one-way journey to Cherokee Sound – only half-way down Great Abaco – can cost as much as $60 for two people. A better bet is to rent an automobile for a day in Marsh Harbour (see p.136). It is too long a trip for rental bicycles, but enthusiastic bicyclists who bring their own racing bikes will find the journey south great fun.

Bahamasair has offered seasonal service to Sandy Point, though it is irregular at best. The *Champion II* mailboat calls at Sandy Point on Tuesday on its eleven-hour journey from Nassau to Great Abaco.

Little Harbour

LITTLE HARBOUR is reached by taking the Great Abaco Highway fifteen miles south of Marsh Harbour, turning west on the hard-pack road for Cherokee Sound and turning two miles down a road marked Dirt Road. The end of this trail isn't much of a town, but the bay itself is quite scenic, with its limestone cliffs backing a crescent bay and beach, its myriad of flowers, and its artist-colony feel. The windswept cliffs and bay are protected by the Bahamas National Trust, and no person may disturb turtle eggs, or any animal or plant. A number of small uninhabited cays nearby are perfect for kayaking, snorkelling and birding.

Little Harbour's main claim to fame is the **Johnston Bronze Art Foundry** and its associated gallery, founded by the Canadian artist Randolph Johnston who came to Great Abaco in 1952 with his wife, the ceramist Margot Broxton. In town, Johnston raised three sons, established an electric generating plant to power his foundry and a furnace to cast huge pieces. His *Monument to Bahamian Women, Sir Milo Butler* and many others are well known. The *Monument* is prominent in Rawson Square in Nassau. Although Johnston died in 1992, his son Peter runs the foundry and gallery (foundry Mon–Sat 10am–noon & 2–4pm; gallery Mon–Sat 11am–4pm; ☎366-2250). The latter not only features works by Johnston, but many elegant pieces by other local jewellers, sculptors and painters. Peter Johnston also runs *Pete's Pub,* a funky **bar** and grill, adorned by T-shirts and pennants of all kinds, near the beach which serves burgers, barbecue and fish cooked on an open grill. Unfortunately there are no inns or lodges in Little Harbour; most overnight visitors are on boats anchored in the harbour.

Cherokee Sound and around

Five miles south of Little Harbour, **Cherokee Sound** is a wonderfully pre-served fishing village which until recently was approachable only by boat and had no electricity, save for generators running on gasoline. These days, the vil-lage is composed of beautifully maintained clapboard and cement houses raised on pillars and each painted in white and pastel colours. Cherokee Sound sports a **BaTelCo** office, a **post office** as well as several churches and a large shallow sound fringed by mangroves. The turquoise-coloured water is great bonefish territory, and the nearby *Different of Abaco* eco-lodge and bone-fish club (see below) uses the sound for its fishing activities in addition to the Marls. Another bonefishing paradise lies on the west side of the sound in the small village of **Casuarina Point**, whose tidal flats are perfect for wading and shelling.

A few miles south of the Cherokee Sound turnoff on Great Abaco Highway lies the short road to **Different of Abaco Nature Park and Bonefish Club** (T366-2150 or 1-800/688-4752, Wwww.differentofabaco.com; 5–8). Located on 300 acres of prime natural habitat for birds, boars and flamingos, *Different* is a premier eco-lodge with 28 nicely furnished cabana rooms, bar, dining room, pool, lake, hot tub, beach, and plenty of activities like boating, bicycles, and billiards. Visitors can rent canoes and kayaks, stargaze through tel-escopes, and go on guided nature hikes. Though most guests come for the fan-tastic bonefishing, the natural habitat of the area is a great draw, as is the friend-ly owner, well known for her hospitality and authentic Bahamian food. Non-guests are welcome to dinner by calling ahead for reservations, and guests of the lodge get free transfers to and from the airport.

Abaco National Park

Ten miles south of Crossing Rocks on the Great Abaco Highway is the turnoff for **ABACO NATIONAL PARK** and the Hole-in-the-Wall Lighthouse. If you wish to drive to the lighthouse, be aware that the serious-ly potholed road traverses fifteen miles of tightly packed pine scrub and pal-metto bush before reaching another dirt track for the final five miles to the lighthouse. For this reason – not to mention the mosquitoes – many people prefer to leave the driving to an **organized tour** under the auspices of Abaco Outback (see box on p.132) or Sand Dollar Tours (T367-2189), both out of Marsh Harbour.

Abaco National Park is 32 square miles of Caribbean pine and hardwood forest laced with nature trails full of wild Atlantic coast scenery. A walk down any of the marked trails will reveal all manner of birdlife: rare egrets, herons, spoonbills, hummingbirds and the **Bahamian parrot**, which is best seen around dawn. An endangered species, found only on Great Abaco and Great Inagua far to the south, the population of Bahama parrots in 1989 was esti-mated between 850 and 1150. The campaign to establish its habitat as a national park in 1994 has been a conservation success, and today it's estimat-ed that the parrot population exceeds 1500. Also visible are plenty of bromeliads and orchids and mangrove swamps – even wild boars. Check at the information centre in Marsh Harbour for trail maps, or with the staff at the lighthouse (see overleaf).

Hole-in-the-Wall Lighthouse

Hardy souls who make it all the way to **Hole-in-the-Wall Lighthouse** will be repaid with a spectacular view of windswept Atlantic headlands and rocky outcrops. Although the lighthouse isn't operating any more, at the time of writing it was leased by the Bahamas Naturalist Expeditions, which has renovated it and uses it as a research station. In the past, BNE offered some hostel-style accommodation at the lighthouse; check in Marsh Harbour for the latest status before planning on staying overnight.

The area around the lighthouse is known as the Hole-in-the-Wall at Lands End, so named because of a 30ft diameter hole that appears in a natural shelf of limestone that extends into the wild Atlantic Ocean off the southern shore. Offshore, **whale and dolphin sightings** aren't uncommon, especially in winter, when humpbacks pass by on their pilgrimage to more southerly waters to calve. On calm days, Hole-in-the-Wall offers good beachcombing and secluded swimming, though the water has a reputation for sharks. A half-hour walk south of the lighthouse brings one to **Alexandria**, a mysterious abandoned settlement of limestone and cement that looks to date back to the early 1800s.

Andros

CHAPTER 4

Highlights

* **Hole in the Wall** A haven for experienced divers, this 80ft-high ledge off Fresh Creek drops off to a pre-Ice Age beach at a depth of 185ft. See p.172

* **Red Bay** On the far northwest shore of North Andros, the descendants of Seminole Indians and escaped black slaves live in this quaint fishing village, weaving traditional palm-thatched straw work. See p.176

* **Snorkelling on the barrier reef** Take a snorkel trip from Small Hope Bay to the Androsian barrier reef half-a-mile offshore, where huge stands of elkhorn, staghorn and brain coral host an astonishing variety of marine life in 12–20ft of clear water. See p.171

* **The Androsia Batik Works** A much-visited factory in Fresh Creek and where artisans create the bright, colourful batik fabrics that are sold throughout the Bahamas. See p.179

* **Bonefishing on Cargill Creek** Enjoy a day of bonefishing on one of North Andros's favourite sites, then relax with a barbecue dinner at one of the rustic lodges in the area. See p.179

* **The Bluff** Get away from it all at this South Andros beach, where coconut palm-lined beaches give way to hinterlands choked with wild orchids and bromeliads. See p.183

Andros

Often called the "Big Back Yard" of the Bahamas, **ANDROS**, located
midway down the archipelago, is the largest island of the entire chain
– one hundred-plus miles north to south and forty miles east to west.
A dense, largely impenetrable tract of pine forests, mud flats and mangroves, it is bisected by all manner of tidal creeks, large brackish bights and
rivers running east to west, cutting off whole chunks of land. At high tide, the
water covers much of that land with a shallow film of saltwater, and when the
tide wanes, the muds become visible, and glisten against a sun that always
seems to shine.

It is not surprising, then, that what lies offshore is of more interest than what's
on the island. Visitors come for the **diving**, **snorkelling** and **bonefishing**,
each of which ranks among the best of its kind in the world. In addition, the
magnificent **Androsian barrier reef**, running the length of the island's east
coast and then some, is reportedly the third longest in the world after
Australia's Great Barrier Reef and the barrier reef off the eastern coast of
Central America. Home to many species of marine life, particularly southern
manta rays and grouper, it is composed of a massive inner barrier of elkhorn
coral, which protects Andros from the brunt of bad weather, tides and hurricane surges.

Andros proper is divided into three zones. **North Andros** contains the
island's most substantial towns, Nicholl's Town and Fresh Creek, and much of
its population – only some 8000 all told. It is separated by a wide bight of saltwater from **Central Andros**, generally called **Mangrove Cay**, which offers
lovely beaches, lagoons, coconut trees and caves. Across the southern bight
from Mangrove Cay, **South Andros** is very lightly populated, has little commercial development and, consequently, is a great place to escape the cares of
civilization. In fact, some parts of central and South Andros have seen electricity only in the last twenty years, and the road system is poor, lending a charmingly isolated aspect to the region – augmented by the lack of any real industry, save for fishing and family farming plots.

Some history

Following the landfall of Columbus on San Salvador in 1492, Andros was
passed over by other Spanish expeditions to the southern oceans until around
1550, when one such expedition arrived seeking slaves. After twenty years of
enslavement, suicide and disease, any natives had completely disappeared from
the island. Virtually bereft of any agricultural base because of a lack of soil, and
totally unsuited to colonial-style plantation exploitation, Andros became a
backwater in the Spanish empire. The original Spanish name for the island, **La**

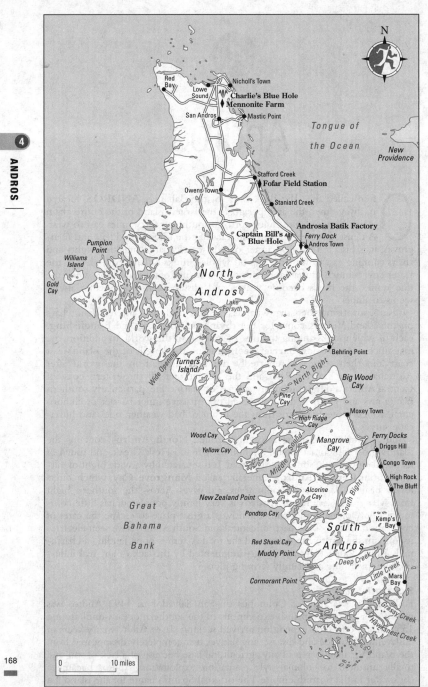

N

Red Bay

Lowe Sound

Nicholl's Town

Charlie's Blue Hole
Mennonite Farm

San Andros

Mastic Point

Tongue of

the Ocean

New
Providence

Stafford Creek
Fofar Field Station

Owens Town

Staniard Creek

Androsia Batik Factory

Captain Bill's
Blue Hole

Ferry Dock
Andros Town

Pumpion
Point

Williams
Island

Gold Cay

North

Andros

Fresh Creek

Lake
Forsyth

Queen's Highway

Behring Point

Turners
Island

Wide Opening

North Bight

Big Wood
Cay

Pine
Cay

Moxey Town

High Ridge
Cay

Mangrove
Cay

Ferry Docks
Driggs Hill

Wood Cay

Yellow Cay

Middle Sound

Congo Town
High Rock
The Bluff

Great

Bahama

Bank

New Zealand Point

Alcorine
Cay

Pondtop Cay

South Bight

South

Andros

Kemp's
Bay

Red Shank Cay

Muddy Point

Deep Creek

Little Creek

Mars
Bay

Cormorant Point

Grassy Creek

Hawksnest Creek

0   10 miles

Isla del Espiritu Santo, alludes to Andros' seemingly providential supply of freshwater for sailors in an area that was sorely lacking it.

Sitting astride the Great Bahama Bank on one side of the Florida Straits, Andros soon became an ideal perch for pirates, who preyed on Spanish shipping circling back to Spain. Because of the island's abundant supply of freshwater and its vast stands of mahogany and pine, the infamous **Sir Henry Morgan** made northern Andros his special base during the middle of the eighteenth century, raiding Spanish shipping on a regular basis.

By the nineteenth century, Andros was primarily home to freed or **runaway slaves** who fished and farmed in small settlements up and down the east coast, having found protection from the weather and tides behind the barrier reef. These tiny settlements were isolated from the rest of the Bahamas, and their residents made a small subsistence living raising corn, plantains, yams, potatoes and peas, supplementing this meagre living with fishing. During the 1830s and 1840s, many **Seminole Indians** fled Florida, took up residence in Red Bay, intermarried with descendants of freed slaves and continue to this day a culture noted for its straw-weaving and fishing in their isolated hamlet.

When, in 1841, a shipwrecked Frenchman noticed that Androsian **sponges** were of higher quality than those found in the Greek isles, the Androsian sponge industry took off. Soon hundreds of Greek schooners and thousands of spongers made Andros their centre of operations, and by 1917, as much as one and a half million pounds of sponges from the forty-mile-wide shoal off the west coast had been harvested. Overharvesting weakened the remaining beds, which led to the harvesting of juvenile members of the species.

During the late nineteenth century, the English attempted to cultivate crops like cotton and sisal for export. It took only two crops of cotton before the thin soil of Andros stopped producing. Indeed, Sir Neville Chamberlain, later Prime Minister of Great Britain, started a sisal plantation on north Andros during the 1890s; its subsequent failure was blamed by the local population on mythical elfin creatures known as chickcharnies.

In 1938, a blight struck the sponge beds, killing most commercial activity. Today, while some Androsians still sponge as a sideline, and sponges can be purchased in roadside shops and certain gift shops in hotels, the activity is largely a memory and a cautionary tale about ecological irresponsibility.

Getting there

Only 25 miles due west of New Providence, **Andros** is easily reached by airplane or ferry from Nassau or mainland Florida. Bahamasair (☎339-4415 or 1-800/222-4262) is the main carrier between Nassau's International Airport and the **four airports** on Andros: San Andros Airport (☎329-4224), near Nicholl's Town; Andros Town Airport (☎368-2030); Mangrove Cay Airport (☎369-0083); and Congo Town Airport (☎369-2640). In general, Bahamasair operates two flights a day to San Andros, Andros Town and Congo Town, primarily early morning and mid-afternoon, though times can vary. Flights from Nassau to Mangrove Cay on Bahamasair are scheduled daily except Tuesday and Wednesday, though it's worth checking the latest schedule. The small carrier Congo Air (☎377-8329) flies a varying schedule between Nassau and Mangrove Cay and Congo Town, while Lynx Air International (☎1-888/596-9247) flies from Fort Lauderdale to Congo Town at least three times a week in high season. Major Air (☎352-5778), based in Freeport, flies into all four airports.

Mailboats ($30 one-way; T393-1064) make the trip from **Potter's Cay** on Nassau's waterfront directly to **Fresh Creek** on North Andros every Wednesday morning in a shade under three hours, though you may be on the ferry for up to seven hours depending on your final destination.

Anyone contemplating a **ferry journey** ($30 one-way) to Andros from Nassau should first contact the Dockmaster's Office (T393-1064) at Potter's Cay for an exact schedule. In general, the M/V *Lisa J II* leaves Potter's Cay, Nassau every Wednesday morning, calling in North Andros at Morgan's Bluff, Mastic Point, and Nicholl's Town, taking about six hours to reach the final stop. It returns to Nassau the following Wednesday. The M/V *Lady D* departs Nassau every Tuesday morning, heading directly for Fresh Creek. The ferry proceeds on to Staniard Creek, Blanket Sound and Browne Sound, for a total trip, again, of about six hours.

The most comfortable ferry from Nassau to Andros is the three-hour **Searoad Express Ferry** ($30; T323-2166), to Fresh Creek, North Andros. The Fresh Creek ferry leaves every Tuesday and Wednesday (10am), Friday (1pm), Saturday (8am) and Sunday (10am), returning to Nassau the same day. Before making plans to go, call for current schedules.

Yachters have only two **marinas** to tie up at on Andros: the eighteen-slip *Lighthouse Yacht Club and Marina* in Andros Town (see p.178) and the *Chickcharnie Hotel* in Fresh Creek (see p.178), which has half a dozen slips for guests of the hotel.

Getting around

Getting around the island is a simple matter, for there is only one main road, the **Queen's Highway**, a narrow strip of paved road that runs along the east coast of North Andros, Mangrove Cay and South Andros. The major settlements on Andros are widely spaced along the highway, whose traffic is light at best.

Public transportation is limited to spotty local taxi service, **mailboats** which call at the major settlements, and a **government ferry**, which runs from Lisbon Creek on Mangrove Cay to Driggs Hill on South Andros but does not connect with North Andros. A locally owned, irregular **minibus** service connects the major settlements of South Andros, but you must consult locals for information before relying on it for service.

Car rental

If you wish to **rent a car**, phone ahead well in advance, as choices are limited. In truth, unless you are going to spend a lot of time here, the cost – an average rate of $65–75 per day – and bother aren't worth it, especially compared to taxi and bike options. On North Andros, Executive Car Rentals Conch

Sound (℡329-2081) and Tropical Car Rentals Nicholl's Town (℡329-2515) are the major car rental operators; in Mangrove Cay, try Brian Moxey's Car Rental (℡369-0353) or King's Supply (℡369-0478); on South Andros, cars are available at Rahming's Rental (℡369-1608) or Mal-Jack's Rental (℡369-3679).

Taxis

No matter at which airport, marina or mailboat landing you arrive, **taxis** will be waiting. Every driver knows the airline and mailboat schedules like the back of his hand, and most double as guides, particularly on North Andros. This service is expensive, and taxi drivers usually quote a price of about $300 per day for two people, though you might try negotiating for a cheaper rate. Many hotels and resorts include a taxi ride from the airport to the lodge as part of the first day's service.

Taxis are owned by individuals and come in all shapes, sizes and states of repair. They are usually dispatched from airports, though you can get a taxi on North Andros in San Andros (℡329-2272) or Fresh Creek (℡368-2579); on Mangrove Cay (℡369-0312 or 0164); and on South Andros in Congo Town (℡369-4548).

Bicycles

Bicycles can be rented from a number of major resorts and hotels, including *Andros Lighthouse Yacht Club and Marina, Small Hope Bay Lodge, Mangrove Cay Inn*, and *Seascape Inn* on Mangrove Cay. You can usually rent one for as little as $10 per day for guests, though most models have balloon tyres and no gearing systems. Bear in mind that the Queen's Highway is narrow, with almost no shoulder, and lined in the north by tall pines, making bicycling long distances a nerve-wracking activity. Avoid biking at night at all costs.

Ferries and mailboats

While there is no scheduled passenger ferry service from Mangrove Cay to North Andros, you can take the small government-run passenger ferry from Lisbon Creek on Mangrove Cay to Driggs Hill on South Andros. The ferry is free and runs twice a day, departing South Andros at 8am and 4pm and returning from Mangrove Cay at 8.30am and 4.30pm, but if you are unable to make the scheduled departure, the operator will almost always make the trip for a fee.

Diving and watersports

Divers from all over the world come to explore the outer wall of the **barrier reef**, which plunges spectacularly straight down to the bottom of the Tongue of the Ocean in a myriad of canyons, caves, blue holes, and sand chutes. Even a mile offshore, snorkellers can find areas as shallow as fifteen feet in which to swim and survey deep-reef structures.

Andros also offers the highest concentration of **blue holes** (see box on p.173) anywhere in the Bahamas. The most famous of these is the **Ocean Blue Hole**, a vast circular cavern entrance about a mile off the coast of North Andros and exactly opposite the lodge operation on Small Hope Bay. The cavern's entrance

Recommended diving spots and dive operators

While there are hundreds of deep and shallow dives along the 140 miles of reef front off the east coast of Andros, several **diving spots** stand out.

Conch Sound Blue Hole, just south along the beach at Nicholl's Town. Located only a dozen feet offshore in a bed of eelgrass, this blue hole is a specialty dive offered by *Small Hope Bay Lodge* and should be attempted only by experienced divers with a guide as the variable tidal flow in the hole makes it dangerous.

Diana's Dungeons, due east of Love Bay on the outer wall about a mile and a half southeast of Staniard Creek. Drops off at about 60ft into passageways and canyons that lead through coral caverns, sand chutes and gullies. The reef throbs with colourful sponges and parrotfish.

Hole in the Wall, northeast of Staniard Creek on the outer wall. Accessible only by boat, this spot is a specialty dive of *Small Hope Bay Lodge* and consists of a wall, tunnel and trough. Considered one of the most spectacular dives on Andros, it is a one-on-one specialty dive for experienced divers and a guide.

Ocean Blue Hole, off Small Hope Bay (see above).

Shark Buoy, northeast of Fresh Creek, 20min by boat. For this ocean dive, a submarine tracking device produces vibrations, which attract pelagic fish, and in turn, pelagic silky sharks. Some New Providence dive shops offer this dive as an option.

Local dive operators

Greem Windows Inn Nicholl's Town, North Andros ☎329-2194, ℻329-2016, @androsfishing@hotmail.com. This new ten-room lodge is primarily a bonefishing operation, but does have a small dive shop which rents equipment for certified divers.

Seascape Inn Moxey Town beachfront on Mangrove Cay ☎369-0342. A full-service dive shop in the lodge offers dive and snorkel trips, as well as instruction and kayaking.

Small Hope Bay Lodge Three miles north of Fresh Creek, North Andros ☎368-2013. This complete, full-service dive centre and lodge is superb for its attention to safety, its knowledge of the surrounding areas and specially guided snorkel and dive trips. It can also arrange for island-hopping charters; most trips start at 9.30am on the excellent dive boat and last most of the morning.

gives onto a vast system of lateral and vertical caverns underwater, and snorkellers who accompany the divers are able to see the 100ft-diameter circular rim of the crater, and watch while divers descend into the sulphurous depths. Anyone wishing to do blue-hole diving should contact Rob Palmer's Blue Holes Foundation (PO Box F-40579, Freeport, Grand Bahama Island, Bahamas; ☎373-4483, @1000432@compuserve.com).

While reef fishing and deep-sea fishing are good off the coasts of Andros, perhaps nowhere else in the world do **bonefish** grow to such large size as on Andros. They are abundant too – enough so that even a novice can hook one. Any hotel should be able to recommend a good bonefish guide, or you can start with the Andros Bonefishing Guides Association in Nicholl's Town (☎329-7372 or 368-4261) or Jolly Boy Enterprises in South Andros (☎369-2727 or 2696), which arrange boats and guides for bonefishing, reef fishing, or deep-sea fishing. The standard package for a day of bonefishing is $350 per day per person, with boat and lunch provided, $250 per half-day. Deep-sea fishing packages usually start at $500 per day for two people. *Charlie's Haven* (☎368-4087), a rustic hotel at Behring Point, North Andros, is a highly recommended bonefishing lodge, and supplies guides and trips for $180 half-day, $300 full day. Bonefishermen may choose either spinning or fly equipment,

Blue holes

The Bahamas contain the largest number of **blue holes** in the world, none as spectacular as those on the eastern portion of Andros. During the Ice Age, when water levels were significantly lower, large circular pits were carved in the limestone owing to erosion from rainwater and carbon dioxide. The blue holes of Andros are now underwater entrances to those holes, entrances that reveal a spider web of caverns covering many square miles in length. They range from around thirty to several hundred feet deep. Tidal action, currents and surf well below the surface cause strong updrafts of water that are known as blowing, or **boiling holes**.

These boiling holes are probably the source of the myth of the **Lusca**, creatures that purportedly inhabit blue holes and kill intruders. Androsians claim these gigantic lobsters will feed on any human silly enough to swim or dive into their domain. But the hazard of blue holes is no myth: boiling effects and strong currents can make subterranean passage exploration treacherous – particularly at the reef's edge, where tides and sulphur eruptions complicate matters – unless you are properly qualified and proceed with extreme caution. Best to always do so in the company of very experienced divers.

but should plan to come to Andros with a complete supply of equipment, tackle, lures and line, as there are no real fly shops here in which to buy local equipment.

Kayaking

Escorted or self-guided **kayaking** tours are a unique way to come up close to the island's ecosystem. Most tours parallel the white beaches, explore mangroves, or paddle toward uninhabited cays offshore. Kayaks are available for free to guests at *Seascape Inn* (see p.181) on Mangrove Cay, the *Kamalame Cay* resort (see p.177) in Staniard Creek, or at the *Small Hope Bay Lodge* (see p.177) on Small Hope Bay. Non-guests can usually rent a kayak, depending on availability, from the resorts for about $35/day.

Small Hope Bay Lodge also offers a half-day **boat safari** by kayak up Fresh Creek for $40 per two people, on which you can sometimes catch sight of turtles, ospreys and dolphins.

Other outdoor activities

If you've had your fill of watersports, **nature walks** can be arranged through several hotels on Andros, particularly *Small Hope Bay Lodge* and *Seascape Inn*. The tourist office on South Andros also has some information on walks. Be advised that many of the nature trails (as advertised) are actually old logging roads, or paths hacked away from logging roads by hotel crews for the convenience of guests. Many have long since fallen into disuse, or are grown over in spots and hard to follow.

In the face of a healthy mosquito population and some fierce heat, **birding** on Andros demands great fortitude. Services of a birding guide may sometimes be obtained through one of the many resorts or hotels, but most birders come to Andros as part of an organized tour from North America or Europe, though some simply guide themselves, trusting to luck and good sense. The most prized of sights for birders on Andros are the Cuban emerald, Bahama wood-star and the black-cowled oriole. Andros is also prime hunting ground for white-crowned pigeons, and there have been reported sightings of flamingos in the far southwestern corner of South Andros.

North Andros

The biggest island in the Andros chain, **NORTH ANDROS** also has the larger towns (though none is what you'd call large), most of the tourist sights and a good percentage of the diving and fishing operations that are Andros' focal point. Though every creek, flat, bight and river sports large numbers of hungry bonefish, many of the unique bonefishing sites are located on North Bight about thirty miles from Andros Town Airport,

A good base for exploring northern North Andros, **Nicholl's Town** is within easy distance of the twee fishing villages of **Lowe Sound** and **Red Bay**, as well as **Charlie's and Benjamin's blue holes**. Further swimming and diving opportunities are available in **Small Hope Bay** as you head south along the east coast toward **Fresh Creek**, just south of San Andros Airport and the last major settlement on North Andros before Mangrove Cay.

Nicholl's Town and around

While there isn't much to see in the coastal village of **NICHOLL'S TOWN**, it is the centre of activity for divers and snorkellers in North Andros, especially those exploring the coast along Conch Sound or hoping to dive the **Conch Sound Blue Hole** (see p.172) one mile offshore. The town is also a base for local trips north to Lowe Sound for bonefishing, west to historic Red Bay and south, along the eastern coast, to the tremendous Charlie's Blue Hole and Benjamin's Blue Hole.

The town itself has about 600 permanent residents, including a few retired expatriates, who live in breeze-block and tin-roofed homes as well as scattered wooden shacks. Just as interesting to gaze at is the **Administrator's Office**, attractively Georgian in style, and facing the curiously named "International Square"; elsewhere, you'll find a post office (Mon–Fri 9am–5.30pm), supermarket, and several bars and restaurants serving simple Bahamian fare. Fringed by tall palms, the **beach** is marked by a wharf that hosts a melange of fishing boats used in the busy conch and grouper trade.

Lowe Sound and Morgan's Bluff

Two miles west of Nicholl's Town lies the pleasant fishing village of **LOWE SOUND**, which doesn't have much more than a few bar-restaurants and some bonefishing guides, notably Arthur Russell (☎329-7372), who can lead you to excellent fishing in the nearby creeks and marshes. Most locals make their

Bonefishing clubs

Most **bonefishing clubs** on Andros are rustic, with a minimum of amenities, and are places devoted almost solely to the pursuit of bonefish. They offer packages for one or two fishermen which include lodging, food, guide and boat. Usually, such clubs offer little entertainment beyond a small bar.

Andros Island Bonefishing Club Cargill Creek ☎368-5167 or 1-800/688-4752, ☎020/7493-0798 in UK, ℗368-5235, ⓦwww.bahamas-mon.com/hotel/abone. With twelve cabins, some wood, some breeze-block, but all have two double beds, private bath, fridge and fans. There's a restaurant on site with a bar with TV. The club prefers to sell weekly package trips, with the basic package about $1490 single/$1000 per person double. ❻

Cargill Creek Fishing Lodge Cargill Creek ☎368-5129, ℗329-5046. An all-inclusive fishing club with ten rooms and a cottage located near the creek, with access to tremendous fishing flats. There is a small pool and a decent restaurant and bar on the premises. Packages are available for fishermen. ❺, with fishing going at $300 per day per person with boat and guide.

Charlie's Haven Behring Point ☎368-4087 or 1-888/262-0700. Many stories about bonefishing are passed around this perennial favourite rustic lodge, which has ten basic rooms, some with a/c, some with fans. There is a small bar and meals are included in the price of the room, though what is most important here is the guidance of owner Charlie Smith and his sons, some of the best guides in the region, who offer trips for $300 per day. *Charlie's* sits right on the edge of the bight, looking out at the vast lustrous river that separates North Andros from Mangrove Cay and has an end-of-the-world feel. ❼

Daisy Nottage's Cottages Behring Point ☎368-4293. While not a bonefishing club *per se*, the guests here are almost all bonefishermen. On site, there are ten basic rooms with an additional five two-bedroom cottages for self-catering. There is also a good restaurant and bar where Daisy herself prepares conch, seafood, and Bahamian fixings like macaroni and cheese and mashed potatoes. Meals are extra. ❽

Moxey's Guesthouse and Bonefish Lodge Moxey Town, Mangrove Cay ☎369-0023 or 1-800/688-4752, ⓦwww.moxeybonefish.com. This classic lodge has ten rooms and two self-catering cottages and sits on a rise above a good harbour north of Moxey Town. The restaurant features both Continental and Bahamian cuisine and the harbour has good snorkelling and diving as well as flats fishing. Packages come in all types, but a basic fly-fish package averages $400/day single.

living from conch, sponging or fishing, save those doing small-scale vegetable farming in the surrounding triangle of countryside – there really isn't much to do here but relax and watch the water.

If you turn right, or north, at the crossroads outside of town, you'll find yourself at **Morgan's Bluff**, which looms two miles ahead where the road ends at the beach. It is said to be where Henry Morgan secured his headquarters during the eighteenth century, and visitors have spent countless hours searching in vain for the pirate's buried loot. Coming here is also largely an unfruitful exercise, for outside of a nice stretch of white sand, some nice views of the Atlantic Ocean breakers, and a few tidal-action limestone caves – one of which is the garbage- and graffiti-strewn **Henry Morgan's Cave** – there's little doing here.

The biggest deal around here is July's annual **All Andros and Berry Islands Independence Regatta,** for which people come to the small harbour to celebrate the holidays and watch the colourful boat races that take place. Food stalls, craft displays and music highlight the onshore festivities, while locals participate in darts, dominoes and bonefishing competitions.

Red Bay

RED BAY, the only settlement that can really claim to cling to Andros' swampy, bug-infested west coast, can be reached by a bumpy, unpaved road leading west from just north of the San Andros Airport, and rocking along for fifteen hard miles. The population is largely descended from Seminole Indians who fled Florida during the 1840s or who joined with black slaves fleeing Florida, taking canoes all the way to Andros where they set up a small fishing village and intermarried with locals. These days, Red Bay is a rather weather-beaten village with a rich cultural heritage centred on straw-basket weaving. Ovoid and watertight, these baskets derive from the Seminole tradition, which is significantly different from palm and raffia weaving styles used by other Out Island Bahamians. Some locals still sponge for a small living, and a couple of small bars serve snacks, but there are **no hotels** or other services at all.

Charlie's and Benjamin's blue holes

Take the Queen's Highway along the coast one mile south of Nicholl's Town and, just before you get to San Andros, you'll see a battered sign to the east of the highway. A rugged track leads a couple of hundred yards into the bush, where you'll see **Charlie's Blue Hole**. This spectacular limestone cavern near the tiny fishing village of Conch Sound is famous for its rapid "boiling", the signal that water is rushing in and out of the hole during tides. Boats can be pulled underwater, or out to sea, by the force of this tide.

Benjamin's Blue Hole is half a mile inland toward Conch Sound from Charlie's. On a dirt track that is largely overgrown, you'll probably need local guidance to find it, yet the stalagmites and stalactites for which it is celebrated are well worth the effort. Diving these spots should be carefully planned (see p.173), though many people come to kayak and swim in their environs.

Practicalities

If you are looking for a **place to stay** in Nicholl's Town, the *Green Windows Inn* (T 329-2194, F 329-2016; **❸**), a ten-minute walk from the beach, has ten rooms, and four suites with bath, all of which are above the bar and restaurant, so noise can be a problem at times. It's a gathering spot for bonefishing freaks, and its restaurant serves basic Bahamian fare. *The Conch Sound Resort*, two miles south of town on Conch Sound Highway (T 329-2060 or 2341) is ten minutes from the beach. Surrounded by a thick pine forest, it has fourteen pleasant enough rooms done up in brown and beige carpeting, mahogany furniture and satellite TV; all have private baths. Some of the rooms are motel-style, some free-standing concrete cottages. Diving, snorkelling, and bonefishing are arranged by the staff. No credit cards. Rooms **❸**; cottages **❼**.

The best **dining** can be found at *Big Josh's Seafood Restaurant* (T 329-7517) in Lowe Sound. Serving breakfast, lunch and dinner, *Big Josh's* specializes in seafood, though good steak, pork chops and fried chicken are also available for around $10. Its *Twilight Zone* bar/restaurant combination stays open late to the throb of satellite TV. The prime option for **eating** in Nicholl's Town, *Eva's Picaroon Restaurant* (T 329-2582), serves standard Bahamian dishes like grouper, peas and rice, and fried chicken, and sometimes has a local band in for entertainment on weekends.

Listings

Government offices Nicholl's Town ☎329-2278
Medical clinics Nicholl's Town ☎329-2055

Police and fire Telephone in general ☎919;
Nicholl's Town ☎329-2278

The east coast toward Fresh Creek

The Queen's Highway hurtles south through thick pine forest and the stretch is riddled with deep potholes. Just past abandoned Owen's Town, the road turns due east toward the ocean, skirts a creek, and winds up at non-descript **Stafford Creek**, which hunkers down on the north side of the creek of the same name. One mile south on the highway, the **Fofar Field Station** caters to North American students of marine biology, geology and ornithology.

Further south along the highway, **Staniard Creek** is a wonderland of flowering plants, including wild orchid, hibiscus and wild lilies, though the dispersed settlement itself is scruffy at best. People come mainly for the mile or so of stirring white **beach**, which runs from the mouth of the creek at Blanket Sound until just north of Small Hope Bay and is often deserted, while those who can afford it stay at the expensive *Kamalame Cay* resort (see "Practicalities" below). Further south near Love Hill, you find the turnoff to **Captain Bill's Blue Hole**, a popular swimming place and a diver's haven. About a mile offshore from Captain Bill's is the **Hole in the Wall** (see p.172), one of the most astonishing dives in the Bahamas.

The highway after Love Hill opens to views of **Small Hope Bay** – sometimes called **Calabash Bay** – a lovely stretch of coastal settlement, white-sand beach and casuarina trees about three miles north of Andros Town itself. Hereabouts the pines of North Andros give way to vast seas of coconut palms, and the coastal beaches are both wide and empty. The bay here is wide, shallow and subject to great tidal movements, superb for snorkelling, diving and swimming.

Practicalities

While there is little **accommodation** between Nicholl's Town and Fresh Creek, two resorts stand out. *Kamalame Cay* (☎368-6281 or 1-800/688-4752, ⑤368-6279; ❽) is a very private resort located on an island off Staniard Creek. With twelve rooms, the main house is expensive and nice, with "stone-wrapped Roman tubs", books, games, but no phones or TVs in the room. A Boston Whaler is available for guests, and the dining room features steaks and chops as well as local seafood prepared Bahamian-style. The main house can sleep up to ten people, and all bedrooms have mosquito nets and king-size beds. Separate villas and guesthouses have kitchenettes. Outside, hammocks hang between palm trees, and there is a small pool and private beach. Snorkelling and eco-tours are included in the package.

Built in 1960 out of native limestone and pine, *Small Hope Bay Lodge* (☎368-2013 or 1-800/223-6961, ⓦwww.SmallHope.com; ❽) is the oldest and one of the best resorts in the Bahamas, offering twenty cottages for families, couples and singles. Some have private bath, some shared bath, and the decor features batik hangings. Guests may dive and snorkel, but there is a hot tub up the beach, as well as kayaks, nature walks, bonefishing, saltwater fly-fishing and reef fishing. Drinks, hors d'oeuvres, airport transfers, and taxes are included in the price of the stay. Dive packages are available as well. Rates vary, but average $240/180 per day diver/non-diver high season, $225/160 offseason.

On Small Hope Bay, *Central Andros Inn Motel* (☏ 368-6209; ❷) is a small, ten-room motel ideal for the budget-conscious traveller. It has a restaurant, a simple bar and TV.

Even if you don't stay at *Small Hope Bay Lodge*, it presents your best **dining** option in the area. The menu features absolutely first-rate stuff, anything from grilled scampi and local lobster on the outdoor open-air charcoal grill, to lamb chops, sea bass, and an out-of-this-world buffet. All the vegetables are garden-fresh, and main dishes are prepared with creativity and flair by a live-in chef. Desserts like melt-in-the-mouth carrot cake and guava duff round out every meal in style.

Fresh Creek and around

Two miles south of Small Hope Bay, the big – for Andros – settlement of **FRESH CREEK** encompasses **Coakley Town** to the north of the creek and, connected by a lovely single-lane bridge, a small collection of buildings to the south that has come to be called **Andros Town**. The creek itself gradually widens heading inland for about ten miles, becoming a wide bight with uncounted interruptions by mud flats, islands, and small creeks. Closer to shore, the tidal estuary supports lovely stands of bougainvillea, pine, palm and palmetto. For isolated swimming, visitors can go south of town to **Somerset Beach** at low tide, which is long and wide and quite handsome.

Near Fresh Creek, the US operates a naval base for submarine testing and evaluation known as **AUTEC** (Atlantic Undersea Testing and Evaluation Center), which employs a few locals but is off limits to visitors. A frequent sight at the **Andros Town Airport** is squads of enlisted men and officers of the US Navy, anxiously waiting their charter or scheduled flights to Miami for their R and R.

Swedish industrialist Axel Wenner-Gren (see p.87), who developed Paradise Island, also had a hand in the initial development of the **marina** at Fresh Creek in the 1940s. Refurbished and largely rebuilt on the same spot, the new marina, the only full-service one on Andros, now boasts eighteen slips and can accommodate vessels up to 150ft.

Accommodation

Andros Lighthouse Yacht Club and Marina Fresh Creek ☏ 368-2305 or 1-800/688-4752, ⓕ 368-2300, VHF Ch 16. With a patio overlooking Fresh Creek and an eighteen-slip marina, the club offers twelve rooms with king-size beds and eight with two double beds, all featuring private baths and cable TV. Although many yachties call in here, it is also good for bonefishing and island tours. ❺
Chickcharnie Hotel Fresh Creek ☏ 368-2026 or 1-800/688-4752, ⓕ 368-2492, VHF Ch 16. On the water about two miles northeast of the airport and half a mile from the barrier reef, *Chickcharnie* has eleven rooms with a/c, TV and private bath, as well as five rooms having a shared central bath. The

pine forest is nearby for hiking, and the staff can arrange bonefishing. The hotel has a few slips for modest yachts. Rates are $80 a/c, $50 fan.
Coakley House Fresh Creek ☏ 368-2013/2014 or 1-800/223-6961, ⓦ www.CoakleyHouse.com. Operated by the owners of *Small Hope Bay Lodge* (see above), this large villa is a self-catering world unto itself at the mouth of the creek. Easily sleeping six, this lovely place features a master bedroom, two other bedrooms, a lounge, patio, dining room and full kitchen, plus a 120-foot. dock and landscaped grounds. Groups can share expenses and live like kings. Rates are $300/1750 per day/week peak season, $250/1500 day/week off-

4

season. Excellent access to fishing, and easy transport between here and Small Hope Bay. **Point of View Villas** Fresh Creek ☏ 368-2750 or 1-800/688-4752, ☏ 368-2761, Ⓦ www.pointofviewbahamas.com, Ⓔ cnonam@batelnet.bs. These fourteen newly built villas are located on five acres of landscaped gardens overlooking the ocean. They are wood-built, surrounded by flowered grounds and cater to families and groups. Staff can arrange for bone-fishing guides. Villa $300 (up to four persons), suite $350.

Skinny's Landmark Motel Fresh Creek ☏ 368-2082. A decent place for a short stay, this fifteen-room budget choice has decent rooms walled in pine, a popular local restaurant and bar. ❷

Coakley Town

A quiet place, **COAKLEY TOWN** was named for **Coakley House**, a fabulous villa built by Wenner-Gren, now operated by the folks at *Small Hope Bay Lodge* as an inn (see opposite). The town is a not unpleasant collection of breeze-block and concrete homes, a few shops, restaurants, bars and a sixty-foot-tall white limestone lighthouse at the point, from which the views look down over cliffs to the blue sea.

Andros Town

Hardly a town at all, **ANDROS TOWN**, across the bridge from Coakley Town, has a very small **tourist office** (Mon–Fri 9am–4pm; ☏ 368-2286, Ⓦ www.androsia.com) and a lovely little park with some disused tennis courts, all in the same shady hundred-yard square, but is only marginally of more interest than its neighbour.

Across the street from the tourist office and down an unpaved lane stands the **Androsia Batik Factory** (Mon–Sat 8am–5pm; free; ☏ 352-2255), which constitutes about the only commercial enterprise on Andros besides truck farming and tourism. Operated by the Birch family, which also owns *Small Hope Bay Lodge*, the factory produces colourful batiks, which make fashionable dresses, blouses, pants, T-shirts and scarves, as well as excellent wall hangings. The batik-making process, which visitors can view, begins with plain white fabrics on which wax-dipped sponge cutouts of patterns are impressed, then the whole is dipped in dye. The wax is melted in hot water and the fabrics, with attendant patterns, are sun-dried.

The factory itself, which employs some forty to fifty islanders, and its **gift shop** look a little careworn, but on most days production is in full, if somnolent, swing. Visitors seldom find a guide, the workers aren't particularly interested and the gift shop attendant is silent – still, there are some excellent bargains in the shop, remnants of fabric, T-shirts on sale, and the occasional dress at a good price, or overstocked goods.

South of Fresh Creek

The road **south of Fresh Creek** runs through bush and pine scrub, and there are no real settlements to speak of. Driving the road is pleasant enough, despite its big potholes. Ten miles south of Fresh Creek, **Little Cargill Creek** and its sister hamlet, **Behring Point**, are in the midst of prime bonefishing country, probably the most prominent activity in this part of North Andros. Both towns have a few rustic, but delightful, fishing lodges, some small restaurants and bars serving Bahamian fare, and little else. The Queen's Highway potholes on for another mile beyond Behring Point, then stops at the bight. Twenty-five miles south leads you to the Bight of Andros, a wide estuary and swamp across which lies Mangrove Cay.

Eating

Chickcharnies Hotel Fresh Creek ☎ 368-2026. Overlooking the water, the hotel's dining room rivals *Hank's Place* in popularity. The steamed conch and crawfish are especially good. Basic dinner entrees run from $8 to $15.

Dig Dig's South of Cargill Creek ☎ 368-5097. Located in a small pink house, this crowded eatery offers excellent entrees like smothered grouper and lobster for $15 and up and a potent house cocktail made from gin, milk and coconut water. Open for lunch and dinner only.

Hank's Place Fresh Creek ☎ 368-2173. Easy to spot right near the water in the centre of the village, *Hank's* is an airy place with a deck over the water for enjoying its inexpensive good fried chicken dishes, buffalo wings, grouper and conch.

Lighthouse Club and Marina Fresh Creek ☎ 368-2305. With the only elegant dining on the island, the marina features a mix of American specialties like steaks and chops, with Bahamian fare like lobster, steamed conch and a hearty conch chowder. The restaurant overlooks the marina and is especially nice at night when the yachts are lighted. Dinner $17 and up.

Drinking and nightlife

While all of the hotels and motels (see "Accommodation", p.178) have **bars** where one can get a cold Kalik, or a rum-soda, there is a paucity of **nightlife** hereabouts. There is literally no nightlife to speak of in Nicholl's Town beyond hotel bars where locals gather to watch cable TV and play dominoes. The *Conch Sound Resort* (☎ 329-2060) on Conch Sound Highway sometimes has live music on weekends, while *Donnie's Sweet Sugar Lounge* (☎ 368-2080) in Fresh Creek features an odd facade of conch shells, a dim low-ceilinged bar and a decrepit dance floor that is often crammed with locals on weekends. In Cargill Creek, *Leadon's Creekside Lounge and Disco* (☎ 368-4167) is open 9am-11pm weekdays, 9am-3am on weekends, and often hosts local bands, with a once-monthly performance by big names in Bahamian music.

Listings

Banks Royal Bank of Canada (Wed 9.30am–3.30pm; ☎ 368-2071) in Andros Town
Government offices Island Administrator, Fresh Creek ☎ 368-2010; Bahamas Customs, Andros Town ☎ 368-2030
Medical clinics Fresh Creek ☎ 368-2038
Police and fire Telephone in general ☎ 919; Fresh Creek ☎ 368-2626

Mangrove Cay

Most people come to eighteen-mile-long **MANGROVE CAY** for its isolation. In fact, getting there from nearby North Andros is impossible except by air or mailboat via Nassau or by private yacht. The reef offshore is near enough that snorkellers can easily swim out, spend some time and enjoy excellent views of Caribbean spiny lobster and natural sponges, which are particularly abundant on this part of the coast.

If you fly into the Mangrove Cay Airport, you'll find a couple of local taxis ready to transport you into **Moxey Town**, which has several hotels, and some good Bahamian restaurants, or south to **Lisbon Creek**, a modestly scenic settlement known for its boat building. The drivers are always ready with a card if you need further transport. Every hotel, resort, or restaurant can phone one of the two or three taxis on the cay.

Accommodation

Most of the hotels and resorts on Mangrove Cay are located right on the beach. The cay's narrow and sometimes potholed version of the **Queen's Highway** runs from the far north at Moxey Town to Bastin Point and Lisbon Creek in the south. The interior is dense scrub palmetto and mangrove swamp. The beach opposite the highway is, however, wide and lovely, and lined by coconut palms.

Helen's Motel Complex Mangrove Cay ☎ & ⓕ 369-0033 or 1-800/688-4752, ⓔ helensmotel@bahamas.net.bs. One mile south of Moxey Town, this modern motel-style place has ten rooms with bath and both a/c and fan, as well as a small restaurant and bar with cable TV. It's basic but clean, and popular with locals. Rates $65–80.
Mangrove Cay Inn Moxey Town ☎ 369-0069, ⓕ 369-0014. Twelve air-conditioned rooms that are darkish, but nicely furnished and carpeted. A good restaurant features an eclectic menu, including conch, lobster, pasta or hoagies. The beach is a 200yd walk away, and the grounds are lush with orchids. You can rent a bicycle, take a nature walk, or play games in the parlour. There's a laundry on site. Basic rates are about $120.
Moxey's Guesthouse and Bonefish Lodge Moxey Town ☎ 369-0023 or 1-800/688-4752, ⓕ 369-0726, ⓦ www.moxeybonefish.com. On the edge of the Middle Bight, a sheeny stretch of water that separates Mangrove Cay from Big Wood Cay to the north, this little inn has ten rooms and two cottages (with two bedrooms each) and pro-

vides mud-flats bonefishing close by. The popular restaurant features Bahamian and American dishes, and affords a good view of the water. Rates $85–125.
Seascape Inn Moxey Town beachfront ☎ 369-0342 or 1-800/688-4752. All in all, a delightful spot, these five beautiful, upscale and new beachfront cabins feature individual decks that are quite private. The owners have put handmade wooden furniture and original art in the rooms, and have created an elevated restaurant. The lunch menu contains chicken, steaks and Bahamian specialties, with excellent desserts. Activities include snorkel trips, diving excursions, nature walks, guided bonefishing, and special backcountry trips too. $100–125.
White Sand Beach Hotel South of Moxey Town ☎ 369-0159. Serviceable for on-the-cheap fishermen, this rather drab older hotel has 25 rooms that sleep six if necessary. They face the flats, just down the street from *Helen's Motel Complex*. Rates $70–90.

The island

The main northern settlement on Mangrove Cay, Little Harbour rests at the northern tip of the island and is generally referred to by the name of its northern section, **Moxey Town**, in honour of its founding family. The town has a beach and a tiny dock where local catches are hauled in and where a ferry calls; the settlement also has a couple of local restaurants and bars for those just passing through. Otherwise, there's little to waylay you here except a pharmacy, from which you'll doubtless want to pick up some mosquito repellant. The only other actual settlements on Mangrove Cay, Burnt Rock and Grant's Town, are quite tiny, almost specks on the roadway. As the Queen's Highway runs south toward South Andros, it becomes even worse, with carriage-rattling potholes and unpaved sections.

The centre of **diving** life on Mangrove Cay is at the *Seascape Inn* (☎ 369-0342 (see above). Prices are negotiable, but one-tank dives cost $40.

Bonefishing guide Dennis Leadon (☎ 368-5156) knows the flats above the cay, while Moxey's (☎ 369-0342) is a central clearing house on the cay for other bonefishing guides. Many fishermen skiff over from Moxey Town to **Bigwood Cay Flat**, a fifteen-minute putt-putt away from Mangrove Cay, where fishing flats stretch for miles in an utterly isolated environment.

There are more than twenty **blue holes** on inland Mangrove Cay, most of them buried deep in the interior, reachable only by scrubbed-over logging roads and trails. In order to dive a blue hole, you'll need to contact the dive master at the *Seascape Inn*, and get information on them.

At **Lisbon Creek**, the southernmost point on Mangrove Cay, the road ends, and one can catch a ferry for Driggs Hill on South Andros. The best Androsian sloops were built at Lisbon Creek, though the art has fallen into desuetude of late. The biggest social-sporting events come in August, when there are two separate regattas in Lisbon Creek.

Eating and drinking

All of the hotels and resorts on Mangrove Cay have pleasant enough **bar-restaurants** where tourists and locals pass the hours in conversation, playing dominoes or throwing darts.

Aquamarine Club Lisbon Creek, no phone. A small restaurant in a home where a good local cook serves up Bahamian seafood like grouper and snapper. The decor is no more than a few tables and chairs, but the meals are inexpensive and good.

Dianne Cash's Ultimate Delight Moxey Town ☎ 369-0430. For a special treat, try *Dianne Cash's*, where the owner has put together four simple tables made of rattan and offers great pork chops, conch salad or stuffed baked crabs – a real specialty. She'll even fix you whatever you want (within reason). Meals cost $5–20. Call ahead for breakfast, lunch or dinner.

Hellen's Moxey Town, no phone. A local restaurant and lounge where special versions of stewed conch, fish and chips, and grits and cheese, all go for under $7.

Nakita's Restaurant and Lounge Victoria Point ☎ 368-2447. *Nakita's* is a good restaurant outside the hotel and resort circuit, with a menu featuring conch, lobster and crab.

Seascape Inn Two miles south of Moxey Town ☎ 369-0342. The timbered restaurant and bar of this resort sits on stilts and features large breakfasts, burger and conch lunches, and Continental and Bahamian-style seafood dinners that run from $15 to $20.

Listings

Airlines Bahamasair ☎ 369-0470; Congo Air ☎ 377-3362
Government offices Island Administrator, Mangrove Cay ☎ 369-0331

Medical clinics Mangrove Cay ☎ 369-0089 or 0186
Police and fire Telephone in general ☎ 919; Mangrove Cay ☎ 368-0083

South Andros

If Mangrove Cay seems isolated, **SOUTH ANDROS,** composed mostly of mangrove and bush, mud flats and tidal swamps, feels like the absolute end of the world, and you will soon forget you are only about 175 miles from the tip of southern Florida. From **Driggs Hill** – where the ferry from Mangrove Cay disembarks – it is about a 25-mile drive all the way to the southern tip at **Mars Bay**, and the Queen's Highway, though bumpy and terrible, presents several pleasant vistas. Allow all day for a sightseeing drive both ways. In fact, the coast of South Andros is one long white beach, perfect for snorkelling and swimming, though facilities are sparse. Offshore lies a fringing reef, while the interior is premier birding and nature hiking territory.

If you are not taking the ferry (see p.170), you will alight at **Congo Town Airport**, where there are always a couple of taxis waiting to take you to Driggs Hill, three miles north, or to nearby Congo Town itself. There are no public marinas in South Andros.

Driggs Hill and around

While quiet **DRIGGS HILL**, the northernmost point on South Andros, isn't much to look at, it does have a pretty enough collection of pastel-coloured houses, a small church and a grocery store. The point where the ferry from Lisbon Creek disembarks, the town offers little to detain you, and you may only stop long enough to arrange a seat on the informal **minibus** operated by one of the locals that goes up and down the coast.

Congo Town, two miles south of the airport and Driggs Hill, is largely known for the *Emerald Palms by the Sea Hotel*, a major honeymoon destination (see below). The town features an ocean walk through coconut palms and, in the centre, a historical cemetery where many of the island's founding families are buried. The walk through the coconut palms is particularly inspiring early in the morning when sunrise tints the sky pink and coral-coloured. Everything to the west of Congo Town is mangrove swamp and dense bush.

The highlight of the area lies right on the beach just three miles south of Congo Town, where **The Bluff** offers a wonderful view of the many cays and islands lying offshore. This panorama is particularly lovely when the light is soft at night, or in the early morning for one of the nearly daily spectacular sunrises.

Practicalities

Far and away the premier **place to stay** in the area, the palm-fringed *Emerald Palms by the Sea* (☎369-2661 or 1-800/688-4752, ⓕ369-2667; ❺) on the highway between Driggs Hill and Congo Town, offers twenty rooms and two suites, all with air conditioning, king or double beds and TV, French doors, wainscoting on the walls and heavy pine furnishings. Diving, snorkelling, swimming, bonefishing, eco-hiking tours and blue-hole swimming are all featured here, as is a guided kayak tour. The dive centre is small, but you can rent equipment there, and there is a tennis court and shuffleboard. Some of the rooms feature tropical decor and two-poster beds.

For **eating**, the best choice is the restaurant at *Emerald Palms*, which serves meals throughout the day ($5-20). Breakfast features huge portions of johnny-cake, French toast, fluffy omelettes and eggs Benedict, while dinner choices include a number of grilled seafood dishes, and the house specialty of crab-stuffed chicken breast. At The Bluff, the locals favour *Big J's Restaurant* which serves up heaps of sheep's tongue souse if you can stand it, along with standards like grits, sausage and eggs, and johnnycake.

In terms of **nightlife**, the only hot spots – and they aren't very hot – are in Driggs Hill. The *Bluebird Club* sports a bar, TV, and a pool table, and the jam-box music can be loud on weekends. Similar is the *Flamingo Club* (☎369-2671), which also has dishes of cracked conch and grilled fish served at the bar.

The king of **bonefishing** guides hereabouts is Stanley Forbes, who runs Jolly Boy Enterprises (☎369-2767) and guides trips for $300 per day.

Kemp's Bay and around

Small, but reasonably lively, with a grocery, marina and a fishing camp, **KEMP'S BAY**, about ten miles south of Congo Town, is only worth stopping for to see its photogenic Conch Shell House, whose limestone walls are covered by hundreds of pink shells. Grouper school offshore in Kemp's Bay, and the fish are manhandled aboard skiffs, cleaned, then shipped off to Nassau to be devoured by tourists.

Deep Creek and **Little Creek**, both tiny fishing villages just past the *Royal Palm Beach*, a wonderful bonefishing centre, look over ocean blue holes. Deep Creek is particularly known for the conch and crab lurking in its waters. Beyond it, a small bridge over the creek leads to Little Creek and *Bair Bahamas Guest House*, overlooking miles of tidal swamp.

South of Deep Creek is the largely nondescript **Pleasant Bay**, notable for its "Slavery Wall", made of limestone and conch about 5ft high. Constructed by slaves in the eighteenth century, it is probably a surviving section of a plantation wall and is currently home to hordes of giant white crabs that make quite a spectacle during mating season.

Practicalities

The best **accommodation** in Kemp's Bay is the *Royal Palm Beach Lodge* (☎369-1608 or 1-800/688-4752, ⓕ369-1934, ⓔRahmings@batelnet.bs), which has ten air-conditioned rooms, a courtyard, palm trees and a small bar and restaurant that features Bahamian fare and is open for three meals a day. There is a modified American plan for meals if you wish. Not fancy, but the place works. Rates are $65–70; add $30–40 for meals. Just south of the bridge at Deep Creek, *Glato's Apartments* (☎369-4669) offers a budget place to put down on South Andros, with six apartments near the beach at about $60.

Big J's on the Bay (☎369-1954), the most popular **place to eat** in Kemp's Bay, has standard dishes like smothered grouper and peas and rice. Both the *Cabana Beach Bar* and *Lewis' Bar* are grungy local hangouts, where you can get a beer and watch locals play dominoes.

At Deep Creek, just north, is Pure Gold Sports (☎357-2007), a good **bone-fish** camp, with two-room suites for guests fronting miles of sandbars and flats. Call for current rates.

△ Sandbars

Mars Bay

With the pastel colours of its stone houses, miles of ocean views, beached schooner offshore, and spreading sapodilla trees, picturesque **MARS BAY**, near the southern end of the line and 25 miles from Driggs Hill, has an air of permanence and spiritual ease. Bonefishing is the name of the game here, but birders come for the tidal flats and offshore cays, as do divers on the run from more mundane experiences. Relax in the square by the large sapodilla tree, or head down to the town dock to watch the locals cleaning and shelling grouper and conch; either is a pleasant way to while away a few hours.

One mile past Mars Bay is the end of the road, where, standing on a dock, you can get a good view of the massive surrounding tidal flats, birds feeding, and a massive sheen on the water at late afternoon that can be quite astonishing. Some people, mainly birders, make the trip by private hired boat (in Mars Bay) over to **Grassy Creek Cays**, a nine-mile journey southeast of the bay. Others ride over to **Big Green Cay**, where one of the world's largest colonies of white-crowned pigeons makes its home twenty miles east of Kemp's Bay. At one time, the cay was home to 20,000 of these pigeons, though the size of the colony has shrunk in recent years as birds have relocated to other cays. The island is currently protected under the Bahamian Wild Birds Act.

Practicalities

Places to stay in Mars Bay are limited, but good enough. *Bair Bahamas Guest House* in Little Creek (℡369-5060, ℻369-4518; ❹) is a three-bedroom inn where you can take meals. **Bonefishing** is also available here, and the inn has two boats and guides. The best place to **eat** in Mars Bay is the *Fisherman's Paradise*, a local Bahamian eatery, where basic meals of grouper and souse cost about $10.

The Biminis and the Berry Islands

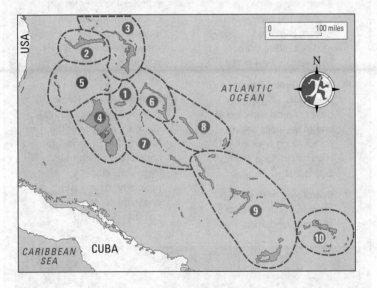

CHAPTER 5

Highlights

✳ **Compleat Angler Hotel**
A can't-miss Alice Town institution; sit down for a lunch surrounded by photos and memorabilia of Ernest Hemingway, who stayed here back in the 1930s. See p.196

✳ **Sport fishing** A major draw for big-time anglers, the nearby Gulf Stream is home to huge marlin, sailfish, dorado and wahoo. See p.198

✳ **Sweet Bimini Bread** This deliciously original bread can be sampled at one of the delis or groceries along the Queen's Highway in Alice Town. See p.201

✳ **Swimming with wild dolphins** Join the folks at Bimini Undersea Adventure for an afternoon cavorting with wild spotted dolphins in the shallow waters just north of North Bimini. See p.197

✳ **Bonefishing** Hire one of Alice Town's knowledgeable and supremely entertaining bonefishing guides and spend the day casting in the mangrove-lined shallows surrounding North Bimini. See p.196

✳ **Mamma Rhoda Rock** This reef system, just off Chub Cay, is one of the finest in the Bahamas for snorkelling owing to its large size, close proximity to land and sheltered southwesterly position. See p.207

The Biminis and the Berry Islands

Bracketing the Andros to the north like dual apostrophes, the **Biminis** and **Berry Islands** are tiny curving remnants of a huge paleo-island that once included all of the Great Bahama Bank, a vast U-shaped platform of limestone indented by the improbably deep Tongue of the Ocean sea-canyon.

Only fifty miles due east of Miami, the Biminis are the closest Bahamian cays to the United States – on a calm night it's possible to see the shimmering glow of Florida's biggest city. Composed of seventeen small, flat islands, the chain occupies a leeward position on the edge of the Great Bahama Bank, which helps explain why the entire eastern (or windward) shore of the two largest islands, **North** and **South Bimini**, are one long white-sand beach. Save perhaps during American college spring break, however, lazing about in the sand is not the main Biminis draw – it's the surrounding waters, and more specifically what's in them, that pulls in the lion's share of visitors. **Divers** and **snorkellers** are attracted to the clear, shallow waters, loaded with colourful reef fish, sunken wrecks and even a few mysterious structures claimed by some

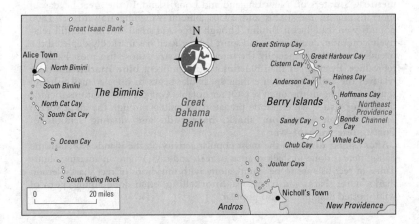

to have come from the lost city of Atlantis. Just as alluring is the opportunity to reel in a record-breaking catch. A favourite casting place of Ernest Hemingway, both the **bonefishing** just off shore and the **deep-sea angling** in the nearby Gulf Stream are world-class, as evidenced by the mass of angling memorabilia hung up in the hotels, restaurants and bars of North Bimini's **Alice Town**.

About 75 miles to the east, due north of Andros and less than forty miles northwest of Nassau, the Berry Islands consist of some fifty small cays and islands, some with rolling hills. Only two of these islands, **Great Harbour Cay** and **Chub Cay**, are inhabited, though, and are rarely visited, despite the exquisite white-sand beaches on most of the northern and eastern shores of each. Save for the South Islands (see p.297), the Berry Islands are among the most difficult of all the Bahamas isles to reach – a fact that brings back the islands' few visitors time and time again.

The Biminis

One popular stylized print shows the **BIMINIS** as seventeen or so small dots against a huge blue background of ocean, while just to the left of each island sweeps a vast brushstroke of deepest turquoise-green. The deeply braided brushstroke represents the Gulf Stream, the lifeblood of the Biminis: without its magical depths the chain could never be called the **Deep-Sea Fishing Capital of the World**. In these deep waters, much to the eternal joy of dedicated anglers, an entire community feeds on plankton and each other in a vast ascending food chain in which the largest predators are large indeed.

The Biminis have built up a sporting industry based on turning the hunters into the hunted. Top prize is the massive **bluefin tuna**, a migratory species that winters in the warm waters of the Gulf Stream before returning in summer to US waters off New England and Long Island. In the great heyday of sport fishing in the 1920s and 1930s, bluefin weighing upwards of 1800 pounds were caught off Bimini. Though large and small bluefin are still relatively common, commercial and sport fishing itself has markedly depleted the overall population, especially the intermediate sizes, those fish most likely to reproduce. Even larger than bluefins, the magnificent **blue marlin** and their relatives the **sailfish** both use their spear-like beaks to impale small fish and squid schooling in the open sea. Other notable Gulf Stream creatures include the **flying fish** – which evade predators by sailing through the air at speeds up to 35mph – **wahoo**, **shark**, **barracuda** and floating schools of **Portuguese men-of-war**.

After fishing, **diving** is the most popular activity on the islands. Much of the diving here is done in shallow areas of reefs and cays, where an amazing abundance of reef fish are to be found, along with squadrons of reef sharks, lemon sharks, nurse sharks and barracuda. **Snorkelling**, often done among pods of wild spotted dolphins, is also popular.

The monk seal

An English traveller to the Bahamas in 1707 wrote "The Bahama Islands are filled with seals. Sometimes the fishers will catch a hundred in a night." The formerly abundant **monk seal** would cavort in masses of up to 500, passing its time basking in the sun, swimming, and diving for food. Columbus had been the first European to describe monk seals, calling them *lobos del mar*, or sea wolves, and he calmly slaughtered eight of the harmless creatures off the coast of Hispaniola in 1494. Over the years, all of these beautiful seals were killed, the oil from their skins often sent off to Jamaica as lubrication for the sugar process – a horrific situation in which a seal species went extinct in the service of human slavery. The last recorded sighting of a monk seal in Bahamian waters was in 1880, and today monk seals survive only in the Hawaiian Islands and in the Mediterranean Sea, though in very small numbers.

Back on land, the main tourist centre in the island chain is **North Bimini**, a flat fishhook-shaped landmass whose slender spine runs nearly seven miles in length before curling back into a wider, marshier stretch dotted with mangrove swamps. Near its southern end sits **Alice Town**, easily the Biminis' largest settlement. Within shouting distance of the town, **South Bimini** is separated from its northern neighbour by a narrow 150-yard-wide ocean channel, and is home to few permanent residents, a tiny international airport amid palmetto-waste flats and a smattering of retirement homes. Busier **North Cat Cay** lies eight miles south of South Bimini. An exclusive resort for the rich and influential, North Cat Cay's other claim to fame occurs every spring in the shallow waters surrounding it, when upwards of 400,000 grouper gather to spawn. Bahamian fishermen follow, at which time a major catch comes about. The **other cays** in the chain are mainly all rocks fringed by sand – suitable to anchor by for a lazy day of uninhibited solitude, but not much else.

If it's solitude that you're after, avoid visiting in mid-March, when college students from across the US arrive to party hard during **spring break**. Late spring and summer are likewise busy, if calmer, due to the large number of fishing tournaments. At these times, hotels are often jammed and reservations, if not made a year in advance, impossible to get. Winter, by contrast, is less crowded and more relaxed, though the weather is cool by Bahamian standards, and the water chilly, divers being required to wear wet suits.

Some history

During the Age of Discovery, the Biminis were of no particular importance to the Spaniards. **Juan Ponce de León** stumbled across the string of islands in 1513 before banging into Florida in his futile search for the Fountain of Youth, but never actually disembarked. Other nameless Spaniards stopped on the Biminis only long enough to enslave the native **Lucayans** living here, transporting them to the nascent gold and silver mines of Hispaniola and Cuba. Beyond these slave expeditions, the only notable visit during this period was made by **Sir Francis Drake**, who halted here in 1586 during one of his West Indian raiding sorties.

It didn't take long for Spanish slavers to strip the chain of Lucayans, and once they did the Biminis were basically forsaken. Since its lack of arable land and tiny freshwater supply created an extremely difficult life, for around two centuries the Biminis were visited only occasionally by wreckers and fishers. In 1835, however, a group of five families of freed slaves made the Biminis their home, a demonstration of both courage and desperation. Legend has it that before they could enter the narrow confines of the inner harbour of what is now **Alice Town**, they had to clear a gauntlet of damaged pirate refuse including cannon, ships' ballast stones, hulls and the like. Four of the salvaged cannon can today be seen on North Bimini, two on the grounds of the *Blue Water Resort* and two in front of *Blue Marlin Cottage*. The primary occupation of the original families was wrecking, though later sponging and fishing joined the list of acceptable ways of making a living.

Life on the Biminis hummed along at this low-key pace until the advent of American **Prohibition** at the beginning of the 1920s, an era that ushered in a boom of smuggling activities, enriching certain businessmen and turning Alice Town into a capital of illegal enterprise. In fact, Alice Town was the main southern jumping-off port – passing through Montreal was the main northern route – for illegal liquor shipments, which headed into the Florida Everglades. The Biminis' fame as a smuggler's den came to an end with the start of the Depression in 1932. It was this crisis that created the opportunity for a Bahamian named **Neville-Norton** to create the sport-fishing industry almost single-handedly. In the mid-1930s, Norton bought a Prohibition-era bar that had fallen on hard times with the repeal of the Volstead Act in 1933, transforming it into the now famous *Bimini Big Game Fishing Club*. Soon, the rich and famous were frequenting the islands, including Martin Luther King Jr and Adam Clayton Powell Jr, a charismatic US Congressman from Harlem, who made the *End of the World Bar* in Alice Town a haunt on his periodic visits to the mistress he kept on the island. The most lasting impression left by a famous visitor, though, is that of **Ernest Hemingway** (see box below). In 1957, an airport was built on South Bimini, opening the door for the tourist infrastructure that exists today.

Old man and the sea

In many ways, the Biminis' truest subtext is that of the legend of **Ernest "Papa" Hemingway**, the great novelist who was also one of America's largest braggarts and he-men. In the mid-1930s, the already famous Hemingway was living life as the kept man of his second wife, Pauline, on Key West. Already having spent much time fishing in the Gulf Stream, he was well on his way towards building his reputation as a master sport fisherman and pursuer of blue marlin. Alice Town and its frontier spirit provided a perfect refuge for the heavy-drinking Hemingway, who would leave wife and children at home for months at a time while he drank, wrote and fished his way around the Gulf Stream.

Stories abound, yet it is true that Hemingway stayed at the *Compleat Angler Hotel*, lived in the *Blue Marlin Cottage* and wrote bits of *To Have and Have Not* – a small, not particularly good novel about a tough-guy smuggler battling the odds – on Bimini. Hemingway also used Bimini as background for another of his lesser novels, *Islands in the Stream*, and he did manage a couple of fistfights on the docks while drunk. "Papa" caught some large marlin and posed for hundreds of photographs, many of which are on display in the bar of the *Compleat Angler*, though a more interesting selection of rare fishing films featuring Hemingway can be seen at the Bimini Museum (see p.196). With a reputation that is larger than life, Hemingway sticks to Alice Town like an overdose of perfume on Ethel Merman.

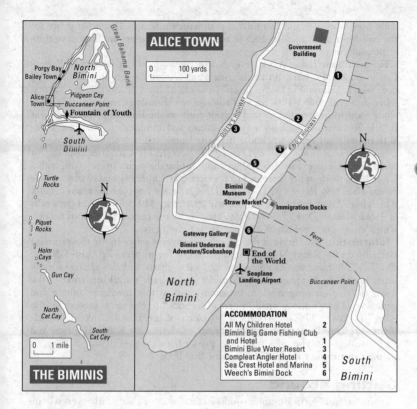

Great Bahama Bank
North Bimini
Porgy Bay
Bailey Town
Pidgeon Cay
Alice Town
Buccaneer Point
Fountain of Youth
South Bimini
Turtle Rocks
Piquet Rocks
Holm Cays
Gun Cay
North Cat Cay
South Cat Cay
THE BIMINIS
0   1 mile

ALICE TOWN

0   100 yards

Government Building

QUEEN'S HIGHWAY
KING'S HIGHWAY

Bimini Museum
Straw Market
Immigration Docks

Gateway Gallery
Bimini Undersea Adventure/Scubashop
End of the World
Seaplane Landing Airport

Ferry

North Bimini

Buccaneer Point

South Bimini

ACCOMMODATION

All My Children Hotel	2
Bimini Big Game Fishing Club and Hotel	1
Bimini Blue Water Resort	3
Compleat Angler Hotel	4
Sea Crest Hotel and Marina	5
Weech's Bimini Dock	6

THE BIMINIS AND THE BERRY ISLANDS | North Bimini

North Bimini

Surprisingly enough, tiny **NORTH BIMINI** is, after New Providence, the most densely settled Bahamian island, its 600 permanent residents crammed onto a narrow strip of land on the southern tip barely wide enough for three city blocks. For years, almost nothing has changed about North Bimini simply because there is little room for growth and because most of the native coppice has been long since chopped down. If the persistent rumours of plans to construct a huge 25-storey hotel and casino complex near Paradise Point on Bimini Bay ever bear fruit, the character of North Bimini will undoubtedly change greatly. Until then, **Alice Town** will continue to be the hub of activity and the island should remain what it has been for some time, a **fishing** and **diving** destination with a considerable – and deserved – reputation.

Arrival and orientation

Though most visitors to the Biminis arrive via South Biminis' international airport (see p.201), it's possible to pull into North Bimini via Alice Town's inner harbour, either at the **Seaplane Landing** or at the **Immigration Docks**. The former is used mainly by Pan Am Air Bridge (☎347-3024 or 1-800/424-2557), which maintains a fleet of seventeen-passenger seaplanes that depart daily from Watson Island Terminal near downtown Miami. Round-trip fare for the half-hour flight is around $200, and baggage allowances are limited to thirty pounds per passenger.

The **mailboat** *Bimini Mack* serves North Bimini (and Cat Cay) from Potter's Cay in Nassau. Be warned that the ride from Nassau, though only costing $45, does take a minimum of twelve hours – and often longer. It also sails to a varying schedule, so call ℡393-1064 for a schedule of weekly sailings, and be sure to bring along food and water. The official port of entry to the Biminis by **private boat** is Alice Town, where yachts must pass customs and immigration. There are several **marinas** from which to choose here, the largest and best equipped being the *Bimini Big Game Fishing Club and Hotel* (℡347-3391, VHF Ch 68; see opposite for room details). The marina has 100 slips and can handle yachts up to 100ft, with a fee of $1.25 per foot per day, plus $15 for electricity. Other marinas nearby include *Bimini Blue Water Resort* (℡347-3166, VHF Ch 68; see opposite for room details), which has 32 slips available at 75¢ per day (electricity $10 per day), and the smaller *Weech's Bimini Dock* (℡347-3028; VHF Ch 18; see opposite for room details), which charges 60¢ per day ($7.50 per day for electricity).

Information is available at the government tourist office in the Government Building on the King's Highway in north Alice Town (Mon–Fri 9am–5.30pm; ℡347-3529). Here you can get maps and a few charts, and also arrange for the services of local historian Ashley Saunders, who leads a **walking tour** of the town ($10), dispensing wisdom on such topics as folk medicine, fishing and genealogy. There's also a small information booth in the straw market on the King's Highway. The only **bank** is a branch of the Royal Bank of Canada (Mon–Fri 9am–1pm), located in the centre of town at the King's Highway and Parliament Street. The dreadfully slow **post office** (Mon–Fri 9am–5.30pm) is by the tourist office in the Government Building.

Getting around

Getting around North Bimini is simple in that you can walk nearly everywhere. There are no rental car agencies on the island, nor need there be, but **golf carts** are available ($40–60 per day) from a number of vendors in Alice Town; these include Capt Pat Rolle's Golf Cart Rental (℡347-3477), Surf Golf Cart Rental (℡347-2438) and All My Children Golf Cart Rental (℡347-3344). **Bicycles** can be rented at Bimini Undersea Adventure (℡347-3089) and South Bimini Yacht Club (℡347-4444), usually for about $20 a day. Bimini Rentals (℡347-3400) and Sawyer's Scooter Rental (℡347-2555) will let you have a **moped** for about $10 per hour. A final transportation option is the red **Bimini Bus**, which cruises mainly up and down the King's Highway. To hop a ride, just flag it down and name your destination – fares are usually around $3.

Two **water taxi** services operate between North and South Bimini. TSL Water Taxi hauls passengers from its dock just south of the mailboat dock for $3 per person. PHK Water Taxi takes passengers from the North Bimini mail dock to South Bimini as well. Neither service has an established regular schedule, but passengers are numerous and taxis run regularly. You should never have more than a twenty-minute wait at either end.

Accommodation

There are under 200 **hotel** rooms on North Bimini, with few budget or self-catering options to choose from, and during the busiest periods – particularly spring, summer and around Christmas and New Year's – it's likely you'll have a hard time finding a room, regardless of price.

Admiral Hotel Bailey Town ☏ 347-2347. Inexpensive by Bimini standards, the two dozen air-conditioned rooms here are used mainly by visiting Bahamians. Doubles, suites and some small efficiency apartments are available. ❸

All My Children Hotel King's Highway, Alice Town ☏ 347-3334. Named for the owner's children (not the popular American soap opera), this plain hotel features modern rooms without much lustre, though all are a decent size and feature good bathrooms. There are some cheaper rooms at an old "inn" next door – basically a run-down house – and a self-catering suite is also available. Better deals are available elsewhere, though in a pinch a night or two here will do. ❸–❺, suite ❽

Bimini Bay Guest House 3.5 miles north of Alice Town ☏ 347-2171. Located on a superb piece of land on a headland overlooking the Gulf Stream – the nearby beach stretches for two miles; developers are hoping to soon rip this establishment down and throw up a mega-resort and casino in its place. For now, the old hotel is a treasure trove of atmospheric Art Deco, though it sadly is quite run-down. The eighteen rooms in the main house are by far the best, with breezy patios and bay windows, and you should avoid being put up in the wooden annex at all costs. There are also six rather dismal free-standing apartments for rent nearby. ❸–❹ weekdays, ❹–❺ weekends, ❽ for apartments

Bimini Big Game Fishing Club and Hotel King's Highway, Alice Town ☏ 347-3391 or 1-800/737-1007, ℱ 347-3392. This Bacardi-run hotel is perhaps the finest accommodation on the cay for those planning a trip around deep-sea fishing and diving. The excellent marina gives quick access to the sea, and the majority of guests are here doing one or the other, meaning there's a nice sportive vibe in the air. Most rooms, all of which have tiled floors and either bay or garden views, are in the main building, though there are a few two-person cottages with grills dotted about the property. Amenities include an assortment of fine bars and restaurants, tennis courts, a swimming pool and lots of watersports options. ❻, cottages ❽

Bimini Blue Water Resort King's Highway, Alice Town ☏ 347-3166 or 1-800/688-4752, ℱ 347-3293. Frequented mainly by anglers, past guests of the *Blue Water* include Hemingway and Mike Lerner, one of the Biminis' most famous fishermen (see p.196). Lerner's old home, now named the *Anchorage*, holds a dozen plainly decorated, but still comfortable rooms with balconies. Rooms in the newer extension are more like motel rooms and less desirable. The *Marlin Cottage*, a three-bedroom house where Hemingway wrote a bit, is also available for rent ($285 a night). The on-site restaurant is excellent (see p.199), as is the friendly bar. ❹–❻, Marlin Cottage ❽

Compleat Angler Hotel King's Highway, Alice Town ☏ 347-3122, ℱ 347-3293. The Biminis' most famous hotel reeks of historic atmosphere. Portions of wooden outer building are made from Prohibition-era rum barrels, fishing knick-knacks are everywhere, and, of course, Hemingway drank, fought and wrote portions of *To Have and Have Not* in Room 1. The dozen rooms are decidedly simple, and the bathrooms cramped, though most guests don't seem to mind. The wildly popular bar is typically heaving, so look elsewhere if you find the idea of live music and caterwauling late into the night disturbing. Guests can use the pool at the *Bimini Blue Water Resort*, which is run by the same owners, and also book fishing charters on site. ❸

Dun's Bayfront Apartments King's Highway, Alice Town ☏ 347-2093. Five simple self-catering apartments offering pretty basic accommodation with a small kitchen, living room, and private bath. Given the location downtown, noise can be a problem, but the units are clean. ❸

Ellis Cottages Porgy Bay ☏ 347-2483. Three cottages in a village one mile north of Alice Town, each with full kitchen and living room. The cottages are handy to nearby food stores and local restaurants, and there is a private dock on the bay. Cheaper rates for long stays. ❹

Sea Crest Hotel and Marina King's Highway, Alice Town ☏ 347-3071, ℱ 347-3495. A pale-yellow three-storey hotel, each room featuring pleasantly tiled floors, cable TV and a balcony with good views, especially in the high-ceilinged rooms on the third floor. There are eleven rooms, with one two-bedroom suite and one three-bedroom suite available. No hotel restaurant or bar, but *Captain Bob's* (see p.199) is downstairs. ❹, suites ❽

Weech's Bimini Dock King's Highway, Alice Town ☏ 347-3028, ℱ 347-3508. The four walk-up rooms at Weech's Dock are clean and big, with bay views through plate-glass windows. Near the action at the marina, *Weech's* also offers a single efficiency apartment with small kitchen. Sunrise is great from these accommodations. ❸, apartment ❺

Alice Town

Essentially two blocks wide, **ALICE TOWN** condenses the Bahamian experience – sun, fishing, food and music – into a diminutive yet dynamic area. The town's main drag, the narrow King's Highway, is home to most of the action, lined with hotels, bars and shops. Running parallel to the King's Highway, and two blocks west, is the Queen's Highway, less a highway than a quiet narrow street that fronts a tranquil beach.

Start your wanderings at its most famous building, the **Compleat Angler Hotel**, right at the heart of the King's Highway. Built in the 1930s, the twelve-room hotel is celebrated for its collection of Hemingway memorabilia – the writer stayed here between 1935 and 1937 – and the bar-lounge is known as the **Ernest Hemingway Museum**. The lounge's dark-panelled walls are hung with photographs of Ernest Hemingway in every conceivable pose, especially those involving proud displays with freshly caught fish. The downstairs lounge has a collection of art prints of Hemingway, and the library has a good selection of first editions of his works. If you're looking for quiet introspection when visiting the museum, come early, as the bar turns boisterous quickly once the sun sets.

A short walk from here is the **Bimini Museum**, where visitors can wander in for free and gaze at the photos of most of the big-game sport fishermen who made Bimini famous, and some of their stuffed catch. Also included in the collection are some rare films of Hemingway himself cavorting on the docks and streets of Alice Town in the 1930s and a number of photographs and other artefacts illustrating Bimini history. The museum contains the Bimini Fishing Hall of Fame whose inductees include Skip Farrington, who recorded the first blue marlin catch off Bimini back in 1933, alongside other local angling legends like Mike Lerner and Neville Stuart, and guides Eric Sawyer, Manny Rolle, Bob Smith and Sammy Ellis.

At the far southern end of Alice Town are the remains of the old **Bimini Bay Rod and Gun Club**, destroyed by the 1926 hurricane that looms large in Bimini folklore. The club isn't much, some ruins, a staircase and an abandoned pool, but it has a certain cachet considering this was a jazz-era hot spot.

North of Alice Town

Towards Alice Town's north end, the King's and Queen's highways merge, then run along a waterfront through the small villages of **Bailey Town** and **Porgy Bay.** In these two small villages live the majority of North Bimini's year-round residents, and though there are no real sights here, there are a number of local restaurants and shops that make for worthwhile diversions. Another three miles on, the road turns to dirt and runs north to **Paradise Point** where the sparkling white beach is excellent for picnicking and snorkelling. Offshore lies the enigmatic Bimini Road (see box opposite). To the east, across the **upper lagoon**, are mangrove shallows and swamps, haunts of bonefish, and the place where guides will lead fishermen for the elusive trophy fish. At the site of the *Bimini Bay Hotel*, a chain bars further access to the dirt road.

Diving and watersports

Easily the most popular outdoor activity on the Biminis is **fishing**, for which it is world-renowned; we've covered all the angling opportunities in detail on the

The road to Atlantis?

Located not far off Paradise Point, opposite the *Bimini Bay Hotel*, is the **Bimini Road**. The "road" consists of rows of limestone blocks constructed in a U shape some 20ft below the water's surface, standing on square pillars that allow the tide to flow underneath. Aerial surveys show that just a few hundred feet southwest of the site a level limestone bench has been "cleared" as well. Although New Agers enjoy claiming the "road" was built by the lost civilization of **Atlantis**, extensive surveys of the site have concluded that there is a link between the stonecutting techniques and those of the Mayan and Incan empires of Central and South America. This connection has led to speculation that the "road" was actually a dry-dock onto which ships were hauled for caulking and refitting.

Just north of Bimini, the **Moselle Shoal** presents another supposedly mysterious site for divers to investigate. The shoals are the site of underwater blocks of granite, which some theorists insist are the remnants of a lost civilization, perhaps again that of Atlantis. One explorer-author, Richard Wingate, has written *The Lost Outpost of Atlantis*, in which he describes evidence of human engineering in the blocks, like drill holes. Some less sanguine theorists have concluded that the granite blocks are ballast from galleons.

box overleaf. **Diving** and **snorkelling**, though, are also justly popular reasons for visiting. Besides the slightly contrived trips out to the Bimini Road and Moselle Shoal (see box above), much of the diving here is done in shallow waters, near and around the shallow reefs and cays found in abundance just offshore. On almost every trip into the water, swirling schools of reef fish and a wide variety of coral formations can be spotted, along with nurse sharks and barracuda. There's also an array of wreck dives, including the *Sapona*, an old rum-running vessel that sank during the huge 1926 hurricane – it now provides a hulk visible from the surface (making it popular with snorkellers too), almost totally covered by coral, harbouring juvenile jacks. The top Biminis **dive shop**, run by Bill and Knowdla Keefe, is Alice Town's Bimini Undersea Adventure (T 347-3089 or 1-800/348-4644, F 347-3079, W www.biminiundersea.com), catering to everyone from dive masters to those looking to get PADI-certified. Their most intriguing trip is a deep-wall dive off the Gulf Stream that the staff claim is straight out of the movie *The Abyss*.

Bimini Undersea is also the best snorkelling outfit around, visiting many of the same reefs the divers do (trips cost around $25). Even more exciting, though, are the **wild spotted dolphin encounters** they run several times a week ($110, kids $70). It takes about an hour to reach the dolphin grounds, and if the pod is encountered snorkellers then get to swim and play side by side with the curious creatures. Encounters with the wild pod are common, though not guaranteed, so if the thought of spending up to five hours circling about the ocean without any luck is overly vexatious, don't sign up.

Those wishing to rent a **kayak** may do so from Bimini Undersea Adventure for around $30 per day, along with a variety of sailboards and two-person kayaks. TLS Water Taxi at the mailboat dock (VHF Ch 68) will take visitors out for a **sunset or moonlight cruise**.

There's a reason the Biminis are considered by many to be one of the world's top **sport-fishing destinations**. For starters, the mangrove flats on the eastern part of North Bimini are incredibly productive bonefishing areas. And, more often than not, anglers seeking tuna, wahoo, sailfish and marlin out in the deep Gulf Stream come back home with at least a decent-sized fish. And lest you think that Bimini fishing is more hype that fact, consider that more than fifty **world records** have been established by catches in the surrounding waters, including those in the categories of marlin, sailfish, bonito, wahoo, mackerel, tuna, barracuda, shark and grouper. The largest marlin caught was a 1060-pound specimen landed in 1979, and a massive 16-pound bonefish catch has been documented.

Because of the intense fishing pressure and overcrowded hotels during fishing **tournaments**, it's probably best to organize your fishing expedition around them. There are nearly a dozen big tournaments every year. The biggest of the bunch are the Annual Bacardi Billfish Tournament in March hosted by the Bimini Big Game Fishing Club, the Annual Midwinter Wahoo Tournament in February, the Bimini Open Angling Tournament in September, and the Bimini Festival of Champions in May.

Anglers who do not have their own **gear** can rent it at several tackle shops or hotels, and every guide can provide tackle and gear for the cost of a day's charter, which averages about $400 per person, $300 half/day, plus tip for the captain and crew.

Deep-sea fishing

Numerous charter boats are available for those who want to go out in the Gulf Stream and after the big pelagic specimens, sailfish, marlin, large wahoo and dolphinfish. We've listed some of the best guides – and their boats – below. The cost to charter with individual guides varies with the kind of expedition being mounted and the number of people tagging along. But count on paying at least $300/400 half/full day for the cost of boat, guide, gear, and snacks. Sometimes, drinks are extra, but bait is always included. On full-day trips, guides usually provide a lunch of sandwiches. It is always best to try to work out as many details of your trip as possible in advance, including your idea of tips, the members of the crew, and the location of your fishing grounds.

In addition to the guides listed below, the major **marinas** all charter vessels with a captain and mate with gear included. Bimini Big Game Fishing Club, Bimini Blue Water Marina, and Weech's Bimini Dock, will charter your trip for around $400–550 half-day, $750–900 full day. Weech's also rents some smaller Boston Whalers around $135 a day/$75 half-day. On South Bimini the Bimini Sands Marina (☎347-3028, ⊛www.bimini.com) is a new 35-slip marina where you can rent a 15ft whaler for $140 per day.

Eating

All of the major hotels, save for *Sea Crest*, have worthwhile **restaurants**, most featuring basic Bahamian fare, seafood, and American specialties, though a few have slightly more eclectic European entrees. Those looking for a faster, cheaper meal have several options as well, with **carry-out** joints located throughout Alice Town, Bailey Town and Porgy Bay, including a classic *Burger Queen*, where you can get a "Little Whopper" without fear of violating trademark laws. If heading out for a dive or snorkel, note that most of the restaurants below will gladly put together a **packed lunch** at a reasonable rate.

Captain Frank Hinzey ☎347-3072, *Nina*, 28ft Bertram
Captain Bob Smith ☎347-2367, *Miss Bonita II*, 51ft Hatteras
Captain Jerome Stuart ☎347-2081, *Nuttin Honey*, 32ft Bertram
Captain Tony Stuart ☎347-2656, *Sir Tones*, 51ft Hatteras

Bonefishing

While deep-sea, or pelagic, fishing is a great draw because of its dramatic essence, **bonefishing** remains popular on North Bimini, and the island boasts a number of the Bahamas' best-known, most informative fishing guides. The fishing guides – known by their first names – listed below are available for angling throughout what are known as the "flats", and in general rates are about $175–250 half/full day, though there are some less experienced guides around who may charge less. Keep in mind that you'll need to bring tackle and that you should always negotiate a complete price before setting off, knowing in advance who is responsible for fuel, food, ice, beer and bait. Most skiffs hold two anglers and a guide, and part of the fun of going out with these guides is their patter, a stream of fishing information, lore, and tall tale that is infectious. There are swarms of mosquitoes in eastern Bimini, so take plenty of repellant and wear long sleeves if necessary.

Bonefish Ansil ☎347-2178
Bonefish Cordell ☎347-2576
Bonefish Ebbie ☎347-2053
Bonefish George ☎347-2198
Bonefish Jackson ☎347-2315
Bonefish Ray ☎347-3391
Bonefish Rudy ☎347-2266
Bonefish Tommy ☎347-3234

Reef and bottom fishing

While bonefishing and deep-sea **fishing** are the "meat and potatoes" of Bimini lore, reef and bottom fishing on Bimini are just as productive and far less expensive. Fishing with bait for amberjack, grouper and snapper is a cheaper thrill than the big-time Gulf Stream experience, and you can hire a little 15ft whaler and a local guide, and have some fun for about $200, plus fuel and lunch. If lucky enough to catch some fish, you can take them back to your hotel and ask the cook to grill the fillets. Note that even for simple reef or bottom fishing, you should try to bring your own equipment.

Anchorage Dining Room *Bimini Blue Water Resort*, King's Highway, Alice Town ☎347-3122. Elegant panelled dining overlooking the entire harbour. Unpretentious main courses include conch, fried chicken, New York sirloin steak, and a good spiny broiled lobster. It's good value (lunch is about $5–10; dinner $12–25) and a nice experience eating on the "hill". Come early to enjoy a cocktail at the bar.

Bimini Bay Restaurant *Bimini Bay Guest House* (p.195) ☎347-2171. Worth the trip for the pleasant ocean view, this hotel restaurant a couple of miles north of Alice Town serves three meals a day, plus an afternoon tea at 3–6pm. Breakfasts are large, featuring French toast and egg platters, while lunches feature sandwiches, seafood salads, and burgers. Dinner typically is locally caught seafood at around $12–20 per entree.

Captain Bob's King's Highway (opposite the *Sea Crest Hotel*) ☎347-3260. At times it can seem as if the entire cay has come here for the renowned early-bird breakfasts, including a delightful fish omelette and superb French toast made from delicious sweet Bimini bread. Lunch is worthwhile as well, featuring ribs, burgers and fresh fish. Open for breakfast (6.30am) and lunch only. Closed Tues.

CJ's Deli Alice Town. A cubby-hole fast-food joint off the docks where you can plop on an orange stool at the bar and savour what's alleged to be the best conch salad on the island, along with a decent sausage and egg breakfast. Closed for dinner.

The Compleat Angler *Compleat Angler Hotel,* King's Highway, Alice Town ☏347-3122. The centre of action for partygoers and fishermen, with live music several nights a week and a menu that includes locally caught fish, steaks, and the ubiquitous peas 'n' rice.

The Gulfstream Restaurant *Bimini Big Game Fishing Club and Hotel,* King's Highway, Alice Town ☏347-3391. The most expensive place in town to eat (entrees $13–26), and arguably the best, *The Gulfstream* is housed in a curved room that ends in the hotel swimming pool, with bright murals decorating the walls. Freshly caught kingfish is a specialty, but there are a number of other good seafood dishes available, including a fine Bahamian gumbo and smoked fish, along with prime rip and lamb chops for those who've had their fill on fish. On some nights, acoustic guitar accompanies dining. Reservations recommended. 7.30–10am & 7–10pm; closed Jan to mid-Feb.

Honey Bun's Bailey Town. Tiny locals' joint just north of Bailey Town, offering burgers and conch dishes at rock-bottom prices.

The New Fishermen's Paradise Alice Town ☏347-3082. Simple restaurant located next to the Pan Am Air Bridge dock, which serves local-style soups and wonderful sandwiches without frills. Daily 7–11am, noon–3pm & 6–10pm.

New Red Lion Pub King's Highway, Alice Town ☏347-3259. Run by Dolores "LaLa" Saunders, this dinner-only pub has a terrific ambience and equally good food. The stuffed Shrimp Delight is a must-try (large shrimp stuffed with conch and fish), but the barbecue ribs are wonderful too, cooked on a brick grill in back. Tues–Sun 6–11pm.

Sandra's Restaurant and Bar King's Highway, Alice Town ☏347-2336. Located in north Alice Town, *Sandra's* is good for no-nonsense Bahamian meals and snacks, including fried grouper, snapper and conch, peas 'n' rice, corn on the cob, macaroni and cheese and simple desserts.

Drinking and nightlife

Nightlife and **drinking** constitute a large part of the lifeblood of the Biminis, and sooner or later everybody passes everybody else doing the rounds of bars and clubs up and down the King's Highway. The centres of activity are the major hotel bars, including those at the *Compleat Angler,* and the *Bimini Big Game Fishing Club and Hotel,* especially its *Barefoot Bar* and *Harbour Lounge.* Perhaps the most notorious nightspot is the *End of the World Bar* near the Seaplane Landing (open until 3am; ☏347-2094), with its sand-covered floors, underwear-hung rafters, and boisterous clientele. A combination bar and tourist sight, the *End of the World* comes most alive after midnight. If looking for a quieter drink, head to Alice Town's "mid-town" area and look out for the *Island House Bar* (11am–3am; ☏347-2439) across from the *New Red Lion Pub,* and *Bimini Breeze,* just down the street. **Bailey Town** sports a few hangouts popular with locals, including *Specialty Paris* near the Anglican church, which often has local rake 'n' scrape music. You can **dance** late on weekends at the *All My Children Hotel,* as well as *Fisherman's Paradise* (0347–3220).

Shopping

The major **shops** on North Bimini are all clustered along the King's Highway in Alice Town. The best place to find authentic **folk art and crafts** is the Gateway Art Gallery (☏347-3131), near Bimini Undersea Adventure in south Alice Town not far from the Seaplane Landing. Located upstairs in the Burns House Building, the gallery sells conch-shell jewellery, locally hand-sculpted figurines depicting Bahamian life and a selection of Bahamian CDs. The **straw market**, located under the arch with the official welcome sign to Bimini in the middle of Alice Town, features crafts as well, but these may be imported, so beware. Nevertheless, it's a fun place to hang out. One of the real buys in Bimini is **fresh bread**, which is justly famous. Try Pritchard's Grocery on the Queen's Highway, allegedly the birthplace of the sweet Bimini bread.

South Bimini

To a large extent, tiny **SOUTH BIMINI**, a five-minute water taxi from Alice Town, is a tangle of tropical hardwoods, low native coppice, and mangrove swamps, some of which can be explored by kayak. The majority of visitors, though, are here to explore the waters surrounding the isle, either diving or fishing while staying at one or the other of two hotels. Yachters pull in as well, docking at either the **South Bimini Yacht Club** (☎347-4444, VHF Ch 68) or the **Bimini Beach Club and Marina** (☎347-3500, VHF Ch 68).

If arriving via the public water taxi, you'll be deposited at the ferry dock at **Buccaneer Point**, from which a road leads south down the western, more developed edge of the island. The road ultimately leads to **Port Royal**, a fancy name for a resort complex of homes owned mostly by wealthy Americans who jet or boat over for long weekend excursions. Running beside the road, almost the entire length of the west coast, is a fine, white-sand **beach**, open to the public; if you are looking for shade, head for the southern end where there's a tiny thatched hut. Bring your water toys along as the **snorkelling** opportunities off the west coast are very good. Near Buccaneer Point, the clear water is good at high tide, when huge numbers of fish, along with eel and octopus, congregate in the shallows. Farther south, around the thatched hut, the water is about 15ft deep and clear as a bell. You can see every reef fish imaginable, along with spotted eagle rays and a few barracuda. Even farther south is **Corner Reef**, whose flats are easy to snorkel, and often reveal rays, crabs, octopus and eels, along with starfish and echinoderms.

Back at the water taxi dock, a second road heads east to the international airport two miles away, and, amazingly, runs through some of the best-preserved **native coppice** on all the Bahamas islands. About midway between the airport and the water-taxi dock is a "must see" – or at least that's what the sign on the road proclaims – the **Fountain of Youth**. As the only sight on the island, it's pretty pathetic, a shallow mud hole with a couple of benches in the shade.

Practicalities

South Bimini's **airport** is serviced by Bimini Island Air (Fort Lauderdale ☎954/938-8991), Island Air Charters (Fort Lauderdale ☎954/359-9942 or 1-800/444-9904), Major's Air (Freeport ☎352-5778), Sky Unlimited (Nassau ☎347-4029) and Taino Air (Freeport ☎347-4033). If heading straight to North Bimini, a minibus service heads from the airport to the ferry for a transfer to Alice Town ($12 total); the trip, though, can take anywhere up to a couple of hours depending on the water-taxi situation in Alice Town.

Getting around South Bimini is easy. Shuttles wait for arriving flights and deliver you to one of the two hotels or the water taxi to North Bimini for $3. **Bikes** can be rented at the South Bimini dock for about $12 per half-day, and you can ride the circuit around South Bimini on a combination of paved and dirt roads in about two hours.

There are only two **accommodation** options on South Bimini, both of them rather expensive. Off Tiki Hut Beach sits the new *Bimini Sands* (☎357-

3500 or 9134, 🖰 www.bimini.com; ❽), home to a marina with room for 35 yachts. Though future plans call for a huge rambling hotel, the only land-based options currently available are ten guest homes, each with full kitchens and patios with good views. The one- and two-bedroom homes, which require a four-night minimum stay, rent on a weekly basis for $750/1550 respectively. Guests also have access to a bar, golf cart and wave-runner rentals, volleyball court and the decent *Petite Conch* **restaurant**. There is also a water-taxi service to North Bimini for guests ($5). For self-catering, one can stock up on groceries at Morgan's Grocery Store and Morgan's Liquor Store nearby. The other overnight option is the *Bimini Beach Club and Marina* in Port Royal (☎ 347-3500, 🖰 bimini@gate.net; ❻), a pleasant motel-style marina built around an L-shaped saltwater swimming pool, with a good lounge and restaurant. The forty rooms are air-conditioned and have rattan furniture, private bath and TV. You can arrange diving and fishing trips through the hotel. Non-guests will want to try the services of the tiny **Scuba Bimini** (☎ 347-4444), with offices in the South Bimini Yacht Club. The operation has two boats and operates a number of one and two-tank dives, averaging $65 per person. Specialty dives are available.

Gun Cay and North Cat Cay

About nine miles south of Bimini Harbour, which curves under South Bimini, is the uninhabited **GUN CAY**, an isolated rocklet known for its excellent fishing, and much visited by boaters. Gun Cay has no facilities, but there is an exquisite stretch of curved sand known as **Honeymooon Bay**. Yachters in the know often anchor off the bay to enjoy its isolation and excellent snorkelling.

One mile southeast of Gun Cay is the larger **NORTH CAT CAY**, a privately owned island purchased in 1931 by the late Louis Wasey as a secluded getaway for himself and his rich friends. Over the years, the club that they formed became the haunt of industrialists, politicians and Hollywood stars, and the cay basically remains the preserve of the **Cat Cay Yacht Club** (☎ 347-3565). Only members and their guests stay at the six-room hotel, or at one of the more than seventy private villas that sit on lush lots on the western and northeastern rims of the island, all surrounded by palms, hibiscus and bougainvillea. Guest have access to a pool, fine beaches and a nine-hole golf course.

About the only way to visit North Cat Cay without being a member or guest of the club is to tie up at the Yacht Club's marina (☎ 347-3565, VHF Ch 16), a relatively new 82-slip facility that's home to the *Cone Bar and Victoria Restaurant*. The marina slips have cable TV hookups, water and electricity, and there's also a small grocery and liquor store; dockage is $1.50 per foot per day and there is a two-day maximum stay. The marina is also a **port of entry** (Mon–Fri 9.30am–5pm). For what it's worth, the Nassau mailboat *Bimini Mack* does call at North Cat Cay on its way to South Bimini, so if you want a quick peak, you can get it by taking the mailboat from Nassau to North Bimini (see p.194).

The Berry Islands

Wholly characteristic of the raised edges of the Great Bahama Bank, the fifty or so mostly uninhabited cays of the **BERRY ISLANDS** form a J-shaped archipelago stretching some 32 miles from north to south. Directly to the south of the Berry chain is the deep Tongue of the Ocean, while all of the territory west is part of the shallow Great Bahama Bank.

The Berrys share several characteristics with the Biminis, including secluded **beaches**, amazing **angling opportunities** and spectacular reefs tailor-made for **snorkelling** and **diving**. Still, the Berrys have far more successfully managed to escape development; indeed, though the southernmost point in the chain is located only 35 miles northeast of Nassau, the cays remain surprisingly isolated.

Over half of the 800 or so permanent residents on the Berry Islands live on the largest island, **Great Harbour Cay**. Located at the northern end of the entire chain, it's still only around ten miles long and no more than one mile wide, deeply indented by a number of salty inlets and lakes. Often referred to simply as "the settlement", the Berrys' largest town, **Bullock's Harbour**, sits on a narrow self-contained cay off the leeward northern edge of Great Harbour Cay, while across a causeway is the chain's largest resort, **Tropical Diversions**. Because nearly the entire leeward edge of Great Harbour Cay is one long sand beach – a practically deserted paradise for sunbathers and snorkellers – *Tropical Diversions* has access to some of the best frontage in all the Bahamas.

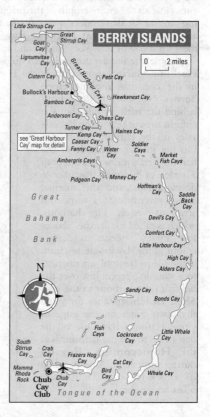

The only other island that can boast anything near a steady stream of visitors is swampy **Chub Cay**, dangling off the southern edge of the chain. On it sits the islands' only other tourist resort, **Chub Cay Club and Marina**, a semi-private resort that boasts the islands' best fishing possibilities.

Several of the remaining cays are privately owned, including two small bumps north of Great Harbour known as the **Stirrup Cays** (Great and Little) – the private province of customers of the Norwegian and Royal Caribbean cruise lines. The rest are home to birds and not much else, and though the idea of sailing out to anchor by one may sound compelling, it's quite unnecessary – even on the Berrys'"populated" cays, solitude is easy to find.

Great Harbour Cay

GREAT HARBOUR CAY guards the northern end of the Berrys chain and is home to around 500 Berry islanders, most of whom live in the sole major settlement of **Bullock's Harbour**, located on its own island separated from the rest of Great Harbour Cay by a narrow causeway. The village is a rundown sort of place, sporting a couple of grocery stores and some small Bahamian restaurants, along with lots of wandering chickens, bantam roosters and peacocks. The town is certainly scruffy, but has its own lackadaisical charm, though you would not need to spend much time here as a rule. Across the causeway to the south is the **Tropical Diversions Resort and Marina**, formerly the *Great Harbour Cay Yacht Club* whose past guests include Brigitte Bardot and Cary Grant. Travellers flock here today not for the star power but mainly for the opportunity to land a load of fish and to play golf on the small attached course.

Beyond here lies the best part of Great Harbour Cay, the **east shore**, made up of eight miles of nearly uninterrupted white beach. A long paved highway runs close to the entire length of the magnificently sandy shore, making searching around for that perfect spot quite simple. To the north lies **Sugar Beach** and in the south, **Great Harbour Bay** holds two grand scallops of sand, all ideal for a day of sun-worshipping and splashing about.

To some, the slender cut with cliffs on both sides where one enters the **Great Harbour Marina**, south of Bullock's Harbour, is one of the prettiest harbours in the Bahamas, rivalling Hope Town's. Not only is the terrain behind the harbour hilly, but the cliffs in the cut set off the boundaries of the harbour beautifully. On the southeastern side of the harbour's tranquil waters are both a series of beautiful townhouse developments, and the marina, which plays host to a wonderful array of vessels. The harbour, which is called locally the "Bay of Five Pirates", seems to change colour as the day progresses, from light blue to tranquil aquamarine, to a stunning green. Just over the hill from the harbour to the east, **Shell Beach** stretches for more than two miles on the edge of Great Harbour Bay. One of the best times to see the harbour is at the **Homecoming Regatta** during the end of August, when it's chock-full of colourful sailboats and yachts.

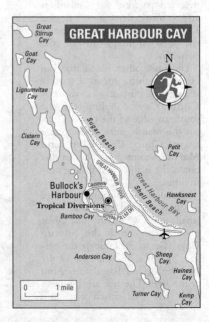

Diving and watersports

Though not as potentially memorable as Gulf Stream angling off the Bimini chain, **deep-sea fishing** here is still top-notch, with possible catches including billfish, dolphinfish, king mackerel and wahoo. Reef fishing and light-tackle bottom fishing is also good as yellowtail, snapper, barracuda, triggerfish and grouper are all present. And the bonefishing here – particularly around Shark Creek, which separates the main body of Great Harbour Cay from its southern cays – is likewise superb. The centre for angling information is the beautifully situated **Great Harbour Marina** (T 367-8005, F 367-8115, VHF Ch 16 and 68). Guides running out of the marina include Percy Darvill and Revis Anderson. Contact them both at the marina on T 367-8119 and expect to pay $350/500 for half/full-day trips. Also in the marina, the eclectic Happy People Rentals (T 367-8117) hire out bonefishing skiffs, fishing rods and tackle, along with jeeps, bicycles, golf clubs and snorkelling gear. As there are **no professional diving or snorkelling services** on Great Harbour Cay, heading out is a do-it-yourself affair. Happy People Rentals, though, is a good place to begin accumulating information on local reefs.

Practicalities

Getting to Great Harbour Cay requires some advance planning. Adventurous souls may try the **mailboat** route: the sea voyage aboard MV *Champion II* leaves Potter's Cay (see p.25) on Thursday evening at 8pm, though this schedule is subject to change, so call the dock (T 393-1064) in Nassau for the latest information. As far as **flights** go, Cat Island Air (T 361-8021) run daily trips from Nassau to Great Harbour Cay for approximately $50; return flights from Great Harbour Cay to Nassau are much longer as they go by way of the Abacos. Charter services include Freeport's Major's Air Service (T 352-5778), Cleare Air (T 377-0341) and Cat Island Air (T 361-8021), the latter two flying out of Nassau. Guests of *Tropical Diversions* often take Tropical Diversions Air (T 954/921-9084), who run puddle-jumper flights from Fort Lauderdale, and also get free transportation to and from the airport. Trans-Island Air (T 954/434-5271), operating out of Fort Lauderdale, is a another charter possibility to both Great Harbour Cay and Chub Cay.

Getting around Great Harbour Cay is pretty simple. A single well-paved road, Great Harbour Drive, runs north to south for about four miles along the eastern shore. Royal Palm Drive leads from *Tropical Diversions* resort, through the golf course, and east toward Bullock's Harbour, while another road links Bullock's Harbour with the main island across the Bay of Five Pirates causeway. Happy People Rentals (T 367-8117) at the marina rents everything you can imagine, including bicycles ($15 a day), small Suzuki Jeeps ($50 day) and motor scooters ($40). Transportation Unlimited (T 367-8466) provides a **taxi** service.

By far the largest **accommodation** option on the island, *Tropical Diversions* (T 367-8838 or 1-800/343-7256, F 367-8115, E tdbahamas@aol.com; ❸–❺) offers both privately owned beach villas ($90–500) on the eastern shore and two-bedroom townhouses ($180–300) on the marina, each with a private dock beneath. All have air conditioning, full kitchens and a daily maid service. The eighty-slip marina accommodates boats up to 150ft, with fuel dock, showers and laundry facilities. Weekly and monthly rates are available, and the marina also has several individual private homes available to rent. In Bullock's Harbour, the *Flower Lady* (T 367-8117; ❸) rents four rooms in her white house on the hill behind the marina. Each room is nicely decorated, has a kitchenette, refrigerator and TV.

Not surprisingly, the marina is the best place to **eat**. The *Wharf* restaurant and bar, open 11am–midnight, is the place to go for breakfast and lunch especially, serving both American and Bahamian-style breakfasts ($4), and simple daily lunch specials like corned beef, burgers, soups and salads. Dinners here range from seafood to pizza ($8–13). Also in the marina is the elegant and rather exclusive *Tamboo Dinner Club* (6–10pm; closed Tues; ℡ 367-8203). The menu is Bahamian-style seafood and chicken, and during weekends local expatriates gather at the elegant bar to play backgammon or watch the huge TV. In Bullock's Harbour, the *Watergate* (℡ 367-8244) is the main sit-down restaurant, dishing out very good pork chops and macaroni and cheese, along with the ubiquitous peas and rice. If you are looking for a quick snack, there are several take-away spots available in town, including *Until Then* and *Cooly Mae's Take Away,* as well as dozens of tiny general merchandise shops. The best **nightlife** option is *Roberts Disco and Lounge* at the north end of town, mainly frequented by locals.

There are no banks or information offices on Great Harbour Cay, though **travellers' cheques** can be cashed at the *Tropical Diversions* resort. If you have pressing travel questions or concerns, the main **island administrative centre** (℡ 367-8291) in Bullock's Harbour can sometimes supply answers on travel along with details on events like the Homecoming Regatta. Also in town is a **post office** (9am–5.30pm weekdays) and a **police station** (℡ 367-8344).

Chub Cay

Long uninhabited, tiny **CHUB CAY** began its development as an embryonic idea of a group of Texas-based anglers and investors who thought it would be fun to own a private fishing island in the Bahamas. Over the years they built makeshift dormitories, imported a permanent support staff and finally built a marina on the most prominent natural lagoon on the western edge of the island. When Hurricane Andrew struck in 1992, the island – along with the *Chub Cay Club* – was brutalized. After being completely rebuilt and refurbished, the *Club* opened again in 1994, this time not only offering private rooms, but also as a public facility.

Named for a fish that inhabits the shallow waters of the Great Bahama Bank, Chub Cay and its twin companion **Frazier's Hog Cay** are today visited mainly for the fine fishing and diving. At only four miles long, the two-island set doesn't invite much inland exploration, though there are two very good **beaches**, both with particularly marvellous shelling for collectors. Still, the **reefs** and rare corals just offshore, along with the deep, fish-filled **Tongue of the Ocean** due south, are the real stars here.

Diving and watersports

Clear visibility in the water – often up to a hundred feet – is a major reason for the high quality of both **snorkelling** and **diving** here, as is the frequent spotting of eagle rays, stingrays, abundant starfish, and sea turtles. One of the best places for snorkelling is **Mamma Rhoda Rock**, located about a mile offshore due southwest from the *Chub Cay Club*. Any day one can look across the straits and see Mamma Rhoda in the distance, where countless roosting birds like Sooty Terns and Brown Noddies make their home. You'll need a boat to get there for snorkelling, about a five-minute ride from Chub Cay. Known for its schools of grunt and yellow trumpetfish, Mamma Rhoda Rock – a designated marine park – is actually one of the best snorkelling reefs in the Bahamas thanks to its large size and sheltered southwestern position. Diving possibilities include deep-wall diving at **Chub Cay Wall**, known for its steep drop-off and huge tiger grouper fish congregations, and **Canyons and Caves**, a shallow reef which lies in only 20–40ft of water.

For information on diving in the area, head to the small **dive shop** located at Great Harbour Marina (☎367-8005). General dive information about diving areas surrounding Chub Cay is obtainable in the US from Neil Watson's Undersea Adventures (☎954/462-4100). There is a small dive shop at the *Chub Cay Club* (☎325-1490 or 1-800/329-1337), offering dives off the Chub Cay Wall and to Mamma Rhoda Rock.

Practicalities

Though a majority of visitors arrive via private yacht, Chub Cay does have its own airport – basically a long concrete runway with enough space to land a 737. Most **flights** are run by Island Express Airlines (☎954/359-0380) out of Fort Lauderdale, though the *Chub Cay Club* can help organize other charter flights from both mainland Florida and New Providence in the Bahamas. There is **no mailboat service** from Nassau to Chub Cay.

One of only two **accommodation** options on the island, the laid-back *Chub Cay Club* (☎325-1490 or 1-800/662-8555, ℱ322-5199, ⓦwww.chubcay.com) has nearly thirty ocean- or pool-side rooms ($140–174), as well as nine two- and three-bedroom villas on the beach ($400–600), all rather plain but still comfortable enough. Amenities include a large swimming pool, a pair of tennis courts and a fine beach, along with a great dive shop and fishing services (see above). The resort can also arrange hiking and biking tours of the island, and has a full-service 96-slip **marina** (VHF Ch 68 and 71). The only other accommodation option hereabouts, *Frazer's Cay Club* (☎305/743-2420; ❹), is a weather-beaten two-storey hotel standing on the southeasterly-facing eastern arm of Chub Cay. Reachable by a dirt and gravel road about two miles from the airstrip, the hotel has ten rooms, a restaurant, and small marina for half a dozen boats. Though it's seen better days, the smallish rooms are still comfortable with fans or a/c.

Dining options are also extremely limited. Best is the *Chub Cay Club's Harbour House Restaurant* (open 7am–9pm), which serves a variety of seafood specialties, including fresh lobster, conch, and grouper. Breakfast starts at $6–8, while dinners are $15–25. Nearby is the *Hilltop Bar*, where tired fishermen watch sunsets and talk about the one that got away. The restaurant at *Frazer's Cay Club* serves Bahamian fare and burgers for lunch. It is much less expensive than the *Chub Cay Club's* restaurant.

Eleuthera

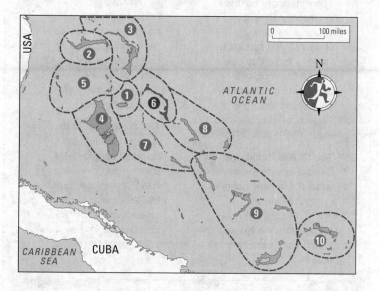

CHAPTER 6

Highlights

✻ **Club Med Beach** One of the most beautiful beaches on Eleuthera, this long expanse of powdery pink sand near Governor's Harbour is backed by a tall forest and features an offshore reef. See p.214

✻ **The Pineapple Festival in Gregory Town** Every year in early June, Gregory Town springs to life for a three-day celebration featuring pineapple-eating contests, a Miss Teen Pineapple Pageant and a Junkanoo Rush. See p.223

✻ **The Devil's Backbone** Snorkel among the many wrecks that have gone down the Devil's Backbone, a three-mile-long reef on the North Eleutheran coast. See p.224

✻ **Dunmore Town** The quaint streets of Loyalist Dunmore Town contain such 200-year-old architectural gems as the Loyalist Cottage and the Little Boarding House. See p.228

✻ **Dinner at The Landing** At *The Landing*, Dunmore Town's best restaurant, you can sample the fresh pasta, choice steaks and squid with aïoli while enjoying the view on the waterfront. See p.232

✻ **The Junkanoo Rush** at Tarpum Bay Join the colourful parade floats, dancers and marching bands that rouse Tarpum Bay every year at dawn on both December 26 and New Year's Day. See p.235

Eleuthera

erived from the ancient Greek word for freedom, the name
"**ELEUTHERA**" was given to the island by a small band of
Bermudans fleeing religious persecution who landed on its beaches in
1648; the original Lucayan inhabitants, long since gone, knew it as
"Cigatoo". Besides the main – and by far the largest – eponymous island, the
Eleutheran chain contains three other populated islands. **Eleuthera** itself
stretches over a hundred miles end to end and is less than two miles wide for
most of its length. Congregating at the northern tip of Eleuthera are tiny
Harbour Island; **St George's Island**, which is more commonly known by
the name of its only settlement **Spanish Wells**; and **Russell Island,** a nondescript hump of land that absorbs the population overflow from Spanish
Wells. These three islands around the northern tip of Eleuthera are flanked by
a handful of smaller uninhabited cays.

The most populous of the Out Islands, Eleuthera has 10,000 residents scattered in a dozen fishing villages spread up and down its long coastline, mainly
along the western shore facing the Bight of Eleuthera, the curve of shallow
water that fills the gentle bow in Eleuthera's coastline. In parts the landscape is
rolling and green, farmed for citrus fruit, tomatoes and vegetables or clothed in
tall grass punctuated by the occasional grove of pine or coconut trees. The
Queen's Highway, which runs from north to south, also cuts through several
stretches of low straggly bush and swamp, but travels mainly along the water's
edge, offering long views of the turquoise sea, and occasionally of both coasts
at once.

Smack in the middle of Eleuthera is the genteel community of **Governor's
Harbour**, its capital and the earliest settlement in the Bahamas. To the north,
Gregory Town, built on a steep hillside surrounding a deep horseshoe-shaped
harbour, is the self-proclaimed pineapple capital of the Bahamas. South of
Governor's Harbour, are the picturesque fishing villages of **Tarpum Bay** and
Rock Sound.

Outside of a handful of comfortable resorts, there are few organized tourist
facilities on the island, which is part of its appeal for many visitors – that and
the many **empty beaches** fit for swimming, strolling, snorkelling, shell-col-
lecting or sunbathing. While the Bahamas are indeed awash with beaches, the
Eleutheran chain offers some of the very finest and most unspoilt in the entire
archipelago (see box on p.214).

By comparison only, pretty Harbour Island – or Briland, as it is also known
locally – bustles with activity. Its only settlement is the historic village of
Dunmore Town, which boasts several luxury resorts, restaurants, bars, dive
outfitters and the stunning, three-mile **Pink Sand Beach**, and is very in with

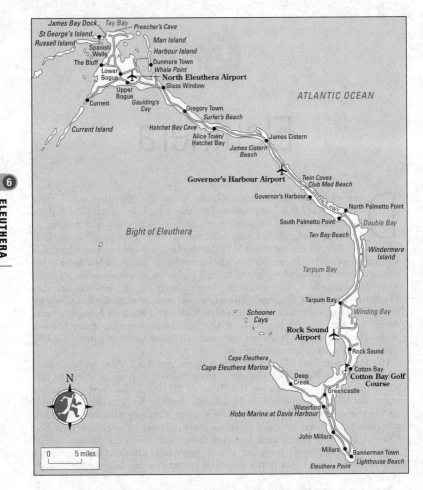

the rich and famous at the moment. Less touristy than Harbour Island, nearby St George's Island offers the working-class settlement of **Spanish Wells**, with a large fleet of fishing and lobster boats. It too has a long white-sand beach, but a far more modest tourist trade.

Some history

Though the British laid claim to the Bahamas in 1629, they did not actually establish a permanent settlement on Eleuthera until 1648, in the midst of the **English Civil War**. Though the bloody struggle between Oliver Cromwell's Roundheads and the Crown reverberated less violently in Britain's colonies, the colony of Bermuda grew so deeply divided that one-time governor William Sayle sought to escape the political intrigue and religious persecution that engulfed the island.

To do so, Sayle obtained British approval to establish a new settlement in the uninhabited islands of the Bahamas and advertised in London for investors in the **Company of Eleutheran Adventurers**. For an outlay of one hundred pounds, investors were entitled to a large plot of land in the settlement and agreed to adhere to its then radical principles of liberty, religious tolerance and an elected government. Sayle set forth from Bermuda in 1648 with seventy settlers bound for Eleuthera, coming ashore at Governor's Harbour.

The historical record of the colony is murky. After an argument with a fellow Adventurer, Sayle set out – probably for Harbour Island – taking most of the settlers with him. One of their ships was wrecked at sea, and they all had a rough first year, and were it not for the emergency supplies sent by the Puritan colonists of New England, they probably would have starved to death on the beautiful white-sand beaches. To repay the gift, the Eleutheran settlers cut and sent a shipload of braziletto, a valuable dyewood, which was sold to help build Harvard College.

When Charles I was beheaded in 1649, republican sympathizers were expelled from Bermuda, and some of them headed for Eleuthera. The Eleutheran colony did not thrive, however, and the inhabitants scraped a meagre living harvesting wood and ambergris – whale vomit, used to make perfume – and wrecking. By 1659, when Cromwell directed the governor of Jamaica to send a rescue ship to take them to Jamaica to be clothed and fed, most had already gone – Sayle himself returned to Bermuda to become governor again. The cannon found on Harbour Island are the only physical remnants of this period.

Seventy-five years later, the combined population of Eleuthera and Harbour Island had grown to 390 (330 Europeans and 60 slaves) living a hardscrabble life that didn't change until the arrival of **Loyalist exiles** and their slaves from the southern United States at the end of the American Revolution. This influx soon established large pineapple, cotton and citrus fruit plantations on Eleuthera, and many of the quaint clapboard cottages in Governor's Harbour, Spanish Wells and Dunmore Town date from this period. Agriculture, fishing, wooden-boat building, sponging and wrecking sustained the small settlements established up and down the coast by freed slaves for the next hundred-odd years.

Eleuthera experienced fleeting glamour in the 1940s and 1950s when British royalty were frequent visitors to Windermere Island, a spit of land lying a few yards off the Atlantic coast, and a number of wealthy expatriates built luxurious winter homes on Eleuthera and Harbour Island. Several resorts were established in southern Eleuthera, including the *Cotton Bay Club*, patronized by Sammy Davis Jr and other members of the Rat Pack. All have since closed, throwing a lot of Eleutherans out of work, and forcing many young people to head to Nassau or elsewhere to make their living.

Getting there

There are three **airports** in the Eleutheran chain, the most often used being Governor's Harbour International Airport (☎332-2321), eight miles north of town. Rock Sound Airport (☎334-2177), two miles north of Rock Sound, handles the south, while North Eleuthera Airport (☎335-1700), on the main island, is only a ten-minute boat ride and five-minute drive from Harbour Island. Daily air service from Nassau to all three airports is available on Bahamasair, from Florida to North Eleuthera and Governor's Harbour on USAir and to North Eleuthera on Continental. Flying time from Nassau is

Much of Eleuthera's long coastline is edged with fine sandy **beaches**, most of which you can have all to yourself on any given day. Listed from south to north, here are ten great destinations to whet your appetite:

Lighthouse Beach Six miles of scoured white sand on the very southern tip of the island, strewn with sand dollars and perfect for picnicking and walking, with good snorkelling on a calm day. Getting there is half the adventure (see p.237 for directions).

Nor'Side Beach A long Atlantic beach backed by high dunes, with a hypnotic surf, good snorkelling from shore and a great beach bar and restaurant on the bluff. From the centre of Rock Sound village, follow Fish Street for about a mile to a T-junction, then turn left. The *Nor'Side Resort* is about 500yd along this road on the right, with access up a steep sandy drive.

Ten Bay Beach A good swimming beach (suitable for small children) located on the sheltered Bight side, fringed by towering coconut palms. Heading north on the Queen's Highway, the turnoff is ten miles past Tarpum Bay. Keep an eye out for a Japanese-style building on your left, and take the dirt road that runs past it a few hundred yards into the parking area.

Club Med Beach Arguably the most beautiful beach on the island; a long expanse of powdery pink sand backed by a tall forest on the Atlantic side of Governor's Harbour. An offshore reef tempers the gentle surf. The *Club Med*, which closed a couple of years ago, is now just a cluster of overgrown buildings set back from sea, and the beach is often empty of visitors.

Twin Coves A secluded double scallop of white sand on the Atlantic side, with good swimming and snorkelling around a small cay about 10yd offshore. Heading north from Governor's Harbour, take the paved road on your right just before you pass the *Worker's Hotel*. Follow it through one intersection, then take a right at the fork in the road, then right again on the road running along the beach (not always within sight). Just past a private home with large landscaped grounds, there is a short track on your left that leads to the beach. You can park your car here.

twenty minutes. Major's Air Service also has regular flights to Governor's Harbour from Grand Bahama several times a week.

Bahamas Fast Ferries ($55 one-way, $100 round-trip; ☎323-2166, ⓦwww.bahamasfastferries.com) operates daily two-hour **ferry** service between Nassau, Harbour Island and Spanish Wells, and service twice a week from Nassau to Governor's Harbour. Searoad/Sealink Ferries ($40; ☎323-2166) has a slower service from Nassau to Governor's Harbour and Current twice a week.

Government **mailboats** call once a week at Rock Sound, Governor's Harbour, Hatchet Bay, Spanish Wells and Harbour Island. See p.25 for details.

Information and maps

There are **Ministry of Tourism offices** in Governor's Harbour on the Queen's Highway in the centre of town (☎332-2142, Ⓕ332-2480) and on Bay Street in Dunmore Town on Harbour Island (☎333-2621), theoretically open during regular business hours, but in practice more sporadically.

The *Eleuthera Advocate* is a free monthly community newspaper carrying local news, published in Nassau and available in island shops in the larger centres, while the free monthly bulletin *Eleuthera Informer* (ⓦwww.eleutherainformer

James Cistern Beach A narrow rocky strand running along the Queen's Highway through the village of James Cistern, ten miles north of Governor's Harbour. Not a swimming beach, but one of the best places on the island for shell collecting.

Surfer's Beach Unlike any other place on the island, this long exposed piece of Atlantic coastline features an exhilarating wild crashing surf backed by high dunes. The turnoff is two miles south of Gregory Town on the Atlantic side.

Gaulding's Cay Beach A picturesque shallow curve of tree-backed beach on the Bight side facing Gaulding's Cay, a lump of land about 50yd offshore that you can wade out to examine. Two miles north of the *Cove Resort*, take the dirt road on the Bight/west side of the highway across from a yellow and white building, then turn left again at the fence strung with buoys (marked).

Tay Bay This secluded dollop of powdery white sand on the very northern tip of Eleuthera is of historical interest as the site of Preacher's Cave, where the Eleutheran Adventurers took refuge after one of their ships was wrecked on the Devil's Backbone reef in 1648. The turnoff is marked from the highway.

Pink Sand Beach The three-mile-long fine sandy strand that put Harbour Island on the map, with a rolling surf, several beach bars and small luxury resorts dotted along its length.

For hardcore sun- and sand-seekers, Geoff and Vicky Wells (© elusive@batelnet .bs) – self-declared beachologists from the frozen north – have published *The Elusive Beaches of Eleuthera*, with detailed directions and ratings for privacy, swimming, shelling, snorkelling and diving prospects at a few dozen more sandy strands; available at Pam's Island Made Gifts in Gregory Town and in other shops around the island. The very detailed four-sheet Tarbox map of Eleuthera available at the *Rainbow Inn* (see p.218) also has marked many beaches and snorkelling spots.

.com) contains advertisements for local businesses and tourist services and is available in hotels and island shops. *Eleutheras* is a pocketsize magazine published annually, containing feature articles on local attractions and businesses, and restaurant and hotel listings. It is less widely available, but might be had from the tourism office.

Tarbox Publications has produced an excellent and very detailed four-sheet **map** of Eleuthera, Harbour Island and Spanish Wells, including their numerous beaches and other local attractions. If you are going to spend any time exploring the island, it is a well-spent $10, available at some gift shops, or at the *Rainbow Inn*, whose owners commissioned it.

Getting around

There is no public transportation on Eleuthera, so to get around, you will need to hire a taxi or rent a car, both of which can be done at the airport upon your arrival. Be sure to book your ticket to the airport nearest to where you are staying as a taxi ride from one end of the island to the other will cost upwards of $100 and take two hours or more. Car rental agencies and taxi drivers serving the areas around Governor's Harbour, Rock Sound and North Eleuthera are listed in the sections on those regions. Car rental costs around $70/$350 a day/week or $400 for a four-wheel-drive, useful if you want to explore the back roads. Lots of people hitchhike up and down the island and this is a reasonably safe and easy way to get around.

North Eleuthera Island and Spanish Wells

The **northern half of Eleuthera** stretches along the Queen's Highway from **Governor's Harbour**, the capital, up to the northern tip. The road passes through a number of small fishing villages, including **James Cistern**, **Hatchet Bay** and the larger hillside settlement and former pineapple-growing centre of **Gregory Town**. Along the way, side roads off the main highway lead to beautiful empty beaches on both the Bight side and Atlantic coast (see box on p.214–215). The underground caverns of **Hatchet Bay Cave** make a great destination on a rainy or sunburned day, while the **Glass Window** – a rocky, wave-doused moonscape further north where Eleuthera is barely a car-width wide – is a sight to behold. North of the Glass Window are several down-at-heel settlements with little to detain a visitor, but you must come this way to catch a ferry to Harbour Island or **Spanish Wells**, a less developed alternative.

Governor's Harbour and around

GOVERNOR'S HARBOUR is a gracious seaside town and working fishing community of a few hundred residents with a distinctly colonial feel and a tangible expatriate presence. The Queen's Highway runs through the centre of town, which is spread out along the waterfront facing the broad, well-used harbour and Cupid's Cay on the Bight side. Quiet, tree-lined residential lanes climb the hillside behind the small commercial district, and lead you in a matter of minutes over the hill and down to the Atlantic coast and the gorgeous pink-sand **Club Med Beach**, about a mile from the town centre.

Located at the midpoint of Eleuthera, with plentiful and charming accommodation, restaurants and several beautiful beaches close at hand, the town makes a good base to explore the island. Governor's Harbour is an ideal point from which to launch day-trips to Harbour Island or Spanish Wells, and there are several points of interest within a twenty-mile radius of Governor's Harbour, notably several fine beaches to the north (see box on pp.214–215) and the caverns of Hatchet Bay Cave.

South of Governor's Harbour, several more fine beaches and a couple of pleasant dining spots in and around Palmetto Point along the Atlantic coast, or a straight shot down the Queen's Highway, make it a good destination for a leisurely day-trip.

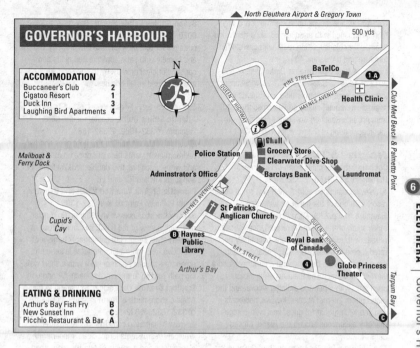

GOVERNOR'S HARBOUR

North Eleuthera Airport & Gregory Town

0 ————— 500 yds

N

ACCOMMODATION

Buccaneer's Club	2
Cigatoo Resort	1
Duck Inn	3
Laughing Bird Apartments	4

BaTelCo

1 A

PINE STREET

HAYNES AVENUE

Health Clinic

QUEEN'S HIGHWAY

Club Med Beach & Palmetto Point

i **2** **3**

Chil

Police Station

Grocery Store

Clearwater Dive Shop

Mailboat & Ferry Dock

Adminstrator's Office

Barclays Bank

Laundromat

Cupid's Cay

HAYNES AVENUE

St Patricks Anglican Church

B Haynes Public Library

BAY STREET

Arthur's Bay

QUEEN'S HIGHWAY

Royal Bank of Canada

4

Globe Princess Theater

C

Tarpum Bay

EATING & DRINKING

Arthur's Bay Fish Fry	B
New Sunset Inn	C
Picchio Restaurant & Bar	A

Accommodation

In addition to the **hotels and inns** centred around Governor's Harbour, more options are available heading north towards Hatchet Bay and south around Palmetto Point. **Holiday rentals** are also available on the beaches around Palmetto Point and in Governor's Harbour in some of the lovely clapboard cottages that climb the hill overlooking Cupid's Cay. For listings of rental agents handling properties in Governor's Harbour, see p.29.

At the time of writing Goodfellows Farm (☎332-2506), just south of Governor's Harbour, had plans to open guest cottages with an organic restaurant; call for details.

Governor's Harbour

Buccaneer's Club Pine St ☎332-2000, ℉332-2888. Halfway up the hill, the *Buccaneer's Club* has five comfortable rooms with glass patio doors, a balcony, TV and a/c in a three-storey wooden house. **4**

Cigatoo Resort Haynes Ave ☎332-3060 or 1-800/467-7595, ℉332-3061, ⊛www.cigatooresort .com. On top of the hill in Governor's Harbour, this recently renovated resort offers 24 clean, bright modern rooms – some with a view of the Atlantic – painted a crisp white with attractive tropical accents in nicely landscaped grounds around a swimming pool. It features tennis courts, a TV lounge, meeting room and an inviting bar and

restaurant with additional tables on the courtyard terrace. Club Med Beach is about a 15min walk away. **5**–**6**; call for special offers.

The Duck Inn Queen's Highway ☎332-2608, ℉332-2160, ⊛www.theduckinn.com. A centrally located treasure on the waterfront, the *Duck Inn* consists of three charming early 1800s wooden cottages set in a verdant garden including Caribbean coconut, starfruit, grapefruit, and several varieties of orchids. Cupid Cottage (**4**) – which has an unimpeded view of the harbour – sleeps two, while the Honeypot Studio apartment sleeps up to four (**4**) in homely rooms with hardwood floors and an unsurpassed view of the sunset and the sea from the private upstairs deck. The larger

217

Loyalist Cottage sleeps up to eight in spare, airy rooms furnished with antiques, polished hardwood floors, cozy colonial sitting room with overstuffed furniture and a veranda (**⑧**).

Laughing Bird Apartments Birdie Lane ☎332-2012 or 1029, Ⓕ332-2358, ⓦwww.vacationspot .com. Four neat, modern studio apartments are available in a quiet shady grove across the road from Arthur's Beach in Governor's Harbour, with hammocks hung in the trees for lolling. **④**

North to Hatchet Bay

Cocodimama Six miles north of Governor's Harbour ☎332-3150, Ⓕ332-3155, ⓦwww.cocodimama.com. A gem of a small beach resort with one of the finest restaurants in Eleuthera (see p.220), *Cocodimama* is located two miles south of the airport. A relaxed, sophisticated retreat, with twelve spacious and beautifully decorated rooms in three two-storey cottages. Each room has a private balcony with a hammock and a view of the sunset. The main house is a casual open area with a bar and a dining alcove, and the resort offers internet access, kayaks, hobiecats and snorkelling gear for guest use, with complimentary excursions around the island. Closed Sept–Nov. **⑧**

The Rainbow Inn Ten miles north of Governor's Harbour Airport ☎ & Ⓕ335-0294 or 1-800/688-0047, ⓦwww.rainbowinn.com. A small, relaxed resort with homely accommodation in hexagonal cottages built around a swimming pool overlooking the sea on the Bight side. Facilities include tennis, free use of bicycles, kayaks, hobiecats and snorkel gear, or the hammocks strung in the trees. Single or double with mini-kitchen (**⑤**); three-bedroom/three-bath cottage sleeping up to six with full kitchen, living room, a screened-in porch with a view of the sea (**⑦**); a two bedroom/one-bath cottage with living room, full kitchen and a sun deck facing the ocean (**⑦**).

Seven Gables Estate Hatchet Bay ☎ & Ⓕ335-0070. *Seven Gables* has four sweet little clapboard cottages for rent on a tidy seaside property. Simple and homely with satin appliqué bed quilts and contains original artwork by the owner, a kitchenette, TV and small porches. **②**

South to Palmetto Point

Atlantic Suites On the coastal road in North Palmetto ☎332-1882, Ⓕ332-1883, Ⓔsuites@batelnet.bs. The five neat one- and two-bedroom apartments here are done up in frilly pink and white. Each has two double beds, satellite TV, and a full kitchen. **⑤** and up

Palmetto Shores Vacation Villas Shore Drive in South Palmetto Point ☎ & Ⓕ332-1305, ⓦwww.ivacation.com/vr-vr-993.htm. On a quiet road with a view of the Bight, this small group of modern-style, simple but comfortably furnished one-, two -and three-bedroom villas is set on a green tree-shaded patch of lawn with a short walking path leading to the private beach. **④** and up

Tropical Dreams On a side road leading to the Atlantic shore north of North Palmetto Point ☎332-1632, Ⓕ332 1278, ⓦwww.bahamasvg.com/Tropicaldream.html. *Tropical Dreams* rents large, clean, modern efficiency units and a couple of two-bedroom apartments. All units have a/c and cable TV, but no view. **③**–**⑤**

Unique Village Resort On the coast near North Palmetto Point ☎332-1830, Ⓕ332-1838, ⓦwww.bahamasvg.com/uniquevil.html. The ten doubles and four one- and two-bedroom villas here are set on a nice piece of powdery beach. The rooms are modern and comfortable with the requisite floral print bedcovers, rattan furniture and beige tiled floors. The perks include a coffee-maker, satellite TV, a/c and a semi-formal dining room with an ocean view serving Bahamian and American cuisine. **⑤** and up

The Town

Although the town centre is dominated by a large, ugly parking lot off the Queen's Highway, around which the grocery store, Shell station, Barclays Bank and several other shops are untidily grouped, the rest of the village is quite picturesque. Daintily painted wooden cottages with gingerbread trim, surrounded by stone walls overflowing with hibiscus and oleander blooms, line the steep lanes climbing the hillside.

Shaded by coconut palms on the triangle of land adjoining Cupid's Cay, the pink and green wooden clapboard **Haynes Public Library** (Mon–Thurs 9am–6pm, Fri 9am–5pm, Sat 10am–4pm; ☎332-2877) was built in 1897 and lovingly restored a few years ago after a narrow escape from demolition. There is public access to the internet here ($5 for 15min, $20 a month), and small exhibits devoted to local history. Nearby stands the Gothic whitewashed **St Patrick's Church** and the hot pink colonial-style **Government Administration** building, where the post office is located.

Dotted with fishing boats and pleasure craft, the harbour itself is enclosed by a curve of white sand joined to **Cupid's Cay** by a narrow causeway. A small hunk of flat rock, Cupid's Cay was the site of the first settlement on Eleuthera, by the Company of Eleutheran Adventurers in 1648 (although a big sign proudly declares it to have been 1646). A church, a few cottages and the ruins of nineteenth-century wooden houses remain. The mailboat and passenger ferries dock at the north end of the cay.

You will miss one of the highlights of Eleuthera if you pass through Governor's Harbour without a visit to **Club Med Beach** (see p.214). Take Haynes Avenue up the hill from the Queen's Highway, past the *Cigatoo Resort* and down the other side, where you come to a T-junction. Park here and take the wooded path just to the right of the junction, which leads to the beach about 200yd in. Back from the T-junction, a scenic, narrow paved road follows the Atlantic coast south for eight miles between Governor's Harbour and Palmetto Point (see below), past several oceanfront holiday estates, rental cottages and strips of sandy beach.

North to Hatchet Bay

North of Governor's Harbour, the Queen's Highway weaves inland and back along the shore to the fishing village of **James Cistern**, ten miles north. If you want to pause here for a quick meal, try *Rosie's Café and Bakery* (see p.221). Three miles further on, Big Rock General Store has a good stock of groceries if you intend to take a picnic at Surfer's Beach (see below).

Continuing north five miles, you come to **Hatchet Bay**, also known as **Alice Town**, a tidy, green settlement with a picturesque protected harbour. Though this sleepy little village does not receive many tourists, you may wish to break at the Gateway service station or at the general store on the highway about a quarter of a mile on where local boys gather to play dominoes under a tree.

Two miles north of Hatchet Bay, a sign on your left – the Bight side – marks the turnoff to the **Hatchet Bay Cave**. This underground cavern of several chambers is filled with dramatic formations of stalactites and stalagmites that extend for a few hundred yards; its entrance is in the middle of a tomato field. The cave walls are adorned with the accumulated graffiti of several hundred years. You need sturdy shoes with a good tread and a flashlight for everyone in your party.

Situated in the midst of a broad expanse of rolling fields dramatically punctuated by tall abandoned grain silos, the cave was once part of a large dairy and poultry farm established in 1937 by Austin Levy. An American textile tycoon, he paid wages above the Bahamian average, for which he was chided by the governor of the day, the Duke of Windsor. The farm went belly-up shortly after the government bought it in 1975.

Three miles past the cave and two miles south of Gregory Town (see p.221), a side road on the Atlantic side leads to **Surfer's Beach**, a wild stretch of dune-backed coastline that draws wave-riders from all over, and is a scenic venue for a picnic.

South to Palmetto Point

Between Governor's Harbour and Palmetto Point, the Queen's Highway cuts inland through bush. The only point of interest along this stretch is **Ten Bay**

Beach (see p.214), well worth the trip south in itself. If you've done the beach, a scenic alternative route from Governor's Harbour to Palmetto Point is the old highway, which runs along the Atlantic coast, emerging in the tatty settlement of **South Palmetto Point**, where you can rejoin the Queen's Highway. **North Palmetto Point**, just a few streets of modern bungalows and a couple of gas stations, sits across the highway on the Bight side. There is a sizeable community of winter residents in and around Palmetto Point; a hotel and a sprinkling of rental cottages along the shore nearby; and a couple of nice restaurants.

Continuing south from Palmetto Point, the Queen's Highway again passes through several miles of straggly bush before it touches the coastline again a few miles north of Tarpum Bay (see p.234). En route, it passes through the settlement of **Savannah Sound**, and the turnoff to **Windermere Island**, site of the exclusive private beach club where Princess Diana was famously photographed several months pregnant in a bikini by paparazzi lurking in the bushes, and Prince Andrew and his former wife Sarah recently spent a joint holiday. Neither place is likely to offer much of interest to the common traveller: Savannah Sound comprises a few houses along the highway and the Atlantic shore, and the Windermere Club, which owns the whole of Windermere Island, is not open to the general public.

Eating and entertainment

There isn't much in the way of **entertainment** in or around Governor's Harbour. *Ronnie's Island Hide-D-Way* (☎332-2307) on Cupid's Cay occasionally has live rake 'n' scrape or rock music by local bands, with dancing every weekend, and pool, drinking, and satellite TV every night of the week. The Globe Princess Theatre (☎332-2735) on the south edge of town is the only **cinema** on Eleuthera, with shows at 8pm several nights a week.

Dining options range from seafood establishments to bakeries offering quick bites to visitors on the go. Most are centred on Governor's Harbour, but there are some choices as you head toward Hatchet Bay or Palmetto Point.

Governor's Harbour

Arthur's Beach Fish Fry On Friday and Saturday afternoons through the evening, cheap, fresh seafood is cooked on an outside grill at this local kiosk.

Pammy's On the Queen's Highway in the centre of town. A popular spot both with locals and winter visitors, *Pammy's* offers mouthwatering home-style Bahamian fried chicken, conch fritters, burgers and sandwiches, with traditional side-dishes like coleslaw, fried plantains, peas and rice and macaroni 'n' cheese. You can eat in the casual diner or take away.

Picchio Restaurant and Bar *Cigatoo Resort* ☎332 3060. *Picchio's* has an Italian chef and a menu that includes seafood dishes like grouper with homemade fries on a bed of lettuce. The highlight, however, is his two new variations on conch – wrapped in puff pastry with soya vinegar, and conch risotto with fresh tomatoes and basil. The pleasant dining room has a view of the garden, white linen tablecloths and fresh flowers.

Lunch $10–13, dinner entrees $22–26. Closed Sun and Mon.

North to Hatchet Bay

Cocodimama Six miles north of Governor's Harbour ☎332-3150. On the wide terrace overlooking the white-sand beach, this is *the* place to watch the sunset with a glass of wine or a Goombay Smash in hand. The cuisine is Italian and Bahamian, featuring fresh seafood, locally grown vegetables and mozzarella imported from Italy. Featured dishes include penne with anchovy fillets, raisins and pine nuts; tuna steak; grouper in a white wine sauce; and vodka lemon sorbet or crepes with Cointreau and ice cream for dessert. The restaurant boasts an extensive wine list with a good selection of Italian and Californian vintages. $50 for dinner. Closed Sept–Nov.

Rainbow Inn Ten miles north of Governor's Harbour Airport ☎335-0294. Among the nicest on the island, the restaurant has a cozy, inviting interior with a central backlit bar, polished wood tables situated with a view of the sea and the sunset, nautical paraphernalia and curios on the walls and a screened-in porch. The food is very good – fried chicken with fresh seafood options like grouper – and the homemade Key Lime pie is sublime. Live music with Dr Seabreeze on Friday nights. Open for dinner only from 6pm. It is closed Sunday and Monday, but a cookout is put on for guests staying at the resort. Closed Sept to mid-Nov.

Rosie's Café and Bakery Across from James Cistern beach in the centre of the village. Rosie's serves a very fine breakfast and lunch at pleasant outside tables and sells delicious homemade bread and banana and pineapple loaf. Open Mon–Sat 7.30am to 3pm.

South to Palmetto Point

Mate and Jenny's South Palmetto ☎ 332-1504. A beacon in the night just off the highway *Mate and Jenny's* has a dark and cozy interior, rafters strung with yachting pennants, a pool table and a jukebox stacked with Jimmy Buffett, Bob Marley and Frank Sinatra. It serves delicious pizza, including a conch-topped version, as well as seafood, steak, sandwiches and immobilizing tropical cocktails. Closed Tues.

New Sunset Inn One mile south of Governor's Harbour. Good moderately priced chicken, burgers and great lobster are presented with friendly service in this slightly barn-like dining room with a prime view of the sunset; order a drink and be prepared to wait a while for your meal.

Run Away Bay Marina, Restaurant and Bar Shore Drive in South Palmetto Point ☎ 332-1744. A nice spot for lunch with pleasant seating on a veranda overlooking the Bight as well as a casual indoor dining room. Tasty seafood meals, sandwiches and salads range $4–8 for lunch and $13–25 for dinner.

Diving and watersports

The Clearwater Dive Shop (closed weekends; ☎ 332-2146) in the town centre near Barclays Bank rents and sells **snorkelling equipment** and can give you the names of local guides who will take you out in their boats. One of them, Gladstone Petty (☎ 332-2280), offers guided **fishing** expeditions. Despite the name, they do not run diving trips.

Listings

Banking Barclays Bank (☎ 332-2300), centre of town on the Queen's Highway; the Royal Bank of Canada (☎ 332-2856), just south of the town centre on the highway. Both are open Mon–Thurs 9.30am–3pm, Fri 9.30am–5pm.

Gas There is an Esso station on the Queen's Highway as you enter town from the south, and a Shell station in the centre of town on the highway near Barclays.

Groceries The Shell station has a well-stocked grocery and general store attached.

Laundry Sands Laundry and Cleaners (Mon–Sat 9 am–5pm, last wash at 4pm) is at the top of National Church Road, accessible by heading north on the Queen's Highway and taking the first right after the primary school as you enter town.

Medical clinic (☎ 332-2774). The clinic at the top of the hill on Haynes Avenue is open 9am–5pm.

Police The local detachment (☎ 332-2111) is on the Queen's Highway in the centre of town across the street from Barclays Bank. In emergencies, call ☎ 911.

Post office (☎ 332-2060). The local branch (9am–4.30pm) is in the pink Government Administration building.

Taxis For excellent taxi service and car rental call Clement Cooper (☎ 332-1726) in Palmetto Point, who rents cars for $280 a week and will meet you at the airport.

Telephone There is a phone booth next to the police station, and a BaTelCo office where you can buy phone cards at the top of the hill near the clinic.

Gregory Town and around

Twenty-six miles north of Governor's Harbour, **GREGORY TOWN** is one of the largest settlements on Eleuthera, a colourful collection of semi-dilapidated wooden houses. The town is built into a steep hillside surrounding a narrow horseshoe harbour, which is flanked by high rocky cliffs on either side.

△ Pineapple store

During the nineteenth century, it became a major pineapple-growing area, with schooners leaving the harbour filled with fruit bound for London's Covent Garden. Since then, although the pineapple is still celebrated here with a three-day festival in early June, the Bahamas has gradually been squeezed out of the pineapple market, and the young men of Gregory Town seem to spend a lot of time these days just hanging around the waterfront.

An interesting selection of locally made **crafts**, Bahamian straw work, clothing, jewellery, books and postcards may be found at Island Made Gifts on the Queen's Highway in the village centre and at Rebecca's Beach Shop next door. Beyond nearby Surfer's Beach (see p.219), there's little in Gregory Town to detain you beyond a gas station and the post office in the pink government administration building by the harbour. There isn't much else going on here, but musician Lenny Kravitz likes the relaxed atmosphere so much he is now a part-time resident.

If you are seeking a beach, the Queen's Highway descends a steep hill and skirts green pastureland for four miles north of Gregory Town before the turnoff to **Gaulding's Cay Beach** (see box on p.215) on your left, opposite a white and yellow house. This sheltered secluded cove is a great place for a picnic and a swim.

Practicalities

For budget **accommodation** around Gregory Town *Cambridge Villas* (T 335-5080, F 335-5308; ❸) on the Queen's Highway on the north side of town has basic no-frills rooms and apartment units. Two miles north of town, *The Cove Eleuthera* (T 335-5142, F 335-5338; W www.thecoveeleuthera.com; ❻) is a casual resort with a sweeping view from the poolside. Set on 28 secluded acres, the resort boasts a sheltered cove with a white-sand beach and good snorkelling from shore. Accommodation is in a handful of cottages housing 24 comfortable rooms with a/c nicely done up with white rattan, ceramic tiled floors and tropical accents. Some have a kitchenette and each has a private patio with an ocean or garden view. *The Cove* offers bicycles, snorkelling gear, tennis courts, and a dramatic coastline to explore by kayak (available free to guests).

The Cove also has the best **eating** in the area, offering three excellent meals from a varied menu of Bahamian and American dishes, featuring fresh seafood and homemade desserts such as pineapple crisp. There is a large, bright dining room, but the choicest tables are on the poolside terrace where a view of the turquoise sea surrounds you. On the south side of town along the highway, *Sugar Apple Restaurant and Bar* and *Millennium Dreams* are bare-bones roadhouses serving Bahamian basics and fried food. Thompson's Bakery, behind the lime-green house at the top of the hill overlooking the harbour, sells bread and pineapple tarts.

North to Spanish Wells

As you continue toward James Bay and water taxis to Spanish Wells and Harbour Island, the landscape becomes more austere, with scrubby bush, stagnant saline ponds along the road, and exposed rock, until the width of the island dwindles away to nothing at the **Glass Window**, five miles north of Gregory's Town. Here, in a rocky moonscape, beneath a narrow, constantly battered bridge, the turquoise plane of the Bight of Eleuthera meets the dark, heaving Atlantic in a dramatic cacophony of crashing waves. The arch of rock that gave the spot its name was smashed in a storm years ago. More recently, on a calm, sunny day in 1993, a huge freak wave known as a "rage" hit the bridge with such force that it shifted it 9ft towards the Bight. Maintaining the one-lane bridge in working condition keeps road crews busy, and, periodically, someone in a big hurry to get to one side or the other in bad weather gets washed into the sea. At the time of writing, it was without a guardrail and missing a few seemingly crucial chunks of concrete, but dozens of cars pass this way every day without incident.

On the north side of the Glass Window, an extremely rocky road on your right leads to the *Bottom Harbour Beach Club and Restaurant* at **Whale Point** one and a half miles away. Inside or on a pleasant wooden deck facing Harbour Island, a ten-minute boat ride away ($10 return by water taxi), you can dine on lobster salad, cracked conch, snapper and sandwiches. There is live rake 'n' scrape music here Friday and Sunday nights.

Continuing further on the highway, you will reach the tatty settlements of **Upper** and **Lower Bogue**, where some residents have attempted to brighten the place up with colourful murals painted on the sides of their cement-block houses, but it's nothing worth stopping for. At Lower Bogue, the road forks, and the road on your left (as you face north) continues for five miles west until it reaches **Current**. A prosperous-looking fishing community with a long stretch of beach, it is home to Eddie Minnis, one of the Bahamas' best-known artists, who is renowned for his distinctive watercolour and oil portraits as well as his depictions of Out Island life.

While there are few amenities in Current, it does contain Pierre's Dive Shop (8am–5pm; ☎335-3284), on the main drag as you enter the village. Visitors enjoy drift snorkelling or diving through Current Cut, a narrow passage of swift-moving water which separates Eleuthera from **Current Island**, where there is a minute settlement, but no roads or any other services.

To continue northward from Lower Bogue to James Bay, take the right at the fork in the road and turn right again at the intersection a short distance further on. A Texaco station marks the turnoff to **Harbour Island** (see opposite) and North Eleuthera Airport. Continuing northward on the highway, you come to a T-junction. The road on the right leads to the large **Preacher's Cave**, where the first settlers on Eleuthera found shelter and held church services after their ship wrecked on the **Devil's Backbone** reef in 1648. It is worth pausing for the excellent Tay Bay beach is here (see box on p.215). The road on the left from the T-junction leads to the wharf at James Bay, where you can catch a water taxi (see opposite for details) to Spanish Wells, one mile and fifteen minutes away.

Spanish Wells

The settlement of **SPANISH WELLS** covers the eastern half of St George's Island, a flat, treeless slip of land two miles long and less than half a mile across. It is an insular but friendly community sustained by a prosperous lobster fishery. The approximately 800 residents are mostly descendants of a small band of Loyalist settlers of British extraction and speak English with a well-preserved Bostonian accent. A growing population of Haitian refugees has been established on nearby **Russell Island**, connected to St George's by a short bridge.

Spanish Wells' neat grid of paved streets is lined with tidy bungalows and clapboard cottages, some of which are over a hundred years old. Although the island boasts a spectacular **white-sand beach** running the length of its northern shore, the economy is not geared towards tourism and there are just a couple of simple restaurants, one motel and a small **museum** (Mon–Sat 10am–noon & 1–3pm; ☎333-4710) devoted to local history. The owner of the Islander Gift Shop next door will unlock the door for you.

Practicalities

A government-operated **ferry** ($4 return; no phone) leaves from James Bay on mainland Eleuthera and returns from Spanish Wells every half-hour, and private **water taxis** ($4 return; ☎333-4291) wait for fares on the dock on both sides. The water taxis, the daily *Bo Hengy* fast ferry from Nassau (an hour and a half away), continuing on to Harbour Island ($100 round-trip, children $60, $55 one-way, children $35; ☎323-2166) and the weekly mailboat all arrive at the main dock on the eastern tip of Spanish Wells.

Once on the island, you can rent a **golf cart** ($9 an hour or $40 a day) at Gemini Golf Carts (☎333-5188) in the little red clapboard house just up from the dock, though it is easy enough to get around on foot unless you have luggage.

If you choose to **stay** on the island, the *Adventurer's Resort* (☎333-4883, ℉333-5073, ⓦwww.bahamasvg.com/adventurers; ❹) is a modern, well-maintained motel on the west side of town with nine double rooms and some one- and two-bedroom efficiency units, each with TV. Diving and fishing expeditions can be arranged and two-seater golf carts are available for $35 a day. Bahamas Vacation Homes Ltd (☎333-4080, ⓦwww.bahamasvacationhomes.com; ❺) handles holiday rentals for several quaint clapboard cottages in the village and along the beach.

For **eating** options, try *Jack's Outback Restaurant* (☎333-4219), a popular spot serving filling simple meals in a retro – perhaps without meaning to be – black and yellow dining room right on the waterfront. The seafood-heavy menu features turtle and fries, lobster, fish, steak or chicken ($13–25), conch fritters and sandwiches ($5–7).

While Manuel's Dive Station on the main street sells watersports equipment, it does not offer guided trips; local Chris Emery (☎333-4238) will take you snorkelling.

Harbour Island

Sitting two miles off the northeast coast of Eleuthera, **HARBOUR ISLAND** – also called Briland, a contraction of Harbour Island formed by dropping the "Har", "ou", and "s" – is the place to be with the rich and famous, and although a number of locals still fish and farm for a living on this tiny green island, the atmosphere is decidedly upscale with a studied casualness. Tourism is the name of the game here – just three miles end to end and less than half a mile across – focused on the spectacular **Pink Sand Beach**, which runs the length of the Atlantic side. The island's only settlement is the picture-perfect village of **Dunmore Town**, which climbs a low hill overlooking the harbour. A clutch of intimate and exclusive beach resorts cater to a wealthy clientele, and tucked in along the shore to the north and south of the village are sumptuous winter homes set in lush, carefully tended grounds.

The moneyed classes come here to let their expensively coiffed hair down and saunter in their designer-label beach togs. Movie stars go for a run on the beach without being accosted, and when local homeowner Elle MacPherson drives her customized golf cart into town to pick up a few things at the market, people don't gawk. Meanwhile, the teenage set transported here by their stockbroker parents cruise the main drag – such as it is – in their golf carts, decked out in bikinis and sarongs with mobile phones in hand, looking for the action.

Arrival

There are several means of reaching Harbour Island. The nearest **airport** is located on North Eleuthera, a mile and a half from the dock on the eastern side of Eleuthera facing Harbour Island, where you can catch a water taxi. Continental (☎1-800/231-0856), Twin Air (☎954/359-8266) and USAir (☎1-800/622-1015) have regularly scheduled flights from Fort Lauderdale, and USAir and Continental also fly daily from Miami. Bahamasair (☎1-800/222-4262 or ☎322-4727) has several flights a day to and from Nassau, and Caribbean Aviation Charters (☎377-3362) also has regular flights from Nassau to North Eleuthera.

All flights are met by **taxis** that will take you to the wharf for about $4 per person from where the water taxi to Harbour Island departs. Water taxis depart regularly for the ten-minute ride to the government dock in Dunmore Town ($4 each way). If you are driving up from southern Eleuthera, there is a parking lot where you can leave your car (no charge).

The **ferry** arrives and departs from the government dock in Dunmore Town, within walking distance of all of the hotels, restaurants and the Pink Sand Beach. Bahamas Fast Ferries ($100 round-trip, children $60, $55 one-way, children $35; ☎323-2166, ☏322–8185, ⓦwww.bahamasferries.com) has service daily between Nassau and Harbour Island aboard the *Bo Hengy*, named for a legendary Harbour Island boat builder. It leaves Potter's Cay in Nassau every morning at 8am, stops at Spanish Wells en route and arrives in Dunmore Town at 10.15am; it departs for Nassau again at 3.55pm except on Sundays, when it leaves for Nassau at 2pm.

Two **mailboats** call at Harbour Island each week from New Providence. *Bahamas Daybreak III* ($30 one-way; ☎335-1163) departs Nassau on Wednesdays at 6pm and the *Eleuthera Express* ($30 one-way; ☎333-4677) leaves Nassau for Harbour Island Thursdays at 7am. Call for the return-trip schedule.

To handle private yachts, there are two **marinas** on the island. Harbour Island Marina (☎333-2427, ☏333 3040, ⓦwww.harbourislandmarina.com, VHF Ch 16) has 32 slips with depths of 10ft or 12ft and the *Hammerhead's Bar and Grill* on site. Dockage fees are $1.25 per foot per day plus services. *Valentine's Resort and Marina* (☎1-800/383-6480 or ☎333-2142, ☏333-2135, ⓦwww.valentinesresort.com, VHF Ch 16) has 39 berths for boats up to 160ft with 12ft draft and an open-air bar. *Valentine's Resort* is across the street, with hotel accommodation, a dive shop, pool and restaurant.

Getting around

Harbour Island is small and Dunmore Town itself is very compact and easy enough to get around on foot. **Taxi** drivers wait for fares on the dock, but most visitors buzz around on **golf carts**, which can be rented on the dock when you arrive, or arranged through your hotel. They are a fun and easy way to explore the far reaches of the island, but the narrow streets of Dunmore Town can be fairly clogged by golf cart traffic jams filled with those out to see and be seen, with a few pickup trucks and minivans mixed in for good measure. Ross's Garage (T 333-2064, F 333-2585) rents well maintained golf carts. A two/four/six-seater costs $35/$45/$65 for 24 hours or $210/$270/$310 for a week. Ross's also rents **minivans** for $75 a day and $450 a week. You can rent **bicycles** at Anthony's Farm (T 333-2567) for $10/$60 per hour/week; and from Big Red's Bike and Cart Rentals (T 333-2045), Dorothea's Bicycle Rentals (T 333-2071) or Michael's Cycles (T 333-2384).

Robert Davis (T 333-2337) offers **historical tours** of Dunmore Town ($100 for a tour lasting an hour and a half for up to three people) as well as horse-back riding on the beach ($30 for an hour, $20 for a half-hour).

Information

The Ministry of Tourism Bureau (Mon–Fri 9am–5pm; T 333-2621, F 333-2622) is located upstairs from the Sugar Mill gift store on Bay Street, opposite the government dock, yet is often unmanned. An informative website (W www .myharbourisland.com) is maintained by Robert Arthur, lifelong resident of Harbour Island and proprietor of *Arthur's Bakery*, offering a virtual walking tour, map and a guide to local restaurants, accommodation, nightlife and local goings-on. Further information is available on the web through W www.briland.com, which has some local history and community news as well as tourist information.

Colourful **maps** of Dunmore Town and Harbour Island as well as a selection of books about the Bahamas can be found at Dilly Dally on King Street.

Accommodation

In addition to its **hotels**, Harbour Island boasts a large selection of charming holiday **cottage rentals** in Dunmore Town and on the more secluded estates fronting the beach and the harbour. Island Real Estate (T 333-2278, E islandrealest@batelnet.bs) handles bookings for over eighty properties ranging from self-catering studio apartments to beachfront villas staffed with a cook and a housekeeper. Generally rented by the week, they range in price from $700 to $7000 a week, with an average rate of $1200–2000 for a one- or two-bedroom cottage.

Bahama House Inn Corner of Dunmore and Hill sts T 333-2201, F 333-2850, W www .bahamahouseinn.com. A charming B&B in a rambling late eighteenth-century mansion set in a large garden with a view of the harbour from the wraparound veranda. The seven guestrooms (one with a kitchen) evoke the colonial era with painted wood floors, high antique beds, polished mahogany wardrobes and colourful scatter rugs. The ground floor is a warm and inviting open space with an old-fashioned kitchen and solid wooden tables where breakfast is served. There are deep comfy sofas for chatting or watching TV and a cozy library nook. ⑤–⑥

Coral Sands Hotel On the beach ☎ 333-2350, ℱ 333-2320, Ⓦ www.coralsands.com. The largest hotel on the island – and the most modern in design – offers 39 guestrooms contained in three two-storey white stucco blocks facing the sea. Most have a private balcony or patio with a view of the ocean or the extensive landscaped grounds. The nicest rooms are in the newly built Lucaya Block, which has spacious and airy doubles and suites featuring floor-to-ceiling views of the ocean, handsome mahogany furniture, four-poster beds, white walls and stone tiled floors. The hotel features tennis courts, a swimming pool and the breezy, inviting *Commander's Beach Bar* with steps down to the beach. ❽

Dunmore Beach Club Facing the beach ☎ 333-2200, ℱ 333-2429, Ⓦ www.dunmorebeach.com. Seven guest cottages on eight acres tucked in among the flowering trees house fourteen double rooms and one-bedroom suites. Newly renovated, they have an old-fashioned elegance with pastel colour schemes, flowered chintz, honey-coloured wood, and white wicker. Each room has a/c, ceiling fans, a 6ft Jacuzzi tub, refrigerator and wet bar, and a private patio with an ocean view. ❽

The Landing On the waterfront overlooking the harbour ☎ 333-2707, ℱ 333-2650, Ⓦ www.harbourislandlanding.com. An elegant and historical inn in a walled garden with deep verandas furnished with upholstered wicker chairs facing the water. The guestrooms are spare and airy, exquisitely restored to evoke the colonial period with four-poster beds and gauzy canopies, crisp white linens and walls, polished dark-wood floors, antique furnishings and dramatic original artwork. Some rooms have private balconies. The inn has one of the finest restaurants on the island, a cozy and popular bar, and a quiet upstairs sitting room for guests which opens onto the veranda. ❽

Pink Sands Hotel Pink Sand Beach ☎ 333-2030 or 2061, ℱ 333-2060, Ⓦ www.islandoutpost.com. Part of Island Records founder Chris Blackwell's collection of luxury boutique hotels, the *Pink Sands'* main building is an artfully weathered dusty pink stucco trimmed with queen conch shells and vaguely Moroccan and Balinese accents. Twenty-one one- and two-bedroom guest bungalows are nestled in secluded nooks around the sixteen-acre property, some boasting ocean views while others have private garden terraces. The interiors are bright and airy, with rough marble floors, walls painted in soft pastels, and furnished with a mix of custom-made wood pieces and exotic accents like Indian tapestries and carved stone lanterns. ❽

Ramora Bay Club Colebrook St ☎ 333-2325 or 1-800/688-0425, ℱ 333-2500, Ⓦ www.romorabay.com. Cottages housing thirty guestrooms and suites are staggered down a gentle green slope facing a private dock with a view of Eleuthera across the water. The main house has an inviting and open Mediterranean feel, with rough painted ochre and terracotta walls, rosy stone floors, dark-wood accents, deep leather sofas and a view of the turquoise water through the vine-covered archways of the loggia which opens onto a broad terrace. There are tennis courts, a swimming pool with lounge chairs facing the harbour, an open-air bar and watersports. Includes free transfers to and from North Eleuthera Airport for stays of three days or more. ❽

Tingum Village Hotel Colebrook St ☎ & ℱ 333-2161. Several rustic and homely self-catering cottages and apartment units set in a quiet grove of coconut palms and flowering bushes with access to the beach a short distance away, and the famous *Ma Ruby's* restaurant a few steps up the path. ❸

Valentine's Resort and Marina On the waterfront on the harbour side of the island ☎ 333-2080, ℱ 333-2135 or 1-800/383 6480, Ⓦ www.valentinesresort.com. Not the place for honeymooners, but a decent budget option patronized primarily by divers. The utilitarian but pleasant air-conditioned rooms are done up in wicker furniture and floral bedcovers and set around a small swimming pool with a view of the marina beyond. There is no TV or phone in the rooms, but these are available in the attached bar and lounge. There is also a dive shop on site. ❸

Dunmore Town and around

With neat narrow streets lined with freshly painted clapboard cottages, flower boxes and white picket fences, **DUNMORE TOWN** – with a population of 1500 – evokes a small New England seaside town. It is a pleasant place to stroll around, with judiciously placed cafés and bars for refreshment along the way. When the sun goes down, people gather at one of Dunmore Town's several atmospheric bars and fine restaurants, and the more energetic stay up to catch some live music and dancing at one of the local clubs.

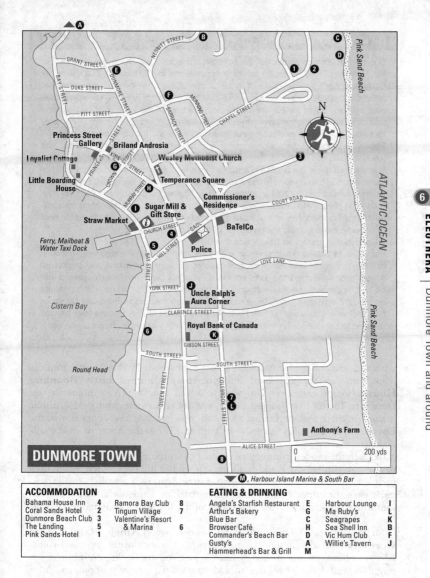

DUNMORE TOWN

*Ferry, Mailboat &
Water Taxi Dock*

Cistern Bay

Round Head

ATLANTIC OCEAN

Pink Sand Beach

Pink Sand Beach

N

Princess Street
Gallery
Briland Androsia
Loyalist Cottage
Wesley Methodist Church
Little Boarding
House
Temperance Square
Commissioner's
Residence
Sugar Mill &
Gift Store
Straw Market
BaTelCo
Police
Uncle Ralph's
Aura Corner
Royal Bank of Canada
Anthony's Farm

▼ M, Harbour Island Marina & South Bar

ACCOMMODATION			
Bahama House Inn	4	Ramora Bay Club	8
Coral Sands Hotel	2	Tingum Village	7
Dunmore Beach Club	3	Valentine's Resort	
The Landing	5	& Marina	6
Pink Sands Hotel	1		

EATING & DRINKING			
Angela's Starfish Restaurant	E	Harbour Lounge	I
Arthur's Bakery	G	Ma Ruby's	L
Blue Bar	C	Seagrapes	K
Browser Café	H	Sea Shell Inn	B
Commander's Beach Bar	D	Vic Hum Club	F
Gusty's	A	Willie's Tavern	J
Hammerhead's Bar & Grill	M		

Just up from the government dock, directly across the street from the **Straw Market**, where local craftspeople sell handmade straw work and souvenir knick-knacks, stands the **Higgs Sugar Mill** on Bay Street. This small, white clapboard building houses the Sugar Mill gift store and the Tourism Bureau. No longer in use, the mill was owned and operated by a certain Hoppy Higgs in the early nineteenth century and was one of three on the island at the time. Sugar and syrup were made here from cane grown on the southern end of the island and exported to the United States.

Bay Street, which runs along the waterfront, is lined with well-kept cottages

An unworthy namesake

Dunmore Town was named for the Scottish aristocrat **Lord Dunmore**, governor of the Bahamas (1787–96), who built a summer home in 1791 on the rise where the Commissioner's Residence (built in 1920) now stands. He laid out a neat grid of streets and divided the remainder of his estate into 190 lots, which he sold to prominent settlers. Using slaves, they farmed sugar cane on the south end of the island and pineapple plantations over on north Eleuthera. Briland also became an important boat-building centre, turning out fishing smacks and the schooners that carried Bahamian sponges, pineapples, sugar and timber to Europe and America. The wooden buildings seen now were built mainly between 1800 and 1860.

Apart from being the original titleholder to the land on which it was built, Governor Dunmore did little to prove himself worthy of being lastingly honoured. Before arriving in the Bahamas, he had an undistinguished career as governor first of New York then of Virginia. When the American Revolution broke out, he abandoned his capital and fled to the safety of a warship anchored offshore, which he declared the seat of government, incurring the contempt of both Loyalists and republicans.

Upon being appointed to office in the Bahamas in 1787, Dunmore developed a mania for fort building and sleeping with other men's wives. He appointed his sons to lucrative offices and suspended the elected Assembly for over a year to prevent it from passing legislation he did not like. One of his contemporaries observed that he had "a capacity below mediocrity" and another charged that he was "obstinate and violent by nature". In 1796, a resident of Harbour Island testified that Dunmore had broken a stick over his head without provocation, and nine days later he was recalled to London, never returning to the pretty little village that bears his name.

with verandas and gabled windows facing the harbour. Walking north from the dock, you pass the clapboard and gingerbread-trimmed **Little Boarding House** (signposted), over 200 years old and now a private home. It was Dunmore Town's first lodging house, run by two sisters who held Catholic masses in their parlour before a church was built. A few doors down, the **Loyalist Cottage** (also marked) was built in 1797 as the home of a local sailmaker.

To reach the modest commercial centre of Dunmore Town, retrace your steps to the government dock and head straight up the hill on Church Street, then turn left onto Dunmore Street. **Temperance Square** is actually a small triangular park surrounded by a picket fence marking a memorial to Dr Thomas Johnson, who died in 1893 and was one of the first Harbour Islanders to qualify as a doctor.

On the corner of Dunmore and Clarence streets, **Uncle Ralph's Aura Corner**, a colourful and growing collection of licence plates and hand-painted signs offering words to live by like "When you are skating on thin ice, you might as well dance." Feel free to add your own piece of wisdom, and leave some change in the bucket. The originator, local resident Ralph Sawyer, donates it to the medical clinic. A block further south on Dunmore Street, is the Sir George Roberts Library, built in 1969, a rather grand edifice set back on a broad lawn. These days, the library amounts to a couple of shelves filled with old novels and textbooks, and the museum which used to be here is now closed. There are a few etchings and interesting old photographs of Dunmore Town on display.

From Dunmore Street, head back along Bay to the south end of the town and you will happen upon an area called Roundheads, after the rebels who dethroned Charles I in England in 1649. Here, you will find the remnants of a battery of **cannon** mounted to protect the small settlement from pirate attacks.

The rest of Harbour Island

By far, the biggest draw on the island is the undeniably lovely **Pink Sand Beach** (see box on p.215), which can be reached by following either Chapel Street or Court Road over the dunes and right onto the sand. The beach offers sweeping vistas, miles of walking, a gentle rolling surf and a sprinkling of beach bars where you can sit and decide for yourself if the faintly rosy hue of the sand really *is* pink.

If you continue south on the Queen's Highway from the Harbour Island Marina, you reach the gated residential community of **South Bar**, which encloses the treed southern end of the island. If you want to follow the dirt track – passable by golf cart – to the **ruins** of the seventeenth-century battlements at the far end, you must stop at the administrative office (℡ 333-2293) to ask for permission. The one cannon mounted here seems feeble protection from the pirate ships that cruised the channel for booty and periodically raided the settlement.

For a good walk, follow Bay Street north into Nesbitt Street along a wooded trail, flanked by rather grand oceanfront estates. The track narrows to a small rocky point at the southern end of the island – about a mile and a half from the centre of the village – ending on a rocky shore with a view of Jacobs Island and the slightly larger Man Island beyond.

Eating

There are more **dining** spots on Harbour Island than anywhere else in the Eleutheran chain, and the variety of options is understandably greater here. You will find several **kiosks** on Bay Street along the waterfront selling fresh conch salad, hamburgers and chips, and wooden benches are situated with a fine view of the harbour. The town's **restaurants** range from the elegant and sophisticated dining rooms in the tony hotels to casual cafés, beachfront bars and local diners. Dinner reservations are recommended for all restaurants, and required if you would like to sample the fine gourmet fare at one of the hotels, where you are generally expected to dress for dinner.

Angela's Starfish Restaurant On top of Barracks Hill ℡ 333-2253. While this simple, inexpensive local restaurant's unfortunate proximity to the local dump over the hill can occasionally be a problem when the wind blows the wrong way and you want to sit outside, the dining room is scrupulously clean. Specializes in seafood. Note – "no bare backs and no profanity".

Arthur's Bakery Corner of Crown and Dunmore sts. Scrumptious cinnamon buns, rich chocolate brownies, fresh-baked pies, pastries and breads fill the display cases. The aroma and soft jazz music waft through the sunny café serving tasty breakfasts and lunches. Closed Sun.

Blue Bar On the beach at the *Pink Sands Hotel* ℡ 333-2030. This relaxed open-air beach bar and grill painted a bright cobalt blue serves burgers, fries and conch fritters and drinks during the day.

Browser Café Murray St ℡ 333-3069. A charming, inexpensive little courtyard café attached to the Briland Brush Strokes Art Gallery, with extra seating on a shaded wooden deck upstairs with a view of the harbour. The weathered grey wood of the gallery wall is dressed up with lilac trim, and fresh hibiscus flowers deck each wooden table. The owner dishes up absolutely amazing coconut French toast, omelettes and fresh squeezed orange juice as well as Bahamian platters of tuna and grits, boiled fish and souse for breakfast, with homemade soups and chowder, salads and sandwiches for lunch, and daily specials like grouper served with fried plantains. Open 7am–3pm.

Commander's Beach Bar *Coral Sands Hotel* ☎333-2350. Enjoy the sweeping view of the beach at this beach bar open for lunch and cocktails. The tasty lunch menu features a rock lobster salad sandwich, salads, burgers including a vegetarian burger, seafood nibbles and yummy frozen drinks.

Dunmore Beach Club Facing the beach ☎333-2200. Has a small formal chintz and white-wicker dining room with a view of Pink Sand Beach. Selections from the constantly changing menu include such creations as coconut milk soup with lemon grass and kafir; followed by seared tuna with green curry and seaweed or spaghetti squash, zucchini, apples and black-eyed peas with green curry; with baked pineapple and vanilla coconut ice cream for dessert. You must make your dinner reservations and choices from the menu by noon.

Hammerheads Bar and Grill Harbour Island Marina ☎333-3240. On a deck overlooking the marina, this attractive lunch and dinner spot serves finger food, salads, sandwiches, jerk chicken, strip steak, veggie quesadillas and great drinks.

Harbour Lounge Bay St facing the government dock ☎333-2031. With tables on a wide veranda, this popular spot for people-watching features such specialties as spicy tequila shrimp, a grouper sandwich, pumpkin soup and other entrees from $10 to $35. Closed Mon, open for dinner only on Sun.

The Landing Bay St, south of the government dock ☎333-2707. An elegant and romantic candlelit dining room with dark hardwood floors and a gourmet menu that centres on fresh pasta, lobster, choice steaks and squid with aïoli. Closed Wed.

Ma Ruby's at Tingum Village Colebrook St ☎ & ⓕ333-2161. Justly popular eatery famous for its hearty cheeseburger, *Ma Ruby's* also serves generous and tasty plates of grouper fingers, lobster, pasta and a scrumptious Key Lime pie, on a casual roofed patio surrounded by greenery.

Pink Sands Hotel Pink Sands Beach ☎333-2030. A casually elegant bar and dining room done up in weathered pink stucco with teak furniture, Balinese accents and lots of candlelight, opening onto a garden, where café tables are set for breakfast under the trees. The expensive dinner menu changes daily, with delectable offerings like smoked salmon or warm goat's cheese with asparagus and tomato in pastry as an appetizer, followed by grilled yellowfin tuna or a sautéed local grouper fillet, and mango cream pie or rum and coconut crème brûlée for afters.

Ramora Bay Club Colebrook St ☎333-2325. Breakfast and lunch are served at wrought-iron café tables in a sunny alcove adjoining the terrace, and dinner is served by candlelight in an intimate dining room with a sunset view. The expensive yet imaginative French cuisine incorporates fresh local seafood and produce into dishes like an organic arugula salad with prosciutto Parma ham and grapefruit; mahimahi cooked with white wine, lemon and herbs; and homemade passion fruit sorbet for dessert.

Sea Shell Inn Nesbitt St ☎333-2361. A pleasant, simple and casual peach-stucco bar and restaurant serving moderately priced Bahamian and American meals such as cracked conch, fried chicken and fish, with live music Sunday nights. $20–25 each for dinner.

Drinking and nightlife

While you can sip a frosty cocktail at any of the appealing beach and waterfront **bars** and **restaurants** listed above, there are atmospheric watering holes at three of the nicest hotels in Dunmore Town. The cozy, warmly lit bar at *The Landing* (☎333-2707) has overstuffed sofas, fine wines, whiskies and rum, evoking an earlier, more glamorous age; the bar at the casual chic *Pink Sands Hotel* (☎333-2030) features live music Tuesday and Saturday nights; and the deep leather sofas at the *Ramora Bay Club* (☎333-2325) are a relaxing setting for a cocktail or a nightcap.

Gusty's (☎ 333-2165) has **live music** a couple of nights a week, while *Seagrapes* (☎333-2439), a cavernous concrete block on Colebrook Street, is a venue for live music most weekends. The *Vic Hum Club* (☎333-2161), on the corner of Munnings and Barrack streets, is a local institution. Home of what is supposedly the world's largest coconut – kept in a cardboard box near the bar – and a bartender with the unfortunate name of Hitler, it features all manner of entertainment, including a ping-pong table, a miniature basketball court that becomes a dance floor as the night wears on and yellow and black striped walls plastered with old album covers and licence plates from all over. *Willie's Tavern* (T 333-2021), on Dunmore Street, established in 1947, is also a popular local hangout, with a pool table and live music on the weekends.

Diving and watersports

The premier local attraction for experienced divers is a high-speed drift dive through **Current Cut**, where you are swept along at speeds of up to ten knots through a narrow underwater canyon. The **Devil's Backbone**, a reef that extends for three miles along the northern edge of Eleuthera, has claimed many a ship over the centuries, including that of the Eleutheran Adventurers. While their vessel has not been found, the area is littered with wrecks, including that of a steam train locomotive that fell off a ship bound for Havana and is now a popular dive site. There are also plenty of other reefs and sea gardens to explore, although most must be reached by boat. Two dive shops in Dunmore Town can set you up for a day of diving or snorkelling and/or rent you a boat. If you'd rather catch a fish than look at it, they can also arrange that.

Dive operators

Ocean Fox Dive Shop Harbour Island Marina T 333-2323, F 333-2500. The Ocean Fox offers daily snorkelling excursions for $35, including equipment. Other diving options include a resort course for $95 including equipment; a single-tank dive for $45; two-tank dive $75; and a night dive for $65. Equipment rental costs $15 for snorkelling gear; $35 for scuba equipment. The owner, Jeff Fox, will also take you deep-sea fishing for $750 for a full day, $450 half-day, including all gear. Deserted Island Beach Picnic $40 per person. Boat rentals are also available.

Valentine's Dive Center *Valentine's Resort and Marina* T 333-2080, W www.valentinesdive.com. Snorkelling trips go for $35, including gear; $65 for a two-tank dive; $125 for a high-speed drift dive through Current Cut. They also do wall dives and night dives or you can charter the dive boat for the whole day for $650. The PADI Open Water Certification is a four-day course from $450 including video and textbook, dive equipment, pool sessions and four open-water dives. They offer the PADI Rescue Diver Course for $450, a nine- to ten-day PADI Dive Master Course for $875; and a number of other specialty courses including search and recover, underwater navigation and night diving. Deep-sea fishing charters go for $750 for a full day, $550 for a half-day including boat, bait, tackle, captain and mate.

Shopping

There are several upscale gift shops and clothing boutiques in Dunmore Town catering to vacationers where you can find a souvenir or something to wear. Miss Mae's Fine Things, on Dunmore Street (T 333-2002), sells pretty frocks, swimwear and gifts, while Island Androsia, on King Street (T 333-2342), deals in the distinctive and colourful batik fabric primarily produced on the island of Andros. Visitors seeking original Bahamian artwork, including paintings and prints by Eddie Minnis (see p.224), can find them at the Princess Art Gallery on Princess Street (T 333-2788) and the Briland Brush Strokes Gallery.

Listings

Banking The Royal Bank of Canada (Mon–Fri 9.30am–5pm; ☎ 333-2250) is located on Murray St. There is a 24-hour ATM connected to Plus and Cirrus.

Groceries The Piggly Wiggly on King St at Crown, and Johnson's Grocery on Dunmore St near Munning St, have a good range of foodstuffs. Pineapple Fruit and Veg on Bay St near Pitt St sells produce. You can buy it fresh from the field at Anthony's Farm.

Internet access Sporadically available through a volunteer-run community project at the Sir George Roberts Library on the corner of South and Dunmore sts.

Laundry Seaside Laundromat (☎ 333-2066) is on Bay St.

Medical attention The Harbour Island Health

Clinic (☎ 333-2227) is the pink building on the corner of South and Colebrook sts.

Pharmacy A pharmacist is on duty at Bayside Drugstore (☎ 333-2174) on Bay St.

Police ☎ 333-2111 or 2327. Located in the Government Administration Building on Goal St. Dial ☎ 911 in an emergency.

Post office Located in the same building and open 9am–5pm weekdays.

Taxis Taxis wait on the government wharf in Dunmore Town, or call Wayne's Big M Taxi (☎ 333-2147) or Jena's Taxi (☎ 333-2116).

Telephone BaTelCo (☎ 333-2375) is on the corner of Colebrook St and Goal Lane and is open 8am to 5.30pm. There are pay phones, prepaid phone cards for sale, and a fax service.

South Eleuthera

South Eleuthera, from Palmetto Point to Eleuthera Point, is the least developed part of the island, the largest settlement down this way being sleepy, prettily painted Rock Sound, with its "international" airport. Also serving as a possible base is the picturesque fishing village of **Tarpum Bay**; the remaining highlights are in the form of stunning beaches, including Winding Bay, Cotton Bay and Lighthouse Beach. There is not much to do in the region other than listen to the sound of the waves from the vantage point of any number of well-sited beachfront cottages, but that's basically the point.

Tarpum Bay

Twenty miles south of Governor's Harbour the Queen's Highway runs through the centre of **TARPUM BAY**, a colourful fishing village nestled alongside a sweeping curve of turquoise water and white-sand beach, just five miles north of **Rock Sound International Airport**.

On the waterfront, the whitewashed **St Columba's Anglican Church** is one of Eleuthera's most photographed sites. Originally settled by the descendants of freed slaves and now home to a small Haitian community, the village has several brightly painted wooden cottages and numerous examples of traditional Bahamian architecture in various states of repair lining its few narrow lanes. Surrounded by flowering trees and roaming chickens, they are picturesque in their decay, at least to a visitor. Roosters provide an early-morning wakeup call for the fishermen and women who sell their catch in the early afternoon on the wharf. Several nights a week the otherwise quiet side streets of the settlement ring with exhortations and hallelujahs from the pulpit of one of its many churches.

On the north side of town you can see the **castle** built by the self-titled Lord Macmillan Hughes, an oddball British artist who lived here thirty years until his recent death. The narrow sandy **beach** at Tarpum Bay extends two miles northward on the Bight side, and there is another fine beach on the Atlantic side at **Winding Bay**, one mile south of town. A fun time to visit Tarpum Bay is for the **Junkanoo** rush-out on either December 26 or New Year's Day, when colourful parade floats, traditional dancers and marching bands with drums, whistles and cowbells take to the streets in the early dawn.

Practicalities

If you are looking for **accommodation** in Tarpum Bay, *Cartwright's Oceanfront Cottages* (☎334-4215; ❹) has three cozy two- and three-bedroom cottages on the waterfront at the western edge of town, with a homely and eclectic decor of crocheted doilies, china cats and a great view of the sea. *Hilton's Haven* (☎334-4231, ☎325-2212, ✉acleare@yahoo.com; ❹) on the waterfront in the centre of the village rents ten simple motel rooms. *Island Dreams* (☎334-2356, ⓦwww.bahamas-island-dreams.com; ❸) has several appealing cottage rentals in and around Tarpum Bay and Rock Sound.

Eating is a bit of an afterthought in Tarpum Bay. Filling deep-fried and Bahamian fare can be procured at *Barbie's* (closed Sun), which has a couple of tables, or at *Bertha's Go Go Ribs* takeaway. The adventurous might seek a drink at the rough-and-tumble *Pink Elephant* on the west side of town.

Rock Sound

Eight miles south of Tarpum Bay, **ROCK SOUND** is a green and tidy little waterfront village of well-kept cottages with fenced gardens and several candy-coloured buildings, including the medical clinic, a colonial-style government administration building and a BaTelCo office. The rainbow-coloured clapboard cottage on the main street houses the delightful Luna Sea Gift Shop, run by the equally charming Janice Gibson, with an imaginatively displayed collection of original Bahamian artwork and crafts. Born and raised in South Eleuthera and back home now after several years of working off the island, Janice is also an avid scholar of local history. Vast quantities of pineapples were shipped from here in the nineteenth century, but there really is not much doing in sleepy Rock Sound these days; many inhabitants are retired or work in the civil service. Its peaceful streets and the constant view of the blue-green sea make for a pleasant stroll.

Other sights include the **Ocean Hole** off Fish Street, a rock crater about 50yd across and 50yd deep filled with rather murky saltwater and a population of fish that like to be fed bread. Further towards the Atlantic coast on Fish Street, the **Nor'Side Beach** (see p.214) is a dramatic stretch of sand with a nice spot for a drink or a meal (see below).

Practicalities

The only real **place to stay** in Rock Sound is *The Nor'Side Resort* (☎334-2573; ❹), which has a spectacular setting perched on a bluff overlooking a long lonesome stretch of beach on the Atlantic side of Rock Sound. To get there from the centre of Rock Sound village, follow Fish Street for about a mile to a T-junction, then turn left about 500yd. A cluster of four hexagonal cottages house eight studio apartments beautifully decorated in soothing neutral shades accented with floral fabrics. The rooms are bright and airy, each with a Jacuzzi tub, TV, kitchen and dining nook. There is good snorkelling from the beach, and a cozy sand-floored bar and a restaurant serving the best home-cooked Bahamian meals on the island, including grouper fingers, cracked conch, barbecue chicken and generous helpings of traditional side-dishes.

Your other **eating** options in Rock Sound are restricted to the *Haven Bakery* (T334-2155; closed Sun) in a bright-green building in the middle of the village, where Julian Haven turns out yummy pastries, pies and sweet Bahamian bread and will prepare special meals on request. *Sammy's Place* (T334-2121) serves tasty and filling deep-fried fare, pizza and fresh seafood done Bahamian-style in a casual diner on a back street near the primary school. The Rock Sound Marketplace on the north edge of town has the biggest grocery store on Eleuthera, a pharmacy, liquor store, gas station and a branch of the Bank of Nova Scotia.

For friendly and reliable **car and SUV rentals** of well-maintained vehicles, call Wilfred Major (T334-2158, F334-2517). Rates start at $350 a week. **Taxi** drivers meet every flight at Rock Sound Airport, or call Friendly Bob (T334-8112, 334-8184 or 359-7806).

South from Rock Sound

Heading south of Rock Sound, you have the ocean on your right for a while before the road cuts inland through low undulating bush. The island broadens into a wide inverted triangle at its southern end, encompassing several small inland settlements and stretches of mangrove swash. There are a few points of interest down this way, notably Cotton Bay for golfers, Lighthouse Beach for beach aficionados, and the Island School for young aspiring marine biologists.

Seven and a half miles south of Rock Sound, you pass the turnoff to the now defunct **Cotton Bay Club** (T334-6156) on your left. Nine of the eighteen holes on the golf course are still open, and the pretty curved beach can be accessed by a short path about 20yd south of the guard house, where you can rent clubs and pay the greens fees ($70 for nine holes, $100 for eighteen holes; $15 to rent clubs).

If you continue a mile further south on the Queen's Highway, the road divides at Greencastle, with the Queen's Highway heading southeast to Eleuthera Point and a paved road veering southwest out of town. The latter reaches a T-junction, where, if you continue right a few miles you reach **Deep Creek**, a smattering of houses and several churches strung along the road facing an expanse of waterlogged mangrove swash. The highlight here is the bone-fishing, for which Alfred McKinney (T334-8097 or 8184) serves as the local guide.

A couple of miles past Deep Creek is the **Island School** (PO Box 6008, Lawrenceville, NJ 08648; T609/620-6700, F895-2093, Wislandschool.org, Eischool@batelnet.bs), a private school offering a semester abroad for high school students interested in environmental conservation and community service projects. The school's dive shop is located nearby at the Cape Eleuthera Marina (T334-6327), and when the equipment is not in use, you can rent it. They charge $175 for full scuba gear including a two-tank dive; $7 to fill an air tank; and $7 to rent snorkelling gear for the day. You can charter a boat and guide, and sea kayak rental can be arranged; call the school for details.

If you are heading for **Lighthouse Beach** (see p.214), stay on the main highway until you come to a sharp right-angle turn leading to Bannerman Town. Don't make this turn, but take the dirt road straight ahead of you. It is three miles of extremely rough, rocky track leading to this absolutely stunning beach. En route, you pass a turnoff to the right, but keep going straight. The road is passable in a car, but a four-wheel-drive is best – the first two miles are worse than the last. You should allow half an hour to cover the distance in from Bannerman Town. Your reward is six miles of pristine pink and white sandy beach and a turquoise surf with the dark shadows of coral reefs and heads visible beneath the surface. On a clear day, you can see Cat Island and San Salvador on the horizon. The jutting headlands at the south end of the beach are topped by a derelict but picturesque modern lighthouse. You can park below the lighthouse, and follow the path up over the dunes and onto the beach.

Practicalities

The only place to **stay** south of Rock Sound are the rooms above *Kell's Take Away and Gas Station* (℡334-0104; ❶) in Wemyss Bight (not the place for a holiday), but the area is easily visited on day-trips from elsewhere on the island. **Eating** options are negligible down this way – it is best to pack a lunch if you are coming for the day. In addition to *Kell's Take Away*, *DJ's Pizza* (℡334-9401) in Waterford does takeaway (open sporadically), and you can grab a bite at *Sharil's Inn* (closed Sun) in Deep Creek, which serves your basic deep-fried fish dinners.

The Exumas

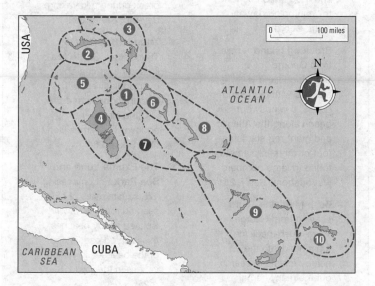

CHAPTER 7

Highlights

✳ **The Out Island Regatta** George Town's Elizabeth Harbour brims with life for several days at the end of April when this annual regatta celebrates the Bahamian tradition of wooden boat building. Rake 'n' scrape music and food stalls keep the town jumping day and night. See p.251

✳ **Stocking Island** A mile from George Town, Stocking Island is blessed with high sand dunes, a windswept beach along the Atlantic and giant red starfish a foot or more in diameter found in large numbers just offshore. See p.251

✳ **Bush Medicine Tours** Leaving from George Town, bush medicine tours head into the nearby forests to search out the many herbal remedies that have been passed down through generations. See p.259

✳ **Leaf Cay** Home to a colony of yard-long giant iguanas, this small isle in the southern Exuma Cays features an isolated beach on the leeward side that is great for a break during a kayaking day-trip. See p.262

✳ **Thunderball Grotto** Thunderball Grotto is a limestone vault arching over pools filled with colourful corals and fish and the site of the eponymous James Bond film. See p.264

✳ **The Exuma Land and Sea Park** Encompassing 176 square miles of blue sea and rocky cays with isolated sandy beaches, this isolated park is one of the best sea kayaking venues in the world. See p.265

7

The Exumas

With a name like a contented sigh, the laid-back **EXUMAS** suit their label. Some 365 islands, cays and rock outcroppings of various sizes make up the island chain, which lies in a narrow band stretched over one hundred miles along the eastern edge of the Great Bahama Bank. The islands are bound on one side by the shallow, clear waters of the bank, and on the other by the deep heavy waves of Exuma Sound. It's not surprising that human life here is very much oriented towards the sea, and those Exumians not engaged in fishing, farming or government services cater to a small yet growing tourist trade here.

The shallow protected waters and deserted beaches make the Exumas ideal for **sea kayaking**, and several outfitters run expeditions through the cays and in the pristine **Exuma Land and Sea Park**. Great and Little Exuma and the islands south of the park boundaries are flanked by prime bonefishing and deep-sea **fishing grounds**, and throughout the region the seas teem with multicoloured life that ensures memorable **diving** and **snorkelling**.

On the bigger, settled islands of **Great and Little Exuma** at the south end of the chain, land has been cleared and planted over generations, giving them a more pastoral air. Blessed with a fine natural harbour, the capital **George Town**, located in the centre of Great Exuma, is a popular destination for boaters and contains most of the chain's hotels, restaurants and outdoor outfitters. To the north and south of the capital, several small fishing and farming settlements, such as **Williamstown** and **Rolle Town**, offer a picturesque glimpse of Out Island life, and make a pleasant day-trip from George Town by car or bicycle.

North of Great Exuma, the **Exuma Cays** stretch out for forty miles. The showstopper here is the remote Exuma Land and Sea Park, an area of extraordinary beauty. There are, though, several other worthwhile stops, including the small fishing settlements on sleepy **Little Farmer's Cay** and pretty **Staniel Cay**, which draws a yachting crowd and hosts a good-time New Year's Day Regatta that lasts for three days.

Some history

Although no archeological evidence has been unearthed, it is quite likely that there were Lucayan settlements here before the **British** laid claim to the Exumas in the seventeenth century. Sometime around 1700, the whole of Great Exuma was granted to Englishman **Henry Palmer**, who never lived on the island chain but sent his ships to gather salt and braziletto, a valuable hardwood used in cabinetry and to make a red or purple dye. While others soon came to hunt whales and rockfish off the islands, the most frequent visitors

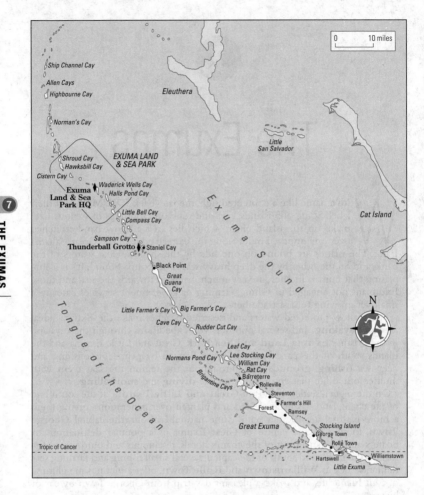

were pirates and privateers, who plied the waters of the Bahamas in their dozens; in any case, no more than thirty settled permanently on the Exumas.

As elsewhere in the Bahamas, the population jumped drastically with the arrival of **Loyalist** exiles from the southern United States at the end of the American Revolution. Among them was wealthy English aristocrat **Denys Rolle**, who years earlier developed a grandiose vision for a model town in the New World. He gathered three hundred unfortunates from the slums of London and shipped them to Florida, where he built a mansion for himself and laid out a tidy little settlement that he first called Charlotia, after the queen, then modestly renamed Rolleton. When most of the English settlers fled the arduous daily grind of the humid settlement, Rolle replaced them with African slaves.

When the peace accord of 1783 returned Florida to Spain and the Bahamas to England, Rolle loaded his 140 slaves, dismantled houses, livestock and other possessions aboard the *Peace and Plenty* and set sail for Great Exuma. The British government granted Rolle two large tracts of land in the north and south of the island, totalling 2000 acres, which he proclaimed Rolleville and Rolle Town, respectively. Rolle was by far the biggest landowner in the Exumas and the biggest slave-owner in the Bahamas, and by 1789, the population of the Exumas had exploded to 704 (66 European and 638 African). When his cotton farms failed owing to rapid soil exhaustion and the damage caused by the chenille bug, Rolle packed up and went back to England, leaving his properties in the hands of overseers.

In 1820, his son Lord John Rolle tried to move his Exumian slaves to his more productive enterprises on Trinidad, but the slaves, who had made homes on Exuma, were adamantly opposed. Under the leadership of **Pompey**, a group of them took to the woods for over a month to avoid being transported, then commandeered Rolle's boat and defiantly set sail for Nassau. The rebels were captured in the harbour, flogged and sent to the workhouse, yet when they returned home, they were greeted with cheers from their fellow slaves, who immediately staged a strike. Pompey was caught and cruelly whipped, and the slaves returned to work. Nevertheless, they refused to labour more than half of each day for their masters. Troops were called out three more times before the Emancipation was proclaimed in 1834.

Well into the mid-twentieth century, Exumians got along on a combination of sponging, fishing, subsistence agriculture and wrecking – the salvaging of valuables from sunken or abandoned ships. Following World War II, the Exumas were discovered by the international yachting set. Cruising through the cays became the thing to do for the in-crowd, and a handful of swanky resorts opened to cater to them. Although the relatively modest tourist trade here is a far cry from the wall-to-wall carnival of Paradise Island or Freeport/Lucaya, it provides a vital source of income for many Exumians.

In the 1970s, a less welcome form of economic growth emerged as **drug smuggling** boomed throughout the Bahamas, and George Town was the scene of what was, at the time, the largest seizure ever of pure cocaine – 247 pounds worth over two billion dollars. The Bahamian government subsequently launched an intensive campaign to rid the islands of drug runners, and things have calmed down considerably since then. Today, the islands have resumed their simple, sleepy way of life.

Great and Little Exuma

The two biggest islands in the Exumas, **GREAT EXUMA** and **LITTLE EXUMA**, lie head to toe only 200yd apart at the southern end of the chain, joined by a narrow bridge. All but a few hundred of the Exumas three thousand residents live on these two isles, most in the capital **George Town**, located in the centre of 35-mile-long Great Exuma. With plenty of accommodation, restaurant and evening entertainment options, George Town makes a good base for exploring the surrounding area, but its most appealing features are the emerald depths of **Elizabeth Harbour** and the cays that lie offshore. Two of

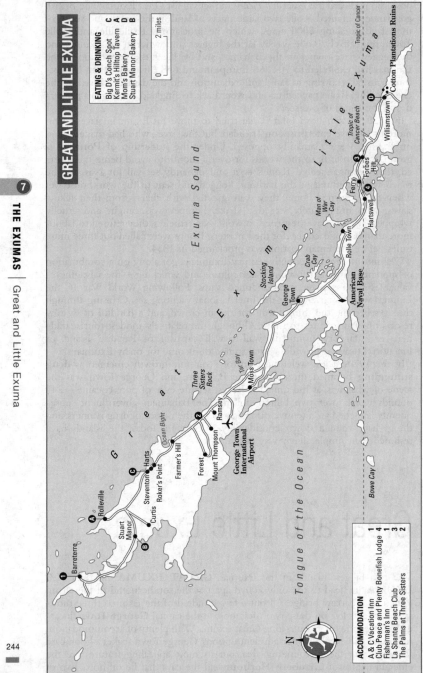

GREAT AND LITTLE EXUMA

EATING & DRINKING

Big D's Conch Spot	C
Kermit's Hilltop Tavern	A
Mom's Bakery	D
Stuart Manor Bakery	B

0   2 miles

ACCOMMODATION

A & C Vacation Inn	1
Club Peace and Plenty Bonefish Lodge	4
Fisherman's Inn	1
La Shante Beach Club	3
The Palms at Three Sisters	2

N

the best, both perfect destinations for a picnic outing either alone or with a guide, are **Stocking Island**, with a long dune-backed beach on its Atlantic side and a couple of casual beach bars, and **Crab Cay**, where there are ruins of a Loyalist plantation. Heading north from George Town, you have your pick of inviting beaches at **Hooper's Bay**, **Jolly Hall**, and **Tar Bay**. The less pictur-esque northern part of Great Exuma has little to offer other than **Barreterre**, which is the jump-off point for trips into the southern Exuma Cays.

Six miles long and two miles wide, Little Exuma to the south is hilly and green. Here you'll find a handful of quiet rural hamlets and a few pretty strands of powdery white beach that make for worthwhile day trip destinations from George Town. Highlights include the seaside settlement of **Rolle Town**, the beach and hilltop ruins on **Man of War Cay**, long and sandy **Tropic of Cancer Beach** and the **Hermitage**, a Loyalist plantation ruin in peaceful **Williamstown**, at the south end of Little Exuma.

Getting there

Eight miles north of the Exumas capital sits **George Town International Airport**. Bahamasair (☎377-5505 or 1-800/222-4262) runs two flights a day here from Nassau, while American Eagle (☎345-0124 or 1-800/433-7300) flies directly to and from Miami once a day.

Unless arriving via private yacht, your port of entry by water will most likely be the government dock in the centre of George Town, within walking distance of most hotels. The *Sealink* ferry ($40 one-way; ☎323-2166) leaves Nassau on Tuesday at 2am, arriving at George Town at 12.45pm, and departs George Town Tuesday at 6pm, arriving in Nassau at 4am on Wednesday morning.

Two **mailboats** service the Exumas from Potter's Cay in Nassau. The well-maintained *Grand Master* mailboat ($40 one-way; ☎393-1064) departs on Tuesday at 2pm, arriving in George Town early Wednesday morning. Depending on the tides and the amount of cargo to be loaded and unloaded, it leaves Wednesday night or Thursday morning, arriving in Nassau twelve hours later. The new *Captain C* mailboat serves the communities of the Exuma Cays. It leaves Nassau on Tuesday afternoons and calls at Staniel Cay, Black Point, Little Farmer's Cay and Barreterre on Wednesday, the Ragged Islands on Thursday, Barreterre, Little Farmer's Cay, Black Point and Staniel Cay again on Friday, and returns to Nassau on Saturday around noon. Round-trip fare is $120. Again, the schedule varies somewhat week to week. Call the Potter's Cay dockmaster (☎393-1064) ahead of time.

Note that if your primary interest is visiting the Exuma Land and Sea Park, you're better off landing at Staniel Cay, just outside its southern boundary (see p.264). If you plan to explore all of the Exumas, it is difficult – though not impossible – to get from George Town to Staniel Cay. There are no commer-cial flights connecting the two, and it requires a combination of cars and boats or an airplane charter.

Information

Located in the centre of George Town above Sam Gray's Car Rental, the Ministry of Tourism's **tourist information centre** (Mon–Fri 9am–5pm;

336-2440, (F) 336-2431) offers a selection of maps, brochures and glossy magazines for the taking. If looking for something more substantial, head for Sandpiper Gifts, across from *Club Peace and Plenty*, which stocks a good selection of books about the Bahamas. A community newspaper, *The Exuma Sentinel*, is published monthly out of Nassau by the *Nassau Guardian* and is available for free at shops and hotels. Bahamas Broadcasting Corporation transmits on Radio frequency 1540 AM, though more entertaining information can often be garnered by tuning a VHF radio onto the locally monitored Channel 16.

Getting around

There is **no public transportation** in Great and Little Exuma. To explore the islands, it's easiest to arrange transportation in George Town, though if arriving by mailboat at Barreterre on the northern tip of Great Exuma land and water taxis can also be had there (see p.255). Taxis are easily accessible, but unless you prefer to have a chauffeur it's more economical to rent a car. The relatively flat and quiet island roads make car, scooter or bicycle a fun way to get around, especially heading south from the capital. Keep in mind, though, that most hotels and restaurants on the outskirts of George Town offer complimentary transportation between their establishments and George Town for their guests. You can also rent a motor boat, sailboat or kayak to explore the coastline and the numerous cays offshore. **Hitchhiking** is easy on Exuma, and a lot of people rely on it to get to work and around.

Taxis

Taxi drivers meet every flight, and the trip into George Town costs around $25 for two passengers. Two reliable and courteous operators are J.J. (T 345- 5005, cell 357-0757), who drives a superannuated white limo, and Leslie Dames (T 357-0015), who pilots a minivan decked out like the *Starship Enterprise*.

Rental cars, bicycles and scooters

None of the major **car rental** companies operates in the Exumas, and available rentals range from perfectly fine to downright dodgy. Three companies with decent vehicles are the aptly named Airport Rent-a-Car (T 345-0090 or 358-8049); Thompson's Rentals (T 336-2442) on the Queen's Highway in the centre of George Town; and Uptown Rent-A-Car (T 336-2822) across the street from Thompson's. All charge around $70 a day, plus a $200 deposit.

Heavy truck traffic and narrow roads make **cycling** in the area immediately surrounding George Town a bit of a hair-raising experience. However, the roads south of town or north past the airport turnoff are quiet and offer scenic vistas to savour. You can rent well-maintained 21-speed bikes at Starfish (see p.257) for $15/25/100 a half-day/full day/week. The Exuma Dive Centre (T 336-2390) and Prestige Cycle Rentals (T 345-4250) opposite Regatta Park rent motor **scooters** for $35/175 a day/week.

Bus and boat tours

For a **bus tour** around the island, you couldn't do any better than Christine Rolle's Island Tours (T 358-4014 or 336-2551 and ask for Taxi #25). Two tours are offered daily at 10am and 2pm (depending on demand), one of which heads southeast to Little Exuma, the other northwest of George Town. Both include visits to rural settlements, local history and bush medicine, and lunch at a local restaurant; either tour costs $15 per person. Starfish the Exuma Activity Centre (℡336-3033) and Exuma Dive Centre (℡336-2390) offer guided **boat tours** (see p.257) of Elizabeth Harbour and the surrounding cays. Renting your own motor boat is another option. Both the Exuma Dive Centre (℡336-2390) and Minns Water Sports (℡336-2604, ℱ336-3483) rent 17- to 22-foot boats for around $80–150 a day ($400–750 a week). Minns also offers boat and engine sales and service, a dock fuelling service, dock space rental and dry storage, and snorkel gear sales and rental. Both companies restrict use of their boats to Elizabeth Harbour. If you want to travel further afield, you must make special arrangements.

Accommodation

You won't find the polished, mints-on-your-pillow type of resort experience in George Town, where most of Great and Little Exuma's **accommodation** is concentrated, though hotel rates tend to be higher than for comparable rooms in North America. However, there is an ample range of comfortable accommodation available. Note that most of the larger hotels add a mandatory service charge of ten to fifteen percent – ask before you book. If there are two or more of you travelling together, often the most economical as well as the most pleasant option is to rent a cottage. In addition to those listed below, see p.29 for a list of companies handling cottage rentals throughout the Bahamas including the Exumas. If you are planning to visit during the Out Island Regatta in late April, you must book months in advance or be prepared to rough it on the beach.

The advantage to staying in the centre of George Town, where there are half a dozen hotels and guesthouses, is easy proximity to services and entertainment in the evening. There is no beach, although there is a regular ferry service to the beaches of Stocking Island (see p.251). Within the immediate area surrounding George Town are several beachfront hotels that offer a quieter, more private retreat, most of which have free transportation to and from George Town. Beyond a mile radius of George Town are several other nice options ranging from simple and homely to rather luxurious. If you stay outside the capital, you will need to rent a car to get around unless you are content to stay put with few diversions besides the beach or the bonefishing flats.

George Town

Bahamas Houseboats ℡336-BOAT, ℱ336-2629, ⓦwww.bahamashouseboats.com. These bright, airy floating apartments are an appealing and economical option for families, a romantic retreat for couples, or simply a fun way to explore Elizabeth Harbour. The 35ft houseboats claim to sleep "two in luxury, four in comfort, and six at a squeeze". Each has big windows to let in the view, a/c, a fully equipped galley, a CD player and an outdoor barbecue. Most boats have a waterslide off the top deck and they all have a motorized dinghy to get to shore. Weekly rate around $2000, daily rate (three-day minimum) $300. Longer 43' boats and a deluxe 46ft boat are also available. ❽

Club Peace and Plenty ℡336-2551 or 1-800/525-2210, ℱ336 2093, ⓦwww.peaceandplenty.com. A historic hotel overlooking Elizabeth Harbour with 35 comfortable peach and white rooms, each with a balcony. A/c, and satellite TV available in all rooms. ❻

Marshall's Guesthouse ℡336-2328, ℱ336-2081. Recently renovated, *Marshall's* offers ten basic rooms and a single one-bedroom apartment in the centre of town. Rooms ❷, apartment ❸

Regatta Point ℡336-2206, ℱ336-2046, ⓦwww.regattapointbahamas.com. A pleasant choice for those who like to have the option of cooking, *Regatta Point* is centrally located, but still private and secluded thanks to its location past the government dock in a stand of coconut palms on a tiny point of land at the end of Kidd Cove. Each of the six apartments has a kitchen and a private balcony. **6**

Two Turtles Inn ☎336-2545, ℱ336-2528, ⓦwww.twoturtlesinn.com. Way overpriced, the carpeted rooms at this inn are dark, dingy and devoid of aesthetic appeal. The establishment's only advantage is its central location, if all you want is a place to lay your head. Note that noise from the patio bar filters up to the rooms. **4**, **5** with kitchenette

George Town's outskirts

Coconut Cove Hotel ☎336-2659, ℱ336-2658. A mile and a half north of town, this pleasant, small beachfront hotel has twelve modern rooms done up in an island theme with private balconies, most with a view of the ocean. There is a restaurant (see p.256), a palm-shaded terrace, a beach bar and a shuttle bus service for guests that runs to and from George Town. **5**, efficiency unit **6**

Coral Gardens Bed and Breakfast ☎ & ℱ336-2880, ⓦwww.bahamasbliss.com. An agreeable and economical option, this B&B, only a five-minute walk from the beach, is run by a friendly English couple. Perched on a breezy hilltop at Hooper's Bay with views of both the east and west coasts of Great Exuma, it has three bright, airy rooms (one double and two twins), with a small refrigerator and private or shared bath. A rental car is available for $40 per day, and there is a discount for stays over fifteen days. Breakfast included. **2**

Hooper's Bay Villas ☎336-2091, ℱ336 2982. Perhaps the best true budget option in the George Town area, though you get what you pay for. The three new, nicely appointed one-room cottages have kitchens and TV, but the bathrooms are grubby and the water flow erratic. The cottages are poorly situated, just a few yards off the Queen's Highway, and built back to front so that sitting on the veranda of the two furthest from the road, you stare directly into the back of the next building. **2**

Hotel Higgins Landing ☎ & ℱ336-2460, ⓦwww.higginslanding.com. Located on Stocking Island, this hotel is a luxurious secluded retreat with five timber guest cottages furnished with antiques, each with a private ocean view. The $495 a night fee includes transportation to and from the airport, breakfast, supper and water-sports. **8**

Minns Cottages ☎336-2033, ℱ336-2645. A delightful respite from the bustle of George Town, these cottages are set in a shady grove on the northern outskirts of town but still within walking

distance. Each of the three rainbow-coloured clapboard structures has a screened-in porch looking out over the ocean. The interiors have cool white tiles with fully equipped kitchens, satellite TV and a/c. One-bedroom cottage **4**, two-bedroom **6**

Mount Pleasant Suites ☎336-2960, ℱ336-2964. These suites are set back from the highway in a modern two-storey building on a wide expanse of lawn at Hooper's Bay. There are 23 comfortably furnished one-bedroom suites and one two-bedroom townhouse, each with a fully equipped kitchen, satellite TV, a/c and a patio or balcony. **3**

Palm Bay Beach Club ☎336-2787 or 1-888/396-0606, ℱ336-2770, ⓦwww .palmbaybeachclub.com. A newish holiday home development with cheerily painted studio and two-bedroom cottage units all within steps of the beach. Some have ocean views, and each is tastefully decorated in warm neutrals, handsome dark wicker furniture and colourful accents. The cottages have a/c, ceiling fans, satellite TV and fully equipped kitchens. There is also a laundry on site and a swimming pool, tennis courts, spa, a clubhouse with a restaurant and a beach bar and grill. The grounds are nicely landscaped, but a dearth of mature trees leaves the resort somewhat exposed to passing traffic at its back end. Studios **7**, two-bedroom units **8**

Peace and Plenty Beach Inn ☎336-2250 or 1-800/525-2210, ℱ336-2253, ⓦwww .peaceandplenty.com. A quiet retreat located a mile and a half north of town, featuring sixteen very nicely appointed rooms, each with a private balcony and an ocean view. Amenities include a pool, a small swath of white-sand beach and an outdoor bar. A shuttle service is available to transport guests to and from George Town. **6**, efficiency unit **7**

South of George Town

Club Peace and Plenty Bonefish Lodge Hartswell ☎345-5555 or 1-800/525-2210, ℱ345-5556, ⓦwww.ppbonefishlodge.com. This handsome timber and stone lodge, complete with wraparound veranda overlooking Little Exuma, is the most luxurious hotel on Great Exuma. The eight airy, nicely appointed rooms have tile floors, a/c, deep balconies and windows looking out onto the turquoise waters of the shallow bonefishing flats nearby. A broad wooden deck extends out over the water with covered areas for dining alfresco or relaxing and hammocks strung in the shade of trees. Rates include meals, a bonefishing guide, taxes and gratuities, and use of kayaks, bicycles and snorkelling equipment. Three nights and two days fishing runs around $1000 per person based on double occupancy. ⑧

La Shanté Beach Club Forbes Hill ☎345-4136. Without the luxurious touches of the *Club Peace and Plenty* but with an even more spectacular setting and welcoming hosts, *La Shanté* fronts a powdery white-sand beach in a secluded cove. The three double rooms (one with kitchenette) and one-bedroom apartment are simply furnished but spacious and comfortable. All are air-conditioned and have TV, and while they do not have ocean views, they are steps from it. The on-site restaurant serves lunch and dinner on a terrace overlooking the beach, and picnic outings to Pigeon Cay, a smidgen of white sand offshore, can be organized. ④–⑤ with kitchen, apartment ⑥

Master Harbour Villas Master Harbour ☎345-5076 or 357-0636, ⓕ345-5140, ⓦwww.exumabahamas.com/masterharbour.html. Three miles south of George Town sit these three white clapboard cottages, set in a green grove of coconut palms and blooming trees on a rocky shore looking out on Crab and Redshank cays. The high-ceiling villas are nicely furnished and equipped with both a/c and ceiling fans. Weekly rates available. One bedroom ⑥, two-bedroom ⑦, four-bedroom ⑧

North of George Town

A&C Vacation Inn Barreterre ☎355-5024. Notable mainly for its handy location near the government dock, this somewhat overpriced inn has six bright, modern rooms that share a kitchen, bathroom and sitting room. ④

Bougainvillea House Tar Bay ☎345-0005, ⓦwww.bougainvilleahouse.com. A luxurious two-storey timber beach house worth noting on the off chance you're travelling with a large entourage, perhaps a wedding party or a family reunion. The home, which can accommodate up to sixteen, has its own spectacular palm-fringed beach, four double bedrooms and additional fold-out couches, several bathrooms stocked with Aveda toiletries, a fully equipped kitchen, outdoor hot tub, and a rooftop wet bar with a driving range. The honeymoon suite has floor-to-ceiling glass on three sides. Rates range from $10,000 a week for the largest wing of the house to $5000 for the honeymoon suite area; all rates include rental car and use of a catamaran, tennis rackets and beach toys. ⑧

The Fisherman's Inn Barreterre ☎355-5017. Two basic doubles that are adequate if you are coming or going on the mailboat, but not the place for a tropical holiday. There is a simple restaurant serving traditional Bahamian and deep-fried fare. ②

The Palms at Three Sisters Near Mt Thompson ☎358-4040, ⓕ358-4043, ⓦwww.thepalmsat3sisters.com. Nicely maintained, modern motel located on a good beach. Its sole disadvantage is its isolation, which is desolate rather than splendid, surrounded by scrubby bush and the odd building along the road. ③

George Town and around

With a population of around a thousand, **GEORGE TOWN** is a bustling little hub of commercial activity with a constant stream of cars on the circular main road, an extension of the Queen's Highway, which runs along the waterfront and through the centre of town. Happily, though, it's not such a rat race that you can't still do your banking on bare feet with a cocktail in hand, if you so choose. And just as refreshingly, it's a town with a sense of humour – note the sign on the small bridge over the channel connecting Victoria Pond to Elizabeth Harbour that reads "This bridge freezes before the road."

Settled in the late eighteenth century and formally incorporated in 1793, George Town's location was selected for its excellent natural harbour. A pleasant if slightly ramshackle settlement with few landmarks, the town is made up of mainly modern cinderblock buildings of various sizes, colours and states of repair that line the main road. The residential areas lie on the flat land east of the town centre and climb the hill behind Victoria Pond. Views of the brilliant turquoise sea and Stocking Island greet you at every turn and you can walk from one end of the village to the other in about fifteen minutes. Alternatively, from a seat at the *Two Turtles Inn* (see p.256) patio bar in the centre of town, you can survey almost all of its primary attractions.

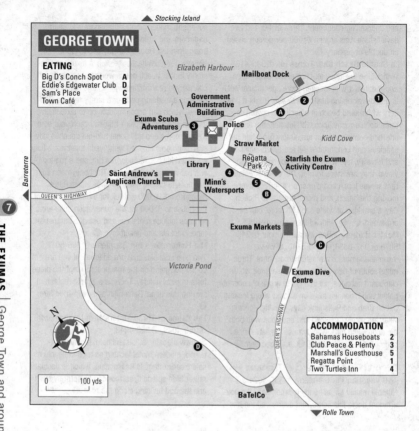

GEORGE TOWN

EATING

Big D's Conch Spot	A
Eddie's Edgewater Club	D
Sam's Place	C
Town Café	B

Stocking Island

Elizabeth Harbour

Mailboat Dock

Government Administrative Building

Exuma Scuba Adventures

Police

Straw Market

Kidd Cove

Regatta Park

Starfish the Exuma Activity Centre

Library

Saint Andrew's Anglican Church

Minn's Watersports

Barreterre

QUEEN'S HIGHWAY

Exuma Markets

Victoria Pond

Exuma Dive Centre

QUEEN'S HIGHWAY

N

0   100 yds

ACCOMMODATION

Bahamas Houseboats	2
Club Peace & Plenty	3
Marshall's Guesthouse	5
Regatta Point	1
Two Turtles Inn	4

BaTelCo

Rolle Town

On the northern edge of town on a rise of land overlooking the sea is **Saint Andrew's Anglican Church**, which was consecrated in 1802, but burned to the ground twice since then. Across the street and toward the centre of town stands the peach and white **Club Peace and Plenty**, looking like a Cotswold country cottage with its steep-pitched roof, dormers and picket fence. The residence of a prominent local family, it was converted to an inn in the 1940s and has hosted celebrities and royalty (including the King of Greece and Duke of Edinburgh) over the years. The hotel bar, now a popular watering hole with yachties, is thought by local historians to be on the site of **Bowe's Tavern**, where slaves from West Africa were auctioned off two hundred years ago.

Walking east from the inn, you'll pass the **Government Administration Building**, which houses the Commissioner's office, the police station and the post office. The building overlooks the government dock on **Kidd Cove**, named for the pirate captain who may or may not have ever visited it. It is here that the mailboat calls. Directly in front of the *Two Turtles Inn*, looking out towards the dock, lies **Regatta Park**. This forlorn patch of grass and dirt comes into its own during the Out Island Regatta and the George Town Cruising Regatta, when it is filled with food stalls, musicians and revellers (see box opposite). In one corner rests the *Patsy*, a small wooden dory of the kind that has been built in the islands for generations. At the other end of the park is the

The Out Island and George Town regattas

Usually sleepy, George Town's Elizabeth Harbour quickly fills up with upwards of four hundred boats during the **Out Island Regatta**, which lasts for several days at the end of April. The regatta has been held every year since 1954 as a celebration of the long tradition of wooden-boat building in the Bahamas – indeed, the race only involves Bahamian-designed, -built, -owned and -sailed vessels – and draws racing crews from all over the Out Islands. It's one of the premier social events of the year, and government mailboats are diverted from their regular routes to carry the racing sloops to George Town. On land, the festivities continue day and night, with rake 'n' scrape music, food stalls, games and dancing.

Foreign yachts get in on the action during the **George Town Cruising Regatta**, held in early March. This week-long regatta features races, a beach volleyball tournament, sandcastle-building contest, live music as well as copious amounts of eating and drinking. Contact the Ministry of Tourism (☎336-2440, ℻336-2431) for details.

open-air **Straw Market** (daily 9am–6pm), where local women sell handmade straw hats, bags, and baskets as well as mass-produced jewellery and tropical-print beachwear.

Stocking Island

A string of small cays along the windward coast of Great Exuma encloses fifteen-mile-long Elizabeth Harbour. The largest of these – though still only three miles end to end and just a few hundred yards across – is **STOCKING ISLAND**, a mile off George Town, its high white sand dunes shimmering in the sunlight. It's an idyllic place to while away the day, with a long windswept beach that runs almost the length of its Atlantic side, while crescents of soft sand are found on the protected shore facing George Town. Keep an eye out for giant red starfish a foot or more in diameter that can be found in large numbers in the shallows. There are no roads on the island and just a handful of luxurious winter homes tucked into sheltered coves. The *Club Peace and Plenty* operates a twice-daily ferry service (free for guests, $8 round-trip for others) that leaves at 10am and 1pm from the club and goes to Hamburger Beach. During the Out Island Regatta and the George Town Cruising Regatta, this is the scene of a beach volleyball tournament. You'll have to bushwhack or swim across Turtle Lagoon to get here from the north end of the island.

The most prominent feature of the island is the **beacon** that tops its highest hill, erected in the nineteenth century to guide ships into the dock. If you head toward it from the snack bar at **Hamburger Beach** (open 10am–3pm), you will pick up a sandy track that's a ten-minute hike up to the peak, from which there's an amazing view of Elizabeth Harbour. A steep path down the far side of the hill takes you to the Atlantic beach.

Crab Cay

Shaped like its namesake, the uninhabited **CRAB CAY**, just south of George Town, has a shoreline that twists and turns around small sheltered coves and a couple of beaches. On the north end of the island are the ruins of a plantation established by the Loyalist exile William Walker in 1784. The foundations of the main house and some outbuildings are still standing on the crest of a hill offering another great view of Great Exuma and the harbour. To reach these ruins, you'll pass through two sets of tall rounded pillars that enclosed Walker's **botanical garden**. An enthusiastic amateur botanist, he collected specimens of exotic plants, which he propagated in his garden on the cay. He obtained breadfruit plants – which he thought could be grown in the Bahamas to reduce the dependency on supply ships that often fell prey to pirates – from Captain William Bligh of *Mutiny on the Bounty* fame after Bligh's return from Tahiti. In 1789, Walker was elected to the House of Representatives, but gave up his seat a year later and moved back to St Vincent. Abandoned by 1830, Crab Cay reverted to the Crown. The best way to see the cay is with Starfish (see p.257), which offers half-day guided tours, and if you really like the view keep in mind that the island is for sale and can be yours for $7 million.

South to Williamstown

Heading **south from George Town**, the Queen's Highway weaves in and out from the shore until it reaches Williamstown, on the southern tip of Little Exuma seventeen miles south. Along the way are the scenic hilltop settlements of Rolle Town, Forbes Hill and Ferry, as well as several inviting deserted beaches, but Williamstown, with its ruins of a Loyalist plantation, salt ponds, and a couple of cheery spots for refreshment, is the prime target.

Rolle Town and around

Leaving George Town, the road climbs a steep hill that curves around and down to follow the water's edge, passing the posh new resort community at February Point on Flamingo Bay. Major construction is still under way, but the *Bistro* down on the waterfront is open for lunch and dinner (see p.256). From the highway, a wide paved road on your right leads to the American naval base, established in 1940, and the otherwise uninhabited south side of the island. The old naval base is now the site of a government-sponsored open-air food fair, with about twelve kiosks serving a range of native foods, fish fries, drinks and music. Past February Point, the Queen's Highway runs along the rocky shore edged with mangroves and dotted with small cays, then cuts inland. On this stretch of road, two stone pillars stand on either side of the highway, marking

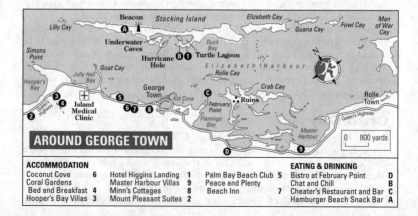

AROUND GEORGE TOWN

ACCOMMODATION						EATING & DRINKING	
Coconut Cove	6	Hotel Higgins Landing	1	Palm Bay Beach Club	5	Bistro at February Point	D
Coral Gardens		Master Harbour Villas	9	Peace and Plenty		Chat and Chill	B
Bed and Breakfast	4	Minn's Cottages	8	Beach Inn	7	Cheater's Restaurant and Bar	C
Hooper's Bay Villas	3	Mount Pleasant Suites	2			Hamburger Beach Snack Bar	A

the western boundary of Lord Rolle's former estate, now the commonage of Rolle Town, although the village itself is several miles further south.

Seven miles from the capital, you reach the pretty hilltop settlement of **ROLLE TOWN**. Turn off the main highway here for one of the most spectacular views in the Exumas. From the top of the hill, look out over **Man of War Cay**, where the shallow waters that surround it help create a beautiful multi-hued panorama of turquoise and bright white. From the junction at the top of the hill facing the water, turn right onto a road that leads down to the shore. A short distance along the road, a grassy path on your left leads to a grave enclosed by a high rock wall. Interred here is the 26-year-old Loyalist settler Ann McKay and her infant son, who died in 1792; their graves are one of the few physical reminders of the Loyalists who came to make a new life on the island. At the bottom of the hill, an overgrown cemetery at the edge of the sea is the final resting place of several generations of Rolles. When the tide is low, you can walk out onto Man of War Cay to explore its tantalizing stretches of white sandy beach and the fortifications on the bluff.

Williamstown and around

Past Rolle Town, the highway drops down to the water's edge, passing through the eastern gates of the Rolle estate at Hartswell and over the short, narrow bridge, built in 1966, that connects Great Exuma to Little Exuma. The appropriately named hamlet of **Ferry**, where the ferryman lived before the bridge

The Jumento Cays and the Ragged Islands

Strewn in a long wisp off the southern tip of Little Exuma, the stony **Jumento Cays** and **Ragged Islands** mark the southeast edge of the Great Bahama Bank. Remote and undeveloped, they get few visitors apart from migratory birds, part of their appeal for the rare passing boat cruiser. The only way to visit is on your own plane or yacht, or on the brand-new mailboat, the *Captain C*, which sails from Nassau on Tuesdays and calls at the sun-baked outpost of **Duncan Town** at the southern end of the chain. Home to all the archipelago's fewer than one hundred residents, most of whom make a hardscrabble living from the sea, the settlement is named for Duncan Taylor, a Loyalist exile who, with his brother Archibald, established a briefly thriving salt-harvesting operation here in the mid-nineteenth century. In those days, it was a lively village of several hundred workers, many of them Africans freed from illegal slave-trading vessels captured on the high seas after Emancipation. Rather than being repatriated, they were deposited at Duncan Town and left to start over. Given the isolation, the barren landscape of the islands and the backbreaking exertion of salt raking, it must have seemed a dubious deliverance to some, and when the demand for Bahamian salt declined, most left Ragged Island.

The peaceful rhythm of daily life was violently shattered in May 1980, when Cuban MiG fighter jets attacked and sank a Bahamian naval vessel while it was in the process of arresting two Cuban boats fishing illegally in Bahamian waters. Four Bahamian marines were killed, and under a hail of bullets, the rest escaped in rubber dinghies, coming ashore at Duncan Town. Cuba eventually issued an official apology and offered a financial settlement to replace the ship, and for the families of the killed marines. The intervening years have passed in a calm interrupted only by the weekly arrival of the mailboat. The only place to stay is at the cement-block *Ragged Island Bonefish Club* (☎772/466-8369, ☏772/466-1717, ⊛www.raggedisland.com), which caters exclusively to fishers. One week of guided fishing, including bed and board, and use of a golf cart costs $2440 per person based on double occupancy. Charter flights from Nassau are arranged for guests at $365 round-trip.

was built, holds St Christopher's Church, perhaps the smallest church in the Bahamas – its about the size of a garden shed – built in 1946 for the devoutly Anglican Fitzgerald family. Further on, **Forbes Hill** is a shady, hilly little settlement named for a Loyalist planter. Note the unexplained cannon hidden in the bushes next to the Variety Store on your left as you enter the community. The pretty curved beach at *La Shanté Beach Club* merits a look-see or, better yet, a leisurely lunch on the terrace and a swim. Two miles past Forbes Hill, a road on the left leads to a beautiful stretch of beach that straddles the Tropic of Cancer, known appropriately enough as **Tropic of Cancer Beach**.

At the southern tip of Little Exuma is **Williamstown**, a peaceful settlement of 300 residents set between the intensely turquoise sea and two large saline ponds, whose edges are rimmed with salt glinting in the sunlight. There is no accommodation in the town, and goats, chicken and sheep roam freely, some taking up residence on the steps of the abandoned Batelco building. At the south end of the settlement, **The Hermitage** – the ruins of the Kelsall Plantation house – stands overgrown in tall grass at the top of a steep knoll overlooking the salt ponds and the sea, too dilapidated to enter, but picturesque in its decay. A modest one-storey affair built in traditional Bahamian style with a steep-pitched roof and deep veranda, the house is a testament to the very limited success of the Loyalist plantation owners during their short stay in the Bahamas – a far cry from the opulent lifestyles many left behind in the southern US states. A row of tiny mud and limestone rooms that were slave quarters still stands downhill from the main house.

North to Barreterre

North of George Town, the Queen's Highway runs close to the shore, though much of the beach is blocked from public access. Leaving town, you pass in succession Jolly Hall Bay (public access to beach via path across from the Island Medical Clinic), Hooper's Bay (beach currently accessible through a vacant lot across from *Hooper's Bay Villas*) and the exquisite pearly beach lining Tar Bay (lined with vacation homes, but accessible by walking over the dunes from the highway).

Further north, **Ramsey** and **Mt Thompson** are farming communities where onions, bananas and other vegetables are grown and readied for market at the Government Packing House. The *Palms at Three Sisters Hotel* (see p.249) is set on the beach at Mt Thompson, with a view of the three big rocks in the sea which gave it its name. At the next settlement heading north on the Queen's Highway, **Farmer's Hill**, stand the beginnings of a major resort development, *Four Seasons at Emerald Bay*, on a lovely cove called Ocean Bight.

Up next is the nondescript roadside settlement of **Steventon**, notable only as the site of a slave revolt in the nineteenth century. A few miles past Steventon, the road forks. To the right is **Rolleville**, the largest slave settlement on the island in Lord Rolle's time, and the site of several slave uprisings in the 1820s and 1830s. Today, the local residents, many of whom are descendants of those slaves, hold a **regatta** on Emancipation Day, the first Monday in August. Despite its evident poverty, the village is quite attractive, running over a hill down to a stretch of sandy beach.

The road that forks off to the left may be less interesting, but there's a payoff at the end. It heads north through **Stuart Manor**, a pleasant farming community on a hill situated inland from the coast. The Stuart Manor Bakery

Bowe Cay

Lying off the southwest side of Great Exuma opposite George Town, at the end of a row of small islands extended like an arm towards Cuba, is **Bowe Cay**, a flat 200-acre area covered in low, dense bush and mangrove swamp. Bowe Cay achieved brief notoriety in the mid-1990s when two writers for *Condé Nast Traveller* magazine were marooned on the island for a week to fend for themselves *Robinson Crusoe*, or maybe *Lord of the Flies*, style. It was a grand publicity stunt staged by a New York company that hoped to market the island as the ultimate getaway destination, and the island was subsequently featured in several magazines – indeed, soon after *Men's Journal* named Bowe Cay one of the top ten great island escapes. Unfortunately for the company, they hadn't asked permission of the island's owner, Glenville Clark, who soon put a stop to their plans.

Mr Clark's family has owned the island since 1843 when it was acquired by his great-great-grandfather, a freed slave named John Rolle. Though never inhabited by the Clarks, it has been used intermittently for farming and grazing. The original deed to the cay was discovered in the 1970s among the papers passed down to Mr Clark's grand-mother, who could not read. Also among them was a Certificate of Indenture dated 1839 binding John Rolle to a man from New Providence for a debt incurred, the full repayment of which was to be symbolized by a final payment of one peppercorn.

The western side of the cay has a small pretty curve of white sandy beach and a mangrove creek that beckons exploring by dinghy or kayak. A coral outcropping just off the beach offers good snorkelling on a calm day, yet the plywood cabana inhab-ited by the Condé Nast castaways was destroyed in a hurricane, and an unsightly pile of empty insect repellent cans mars its appeal as an island paradise. Perhaps encouraged by the spate of media attention, Glenville Clark (☎345-0054) is asking a **rental fee** of $1500 a week for the island, but you might be able to negotiate a more reasonable rate. He hopes to eventually develop a resort on the beach, but for now be prepared to camp and to bring all of your food and water. If roughing it on a deserted island appeals to you, note that there are a dozen in the Exuma Land and Sea Park (see p.265) where you can camp for a slightly more affordable $5 a night.

(7am–4pm; ☎345-2313) sells sweet Bahamian bread and banana loaf here. There is little of scenic interest between Stuart Manor and **Barreterre**, a for-lorn collection of buildings spread along a rocky shore. The only reason for venturing this far is because it is the jumping-off point for excursions into the cays. From Barreterre, Captain Martin (☎358-4057 or 345-6013) and Rev A.A. McKenzie (☎355-5024) both offer snorkelling, fishing and sightseeing outings in the cays north of Great Exuma, including a visit to the giant igua-nas on Leaf Cay (see p.262). Both also offer a water-taxi service and could take you up to Staniel Cay or to the Exuma Land and Sea Park headquarters on Warderick Wells Cay twenty miles north, but it'll cost you $150–200 for a boatload of four to six people. McKenzie also has a seventeen-foot Boston Whaler for rent. If needed, you can buy gas at the pump next to the *A & C Vacation Inn*. If you arrive between 9am and noon, toot your horn three times – the owner is working on his farm, but will hear you.

Eating

As might be expected, seafood dominates **restaurant** menus on Great and Little Exuma, be it conch, lobster, or fish just hours or even minutes out of the ocean. In the settlements up and down the islands, simple local diners prevail, serving traditional Bahamian meals like boiled fish and grits for breakfast and conch fritters or fried chicken with tasty sides of peas 'n' rice, coleslaw and macaroni and cheese later on. Beyond these diners, the majority of dining options are in George Town and its environs, primarily in the hotels. Most of the hotel restaurants dish out a vegetarian option of some kind; elsewhere non-meat eaters will have to rely on standbys like grilled cheese sandwiches and omelettes, or delicious home-style Bahamian side-dishes like macaroni and cheese.

George Town

The Chat and Chill Stocking Island, no phone (VHF Ch 16). Open-air beach bar fronting Stocking Island's Volleyball Beach that makes for a breezy and inexpensive place for a burger, fresh seafood or just a cool drink and a swim. Open 11am–7pm.

Club Peace and Plenty Restaurant *Club Peace and Plenty* ☎ 336-2551. Set in a glassed-in alcove off the hotel's lobby with a nice view of Stocking Island, this expensive restaurant features fish, lobster and steak prepared by an American chef. The dining experience is marred by poor service. Open for breakfast.

Eddie's Edgewater Club On Victoria Pond ☎ 336-2050. A popular, inexpensive local spot overlooking Victoria Pond. Come here to sample delicious native dishes such as steamed turtle or to just hang around playing pool. Live music Mondays and Saturdays.

Mom's Bakery Several mornings a week around 10am, Doris "Mom" Rahming parks her van across from Exuma Markets to sell her delicious coconut bread, banana cakes and other home-baked goodies. If you happen to miss her, you can go to the source in Williamstown.

Sam's Place On the waterfront ☎ 336-2579. Located upstairs in a grey timber two-storey building overlooking the marina, *Sam's* is the best place in George Town for breakfast, specializing in Bahamian boiled breakfasts and American-style platters including bacon and eggs and pancakes. At lunchtime, the inexpensive seafood plates and burgers served on the deck overhanging the marina are pretty good too. Open 7.30am–3pm.

The Town Café Queen's Highway ☎ 336-2194. Beside the Shell gas station, this inexpensive café doles out Bahamian and American standards, mainly of the deep-fried variety, along with fresh-baked goods. Though the view of the parking lot is not great, the bright white interior, fresh flowers and hearty meals make it a local favourite. Open 7.30am–5pm.

Two Turtles Inn Queen's Highway ☎ 336-2545. The outdoor patio bar overlooking the main drag and the wharf is a great place to watch the world go by while sampling tasty fare such as conch

done every which way, along with burgers and salads. On Friday nights there is an outdoor barbecue with live entertainment.

George Town's outskirts

The Bistro at February Point ☎ 336-2661. One mile south of George Town, this moderately priced beachside bistro serves both lunch and dinner, either in a casual dining room or out on a lovely terrace. The menu features delicious, beautifully presented plates of seafood, meat dishes and a vegetarian option. Wednesday night is pizza night with a two-for-one deal. Free transfers to and from George Town for dinner.

Cheater's Restaurant and Bar ☎ 336-2535. A no-frills roadhouse two miles south of town on the Queen's Highway serving delicious home-style Bahamian meals like fresh fish and fried chicken with sides of coleslaw, peas 'n' rice and macaroni and cheese. Tuesday nights feature a fish fry with rake 'n' scrape music. Open for breakfasts on Sat, closed Sun.

Coconut Cove Restaurant *Coconut Cove Hotel* ☎ 336-2659. Easily one of the best restaurants in the Exumas, with a cozy atmosphere and attentive service. The moderate-to-expensive menu has delicious pizza, pasta dishes, steak and seafood platters. Open daily for breakfast (7.30–9.30am); dinner 6–9pm Tues–Sun; reservations recommended.

South of George Town

Club Peace and Plenty Bonefish Lodge Hartswell ☎ 345-5555. Appealing restaurant with a decor of terracotta tiled floors, cozy wooden booths with hunter-green upholstery, and windows looking out over the bright blue-green water. The menu features (not surprisingly) local seafood, and traditional American cuisine like steak, chicken and pasta. Open for dinner only to outside guests; reservations required. Free transportation available from George Town.

La Shanté Beach Club Forbes Hill ☎ 345-4136. Simple lunches and dinners – burgers, fresh-caught seafood – served on a pleasant terrace overlooking a beautiful curved beach.

North of George Town

Big D's Conch Spot Steventon ☎358-0059. A popular local spot for conch, with outdoor beach seating on a covered wooden deck.

The Fisherman's Inn Barreterre ☎355-5017. Simple local place with a minimalist approach to interior decor serving your basic seafood and deep-fried stuff.

Kermit's Hilltop Tavern Rolleville ☎345-6006. Located in a hot-pink building with a commanding view of the sea, *Kermit's* doesn't get enough business to keep the fryer on all day, but the friendly staff will whip you up a hearty Bahamian meal if you call ahead.

Drinking and nightlife

Although sizeable quantities of rum and other tropical libations are consumed on the foredecks and poolside in the Exumas (mainly by visitors), **nightlife** is pretty low-key and non-existent outside of George Town. Any night of the week in George Town, though, you can usually find an interesting conversation, a game of pool and/or some rake 'n' scrape music at one or another of a handful of local watering holes. Occasionally one of the area hotels hosts a dinner and dance, and at regatta time, the place is a 24-hour a day party.

The tiny, cozy English country pub at *Club Peace and Plenty* (see opposite) is a gathering point for the boating crowd in the evenings, and its outdoor pool bar overlooking Stocking Island is a pleasant place for a sunset drink. On Wednesdays and Saturdays, there's usually also live music. On Fridays, the action shifts to the outdoor patio bar at the *Two Turtles Inn* (see opposite), when live music is normally put on. *Eddie's Edgewater Club* (see opposite) is a popular local hangout for a game of pool and live music on Mondays and Saturdays.

Watersports and other outdoor activities

Though typical tourist sights are thin on the ground on Big and Little Exuma, the wealth of outdoor adventures available easily picks up the slack. Located in a bright-blue two-storey building on the main drag overlooking Kidd Cove in George Town, **Starfish, The Exuma Adventure Center** (☎336-3033 or 1-877/398-6222, VHF Ch 16 "Starfish", ⓦwww.kayakbahamas.com) is the Exumas' top multipurpose outfitter. The highly qualified and knowledgeable staff run a wide variety of day-trips, including guided historical and eco-tours by skiff of Elizabeth Harbour, Crab Cay and Stocking Island. They also offer cycling trips on quiet island byways and paddling excursions through the little-explored cays off George Town, including the recently named Moriah Cay National Park, which is at the moment just a line on a map enclosing several cays at the southern end of Great Exuma. Starfish also organizes full-moon, sunset and sunrise guided paddles, and Romantic Castaway Getaways, where you and your sweetheart are dropped on a deserted island with a bottle of wine and a picnic lunch to while away the hours. Two- to six-day guided kayaking and camping trips in the Brigantine Cays (see p.261) can also be organized on request and all trips can be customized to suit children, seniors, and beginners. If you want to explore the area on your own, Starfish rents well-maintained kayaks, Hobie Wave sailboats, bicycles, snorkelling equipment and camping gear at reasonable rates. **Prices** for guided trips range $30–45 for half a day including lunch for an adult, $60–75 for a full day. Bicycles rent for $25 per day and $100 per week; decked kayaks from $35 per day and $175 per week; and Hobie Wave sailboats for $75 per day and $300 per week. You can also take a sailing or kayak lesson from certified instructors for $35. Snorkel gear rental is $15 per day and $25 per week; and full camping gear (no sleeping bags) rents for $175 a week.

For more on **kayaking** throughout the Exumas, see the box on pp.266–267.

Diving and snorkelling

With scores of pristine coral reefs and sea gardens, underwater valleys and caverns, wrecks and blue holes to explore, the Exumas are one of the best places in the Bahamas to **dive** or **snorkel**. One of the top dive shops hereabouts is Exuma Scuba Adventures (☎336-2893 or 357-2259, ⓦwww .exumascuba.com), based out of *Club Peace and Plenty* in George Town. Snorkelling trips by reef boat cost from $15 to $65 for an all-day outing including a picnic lunch on a deserted cay. Diving rates range from $45/55 for one-tank/two-tank dives; $55 for a one-tank night dive; $120 for a full day of diving including a boxed lunch. Diving equipment can be rented for $29/45 for half-day/full day. The shallow waters of the Exumas are a great place to learn to dive, and the very experienced dive master runs full scuba certification courses for $310. An introductory snorkelling or scuba lesson (including a free snorkel trip or one-tank dive) is offered for $15 and $45 respectively, including use of equipment. The only other dive shop on the islands is the Exuma Dive Center (☎336-2390, Ⓕ336-2391, Ⓔexumadive@BahamasVG.com), also run out of George Town. A three-hour snorkelling trip with the Center is $35 including equipment rental, and gear alone can be rented for $15 per day. Diving excursions cost from $65 for a two-tank dive plus $15 for full scuba gear rental. The Center offers scuba certification for $405 and an introductory resort course for $100. You can take a guided tour of the harbour with snorkelling for $250 a boatload; banana boat rides for $10; and water-ski for $25 a spin. The Dive Center also rents a variety of watercraft including glass-bottom dinghies, Sunfish, and windsurfers for $20–25 per hour; and Misty sailboats for $80 per day.

Fishing

The Exumas are well known to serious fisherman for superb **deep-sea and bonefishing grounds**, and a number of fishing guides are based in and around George Town. Rates are in the range of $240 for a half-day to $400 for a full day of fishing, equipment included. Cely's Fly Fishing (☎345-2341), based in Stuart Manor north of George Town, specializes in bonefishing, deep-sea fishing and reef fishing. Cely will also take you snorkelling or sightseeing by boat. Cooper's Charter Service, run by Captain Wendell Cooper from George Town (☎336-2711), offers deep-sea fishing and bottom-fishing expeditions as well as guided snorkelling trips, harbour tours, and sightseeing excursions. Fish Rowe Charters (☎345-0074) runs half-day, full-day and week-long sport-fishing charters. They do both bonefishing and deep-drop fishing and offer scuba, snorkelling, sightseeing and shelling outings as well. A half-day fishing is $550 and a full day is $750 for up to six people. Two other bonefishing guides whose services are worth looking into are Abby MacKenzie (☎345-2312), known as the "The Bonefish Cowboy", and Garth Thompson (☎345-5062 or 336-2390).

Bush medicine tours

One of the highlights of any trip to George Town is a **bush medicine tour** into the nearby forest given by Joseph A. Romer (call ☎345-7044 for prices). A herbal bush medicine practitioner, Mr Romer will explain the traditional uses of various indigenous plants as well as the remedies that have long been used in the Bahamas to treat a variety of ailments ranging from the common cold to infertility.

The practice of bush medicine was brought to the islands by African slaves and relied upon in the Out Islands when Western-trained doctors were rarely available. More than two hundred plants in the Bahamas have traditional medicinal uses, including cascarilla – also known as sweetwood – which is used as a tonic to treat stomach upset and these days as a flavouring agent in Campari liquor. Resin from the heavy, dense wood of the lignum vitae, the national tree of the Bahamas, can be applied to strengthen a weak back, while an infusion of buttercup is used to treat colds, adult stomach pains and infant constipation. Hurricane weed is believed to eliminate kidney stones; kalanchoe, a plant with small, shiny oval leaves, is used in a tea or poultice to treat such diverse ailments as asthma, headaches and ulcers. One of the best-known wildflowers in the Bahamas, periwinkle is used in the treatment of leukaemia. If you are feeling seasick, sniffing crushed orange peels is said to quell a queasy gut. A bush tea made from the leaves of the gamalamee tree is reputed to be Mother Nature's version of Viagra, known as "Twenty-one gun salute" on Cat Island and "Strongback" in the Exumas.

Listings

Airlines American Eagle (☎345-0124) and Bahamasair (☎345-0035) both have desks at George Town International Airport.

Bank The Bank of Nova Scotia (Mon–Thurs 9.30am–3pm, Fri 9.30am–5pm) is located in the centre of town by the bridge. There is an ATM, but be prepared for it to be out of service.

Gas The Esso station on the waterfront behind Thompson's Car Rental is open 8am–7pm. There is no gas available south of George Town. You can fill up north of town at Farmer's Hill and Barreterre.

Groceries Exuma Markets, across from the bank, has well-stocked shelves, a paperback-book exchange and fax service. Groceries also available at Shop Rite Mart a few doors down.

Health clinic The government clinic is located on the north edge of town (Mon–Fri 9am–1pm; ☎336-2088, after-hours emergencies ☎336-2606).

Internet Access is available at the College of the Bahamas (☎336-2790 or 2792), four miles north of town. Call ahead to make sure the system is working.

Laundry There's a laundromat at the marina next to the Esso station; dry-cleaning and laundry service is available from Exuma Cleaners on the main street.

Library Run by volunteers out of a small wooden building sandwiched between the primary school and the *Two Turtles Inn*. There is a book exchange.

Open Mon–Sat 10am–noon.

Police Located in the pink Government Administrative Building on the waterfront (☎336-2666, ☎919 in emergencies, VHF Ch 16 "Boys in Blue").

Post office Housed in Government Administrative Building (Mon–Fri 9am–5pm).

Shopping Great and Little Exuma offer slim pickings for diehard shoppers. George Town's Sandpiper Gifts, across from *Club Peace and Plenty*, has a tasteful selection of jewellery, Caribbean-made crafts, Androsia print clothes and other resort wear, original artwork, postcards and a good selection of books. The Peace and Plenty Boutique next door also sells Androsia fabrics, souvenirs and gifts.

Local artisans sell handmade straw work, souvenir trinkets and textiles at the Straw Market in the centre of town. Starfish, The Exuma Activity Center and Minns Watersports all sell watersports gear.

Telephone Batelco (Mon–Fri 9am–5.30pm) is located at the south end of town, and you can send and receive faxes here. There are pay phones at *Club Peace and Plenty* and in front of *Two Turtles Inn*. Prepaid phone cards are on sale at the Exuma Markets.

Travel agency H.L. Young Travel (Mon–Fri 9am–5pm; ☎336-2703) is located above the Bank of Nova Scotia in George Town.

△ The perfect seat for an ocean view

The Exuma Cays

Off the tip of Barreterre, the **EXUMA CAYS** stretch along a northwest trajectory for approximately forty miles. Uninhabited for the most part, this string of a couple of hundred islands and cays of various shapes and sizes shares a similar topography of white sand, honeycombed black coral rock and hardy vegetation, surrounded by a rich marine environment.

The southernmost portion is known as the **Brigantines**, frequented mainly by kayak day-trippers. The only permanent settlements in the Exuma Cays are found north of here on sleepy **Little Farmer's Cay**, **Great Guana Cay** – in the scruffy village of Black Point – and at pretty **Staniel Cay**. The latter is also the easiest access point to the magical **Thunderball Grotto**, a top snorkelling and diving destination. There are dozens more islands sporting sandy beaches hereabouts, the most notable being **Leaf Cay**, home to a colony of giant iguanas situated about five miles from Barreterre.

In the centre of the Exuma Cays chain lies the impressive **Exuma Land and Sea Park**, a marine conservation area encompassing 175 square miles of serene and pristine natural beauty. Within its boundaries are fifteen sizeable cays – and a seemingly infinite number of smaller ones – offering empty powdery white beaches and hiking trails, and around which there's fabulous sea kayaking as well as an astounding variety of marine life to delight both snorkellers and divers.

Beyond the park's boundary, the northern tip of the Exuma Cays lies closer to Nassau than to George Town and is easily accessible on day-trips from Paradise Island. Most trips take in the beaches and hiking trails of **Ship Channel Cay** and a visit to the iguanas on **Allan's Cay**. Also worth a visit are **Highbourne Cay** and **Norman's Cay**, both home to more beaches, nature trails and marinas.

The Southern Cays

The **SOUTHERN CAYS**, extending from just off Barreterre northwards to Staniel Cay, which sits near the southern boundary of the Exuma Land and Sea Park, are the most settled part of the cay chain. About five hundred people in all live in the three settlements of Farmer's Cay, Black Point and Staniel Cay. Several of the surrounding small cays are privately owned, capped with vacation villas occupied by seasonal residents.

Directly off the leeward side of Great Exuma near Barreterre lies a short strand of little cays known as **The Brigantines**. Starfish (see p.257) offers guided camping and kayaking expeditions in the islands departing from George Town, travelling by van to Barreterre and putting the boats in there.

Arrival and getting around

The main tranport hub in the Exuma Cays' southern end is Staniel Cay, which can be reached from Great Exuma via a **water taxi** from Barreterre (see p.255). A more expensive option is to charter a plane from George Town; Island Air Service, based in both Florida and Staniel Cay (☎305/944-3033, ℉944-8033, ℮flyisleair@aol.com), charges around $450 for chartered flights in a five-seat airplane.

If heading over **from Nassau**, look into a trip on the *Captain C* **mailboat** ($120 round-trip). Though the schedule can vary greatly depending on weather and cargo, the mailboat typically leaves from Nassau on Tuesday afternoons, calling at Staniel Cay, Black Point, Little Farmer's Cay and Barreterre the next day. After heading down to the Ragged Islands on Thursday, the mailboat calls in again at Barreterre, Little Farmer's Cay, Black Point and Staniel Cay Friday, and is back in Nassau on Saturday around noon. Call the dockmaster at Potter's Cay (☎393-1064) for the latest. Another option from Nassau – just as affordable though less atmospheric – is a **flight** on Flamingo Air ($60 one-way; ☎377-0354), who operate three scheduled flights a week to Staniel Cay.

Once in Staniel Cay, you can rent or charter a **boat** to head over to any of the nearby cays, Thunderball Grotto, the national park to the north or even south to Barreterre on Great Exuma. The Staniel Cay Yacht Club rents thirteen- and seventeen-foot Whalers for $85 and $235 per day respectively, including fuel. You might also ask on the dock for a local fisherman who could run you where you want to go, or try Captain Bill Hirsch (see p.226) who runs frequent boat charters in the area.

Lee Stocking Island

Six miles north of Barreterre sits the densely forested **LEE STOCKING ISLAND**, owned by American philanthropist John H. Perry Jr, who in 1984 funded the establishment of the nonprofit Caribbean Marine Research Center (☎561/741-0192 (Florida), ⊛www.cmrc.org, VHF Ch 16 "Research Center"). Every year, scientists from all over the world come here to study various aspects of tropical marine ecology, ranging from animal population trends and the effects of coral bleaching to the nutrient value of sea grass for turtles. Pristine waters as deep as 6000ft in nearby Exuma Sound make it an ideal environment for marine research.

As there are sensitive ongoing experiments on the island and in the waters surrounding it, the CMRC asks that you respect a half-mile no-wake zone around the island and call ahead for permission to come ashore. There are no public facilities on the island, and access to most areas is restricted, but there is an impressive view down the length of the Exuma chain from **Perry's Peak**, the highest point in the Exumas at 123ft. A well-defined trail begins at the south end of Coconut Beach in the middle of the island, and it takes only ten minutes to reach the lookout. If you are a student or amateur with a serious interest in marine biology, the CMRC runs a six-week internship programme – see their website for details.

Leaf Cay

Just south of Lee Stocking Island, tiny, sandy **LEAF CAY** is home to a colony of giant iguanas, one of the few places in the Bahamas this endangered species can still be found. The hefty yard-long lizards sun themselves on a small, pretty curve of beach on the leeward side of the cay. Beyond the low ridge behind the beach is a freshwater pond encircled by dense leafy trees that allows the iguana population to thrive here. The beach is a spectacular venue for a picnic, with views of both the deep dark waters of the sound and the bright blues and greens of the shallow banks. Just remember to take a good last look around before you leave, removing any garbage that may be hazardous to the health of the dwindling giant iguana population.

Musha Cay

If your latest movie is doing well at the box office but life in the public eye is getting you down, a week or two on sumptuous and remote **MUSHA CAY** (℡355-4040, Ⓕ355-4039, Ⓦwww.mushacay.com), north of Lee Stocking Island, could be just the right pick-me-up. This fantasy island, with its palm-shaded beach, mosaic-tiled pool, exercise studio, tennis courts, TV station and a staff of 35 – including a masseuse and a pastry cook – is available for parties of up to fifteen for just under $350,000 per week. While remnants of old stone walls suggest the cay may have once been the site of a Loyalist plantation, these days, sun-kissed celebrities like Oprah Winfrey and Tom Hanks gather in the evening for cocktails and dinner in the wood-panelled dining room overlooking the dock. The four guest cottages are furnished with polished marble floors and antiques, and each has a hot tub and a fireplace or two. However, some celebrity guests prefer to bunk down in the relative austerity of the one-room beach cabana with its outdoor toilet and shower. You can park your jet on nearby **Rudder Cut Cay**, where there are plans to build a golf course.

Little Farmer's Cay

Immediately north of Musha Cay, **LITTLE FARMER'S CAY** is a pretty, peaceful fishing village of less than a hundred residents built on a low green hillside around a small horseshoe-shaped harbour. Many of the gaily painted houses are built in the traditional Bahamian style with steep-pitched roofs and deep verandas. The first weekend in February the community bursts with partygoers who come for the Farmer's Cay Festival and Regatta.

A short walk up the hill overlooking the wharf, the spotless and informal *Ocean Cabin Restaurant* (℡ & Ⓕ355-4006) serves breakfast, lunch and dinner. It has tables inside and out, a cozy bar and a book exchange. On Tuesday night, owners Terry and Ernestine Bain host a potluck dinner (bring anything but pork), and on Wednesdays during the tourist season cookouts and crab races are held. You can rent two cottages (❺) on top of Dabba Hill, the highest point on the island, or a whole island, **Hattie Cay**, with four cottages and room for two to sixteen people for $1000–2000 a week. Contact the *Ocean Cabin* for details.

About a mile from the wharf (you have to drive down the landing strip to reach it) is the Farmer's Cay Yacht Club and Marina (℡355-4017, Ⓕ355-4017). The *Captain C* mailboat calls here every week, the main harbour being too shallow. A rustic **restaurant** and bar is located directly on the water, serving traditional Bahamian dishes. There are four cramped but adequate twin rooms in the back equipped with satellite TV and air conditioning (❹). For guided **snorkelling trips** or a **water taxi**, call "Little Jeff" over on the wharf (℡355-4003).

Great Guana Cay

Continuing northward, twelve-mile-long **GREAT GUANA CAY** is the largest cay in the chain, and **Black Point** at its north end is the largest settlement with a population of 300. It is named for the long finger of dark rock that juts toward Staniel Cay, visible across the water. The village, strung out along a strip of pavement that follows the shore, has the dissipated and depressed atmosphere of a forgotten outpost, and fishing provides a meagre living. *Lorraine's Café* (℡355-3012) is a cheerful oasis, serving traditional

Bahamian **meals**, such as grouper fingers, conch fritters, and home-baked goods like banana bread, and is a favourite with passing boat cruisers. *De Shamon's* (☎355-3009) also serves native dishes in its small, neat dining room. The mailboat *Captain C* calls every week, and if for some reason you want to linger in Black Point, there are four spacious double rooms over *De Shamon's*, each equipped with a fridge (❷).

Staniel Cay and around

The contrast between Black Point and the tidy, green settlement on **STANIEL CAY** is striking. Though still a sleepy fishing village, the latter has a more prosperous air thanks to its popularity with yacht cruisers and an expatriate presence that infuses money into the local economy. The **gateway** to the Exuma Land and Sea Park, Staniel Cay has an airstrip, with regularly scheduled flights from Nassau (see p.262 for details on getting to Staniel Cay), two marinas, a couple of restaurants (see p.265) and several shops selling provisions. The action is centred on the two marinas – the Happy People Marina and the Staniel Cay Yacht Club – that sit about a quarter of a mile apart. The marina and club are connected by a flat, narrow paved road lined with small stucco cottages, which runs by the public beach. What little traffic exists is of the golf-cart variety. A particularly fun time to visit is over New Year's, when Staniel Cay hosts a well-attended regatta. Warm-up events include a cookout on the public beach, a children's boat race, fireworks and a Junkanoo rush-out early New Year's morning. Another great time to visit is in August during the Bonefishing Tournament, held in conjunction with the Staniel Cay Homecoming. Staniel Cay is also the closest isle to the celebrated Thunderball Grotto (see box below).

Besides the **accommodations** on Staniel Cay listed opposite, those with a bit of extra money to burn should keep in mind the small, privately owned cays bordering the Exuma Land and Sea Park to the north. The most expensive is **Fowl Cay** (☎1-866/369-5229 in the US, Ⓦwww.fowlcay.com; ❽), a fifty-acre cay located a mile and a half north of Staniel Cay, with accommodations in three attractive rental cottages. In high season, a one-bedroom cottage sleeping two is $5500 a week, including all meals and liquor; a three-bed/three-bath cottage sleeping six runs $10,700. Less expensive is a house on the 450-acre **Compass Cay**, home to a beautiful, long white-sand beach. The *Compass Cay Marina* (☎355-2064; VHF Ch 16; ❽) rents a three-bedroom cottage here sleeping up to four people, with a full kitchen, satellite TV, VHF radio and use of a thirteen-foot

---

Thunderball Grotto

Just offshore from Staniel Cay is the spectacular **Thunderball Grotto**, one of the Bahamas' most enchanting places: a hollowed-out island with a limestone vault arching over pools filled with colourful corals and fish, with shafts of sunlight pouring in through openings in the roof. It boggles the mind that a whole film crew got down here to film scenes from the James Bond movie that gave the grotto its name – and then did it again to film *Never Say Never Again*. You have to dive or snorkel into the undersea cavern through a current, and unless you are an expert go with a guide – or just rent the movie.

In Staniel Cay, you can **rent or charter a boat** to take you to the Thunderball Grotto, into the national park or down to Barreterre on Great Exuma (see p.255). You might also ask on the dock for a local fisherman who could run you wherever you want to go.

motorboat. Rates are around $1650 a week for two people, plus $100 each for up to two more guests. A final option is a cottage on 31-acre **Sampson Cay**, located three miles north of Staniel Cay. The recently renovated *Sampson Cay Club and Marina* (☎355-2034, ⓕ357-0824 ⓦwww.sampsoncayclub.com; ❺) features five cottages that rent for $300 a night, a marina, grocery store, restaurant and bar. The marina has sailboats and snorkelling gear for guest use, or you could rent a thirteen-foot Boston Whaler here to explore the area for $80 per day.

Practicalities

The cheapest **place to stay** on Staniel Cay is the *Happy People Marina* (☎355-2008, ⓕ355-2025; rooms ❸, apartment ❼) which, though showing its age, has adequate motel-style rooms on the waterfront and a two-bedroom apartment for rent. The nicer *Staniel Cay Yacht Club and Marina* (☎355-2024, ⓕ355-2044, ⓦwww.stanielcay.com; ❺) features five cute wooden cottages, each with its own veranda overlooking the water and equipped with a coffeemaker and a small refrigerator; weekly specials and a cottage sleeping four and one sleeping up to seven are also available. The *Atlantica* and *Shipwrecked* (☎355-2043 or agent Marty Wohlford at ☎954/525-5198 (US), ⓦwww.a1vacations.com; ❹–❼) are two cozy, colourful rental cottages on stilts topping a little knoll just across the road from the public beach. The one-bedroom cottage rents for $600 a week, while the two-bedroom goes for $950.

When it comes time to **eat**, the *Happy People Restaurant and Bar* (☎355-2008), located next to the hotel and marina, is a popular local hangout that's open for breakfast, lunch and dinner, serving Bahamian dishes, sandwiches and burgers. Known for impromptu performances by singer Jimmy Buffett, the interior is dark, and the rafters strung with yachting pennants. The colourful, relaxed *Staniel Cay Yacht Club Restaurant and Bar* (☎355-2024) has one of the most pleasing and inviting interiors in the Exumas, dressed up with a nautical theme. Standard Bahamian and American dinners are served daily in one sitting at 7.30pm (reservations required by 5pm), while breakfast is served daily starting at 8am and lunches Monday–Saturday 11.30am–3pm. North of the settlement, overlooking Thunderball Grotto, is the *Club Thunderball* (closed Mon), serving native dishes for lunch and dinner and offering a pool table, and dancing on weekends.

The Exuma Land and Sea Park

Beginning five miles north of Staniel Cay, the **EXUMA LAND AND SEA PARK** encompasses fifteen substantial cays – including **Warderick Wells Cay**, home to the park's headquarters – and numerous smaller outcroppings stretched over 22 miles of the Exuma chain. The park covers an area of 176 square miles, bound to the east by the deep cobalt waters of Exuma Sound, and in the west by the endless jade and sapphire shallows, reefs and sandbars of the Great Bahama Bank, both sides brimming with tropical marine life. The low rocky islands are rimmed by stretches of brilliant white sandy beach, some windswept and backed by rolling dunes, others sheltered by tall stands of coconut palms. As there is no commercial development of any sort within park boundaries, visitors should bring their own food and shelter, and be able to entertain themselves – not particularly hard with the spectacular sunrises and sunsets, and at night an opulent canopy of stars that appears close enough to pluck one.

Sea kayaking in the Exumas

One of the best and increasingly popular ways of exploring the Exumas is by **sea kayak**. If you want to explore the Exuma Cays and the Land and Sea Park **on your own**, your easiest option is to rent sea kayaks and camping equipment from George Town's Starfish outfitter (see p.258 for rates). Though the sunny skies and generally placid turquoise sea can make one forget, this is a remote wilderness area and you'll need to be experienced, fit, and well equipped. There are few visitors, even fewer places to replenish drinking water, and in high winds the sometimes wide cuts between the cays become extremely dangerous. It is essential to carry the following **safety equipment** if travelling independently: a first aid kit; nautical charts and a compass; a VHF radio with a range of at least five miles and extra AA batteries. You also need a GPS (Global Positioning System); an EPIRB (Emergency Position Indicating Radio Beacon) signalling device for extreme emergencies; and flares, smoke signals and a horn for attracting the attention of passing boats. Only a few cays at the southern end of the chain are permanently inhabited and in the Land and Sea Park, one park ranger is responsible for patrolling its entire 176 square miles. It could be a long time in an emergency before being spotted by a passerby. You will also need to bring sufficient food and drinking water for the duration of your trip – at least a gallon of water a day per person. Only small cooking fires are permitted, and the use of camp stoves is encouraged.

Another point to keep in mind is that several of the islands in the chain are **privately owned**. The owners have paid millions of dollars for their privacy, and do not appreciate uninvited campers on their beaches. This means that you have to plan your route carefully. When you come into the national park, call "Exuma Park" on VHF Ch 16 and let the warden know where you are camping and your intended route through the park. If you are travelling outside the park boundaries, it is a good idea to check in with the police detachment in George Town or Staniel Cay beforehand. On a more positive note, don't forget your snorkelling gear and sturdy closed-toe shoes so you can to explore the islands and reefs.

The warden of the Exuma Land and Sea Park recommends that kayakers and sailors alike equip themselves with Stephen Pavlidis's *Cruising Guide to The Exuma Cays*. Nautical charts for the area can be found in the *Explorer Chartbook: Exumas and the Ragged Islands* by Monty and Sara Lewis and *The Yachtsman's Guide to The Bahamas*.

Arrival and getting around

Unless you are piloting your own watercraft, getting to the park takes some money and effort. The park is most easily accessed from Staniel Cay (see "Getting around" details on p.262), from where you can **rent or charter a boat** to take you into the park. Often in the area is Miami-based Captain Bill Hirsch, (☎305/944-3033, ☎944-8033, ⓦwww.myknottymind.com) who will run trips up to Warderick Wells for $100; he also offers guided tours of the park aboard his yacht *Knotty Mind* for $450 per day, all-inclusive. The yacht, which sleeps four guests, has an air compressor on board to refill diving tanks as well as a gourmet cook. An expensive, though undoubtedly memorable option, is a tour on the sailboat *Cat Ppalu* (Miami ☎305/888-1226 or 1-800/327-9600, ⓦwww.blackbeard-cruises.com). From Nassau, the boat heads out on guided diving trips through the park several times a year, with plenty of time made for exploring the cays topside.

From Nassau, Captain Paul Harding of Diving Safaris Ltd (☎393-2522 or 1179) can fly you directly to Warderick Wells or any other place in the park in his **floatplane**.

Guided tours and programmes

Several outfitters run **guided expeditions** through the cays. Starfish (see p.257) offers kayaking day-trips that involve a leisurely paddle followed by a picnic lunch on one of the several small islands that enclose Elizabeth Harbour. Starfish's knowledgeable guides also lead two- to five-day camping trips in the Brigantines off the north tip of Great Exuma.

For those who have never sea-kayaked before, North Carolina Outward Bound (2600 Niceville Rd, Asheville, NC 28805; ☎828/299-3366, ⓕ299-3928, ⓦwww .ncobs.org) offers an eight-day sea-kayaking course in the southern cays. The expeditions, which cost around $1700 excluding airfare to George Town, are run once a month December through April. Days are spent practising strokes and rescue techniques, learning chart navigation, snorkelling and paddling from island to island. Contrary to popular Outward Bound myth, you won't be stranded alone on a deserted island with only a safety pin and a magnifying glass to save you, though the course does include a "solo" period for reflecting on the beauty of the surroundings. Highlights include visiting the giant iguanas on Leaf Cay and hiking to the lookout at Perry Peak on Lee Stocking Island.

Also available are eight-day guided expeditions ($1600) run by Ibis Tours (PO Box 208, Pelham, NY 10803; ☎914/738-5334 or 1-800/525-9411, ⓔinfo@ibistours .com), which head through the Exuma Land and Sea Park in March, April and May. Paddlers put in at Staniel Cay and leisurely wend their way up towards Norman's Cay at the south end of the park, with plenty of time made for snorkelling, swimming, fine dining, and lolling on the many beaches which beckon along the way. The kayaks are equipped with sails to lessen the level of exertion required. Another outfitter with similar sail-equipped kayaks is Ecosummer Expeditions (PO.Box 1765, Clearwater, BC, Canada V0E 1N0; ☎250/674-0102 or 1-800/465-8884, ⓦwww.ecosummer.com), who offer a nine-day trip through the heart of the Exuma Land and Sea Park (March & April; $1600) as well as a more strenuous fifteen-day traverse of the entire Exuma chain from Barreterre to Norman's Cay (February; $2300).

Accommodation

Most visitors to the Exuma Land and Sea Park arrive on their own sailboats or with organized kayaking and camping expeditions. There are 22 moorings at the north anchorage of Warderick Wells by the park headquarters (see overleaf), and four more at the south anchorage. The mooring fee is $15 a night, and the park asks that you call (VHF Ch 16 "Exuma Park") the morning before you intend to arrive. There are no hotels within the park boundaries, but there are dozens of soft sandy beaches on which to pitch your tent. **Camping** fees are $5 a night, and the park relies on campers to drop their payment at the park headquarters or mail it in after they leave. There are also accommodations available just outside the park boundaries on Compass Cay and Sampson Cay to the south (see pp.264 and 265); on Norman's Cay and Highbourne Cay to the north (see p.270); and in the nearby settlement of Staniel Cay (see p.264).

The Exuma Land and Sea Park was established in 1958 by the Bahamas National Trust (BNT) as a **marine conservation area**. The nonprofit BNT, alarmed at the destruction of the historically abundant diversity of plant and animal life in the islands, successfully lobbied to have this part of the Exumas set aside to protect and replenish species of fish and wildlife. Local fishermen were allowed a limited catch in park waters until 1986, when it became a no-take zone for fish, lobster, coral and even seashells. Ten years after the ban took force, grouper and lobster were around fifty percent larger and fifty percent more plentiful than those found outside park boundaries.

Nevertheless, the no-take policy is resented by some local fisherman, and **poaching** is a continuing problem. After the park's sole warden began strictly enforcing the no-take policy, poachers brought death threats against him and Bahamian Defence Force officers were stationed on Warderick Wells Cay to both protect him and his family and arrest violators.

As you travel through the park, you may see "For Sale" signs on various lonely humps of land. Some of the cays in the park were owned by wealthy foreigners before it was established and remained in private hands, in some cases jeopardizing conservation efforts as the park's authority does not extend beyond the high-water mark on privately owned cays. In the mid-1990s, for example, a developer bought **Hall's Pond Cay**, planning to establish a resort community on the island. In cutting roads and digging foundations, vast quantities of loose earth were washed into the sea, and the coral reef located 400yd offshore began to die. Eventually, the Bahamian government repossessed Hall's Pond Cay, but considerable damage had already been done.

Volunteer programmes

For those interested in helping out, the Land and Sea Park runs a **volunteer programme**. With limited support from the government – the park currently relies completely on private donations for its day-to-day operations – the park depends heavily on volunteers to staff the office on Warderick Wells and maintain the park facilities. Each year, passing boaters, school groups and a small cadre of long-term resident volunteers put in some 27,000 hours of unpaid labour. The tasks are often far from glamorous. Projects include cutting hiking trails, beach clean-up, machinery maintenance and sorting nails and screws, even babysitting the warden's children. Facilities at Warderick Wells are limited, so you must be prepared to sleep on your boat or bring a tent (mooring and camping fees are waived). There is drinking water, showers and a kitchen for use by volunteers, but you will need to bring your food. Periodically, a boat goes to Staniel Cay or Nassau for supplies. Contact the warden at least a month in advance outlining your skills and availability (see park headquarters details below for contact information). If just passing through the park, the headquarters has a long "To Do" list of jobs requiring a few hours or a few days; any help is appreciated.

Warderick Wells Cay

In the middle of the park sits **Warderick Wells Cay**, home to the park's **headquarters** (Mon–Sat 9am–noon & 3–5pm, Sun 9am–1pm; c/o Bahamas National Trust, PO Box N-3189, Nassau, Bahamas; ☎359-1821, ©exumapark @aol.com, VHF 16 "Exuma Park"). The visitors' centre, housed in a wooden building at the cay's northern end, holds an interesting display on the natural history of the Exumas, along with maps, information sheets and reference books to guide your explorations. The office also has a book exchange and sells postcards and T-shirts, but does not stock food of any kind. On Saturdays through the winter, the park hosts a happy hour for visitors on the veranda.

Notable for more than just the visitors' centre, Warderick Wells is well worth the considerable effort it takes to reach it. The isle's undulating ridges and valleys offer relief to eyes accustomed to the generally flat topography of the Bahamas, and seven miles of well-marked hiking **trails** crisscross the island, leading through groves of thatch palm and silver buttonwood, past limestone sink holes, and along a broad tidal creek bed to impressive lookout points and Loyalist plantation ruins. A dozen soft white-sand beaches dot the windswept Atlantic coast and secluded palm-fringed coves of the leeward side of the island, while the coral reefs and sea gardens surrounding the island teem with life.

In the days of pirates and privateers, the cay was a source of freshwater for passing sailors. At the southern end of the island, opposite Hog Cay, a conch-shell-lined path marks the way to **The Pirate's Lair**, a secluded stand of tall cabbage palms with a floor of soft sand used as a rest stop by Blackbeard and his ilk. Some of the grasses growing here are not indigenous to the Exumas and are found only on the coast of Louisiana, leading historians to believe that their seeds were brought in the sleeping mats of the pirates who gathered here to plan raids and collect water from the nearby spring. Sometime in the late eighteenth century, unknown Loyalist exiles settled on the island. **Anita's Trail** leads to the ruins of a stone house discovered in 1995, about a two miles south of the headquarters (trail maps are available from there). Just south of the ruins, a waist-high stone wall runs across the width of the whole island, from the windward to leeward shores. It is likely that the settlers built it to confine their cattle to the southern part of the island. Follow the wall to its western end, and you arrive at **Beryl's Beach** in a lovely, sheltered cove.

A fifteen-minute hike from the park headquarters, **Boo Boo Hill** marks the highest point on a limestone ridge at the north end of Warderick Wells and has a commanding view down the length of the island and of both coastlines. A path at the east end of **Powerful Beach** near the park office leads to the rocky summit where it is believed a cairn was erected in the nineteenth century by survivors of a shipwreck, missionaries en route to save wayward souls. For years, passing boaters have made a pilgrimage up Boo Boo Hill to leave a marker of their voyage, some of them quite elaborate, and they make for interesting reading. Just below the steps to the park office, at the south end of Powerful Beach, rests the mounted skeleton of a huge sperm whale, 52ft long and over 6ft high. The whale washed up on Shroud Cay in 1995.

In another conservation effort, 25 **hutias**, small hedgehog-like creatures, were introduced on Warderick Wells in 1985. They were, and are still considered to be, an endangered species, though there are now an estimated 2500 on the island. You are unlikely to see the hutias as they are nocturnal, but you might smell them – they have a scent akin to decaying leaves. The cay is also home to all kinds of birds, lizards and a wide variety of plant life, not to mention three lemon sharks and a five-foot-long barracuda named Bubba, which have taken up residence in the shallow waters near the park headquarters. They have acquired a taste for food scraps, and may often be seen drifting motionless between the docks on hot afternoons. By all accounts quite timid, they disappear when anyone else is in the water but are fascinating to observe – though more than a bit unnerving if you fancy a swim or snorkel around the reef.

The rest of the park

Just to the north of Warderick Wells is **Alligator Cay**, where the resident giant iguanas can be found sunning themselves on the beach. Further north, the long and narrow **Hawksbill Cay** boasts inviting stretches of beach on both sides. Besides sun-worshipping, you can also explore the ruins of a Loyalist settlement set in a grove of tamarind trees; a marked trail begins from the beach midway along the west side of the island. Historically a watering place for pirates, spongers and fisherman, **Shroud Cay**, north of Hawksbill Cay, is traversed by several tidal creeks and mangrove swamps that are breeding grounds for various species of fish and birdlife. These may be explored carefully by kayak or dinghy. On the north end of the cay, overlooking Exuma Sound, is Camp Driftwood, a structure constructed incrementally by passing boaters out of flotsam and jetsam. In the 1980s, it was used by US drug agents to spy on Carlos Lehder's smuggling operations close by on Norman's Cay (see below).

At the southern end of the park, **Little Bell Island**, also known as **Cambridge Cay**, is a popular stop-off for boat cruisers. It is privately owned, but visitors are welcomed ashore. Towards the north end of the cay, a trail from a beach on the leeward side takes you to a lookout where you can make out the length of the island and a chain of cays extending north and south. Immediately south of Cambridge Cay are the **Rocky Dundas**, two tall rocky piles that house grottoes dripping with stalactites and stalagmites that visitors claim rival the more famous Thunderball Grotto. The Rocky Dundas stand exposed to Exuma Sound in Conch Cut, which can be rough in windy weather, and as there is a strong northward current on the incoming tide, it is recommended that you visit in calm weather at low tide.

The Northern Exumas

Although the northern boundary of the Land and Sea Park was placed arbitrarily at the Wax Cay Cut, the Exuma chain continues on a northwest trajectory for another ten miles. From the relatively sizeable islands of Norman's Cay and Highbourne Cay just outside the park boundary, the string of cays gradually peters out to a series of rock outcroppings forty miles southeast of Nassau. In between, numerous cays and rocks of various shapes and sizes, inviting strands and crescents of beach and great opportunities for diving, snorkelling and birdwatching are all yours to explore. Note, however, that many of these cays are privately owned, as marked on nautical charts for the area.

Just north of the Land and Sea Park, remote **Norman's Cay** was the focus of international attention in the early 1980s when it was revealed that drug lord Carlos Lehder was using it as a base of operations for running cocaine. After terrorizing the other wealthy residents of the cay into abandoning their properties, he smuggled billions of dollars of contraband into the United States from here before being caught and jailed. These days, with its long beach and gracefully swaying palm trees, the cay is once again a popular stop-off for yachters cruising the Exumas.

A few miles to the north, **Highbourne Cay** is the only other permanently inhabited cay in the chain. It's privately owned, but boaters are permitted ashore at the Highbourne Cay Marina (☏355-1008, Ⓕ355-1003, VHF Ch 16), which has a grocery store, pay phone, and berths for boats up to 130ft.

Practicalities

The Northern Exumas are most easily reached from Nassau, which lies forty miles to the west. Captain Nigel Bower of Powerboat Adventures (☎393-7116 or 7126, ⓕ393-7029, ⓦwww.powerboatadventures.com) leads an action-packed full-day outing that includes a visit to the resident Bahamian dragon iguanas on Allan's Cay, snorkelling, a nature hike, and a barbecue lunch on the powdery white beach on Ship Channel Cay ($175, children $100). Apart from organized excursions, visiting the northern cays is logistically difficult and expensive unless you have your own yacht or airplane. You will have to charter a water taxi or airplane from Nassau or Staniel Cay. There is an airstrip on Norman's Cay.

Accommodation options on the Northern Exumas are limited. On Norman's Cay, *MacDuff's* (☎357-8846 or 937/845-0498 in the US, ⓕ937/845-7351, VHF Ch 16) rents one-bedroom beachfront cottages (❽), and there is also a restaurant and bar patronized by passing boaters. *Highbourne Plantations* (contact the marina) rents four seaside cottages (❽) nearby that sleep up to six people.

Cat Island and San Salvador

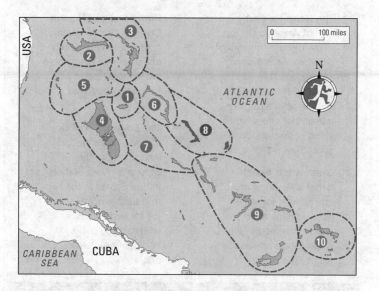

CHAPTER 8

Highlights

✳ **Annual Cat Island Regatta** If you are here in August, pick a spot on New Bight's harbourside to scope out this regatta, which draws hundreds of yachters to the island for music, food and, of course, sailing. See p.280

✳ **The Hermitage on Mount Alvernia** On top of the highest "mountain" (206ft) in the Bahamas, just outside New Bight in central Cat Island, The Hermitage is a religious retreat that offers terrific views of the Atlantic coast. See p.281

✳ **Greenwood Beach** Swim and sun on this spectacular ten-mile patch of pink sand, which rivals any in the world for beauty and isolation. See p.282

✳ **Diving** The south shore of Cat Island boasts some great diving spots, including the Black Coral Wall, Vlady's Reef and the Anchor, which feature massive sheets of coral and sea fans as well as plentiful tiger fish and parrotfish. See p.285

✳ **Bonefishing at Pigeon Creek** A classic casting spot located just south of Fernandez Bay, where the fish are huge and access is easy. See p.286

✳ **The Lucayan Trail** One of many hikes that emanate from the Bahamian Field Station in San Salvador, the two-mile Lucayan Trail is a joy for birdwatchers, who can see ospreys and cormorants. See p.294

Cat Island and San Salvador

CAT ISLAND and SAN SALVADOR still retain the traditional farming and agriculture of the old Bahamas. While their population's youth leaves in droves for service jobs in New Providence and Grand Bahama and the population has shrunk to new lows in the last few decades, visitors still come for the islands' splendid stretches of pink-sand beaches and exquisite snorkelling and diving possibilities.

On the extreme eastern edge of the Great Bahama Bank, 130 miles southeast of Nassau, Cat is seventy miles west of San Salvador, which rests in the Atlantic Ocean. The two are forever linked not only by their relative proximity but by the enduring controversy surrounding Columbus's first landing in the New World. The two islands have long claimed this historic yet unverified spot as well as the name "San Salvador", which the explorer gave it in his journals. Until the twentieth century, Cat Island was widely accepted as the island of his landfall and, consequently, known as San Salvador, while modern San Salvador was known as Watling's Island. However, after detailed

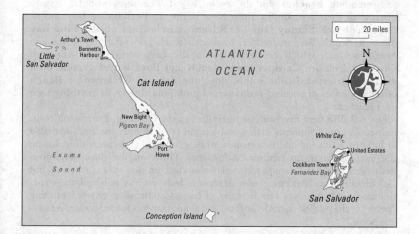

studies of the sixteenth-century Spanish missionary Bartolomé de Las Casas's version the Columbus journals, the consensus shifted. On May 6, 1926, the Bahamian legislature formally renamed the islands the way they are now. To this day, some Cat Islanders still claim that Cat was the original landfall for Columbus.

Cat Island

Cat Island is a slender 48-mile-long boot-shaped slice, no more than four miles wide at any one point until it reaches the sole in the far south, where its width triples. Lush and hilly by Bahamian standards, Cat has some of the best soil for farming in the Bahamas, and consequently boasts more vegetation and animal life than other islands. These days, small-scale farming is far more important than fishing as a source of livelihood for its roughly 2000 permanent residents, and the island has a deserted feel that is quite comforting to visitors seeking a refuge from fast-paced modern life.

North to south, a single smooth and well-paved **Queen's Highway** runs the entire length of the island and is punctuated here and there by ramshackle villages and plantation house ruins. Along the highway, you can plainly see the ridgeland that dominates the topography, a series of rising platforms that were once dunes, but have now solidified.

South Cat is centred on **New Bight**, a relatively sprawling settlement two miles in length, which features the **Mount Alvernia Hermitage** on the highest peak of the Bahamas, serves as Cat's administrative centre and is the gateway to the boot of Cat Island. North Cat is anchored by the charming settlement of **Arthur's Town** and its nearby sister **Orange Creek**. The whole north coast is one continuous beach, though often fronted by dramatic steep cliffs and broken by isolated coves.

Outstanding **beaches** dot the entire island. The most popular, largely because of their accessibility from New Bight, are **Fernandez Bay** and its tiny sister beach, **Skinny Dip**. The Atlantic coast beaches, notably **Fine Bay** opposite Smith Bay, are wilder, harder to reach and offer big waves and rough weather, which can make for challenging surfing. Just north of Orange Creek are **Camperdown Beach** and **Port Royal Beach**, both wild and deserted. In the south, along the Atlantic, **Greenwood Beach** offers ten miles of isolated and deserted pink sand that rivals anything seen on Eleuthera.

The **wildlife** here may well be unrivalled in the Bahamas. Burrowing owls, numerous non-poisonous snakes and a number of amphibians are observable in interior scrubland and near ponds, while giant land crabs are visible during the evening hours in oceanward lowlands. However, the once-ubiquitous freshwater turtle (*Chrysemys felis*), once abundant on not only Cat Island, but also Eleuthera and Andros, is now in serious decline. On Cat Island, these turtles are found in only a few hectares of lakes. Cat Islanders enjoyed hunting "peter" as they called it, both for food and as adornments for freshwater reflecting pools.

Obeah

In addition to the Out Island bush medicine (see p.259), which resembles the indigenous medicine of other cultures that have had little experience with modern physicians, some Cat Islanders still practise **obeah**. This form of witchery concentrates on the application of "cures" and "spells" to guard against evil eyes or thefts. Empty bottles are a particular fetish of obeah, and you can see them dangling from the occasional tree, or littered about graveyards, all in homage to the spirits of the dead, who are said to enjoy a libation in preference to more destructive behaviour. Farmers fill their bottles with hair, dirt or fingernails, and place them at strategic spots in their fields to protect crops. Another manifestation of obeah is the placing of lightning rods on some Cat Island houses, particularly in New Bight, to protect against ghosts and spirits.

Some history

While the Spanish established a number of settlements on the island, it is widely accepted that the island is named for **Arthur Catt**, a seventeenth-century pirate who was based on Cat Island. Locals often say that the name of the island is derived from the large numbers of feral cats abandoned on the island when the Spanish left, but serious historians are sceptical.

In any event, the first significant influx on Cat was made up of **American Loyalists** fleeing the American Revolution in 1783, and the number of Hepburns, Deveauxs, McDonalds, Campbells and Sutherlands on Cat Island today attests to those early families. They set up cotton plantations and cattle farms; at the height of plantation agriculture, there were perhaps forty slave-labour farms on the island, the remains of which can still be found scattered about the bush.

The land was soon depleted, however, and the slave-plantation culture pretty much ended in 1831 with widespread slave revolt. When Britain abolished slavery in 1834, many slave owners fled the island, and the newly emancipated settlements were taken over by the former slaves. (New Bight, for instance, began its life as Freetown, where freed slaves settled after the British banning of the slave trade.) Soon, a new form of colonial agriculture began to dominate Cat Island with the establishment of huge pineapple and sisal farms on the interior. In the mid-1850s, the population of Cat hit five thousand, a railroad was built to carry produce to shipping points and the production of ethereally sweet pink pineapples rivalled that of Eleuthera.

Only fifty years later, however, with the emergence of world markets, Cat's relative isolation and constant competition from American and British conglomerates drove both the pineapple and the sisal business into bankruptcy. Since then, Cat Islanders have lived a traditional and quiet life, farming small pothole plots in the deep interior of the island, fertilized with guano gathered from bat caves. The most successful of these plots grow tomatoes, onions and pineapples, though only for local consumption. For most of the island, electricity only came about a decade ago, and the effects of tourism are still minimal.

Arrival

There are two **airports** on Cat Island: the small Arthur's Town Airport (☎354-2049) in the north and the more widely used New Bight Airport (☎342-2017) servicing the south. Bahamasair (☎1-800/222-4262) departs for Arthur's Town ($70 round-trip) every Tuesday, Thursday and Sunday from Nassau and

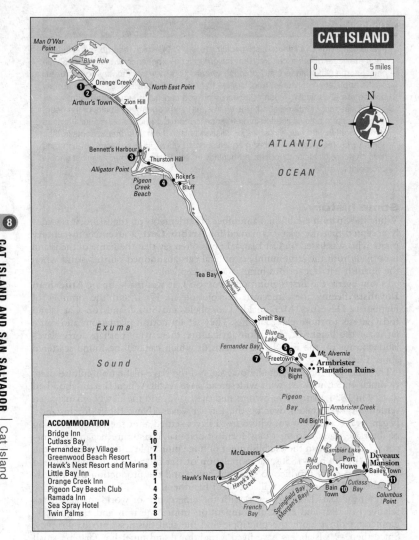

ACCOMMODATION

Bridge Inn	6
Cutlass Bay	10
Fernandez Bay Village	7
Greenwood Beach Resort	11
Hawk's Nest Resort and Marina	9
Little Bay Inn	5
Orange Creek Inn	1
Pigeon Cay Beach Club	4
Ramada Inn	3
Sea Spray Hotel	2
Twin Palms	8

for New Bight (also $70 round-trip) Monday and Friday from Nassau. Smaller carriers fly from Fort Lauderdale to New Bight, including Air Sunshine (☎1-800/327-8900) and Island Express (☎954/359-0380). Local lodges like *Fernandez Bay Village* near New Bight and *Greenwood Beach Resort* in Port Howe offer private charter service into New Bight for their guests for $100 per person one-way.

The more adventurous may prefer the **mailboat** to the plane. The MV *North Cat Island Special* departs Nassau's Potter's Cay dock (☎393-1064) on Wednesday afternoon at 1pm with a one-way fare of $40, returning to Nassau on Thursday. It calls at New Bight, Bennett's Harbour and Arthur's Town during a fourteen-hour trip. Likewise, the MV *Sea Hauler* departs Nassau on Tuesday at 2pm, arriving in Old and New Bight, to return to Nassau on Saturday. Better and more comfortable is the *North Cat Island Special*. If you plan to take the mailboat, be sure to call Potter's Cay dock to check on exact departure times.

The only formal **marina** is the eight-slip facility at Hawk's Nest Resort Marina (☎342-7050 or 1-800/688-4752, ⓕ342-7051, VHF Ch 16) with gas, diesel and groceries. Yachters regularly anchor in shallow Fernandez Bay and spend a few days in idleness, taking dinghies ashore during the day and spending evenings on board their vessels. Given the lack of marina facilities on Cat, this is a logical choice for boaters.

Getting around and information

Cat is difficult to negotiate for there are no taxis or buses on the island. A few enterprising individuals have attempted to set up their own private cars as **taxis**, but these are quite unreliable, expensive, and often unavailable; however, if you've booked a room at one of the major resorts, management will almost always arrange transportation for you from the airport.

If you are spending significant time on the island, you can **rent a car**, though options are few and costly. In New Bight, the Russell Brothers who own and operate the New Bight Shell station (☎342-3014) rent a few cars at the expensive rate of $80–100 per day, with the proviso that the renter is responsible for all damage. Guests of the *Bridge Inn* (☎342-3013) in New Bight get a special rate of approximately $65 for weekly rentals, though it is still no bargain. In Orange Creek, both the *Sea Spray Hotel* (☎354-4116 or 1-800/688-4752) and the *Orange Creek Inn* (☎354-4110) rent a few cars at the same rate as those in New Bight.

The most economical way to see Cat Island is to rent a **scooter** or a **bicycle**. In Arthur's Town, a little market called Cookie House (☎354-2027) rents them for $20 per day, while the rental agencies often have one or two scooters available for rental as well. The best place to find bicycles is at the major resort hotels, where guests have the use of bikes for free, while others may make arrangements for rentals by phoning ahead. The *Sea Spray Hotel* (☎354-4116 or 1-800/688-4752) rents bicycles for about $7 per day.

There are no **information centres** on Cat Island.

South Cat Island

Two-thirds of the way down Cat, **New Bight** serves as the island's tourism and administrative centre, containing police station and a BaTelCo office in its Government Administrative Complex. Home to Father Jerome's celebrated **Mount Alvernia Hermitage**, it has access to several beaches, most notably **Fernandez Bay**. Three miles south, **Old Bight** is the base for trips to Greenwood Beach as well as several blue holes. South Cat is rounded off by **the boot**, which features some of the island's best **diving** and **snorkelling** between Columbus Point and Hawk's Nest Point.

Accommodation

Most South Cat hotel options are situated in the settlement of New Bight, though the *Greenwood Beach Resort* and *Fernandez Bay Village Resort* offer more upscale oceanfront accommodation.

Bridge Inn New Bight ☎ 342-3013, ℱ 342-3041.
This motel-style twelve-room affair features single,
double and triple rooms with access to a swimming pool, bar and restaurant, volleyball and tennis. The owners can arrange bonefishing and boat
trips, as well as excursions. Rooms are comfortable but modest with private bathrooms and TV. ❷

Cutlass Bay West of Bain Town ☎ 342-3085 or
1-800/723-5688. As a "clothing optional" all-inclusive, *Cutlass Bay* is the only nudist colony in the
Bahamas and is for adult couples only. Its eighteen
Spartan villas have no TV or phone, but there is a
delightful area of lawns and gardens, a great
beach, tennis court, pool, nature trails and game
room. Breakfast and lunch are served on the
veranda, dinner in the clubhouse. *Cutlass Bay* sells
expensive exclusivity. ❽

Fernandez Bay Village Resort New Bight
☎ 342-3043 or 1-800/940-1905, ℱ 342-3051,
Ⓦ www.fernandezbayvillage.com. An old reliable
twelve-villa resort only a mile from New Bight
Airport. Villas are stone and timber with brick
floors, gardens and private bath, and guests have
access to canoes, kayaks and snorkelling on
Fernandez Bay or Skinny Dip beach nearby. Mrs A,
now well into her 80s, is often in attendance at
meals served buffet-style on the patio or in the
dining room, and she can regale you with stories
about Father Jerome and obeah. Meals are freshly
prepared and there is often a bonfire at night on
the beach. ❽

Greenwood Beach Resort Port Howe ☎ & ℱ
342-3053 or 1-800/688-4752, Ⓔ gbr@grouper
.batelnet.bs, Ⓦ www.greenwoodbeachresort.com.
These isolated sets of twenty rooms are located on
ten miles of pink sand beach with access to excellent snorkelling and diving. Each room has king-
size beds, private bath and patio. On the grounds
are a swimming pool, dive shop, restaurant and
bar and a private sandy beach. Double rooms have
ocean views. ❹

Hawk's Nest Resort and Marina Devil's Point
☎ 342-7050 or 1-800/688-4752, ℱ 342-7051,
Ⓦ www.hawks-nest.com. Four hundred acres of
beachfront with ten oceanfront rooms and one
two-bedroom beach house. Rooms have king-size
or two queen beds, private baths, ceiling fans and
patio. The house is fully equipped and has maid
service. A good dive service is on the grounds, as
well as volleyball, mopeds, golf carts and fishing.
Rooms rent for $135 per person double. The house
costs $370/2200 daily/weekly. *Hawk's Nest* has a
4600ft private airstrip and an eight-slip marina. ❽

Little Bay Inn New Bight ☎ 342-2004. Located
just below Smith's Bay, this motel-style place has
six rooms with shared kitchens; a bit pricey for
what you get. ❸

Twin Palms Beach Resort New Bight ☎ 342-
6008. Just a block from the *Bridge Inn*, this small
guesthouse has but a handful of rooms – though
cheap and on the beach. ❶

New Bight and around

For most visitors, sprawling **NEW BIGHT** is the disembarkation point
because of its airport and proximity to Fernandez Bay, and is the most devel-
oped part of the island, thus a logical place to base yourself for a few days.
There is little of interest sight-wise beyond Father Jerome's hermitage on
Mount Alvernia, so it's perhaps best to try to coincide a trip with the local
rake 'n' scrape Festival, which takes place in late June, or the **Annual Cat
Island Regatta**, which draws hundreds of yachters to New Bight every
August.

Just past the sprawling Government Administrative Complex on the Queen's
Highway south of New Bight, the **Armbrister Plantation Ruins** consist of
some crumbling stone fences and the remains of Henry Hawkins Armbrister's
house, which was built in the pre-Loyalist 1760s. Much of the land around here
is owned by the Armbrister family, and Frances Armbrister, widow of a Cat
Island landowner and 1930s Hollywood producer Cyril Armbrister hold family deeds to their property that go back to the 1780s. A former radio actress,
Frances and her husband returned to Cat Island in the 1950s, when she con-
vinced her husband to "do something with all that worthless land in the
Bahamas".

One of the results was the *Fernandez Bay Village* (see above), three miles north
of New Bight. Today, Frances' son, Tony, owns and operates this resort, which

dominates **Fernandez Bay**, its sister beach Skinny Dip and their surrounding shoreline, offering lovely white sand lined with casuarina trees. Perfect for sunbathing and snorkelling, this bit of coast is free and open to all, guests of the resort and non-guests alike. Nevertheless, you'll never find it crowded.

On the way back to New Bight, stop off just north of Smith Bay, where you'll find several ponds near the Queen's Highway that are good for birdwatching and hiking, especially **Tea Bay Ponds**. Five miles north of Smith Bay just off the east side of the Queen's Highway, the twin Tea Bay Ponds are home to many herons and moorhens, and are especially noted for their populations of ducks, grebes, paired white-cheeked pintails and some sandpipers. Tea Bay Ponds are also some of the few left on Cat Island where you might catch a glimpse of the endangered Cat Island turtle. From Smith Bay, dirt track roads run to **Fine Bay**, a good surfing destination with nearly ten miles of pink-sand beach, and another to **Turtle Cove**, where you can watch – what else – turtles frolicking in shallow water.

Mount Alvernia Hermitage

The highlight of any visit to New Bight is undoubtedly the 206-foot climb to Father Jerome's celebrated **Mount Alvernia Hermitage**, perched atop Como Hill, the highest point in the entire Bahaman archipelago. Born John Hawes to an English middle-class family in 1876, Father Jerome was an ordained Anglican minister who first came to the Bahamas in 1908 on a mission to rebuild churches destroyed by a recent hurricane, and his St Paul's Anglican Church in Clarence Town on Long Island (see p.305) still stands as a testament to his zeal. Though his staunch belief in racial equality did him little good with the entrenched aristocracy near Marsh Harbour on Abaco, he still spent several years on his mission in the Bahamas before leaving for Rome in 1911, where he converted to Catholicism. After two decades preaching in Australia, he returned to the Bahamas in 1939 and spent the last seventeen years of his life on Cat Island, living as a hermit and ministering to the needs of the desperately poor. He did manage to find time to construct the Hermitage, which served as a medieval-style sanctuary and retreat.

The laborious climb – best done to coincide with either sunrise or sunset – begins at a dirt track just behind the Government Administrative Complex. The rock staircase was carved by hand into the hillside by Father Jerome himself, and includes hand-carved statuettes representing the fourteen stations of the cross. Once on top, you're rewarded with a panoramic view of both the Atlantic Ocean on the east and Exuma Sound on the south and west, as well as wide-angle views of the island's crown of coppice north and south. The midget-size hermitage itself comprises only three Spartan rooms, including a cloister and chapel, sparsely furnished, though there is a cone-shaped bell-tower rising from one side. To one side of the tiny chapel, Jerome's tomb is a simple stone sarcophagus kept free of weeds by a loving caretaker. The hermitage itself is topped by a peak-cap bell-tower and contains a tiny cloister.

Old Bight and the north boot

The boot of Cat Island begins at **OLD BIGHT**, a slightly seedy settlement four miles south of New Bight, and encompasses an area that is ten miles long and five miles wide. Old Bight serves as the starting point for one of the island's most scenic hikes as well as the base for a visit to three blue holes. The town is also home to two small churches – St Francis of Assisi Catholic Church, one of Father Jerome's Gothic stone fabrications, which is decorated by oddly camp frescoes, and St Mary's Church, a monument to Emancipation, which was given to the Cat Islanders by the family of Blaney Balfour, a British governor during late slave days.

From Old Bight, a dirt path leads out to **Gambier Lake**, skirts its north shore, and then continues on to beautiful Greenwood Beach, a total trek of about five miles, one-way. At Gambier Lake, birdwatchers can see a number of colourful species including grebes, cormorants, herons, egrets, and terns. Land birds include Bahama mockingbirds, Bahama woodstars, and Greater Antillean bullfinches. The road, an old logging track, peters out at **Greenwood Beach**, the loveliest on the island and maybe in the entire Bahamas, just north of *Greenwood Beach Resort*. The hike to the lake and the beach and then back is a full day's work, and should be undertaken only with adequate supplies of water, plenty of mosquito repellent, and directions. Services of a local guide are highly recommended, and both the *Bridge Inn* and *Fernandez Bay Village* can suggest some reliable ones to accompany you on your walk.

The sole of the boot

Essentially a flat, hot, palmetto scrub riddled with lakes and salty depressions, the boot itself isn't very hospitable country. However, off the south coast, or **sole of the boot**, you will find most of Cat Island's dive sites and the two hotels on the boot.

Just south of town, Armbrister Creek, a mangrove-lined tidal estuary replete with birdlife, leads to the *Boiling Hole* – a tidally influenced blue hole – that invites local speculation about magical forces and ghosts. Just outside *Bain Town*, which is fifteen miles south of Old Bight via the somewhat confusing Deep South Roundabout from which you must head east, are a couple of those dive sites. Just behind the St John the Baptist church in Bain Town, you'll find **Lotto-Man Hole**, a cave that opens into numerous underground passages, some of them water-filled. Lotto-Man is dangerous at distances beyond the entrance. **Mermaid-Hole**, located half an hour's walk to the east of Bain Town, has several underwater passages that are divable by experts only. Anyone interested in exploring either the cave or the blue hole near Bain Town should consult with the *Greenwood Beach Resort* for advice (see p.280), and should consider hiring a guide through the resort.

To the east of Gambier Lake, or five miles south of the Deep South Roundabout, sits the picturesque village of **Port Howe**. Not much more than a collection of village limestone homes these days, Port Howe is believed by some to have been a Spanish settlement for the transshipment of Lucayan Indian slaves to Hispaniola in the sixteenth century. During the 1700s, English wreckers established a village that was regularly attacked by Spaniards and pirates, and by 1783 English Loyalists had arrived and established several important plantations. It came to be called Port Howe after the British naval commander of the same name during the American Revolutionary War.

Five miles up the coast from Port Howe, just before the entrance to the *Greenwood Beach Resort*, lie the ruins of the **Deveaux Mansion**. A large, stark stone building, it looms like an apparition out of the lush foliage that entangles it. The main house of a cotton plantation owned by Captain Andrew Deveaux of the British Navy who recaptured Nassau from Spain in 1783, the mansion copied the contemporary style of American plantation houses in the Deep South, and its interior was created by French craftsmen in the late 1780s. Its wood galleries overlook the sea, and it has a surviving grandeur despite the fact that what remains is mostly the roof and heavy wood floors. Near the still-standing kitchen – marked by a chimney, fireplace and an ablution block – are the slave quarters.

A dirt track runs from Port Howe east to **Columbus Point**, the heel of the boot and the southernmost point on Cat Island. The track can be accessed from Port Howe toward Bailey Town, an abandoned Loyalist village just to the east. At Zion Church the track forks, one path leading slightly north to Winding Bay, from where you'll have to trek south to the point, another leading toward Churney Bay and Columbus Point, which provides a spectacular wide-angle view of breakers crashing on a near-shore coral reef, several indented creeks, and shallow pools full of starfish and other echinoderms. It is a long, hot walk from Greenwood Beach to Columbus Point for a view that might best be seen from a dive boat.

The rest of the boot is pretty isolated and haggard, and the rewards are snorkelling and diving (see p.285 for sites). The snorkelling is especially good in the neighbourhood of **Morgan's Bay** because the reef is so close, and a rough potholed road leads from here to **Devil's Point**, a slumberous but pretty fishing village named in the local belief that "cork did sink and iron did float" in its adjacent waters. You can turn off on an unmarked side road north toward the scruffy settlement of **McQueen's**, where the dirt road to **Hawk's Nest Point**, the farthest west tip of the boot, begins. The creek and estuary that cut hard into the point are brimming with prime bonefish; inquire at *Hawk's Nest Resort* see (p.280) for guides and boats.

Eating

All of the major South Cat resorts, except *Cutlass Bay*, welcome guests at their **restaurants**. The major settlements each have small bar/restaurants that serve decent Bahamian specialties like fried chicken, grouper and snapper. Few dining experiences are as pleasant as the buffet-style dinner for $30 at *Fernandez Bay Village* (☎342-3043), with its torch-lit patio and marvellous sunsets augmenting excellent food, including delicious barbecue ribs done outside on an open fire, great crab legs, and fried chicken. Every diner should try the famous conch chowder here, for it sets the standard in the islands. The *Bridge Inn* restaurant (☎342-3013) is decent for such Bahamian standards as fish stew, lobster, johnnycake, fried chicken and the ubiquitous Bahamian grouper, peas and rice. The restaurant features barbecue on Friday nights. The *Greenwood Beach Resort* (☎342-3053) offers call-ahead seating for non-guests at their evening outdoor buffets, which usually consist of an array of grilled seafood specialties, barbecue chicken and one pasta dish each night. The *Hawk's Nest Resort* (☎342-7050) restaurant is smaller, but the food is a good mix of European and Bahamian entrees, with the specialty being lobster/shrimp-stuffed mutton fish, a gargantuan meal serving at least four.

Drinking and nightlife

Around New Bight there are several great places to mix while listening to **live music** and drinking cold beer. Try Iva Thompson's *First and Last Chance Bar*, located between the airport and town, or *Twin Palms* (☎342-3184), an ocean-front **bar** on the outskirts of town that sometimes features the rake 'n' scrape music of Blind Blake. rake 'n' scrape is also featured at times on Saturday night at the *Bridge Inn* (☎342-3013). Very popular with New Bight locals, the *Blue Bird Restaurant and Bar* (☎342-3095), specializes in gossip and fried chicken. Still in New Bight, along Queen's Highway, the popular *Sailing Club* bar and restaurant serves food from 8am to 10pm, though you must make reservations for dinner. It gets wild on Saturday night, with dancing until very late. In Smith's Bay, *Hazel's Seaside Bar* is a simple oceanside shack with a relaxed atmosphere for a cold beer. Dominoes is the main attraction of the *Pass Me Not Bar* in Old Bight (☎342-4016), though you can get a cold beer here and rest your bones.

North Cat Island

Arthur's Town and nearby **Orange Creek** are the main settlements in less populated North Cat, which is studded here and there by ruins, many thought to predate even Loyalist settlement. Smaller villages, such as **Bennett's Harbour**, are just isolated settlements with no services or amenities, but it is particularly pleasant to pass by these traditional villages on a bright, windy day.

Arthur's Town and around

Thirty miles north of New Bight, **ARTHUR'S TOWN**, near the end of the Queen's Highway, is the administrative headquarters for northern Cat, housing not much more than a BaTelCo telephone station, a medical clinic, a police station and a coral-coloured Commissioner's Office. A small village of only a few hundred people, it was the boyhood home of **Sidney Poitier**, yet there is surprisingly no museum or monument to him, and his boyhood home is decrepit and abandoned. Oddly, the lesser-known Sir Roland Symonette, a local historian, politician, and major landowner on the island, has a decent little park named for him right in the centre of the village. The only real building of note, on the main road to the airport, is **St Andrews Anglican Church**, built of stone in the 1870s. Continue along the airport road and you will find **Camperdown Beach** on the Atlantic coast, favoured by locals and lined by sea grape and coconut palms.

Just up the road three miles is the tiny two-part village of **ORANGE CREEK**; the older section, north of the actual creek, is a bit more interesting, composed of attractive limestone and pastel-painted clapboard houses. There isn't much to see or do on either side, and those who come do so mainly to snorkel in the nearby reefs or go bonefishing, at much cheaper rates than elsewhere in the Bahamas (see p.286 for details).

North of Orange Creek, the land filters out into a series of creek beds, muddy mangroves and palmetto bush. Several paths out of Orange Creek are good for hiking. One, just north of town, forks west for about half a mile to **Port Royal Beach**, an isolated stretch running to Man O' War Point that is good for snorkelling and swimming. A second easily followed track heads north a mile to **Oyster Lake** and then branches off north for half a mile to **Glass Hill**, which overlooks a nice blue hole. East of Oyster Lake, lies **Griffin Bat Cave,** where you can find leaf-nosed bats in the dark. It is very tough going, hot and buggy; the Cleare brothers will act as a guide.

Practicalities

Arthur's Town has only a couple of choices for **lodging**, such as *Dean's Inn* (☎354-2121; ❷), which has ten apartments to let. Most people opt to stay in Orange Creek at either *Orange Creek Inn* (☎354-4110, ☞354-4042; ❷) which has sixteen rooms with fans, no restaurant or bar, but a food store, or the

Sea Spray Hotel (℡354-4116 or 1-800/688-4752, ℻354-4161; ❸), which over-looks the blue water of Exuma Sound. Convenient to the airport, *Sea Spray* offers sixteen rooms, most with air conditioning and TV, and one suite; they can also arrange bonefishing and snorkelling trips.

Near Symonette Square in the centre of Arthur's Town, Pat Rolle's *Cookie House Bakery* (℡354-2027) is a great **place to eat** for lunch or dinner if you're in the mood for basic fried-fish dishes or burgers. Also near the square is *Gina's*, a tiny take-out for hotdogs and burgers with chips.

Bennett's Harbour and around

About fifteen miles south of Arthur's Town along the Queen's highway, **BEN-NETT'S HARBOUR** lies hard against a wonderful half-mile sweep of pic-turesque bay. Initially a pirate hiding place, the actual settlement was founded by slaves freed by British naval vessels, and Bennett's earned its income by exporting hundreds of tons of salt from evaporating ponds nearby. These days, Bennett's looks weather-beaten and rough, with clapboard houses that have seen better days, but the bay is beautiful, and the area does have a few rooms to let. Bennett's Harbour is also a departure point for birding or bonefishing trips to Little San Salvador (see box on p.287).

Just south of Bennett's Harbour is Roker's Bluff, often called simply **the Bluff**, once reputed to be one of the wealthiest settlements on the island. It is the site of former cotton plantations that took advantage of its high ground and thus of its good soil and excellent drainage. Many of its original inhabitants were Scottish Loyalists who migrated from Virginia following the American Revolution. On the north side of the Bluff is a sign about a quarter-mile out of town indicating "Pigeon Cay". A dirt road leads to the lovely **Pigeon Creek Beach**, a curved mile of white sand on the south-facing side of Pigeon Cay. The beach is backed by palms and casuarinas and affords visitors ultimate solitude.

Practicalities

In the Bluff/Pigeon Cay area the **place to stay** is the intimate *Pigeon Cay Beach Club* (℡ & ℻354-5084 or 1-800/688-4752, ✉pigeoncay@aol.com, ⓦwww.igeoncaybahamas.com; ❻). With five rooms and eight thatch villas of stone and stucco with Mexican tile floors, *Pigeon Cay* is an excellent quiet get-away. There is a good restaurant and bar, as well as canoes, bikes, snorkelling and fishing. On the Bluff itself, the *Remanda Inn* (℡354-6973; ❷) has seven small motel-style rooms with fans and shared or private bath as well as a tiny restau-rant and bar.

For **eating**, Bennett's Harbour has a good grocery in Len's Grocery, and the *Beverage Restaurant and Disco*, which has decent souse and music on weekends.

Diving and watersports

While the Atlantic or "north coast" is storm-tossed and rough and the west coast unnavigable, the south coast of the boot, from Columbus Point in the east to Devil's Point in the west, is one of the most spectacular **diving sites** in a region filled with spectacular ones. Here along the coast, the reef wall begins at only around 50ft and drops off steeply into gulleys, chimneys, canyons and troughs. The best dive sites along the south shore of the boot include **Black Coral Wall**, **The Maze**, **Vlady's Reef**, **The Anchor**, **The Cut** and **The Cave**. Only The Cut is reachable from shore, the others are regular stops on the itinerary of Cat Island dive shops. Most feature massive sheets of coral, along with plentiful tiger fish, snapper, grunt, parrotfish and flamingo tongue shells, among hundreds of other species of flora and fauna. Elsewhere the seagrass beds are alive with wrasse, hermit crabs and sand gobies. At The Cave one can sometimes spot reef shark, though they are skittish.

A must-see for experienced divers, **Tartar Bank**, an offshore pinnacle that doesn't so much feature coral as huge schools of pelagic triggerfish, many sharks, spadefish, barracuda, jacks and eagle rays, lies sixteen miles southeast of Cat, a boat ride of at least 45 minutes that can be arranged by any of the dive shops. The best time to dive Tartar Bank is November to January for the fish, though the weather can be wild.

All of the major resorts in the south assist with **snorkelling** as well as diving. For the most part, snorkellers are welcome to go out on dive boats, and in most places in-shore snorkelling in grass beds and shallow reefs presents the opportunity to see starfish, rays and small fish.

Dive operators

Fernandez Bay Village Dive Resort Fernandez Bay ☎342-3043 or 1-800/940-1905, ℉305/474-4864, ⓦwww.fernandezbayvillage.com. The resort has complete dive facilities and offers many dives, as well as introductory training courses on a personal basis. Open-water dive courses cost $380, with cave dives $25 and night dives $85.

Greenwood Dive Centre *Greenwood Beach Resort* ☎ & ℉342-3053, ℮gbr@grouper .batelnet.bs, ⓦwww.greenwoodbeachresort.com. The largest dive operation on Cat, this is comprehensive in every way, with two dive boats that can carry twenty divers. Courses are conducted in both English and German, and the dives offered include a complete array of south shore dives. Dives cost about $65 for one- or two-tank dives, open-water certification $370, with both PADI and resort courses offered. Greenwood takes snorkellers on their boats for $20.

Hawk's Nest Resort and Marina Hawk's Nest Point ☎342-7050 or 1-800/688-4752, ℉342-7051, ⓦwww.hawks-nest.com. This small operation uses *Greenwood*'s facilities. *Hawk's Nest* specializes in dives on the offshore reef, a spot that is also good for snorkellers, as well as areas on and around Devil's Point, where massive stands of elkhorn and staghorn coral punctuate the reef. Basic one- or two-tank dives start at $70 and $80.

Fishing

With its mud creeks, shallow sandbanks and mangroves, the entire west coast is best suited to **bonefishing**. Near Fernandez Bay, **Joe's Creek Sound** and **Pigeon Creek** are great bonefishing sites, and the best place to find guides is at Fernandez Bay Village Dive Resort (☎342-3043), which charges $150/200 for half-day/full-day trips. Bonefishing in North Cat is just as good and you can contact Wilson or Lincoln Cleare in Orange Creek (☎354-4042) for both bonefishing ($300/day) as well as some sightseeing. Additional information on sightseeing, bonefishing, and trips to Little San Salvador (see opposite) can be had by contacting personnel in Arthur's Town at the tiny Commissioner's Office at the harbour. In Bennett's Harbour, bonefishing guides and sightseeing can be arranged by checking with Patrick Cooper at the *Remanda Inn* (☎354-6973). In Arthur's Town, Dell Rolle at the *Cookie House Bakery* (☎354-2027) knows the score for guides and sightseeing, or drop by *Dean's Inn* (☎354-2121).

Sport fishing has had a slow start on Cat Island, though it is quite spectacular. The hot spot is the south shore of the boot, which can be great for wahoo, white marlin and yellowfin tuna. Fernandez Bay Village Dive Resort (☎342-3043) is probably most experienced with sport-fishing trips although each of the south island resorts can provide guides and boats. Most sport-fishing trips to the twelve miles of excellent fishing grounds cost $300 full day, extra for tips and drinks.

Little San Salvador

Small, uninhabited, privately owned **Little San Salvador** lies about fifteen miles due west of Bennett's Harbour on Cat Island. Nine miles long, Little San Salvador is wrapped around a large inner lagoon, which serves as a comfortable anchorage to yachters and fishermen in bad weather. In 1996 it was sold to Holland America Lines and is now used as a landing spot for some of its cruises through Bahamian and Caribbean islands. The elliptical lagoon is a favourite with birders, who can often spot white-tailed tropicbirds and four species of terns. Resident land birds include burrowing owls, ospreys, vireos, bananaquits and black-faced grassquits. The bonefishing in its mangroves is widely celebrated.

Those with a yen for adventure can try to arrange transport to Little San Salvador by visiting the Commissioner's Office in Arthur's Town in person, or by boldly approaching a fishing captain on the docks of Arthur's Town or Bennett's Harbour. The Cleare brothers (see "Fishing", opposite) can arrange trips there as well, even though the island is privately owned. The average birdwatching expedition is around $200 per day, while bonefishing, given the distance and permissions required, is slightly more expensive than on the main island of Cat.

San Salvador

Only twelve miles long and five miles wide, **SAN SALVADOR** is low and hot, with a swampy interior dominated by large saline lakes and brine ponds surrounded by scrub palmetto bush. The shore is an almost uninterrupted stretch of empty white beach, and visitors come for its offshore western reef, which provides some of the finest **diving** and **snorkelling** in the Bahamas. The island also offers **hiking** and **birding** opportunities.

San Salvador's population hovers around a thousand, most of whom are involved in either tourism or small-scale farming and live in the capital of **Cockburn Town**, in **Victoria Hill** in the northeast or in **United Estates** in the northwest. The Queen's Highway circles the island, touching **Sandy Point Beach**, home to the former plantation Watling's Castle, on the southwest tip, and **Graham's Harbour** on the northeast point.

In the interior of San Salvador, **Great Lake** connects Cockburn Town with United Estates, and was once the main thoroughfare for islanders. **Little Lake**, very near Cockburn Town, is accessible by dirt road, and is worth a visit for its birdwatching opportunities. Offshore, several cays offer excellent naturalist encounters, including the rock iguanas of **Green Cay**, while the unspoiled beaches of **Rum Cay** should appeal to anyone.

Some history

San Salvador was originally home to **Lucayan Indians**, whose refuse piles and cave dwellings remain on the island. They fished for tuna from canoes, hunted large squadrons of turtle in the lagoon sea-grass beds, gathered conch and even snared or trapped birds like heron, grebe and osprey. They also had the grave misfortune to be the first inhabitants of the New World to meet with Christopher Columbus on his voyage of European discovery in October of 1492. In his journal, Columbus identified his landfall by the

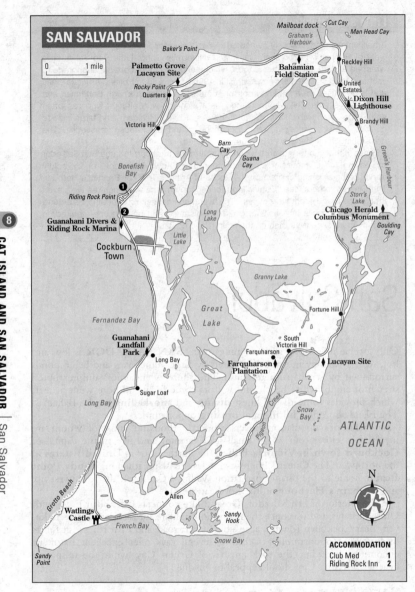

SAN SALVADOR

Indian name **Guanahani**, and while scholars have debated its exact location, most have settled on present-day San Salvador – though some still plump for either Cat Island or uninhabited Conception Island some thirty miles southwest. In any event, within fifty years of his arrival, the Lucayans of San Salvador had disappeared, victims of disease and transshipment for slavery on Hispaniola.

After the pirate George Watling claimed the island during the late sixteenth century, San Salvador was dubbed **Watling Island**, yet until the Loyalist influx in the late 1700s, there was almost nothing on it. Thereafter, a few cotton plantations were established but failed to thrive. During the middle 1800s, there were attempts to grow sisal, but these were failures as well, and were completely wiped out with the advent of synthetic fibre, and the island was largely uninhabited when it was renamed San Salvador in 1926.

The island remained a backwater until the 1970s' discovery of wall diving and international tourism. A retired diver named Bill McGehee plunged into the water off the west and south coasts of the island and was astonished by the reef's beauty and complexity, the inspiration for a more-than-modest industry and the odd modern resort.

Arrival

The only **airport** on the island, San Salvador Airport is only one mile north of Cockburn Town, and Bahamasair (☎377-5505) has two flights a week from Miami on Thursday and Sunday, as well as scheduled service from Nassau to Cockburn Town on Friday and Saturday. Air Sunshine (☎1-800/327-8900) also flies from Fort Lauderdale to Cockburn Town, and *Club Med* provides charter service from Miami or Eleuthera. *Riding Rock Inn*, the other tourist facility on San Salvador, also provides a charter flight every Saturday from Fort Lauderdale.

Visitors by sea have fewer options. The **mailboat** from Nassau's Potter's Cay dock makes a rather uncomfortable weekly eighteen-hour crossing ($40) on the MV *Lady Francis* to the government dock in Cockburn Town, departing on Tuesday evening at 6pm. Contact the Potter's Cay dockmaster (☎393-1064) for exact sailing times. The nine-slip **marina** at the *Riding Rock Inn* (☎331-2631, ✉ridingrock@aol.com, VHF Ch 16) is the only one on the island.

Getting around and information

A few **taxis** are always on hand to meet arriving passengers at San Salvador Airport. **Car rental** is available at the airport from a few stalls and rates average $85 per day. *Riding Rock Inn* rents cars, as does C and S Car Rentals (☎331-2714 or 2631) in Cockburn Town. C and S also rents bicycles. Also in Cockburn Town, Dorret's Car Hire and Grocery Store (☎331-2184) has both jeeps and cars for rent at about $85 per day. *Riding Rock Inn* also rents **bicycles** for $10 a day. The entire island can be biked around in five or six hours, and many people try it even in the heat. If you do, go prepared with water because many food shacks on the west and north coasts are often closed.

With an increase in tourism, both the *Riding Rock Inn* and *Club Med* have begun providing **island tours**. The particulars are changeable; you'll need to consult the resorts for what's on offer. There are no government-run information centres on San Salvador.

Diving and watersports

Famous for its calm, clear water, as well as its incredible wall reefs, San Salvador has become the top wall-**diving** destination in the Bahamian chain. Dive spots number in the hundreds from the northwest coast to Sandy Point in the south, and operators have spotted 48 mooring buoys around the island, with another twenty placed in sheltered sand holes clear of reefs, which are used primarily for snorkelling.

Most famous of the dives is the **Frascate** wreck north of the airport. This huge steel-hulled vessel (262ft long) broke up on January 1, 1902, and its wreck is strewn over half an acre of reef. It is home to parrotfish, wrasse and surgeonfish. Other good spots to dive include **Riding Rock Wall, Telephone Pole, Vicky's Reef, Snapshot, Double Caves** and **Great Cut**. All the dive sites are located at or near the drop-off into deeper water, and the majority are just off Cockburn Town in a two-mile stretch on Fernandez Bay. Double Caves is at Sandy Point, while Great Cut is located at the southwest tip of the island near Hinchinbroke Rocks.

Midway down Fernandez Bay is the shallow spot **Snapshot**, a particular favourite of **snorkellers** and photographers, where a series of coral patches on a white-sand bottom is home to yellowhead jawfish and squirrelfish. The many gulleys, vertical walls, canyons and shallow reefs are home to a seemingly infinite variety of sea life including eels, barracuda, starfish, lugworms, golden stingrays, peacock flounder, shrimps, reef sharks, surgeonfish, turtles and damselfish, among others.

While the possibilities for **sport fishing** have barely been tapped on San Salvador, the northern hump of the island is a major winter collection point for flying fish, which are food for both tuna and wahoo, making it a hot spot for sport fishing. During the winter season – September through April – there are regular catches of large marlin as well. Both *Club Med* and Guanahani Divers offer sport-fishing trips on thirty-foot charters for $300/500 half/full day.

Dive operators

Columbus Isle Dive Centre *Club Med* ☎ 331-2000 or 1-800/258-2633, ℱ 331-2222. Catering to *Club Med* guests, the centre includes all costs in the *Club Med* price. They have four dive boats with a capacity of 170 divers and fifty snorkellers. With that many people, the operation is rather impersonal, but it does have the latest equipment. Its retail shop is rather small.

Guanahani Divers   ☎ 331-2631 or 1-800/272-

1492, ℱ 331-2020, ℰ RidingRock@aol.com. Unaffiliated divers use this operation, which has three dive boats and offers a complete instruction course as well as classes in underwater photography. The basic one- and two-tank dives are $40 and $60, with certification at $400. Guanahani has a resort course that costs $105. On site is a large retail store where you can also see weekly slide shows and enjoy a nice clubby atmosphere and good food.

Cockburn Town

Though not the largest settlement on San Salvador – that prize goes to United Estates on the northeast coast – **COCKBURN TOWN** is nonetheless its centre of island activity. With both major resorts located just north of town, as well as having the airport, government complex and medical clinic, Cockburn Town is as close as it gets to urban convenience on San Salvador.

The town itself is three blocks square and contains an odd admixture of old stone houses, tumbledown clapboard homes and modern structures. The centre of life is the **government dock**, where the weekly mailboat delivers island supplies and mail, and its arrival creates a stirring of expectation and excitement. Near the dock, across from the BaTelCo building, you can stroll on the **fossil coral reef**, where you can see old brain coral and various staghorn corals, as well as molluscs imbedded in the reef.

Just north of First Avenue, which holds most of the local administrative offices, is the **San Salvador Museum**. In the neighbourhood of Victoria Hill, this musty museum is free to the public, but you'll have to ask at nearby residences for someone to come unlock the doors. Located in a nineteenth-century jailhouse, this mouldy collection of artefacts includes Lucayan archeological finds, and some replicas of the Columbus and the plantation periods. While not much of a museum, it is worth a brief look for the strange folk-art mural adorning the outside wall.

Cockburn Town is near two lakes of great interest to birdwatchers. Follow First Avenue to the east: it ends only half a mile away at **Little Lake**, where there is a pier from which one can see numerous cormorants, herons, ducks and grebes. Going north from town you'll encounter a dirt road that runs east toward the end of the airport runway near *Riding Rock Inn*. With a right turn inland on an old dirt road, you pass the city dump, a construction vehicle parking area, then the north shore of Little Lake, finally ending up at a rather flimsy observation platform on **Great Lake**. Birders come for glimpses of cormorants, reddish egrets and herons. Beware of the observation platform. It is not well maintained, and you should test it carefully before climbing.

Practicalities

Accommodation on the island is centred on two main resorts near Cockburn Town. One of the best dive resorts in the world, *Club Med Columbus Isle* (T331-2000 or 1-800/453-2582, F331-2222; **③**), the French outfit's flagship, is sprawled across eighty acres with a great beach. There is a huge swimming pool around which are entwined 286 double rooms, three restaurants, twelve tennis courts, a fitness centre and just about every recreation imaginable (no children under 12 allowed). *Riding Rock Inn Resort and Marina* (T331-2631 or 1-800/272-1492, F331-2020, Eridingrock@aol.com; **④**) is located southwest of the airport and has 42 furnished rooms with a/c, TV, patios and five deluxe cottages. *Riding Rock* has a pool and tennis court, offers some special dive packages and rents cars and bicycles. Elsewhere, in quiet Victoria Hill, the *Ocean View Apartments* (T331-2676; **④**) are three a/c stucco one-bedroom cottages with small kitchenettes that are perfect for longer stays.

Visitors will have no real reason to seek out **bars** and **restaurants** outside of Cockburn Town, which has the good *Three Ships Restaurant* (T331-2787), featuring Bahamian dishes like fish and grits; reservations required for dinner. Another good bet is the restaurant at *Riding Rock Inn*, which serves expensive but good Bahamian dishes like conch, smothered grouper and broiled snapper for $25. The breakfasts with heaping piles of pancakes, johnnycake, and delicious omelettes run $10. *Club Med* allows non-guests on their grounds for an evening buffet dinner and entertainment, all for $40.

The main local hot spot in Cockburn Town is *Harlem Square Club* (T331-2777), a sleepy domino parlour during the week, but which heats up on Friday and Saturday nights when rap music and dancing are featured.

The southwest coast: toward Sandy Point

The **southwest coast** of San Salvador was once home to cotton and citrus plantations, whose place was taken by a number of small villages. These too have largely been abandoned, with only ghostly remnants of stone houses standing vacant along beautiful sweeps of beach like **Grotto Beach** and **Sandy Point Beach**.

Long Bay, just two miles south of Cockburn Town on Queen's Highway, is the supposed site of Columbus's original landfall. Here you'll see **Guanahani Landfall Park**, really a modest stretch of scrub and beach punctuated by four monuments, none of which is particularly inspiring. One monument commemorates the 1968 Olympic games in Mexico, while another is the much photographed concrete cross near a plaque presented by Spain on the occasion of a visit by three caravel replicas to the island on February 10, 1992. Travelling further south, you will come to **Grotto Beach**, near Sandcliff Avenue off Queen's Highway, an extremely pretty stretch of white sand good for swimming and snorkelling.

The island's southwestern tip is called **Sandy Point**. Of particular interest here is **Owl's Hole**, reached by going east and taking the first left on a dirt road, then stopping at a T in the road, and walking into the bush about 50ft. This sinkhole is home to barn owls and the remains of a huge fig tree that was toppled by Hurricane Lily in 1996. The only sign of life near Sandy Point is **Columbus Estates**, a tiny subdivision where wealthy Americans have built vacation homes. On a hill in the estates is **Watling's Castle**, the crumbling remains of a plantation established by Loyalist settler Cade Matthews, who named it for San Salvador's famous pirate. While the plantation, operated until 1925, is now defunct, a watchtower and some slave quarters provide a good and breezy view of the sweep of Sandy Point.

The east coast

Continuing along the Queen's Highway brings you to the **east coast**, which begins with the **High Cay Land and Sea Park**, harbouring three cays, High Cay, Porus Cay and Low Cay. Important nesting sites for ospreys and boobies, these cays can be reached only by hired boat, and you should check with the authorities at the government offices in Cockburn Town about visiting. The rocky cays are a critical habitat for nesting ospreys, terns, boobies and a handful of endangered iguanas, and are off limits to visitors at certain times.

Heading north, off a rough dirt turnoff to a subdivision of Columbus Landing called **Sandy Hook**, you will find a dirt road to beautiful **Snow Bay Beach** off the mouth of **Pigeon Creek**. Both Snow Bay and Pigeon Creek present good opportunities to watch wild birds like Roseate, Sooty, and Bridled terns, Brown noddies and Audubon's shearwaters, along with rails and herons. The entire five-mile dirt track stretching from Blackwood Bay to Pigeon Creek is good bonefishing territory, and baby sharks can sometimes be seen in the creek itself.

Pigeon Creek heads toward the sea, revealing the ruins of the **Farquharson Plantation**, established in the 1820s by a justice of the peace, but long abandoned. The ruins are rather extensive, and include parts of the Great House, the kitchen, which has a fireplace and brick oven, and several estate buildings north of the Great House, as well as slave quarters to the south. The estate, which had 56 slaves two years before Emancipation, grew mostly guinea corn, a subsistence crop, as well as pigeon peas, sweet potatoes, cabbage and pumpkins.

A mile past the ruins lie the remains of Pigeon Creek Indian site where archeologists have conducted numerous digs that are now nothing more than piles of rubble, a few cave sites, and some barely decipherable petroglyphs. Artefacts like pottery shards and shell ornaments and weapons, along with a few tools, have been carted off. More ruins lie north of the Pigeon Creek area:

Fortune Hill and Polly Hill once held nineteenth-century plantations, the former perhaps the largest and grandest plantation ruins in the Bahamas, with two octagonal buildings which probably served as work areas, and, if you're interested, a latrine. The ruins of the estate houses are in a tumbledown state, but their outlines are clearly visible, as are the ruins of slave quarters. Amid the palmettos and shade trees, they are a sad reminder of the brief period of slave agriculture in an eerie, hot, forlorn spot on the island.

The rest of the east coast is rather lonely, but punctuated here and there by excellent and empty beaches for swimming and sunning, especially five-mile-long **East Beach**, a stretch of exposed white sand that lies four miles north of the Indian site.

The northeast coast: toward United Estates

Continue up the east coast on the Queen's Highway and, just before coming to **UNITED ESTATES**, the largest settlement on San Salvador, you'll reach Crab Cay, three miles southeast of town. Follow signs for Storr's Lake and East Beach, then follow a path to the beach, which brings you to the **Chicago Herald monument** to Columbus. Placed in 1891 by the newspaper, it's a rugged affair – a stone marker topped by a weather-pitted globe that supports a plaque commemorating the supposed first landfall of the explorer – and the lack of any historical confirmation that this is the spot makes it a rather bogus monument.

A few miles north, and far more impressive, the **Dixon Hill Lighthouse** (9am–noon & 2–5pm; free) is a towering structure that dominates the immediate landscape. A genuine delight, this smooth, white stone tower slopes gently to a capped top where visitors can roam the first balcony for views. Virtually alone on a bluff overlooking the Atlantic Ocean, the lofty structure stands 163ft above sea level, rising 67ft from its base.

The ragtag collection of hovels, homes and shacks called **United Estates** is the most populated settlement on San Salvador, but you may wonder why you came; there's little to do here and little reason to base yourself in the area.

Graham's Harbour and around

From United Estates, the Queen's Highway sweeps along to **GRAHAM'S HARBOUR** on the northeast tip of San Salvador, where, it is widely believed, Columbus anchored his ships and surveyed his discovery, sometime after first making contact with the Bahamas on San Salvador. The harbour beach itself is nothing special, but it is a quiet stretch good for swimming and sunning, and at the end of North Point to the east is the large wreck of the *Columbia*, which ran aground in 1980. The highlight of the year, the Columbus Day Regatta, is held in Graham's Harbour every year on October 12.

In the centre of Graham's Harbour, the **Bahamian Field Station** (free; ☎331-2520, ⒻFax 331-2524) is a research and educational facility on the site of a former US Navy base. On site is a small library, a herbarium and an insect collection. Serious birders and naturalists often make the field station a stop before taking to the nature trails with its free checklist of local birds, plants, insects, bats and underwater invertebrates. South of the station grounds, the field station has a series of trails of interest to birders who can see many species of ducks like pintails, along with Zenaida doves, woodstars, warblers, grassquits, and, on the ponds, species like osprey and cormorants. In winter, Indigo buntings and Grey kingbirds are common. The circular **Lucayan Trail** runs through almost two miles of coppice and swamp. The field station sells a trail guide that lists birds and other points of interest, including several fossil beds.

Another highlight for naturalists is the half-day boat trips to the **Green Cay**, **White Cay** and **Gaulin and Cato cays**, just offshore from Graham's Harbour. The approximately 250 rock iguanas on Green Cay have become somewhat tame because of human feeding and there is excellent snorkelling off Gaulin Cay. Both White Cay and Gaulin Cay host large populations of Brown boobies, which nest on the ground, and Magnificent frigatebirds which nest in sea lavender bushes. Check with the Bahamian Field Station for advice on guides and boats for the crossing.

There's little on the ride back from Graham's Harbour to Cockburn Town to detain you.

Outlying cays

Twenty-five miles southwest of San Salvador, **CONCEPTION ISLAND** is now officially a national land and sea park and only visited by intrepid yachters who get permission to land from the Bahamas National Trust (☎393-1317, The Retreat, PO Box N4105, Nassau, or ☎352-5438, Rand Memorial Nature Centre, Freeport). Visitors to Conception Island must make their own arrangements with local boat owners. The island, which is uninhabited but for green turtles, boobies and migratory seabirds, is three miles long and one mile wide and sits on its own shallow bank surrounded by a fringing reef and circled on all sides by fabulous beach. Under good weather conditions, you can sometimes see it from San Salvador.

Far more accessible is **Rum Cay**, a small island 25 miles southwest of San Salvador whose name is said to memorialize the wreck of a freighter loaded with rum, which foundered on the coral reefs offshore. Only ten miles long and five miles wide, it contains the village of **PORT NELSON**, with a couple of restaurants and bars and a few hundred hardy souls hanging on amid coconut palm groves and salt ponds.

Rum Cay is fringed all around with a reef that is perfect for snorkelling, and while its beaches are delightful, you will need a boat to access most of them as there are no roads in the wild interior. Divers will particularly enjoy the wreck of the 101-gun man-of-war HMS *Conqueror*, which was built in 1855 and sank near Rum Cay in 1861. There are no scheduled **flights** here, though there is a 2500-foot private airstrip and the eighteen-slip Sumner Point Marina has a restaurant and is a port of call for the MV *Lady Francis* **mailboat** once a week.

The south islands

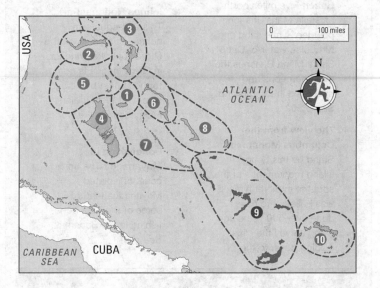

CHAPTER 9

Highlights

✳ **The Stella Maris Resort** One of two major resorts on Long Island, the unpretentious *Stella Maris* commands a cliff with views of the Atlantic and Exuma Sound. See p.302

✳ **Cape Santa Maria Beach** Five miles north of Stella Maris, the long powdery white sand and turquoise water of Cape Santa Maria Beach is the most gorgeous and unspoiled in Long Island. See p.303

✳ **The view from the Columbus Monument** Stand by this Long Island monument – at the spot the explorer himself was believed to have done over 500 years ago – and survey the cliffs leading down to the Atlantic and to Exuma Sound. See p.303

✳ **Hamilton's Cave** Tour this elaborate cave in Long Island and see Lucayan pottery artefacts as well as the stalactites and stalagmites. See p.304

✳ **Inagua National Park** This 287-square-mile conservation area on the shores of Lake Windsor in Great Inagua is home to the largest breeding colony of West Indian Flamingoes in the world. See p.311

✳ **Bonefishing in Mayanagua** The north coast of isolated Mayanagua features some of the best bonefishing in the Bahamas. See p.313

9

The south islands

The most remote islands of the Bahamian archipelago, the **SOUTH ISLANDS** lie about 250 miles southeast of Nassau. Consisting of Long Island, Crooked and Acklins islands, Great Inagua and Mayaguana, the south islands are comparatively free of tourist development and offer a taste of the slowly vanishing traditional Out Island life.

Of this group, **Long Island**, a narrow sliver of land dividing the Great Bahama Bank from the deep Atlantic Ocean, is both the most populated and visited. It has the double virtue of unspoiled natural beauty and a couple of lovely small resorts offering appealing accommodation, fine dining and a full range of activities, including excellent **diving** and **snorkelling** options. Owing to its fortuitous position along the North Equatorial current, Long Island also boasts superb **fishing** all year round.

Further south, the less developed **Crooked and Acklins islands** are known for their matchless tarpon and bonefishing, while at the southern extremity of the archipelago – actually closer to Cuba than to Nassau – the islands of **Mayaguana** and **Great Inagua** are largely untouched by human hand. Home to a large diversity of flora and fauna, including nesting sea turtles and the largest colony of West Indian flamingos in the world, Mayaguana and Great Inagua offer long stretches of virgin beach, trackless interiors and coral reefs.

All of the southern islands have regular air service from Nassau on Bahamasair, and a weekly passenger service from Nassau on the government mailboats. A large percentage of visitors to the southern islands arrive by private plane or yacht, and there are airports and marinas on each island, as detailed below.

Some history

During his two-week cruise through the Bahamas in October of 1492, Christopher Columbus paused long enough to admire the scenery of Long Island – which he named "Fernandina" in honour of the king of Spain – and to catch a whiff of the cascarilla growing on Acklins and Crooked islands, which he duly called "the fragrant islands". As with the rest of the Bahamas, if he spent any actual time on the south islands, it was probably only to size up the Lucayan natives as potential slaves.

Following the American Revolution, the Long, Crooked and Acklins islands were carved up into **Loyalist** estates. The exiles who washed up on their shores were of a more modest economic status than those who settled elsewhere in the Bahamas and farmed cotton, pineapples and livestock on small acreages. Most of the settlements in Long Island were named for these Loyalist settlers, who for the most part had abandoned their plantations by 1803, having exhausted the thin soil.

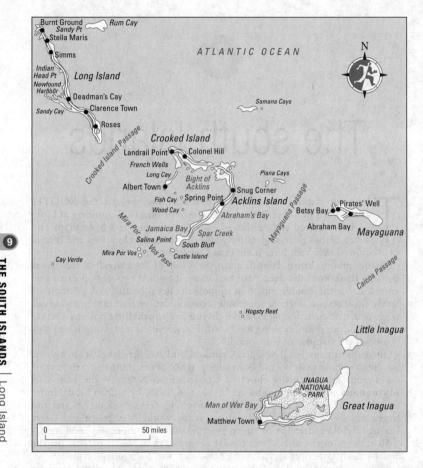

As elsewhere in the Out Islands, for most of the past two hundred-odd years, Long Islanders have scraped a modest living from fishing, subsistence farming, salt production and boat making. At the height of the thriving **sponge trade** in 1921 (see box p.305), Long Island had a population of 4600. However, with the collapse of traditional local industries like sponging, salt raking and wooden boat building, the island's population has since been in steady decline. **Tourist** development began on a small scale in the 1960s with the opening of the *Stella Maris Resort* at the north end of the island.

Long Island

Despite a wealth of lovely beaches, fine diving and snorkelling and some of the prettiest scenery in the Bahamas, **LONG ISLAND**, about thirty miles south of Cat Island, is still well off the beaten track. It is home to roughly 3200 residents who earn their living from the sea and live in a dozen or so small fishing settlements that dot its seventy-mile-long coastline. From Seymours on the north tip to Gordon's in the south, the **Queen's Highway** runs the length of the island, directly along the seashore for much of the way. Whether you base yourself here at one of the two resorts in the north, or at one of the smaller lodges and guesthouses to the south, it is possible to explore the whole of the island on day-trips by car, or a good portion of it by bicycle.

The majority of visitors to Long Island assemble around **Stella Maris**, at the island's north end, where most accommodation and tourist services are located. In the immediate vicinity are several worthwhile beaches – notably the spectacular three-mile-long **Cape Santa Maria Beach** – as well as the **Columbus Monument**, which tops a rocky bluff at the northern tip of the island and offers an impressive view.

As you head south on the Queen's Highway from Stella Maris, the island's landscape begins to switch from rocky cliffs and cactus-covered sand flats to pastoral seaside villages interspersed with stretches of dense bush. Around **Salt Pond**, an unpretentious village in the island's centre, are more enticing beaches, including **Guana Cay**, which is home to good snorkelling. A break from the beaches is afforded by nearby **Hamilton's Cave**, where several underground chambers are filled with stalactites and stalagmites as well as recently found Lucayan artefacts.

While the sparsely populated southern end of Long Island is given over to farming, the area boasts an exquisite beach on **Lochabar Bay**. The main settlement in the south of the island, **Clarence Town**, features little more than two photogenic historic churches and the secluded **Lowes Beach**. In general, Long Islanders tend to be a devout lot, and on Sunday mornings, the numerous **picturesque whitewashed churches** up and down the island fling open their doors and the air is filled with hymns and birdsong.

Getting there

There are two **airports** in Long Island, the most widely used being the one at Stella Maris (☏338-2015) at the northern end, while Deadman's Cay (☏337-0877) serves the island's centre and southern tip. Bahamasair (☏352-8341) operates one flight a day from Nassau to Long Island at midday, stopping first at Stella Maris, then Deadman's Cay. The *Stella Maris Resort* (☏338-2050) operates a plane for guests that flies several times a week to George Town on Great Exuma and to Nassau. Bear in mind that both airports are a couple of miles from the nearest hotel, so be sure to book your flight to the one closest to where you are staying as long-distance taxi fares can be very expensive.

Two government **mailboats** serve Long Island. The *Mia Dean* ($45 one-way) departs Potter's Cay in Nassau (for the dockmaster, call ☏393-1064) on Tuesday at noon, reaching Clarence Town at the southern end of Long Island twelve hours later and departing for Nassau on Wednesday or early Thursday morning. The *Sharice M* ($45 one-way) departs Nassau Mondays at 5pm, calling at Deadman's Cay, Salt Pond and Seymours in north Long Island after a fifteen-hour crossing; it also heads back for Nassau on Wednesdays.

If arriving by private yacht, there are two full-service **marinas** on the island. The Stella Maris Marina (☏338-2055, VHF Ch 16), located near the *Stella Maris Resort* at the north end of the island, features fifteen boat slips and offers access to the resort's amenities. The Flying Fish Marina (☏337-3430, ℻337-3429, ✉flyfishmarina@batelnet.bs, VHF Ch 16) in Clarence Town also has fifteen slips, as well as a provisions store.

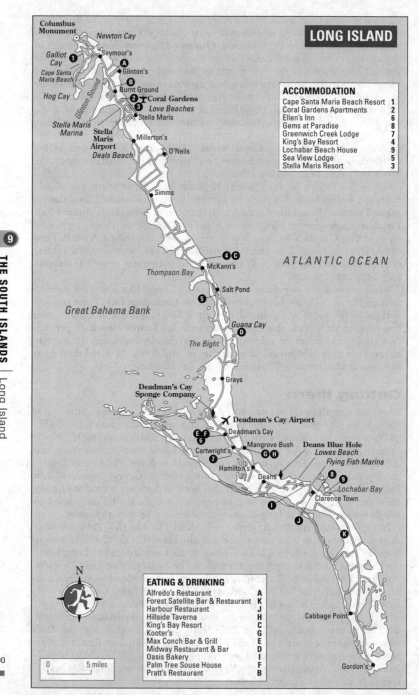

Columbus
Monument

Newton Cay

Galliot
Cay

Seymour's

Cape Santa
Maria Beach

Ⓐ

Glinton's

Hog Cay

Ⓑ

Burnt Ground

Coral Gardens

Ⓖ Ⓐ

Love Beaches

Stella Maris

Stella Maris
Marina

Stella
Maris
Airport

Millerton's

Deals Beach

O'Neils

Simms

ACCOMMODATION

Cape Santa Maria Beach Resort	1
Coral Gardens Apartments	2
Ellen's Inn	6
Gems at Paradise	8
Greenwich Creek Lodge	7
King's Bay Resort	4
Lochabar Beach House	9
Sea View Lodge	5
Stella Maris Resort	3

Ⓓ Ⓒ

McKann's

ATLANTIC OCEAN

Thompson Bay

Salt Pond

Ⓔ

Great Bahama Bank

Guana Cay

Ⓓ

The Bight

Grays

**Deadman's Cay
Sponge Company**

✈ **Deadman's Cay Airport**

Ⓔ Ⓕ

Deadman's Cay

Ⓕ

Cartwright's

Mangrove Bush

Deans Blue Hole

Ⓖ Ⓗ

Lowes Beach

Ⓖ

Hamilton's

Flying Fish Marina

Deans

Ⓗ Ⓘ

Lochabar Bay

Clarence Town

Ⓘ

Ⓙ

Ⓚ

N

Cabbage Point

Ⓢ **THE SOUTH ISLANDS** | Long Island

0   5 miles

EATING & DRINKING

Alfredo's Restaurant	A
Forest Satellite Bar & Restaurant	K
Harbour Restaurant	J
Hillside Taverna	H
King's Bay Resort	C
Kooter's	G
Max Conch Bar & Grill	E
Midway Restaurant & Bar	D
Oasis Bakery	I
Palm Tree Souse House	F
Pratt's Restaurant	B

Gordon's

Getting around

There is no public bus service in Long Island, but **taxis** meet every flight and are a dependable means of transport. For reliable service in northern Long Island call Shervin Smith (T 338-6009 or cellular 357-1408). In Deadman's Cay, Olivia Turnquest, the proprietor of *Ellen's Inn*, runs an efficient taxi service (T 337-0888). To travel long distances or tour the island, it is more economical to rent a car; a taxi ride from Stella Maris to Deadman's Cay will cost about $80, while going from one end of the island to the other is around $150.

If you plan to do some exploring on your own, you will need to **rent a car** or **motor scooter**. At the northern end of Long Island, Alfred Knowles (T 338-5009, F 338-5091) and Joe Williams (T 338-5002) in Glinton's both rent cars for $65 a day including unlimited miles; delivery to the Stella Maris Airport or your hotel can also be arranged. Inell Ditez (T 338-7049) in Burnt Ground rents scooters for $40 a day, while the *Stella Maris Resort* (T 338-2052) rents them out only to guests at a similar rate; the resort also rents out cars to guests for $75 a day, including gas but charging 35¢ a mile, which can add up quickly.

With varied scenery and little traffic, Long Island is a wonderful place for **cycling**. A few gentle inclines in the generally flat roads offer the reward of beautiful views up and down the coastline. The two biggest resorts on the island have serviceable touring bikes for guest use – *Cape Santa Maria Beach Resort* (T 338-5273) charges $10 per hour, while *Stella Maris Resort* (T 338-2052) rents bikes for free. It is reasonably safe to **hitchhike** in Long Island, but not many people do it.

Accommodation

Accommodation in Long Island ranges from two fine small-sized resorts at the north end of the island to a couple of secluded self-catering beach lodges on lovely Lochabar Bay south of Clarence Town, with a handful of less expensive local guesthouses situated in the settlements in between. For diving, snorkelling and other organized activities as well as fine dining, the *Stella Maris Resort* or the *Cape Santa Maria Beach Resort* are your best bets. While you can save by staying at one of the other guesthouses listed below – especially if you are staying for a week or more – you may have to sacrifice the ocean view and room space and will probably need to rent a car to get around.

Stella Maris and around

Cape Santa Maria Beach Resort Long Island's northern tip T 338-5273 or 1-800/663-7090, F 338-6013, W www.capesantamaria.com. Situated on a pristine strand of powdery white beach on a flat, sandy peninsula, this is surely one of the most beautiful locales in the Bahamas. Twenty attractive double rooms in ten beachfront cottages are decked out with colourful tropical fabrics, clay-tile floors and rattan furniture, each with a screened-in porch just steps from the water's edge. There is an appealing dining room and bar (see p.307), a fitness centre, bicycle rentals and the resort offers a full range of watersports as well as fishing trips. Double rooms go for $295 and up. Closed Sept & Oct. ❽

Coral Gardens Apartments Stella Maris T 338-5009 or T & F 338-5091. Located on an inland road a quarter of a mile from the ocean and the *Stella Maris Resort*, the *Coral Gardens* offer four simply but nicely furnished and well-maintained two-bedroom apartments that sleep four and have full kitchens. ❺

King's Bay Resort McKann's T 338-8945, F 338-8012. Despite its spectacular setting on an isolated, windswept stretch of beach on the Atlantic side, the ten small carpeted rooms here are skimpily furnished and somewhat dingy. There is, though, a pleasant restaurant and bar serving traditional Bahamian dishes, seafood and cool drinks, with tables on the veranda overlooking the ocean. ❷

Stella Maris Resort Stella Maris ☎ 338-2052 or 1-800/426-0466, ⓦ www.stellamarisresort.com. Sitting on a green hilltop with views of both coasts, this friendly, unpretentious resort offers two dozen bright comfortable guestrooms – each with a private veranda – housed in a couple of one- and two-storey buildings. The resort contains three swimming pools, a hot tub, tennis courts (with a pro on staff), a fitness centre and children's play area, and the scenic oceanfront drive leads to several secluded beaches within walking distance. There are bicycles, sunfish sailing and snorkelling gear available for guest use at no charge and a free all-day boat trip twice a week. ❻

Salt Pond to Deadman's Cay

Ellen's Inn Deadman's Cay ☎ 337-0888 or 1086, ⒻⒻ 337-0333, Ⓔ ellensinn@batelnet.bs. This inn on the highway has sparkling clean, homely rooms with a shared kitchen and sitting room. Weekly rates are around $450. ❹

Greenwich Creek Lodge Cartwright's ☎ 337-6278, Ⓕ 337-6282, ⓦ www.greenwichcreek.com. Situated on a mangrove-edged shore, the lodge caters to serious bonefishermen. Its well-maintained two-storey timber lodge with wraparound verandas houses eight nicely furnished doubles (containing two beds) and four king rooms, some with TV. There is a small dipping pool and a common room where meals are served. Based on double occupancy, a week of bonefishing including accommodation, meals and a guide costs $2100. ❼

Sea View Lodge Southern edge of Salt Pond ☎ 337-7517 or 0100. A good budget option locat-ed within sight of the mailboat dock. Three airy, tastefully appointed one- and two-bedroom cottages with fully equipped modern kitchens and satellite TV sit on a treeless expanse of lawn between the Queen's Highway and the rocky water's edge. Guests get a choice view of the sailing races during the Long Island Regatta in mid-May. ❸

Clarence Town and around

Gems at Paradise Lochabar Bay ☎ 337-3019, Ⓕ 337-3021, ⓦ www.gemsatparadise.com. High on a bluff overlooking a string of cays just south of Clarence Town, this large three-storey gabled house has six beautifully furnished en-suite double and twin rooms sharing a small kitchen, as well as three self-contained one-bedroom apartments. Half of the rooms have private balconies with a view of the sea, and all of them have TV and phone. There is a small beach with kayaks and a bar. ❻

Lochabar Beach Lodge Lochabar Bay ☎ 327-8323 or 337-3123, Ⓕ 327-2567, ⓦ www.thebahamian.com/lochabarbeach. On an exquisite curve of white-sand beach, this lodge is a secluded idyll for those who really want to get away from civilization. The two-storey timber and stucco structure, housing two studio apartments and a one-bedroom apartment sleeping up to five, lies directly on the beach. The rooms feature clay-tile floors and whitewashed walls or rustic wood panelling and floors, and French doors that open onto a balcony or patio. Neither the owners nor the manager live on site, so call ahead. ❺

Stella Maris and around

About a mile north of the airport and two miles from the marina, **STELLA MARIS** encompasses the *Stella Maris Resort* and a smattering of vacation homes built along the rocky hilltop overlooking the Atlantic. The resort itself lies on the site of English settler William Adderley's nineteenth-century cotton plantation; the stone ruins are still visible along the shore just north of the airport. After Adderley's demise, the cotton fields returned to bush until a large chunk of the area was purchased in the 1960s by the German developer whose estate encompasses the resort.

For those who crave a crashing surf and solitude, Ocean View Drive, which follows the Atlantic for three miles from the front of the resort, offers cliff-top views, rock pools and secluded beaches. The **Love Beaches**, three small rocky coves backed by high dunes at the southern end of the drive (signposted from the road) are a great destination for a picnic and a dip in calm weather. At the north end of the road are the **Coral Gardens** snorkelling grounds (the path is signposted from the road). Note that the surf along the Atlantic coast can be treacherous in breezy or inclement weather.

To the north

While Stella Maris itself has little to detain you unless you're staying at the resort, the lightly populated area to its immediate north contains several of Long Island's highlights. For swimming and beaching, you cannot beat the gorgeous long, powdery white-sand beach and turquoise water at **Cape Santa Maria**, five miles north of Stella Maris and a great destination for a bike excursion. Cape Santa Maria runs the length of the western side of Galliot Cay, a thin, flat, sandy and treeless peninsula set in the calmer waters of the island's leeward coast. To hit the beach, head north from Stella Maris on the Queen's Highway, passing through **Burnt Ground** and **Glinton's**, two rather down-at-heel roadside settlements where you can stock up on provisions for a day at the beach. The turnoff to the beach is on the left side of the highway (signposted) after you cross a short causeway built over a salt pond at **Snow Hill**, a small collection of cottages topping a low knoll.

Retrace your steps to the Queen's Highway and head north for a pit stop in the quaint hilltop hamlet of **Seymour's**, a small cluster of cottages with goats and fruit trees in their yards that boasts a lovely panoramic view from the steps of its tiny whitewashed church. Heading two miles still further north, a rough dirt road on your left just before you reach the church leads to the **Columbus Monument**. The track is steep in places and alternatively sandy or very rocky, passable by four-wheel-drive, but otherwise best traversed on foot or bicycle. About halfway up, you pass a turnoff on the left, which leads to a **lighthouse** overlooking Galliot Cay, about a mile away. Continue straight on the main path to reach the monument, a concrete and iron obelisk that sits atop a steep rocky headland. It is believed that Columbus stood here over 500 years ago, taking in the same breathtaking cliffs and small rocky cays rimmed with white sand and blue-green water. The north side of the bluff on which the monument sits is an abrupt drop off into the deep Atlantic – take care, it is often windy up here – but the view to the south takes in a shallow, sheltered emerald-green bay edged with white sand, ideal for swimming and bonefishing.

Back on the Queen's Highway at Seymour's, the road continues north over a hill and down to the water's edge overlooking **Newton's Cay**, a small uninhabited island joined to the mainland by a short bridge across the narrow tidal creek. A three-minute walk across the bridge and up the path on the other side leads you to a small bush-backed beach on the far side of the cay, rather ho hum in comparison with other Long Island beaches but still a decent spot for a swim and usually deserted. The beach on Newton's Cay is also the site of a model boat regatta in October (contact the *Stella Maris Resort* ☎ 338-2050 for details), with a barbecue and volleyball tournament.

To the south

South of Stella Maris, the Queen's Highway hugs the western shoreline on the way to **Millerton's**, where there is a school and a beautiful old whitewashed church set behind a stone wall, and a roadside straw works where you can buy handicrafts made by local artisans. One mile south of Millerton's, **Deal's Beach**, fringed by casuarina trees, runs for a mile alongside the road, then sweeps out to a more secluded point of land. It is a pleasant place for a swim and picnic, with good snorkelling over a sea fan garden off the point at the beach's south end. Heading south from Deal's Beach, a dirt road on the right leads to **O'Neil's** on the Atlantic coast, where there are a couple of houses and a secluded beach on a double bay.

Back along the Queen's Highway, the pretty hamlet of **Simms**, where a few tidy cottages are shaded by tall fruit trees, features a tiny stone prison (no longer in use) and a pink-painted post office dating from the early nineteenth century. From Simms, the highway heads inland over gently undulating terrain, passing a few scattered houses along the way. At the settlement of **McKann's** – really just a few houses along the road – a sign marks the turnoff to the *King's Bay Resort*, with a simple casual restaurant and bar on a scenic piece of Atlantic beach, a great place for a pit stop. South of McKann's, the road climbs a steep hill topped with another pretty little church, with a spectacular view of **Thompson Bay**, and moves inland again, travelling through flat scrubby bush until it reaches the settlement of Salt Pond, three miles further on.

Salt Pond to Clarence Town

Named for the saline ponds that lie behind the settlement, **SALT POND** is now a small hub of low-key commercial activity stretched out along the highway, with a large general store, a few dozen modern bungalows, a fish processing plant and a busy dock. In mid-May, Salt Pond hosts the **Long Island Sailing Regatta**, one of the most popular events in the Out Islands for the past 35 years (call ℡393-8725 for information), otherwise there is little to keep you in the settlement.

The 25 miles between Salt Pond and Clarence Town to the south are the most heavily populated area of Long Island. A string of roadside settlements, none with more than a few dozen residents, merge one into another along the rocky leeward shore, interspersed with a few stretches of dense bush. The highest concentration of settlement and economic activity is in **Deadman's Cay**, where there are several shops, schools, service stations and a bank, but little of scenic interest. You can, however, spend an enjoyable day or two exploring the area, where there are several enticing beaches along the Atlantic coast, a few sites of cultural interest, as well as some pleasant places to stop for a bite.

If you head south on the Queen's Highway, the road on your left just past the Harding's Supply store leads to a picturesque double bay suitable for swimming and beachcombing. Four miles south of Salt Pond, a wide dirt road on your left leads to a cove edged by a soft golden-sand beach overlooking **Guana Cay**, about 500yd offshore. There is good snorkelling in the shallow protected bay between the beach and the tiny hilly cay, on which there is another sandy beach, a grove of tall coconut palms, an abandoned hut perched on the hilltop and a colony of curly-tailed iguanas.

Further south, the small settlement of Hamilton's is notable as the site of **Hamilton's Cave**, an extensive cave system where Lucayan artefacts were discovered in 1935. The cave is on private land, but Leonard Cartwright (℡337-0235 or 6228) offers guided tours through the underground chambers filled with stalactites and stalagmites for $8 per person. Also in Hamilton's is a pretty little whitewashed Catholic church – Our Lady of Mount Carmel – built in 1938, which is bare inside but has a lovely tiled floor and compelling rounded architecture. In sharp contrast right next door, a huge modern **Jehovah's Witness Temple** attests to the rapid growth of evangelical churches in Long Island in recent years. Also near Hamilton's is Wild Tamarind Pottery (℡337-0262; signposted from the highway), where you can purchase whimsical little pottery houses and handcrafted knick-knacks from artist Denis Knight and his wife Marina, a friendly English/Bahamian couple.

At Deans, a few minutes further south, there is a nice long stretch of beach with a picnic shelter and a barbecue pit. The primary attraction, however, is the **world's deepest blue hole**, surrounded on three sides by a rocky ledge, and plunging 600ft to the ocean floor just a few yards from shore.

The sponge trade

The harvesting of **sea sponges** has provided an important source of income for many Bahamians since the 1840s and was one of the islands' primary exports until the double whammy of fungal blight and the invention of artificial sponges wiped out the local industry in the late 1930s. At its height around 1905, sponging employed up to one third of the Bahamian work force, although few got actually rich in the business. During the industry's heyday, bales of Long Island sponges were sold at auction in Nassau to Greek merchants, and a sponge sold in a London shop might fetch up to twelve times what the fisherman was paid for harvesting it.

Anchored over the sponge beds, where the water ranged between 8ft and 24ft deep, crews would hook the sponges from their moorings, sometimes using a water glass or oil spread on the surface of the water as a lens through which to find a lush clump for harvesting. They would then skin-dive to collect the clumps where necessary, and the sponges were left in saltwater "kraals" on nearby cays to be washed clean, before being trimmed and strung in the boat rigging to dry on the voyage home.

With the gradual recovery of the sponge population and a growing international market for natural health products, there has been a modest revival in Bahamian sponge harvesting in recent years. In Long Island, Roland McHardy runs the **Deadman's Cay Sponge Company**, Lower Deadman's Cay (☎337-0013), harvesting the sponges himself and exporting them around the world. He welcomes visitors to stop by and have a look around and a chat. You can buy natural sponges of several types from the drying sheds.

Further south on the Queen's Highway, a rough dirt road on your left before you pass the *Oasis Bakery* leads to **Lowes Beach**, marked by a sign for the *Compass Rose Guesthouse* (which is closed). The view south along the narrow, scoured sand beach reveals white rollers pounding the shore all the way to Clarence Town, visible in the distance. The beach itself makes for a good walk, but if instead you take the sandy path on your left as you face the water, it leads you to a hidden treasure 200yd away – a perfect oval pool almost enclosed by a low wall of coral rock and rimmed by a powdery white-sand beach. The water drains from the pool at low tide, but otherwise forms a completely private, calm, sandy-bottomed pool, with a view of the crashing surf through a narrow gap in the rock barrier.

Clarence Town and around

Hilly, green **CLARENCE TOWN** is built around a small natural harbour on the Atlantic coast, sustained by fishing, farming and its role as the seat of government for the island. It is notable primarily for two picturesque whitewashed stucco **churches** built by Father Jerome, the hermit of Cat Island (see p.281). Originally ordained as an Anglican minister, he built the red-trimmed, traditional Gothic St Paul's Anglican Church first and the blue-trimmed, Spanish-looking St Peter's Catholic Church after his conversion to Catholicism in 1911.

South of Clarence Town, the Queen's Highway travels inland through flat, scraggly bush until it reaches the minute settlement of Gordon's – just a couple of buildings – at the southern tip of Long Island, eighteen and a half miles from Clarence Town. Few people live down this way, and there is not much of scenic interest to attract a visitor, with the exception of **Lochabar Bay**, a pristine curve of white sand surrounding a deep blue hole two miles south of

△ Long Island sponges

Clarence Town, and the long lonely beaches at **Cabbage Point** and **Gordon's**, which are promising destinations for shell collectors. This area was, for a short period in the 1970s, a hub of salt production until several seasons of heavy rains and falling world prices wiped out the market for Long Island salt. You can see the abandoned saltpans along the highway, now used seasonally to farm shrimp and fish.

Eating

If fine **dining** is what you are after, head for the *Stella Maris Resort* or *Cape Santa Maria Beach Resort*, which both have relaxed but elegant dining rooms and gourmet menus. Otherwise, your options are generally limited to deep-fried fast food and simple but tasty Bahamian fare in one of several roadside diners and cafés up and down the island.

Stella Maris and around

Alfred's Restaurant, Bar and Ice Cream Parlour Glinton's ☎ 338-5009. A clean and simple chrome and tile eatery serving deep-fried food, liquid refreshment and – what else? – a variety of ice cream.

Cape Santa Maria Beach Resort Northern tip of Long Island ☎ 338-5273. The resort has a beautifully atmospheric dining room set in a glass-walled two-storey timber beach house facing the white-sand beach. The expensive menu features gourmet seafood dishes and imaginative American cuisine. Reservations required.

King's Bay Resort Near McKann's ☎ 338-8945. *King's* serves traditional Bahamian dishes and fresh seafood in a simple, casual dining room or on the deck with a spectacular oceanfront setting.

Pratt's Restaurant Burnt Ground ☎ 338-7022. Another simple, tidy local restaurant serving Bahamian dishes, seafood and deep-fried fare.

Stella Maris Resort Stella Maris ☎ 338-2050. A bright airy hilltop dining room with a sunny sophisticated decor of potted greenery, honey-coloured rattan and huge windows on three sides with pleasing views of flowering trees and the ocean beyond. The lunch menu features soups, sandwiches, salads, seafood specials and a spinach tortilla. Dinner selections include seafood, steak, stuffed Cornish hens, and apple fritters with brandy sauce for dessert. Reservations recommended.

Salt Pond to Deadman's Cay

Coco's Restaurant and Lounge Hamilton's ☎ 337-6242. A dark, sparsely furnished restaurant fronted by a huge parking lot, serving cold drinks and native dishes.

Hillside Tavern Mangrove Bush ☎ 337-1628. A popular local watering hole with a small restaurant attached serving traditional Bahamian and deep-fried fare.

Kooter's Mangrove Bush ☎ 337-0340. Legendary in Long Island for its conch burger, *Kooter's* has shaded picnic tables on a wraparound wooden veranda directly on the water. It also serves sandwiches, conch, salads, ice cream and soft drinks. Sunday open for ice cream only.

Max Conch Bar and Grill Deadman's Cay ☎ 337-0056. Specializing in conch cracked, frittered and marinated, this colourful local favourite also offers fried chicken, burgers and fries at an outdoor kiosk with bar stools and tables.

Midway Inn Restaurant and Bar Bight ☎ 337-7345. A scruffy but friendly roadhouse offering simple unexceptional refreshment in the middle of a long stretch of unbroken bush between Salt Pond and Deadman's Cay.

Palm Tree Souse House Deadman's Cay ☎ 337-0023. Right across from *Ellen's Inn*, this unadorned wooden shack lets you do like the locals do, serving sheep's tongue souse and other traditional Bahamian specialties.

Clarence Town and around

Harbour Restaurant Clarence Town ☎ 337-3247. Right near the government dock, this clean and pleasant lunch room has windows overlooking the harbour and a menu with tasty versions of your basic seafood, deep-fried food and sandwiches.

Oasis Bakery and Restaurant A mile north of Clarence Town ☎ 337-3003. A lovely spot for breakfast or lunch with tables set on a deep wooden veranda overlooking a small pond. The *Oasis* offers fresh-baked bread, pastries and cookies to eat in or take home as well as inexpensive sandwiches, pizzas, burgers and conch done several ways for lunch.

Nightlife

There is really no **nightlife** to speak of in Long Island, though the *Stella Maris Resort* organizes happy hours, barbecues and a cave party every week, with live music some evenings. Each community has a roadside bar where a predominately male crowd gathers to play pool or dominoes, and the *Forest Satellite Bar and Restaurant* south of Clarence Town is a popular hangout for the younger set.

Diving and watersports

The pristine waters surrounding Long Island hold some of the best and most varied **diving** sites in the Bahamas, including the **world's deepest blue hole**, nineteenth-century wrecks, lush reefs and coral gardens. There are also gorgeous **snorkelling** grounds accessible from shore surrounding the island, notably from the beach overlooking **Guana Cay**; the **Coral Gardens** on the Atlantic coast at Stella Maris; and over a sea fan garden at the south end of **Deal's Beach**.

Dive resorts

Cape Santa Maria Beach Resort Northern tip of Long Island ☎338-5273 or 1-800/663-7090, ⓦwww.capesantamaria.com. Among its many amenities, the resort offers reef, wreck, wall and shark dives, charging $75 for a two-tank dive, plus equipment rental ($33). A resort course costs $85. Closed Sept & Oct.

Stella Maris Resort Stella Maris ☎338-2050 or 1-800/426 0466, ⓦwww.stellamarisresort.com. One of the longest-established dive operations in the Bahamas, *Stella Maris* offers a variety of dives that explore coral reefs, blue holes, a shipwrecked 1848 British Navy vessel and the San Salvador and Conception Island walls. They also offer night and shark dives, as well as a full three-day PADI certification course for $405, with a deep saltwater training tank at the marina. A full day of diving (two to three dives) costs $75, including equipment rental; a six-day package is $405. They will tailor a diving package according to where you want to go, travelling as far afield as Crooked and Acklins islands, the Ragged Islands, Rum Cay, San Salvador and Conception islands and the Exumas. The dive shop also offers daily snorkelling trips ($30 per person), with free all-day guided excursions for guests twice a week, and free use of the equipment any time.

Fishing

Long Island boasts good **fishing** all year round, with excellent deep-sea, reef and bonefishing. While most visitors make use of the resorts, in northern Long Island Shervin Smith (☎338-6009 or cellular 357-1408) is a particularly adept deep-sea fishing guide, while The Flying Fish Marina in Clarence Town (☎337-3430, ⓔflyfishmarina@batelnet.bs) runs sport-fishing charters.

Fishing guides

Cape Santa Maria Beach Resort Northern tip of Long Island ☎338-5273, ⓦwww.capesantamaria.com. Deep-sea ($550 a half-day) and reef-fishing ($450 a half-day) charters are available for up to six people, while bonefishing ($200 a half-day) charters can be arranged for one or two.

Greenwich Creek Lodge ☎337-6278, ⓦwww.greenwichcreek.com. The lodge offers all-inclusive deep-sea, reef and bonefishing packages from $2100 a week.

Stella Maris Resort Stella Maris ☎338-2050, ⓦwww.stellamarisresort.com. Docky Smith offers guided fishing expeditions and packages, including a full day of bonefishing ($275) for two; bottom or reef fishing from $350 a day; and deep-sea fishing from $650 a day.

Listings

Airlines Bahamasair can be reached at Stella Maris Airport (☎338-2015) and at Deadman's Cay Airport (☎337-0877).

Banking There are branches of the Bank of Nova Scotia at the Stella Maris Airport (☎338-2057) and at Buckleys (☎337-1029); and of the Royal Bank of Canada at Grays (☎337-1044) and Cartwright's (☎337-0001), all open Mon–Thurs

9

9am–1pm and Friday 9am–5pm. Note that outside the larger resorts, credit cards are generally not accepted.

Gas You can buy gas in Simms, Salt Pond, Deadman's Cay and Clarence Town; service stations are closed on Sunday.

Groceries There are general stores selling groceries in Burnt Ground, Stella Maris, Simms, Salt Pond, Deadman's Cay and Clarence Town, also closed Sundays.

Laundry There are laundromats in Stella Maris across from the marina and in Deadman's Cay.

Medical services There are government clinics in Clarence Town (☎337-3333), Deadman's Cay (☎337-1222), and Simms (☎338-8488). In emer-gencies, a doctor can be reached at home in Deadman's Cay at (☎337-0555) or in Stella Maris (☎338-2026).

Police There are police detachments in Clarence Town (☎337-3919), Deadman's Cay (☎337-0999), Simms (☎338-8555) and at the Stella Maris Airport (☎338-2222).

Post office Located in Clarence Town, Deadman's Cay, Simms and at the Stella Maris Airport.

Telephone There are BaTelCo offices and call boxes in Clarence Town (☎337-3000), Deadman's Cay (☎337-1337) and Simms (☎338-0841), and phone booths in Salt Pond, at the Stella Maris Marina and Resort. Be prepared for patchy service. The island is not wired up to the internet.

Crooked and Acklins islands

A destination for anglers and few others, **CROOKED** and **ACKLINS ISLANDS** lie close together, about sixty miles east of Long Island, and are connected to each other by a daily ferry service. While there were around fifty Loyalist cotton plantations on the islands two hundred years ago, today the islands are sparsely populated and barely developed. One of the few industries left on both islands is the harvesting of cascarilla bark, exported to Italy to make the aperitif Campari. Roughly four hundred people live on each of the two islands in a smattering of small coastal villages, most without electricity or running water. While they lack traditional sights or even the typical beaches you might expect to find in the Bahamian chain, they are home to some of the finest **tarpon** and **bonefishing** around and dedicated anglers should serious-ly consider visiting the islands. For non-fishermen, there are several nice stretches of beach to explore, though in truth they're not spectacular enough to draw you here on their own. Note that most residents are devout Seventh Day Adventists, so no pork or alcohol is sold in the islands, and things shut up tight on Saturdays.

Practicalities

Bahamasair (☎377-5505) **flies** to Crooked Island's Colonel Hill twice a week from Nassau with onward service to Spring Point in Acklins. The *United Star* **mailboat** sails to the Crooked and Acklins islands once a week from Nassau calling at Pittstown Point, Long Cay and Spring Point ($70 one-way; ☎393-1064). A government-operated **ferry** ($5) runs twice daily from Cove Point on Crooked Island and Lovely Bay on Acklins.

The nicest **place to stay** on either island is *Pittstown Point Landings* (☎☎561/799-1673 or 1-800/752-2322, ⓦwww.pittstownpointlandings.com; ❼), on a white-sand beach at Landrail Point on Crooked Island. There are twelve bright, airy rooms, some with a/c, some with ceiling fans. The dining room is situated in what was once the local post office – the first in the west-ern hemisphere – built in the eighteenth century. The resort offers diving and snorkelling and will arrange guided fishing expeditions. A meal plan is available for $60 per person a day. On Acklins Island, there are a few simple guesthous-es catering mainly to fishermen, including *Grey's Point Bonefish Lodge* (☎344-3210 or 326-2686; ❷) in Pine Fields; and *Nai's Guesthouse* (☎344-3089; ❷) in

Spring Point. There are no banks on Crooked or Acklins islands, but there are a few small shops in Cabbage Hill and Spring Point, a medical clinic in Landrail Point, and a post office and BaTelCo office in Colonel Hill.

Great Inagua

GREAT INAGUA lies at the southern tip of the Bahamian archipelago. Forty miles long and twenty miles across at its widest point, it is the third largest island in the Bahamas, behind Andros and the Abacos. The island's name is probably a corruption of its Lucayan name "Inawa", meaning "small eastern land", though it may well derive from the Spanish words "Ileno" and "agua", or "full" and "water".

The shallow waters of Lake Windsor cover one quarter of the interior, and much of the remaining area is low, flat bush and swamp. The island sits squarely in the path of the relentless trade winds, which combined with a strong, hot sun provide ideal conditions for solar salt production. There is only one settlement on Inagua, **Matthew Town,** at the southwest corner of the island.

The landscape of Inagua has also been described as stark and forbidding, but when Gilbert Klingel, a young American biologist, was shipwrecked on the island in 1930, he found it to be a magical world bursting with life, and stayed on for many months studying the unique flora and fauna of the island, returning several times throughout his life. His *Inagua, Which is the Name of a Lonely and Nearly Forgotten Island* (see "Literature" p.369) describes the vegetation of the island as of a type "that tends to show its beauty in the sharpness of thorns, highly colored bark, spiny cacti and thick padded leaves… thorns, speaking mutely of a scanty existence, of the scorching hot sun, of searing winds and dry soil….A few thatch palms dotted some distant ridges and stood out starkly against the sky….Yet they were not devoid of flowers, for even on the cacti pads bloomed scarlet and yellow blossoms. A subtly pleasing scene, tropical, yet not gaudy, the sort of thing that does not tire one too quickly."

As Inagua has changed very little since then, nature lovers and birdwatchers will enjoy it most. The bulk of the island – 127 square miles – has been set aside as **Inagua National Park**, a protected conservation area for a large colony flamingos which nest on the shores of Lake Windsor. Inagua is also home to a profusion of birds including the endangered Bahamian parrot, pelicans, the roseate spoonbill, herons, egrets, warblers, Bahama pintail ducks, burrowing owls, kestrels, sandpipers and ospreys. There are also herds of wild donkeys roaming the island, boars, and several species of iguanas. While nature is the main attraction on Inagua, the nineteenth-century **Great Inagua Light House** (☎339-1370), still operational on a point of land a mile south of Matthew Town, makes a great destination for a short hike. From the top of it, you'll get a wonderful panoramic view of the entire island and the lush blue sea.

Five miles to the north of Great Inagua, **Little Inagua** is thirty square miles of wilderness, uninhabited except for herds of feral goats and wild donkeys, nesting sea turtles, and varied birdlife including a rare species of heron. Its seclusion is ensured by a vast barrier reef that encircles the island, making it difficult for boats to come ashore.

Arrival and getting around

Great Inagua is a ninety-minute **flight** from Nassau. Bahamasair (☎377-5505, ⓦwww.bahamasair.com) flies to Matthew Town three times a week, with a stop-off on Mayaguana (see overleaf) en route. Air Sunshine (☎954/434-8900 or 1-800/327-8900, Ⓦwww.airsunshine.com) flies from Fort Lauderdale to Great Inagua twice a week. The *TransCargo II* **mailboat** pulls into Matthew Town once a week ($70 one-way); departures vary from week to week, so call the Nassau dockmaster at Potter's Cay (☎393-1064) for up-to-date information. Windjammer Barefoot Cruises' (☎1-800/327-2601, Ⓦwww.windjammer.com) supply ship, the *Amazing Grace*, also stops at Inagua on its **cruises** through the Bahamas and the Caribbean.

There is no public bus service on the island, but **taxis** can be hired at the airport or mailboat dock upon arrival. The airport is two miles north of town, while the mailboat dock is on the north edge of Matthew Town within walking distance of in town accommodations. There are only about eighty miles of road on Inagua, most of it rough bush tracks, but should you want to **rent a car** to do some sightseeing, call Ingraham Rent a Car (☎ & Ⓕ339-1677).

Accommodation

Accommodation on Inagua is simple but comfortable, amounting to a few basic guesthouses in Matthew Town offering running water and a/c but little else, and a rustic bunkhouse in the national park.

Camp Arthur Vernay c/o Park Warden Henry Nixon ☎339-1616, Ⓕ339-1850, VHF Ch 16 "Inagua Park". A simple camp in an isolated spot on the shore of Lake Windsor in Inagua National Park. The cement-block bunkhouse sleeps nine, with a shared shower and outdoor kitchen with a wood stove (a better idea is to bring a gas camping stove). Sheets and mattresses are provided but you must bring your own food and drinking water. $25 per person, and reservations are essential. **❶**

Morton Salt Company Main House Kortwright St, Matthew Town ☎339-1267, Ⓕ339-1265. Six simple, clean rooms in a two storey wooden house in the centre of town; with private baths and TV,

and the upstairs rooms have air conditioning. Guests share a common sitting room equipped with a phone. Note that the power plant is located across the street so it can be noisy. **❷**

Pour More Motel Kortwright St, Matthew Town ☎ & Ⓕ339-1659. Six modern air-conditioned rooms with private bath and TV; a restaurant and bar is attached. **❸**

Walkine's Guest House Gregory St, half a mile south of Matthew Town ☎339-1612. Across the road from the beach, this modest guesthouse offers five air-conditioned rooms with TV; three with private bath. **❷**

Matthew Town and around

MATTHEW TOWN's population is about 1200, most of whom are employed at the **Morton Salt Works** just north of town. The "town" itself is about a square block long, and contains the island's administrative centre and a grocery store. The saltpans cover 12,000 acres and produce a million pounds of salt a year, exported around the world. This thriving revived industry gives Matthew Town an air of prosperity not found on most other Out Islands. The **Erickson Museum** (☎339-1863) in Matthew Town is devoted to the history of the salt works. You can also arrange a tour of the works (call ☎339-1847).

Inagua National Park

A 287-square-mile protected conservation area for **West Indian flamingos** founded by the Bahamas National Trust in 1962, **INAGUA NATIONAL PARK**, on the shores of Lake Windsor, is home to the largest breeding colony of the birds on earth. Within the national park is the **Union Creek Turtle Reserve**, a protected habitat and research station devoted to giant sea turtles. The park entrance is twenty miles east of Matthew Town, and to visit you must first make arrangements with the Park Warden, Henry Nixon (℡339-1616, Ⓕ339-1850, VHF Ch 16 "Inagua Park"); they'll set you up with **guided tours**, too.

Upwards of 80,000 flamingos live in Inagua National Park, nesting and hatching their fluffy white chicks on the shores of Lake Windsor throughout March and April. Traditionally, both flamingo meat and eggs were considered Bahamian delicacies, and they were hunted nearly to extinction on Inagua in the 1930s and 1940s. The colony did not recover for several decades, and its resurgence was due in large measure to the establishment of the national park.

Eating and drinking

Eating on Inagua can be an adventure for the health-conscious. Fresh vegetables and fruit are often scarce, and what's on offer in local restaurants depends heavily on what the mailboat brought. There are a handful of simple local diners around Matthew Town serving a similar menu of deep-fried fare and traditional Bahamian dishes like boiled fish and pig's feet souse. Try the *Cozy Corner Restaurant and Bar* (℡339-1440) on North Street; the *Last Stop Takeaway* (℡339-1740) on the corner of Russell and Meadow streets; or *Topp's Restaurant* (℡339-1465) on Astwood Street. Both *Cozy Corner* and *Topp's* have bars for a casual drink.

Outdoor activities

Great Inagua Tours run by Marianne and Larry Ingraham (℡339-1862 or 305/478-1833) offer **snorkelling** excursions, **birdwatching** and **nature tours** of the island including the national park, and can also arrange for you to camp in the park. Inagua is surrounded by rich, teeming coral reefs which are largely undisturbed and unexplored. Unfortunately, there is no dive operator on Inagua, so if you want to **dive** in the area you'll have to charter a dive boat from elsewhere.

Listings

Banking Bank of the Bahamas (℡339-1264; 9.30am–2pm; closed Wed).
Groceries There are several small stores in Matthew Town, but be prepared for a skimpy selection of foodstuffs.
Medical clinic ℡339-1249; doctor's residence ℡339-1226.
Police On Gregory Street in the centre of Matthew Town (℡339-1444; ℡919 in an emergency).
Post office In the Government Administrative Building on Gregory Street in the middle of Matthew Town.
Telephone The BaTelCo office (9am–5.30pm; ℡339-1000) is located north of the mailboat dock, a half-mile from the centre of Mathew Town. There are also public phone booths in town.

Mayaguana

About as far off the beaten track as you can get in the Bahamas, **MAYAGUANA** receives few visitors apart from the occasional passing yachters, sport fishermen and scientists who come to study the unique bird and lizard life on the island. Sitting alone in the ocean roughly fifty miles from Acklins Island to the west, and sixty miles from the Turks and Caicos to the east, Mayaguana is almost completely undeveloped, having only had electricity and telephone service since 1997.

The island is home to a much larger population of birds – flamingos, booby birds, and osprey among others, and is a nesting site for sea turtles. On **Booby**

Cay, which sits a few hundred metres off the eastern shore of Mayaguana, there is a colony of Bartschi's rock iguana, an endangered species found nowhere else in the world.

The island's 320 or so residents live in three small settlements tucked in along the shore on its western half. The village of **Abraham's Bay** is the administrative capital, located slightly inland from the waterlogged south shore, with a couple of small shops, three simple guesthouses (see "Practicalities" below), a post office and BaTelCo office. **Betsy Bay** is where the mailboat docks each week, and **Pirate's Well** on the north coast is a pretty little settlement of a few houses in a clump of palm trees fronting a long white sand beach. **Curtis Creek**, almost directly due north of Abraham's Bay on the north coast and accessible by road, is an inviting vista of white sand and turquoise water threading its way among a handful of small cays in a shallow bay. It's an ideal venue for a picnic, some snorkelling, and a paddle by kayak or dinghy (you will have to bring your own collapsible kayak and snorkel gear).

The main reason visitors come to Mayaguana is to **bonefish** off the isle's north coast. American fishing guides John Pinto and Gary Borger (☎586/445-8874, ⓦwww.garyborger.com) offer bonefishing holidays on canoes; a week's package, including accommodation and meals at the *Baycaneer Resort* (see below) and equipment, runs around $2000, excluding airfare. Alternatively, local fishing guide Leroy Joseph (☎339-3065) can take you out for a day of fishing, snorkelling or sightseeing by boat. If you go to Mayaguana, don't forget insect repellent as the mosquitoes can be fierce in the evenings.

Practicalities

Mayaguana is a 24-hour voyage by the **mailboat** *TransCargo II* from Nassau, with departures once a week, continuing on to Great Inagua ($70 one-way). The schedule changes weekly, so call the dockmaster at Potter's Cay, Nassau (☎393-1064) for departure times. Bahamasair (☎377-5505 or 1-800/222-4262, ⓦwww.bahamasair.com) has three **flights** a week with continuing service to Great Inagua.

Baycaneer's Resort in Pirate's Well (☎339-3605 or 377-2356, ⓕ377-2357, ⓦwww.bahamasnet.com/baycaneerbeach; ➍) is the choicest **accommodation** on the island, with sixteen rooms in a one-storey yellow stucco Spanish-style house situated directly on the white-sand beach which runs for several miles in both directions. There is a restaurant attached and a meal plan is available for $40 a day per person. *Mayaguana Inn Guest House*, in Abraham's Bay (Calvin Brown c/o BaTelCo ☎339-3065; ➊), has five no-frills rooms, and *Paradise Villas* (☎339-3109 or 351-5569, ⓕ339-3109; ➌), also in Abraham's Bay, has four simple but adequate rooms in modest white stucco bungalows around a small swimming pool, with a bar and restaurant. A final lodging option in Abraham's Bay is *Reggie's Guest House and Lounge* (☎339-3065; ➋), which can also organize fishing trips for $125 a day for two people and snorkelling excursions for $100 for two people.

10

The Turks and Caicos Islands

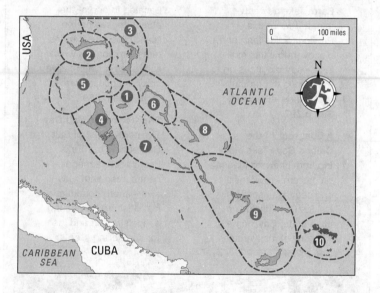

CHAPTER 10

Highlights

* **Grace Bay** On the north coast of Providenciales this six-mile stretch of gorgeous beach along the turquoise Atlantic is the perfect place to while away the hours. See p.322

* **The Caicos Conch Farm** Take a twenty-minute tour of this Providenciales farm and discover how this mollusc – so ubiquitous on the menus throughout the islands – is raised. See p.327

* **A boat tour of the Caicos Cays** Take a day-trip from Leeward Marina on eastern Providenciales and see the unspoiled Caicos Cays, including Little Water Cay, home to a colony of rock iguanas. See p.325

* **The wooden houses of Cockburn Town** Stroll along Duke and Front streets and take in the 1840s wooden houses that align the harbour. See p.338

* **The Turks and Caicos National Museum** Located in one of the oldest houses on the island, this museum features a major shipwreck as well as an impressive array of Lucayan artefacts. See p.339

* **Snorkelling on Salt Cay** The north coast of Salt Cay boasts the Turks' best beach, a magnificent spread with massive elkhorn coralheads just offshore harbouring schools of fish and ideal for snorkelling. See p.344

10

The Turks and Caicos Islands

T hough just twenty years ago the **Turks and Caicos Islands** were one of the quietest and least-known destinations in the West Indies, today, on the back of classy development on Providenciales, and the discovery of great beaches and diving on all of the islands, they have become one of the most fashionable places to visit in the Caribbean.

The country – independent of the Bahamas though part of the same archipelago – comprises two groups of islands (the Turks and the Caicos) of which eight are inhabited and around forty uninhabited. The two groups are separated by the deepwater channel known as Columbus Passage, 22 miles wide and up to 6000ft deep.

To the east, the much smaller group of Turks Islands includes **Grand Turk** and **Salt Cay**, the former the home to government since the eighteenth century, the latter a tiny island named for the salt industry that once dominated the country's economic fortunes.

To the west, the long chain of Caicos Islands includes the inhabited **South**, **Middle** and **North Caicos** – each with its own individual charms – and the fast-developing island of **Providenciales**, known as Provo, and home to most of the nation's tourist development. The Caicos Islands also showcase a string of tiny islands that include the ultra-chic **Parrot Cay** and **Pine Cay**, where two exclusive hotels have been established and the rich and famous have put up their winter homes.

The reason people visit the Turks and Caicos is for the truly sensational white-sand **beaches** that stretch for miles on all of the islands, and for the world-class **diving** and **snorkelling** as well as **deep-sea** and **bonefishing**. None of the islands offers a great deal to look at as you go inland. The dry and dusty interiors are characterized by low-lying scrubby vegetation and, particularly in the Turks Islands, large expanses of rather featureless salt ponds.

Where and when to visit

The likelihood is that you'll be heading to **Providenciales**, which receives nearly all of the country's international flights and has the major hotels, guesthouses and restaurants. Even if you plan to stay there, however, you should certainly consider excursions to one or more other islands. Particularly recommended are the thirty-minute flight to **Grand Turk** – a terminally calm, easy-

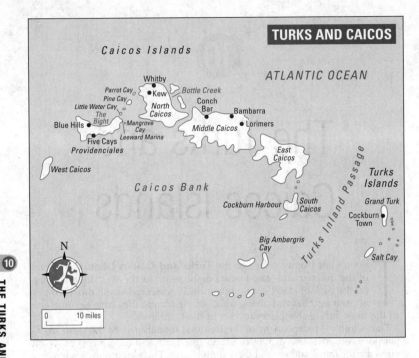

going place characterized by great colonial architecture, the National Museum and fantastic diving and beaches – or a boat trip around the spectacular **Caicos Cays** to **Middle** or **North Caicos**, where you can check out some dramatic caves or the remains of an old plantation house before crashing on a beach.

The average **temperatures** are in the low 80s (°F) year- round, the coolest months being from December to April when you might need a light sweater in the evening. The hottest time is from September to November, when the trade winds drop and it can get a bit sticky. As in the Bahamas, hurricane season is officially from June 1 to October 31, though direct hits are thankfully rare.

National holidays

New Year's Day
Commonwealth Day (second Monday in March)
Good Friday
Easter Monday
National Heroes Day (last Monday in May)
Queen's Birthday (nearest Monday to June 16)
Emancipation Day (August 1)
National Youth Day (last Friday in September)
Columbus Day (second Monday in October)
International Human Rights Day (October 24)
Christmas
Boxing Day

Some history

The earliest inhabitants of the Turks and Caicos Islands were **Amerindians**, who originally made their way up the Eastern Caribbean chain in long dug-out canoes many centuries BC. They were simple, peaceful people who survived on basic farming and fishing, but over the centuries they were driven further and further north to escape the more warlike Carib Indians, who followed their route. Amerindian sites and relics have been found dotted across the islands; particularly important finds include those at the Conch Bar caves in Middle Caicos (see p.334) and a canoe paddle recently discovered in North Creek on Grand Turk. The Amerindian period is well documented at the National Museum in Grand Turk (see p.339).

There is a major debate about the first European visitor. While the island of San Salvador in the Bahamas (see p.287) has probably the strongest claim to be the place where **Christopher Columbus** first set foot in the Americas in 1492, there are many exponents of the theory that it was in fact Grand Turk that saw the *Santa Maria* pull up to shore. The debate goes on as to which of the two was the "bean-shaped, low-lying island surrounded by reef with a good anchorage to the south", as described by Columbus in his diaries.

Whoever the first visitors were, they didn't stay long. Spanish slaving ships raided the island for Amerindian labour for the gold mines of South America and by 1513 the population had been reduced to zero. As for the colonial powers, ownership of the islands passed between Spain, France and Britain, but no one was very interested in setting up camp on them; they were perceived as offering poor water supply and little shade, and only pirates took up occasional refuge. During what became known as the **Golden Age of Piracy** from 1690 to 1720, Providenciales and the Caicos Cays were used as hiding places by great pirates like Calico Jack Rackham, Mary Read and Anne Bonny, and stories of buried gold and jewels still bring treasure-hunters to the islands.

By the later seventeenth century, though, it was a new "treasure" that attracted occasional visitors – **salt**. Soon, rakers came from Bermuda, having discovered the ease with which salt could be produced from shallow saltwater ponds, or salinas, which were constructed across the islands. This was particularly evident in Salt Cay, Grand Turk and South Caicos, where large numbers of trees were chopped down to discourage rainfall (resulting in the largely bare landscape that endures today). "White gold", as the stuff came to be known, was a highly lucrative crop, much of it sent off to Newfoundland for salting cod, and some of the remaining grand houses on Salt Cay are testament to that profitable era. By 1781, the rakers had established a permanent settlement in Grand Turk.

Meanwhile, the Caicos Islands became inhabited only after the American Revolution, when thousands of defeated **Loyalists** fled from the southern states, particularly Georgia and the Carolinas. Some were granted large tracts of land by the British government, from Providenciales to Middle Caicos, in

Why the name?

The Turks Islands were named for the Turk's-head cactus that grows wild across the islands, itself deriving its name from the red fez-shaped flower that it bears when in bloom. Caicos almost certainly comes from the Spanish word "cayos", for small islands or cays.

recompense for what they had lost in North America. Around forty Loyalists arrived during the 1780s, bringing with them more than one thousand slaves, and began farming cotton. Though immediately successful – **Caicos cotton** was said to be some of the finest in the world – the cotton industry went into decline after just a generation, with hurricanes and pests taking a heavy toll. Though a few planters moved to the Turks Islands and went into salt, most had left the country by the mid-1820s, leaving their slaves behind to a subsistence existence of farming and fishing.

Things began to change only with the arrival of a group of American investors in the 1960s. They laid the foundations for the tourist development that was to follow, building a small airstrip on Provo and erecting the first hotel – the *Third Turtle* – in Turtle Cove. A trickle of foreign visitors began to arrive, turning into a steady stream once **Club Med** insisted on a proper airport to service their Grace Bay resort in the mid-1980s.

Today, **Provo** has steamed ahead of the other islands, with almost all of the major development focused there. That development has given wealth to a large number of Turks Islanders and – to the government's great delight – brought back a number who had grown up away from home, particularly in the Bahamas and the US. Though the country could now probably afford independence, it remains a British crown colony.

Development has brought undoubted problems for the islands. Young people from all of the other islands have come to Provo to make their money, leaving places like South Caicos almost moribund. Also, the arrival of large numbers of expats, whether migrant labour from nearby Haiti and the Dominican Republic, or professionals from Europe and North America, has meant that Turks Islanders often feel like a minority in their own country; there is a major political schism between those who seek rapid development at any cost and those who wish to preserve a clear national identity.

The area code for all Turks and Caicos phone numbers is ☏**649**.

Getting there

Unless you've got your own boat, the only way you're going to arrive in the Turks and Caicos Islands is by **plane**. A decade ago, there were just two scheduled international flights a week to Providenciales. Today, getting there is much easier, though to reach the other islands you'll need to stop in Provo and jump on one of the inter-island shuttle flights.

American Airlines flies to Providenciales three times daily from Miami, a ninety-minute flight, and offers weekend flights from New York. British Airways flies to Providenciales once a week from London, stopping in Nassau en route. Air Canada makes the four-hour flight in from Toronto on Saturdays. Bahamasair leaves Nassau for the two-hour flight to Provo on Tuesday, Thursday and Saturday. Finally, Air Jamaica offers a ninety-minute flight in from Montego Bay daily from Friday to Monday. All five airlines turn around and fly out the same day.

If you are flying into Providenciales from the Dominican Republic, Skyking (☏649/946-4594, ⓦwww.skyking.tc) has four flights per week from Puerto Plata and two from Santo Domingo. It also operates six flights a week to and from Cap Haitien in Haiti.

If you're planning to arrive by yacht, the largest **marina** is at Turtle Cove in Provo (℡649/941-3781; VHF Ch 16) where there are over a hundred slips. Other marinas in Provo include the much smaller Leeward Marina (℡649/946-5553; VHF Ch 16) and the Caicos Marina on the south side of the island (℡649/946-5416; VHF Ch 16). In South Caicos and Grand Turk there are a handful of slips at Seaview (℡649/946-3508; VHF Ch 16) and Flamingo Cove (℡649/946-2227; VHF Ch 16) respectively.

Customs and red tape

Citizens of the US do not require a passport to enter the country, provided they can produce some proof of citizenship as well as a photo ID. Other nationalities only require a valid passport. Everyone should have proof of onward travel. Customs duty-free allowances include 200 cigarettes or fifty cigars and 1.1 litres of wine or spirits.

There are no foreign embassies or consulates in the Turks and Caicos, and anyone seeking diplomatic assistance should contact the relevant authorities in Nassau in New Providence (see p.16).

Money and costs

The currency in the Turks and Caicos Islands is the **US dollar**. Major credit cards are accepted at all of the main hotels and restaurants. Prices are high, not least because almost everything that is consumed is imported from America. The **departure tax** is US$23.

Getting around

Getting between the islands of the Turks and Caicos is relatively easy, especially if you're starting from Provo; three local **airlines**, TCA (℡649/946-4255), Inter-Island (℡649/946-4381, ⓦwww.interislandairways.com) and the generally more reliable Skyking (℡649/946-4594 or 941-5464, ⓦwww.skyking.tc) offer frequent connections. Skyking has nine daily scheduled flights each way between Provo and Grand Turk taking thirty minutes, three stopping in South Caicos to pick up and drop off en route in both directions. Round-trip fares cost around US$120. Normally, there are daily flights, too, between Provo and North and Middle Caicos (around US$60 round-trip) and between Grand Turk and Salt Cay (US$30), though the times of these seem to vary from day to day.

Each of the islands has a **taxi** service, and there will invariably be a taxi waiting for passengers at the airports. For **car and jeep rental**, typically around US$60 a day, it's best to try in Providenciales or Grand Turk. Elsewhere you may struggle to get a rental; it's worth asking at your hotel.

The Caicos Islands

THE CAICOS ISLANDS form a rough semicircle, running from the lovely and soon to be inhabited island of West Caicos up through the major tourist centre of Providenciales and a chain of tiny islands – the Caicos Cays – to North Caicos, then back down again through the largest island of Middle Caicos and uninhabited East Caicos to the once busy but now largely ignored island of South Caicos.

North, Middle and South Caicos can be easily accessed by plane from Providenciales, while North and Middle can also be visited via a fabulous boat trip from Leeward Marina that takes you round the Caicos Cays.

West Caicos is a popular site for divers, who make the trip from Turtle Cove Marina in Provo; in January 2002 building work began on a marina, airport, five-star hotel and a series of exclusive private homes. East Caicos is home to a posse of stray donkeys and swarms of mosquitoes; enthusiastic talk in the islands of a major cruise-ship port here seems highly optimistic.

Providenciales

Nowhere has the Turks and Caicos tourist industry boomed as evidently as **PROVIDENCIALES**, a flat island some twenty miles long and for the most part just a couple of miles across. With little in the way of cultural life or historical interest, only the hardcore diving and fishing cognoscenti used to make their way here. Tourism began to heat up in the 1980s, with the arrivals of *Club Med* and a proper airstrip, and rocketed through the 1990s as investors spotted the great potential for resorts. The opening of *Beaches* in the late 1990s (one of the enormously successful Sandals resorts) really put Provo on the map as far as large-scale tourism was concerned.

Many of the residents who came to Provo in the 1960s and 1970s when it was barely developed, with a subsistence economy based on fishing, speak with undisguised dismay at the recent arrival of crowds and traffic on the island. Yet, for all their complaint, the island is far from busy; it's hard to go far without discovering a magnificent beach to yourself, and Provo remains a relaxed and easygoing getaway.

There's no real town to speak of on the island. **Downtown**, as the business centre is known, is a rather ugly grouping of shops and offices that you'll pass through on your way from airport to hotel. The three traditional areas of settlement (which can loosely be described as villages) are little visited by tourists. They include **Blue Hills**, a pretty residential area that runs alongside the sea north of the airport; **Five Cays**, a rather drab collection of homes and shops on the south of the island; and a series of homes and churches around the *Beaches* resort known as **The Bight**.

For many visitors, particularly those staying at the all-inclusives on the north coast, the only sightseeing worth venturing out for is a wander along the six miles of magnificent beach on **Grace Bay**. It's a spectacular stroll beside a turquoise sea, with occasional shade beneath the casuarina trees, and however large the crowd outside the hotels, you'll invariably find a deserted spot to pitch camp. Others will be intrigued by the **Caicos Conch Farm**,

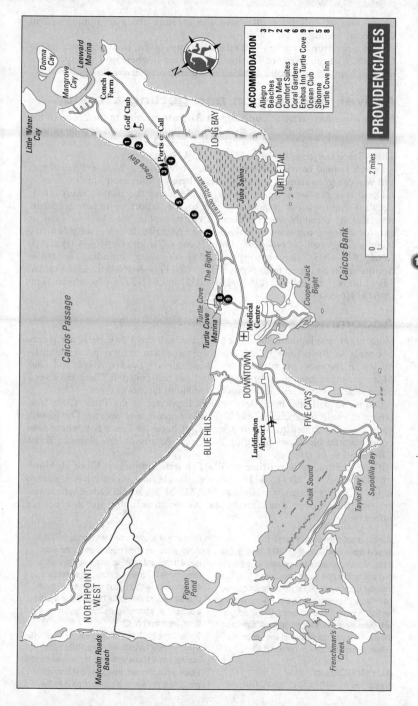

PROVIDENCIALES

ACCOMMODATION

Allegro	3
Beaches	7
Club Med	2
Comfort Suites	4
Coral Gardens	6
Erebus Inn Turtle Cove	9
Ocean Club	1
Sibonne	5
Turtle Cove Inn	8

0   2 miles

Little Water Cay

Donna Cay

Mangrove Cay

Leeward Marina

Conch Farm

Golf Club

Ports of Call

Grace Bay

LONG BAY

Juba Salina

TURTLE TAIL

LEEWARD HIGHWAY

Caicos Bank

Cooper Jack Bight

The Bight

Turtle Cove

Turtle Cove Marina

Medical Centre

Caicos Passage

BLUE HILLS

DOWNTOWN

FIVE CAYS

Luddington Airport

Chalk Sound

Taylor Bay

Sapodilla Bay

Frenchman's Creek

NORTHPOINT WEST

Pigeon Pond

Malcolm Roads Beach

where visitors will learn all about the creature that's so ubiquitous on Caribbean menus.

More adventurous visitors will take advantage of the **boat** trips run to the Caicos Cays from Leeward Marina (see opposite), where you can spot rock iguanas, hunt for sand dollars and make a picnic on a deserted island.

Arrival, information and getting around

Nearly all visitors arrive at **Luddington Airport**, roughly in the centre of the island, recently refurbished and air-conditioned. There's always a string of taxis waiting outside and a couple of car rental desks. A taxi to one of the hotels along Grace Bay costs between US$12 and US$20.

There's a small **tourist office** at Turtle Cove Marina (Mon–Fri 9am–5pm) and you can get a map of the island from there or from most hotels.

There is a bus service that ferries people along the island's main artery, Leeward Highway, but it does not run to the airport or to any particular timetable. It's certainly worth **renting a car** to explore the island for a day or two (or a jeep if you want to make a trip to Malcolm Roads – see p.328); try Rent-a-Buggy (T649/946-4158), Provo Rent-a-Car (T649/946-4404) or Avis (T649/946-4705). Expect to pay US$55–60 a day, including insurance. **Scooters** can be rented from Scooter Bob's (T649/946-4684) for US$30 a day.

For **taxis**, try Nell's (T649/231-0051 or 941-3228) or Provo Taxi (T649/946-5481).

Accommodation

With resort development sprinting along through the 1990s, there are plenty of **hotels** on Provo, though most are at the top end in terms of price and quality. By far the most popular are the all-inclusives – *Beaches*, *Allegro* and *Club Med* – though these are all large-scale and can feel crowded. There are several other smaller and excellent options dotted along the north coast.

The island's original hotel development happened in the Turtle Cove area, where the sadly crumbling *Third Turtle Hotel* awaits new owners. The island's focus has now shifted to the great stretch of beach at Grace Bay where new condominium blocks are going up every year. As a result, the places in Turtle Cove tend to be cheaper.

If you're thinking of **renting a villa**, Lynnette Simpson at Elliot Holdings (T649/946-5355, F946-5176, Wwww.ElliotHoldings.com) has a superb range of places starting from around US$1500 per week. Other villa owners rent their homes out directly, and it's worth scanning the internet for offers.

Around the airport

Airport Inn Airport Road T649/941-3514, F941-3281, Wwww.tcnational.tc/hotel.htm. Near the airport and far from the beach (though they'll lay on a free ride to get there), this is the cheapest option on Provo, with nineteen clean and tidy rooms going for US$75 a day if air-conditioned, US$65 a day if not. Some rooms have kitchenettes, all have cable TV, and there's a local restaurant and bar on site. Fifteen percent discount on car rental. **❸**

Turtle Cove

Erebus Inn T649/946-4240, F946-4704.

Perched just above Turtle Cove Marina, with fine views out to sea, the *Erebus* is one of the older island hotels and could do with a lick of paint to reinvigorate it. For now, though, it's a pleasant enough place, with 21 good-sized and air-conditioned rooms all with cable TV and either a patio or a balcony, clay tennis courts and a restaurant and large, attractive bar. **❹**

Turtle Cove Inn Resort T649/946-4203, F946-4141, Wwww.TurtleCoveInn.com. Right by the marina, and a 10min walk from the nearest decent beach, but a pleasant, easygoing and reasonably priced little place near a couple of good restaurants. The friendly Tiki bar is popular with local residents, particularly at breakfast and lunch, and there's a smallish, shaded pool. **④**

Grace Bay

Allegro ☎649/946-5555, ℱ946-5522, ⓦwww.allegroresorts.com. Rather hideous when approached from the road, the 186-room all-inclusive compensates guests by being on a superb part of Grace Bay. It also features the nation's only casino, aimed at casual blackjack and roulette players rather than the high rollers. There are two restaurants: a casual open-air place on the ground floor and a smart Italian upstairs (make your reservation early), as well as a piano bar. The rooms all have rattan furniture, colourful throws, a/c and fans, there's a large (often crowded) pool, and there are tennis courts, a fitness centre and good watersports facilities. **⑥**

Beaches ☎649/946-8000, ℱ946-8001, ⓦwww.beaches.com. This superb all-inclusive resort – part of the impressive Sandals chain – is aimed at families, with top-class facilities for entertaining children during the day including a Pirate's Island, a Sega centre and their own restaurant and disco. Rooms are spacious, colourful and evenly distributed across a wide area, all within a short walk of the glorious beach and a number of pools. Watersports facilities are top-notch, while nine excellent restaurants range from Italian and French to Caribbean and Japanese, some catering to adults only. **⑧**

Club Med ☎649/946-5500, ℱ946-5501, ⓦwww.clubmed.com. A longstanding and recently refurbished adults-only 300-room resort, *Club Med* has a largely American clientele and heavy emphasis on daily sports and nightly entertainment. Most of the food is laid on in the self-service restaurant, which has a vast and constantly changing selec-

tion of buffet items, and you'll have to book to use the excellent Italian restaurant with waiter service. **⑦–⑧**

Comfort Suites ☎649/946-8888, ℱ946-5444, ⓦwww.comfortsuitestci.com. One of the cheapest options in the Grace Bay area and not a bad spot, the *Comfort Suites* are a 10min walk from the beach and right by the Ports of Call shopping area and restaurants. There are 100 rooms, all with either a king bed or two double beds, plus cable TV, a fridge, phone and a/c. Rooms start at US$145/135 in summer/winter. **④**

Coral Gardens ☎649/941-3713, ℱ941-5171, ⓦwww.coralgardens.com. This small block of smart and good-value one-, two- and three-bedroom condominiums is popular with repeat visitors to the island. All condos are good-sized, starting at 1000 square feet, with private balconies, sea views, fully equipped kitchens and daily maid service. The block is close to a good snorkelling site. **⑤–⑥**

Ocean Club ☎649/946-5880, ℱ946-5845, ⓦwww.ocean-club.com. Luxury all-suites resort whose success has spawned a bunch of imitators along the coast, *Ocean Club* has studios (US$180/225 in summer/winter), one-bedroom suites (US$315/425) and up to three-bedroom suites (US$550/835). There are three pools, three restaurants, a fitness centre with massage, tennis courts, boutiques and on-site dive operator and watersports. **⑦**

Sibonne ☎649/946-5547, ℱ946-5770, ⓦwww.Sibonne.com. One of the best and best-value options on the island, this small boutique hotel sits beside a magnificent stretch of white sand and houses the *Bay Bistro*, one of the finest restaurants on Provo (see p.329). The two-storeyed and attractively landscaped hotel has 27 medium-sized rooms, all with air conditioning, and a tiny pool. **⑥–⑦**

Leeward Marina and boat tours

Perhaps the highlight of any stay on Provo is a **boat tour** exploring the Caicos Cays (see box, overleaf) or merely taking in the surrounding waters. At the eastern end of the island, neat little **Leeward Marina**, two miles from Grace Bay and four from Turtle Cove, overlooks the first of the cays that stretch around to North Caicos. The marina is home to most of the boat tour groups. You can just about make out the mangrove swamps of Mangrove Cay directly across the channel and, looking to your left, the sandy beaches of Little Water Cay (see overleaf) where rock iguanas strut their stuff. If it's a calm day, it's worth renting a kayak from the Big Blue (US$20 per hour for a double; ☎649/946-5034) for an hour or two of cruising across to the cay and stopping on a deserted sandbank or beach to look for shells.

If you're feeling less energetic, there are a number of very professional operators based at the marina who run excellent **sailboat or speedboat trips** to Little Water Cay to see the iguanas and to other nearby cays for shelling and picnics, normally stopping for some excellent snorkelling en route. Even more adventurous and definitely worth trying are the speedboat trips that go around all of the cays to Middle Caicos, where you can visit the Conch Bar caves (see p.334). The journey takes about ninety minutes each way, and you'll stop off to see the iguanas and to do some snorkelling.

The main **speedboat operators** are Silver Deep (T649/946-5612) and J&B Tours (T649/946-5047). Both run similar trips for similar prices; expect to pay around US$50 per person for the visit to Little Water Cay and US$120 for the trip to Middle Caicos. Big Blue (T649/946-5034) runs slightly pricier tours, with more emphasis on "eco-adventures", like visiting mangrove swamps or nature trails on Middle Caicos.

Sailing trips are run by Sail Provo (T649/946-4783) and Beluga (T649/946-4396) on comfortable catamarans or trimarans; as well as trips to the cays and snorkelling and shelling trips, both offer sunset cruises for around US$50 per person.

The Caicos Cays

Strung out in a chain between Providenciales and North Caicos are a dozen tiny **Caicos Cays**, of which all but two are uninhabited. Though there are airstrips for the private planes of the millionaire residents of Pine Cay and Parrot Cay, the most likely way to set foot on any of the cays is by taking a boat trip from Leeward Marina (see p.325). All beaches are open to the public and, on all the uninhabited islands, you're pretty much free to wander around at your leisure.

Five minutes by boat from Provo, the nature reserve of **Little Water Cay** is home to several thousand rock iguanas. These reptiles – unique to the region – were once found throughout the islands, but development and destruction by man and dog has led to their virtual extinction elsewhere. Here, wooden boardwalks have been put up across the cay to allow you access to the heart of their protected habitat. You'll see dozens of them – up to 2ft long – sunning themselves on the beach or foraging around in the scrub.

Northeast of the cay, **Water Cay** is fringed by small sandy cliffs and fantastic white sand, while the adjoining **Pine Cay** has a small hotel and about 35 private homes dotted around its beaches and interior providing winter retreats for their wealthy and mostly US-based owners. The twelve-room *Meridian Club* hotel (T203/602-0300 or 1-800/331-9154, F203/602-2265, Wwww.meridianclub.com; ❽) is one of the finest of its kind in the world, priding itself on being simple but classy ("barefoot elegance" is the appropriate slogan), with nature trails crossing the cay, and kayaks, snorkelling, fishing and diving all available for guests. Rooms cost US$825/650 in winter/summer based on double occupancy, and children under 12 are not allowed.

Beyond Pine Cay as you head east is **Fort George Cay**, which once housed a fort erected in the eighteenth century by the British to deter pirates from concealing themselves and plunder pinched from Spanish galleons sailing further south. The fort itself is long gone, though two of its iron cannons can be seen by snorkellers in shallow water just off the northwestern shore.

Last in the chain and closest to North Caicos, **Parrot Cay** (formerly known as Pirate Cay, and thought to have been a refuge for pirates, including Calico Jack, Anne Bonny and Mary Read) witnessed the opening of the multimillion-dollar *Parrot Cay Resort* (T649/946-7788, F946-7789, Wwww.parrot-cay.com; ❽) in the late 1990s. With fifty rooms and six villas, some with private swimming pools, and a fabulous spa, the place is altogther grander – and, most would say, rather snootier – than the *Meridian Club* on Pine Cay. Prices starting at US$400 a room/US$2000 a villa mean that it's for the rich only, and in true copycat style a bunch of celebrities have beaten a steady trail here since it opened to the likes of Paul McCartney.

The Caicos Conch Farm

Tucked away in the wilds of Leeward east of the marina, the **Caicos Conch Farm**, on Leeward Highway (Mon–Sat 9am–4pm; US$6, children US$3; T649/946-5330), is the only one of its kind in the world. Started in 1984, the farm is responsible for rearing queen conch – a giant sea snail, famous for its gorgeous pink shells and pearls – for export and for sale in the islands. Conch are subject to numerous predators in the sea, including sharks, stingrays, porcupine fish and octopus. At the farm they are protected, first in large hatcheries and then, as they grow towards adulthood at three to five years, transferred out to pens at sea.

Twenty-minute **tours** of the farm are given frequently – if you arrive while one is in progress you can join in and the guide will fill you in on the parts you missed at the end. During the tour you'll see the hatcheries through which the conch progress and you're free to handle them and see the eyes on stalks peering out at you and the foot and toenail that they use to drag themselves along the ocean bottom.

The tour ends with an introduction to Sally and Jerry – two adult conchs who are used to being handled and will pretty much heave their whole bodies out of the shell for you to inspect. Your guide will doubtless reveal the startling fact that, if a crab bites off a male conch's penis, the conch quickly grows a new one. Mulling that over, you're free to have a quick look at the **gift shop**, where inexpensive conch shells, earrings and expensive conch pearls can be purchased.

Long Bay and the Hole

With its entrance just a short drive along the road that runs west of the Conch Farm, **Long Bay Hills** is a developing residential area on the south side of the island, with an impressive stretch of sand. Unfortunately, millions of conch shells washed in by the prevailing winds make access to decent swimming awkward, though you'll notice that some local house owners have tried to clear a path out to the ocean. Even then, however, the water is shallow for some way out and the sand more silty than you'll find on the north shore.

Follow signs to the hidden and rather dramatic **Hole**, where the cap of the limestone rock has crumbled away – probably the result of wave action many centuries ago – leaving an eighty-foot drop down to a wide green pond. You can clamber around the edge – brave souls have been known to scramble down for a swim in the icy water – but beware there are no ropes or other protection, so make sure to keep small children well away.

Blue Hills and Malcolm Roads

West of Long Bay, Leeward Highway cuts straight across the island towards Downtown, the island's tiny commercial centre. Perhaps the prettiest drive on the island emerges after turning off to the right just before you reach downtown and, after about half a mile, taking the right fork that leads you onto a coastal road that passes **Blue Hills**, the most attractive of Provo's original three settlements. As well as an astounding variety of churches, and a graveyard where all the graves face out to sea, there are some great bars on the beach serving fish and conch snacks and lunches.

If you've got a jeep, at the end of Blue Hills you can turn left to join a more substantial road a few hundred yards inland (the continuation of the road you avoided earlier by forking right). Continue west towards Malcolm Roads and Northwest Point. Where the road divides, take the left turn (ignoring signs for the white-elephant Crystal Bay condominium project) down a diabolical track about four miles long to Malcolm Roads. As you crawl down this rocky road, look out for osprey nests (big composites of twigs and sticks), close-ups of the palms and cacti that characterize the island's original vegetation, and great views over the bays and over virtually inaccessible inland ponds where birdlife can be spectacular.

The beach at **Malcolm Roads** is one of the most beautiful spots in the country. The surf often crashes in on the magnificent beach here, and you can expect to have it to yourself, though you may see dive boats moored some way offshore at some great dive sites. Bring water as there's no shelter and no facilities, but the adventurous can clamber around some rocky outcrops to find tiny coves for swimming. Steer clear of the small group of thatched, wooden Tiki huts that were put up here for a French gameshow in the early 1990s; untended since then, and blown about by occasional hurricanes, they have fallen into disrepair, with rotten floorboards and rusty nails a peril to the unwary.

Five Cays, Chalk Sound and the south

There's little in the way of tourist development on the south side of the island, where you'll find one of Provo's original settlements at Five Cays (named for the small group of rocks just offshore) and the gorgeous **Chalk Sound** national park and semicircular Taylor Bay.

To get there from downtown, turn down the main road virtually opposite the airport road. A left turn at the gas station leads to Five Cays – an uninspiring and unkempt jumble of houses, schools and small businesses. Make sure you stop at the excellent *Liz's Bakery* (daily 6am–6pm) on the main road for some freshly baked breads, cakes and pasties.

Continuing south on the main road towards the island's main dock at South Dock, a turn to the right just before you reach the sea leads to the gloriously milky blue Chalk Sound, one of the prime addresses on Provo. It's a stunning lagoon, but bear in mind that it's not a great place to swim because of the silty bottom.

The sound is protected from the sea on its southern side by a narrow peninsula, which is indented with a series of bays, overlooked by grand and very expensive private homes. Sapodilla Bay is the first and largest of the bays, with a handful of yachts normally moored just offshore. At the eastern end of the bay, reached by a rocky path just west of the run-down *Mariner's Hotel*, there are a number of inscriptions in the rock that were carved by shipwrecked sailors in the early nineteenth century. Copies of the inscriptions decorate the walls of the airport.

Beyond Sapodilla Bay, Taylor Bay has a perfect crescent of sand. Like Chalk Sound and Sapodilla Bay, though, it's not a great place to swim as the sea is shallow and the sea-bed silty for some distance from shore.

Eating and drinking

There is a good range of places to **eat** in Provo, from fine French and Italian restaurants to local hostelries dishing up traditional island food. As you'd expect, seafood has pride of place on most menus, but there's plenty to keep you happy if you're a meat-eater. Vegetarians will struggle to find much in the way of variety.

Downtown

Angelas Leeward Highway, opposite turnoff for Turtle Cove ☎649/946-4694. New York-style deli, with a great range of bread, meat, cheese and other goodies, offers sandwiches, muffins and other good munchies all day long. There's a separate branch in the Ports of Call village. Mon–Fri 6am–5pm, Sat & Sun 6am–3pm.

Doras Leeward Highway ☎649/946-4558. Dora has run this place – best of the native restaurants – for over a decade and still dishes out excellent and relatively inexpensive fare from curried chicken, lobster and goat to beef stew and creole snapper or grouper. Monday and Thursday have a seafood buffet where, for US$22, you get a great selection of conch fritters, lobster, turtle and fish. Open all day.

Hey Jose! Central Square, Leeward Highway ☎649/946-4812. Longstanding island favourite for Mexican dishes (enchiladas, burritos and fajitas) and pizzas at US$10–20 per head. Cocktails are excellent, particularly during Friday happy hour (5.30–7pm), when trademark margaritas go for US$3.50 a shot. Lunch and dinner Mon–Sat.

Tasty Temptation Butterfield Square, Downtown ☎649/946-4049. This long-running bakery sells a great selection of plain or filled croissants, rolls and sandwiches from around US$5 as well as giant muffins and good coffee. Mon–Fri 6am–3pm.

Turtle Cove

Banana Boat On the marina ☎649/941-5706. Pleasant family-friendly place, with a moderately priced range of fish and seafood platters, including excellent cracked conch and snapper or grouper in a spicy creole sauce.

Sharkbite Overlooking the marina ☎649/941-5090. This great spot offers tasty meals from almond-crusted grouper in curry sauce (US$17.50) to fish and chips (US$9.95) and burgers (US$10 up). Alongside the restaurant there's a long and busy bar, and a handful of games to keep the kids engaged before their food hits the table.

Tiki Hut On the waterfront ☎649/941-5341.The *Tiki Hut* offers a fine breakfast and is also a popular early evening meeting place – always packed during fishing tournaments – and a pleasant place to catch a drink before heading on to dinner at one of the nearby restaurants. No airs and graces, but friendly and easygoing.

Grace Bay

Bay Bistro *Sibonne Hotel*, Grace Bay ☎649/946-5396. Sip a cocktail at the bar and watch a fabulous sunset before sidling into this easygoing bistro that has quickly earned a reputation as one of the finest places to eat on the island. The fish and lobster are superb whether marinated in ginger and soy or simply pan-fried on the grill, and there's a smaller selection of fine cuts of beef or lamb if you're feeling carnivorous. Finish with the lemon crème brûlée – it's huge, but you'll manage it. Starters cost US$5–10, main courses US$16–35. Lunch and dinner; closed Tues.

Bella Luna Glass House, Grace Bay ☎649/946-5214.Choose your fresh pastas smothered in tomatoes, herbs and anchovies, or turn to the fresh catch pulled out of the sea that morning. Dinner only; closed Mon.

Caicos Cafe Caicos Café Plaza, near Ports of Call, just east of *Allegro Hotel* ☎649/946-5278. Beautifully lit with candles and fairy lights and decorated with Haitian art; the French owners of this semi-outdoors restaurant (somewhat exposed if the weather's bad) serve superb fresh meals. Starters include conch salad (US$9) and tuna *carpaccio* (US$12), while mains always feature fresh local fish and lobster (US$20–27) and imported steaks. Finish things off with a Caicos Coffee, strong and infused with plenty of kahlua and whipped cream.

Lattitudes Ports of Call ☎649/946-5832. Happy hour starts at 5pm after which Californian but long-time resident Jeff Rollings starts dishing out top-notch pizzas, ribs, steaks, fish and burgers in a relaxed and funky setting. All dishes under US$15. Dinner only.

Nightlife and entertainment

Nightlife on Provo is fairly quiet. However, if you're up for dancing, the nightclub *Stardust and Ashes* (on Leeward Highway near the turnoff for the *Allegro Hotel*) has something going on each night from Tuesday to Saturday, including a mellow jazz night on Tuesday, a late late "island party" night on Friday and salsa and merengue at Saturday's Latin night. For more sedate fun, you can head to the casino at the *Allegro Hotel* to try your hand at blackjack and roulette.

The biggest party of the year is held around "Provo Day", which takes place in late July and early August each year. There is a beauty pageant, a regatta and a parade of floats and a big weekend party with live music and stalls (normally around the ballpark in Downtown) selling beer and local food like souse and conch fritters.

Diving and watersports

The **diving** around Provo is as good as you'll find anywhere. True, the best wall diving is a lot further from shore than you'll find in Grand Turk, but there is a great variety of excellent sites here, including those at Northwest Point and at West Caicos, between sixty and ninety minutes by boat from Turtle Cove Marina. There are also good shark and other dives to be found closer by off the island's north shore.

Reputable operators include the longstanding Provo Turtle Divers (ⓣ649/946-4232, ⓦwww.ProvoTurtleDivers.com), Caicos Adventures (ⓣ649/941-3346, ⓦwww.caicosadventures.tc), and Big Blue Unlimited (ⓣ649/946-5034, ⓦwww.bigblue.tc), who also offer **whale-watching** trips in February and March when humpback whales pass by, and kayaking tours of the cays near Provo. Expect to pay around US$55, US$90 or US$130 for a one-, two- or three-tank dive; US$60 for a night dive or US$160 for an introductory resort course that includes a two-tank dive. A four- or five-day open-water certification course, involving four to five two-tank dives, costs US$400-450.

If you want to **snorkel** while you're on Provo, the best places close to shore are near the hotel at *Coral Gardens* and at Smith's Reef, just east of the entrance to the Turtle Cove Marina. At both places you'll find good reefs just offshore. Alternatively, ask the dive operators when they have a snorkelling trip going out (normally US$35 per person) or take one of the island/snorkelling trips offered by the outfits at Leeward Marina (see p.325).

Other watersports are not exactly well catered for, although the larger hotels all have good facilities for their guests. If you're not staying at one of those, your choice is likely to be rather limited, though you can rent windsurfers, hobiecats and kayaks from a rental outlet on the beach outside the Ocean Club on Grace Bay.

Fishing charters offer superb deep-sea fishing for marlin, wahoo, tuna and shark, difficult but exhilarating bonefishing in the shallow flats around the islands and bottom fishing for grouper, snapper and parrotfish. For deep-sea fishing, try Sakitumi (ⓣ649/946-4065) or Gwendolyn (ⓣ649/946-5321) at Turtle Cove Marina and expect to pay US$850 or US$550 for a full- or half-day's fishing for up to six people, or US$150 if they'll take you on your own. For bonefishing or bottom fishing, try Catch the Wave (ⓣ649/941-3047) or Silver Deep (ⓣ649/946-5612), both at Leeward Marina. In July there's a huge billfish tournament, with boats coming from around the world to hunt for the biggest blue marlin in the sea.

Golf and tennis

There is a magnificent **golf** course at Provo Golf and Country Club (ⓣ649/946-5991), where you'll pay US$120 each for eighteen holes and a cart or US$70 for nine holes. Many of the hotels have private **tennis** courts, and the public are welcome to hire the courts at the *Erebus Inn* (see p.324).

Shopping

For **shopping**, the Ports of Call village near the *Allegro Hotel* has a number of stores selling T-shirts, books, postcards and island souvenirs (conch shells are popular), and there are similar stores at Central Square, near *Hey Jose* restaurant on Leeward Highway. The best supermarket is TGA, on Leeward Highway (daily 8am–8pm).

Listings

Banks Both Scotiabank and Barclays have branches in Downtown. Hours are Mon–Thurs 8.30am–2.30pm, Fri 8.30am–4.30pm.
Laundry Pioneer Cleaners, Butterfield Square, Downtown (☏649/941-4402).
Medical services Associated Medical Practices, Leeward Highway (☏649/946-4242; Ⓦwww.doctor.tc); Grace Bay Medical Centre,

Grace Bay (☏649/941-5252).
Photo One-hour photofinishing at Village 1 Hour Photo, Village Cinemas complex, Leeward Highway (☏649/941-4558).
Police ☏649/946-4259, for emergencies ☏911.
Post office Airport Road (Mon–Fri 8am–noon & 2–4pm).

North Caicos

The most lush and in many ways the most beautiful of the nation's islands, **NORTH CAICOS** gets more rainfall than any of the others, so the vegetation here is denser and taller. Many islanders keep vegetable patches and grow fruit trees, including tamarind, papaya and sapodilla. As you'd expect, the beaches are great, too. Although property speculators have pushed land prices to dramatic highs on hopes that North Caicos will become the next Provo, tourist development is pretty low-key to date, with just a few small hotels on the north coast.

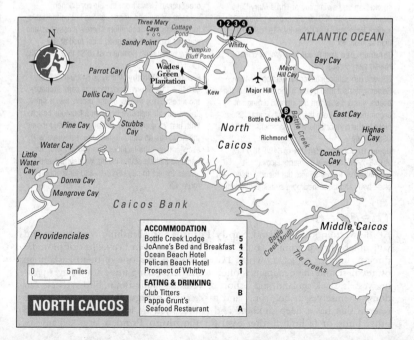

ACCOMMODATION
Bottle Creek Lodge	5
JoAnne's Bed and Breakfast	4
Ocean Beach Hotel	2
Pelican Beach Hotel	3
Prospect of Whitby	1

EATING & DRINKING
Club Titters	B
Pappa Grunt's Seafood Restaurant	A

NORTH CAICOS

Arrival, information and getting around

There are no international flights to North Caicos, and most people arrive by plane from Providenciales with Skyking, TCA or Inter-Island Airways to **North Caicos Airfield**, north of Major Hill on the east coast of the island. There is no longer a scheduled ferry service to the island, though boats do make trips from Leeward Marina as part of **day excursions** from Providenciales (see p.325).

There is **no tourist office** on the island nor any formal car rental facilities, although it's worth asking at your hotel if they can arrange a rental for you (they normally can). There are **taxis** at the airport to meet incoming flights. If you want to tour around by taxi, M&M (☏649/946-7338) charge US$25 per hour.

Accommodation

Most of the **hotels** on North Caicos are scattered along the lovely sandy beaches of Whitby, though the Bottle Creek Lodge is a delightful newcomer on the other side of the island.

Bottle Creek Lodge Bottle Creek ☏649/946-7080,🌐www.bottlecreeklodge.com. Comfortable eco-friendly accommodation in two cottages and an apartment overlooking the turquoise creek that divides North from Middle Caicos. Not ideal for the beach, but a very easygoing place that has sailboats and kayaks to help you explore Middle Caicos and nearby cays. The owners will also arrange expeditions around the island, such as snorkelling and swimming at Three Mary Cays. Based on double occupancy, expect to pay US$130 a night from May 1 to December 15, US$170 in high season. ❺

JoAnne's Bed and Breakfast Whitby ☏649/946-7184; ☏946-7301, 🌐www.turksandcaicos.tc/joannesnbn. JoAnne Selver's modest little place, a short walk from the beach, has a restaurant on site and a range of accommodation, from the fairly basic at US$90 a night to the comfortable villa apartments that cost US$120. ❹

Ocean Beach Hotel Whitby ☏649/946-7113, ☏946-7386, 🌐www.turksandcaicos.tc/oceanbeach. Rather simple but friendly place with one-, two- and three-bedroom suites, most with kitchenettes, on another fine stretch of beach. All ten of the rooms have fans and functional furniture, there's a decent restaurant and the hotel can arrange boat trips and diving. Rooms start at US$120, rising to US$215 for the largest rooms. ❺

Pelican Beach Hotel Whitby ☏649/946-7112, ☏946-7139. Easygoing and longstanding small hotel owned by local pilot Clifford Gardiner, with great ocean views from the air-conditioned upstairs rooms and unpretentious but comfortable furnishings and decoration. There's a cosy bar, and you can expect to find good local food at the roomy restaurant. Rooms cost US$145 to US$225. ❻

Prospect of Whitby Whitby ☏649/946-7119, ☏946-7114, 🌐www.clubvacanze.com. Probably the nicest place to stay on the island, this is an Italian-run all-inclusive hotel on a fabulous beach. With just 23 good-sized and air-conditioned rooms the hotel has an intimate feel, the restaurant is excellent, and the facilities that you get with the package include scuba diving, windsurfing and tennis. Expect to pay US$270–380 for a double room. ❽

The island

At the west end of the island, **Sandy Point** is a small fishing community and your likely arrival point if you're coming by boat from Provo. Just offshore lie three prominent rocks known as **Three Mary Cays**; one of them has a huge osprey nest, and the occupant is often seen there gazing imperiously over passing vessels. Back on land, and a short drive from Sandy Point, birdwatchers can douse themselves in bug spray and make for **Cottage Pond**, a small nature reserve that has a deep sinkhole and is inhabited by local ducks, grebes and other birds, or (a little further east) for **Flamingo Pond**, a large expanse of brackish water, where you can normally spy a flock of flamingos (though, disappointingly, it's hard to get close to them, and you'll need binoculars for a decent view).

On the north side of Flamingo Pond, **Whitby** is home to the island's main hotels and guesthouses and fringes onto a number of excellent white-sand beaches with good snorkelling just offshore. On the western edge of Whitby, the powdery sands of Pumpkin Bluff Beach are quite magnificent while, on the eastern side of the village, Pelican Point is a good place to snorkel.

South of Whitby, the road leads inland to the farming settlement at **Kew** – the only one of the original settlements in the country not based on the coast – named for the botanical gardens in London and home to many of the island's most productive fruit and vegetable growers. There's also a post office, church and general store.

A mile to the west of Kew, the extensive though unspectacular ruins of **Wades Green Plantation** are currently under restoration, and you're free to wander around the remains of the massive kitchen, overseer's house, stables and walled garden plots. Built in 1789 by Wade Stubbs, the plantation developed high-quality cotton and was a rare success story for the area; upon his death in 1822, Stubbs owned over 8000 acres on North and Middle Caicos and Providenciales, as well as 384 slaves, many of whom took his surname. Today, Stubbs is one of the most common names in the islands.

On the eastern side of the island, **Bottle Creek** is the island's largest settlement, with houses spread out along the ridge that overlooks the creek dividing North from Middle Caicos. It's a peaceful and gorgeous spot, especially if you're passing through by boat. A vehicle ferry passes across the creek at weekends; at other times you can ask around in Bottle Creek if someone will drop you over at Crossing Place in Middle (five minutes by boat), though you'll want to arrange a taxi for the other end.

Eating and drinking

Away from the hotels, there's not much in the way of **restaurants or bars**, and nightlife tends to be quiet.

Club Titters Bottle Creek ☏ 649//946-7316. This local place dishes up tasty and inexpensive stuff all day, including grouper with peas and rice and cracked conch, and there's occasional live entertainment at weekends.

Pappa Grunt's Seafood Restaurant Whitby ☏ 649/946-7301. Expect to find lots of local fish and conch on offer at *Pappa's*, served in a variety of fashions, with fried chicken and burgers for those after their meat. Most dishes cost US$6–10.

Pelican Beach Hotel Whitby ☏ 649/946-7112. Good mixture of local and international food, with plenty of fine grilled snapper and grouper served up with peas and rice as well as ribeye steaks and lobster salad for US$15–20. The place can lack atmosphere when it's quiet, but there's a very easygoing vibe.

Prospect of Whitby Hotel Whitby ☏ 649/946-7119. Excellent food, often Italian but far more than basic pizza and pasta, at this all-inclusive, where non-residents can get a pass for dinner. The chef lays on daily specials that might include veal, lobster or fillet steak, and you can expect to pay upwards of US$35 for a three-course meal.

Middle Caicos

Home to just 300 people, **MIDDLE CAICOS** is the largest island in the country and one of the quietest. Despite more great beaches fringing its 48 square miles, especially those at Mudjin Harbour near Conch Bar and further east at Bambarra, tourist development has been very slow and there are few facilities for the visitor. You'll find just a handful of guesthouses and a couple of taxi drivers on the island, but if you're after peace and quiet, you couldn't find many better refuges; if it's action you're after, stay well away.

The island was settled by Lucayan Indians between the eighth century and around 1540, by which time the Spanish had succeeded in wiping out the local population through murder or enslavement in South American mines. Few traces of their settlement were left, and the island remained uninhabited until Loyalists and their slaves arrived from North America after the Revolution. As elsewhere in the islands, the settlers' attempts at growing cotton made little progress and, within a generation, the settlers took off, leaving their former slaves to get on with life in the three north coast settlements that survive today.

Arrival, information and getting around

There are daily flights from Providenciales with TCA and Inter-Island Airways, some of them stopping at North Caicos en route to **Middle Caicos Airfield**, just south of Conch Bar. There is also a ferry from Bottle Creek in North Caicos on Saturdays from 8am (US$2 per person, US$20 for a car), landing at Crossing Place in the west of the island.

You won't find a tourist office on the island or a car rental outlet, but there are a couple of **local taxi drivers** who prowl around the airport and will be delighted to take you on a tour of the island – reckon on around US$25 per hour. Try Earnest Forbes (T649/946-6140) or Cardinal Arthur (T649/946-6107). They'll also be happy to organize fishing trips for you on the shallow waters south of the island.

Accommodation

Other than private villas, there are just a couple of places for visitors to **stay** in Middle Caicos, the small but upmarket *Blue Horizon Resort* or the pleasant little *Taylor's Guesthouse*.

Blue Horizon Resort Mudjin Harbour T649/946-6141, F946-6139, Wwww.bhresort.com. A handful of large and comfortable cottages perch on the hilltops above the harbour, with fine views over the coastline. It's a fabulously relaxed place, a short walk from a superb beach – sometimes pounded with waves, at other times blissfully calm – though don't come expecting much in the way of entertainment or nightlife. The staff will lay on snorkelling or hiking expeditions if you're up to it. Meals available by reservation. ❻

Taylor's Guesthouse Conch Bar T649/946-6161. A good place for those on a tight budget, with inexpensive rooms (US$50 a night) in a large and attractive wooden house, five minutes' walk from the beach, with fans, TV and a small restaurant. ❷

The island

Perhaps the main draw in Middle Caicos is a series of limestone **caves** at **Conch Bar** in the northwest of the island. Formed many millennia ago by the action of water on the soft rock, the extensive network was once the home to Lucayan Indians, almost certainly here at the time of Columbus, and various of their artefacts – including tools and pottery – have been removed to the Turks and Caicos National Museum in Grand Turk (see p.339). Today the caves are home to plenty of bats – bat guano was mined here early in the twentieth century – though they're invariably asleep when you visit.

Tours of the caves need to be arranged in advance, either through a tour company in Provo (see p.324) or direct by phoning one of the Middle Caicos taxi drivers and asking them to organize a tour for you. A guide takes you down into the caves (you're each given a flashlight), and the thirty-minute tour takes you past countless stalactites and stalagmites and deep into the system. Among the highlights are the cave believed to have been used by the Lucayan chief and the "Christmas Chamber", where Middle Caicos residents traditionally used to go on Christmas Eve to sing carols.

If you are over on a tour, it's worth spending some time at **Mudjin Harbour**, a short drive east of the caves. It's a dramatic setting with tall cliffs dropping down to the sea, a rocky promontory just offshore and waves often crashing in to a yellow-sand beach. As you go down to the beach there's a short trail off to the left that leads to the top of the cliff and offers fantastic views down the coast and across the scrubby, undeveloped interior of the island.

East of here the road leads to the small settlement of **Bambarra**, where a large and very quiet white-sand beach is framed by casuarina trees; at low tide you can wade out along a sandbank for half a mile to delightful Pelican Cay. Further east, **Lorimers** – named for a former plantation owner – is one of the most remote settlements in the country, though there's little of note here for visitors.

South of the three main settlements there is no development at all, the island being covered with ponds, creeks, tidal flats and mangrove, while offshore the Ocean Hole (accessible only by boat) is a giant and rather murky sinkhole dropping 200ft and occasionally explored by bold divers. Nearby, the Man-O-War Bush plays home to a host of frigate birds; the mating performance of the males in the spring is quite magnificent as they soar around puffing up their bright-red throat pouches to impress the onlooking females.

Perhaps the high point of the year on the island is its **Middle Caicos Expo**, a great weekend party in August, when former residents return and others flood in to hear live bands and hang out at the beer tents set up on Bambarra Beach.

Eating and drinking

The only real **eating** options on Middle Caicos are at the island's hotels, the most reliable for either lunch or dinner being the *Blue Harbour Café* at the *Blue Horizon Resort*.

Given the tiny population of the island (and the fact that most of it consists of either elderly people or children), there's nowhere much to head to for a night out, though there's a small **bar** in Conch Bar where local guys gather in the evening to drink beer and play dominoes. Plan quiet nights in your hotel, guesthouse or villa and lay in the beer from the grocery store in Conch Bar.

Hiking and biking

The **Crossing Place Trail** is an ancient path that leads from Lorimers in the east around the north coast of Middle Caicos to Crossing Place on the west coast, from where one could cross to North Caicos at low tide. For many years the path was overgrown, but recent clearance work by the National Trust means that you can now follow the track for four and a half miles from Conch Bar to Crossing Place. Part of the path is on the beach and passes through Mudjin Harbour, with trail markers along the way. It's a great way of seeing the island, though you may want to arrange for a taxi to pick you up at the end of the route.

There is also a seven-mile biking trail from Conch Bar to Bambarra Beach, with good snorkelling spots along the way. Bikes can be rented from Sport Shack in Conch Bar for around US$15 a day.

South Caicos

At just over eight square miles, **SOUTH CAICOS** is one of the smaller of the inhabited islands. Before the tourist development in Provo over the last two decades, it was the most important of the Caicos Islands, its economy founded on salt raking and conch and lobster fishing on the nearby banks. Seafood continues to be processed at factories on the island, but many young folk have left for work on Provo or overseas, and South Caicos has lost much of its vigour, the dusty streets of its main town, **Cockburn Harbour**, now roamed by wild cattle.

As in Grand Turk, salinas were developed by Bermudan salt rakers in the seventeenth century, but these now lie abandoned and in decay. As a result, there's little for visitors to do on the island other than wander the quiet streets around beautiful Cockburn Harbour and catch up on more excellent beaches. Best of all, try some fabulous **diving**, including the fuselage of a plane sunk in 50ft of water outside the harbour and now home to a colony of reef fish.

Practicalities

The **South Caicos Airport** is at the west side of the island, and has daily flights from Provo and Grand Turk. There are a couple of **taxis**, which meet all the flights.

There's talk of big hotel development to try to boost tourism on the island, but for now choice of **accommodation** is limited to the *South Caicos Ocean Haven* (℡649/946-3444, 🅕946-3446, 🆆www.oceanhaven.tc; ❹). Right by Cockburn Harbour and popular with divers, *Ocean Haven* has twenty comfortable air-conditioned rooms, a pool and a good, small restaurant.

Food options are strictly limited, too, though you can get a decent meal at *Doras Airport* (℡649/946-3247), which serves low-cost food all day, including a particularly tasty lobster sandwich. *Muriel's,* on Graham Street (℡649/946-3535), has good and inexpensive local food, served all day at this simple but friendly place, ranging from conch fritters and curried chicken to stewed beef and steamed fish. *Ocean Haven Sunset Bar and Restaurant* in Cockburn Harbour (℡649/946-3444), at the hotel of the same name, offers the best food on the island, with seafood the speciality. Look out for pan-fried or baked tuna, wahoo and snapper, served with peas and rice or french fries, for US$12–15.

Activities

Dive boats come across from Grand Turk every now and then in calm weather to take advantage of South Caicos's great sites along the edge of the Caicos Bank to the south of the island, where you can expect to find turtles, sharks and large shoals of eagle rays. The only local operation is at *Ocean Haven* (see above), where you can also rent gear.

The "Big South" comes back to life in May for **Regatta Weekend**, when there are sailing and other sporting contests, live bands playing all night and a great party atmosphere.

The Turks Islands

The small group of **TURKS ISLANDS** has just two inhabited islands: Grand Turk, the home of government, and tiny Salt Cay, with its population of under a hundred. Both places are quiet and quaint, showcasing attractive remnants of the colonial era, with great beaches and diving to keep you entertained during the day but little in the way of nightlife.

Grand Turk

Despite the best efforts of the government, major development continues to elude the small but delightful island of **GRAND TURK**. Frustrating as this is to the powers that be – who see their young people emigrating to Providenciales or abroad to make their money – for those who make the effort to get here, it means that the island remains charming and unspoiled.

A series of expansive, muddy-coloured salinas dominate the centre of the island, testament to the salt trade that first brought development to Grand Turk. West of here and running beside the sea, **Cockburn Town**'s Front and Duke streets house much of the country's finest colonial-era architecture as well as the tiny but superb **Turks and Caicos National Museum**. The diving and fishing on Grand Turk are world-class and the beaches magnificent. Consider renting a car or scooter for a day to tour the island, which will only take you a few hours.

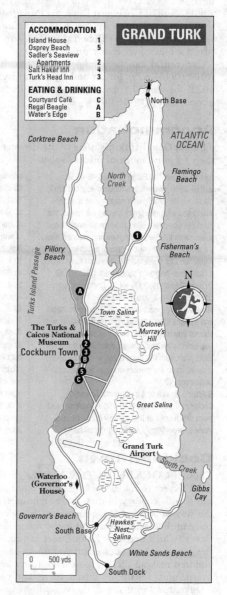

ACCOMMODATION	
Island House	1
Osprey Beach	5
Sadler's Seaview Apartments	2
Salt Raker Inn	4
Turk's Head Inn	3

EATING & DRINKING	
Courtyard Café	C
Regal Beagle	A
Water's Edge	B

GRAND TURK

North Base

Corktree Beach

ATLANTIC OCEAN

North Creek

Flamingo Beach

Pillory Beach

Fisherman's Beach

Turks Island Passage

N

Town Salina

Colonel Murray's Hill

The Turks & Caicos National Museum

Cockburn Town

Great Salina

Grand Turk Airport

South Creek

Waterloo (Governor's House)

Gibbs Cay

Governor's Beach

South Base

Hawkes Nest Salina

White Sands Beach

0   500 yds

South Dock

Arrival, information and getting around

There are no international flights into Grand Turk, although the government is reported to be negotiating desperately with American Airlines for them to provide a service. For now, you'll need to arrive at **Grand Turk Airport**, about a mile south of Cockburn Town, via Providenciales, from where there are more than a dozen flights a day (see p.321) costing US$60 each way.

The only **tourist office** (Mon–Fri 9am–4pm; ℡649/946-2321) on the island is located on Front Street.

Car rental can be arranged from Dutchies (℡649/946-2244) or Tony's (℡649/946-1879) for around US$55 a day; scooters from Val's (℡649/946 1022) for US$30 a day. **Taxis** are found at the airport or can be reached by phone – try K's (℡649/946-2239).

Accommodation

Though Grand Turk has none of the five-star **hotels** that you'll find on Provo, there's a good range of places to stay.

Island House The Ridge ℡649/946-1519, ℱ946-2646, ℗www.islandhouse-tci.com. On a hill above the creek, with great views over the island and a breeze pretty much year-round, the *Island House* offers eight modern air-conditioned suites, with kitchens, balconies and wooden floors. It's a short drive from the beach, but there's a pool if you can't be bothered. Studios start from US$80 a night; one-bedroom suites from US$110. ❹

Osprey Beach Hotel Front St, Cockburn Town ℡649/946-1453, ℱ946-2817, ℗www.ospreybeachhotel.com. This comfortable and tranquil little place is right on the beach, with sixteen tidy rooms each with a patio or a balcony overlooking the sea. There's a small restaurant a short walk from the main hotel, and a tiny pool around which the owners arrange occasional barbecues. ❺

Sadler's Seaview Apartments Duke St, Cockburn Town ℡649/946-2569. There are just three small units at this friendly little pad, a stone's throw from the sea. All rooms have

kitchens and TV and are cooled with ceiling fans. ❸

Salt Raker Inn Front St, Cockburn Town ℡649/946-2260, ℱ946-2817, ℇsnaker@tciway.tc. Under renovation at the time of writing, the faded colonial charm of the *Salt Raker* made it an old favourite for visitors to Grand Turk, just across the road from a good beach and an incredibly peaceful and laid-back place. The best rooms overlook the ocean; others are spread around the garden where the restaurant is located. ❺

Turk's Head Inn Front St, Cockburn Town ℡649/946-2466, ℱ946-1716, ℗www.grand-turk.com. Another charming colonial building from the 1840s, the *Turk's Head* pulls in a mixture of business travellers and tourists for its attractively furnished rooms and period style. At quiet times, it can feel rather soulless, but the bar is normally a busy spot in the evening with local residents and there's a good restaurant on site. A short walk from the beach. ❹

Cockburn Town

Though **COCKBURN TOWN** is the capital of the island and the country, don't expect to find a bustling city. Comprising a couple of streets of (mostly) nineteenth-century homes and warehouses, the town seldom offers much in the way of activity. The government has spent a lot of money to smarten the place up, but it hasn't brought in the masses. Stroll down the main drag of Duke Street (which becomes Front Street as you head north) which runs alongside the gorgeous blue ocean, and you might encounter a gaggle of smartly dressed children making their way to school or a languid cow munching from some overhanging foliage. It's quaint, pretty and very quiet.

Duke and Front streets showcase the island's **architectural highlights**. At the southern end of Front, the *Salt Raker Inn* and *Turk's Head Inn*, two of the best hotels on the island, are examples of the cute wooden houses built in the

1840s by Bermudan shipwrights who came to the island to collect salt. Other colourful examples like the General Post Office line this area of Front Street, many of them constructed with ballast and timbers taken from the trading ships of the time. Purple and orange bougainvillea adorns the exteriors of some of the buildings, and you'll see the occasional Turk's-head cactus (small, with a red flower).

Further north, past the large Cable and Wireless compound, the post office and the legislative council chamber are equally colourful, and a couple of iron cannon from HMS *Endymion* stand in the courtyard of the plaza that surrounds the buildings. A bit north, the large pink **Victoria Public Library** (Mon–Fri 9am–4pm; free) was erected in 1889 to commemorate fifty years of the British queen's reign. Behind it, the nation's old prison was famous for allowing inmates to nip over the wall (and back to their partners) at night, provided they were safely back in their cells by roll call in the morning. Today, discipline is tighter and inmates are held in a modern jail.

The Turks and Caicos National Museum

Continuing up Front Street, the **Turks and Caicos National Museum** (Mon–Fri 10am–4pm; US$5; ☎649/946-2160, ⓦwww.tcmuseum.org), is one of the highlights of any visit to Grand Turk. Housed in the former Guinep Lodge – one of the oldest houses on the island – the museum showcases its exhibits over two floors.

The ground floor is given over to a single **shipwreck** from the Molasses Reef, south of Grand Turk. The wreck is the oldest and most important find of one of the ships of the so-called Age of Discovery. At first, the wreck was thought to be the *Pinta* – one of the flagships on Columbus's first voyage in 1492 – but after extensive research it is now thought to date from around 1515. It was not a treasure ship, although some morons blew parts of it apart with dynamite looking for treasure after it was first discovered in the 1970s. Key parts of the exhibits include the enormous main anchor, cannon and other weapons, hand- and foot-cuffs for prisoners and such tools as a tailor's sewing kit.

Upstairs, the exhibits span the islands' history from pre-Columbian times to the present. One room is given over to artefacts – notably pottery – from the Lucayan Indians, while another presents information on the reefs and fish that surround the islands. There is also an exhibit on famous visits to the island, ranging from astronauts John Glenn and Scott Carpenter, who splashed down near here in 1962 and were brought to Grand Turk for a debriefing, to Queen Elizabeth II and members of the royal family, who have visited periodically over the last forty years.

Look out, too, for features on Columbus's voyages of discovery. Although the orthodoxy has it that his first point of call was in the Bahamas, local historians have made a persuasive case for Grand Turk being where he initially made landfall in the New World. The jury is still out on the issue.

The rest of the island

At the northern end of Grand Turk, a creek runs in from the ocean and provides safe anchorage for fishing and other boats. To the east of here, the main road runs up to North Base – a former military base, now renovated to provide offices and a school. A track leads round to the left of the base to the old **lighthouse**, built in the 1850s to warn ships of the extensive reef that wrecked many over the preceding centuries. The lighthouse-keeper's cottage and the kerosene store still stand alongside it, dating from the same period, and the area

△ Grand Turk Beach

offers great views out across the reef and nearby bays, though sadly you can't ascend the lighthouse.

There are good beaches lining the west and east coasts, though the pick of them is probably **Governor's Beach**. Take water, as there are no facilities on the beach and there's every chance you'll have the beach to yourselves. To get there, head south, ignoring the turnoff to the airport, and keep going towards the governor's residence, known as Waterloo because it was built in 1815, the year of Napoleon's defeat at the battle of that name. The grand house (not open to the public) was originally the home of a Bermudan salt magnate. Just before you reach the imposing white walls of the residence, turn off to the right along a track that runs past the small nine-hole **golf course** in the grounds of the house (☎649/946-2308 to book a round for US$25). At the end of the track, a path leads through the bush to a superb stretch of white sand, backed by casuarina trees and fronting onto a magnificent turquoise bay.

Eating and drinking

There's not much sophistication to **dining** out in Grand Turk, but there are plenty of decent options and prices are reasonable.

Calico Jacks *Turk's Head Hotel*, Front St, Cockburn Town ☎649/946-2466. *Calico Jacks* offers good food from an experimental and eclectic menu, covering everything from grilled lobster (US$25) and fish and chips (US$9) to Thai curry (US$12) and stone-crab claws (US$22). Sit outdoors under the trees at lunchtime but remember the bug spray.

Courtyard Café Duke St, Cockburn Town ☎649/946-2260. At a couple of tables around a small patio outside the *Osprey Beach Hotel*, you can get a light breakfast of cereal, muffins or eggs and inexpensive lunches of conch, fish and chicken.

Regal Beagle Hospital Rd ☎649/946-2274. This shack-like island restaurant dishes up tasty and inexpensive native lunch and dinner, such as conch fritters, stewed beef, goat curry and fried chicken.

Water's Edge Front St, Cockburn Town ☎649/946-1680. Normally the best food on the island, served on a pier poking out into the gorgeous waters off the west coast, and usually busy at lunch and dinner. The bar is well tended and often lively, and the cracked conch, conch salad, grilled fish and tasty "gooburgers" go down a treat. Look out for occasional live music, and expect to pay around US$20–25 for a three-course meal.

Nightlife and shopping

Nightlife is pretty quiet in Grand Turk, though there's usually some late-night music and dancing action at *Nookie Hill* on Friday and Saturday and the occasional mellow guitar courtesy of Mitch Rolling at *The Water's Edge* (☎649/946-1680).

Shoppers will find their options limited, though they should try X's on Duke Street for its impressive collection of Haitian art and wood carvings.

Diving and watersports

Most of the action centres around superb **diving**, snorkelling and fishing. Diving opportunities are world-class, many of them very close to shore. There are fantastic deep and shallow dives to be had at twenty sites along the five-mile wall that starts just 250yd (five minutes in a boat) from the west coast. You'll find magnificent coral formations, abundant reef life and plenty of shipwrecks.

The three operators are Blue Water Divers (☎649/946-2432, ⓦwww .grandturkscuba.com), Oasis Divers, who also offer **whale-watching trips** (☎649/946-1128, ⓦwww.Oasisdivers.com) and Sea Eye Diving (☎649/946-1407, ⓦwww.seaeyediving.com). All offer PADI certification courses and are happy to take snorkellers along if they're going to a shallow site. **Snorkellers** should also make for the old pier at South Dock – not the most attractive place to dive but teeming with fish – and try to get on a boat ride to deserted Gibbs Cay where the snorkelling is fantastic and you'll bump into some friendly southern stingrays.

Fishing trips are a little harder to arrange, but you should try Dutchies (☎649/946-2244) or ask at your hotel or one of the local dive operators. If you can find a boat going out (usually around US$300-400 for a day) you can expect to catch wahoo, tuna, sailfish and barracuda in the deep waters close to shore.

Salt Cay

For many people, tiny **SALT CAY** is one of the loveliest of the islands in the country. Triangular in shape, it measures no more than six and a half square miles and is home to fewer than one hundred residents. The island was an important spot for the Bermudan salt rakers, whose relics still litter the place and provide much of its charm – fabulous old whitewashed houses as well as the saltpans from which the "white gold" was laboriously scraped. Add to that some sugary white beaches, great diving and snorkelling and a small but fine range of accommodation, and you've got another great place to chill out for a while.

Arrival, information and getting around

Flights with TCA and Inter-Island Airways leave daily from Provo for **Salt Cay Airfield**, about a mile and a half northeast of Balfour Town, and cost US$120 return (see p.321). There are also daily flights between Grand Turk and Salt Cay, though these are less frequent and cost US$25 each way. The government ferry runs between Grand Turk and Salt Cay, leaving Grand Turk on Monday, Wednesday and Friday at 3pm and costing US$4 per person.

There is no **tourist office** on the island and just a couple of **taxis**, which are always poised outside the airport awaiting the next plane.

Accommodation

Mount Pleasant Guest House ☎649/946-6927, ⓕ946-6927, ⓦwww.turksandcaicos.tc /mtpleasant. Sensibly priced and superb value, this timber-beamed, former nineteenth-century salt trader's home on the great north coast beach has been catering mainly to divers for over a decade. There's a comfortable lounge/library for guests, and rooms are colourful and quiet. The restaurant and gazebo bar are the most popular on the island. ❹

Salt Cay Sunset House ☎649/946-6942, ℱ946-6942, ⓦwww.seaone.org. Another charmingly restored old salt trader's home, with just three rooms ranging from US$70 to US$100, the house features a big, communal living room where guests can escape from the sun and catch up on their reading. Good food served by the owners on the veranda. ❸

Windmills Plantation ☎649/946-6962, ℱ946-6930, ⓦwww.WindmillsPlantation.com.

Fabulous and fabulously expensive, the *Windmills* is built like a traditional West Indian plantation house. Wooden walkways connect the main house, with its wooden verandas and gingerbread fretwork, to the other guestrooms, all furnished with superb antiques and custom-designed furniture that includes four-poster beds. The restaurant is world-class and, needless to say, the new management team of Jim and Sharon Shafer (recently arrived from the *Meridian Club* on Pine Cay) will arrange whatever activity you need. ❿

The island

Like Grand Turk, the centre of Salt Cay is dominated by the flat shallow **salinas** that brought the island its early development at the hands of Bermudan salt traders in the seventeenth century. Recognizing the commercial potential of raking up the salt, the traders built stone walls and sluice gates to create smaller ponds from which the water would evaporate more quickly under the baking sun. Windmills were built to speed up the process, but it was fiercely hard manual work. Trading ships arrived from Bermuda carrying limestone rocks as ballast (later to be incorporated into the traders' smart houses), then carried the rough salt off to trade along the eastern seaboard of the fledgling United States.

For centuries, this trade was the source of the island's wealth, but the industry was in decline for decades before it finally ground to a halt in the 1960s. Nothing much has happened since, and Salt Cay's population has slowly melted away, the remaining people mostly elderly or children, their numbers supplemented by a trickle of tourists.

On the west side of the island, Balfour Town is the principal settlement, home to the government buildings, local school and a couple of stores. It's also where you'll find the **White House**, which dominates the shoreline, though it's not open to the public. The most spectacular of Salt Cay's two-storey jalousie-windowed limestone houses, it was built by local salt magnate Joshua Harriot after the great hurricane of 1812 had flattened his wooden home with a fifteen-foot tidal wave. Elsewhere, more recent and colourfully painted wooden houses have little courtyards and low stone walls to keep stray cattle at bay.

The island's best **beach** runs along the entire north coast, a magnificent swathe of sand, with massive elkhorn coralheads in a couple of places just offshore harbouring schools of fish and perfect for snorkelling. The rocky east coast is dominated by sharp-edged ironshore limestone, with a series of small bays dotted along it. It also has the island's highest point at **Taylor's Hill** 60ft above sea level.

For **divers** there are a handful of good sites five minutes by boat off the west coast of the island, where you'll find spotted eagle rays and a wealth of colourful fish as well as deepwater gorgonians and black coral trees. Ten miles further south, the wreck of HMS *Endymion*, an eighteenth-century British warship complete with cannon, lies in 30–40ft of water.

Eating and drinking

The hotels and guesthouses are where you'll do almost all of your **eating and drinking**, with particularly good food (particularly seafood) at the *Mount Pleasant*, though you should also have a drink and a game of pool at the *One Down, One To Go* bar in Balfour Town for some local colour.

Diving and watersports

Salt Cay Divers (℡649/649-6906, ⓦwww.saltcaydivers.com), based at the *Mount Pleasant Guest House*, organize **dives.** Five days of three-tank diving costs US$400 per person; with two-tank diving it's US$325 per person. They can also rent you a bike or organize a horse-riding tour of the island. Check their excellent website for special deals.

From January to March, **humpback whales** make their way to the nearby Mouchoir Banks to breed, and while a fortunate few will spot them blowing from the shore, Salt Cay Divers (and their Grand Turk equivalents) organize frequent whale-watching trips to see them for around US$40 per person.

Contexts

Contexts

The historical framework

For three centuries after Columbus touched down on the Bahamas in 1492, the islands became an outpost of the great imperial struggles that consumed England, France and Spain. Because of its strategic position astride the Gulf Stream passage leading toward Europe, Nassau, the deepwater port on the northern side of New Providence, became first a rendezvous for English privateers preying on Spanish galleons and then a rambunctious haven for pirates from many nations. When England finally won control of the islands in 1783, the focus of Bahamian history shifted from Europe to North America, with the American Revolution being only the first wave in a series of influences and distortions that both dovetailed with and determined Bahamian lives. After World War II, the Bahamas achieved its independence and set about defining itself as a free and democratic country with an authentic culture.

For a historical framework of the Turks and Caicos, please see p.319.

Pre-Columbian Bahamas

Many anthropologists believe that the first temporary inhabitants of the Bahamian chain were ancient Siboney Meso-Indians, who migrated from the Greater Antilles for a short period well before the time of Christ. The first permanent settlers were, however, a tribe of Venezuelan Indians who spoke Arawak, and were related to larger groups of **Arawak-speaking peoples**, who had fled their more warlike neighbours, the Caribs. Around 500 AD, hustled along by population pressure and contests for land, a pulse of Arawak migration brought the first true settlers to the Bahamas. They called themselves the *lukki-caire*, a term that evolved into **Lucayan**, meaning simply "island people". Firmly established in Hispaniola and Cuba, these Lucayans practised a basic neolithic Taino culture, living simply by fishing and basic agriculture. By 900, they had had firmly established themselves throughout the Bahamas in large numbers.

According to Columbus's diaries, the Lucayans were light brown in skin colour, with jet-black hair and broad, flat foreheads. They were indubitably peace-loving, played a ball game called *arieto*, smoked tobacco for ritual pleasure, tattooed their bodies and adored body ornaments and jewellery, though they wore few clothes. Although the Lucayans did have weapons like bows and arrows, they had not developed armour.

Their settlements throughout the islands were composed of rectangular or circular huts. Though essentially egalitarian, each settlement was headed by a chief, or *cacique*, who personified the ideal of wisdom. Despite having neither a written language nor the use of the wheel, the Lucayans managed to evolve a culture that made pottery, carved elaborate wooden articles, wove cotton, and built watertight boats.

Little trace of Lucayan society remains in the Bahamas today. Anthropologists have unearthed numerous "sites", but most artefacts are limited to shards of pottery. **Petroglyphs** remain etched into rocks around the islands, but most are badly weathered. Scientific estimates of the Lucayan population on the Bahamas at the end of the fifteenth century put the figure at 40,000–50,000.

The first encounter

It was the Lucayans who greeted **Columbus** on or about October 12, 1492, the explorer having left Spain to search for a route to the East Indies under the commission of Queen Isabella and King Ferdinand. After a 33-day crossing of the Atlantic powered by the trade winds, he landed on what was probably modern-day San Salvador, an island the Indians called *Guanahani*. The one hundred or so Spaniards found the Lucayans very welcoming, so much so, in fact, that Columbus observed that "they should be good servants".

Taking several Lucayans with him as guides, Columbus sailed south and east, discovering other Bahamian islands like Rum Cay, Long Island, Crooked Island, and finally the Ragged Islands, bestowing Spanish names on each as he went. There was little there to bring prosperity, however, and he moved on to Cuba and then Hispaniola. Subsequent waves of Spanish explorers came, and between 1500 and 1520, the Spanish deported most Lucayans as **slaves** to work the mines and plantations of the New World. Many Lucayans succumbed to illness and disease, while others committed suicide in despair. Legend has it that when Juan Ponce de León visited the island of Andros looking for the fountain of youth in 1513, he found but a single native. Within 25 years of their first encounter with European society, the Lucayans had been exterminated.

Imperial struggles

For nearly a century after the initial encounter between Columbus and the Lucayans, the Bahamas came under the nominal **control of Spain**. Despite the Treaty of Tordesillas in 1494, which had divided the western world between Spain and Portugal, the Spanish had little use for their possessions in the Bahamas. Consequently, English freebooters and privateers, such as Sir Walter Raleigh and Sir Francis Drake, were able to use Bahamian waters to hide after plundering Spanish galleons; explorers like Sir John Hawkins and John Cabot also briefly visited the Bahamas during the 1500s. However, dangerous reefs, tricky tides and frequent hurricanes made actual settlement on the islands unfeasible.

In 1629, Charles I of England ignored the Spanish claim on the islands and granted the Bahamas to one of his favourites, Sir Robert Heath, as part of the English effort to colonize the northern and middle Atlantic. At the same time, France's King Louis XIII granted the islands to a member of his court. And while neither Charles I nor Louis XIII sent actual colonists to the Bahamas to cement their claims, the tone of imperial struggle was set, dictating the course of Bahamian history for the next two centuries.

The Adventurers

The first European settlers of any consequence here were **Puritans**. The English Civil War (1642–48) visited great persecution on the country's Puritans, who fled for the American colonies. One, William Sayle, became the first governor of Bermuda, yet after his tenure there he grew dissatisfied with the religious freedom on the island. With the approval of the Crown, he left Bermuda in 1648 with his **Company of Eleutheran Adventurers** and set sail for the uninhabited Bahamas. Sayle's group arrived on the island of Cigatoo, now known as Eleuthera, where it had hopes of establishing large-scale plantations. However, the colonists were quickly disappointed by the thin soil and unreliable rainfall, and also cursed by political faction, ultimately splitting up, with some departing for Virginia and others returning to Bermuda. After more than ten years of struggle, most of the colonists were gone, and those who remained lived at near-starvation levels. Sayle himself returned to Bermuda and was later made governor of South Carolina in 1663, from which position he advocated for the Bahamian colonists, enlisting support for them from Puritan communities as far away as New England.

At the same time that Sayle and the Adventurers were colonizing parts of the Bahamas, **Oliver Cromwell** dethroned King Charles I. Shortly thereafter, Cromwell initiated his "Grand Western Design", an imperial enterprise designed to challenge Spanish supremacy in the Caribbean. He planned to entice settlers with promises of land and to secure the services of privateers against Spanish shipping interests. Government-sponsored Puritan settlers began arriving, as did freed black slaves and even, in 1659, a number of American colonists from New Providence, Rhode Island, who gave their name to an island of major importance in the chain.

Piracy and war

Although the Adventurers had committed a constitution to paper, the colonists lived for decades without any formal government. In 1670, Charles II, newly restored to the throne, parcelled out the islands to six Lords **Proprietors of the Carolinas**. The Proprietors were led by Lord Ashley of South Carolina, who promptly dispatched 300 new settlers who centred their activities on New Providence's Charles Town (renamed **Nassau** in 1695 in honour of King William III of England, prince of Orange-Nassau). The Royal Proprietors were absentee landlords who didn't find much profit in their lands, and when the first governor died en route to the islands, the unruly islanders on New Providence elected their own. The Proprietors soon dispatched other governors, but throughout the 48-year period of Proprietary Government, Nassau was a tumultuous place to say the least, and most of the dispatched governors were easily corrupted, exiled by local residents or even murdered. Perhaps the government's greatest achievement was the first formal census of Bahamian residents in 1671, which revealed a population of 1097, of whom 443 were slaves working plantations of cotton, tobacco, sugar cane and sisal.

By the late seventeenth century, a hundred years of constant warfare between England, France and Spain allowed Nassau to become a haven for **pirates**, outlaws and wreckers. Its many reefs, cays, rocks, shoals and inlets, along with unforgiving tides and bad weather, forced many a ship aground only to be plundered, and allowed the shallow-draught vessels that pirates preferred to effectively hide from imperial navies. Perhaps the most famous privateer of the time was Henry Jennings, who, in 1715, attacked a Spanish galleon and captured five million pieces of eight, returning to Nassau a hero.

Pirates like Edward "Blackbeard" Teach and Calico Jack Rackham became infamous for their cruelty, but were also prominent as de facto island leaders. After thirty years of raiding and wrecking ships, Nassau's outlaws grew even bolder and were beginning to prey on ships of all nations, even going as far as raiding towns in the south Caribbean and the Carolinas. Something had to be done.

Royal government

In an effort to bring order to his disorganized subjects in the Bahamas, King George II took control from the Proprietors in 1718, made the Bahamas a **Royal Colony** and sent out a former privateer and explorer named Woodes Rogers as Royal Governor, with a mandate to clean up Nassau. Rogers sailed into Nassau Harbour in late 1718, advising the pirates they could accept either death or a pardon. Backed by three warships and a cadre of Royal Marines, Rogers executed a few outlaws, chased others away and co-opted still others into royal service. However, just as calm returned to Nassau, a new war between England and Spain broke out in 1720, leaving many residents of the crown colony fearful of attack. Rogers organized militias for defence and fortified Nassau, repelling a Spanish attempt to sack the city. When an epidemic seared through Nassau, many of his supporters died, stripping him of badly needed political support, and he returned to England a poverty-stricken man in 1721. Rogers, though, returned in 1729, again on a mission to root out piracy and corruption that had made a comeback in his absence.

It was during his second period as Royal Governor that Rogers created a **General Assembly** made up of 24 elected land-owning members, which first convened on September 29, 1729. In form, it remained virtually unchanged throughout the succeeding two and a half centuries, until Bahamian independence in 1973. The Assembly of 1729 was notably oligarchic, governed by an elite class of landowners that served its own interests and those of its friends in England. Quite often, though, the interests of the Nassau elite conflicted with the Crown, setting the stage for a series of political battles between royal governors and wealthy landowning whites. This tension was only compounded by the tide of imperial wars between England, France and Spain, which flared anew in 1738, 1748, and 1756, and saw England once again legalizing privateering.

The Bahamas remained a poor outpost in an increasingly wealthy Empire. Its thin calcite soil could not support mass slave-labour plantations as in the southern Caribbean, and tobacco, cotton and sisal failed in turn. Once the islanders had cut down great stands of hardwoods, the trade in forest products dwindled, leaving most Bahamians to scrape a living from subsistence agriculture and fishing, salt farming, turtle hunting and wrecking; indeed, by 1750 more than 300 salvage ships were employed in Bahamian waters.

The American Revolution

Because of its location amid shipping lanes to and from Europe and North America, the Bahamas has always been affected by the tides of North American immigration and colonization. Moreover, many residents of the Bahamas had family and religious ties to American colonists. When the **War for American Independence** broke out in 1776, the Crown responded by blockading trade with its American colony. Bahamians were torn, with many remaining loyal to the Crown while a significant minority supported the American rebels. Almost immediately the American Navy attacked Nassau, capturing Fort Nassau in hopes of spiriting away its huge cache of gunpowder, which had, however, been taken away beforehand. Again in 1778, the American Navy attacked Nassau, and a joint French-Spanish fleet opportunistically captured New Providence for Spain in 1782, just as the Revolutionary War was winding down. With the Spanish in formal control of Nassau at the end of 1783, a pro-British group of 200 mercenaries and British Loyalists sailed into Nassau Harbour led by Andrew Deveaux, a Loyalist American colonel. Deveaux had his men sail to and from their landing vessels repeatedly, inducing a Spanish retreat under the illusion of an onslaught by so many troops. When the Treaty of Versailles formalized the end of the American Revolutionary War, England was granted sole possession of the Bahamas.

The Loyalists and Emancipation

Many American colonists – mostly merchants from New England or planters from the Old South – remained loyal to England during the Revolutionary War and fled the newly independent country for Canada, England or the Bahamas. Between 1783 and 1785, more than 8000 **Loyalists** and their slaves arrived in the islands, tripling the colony's population. While some of the Loyalists soon moved on to more southerly English colonies like Barbados, others stayed, purchased land and set up plantations devoted to cotton and worked with slaves. George III, seizing an opportunity to oversee a more closely-knit colonial government, guaranteed Loyalist settlers free land and sent out an autocratic Scottish earl named **Lord Dunmore** to be the new governor. Corrupt and dissolute, Dunmore had been a former governor of New York and was widely despised in America for having destroyed the port of Norfolk before fleeing George Washington's troops. In the Bahamas, he spent lavishly on himself, building two huge forts, Fincastle and Charlotte, and came close to bankrupting the colony by doing so. Ultimately replaced in 1796, Dunmore left behind an economy that was only marginally successful as well as a political and cultural decadence based on slaveholding, oligarchy, and corruption in public works.

At the beginning of the 1800s, the Bahamian population hovered around 12,000, 75 percent of whom were **slaves**. The rest were whites and black freemen, who themselves sometimes owned slaves. Although some Loyalists were devoted to plantation-style agriculture, the islands could never adequately supported such a system, and the industry quickly went downhill, disappearing entirely shortly after 1800. As no large sugar culture emerged on the islands as elsewhere in Caribbean, many blacks were freed to become farmers, mariners, fishermen, labourers and the like, and slavery never flourished on the islands. Freed slaves were often joined by thousands of slaves liberated from slave ships on the high seas by the Royal Navy, leading to the establishment of towns like Adelaide and Carmichael on New Providence.

The Loyalist era extended until 1834, when the British parliament abolished slavery in the colonies and granted limited freedom to ex-slaves. While parliament hoped a period of adjustment would precede **Emancipation** and that slaves would work as apprentices to their former masters for wages, most slaves owners were simply too poor to uphold the system. Bahamian blacks almost immediately became free men, though some remained as indentured servants and domestics, and those Loyalists opposed to abolition soon fled the islands. The resultant social fabric consisted of a large majority of blacks living subsistence lives, a few wealthy white landowners controlling the General Assembly and commerce in general and an economy surviving on barter and very little trade. A few immigrant Greeks, Jews, Syrians and Chinese joined their fellow islanders in looking for ways to make a living, though they likewise faced difficulties.

In fact, for much of the nineteenth century, the entire West Indies was mired in poverty and disillusionment. In the Bahamas, wreckers still worked their salvage boats, spongers still hunted for dwindling supplies of sponges around Andros and other Out Islands, and some enterprising farmers grew citrus and pineapple on Eleuthera and the Exumas. But when huge American conglomerate interests like Dole persuaded the US Congress to slap high tariffs on fruit imports, the Bahamian fruit industry collapsed. And as the British mapped the islands and erected lighthouses, wrecking as a cash cow dwindled as well.

The American Civil War

The **American Civil War** (1861–65) had an immense impact on the struggling Bahamian economy. When, at the outset of the war, Abraham Lincoln imposed a blockade along the Atlantic that decimated Southern shipping, it drastically curtailed the vital export of cotton from Charleston and Wilmington to Britain. Almost overnight, the Bahamas – and Nassau in particular – became an important cog in the Confederacy's survival, as the South sought to circumvent the blockade by rerouting shipping through the Bahamas. Bahamians of all stripes and sizes became involved in **blockade running**, an adventurous industry that would become the lifeblood of the Bahamas during several episodes in its later history. Shipbuilding received a boost as well, with Bahamian smugglers building specially outfitted vessels designed to outrun Northern gunboats. In return, Bahamians smuggled manufactured goods to the Confederacy, engaging in a lucrative two-way trade.

Between 1859 and 1866, Nassau boomed, the *Royal Victoria Hotel* was built on Bay Street, and the bars, cafés and nightclubs along Bay were jammed with Southerners, Bahamian blockade runners, and English entrepreneurs. But with the end of the war, the Bahamian economy slipped into reverse, and depression conditions returned.

Prohibition and the World Wars

While the end of the Civil War halted Nassau's brief reign as a smuggler's paradise, it brought budding prosperity to the United States, helping create a middle class that had enough disposable income to travel. By the turn of the century, American transportation magnate Henry Flagler had almost single-handedly created Florida as a tourist destination, building roads, railroads and hotels, luring thousands to Florida's warm winter climate. Nassau was beginning to get a spill-over of tourists, which only increased when Flagler inaugurated steamship service connecting Miami with Nassau.

World War I saw some Bahamians entering the British army and serving on the Western Front, and patriotic Bahamians from all walks of life contributed funds to the war effort. Save for supplying fruits, vegetables, medical supplies and clothing, the tiny Bahamian economy, had little impact on the war effort; sadly, the reverse was not true. The devastation of English export ability further depressed an already struggling Bahamian economy, and by the war's end the Bahamas was again in decline, a steady downward trend that was only halted by the passage of the 1920 Volstead Act by the US Congress. This law made the production and sale of alcoholic beverages illegal on the territory of the United States, ushering in the era of **Prohibition**.

Rum-running days

Almost immediately Bahamian smugglers entered the illegal alcohol trade. With their skills at boat building and navigation, and the close proximity to the Miami haunts of American gangsters, Nassau's rum-runners sped across the Gulf Stream to be met by larger boats accepting cargoes of liquor. Between 1920 and 1933, when Prohibition was finally repealed in the United States, Nassau boomed again, with construction projects fuelling a labour shortage, hotels jammed with tourists and gangsters, and many of the Out Islands profiting from shipbuilding and smuggling alike. Riding a crest of profits from whiskey, rum, beer and gin, the British parliament was not eager to clamp down on the trade. For thirteen years, Bahamians got to ride the high end of their boom-and-bust cycle – until the end of Prohibition and the beginning of the Great Depression.

It was an expansive Canadian multi-millionaire who set the course for the Bahamas to escape the Depression. **Sir Harry Oakes**, who made his fortune from mining, came to New Providence in the 1930s looking for a place to invest his money without enduring high Canadian and British taxes. He bought huge chunks of New Providence and Out Islands land, built Oakes Airfield on New Providence, and initiated a round of construction that provided jobs when none were to be found. Though mysteriously murdered in his palatial home outside Nassau in 1943, Oakes managed to plant a fertile seed, being one of the first to envision the Bahamas as a tax haven and winter getaway for wealthy expats.

World War II

What truly helped shock the Bahamas out of its Depression doldrums, though, was the beginning of **World War II**. The conflict brought the Allies to the Bahamas in force, and in the early 1940s five US/UK naval bases were established on the Out Islands, from where ships swept the South Atlantic on anti-submarine duty. Two new airports were built as well, one of which was later to become Nassau's International Airport.

At the outbreak of war, the British government sent out the **Duke of Windsor**, the former Edward VII who had abdicated his throne to marry an American divorcee, to become Royal Governor. While he arrived with a tarnished image, including accusations that he was soft on Fascism, his appeal lay in his celebrity. The duke soon gained a popular following for his work in establishing the Out Island Economic Committee, Windsor Camp at Clifton on New Providence (a camp for kids) and an infant welfare clinic on Blue Hill Road in Nassau. Even so, his most vocal critics saw the duke as yet another prop for the white oligarchy – basicallly the merchants, lawyers, landowners and politicians commonly known as the "Bay Street Boys" – that controlled the General Assembly and business in Nassau since virtually 1729.

At the same time, a formal apartheid existed in public facilities in the Bahamas, and black labourers were paid lower wages than their white counterparts. Eventually, on June 1, 1942, thousands of labourers working on an airport construction project met in Nassau's Over-the-Hill in Nassau and marched down the Burma Road to Bay Street in protest at their poor treatment. The march evolved into a riot, and five people were killed by a company of Cameron Highlander troops and police. With hundreds of injured workers on their hands, the builders granted the labourers a pay rise. Afterwards, their consciousness raised, it was unlikely that black Bahamians were going to return to the days of apartheid without a fight.

Tourism and independence

Save for a small spurt in the early 1900s when wealthy Americans flocked to Henry Flagler's *New Hotel Colonial*, **tourism** in the Bahamas remained the preserve of a few fishermen and wealthy businessmen. All that, though, began to change around 1960 with the advent of the Cuban Revolution and the activities of Sir Stafford Sands.

Before Fulgencio Batista's corrupt dictatorship was replaced by Fidel Castro's Communist regime in 1959, Americans from the East Coast considered Cuba a gambling, swimming and nightclub mecca. **Sir Stafford Sands**, a prominent Nassau businessman and landowner, saw the closing of Cuba as a prime opportunity for the Bahamas and organized the Bahamas Development Board, composed of prominent citizens. Sands's goal was to see the total of 32,000 visitors of 1960 raised to one million by 1970. Aided by government laws modelled on those of Switzerland, Sands oversaw the development of European-style banking secrecy, favourable tax laws and lucrative government subsidy for private business. Soon, capital from highly taxed English sources flowed into Nassau banks, providing a fund from which hotels, roads, airports and infrastructure of all kinds could be financed. The US air base on New Providence was expanded and opened as the **Nassau International Airport**, Prince George Wharf was dredged to allow cruise ships and high-end resorts opened for business. Finally, Hog Island was transformed into Paradise Island, and gambling as an attraction began to take hold. Elsewhere, on Grand Bahama, the new city of Freeport sprang up on land that had been palmetto scrub, and resorts began to appear on a lesser scale on the Out Islands.

The battle for power

Not all, though, revolved around sun and fun during the middle half of the of the twentieth century. It was inevitable that the anti-colonial struggles of Africa and Asia, as well as the Civil Rights movement in the US, would have a profound effect on racial politics in the Bahamas, and by the early 1950s a small black middle class had developed, fuelling calls for representative government and a more even distribution of economic profits. In 1953, a political organizer from Andros named **Lynden Pindling** formed the Progressive Liberal Party (PLP) on a platform of social, economic and political equality leading to independence. The Bay Street Boys formed the United Bahamian Party (UBP), and a country that had seen no political parties in its history all at once had a fight on its hands.

Through the 1950s and early 1960s, the PLP and UBP jockeyed for power and influence. In 1963, a huge national strike brought matters to a head in the British parliament, which drew up a new constitution for the Bahamas with the aim of creating a more representative form of government. When the new **1964 Constitution** was adopted, it replaced the old colonial-style government with a two-chamber House of Assembly elected by Bahamians themselves and headed by a prime minister whose cabinet members would be drawn from the party with the most votes. In national elections in 1964, the leader of the UBP, Roland Symonette, won by a narrow majority. However, discontent was rampant and the election was seen as illegitimate because of restrictive voting laws (only landowners could vote) that diluted black power. Pindling and his PLP adopted a strategy of non-co-operation, resulting in a new election in 1967, which Pindling won.

Independence at last

By 1969, further changes to the Bahamian constitution gave the country control over most of the economy. Now, only defence, foreign policy and internal security were vested in the British parliament. The drive for independence was not without its detractors, however. Joining with the UBP, a number of minority parties formed a new Free National Movement (FNM), which opposed complete independence from Britain. On the Abacos and in Eleuthera, home to the original Loyalists, a wave of anti-independence sentiment developed which led to a proto-secessionist movement. Despite such pressures, the independence movement could not be stopped. At elections held in September of 1972, Pindling's party won overwhelmingly. As a result, on July 10, 1973, Bahamas was granted **independence**. At midnight, the Union Jack was lowered over Fort Charlotte in Nassau, and the Bahamian flag with a black triangle and stripes of aquamarine and gold was raised. Thousands celebrated joyfully in the streets.

Modern-day Bahamas

The **Pindling years** were a mixed bag. At first, there was a great deal of enthusiasm, yet with the Oil Embargo and the high inflation of the late 1970s, too much foreign capital was flowing into the Bahamas for purely speculative purposes. Land was being purchased for resale instead of development, and Pindling's efforts to redress abusive labour practices led to a backlash from developers who refused to negotiate government deals. In addition, the banking system and construction industry was awash in foreign cash, and many government officials succumbed to the lures of bribe-taking and kickbacks.

As the new nation slid into recession, **drug smuggling** from Colombia blossomed, with the Bahamas becoming a major stopover for shipments to Miami. With its many hiding spots, the Bahamas had always been a magnet for outlaws, and the drug trade was no different. Operating out of hidden airstrips, or with heavily laden seaplanes, Bahamians, even those in government, became ensnared in the lure of the drug business. It got so bad that Colombian drug lords managed to bribe the government at its highest levels. The US Drug Enforcement Administration led a massive crackdown in the mid-1980s, by which time the stench of rotting political flesh was pervasive in the islands.

Pindling's time came to an end on August 19, 1992, when the Free National Movement led by **Hubert Ingraham** swept into power by winning 31 of 49 Assembly seats. The new government was conservative, pro-business and anti-corruption, and among its first acts was to sell off inefficient government-run properties and adopt a programme of fiscal restraint. On March 14, 1997, the FNM was returned to power with an increased majority, winning 35 of 40 seats in the Assembly.

Ingraham's conservative FNM government has adopted a business-friendly National Investment Policy, which brings together attractive elements of the banking laws, tax advantages and fiscal restraint, all designed to reduce the national debt, which was $1.1 billion by the end of the Pindling years. By 1996, the debt had been reduced to $358 million, inflation was down to 0.5 percent, and unemployment had been reduced to ten percent.

The current outlook

With its proximity and easy access to North America, tourism is still the major industry in the Bahamas, and employs almost half of the islands' workforce. Many of the Out Islands economies are largely subsistence level, based on fishing and farming, and much of the their youth flocks to New Providence and Grand Bahama to work at the resorts and hotels. Occasionally, this dependence on foreign disposal income has placed the Bahamas in a precarious position – particularly in the immediate aftermath of the September 11 attacks, when worldwide tourism ebbed – yet the islands still appear to be in better economic shape than most of their Caribbean neighbours.

Society and culture

The Bahamas are a somewhat strange amalgamation of Caribbean island life, American influence, Anglo leanings and African heritage. It hasn't necessarily served to make for the most distinctive culture, though a few arts do flourish, among them music. More interesting probably are the people themselves: their ethnic heritage, religious rituals and the like.

People and customs

Almost 85 percent of Bahamians are the descendants of **slaves** imported to the New World from West Africa, often via mainland North America. Some of the slaves moved here through the United States came along with their owners, typically Loyalists who ran plantations in the South and fled during the American Revolution. Similarly, white Bahamians often trace their ancestry back to these **Loyalist migrations**, or even further back to the Eleutheran Adventurers who fled England or Bermuda on account of religious persecution.

The largest minority in the Bahamas are **Haitians** – some twelve percent of the population – many having left Haiti to escape poverty and political repression. Chinese, Hispanics, Greeks and Jews constitute about three percent of the population, and each group tends to remain separate from the others and from Bahamians in general.

Despite the fact that there is somewhat of a divide between black and white here, and more narrowly defined ethnicities too, Bahamians are a largely tolerant people, and have seen quite a bit of racial intermingling over the years. The slang term "Conchy Joe" is often applied to any person whose family has been in the Bahamas for a very long time, and whose resultant racial profile is mixed.

Daily life and rituals

Above all, Bahamian society is generally **laid-back**, which means that enjoying life is more important than any formalities. Punctuality, for example, is not a primary value: events sometimes seem delayed for no real reason; concerts, theatre openings, or mailboat sailings are assigned approximate times only; cricket games in Nassau, scheduled to begin at 1pm on Sunday, often get started an hour later, after the teams exchange pleasantries. That doesn't necessarily translate into a persistent lack of efficiency – buses and taxis in the main cities, for instance, can be quite well run – but you may have to exercise a good deal of patience while on the islands, or getting from one island to another.

On the Out Islands, where most people pursue rural lives on a diurnal or seasonal schedule, rising with the sun, retiring at dark, life proceeds in a fairly consistent manner. Rural Bahamians tend to live on roads without addresses, in houses haphazardly built, and disdain town living in general. They fish, they tend a small field, gather some fruits, pay attention to their families, have fun on Saturday night and go to church on Sunday.

Religion

The overwhelming majority of Bahamians are **Christian**, many of them Baptists or Methodists, though a growing number have adhered to evangelical sects which have proselytized heavily in recent years. The Anglican church, because of its British origin, holds sway with the majority of white Bahamians. Going to church on Sunday is extremely important, quite clearly indicated by the profusion of churches throughout the islands: Roman Catholic cathedrals, stone Anglican churches, small single-room buildings thrown up by a congregation using clapboard. Ministers, always in short supply, often island-hop to serve their flocks, and services take on a form not unlike Southern Baptist proceedings, with music and "testimony" services in which members of the congregation loudly confess their sins. As well, religious processions are common, and the major Christian holidays like Christmas and Easter, are celebrated with fervour.

Despite the widespread acceptance of Christianity in the islands, older **folk superstitions**, part of the African cultural heritage, have a place in Bahamian life. Many superstitions centre on supernatural spirits who put evil spells on people. Bahamians may whisper secret incantations to ward off these evil spells, or may sprinkle guinea grain around a home to keep away illness or death. Love potions derived from *santeria* practices can be found in some markets, particularly cuckoo soup, a dark broth thought to have tremendous power. More pernicious forms of superstition survive as **Obeah**, a variant of Voodoo, which sees some practitioners advertising spiritual powers or psychic ability for the purpose of casting spells or curses. Some Bahamians practise both Christianity and Obeah, particularly those who believe in white magic and keep a dream book in the belief that good spirits which come in dreams will help them be happy, successful and rich.

Language

Although the official language of the Bahamas is **English**, most Bahamians on the street speak a combination of King's English and a dialect that draws heavily on African logisms, Caribbean slang, and Creole. The present tense is often used, even when indicating that something happened in the past, plurals are often dropped and repetition is used for emphasis. Bahamian slang uses cockney English, American forms, and made-up words to form a unique, and often obscure but spirited form of talk. Most people are addicted to proverbs, and can speak quite animatedly when excited.

Words are spoken in a type of patois not dissimilar from the type associated with Jamaican speakers. For example, "thought" becomes "tot", and "child" becomes "chile", and the pronounced words are spoken with a definite island lilt.

Music

Bahamians share a West African oral tradition, as well as a cultural heritage of myth and folktale, which has easily translated into a strong **musical tradition**. The underpinning of all West African oral tradition is the chant, which appears in African music as an all-encompassing storytelling dynamic usually accomplished by a main singer backed by a chorus that provides a dynamic accompaniment. In the Bahamas, this chanting aesthetic, filtered through the slave experience and Caribbean influences from other islands, reappears as rigging or chatting, both of which are forms of musical improvisation. Though neither of the major Bahamian musical expressions has had the worldwide influence of, say, soca or Cuban *son*, each gives a spirited sense of the people. For an introduction to island music, check out either Folkways Records compilation *The Bahamas: Islands of Song*, with its shanty tunes and local renditions of popular songs, or *The Real Bahamas*, notable especially for the wondrous guitar sounds of **Joseph Spence**.

Goombay and Junkanoo

Almost everybody in the Bahamas gets involved with the exuberant New Year's festival called **Junkanoo**, whose roots lie in an improvised slave music called **goombay**. Using all manner of instruments for its various flourishes, goombay features a regular, unsyncopated beat that forms the heart of the fast-paced sustained melodies, often hypnotic in their regularity. At the heart of the beat is the **goatskin drum**, which takes the place of the huge African drums used to convey messages across the vast forests of West Africa, and was developed by slaves as a replacement in the New World. Other instruments contributing to the unique sound include bongos, conch-shell horns, maracas, homemade rattles of all types, click sticks, flutes, bugles, whistles and cowbells, all of which were available or to hand wherever slaves gathered.

Rig and chat, rake 'n' scrape

Rigging and **chatting** are part of the gospel tradition in Bahamian churches, a form of call-and-answer singing that somewhat mirrors what you might find in a Southern Baptist church in the US. Homemade instruments, impromptu lyrics and storytelling, are the foundation of another kind of music called **rake 'n' scrape**, which is popular in nightclubs and on street corners. Starting with a rhythm section composed of seed-pod shakers, musical saws, and other household implements, then laying on instruments like accordions and cheap guitars, rake 'n' scrape has emerged as an authentic popular Bahamian musical form. On almost every Out Island, bands perform the music in small clubs, at regattas and festivals, or simply at get-togethers.

As more and more Bahamians listen to radio or buy CDs, popular imported forms of music like reggae from Jamaica, soca from the southern Caribbean, American rhythm and blues, hip-hop, and rap are heard, and integrated into the musical customs, though no striking new hybrids have arisen.

Flora and fauna

By any standard Bahamian forests are spare. Only species adapted to the stresses of salt soils, wind, and harsh sunlight can survive. Today, 1371 species, varieties and hybrids of **trees** and **flowering plants** grow in the Bahamas, a small number by subtropical standards. Much of the original hardwood forests of mahogany, strangler fig, lignum vitae, and gumbo limbo were felled to clear land and build ships, and even the secondary pine forests on the larger islands have been logged heavily. Salt-tolerant species like the red, black and white mangrove still survive, but their range is diminishing due to development and pollution.

The Bahamas have only thirteen native land mammals, most being bats. But for the elusive hutia, a small rodent-like creature that was hunted nearly to extinction over the years, the rest of the land mammals are semi-domesticated sorts of animals like pigs and donkeys or scavengers like racoons. The islands host a number of reptile species like iguanas and snakes, and there are many land crabs crawling about; **birdlife** is also abundant. It is in the sea, however, that the numbers of species explode. **Marine life** here consists of thousands of types of sea mammals, echinoderms, crustaceans, reef fish, pelagic fish, algae and more, all occupying unique ecological niches in order to survive through adaptation.

Terrestrial habitats

The original **forests** (in Bahamian lingo, the "coppice") that greeted the Conquistadores were magnificent stands of mahogany, horseflesh, mastic, cedar, and poisonwood, among many others. In the remotest areas of islands like Little Inagua, some vestiges of this can still be seen. To better comprehend what you're encountering, it's useful to know a bit about the various categories of forest.

The blackland coppice

The **blackland coppice** makes up the interior of most Bahamian islands, save for the most southerly ones. In this coppice, the understorey is starved of light, making the ground below relatively sterile. Apart from the types listed above, both the gum elemi with its reddish-brown bark and aromatic resins once used as a coagulant for wounds, and the short-leaf fig, which grows to heights of 50ft and more, dominate. Nearly as abundant is the strangler fig, whose wind-borne seeds lodge in the branches of other trees and begin life as an epiphyte, sending roots down to the earth below. Also part of the canopy is the marvellous Bahama **strongbark**, whose brilliant-white flowers in late summer attract swarms of fast-flying ringlet butterflies – in fact, it's sometimes called the butterfly tree. Included in the overstorey of the blackland coppice are easily recognizable trees like the common **poisonwood**, a member of the sumac family along with poison ivy, mango, cashew and pistachios, and the unmistakeable silk cotton tree, remarkable for its flying-buttress-style flanking roots.

The understorey of the blackland coppice contains a number of interesting plant species. Most beautiful is the silvery **satinleaf**, which quakes like aspen in a strong breeze, the leaves undercoated with a soft brown down, the tops a dark, shiny silver. Particularly after abundant rain, or in the spring, the understorey can come alive with pigeon plums, a relative of the sea grape, the blolly, which produces a fleshy red fruit, and the willow bustic, another plant that produces a fruit attractive to birds.

With its humidity and stillness, the coppice provides ideal conditions for **orchids** and **bromeliads**, which cling to the barks of trees. These epiphytes derive their nourishment from wind blown dust and debris, and unlike the strangler fig remain airborne all their lives. Orchids are represented worldwide by more than 20,000 species, and perhaps 800 are known on the Bahamas, ranging from the genus *Epidendrum* with nine species in the northern Bahamas, to the tiny yellow *E. inaguensis*, with its linear leaves. Three native species of vanilla are climbing orchids found in central and southern portions of the islands. Bromeliads are best represented by wild pineapple, Spanish moss and wild pines. Most are epiphytic, and all resemble pineapple in some way; the wild pines, for example, have a rosette of long, green leaves.

Hikers in the blackland coppice should be alert for the signs of the **crab spider**, which spins a massive web that often hangs across trails between the trunks of large trees. A much larger spider, the orange and black Santa Claus spider, also builds a radially symmetrical web in the arching vaults higher up. During the dry summer months green **anolis lizards** can be seen skittering around the dry leaves on the ground, while cicadas chorus wildly and the air fills with mosquitoes, flying beetles and sandflies.

Along with the chattering of cicadas and the buzzing of insects, the frequent silence might be shattered by the call of the **smooth-billed anis**, an aggressive blackbird with a broad high-crowned bill with which it snares insects and lizards. Because they are intensely social birds, they can easily be spotted in flocks of twenty or more where one bird stands sentinel while others feed. The anis even builds its nests socially, constructing huge communal nests in the topmost folds of the canopy where females in a troop lay their eggs in clutches. Less common in the coppice is the **great lizard cuckoo**, a large flightless bird which can be found on Andros, New Providence, and Eleuthera. Preying on lizards, frogs, and large insects, the lizard cuckoo can sometimes be approached to within touching distance as it perches in low-hanging branches. Every dense blackland coppice has a fair abundance of **pigeons**, the most elusive of which is the Key West quail dove, a very lovely small bird with green and purple colouring which allows it to forage almost unseen in the leaves of the floor.

Where some sun does reach the forest floor, or in the low branches of the understorey, one can sometimes see the Bahamian **fowl snake**, a true member of the boa constrictor family. The fowl snake has speciated into many varieties and subspecies, distributed on all the islands save for Grand Bahama and San Salvador. A few grandaddies that survive to old age can reach lengths of up to 6ft.

The whiteland coppice

On lower terrains and usually nearer to coasts, with soils composed of more rock and lime than in the blackland coppice, the somewhat impoverished forests are known as **whiteland coppice**, and are relatively more common in southern islands than in northern ones.

While here and there large shading trees like the mahogany, sea grape, and manchineel do grow, most of the whiteland coppice can best be classified as woody **shrubland**, home to animals like goats and pigs. Hikers in the white-land coppice will find themselves wandering about in stands of **Braziletto**, which resembles the palmetto of Florida, as well as growths of several species of acacias, small trees or large shrubs with large, bipinnate leaves. Some members of the whiteland coppice come armed with spines like the aptly named **haulback**, whose spines are shaped like a cat's claw. Also common to the whiteland coppice is the **common tea**, widely used in the West Indies as an antidote to fish poisoning.

The depredations of goats, the vagaries of rainfall, salty winds, and violent hurricanes all make life difficult in the whiteland coppice. Perhaps no plant is better suited to this terrain than the **cactus**, of which there are dozens of species and subspecies in the Bahamas, some of which produce incredibly beautiful flowers. The largest is the dildo cactus, a columnar candelabra-branched variety that can grow over 20ft in height and incorporates huge amounts of calcium carbonate in its tissues. Cut into one and it seems dry as dust. Another cactus is the Turk's Cap, a non-branching columnar type, which produces a cap of red flowers, a must-see for visitors to the southern islands. The most spectacular cactus, though, is undoubtedly the queen-of-the-night, which grows like a vine on trees and rock walls; it develops a huge bud which soon bursts into an even larger white flower that smells of vanilla and attracts swarms of sphinx moths. As well huge **bat moths** can be seen in the whiteland coppice clinging to the trunks of the acacia or other larger trees. These massive dark-brown moths have geometrical patterns on their wings and tend to favour the balsam tree for their habitats.

Four species of **crab** inhabit the Bahamas, and the density of their populations can be monumental. Some biologists estimate that upwards of 7500 white crabs utilize every acre of whiteland habitat. The species of Bahamian land crab include the commonly eaten **giant white crab**, which can be as much as 2ft from claw to claw in breadth, and the smaller, perhaps tastier, **black crab**. It is hard to tell these species apart when immature because both are blackish-blue; when mature, however, white crabs are larger and turn a dirty yellowish colour. The **hermit crab** has no shell of its own, but adopts places to live, like the abandoned shells of marine animals. Its muscular blue claw is used to open fruits and seeds, as well as for defence.

The windward shore

The **windward shore** comprises a few different ecological zones, moving from the white-, rose- or pink-coloured sand back to an algae-filled quagmire, home to many shrimp, crab and shore flies, which gives way to the dunes, a harder place still for wildlife to flourish.

Perhaps the most noticeable animal around the shore is **birds**, exemplified by the graceful white-tailed tropic bird which flies in pairs or floats on the sea parallel to the shore searching for squid and fish. The tropic bird is startlingly white, with black patches over its eyes, and long central tail feathers. Almost as common are the Bahamian swallows, which dart and course looking for insects.

Harder to spot, inhabiting as it does more lonely coastal areas of the windward shore, is the impressive **fish hawk**, more commonly known as osprey. Fish hawks have long sleek bodies and distinctive black bands behind their eyes, and in colonies build massive nests on isolated cliffs which are often inhabited by generation after generation of birds for forty years or more. The dunes are **high-stress zones** for plants and animals. Without fresh water, subject to harsh sunlight, and driven by winds, only hardy species survive in this niche. Both the sea grape and the cocoplum are rambling shrubs that help to anchor dunes against the wind. The sea grape is a vine, and its purple fruit is made into tarts, jellies and jams by many Bahamians. The large white fruits of the cocoplum are too sour to be edible for humans, but birds and iguanas love them. Perhaps the earliest colonizer of the dune environment is the sea oat, which produces a panicle full of seed, and the beautiful white lily, beloved by beachcombers because of its white blossom that erupts into bloom after any rain. White lilies grow so thickly that some dunes are completely covered in them. Few animals are able to survive for long in the dune zone, although the wing nighthawk, a member of the swift family that feeds on shore insects, lays its eggs in the sand.

Shade is hard to come by on the windward shore. The **geiger** tree graces some Bahamian beaches, as does the common **manchineel**, which has poisonous green fruit and a toxic latex-like sap. The geiger is recognizable by its bushy orange flowers on which numerous nectar-sipping birds perch. Many Bahamian beaches have been planted with stands of Australian **casuarina**, a tall wind-resistant tree with thin needle-like leaves. It does produce some shade, but grows sometimes at the expense of native species, and also drops its needles onto the beaches, ruining the smooth sand texture underfoot.

Just behind the dune zone is the **palm niche**. Here, shimmering silver palms, buccaneer palms, and the more utilitarian **thatch palm**, all stand; the last of these has been put to use for generations, its leaves woven into baskets, rope, shoes, hats, mats, and thatched roofs. Sheltered well enough from wind and storm, the thatch palm can grow to over 40ft in height.

Among all the clutter of palms, downed palm fronds, grasses and dunes, are smaller shrubs like the love-vine and passionflower, where many types of butterfly roam, picking off loads of nectar. Zebra butterflies with their striped black wings often feed on the berries of the guana berry plant, which has clusters of bright red and white flowers, or the pale pink flowers of the common ernoda. One of the great pleasures of the dunes, especially early in the morning or at dusk, or after rain, is to wander under the palms spotting butterflies and blooming shrubs, and even the tiny **worm snake**, its two varieties only a few inches long.

Unfortunately for humans, the windward shore is home to the ubiquitous **sandfly**, an insect no larger than a grain of pepper but which can produce a healthy welt on the skin. There are two species of sandfly: the so-called ferocious sandfly is active during evening and night, while the Becquaert's sandfly operates from dawn to dusk. Only the female sandfly bites, using blood as nourishment to manufacture huge batches of eggs. The males, meek and mild, seldom stray far from their hatching sites, and spend their time sipping nectar from flowers. Researchers have concluded that female sandflies can produce 3000 bites per hour on unprotected flesh. Fortunately for beachgoers, wind provides considerable relief from sandfly activity, and it's a rare day indeed when relief doesn't come in some form.

Tidal pools, cliffsides, and rockbound coasts are less hospitable to life than most other niches on the windward shore. Called the **ironshore**, this rocky saline zone is almost lunar in appearance, with a few ground-hugging shrubs dotting the landscape.

The Carribean pine

The pine forests of the Bahamas are found on only four islands, Grand Bahama, Andros, Abaco and New Providence. The lovely **Caribbean pine**

(*Pinus caribaea*) is a light-demanding relative of Florida's slash pine, and like its Florida cousin thrives on a system of fire and regeneration. Its adaptation to fire includes an ability to release seeds from cones almost immediately after a fire, the seeds colonizing ashy soils in a matter of days, as well as a fire-retardant resiny sap that allows most pines to survive all but the hottest blazes. As in Florida, bush fires in the forest are not uncommon during the dry season or in droughts, but almost immediately after a fire the forest floor is covered with new pine seedlings, orchids and fresh grasses.

Despite its great height, the Caribbean pine allows enough light to the forest floor for a vigorous understorey to develop, which can include beautiful flowering shrubs like the **wild guava**, with its prominently veined leaves, and **five finger**, which produces leaves with five fingers and flowers that range in colour from white to red to purple.. Birdwatchers come from all over the world to catch a glimpse of the rare **Kirkland warbler**, attracted to the flowering plants, or the **Bahamian parrot**, a colourful remnant species found on the south of Abaco; of the many other bird species, note the giant **turkey vulture**, which can often be seen wheeling in the sky above the massive forests of Andros or the Abacos. The understorey is also home to many species of **butterfly** such as the one-inch-long atala hairstreak, known to occur on Grand Bahama, Abaco and New Providence. You can recognize it by its metallic blue colour, brown wings, and an orange spot on the bottom of its thorax.

Meandering through the understorey of a typical Bahamian pine forest provides a chance to observe **sago palms**, which are not palms at all, but descendants of non-flowering cycads, prehistoric plants dating to the Jurassic Age, the time of the dinosaurs. The caterpillar of the atala hairstreak butterfly feeds on sagos, as do large echo moths.

Ocean habitats

A lot of divers and snorkellers come to Bahamian resorts to witness the panorama of colourful tropical fish, sharks and rays that inhabit deeper waters, going so far as to wall-dive to depths of 100ft and more. Many visitors overlook the biological drama of the shallow beds of turtle and manatee grasses, which may be only a fifty-foot swim away from the door of their resorts. Spending an afternoon floating in a shallow bed of turtle grass, with its compliment of tiny lettuce coral, limestone rock and sand bottom, can reward a patient observer with many astounding discoveries.

Turtle grass

Turtle grass is a habitat harbouring many species that have adapted by mimicking the appearance of sea grass itself. Many types of sea horses can be seen floating in the grass, tail down, while pipefish also mimic the look of a piece of grass. Large numbers of shrimp, small crabs, and juvenile cowfish also tend to mimic the colours around them. Equally prevalent are echinoderms like starfish, sand dollars, crinoids, and sea cucumbers. On the beds of sea grass often lurk urchins and sea potatoes, both of which are oval in shape and covered by spines.

The most famous denizens of the shallow grass beds are **sea turtles** and **sponges**. Once mainstays of the Bahamian economy, turtles have been hunted with wild abandon and their numbers are vastly reduced from the multitudinous herds that greeted Columbus. The common green turtle haunts the shallow waters of the grass savannas, feeding on grass, while the larger loggerhead and hawksbill inhabit deep-sea and reef environments respectively, chomping into conchs and other prey with their huge beaks.

Unlike green turtles, sponges are ubiquitous in Bahamian water. Coming in many sizes and shapes, sponges are no more than a gelatinous mass with a soft, crunchy skeleton that filters seawater for tiny organisms on which it feeds. They can be coloured anywhere from pure white to a bright hallucinatory red.

Creeks and mangroves

Almost every Bahamian island has its domain of **creek** and **mangrove** country, mostly on the leeward side, away from the windswept beaches and dunes. Particularly representative of this bio-regime are the western flats of Andros and the northern Abacos, where shallow basins, circular lagoons, wide creeks and mangrove swamps exist in an environment of mud flats and algal plains.

There are no freshwater rivers or creeks in the Bahamas. Instead, thousands of saline tidal creeks drain rainwater from interiors, while other smaller creeks simply rise and fall with the tide. Almost all tidal basins are fringed with either red, white, or black mangroves which, while biologically separate, serve to anchor limey soils while at the same time providing a phenomenally productive habitat for wildlife. Only the red mangrove is a true mangrove, dropping roots into salty water, the only flowering plant that can perform this feat. The mangrove forest not only provides shelter and shade for hundreds of juvenile fish, crustaceans and shark, but provides food in the form of decaying plant matter, fungi and algae.

To penetrate this habitat, you'll often need a kayak or shallow-bottom boat, and the ability to withstand swarms of mosquitoes. Inhabitants include encrusting sponges, mangrove crabs, shells and tunicates, as well as a wide variety of crustaceans. Even larger predators like barracuda and snapper prowl the shallow creek beds and the mangrove fringes. In particular, the lemon shark uses the shallow red mangrove habitat to breed and calve its young, sending the juveniles off among the mangroves to feed on a variety of small bony fish, crustaceans, and other juvenile fish like snapper. Lemon sharks are the colour of dirty mustard, which distinguishes them from other mangrove juveniles like the nurse shark, typically metallic grey, though sometimes mottled as well.

At dusk, creeks and mangroves burst into action. Young lemons, nurses, bonnetheads and blacktips, all sharks, begin to feed in earnest. The juveniles of many common reef fish are present in the evenings as well, including schoolmaster snapper and the mangrove snapper which turns red as an adult, but which is bluish-green in the mangrove. For many, though, the mangrove and creek are the special realm of the bonefish, which spends its early years in the ocean as a tiny eel-like larval form feeding on plankton, but which heads to the shelter of the creeks as a juvenile where it grows to 2-4lb and eats anything that moves.

Large areas of the creek and mangrove regime are composed of **shallow muds**. While generally unpleasant because of heat and insects, the muds play host to an amazing variety of life, including the *Cassiopeia xamanchana*, or upside-down jellyfish, which swarms in the hundreds turning their tentacles down into the mud where they drift and sift for tiny organic debris. Puffer fish, with their boxy body and dark-banded sides, and green morays can be seen in the shallow muds beside black mangrove growths, and the creek bottoms are filled with variegated urchins, young crawfish and juvenile land crabs.

Lagoons and patch reefs

The **tidal foreshore** is much overlooked by visitors to the Bahamas, a place where the water is only a few feet deep in most spots, sometimes dropping off to four or five feet, where coastlines give way to inlets and lagoons, and small waves ripple shoreward. Where the water is a little deeper, sandy bottoms give way to patches of sea grass which provide some stability, and the bottom is littered with debris like rock, coral fragments, and what is known as patch reef.

Much of the foreshore is the domain of the calcareous alga, a tiny plant that looks like a cross between a lichen and a coral, and which secretes coloured calcium that often tints Bahamian beaches pink. Even the sands of shallow seawater are teeming with life – hundreds of varieties of tiny bivalve shelled animals, crustaceans, and various marine worms. In slightly deeper water, or in **shore lagoons**, the rose coral attaches itself to the bottom by a short pointed stalk, and the clubbed finger coral grows in a clump of stout branches that may form extensive beds. A snorkeller floating in 3ft of water on a clear day can see a host of life, including small filter-feeding shrimp, sea horses, urchins, sea cucumbers, sponges, gorgonians, bryozoans and even a bizarrely big-mouthed yellowheaded jawfish or two.

Perhaps the most fun of all in shallow water comes from spotting **starfish**. Probably the most prominent of all in the shallows is the *Oreatus reticulatus,* or orange starfish, a huge specimen which can be as much as 2ft across fully grown. With five stumpy arms radiating outwards, it propels itself slowly through this habitat by spines located on the underside of its body. Less obvious is the slender-limbed brittle star. Half a dozen kinds make their homes in shallow grasses or amid gorgonians, where it takes on a lavender colour and is characterized by long slender arms with a stripe of purple or red along each.

Above sandy bottoms inhabited by sand dollars, sand biscuits, and heart urchins, evening feeders like primitive bonefish, pompanos, pompano jacks and permits often cruise looking for marine invertebrates and small fish. The jacks and permits have narrow oval bodies and long dorsal and anal fins, with deeply forked tails. They travel in small groups close to shore, or in the warm-water inlets of lagoons. Once ubiquitous in shallow water, the famous Bahamian **conch** is almost synomymous with the islands. The most famous is the queen conch (*Strombus gigas*), a huge coral-coloured specimen with the famous curved shell out of which is made jewellery, tools and other ornaments. The overfishing and overexploitation of conch in the Bahamas has led to progressively smaller and smaller conch being taken for food, and a deterioration in the species in general.

In slightly deeper water begins the **patch reef**, composed of small areas of dome coral, elkhorn, star and brain coral, as well as patches of staghorn, which stand like stone trees. Wave action and occasional hurricanes reduce the patch reef to a flat-topped and highly buttressed form that has valleys of pillar coral, finger coral, and lettuce coral, which forms an underpinning for the patchy beds. Marine life here includes numerous species of fish, anemones, sponges, crustaceans and worms, such as the slightly poisonous bristleworm, a bright-orange worm that crawls over brain coral and can burn and sting human skin. The predators of the patch reef include bright schools of French and blue-striped grunts, blue tang, and snapper, all of which hunt invertebrates. Every patch reef in shallow water seems to have its resident barracuda, the long (up to 2ft), slender silver fish with a mouthful of sharp teeth and a forked tail. Genetically designed as a speedy killer, the barracuda isn't particularly dangerous to snorkellers or divers, though eating one can subject you to ciguatera poisoning.

Another visually upsetting member of the patch reef community is the **moray eel**, which ranges in type from the plain green moray, which is quite common and reaches a length of up to 6ft, to the smaller spotted moray and goldentail.

Not uncommon in the shallow water of the foreshore, or in the patch reef, is the **stingray**. Lying partly buried in sand, eagle rays have pointed wings, a spotted back and long graceful tail, while southern rays have grey bodies and rounded wings. The smaller yellow stingray is usually only about 1ft in diameter, with bright blue spots on yellow skin. Stingrays aren't particularly aggressive, but they do have a poisonous spike at the end of their tail, to be avoided at all costs. Feeding mostly at night, two cephalopods, the **octopus** and the **squid**, can sometimes be seen at dusk by intrepid snorkellers, or by night divers. The reef octopus is a feeder on molluscs and crustaceans, which it crushes with strong jaws and teeth, while its smaller cousin the Joubin's octopus feeds on bivalves.

As every snorkeller knows, the patch reef is teeming with **reef fish**, varieties that often show up in home aquariums. Starting with the damselfish, which comes in dozens of varieties from the ubiquitous sergeant major to the blue-bodied, yellow-tailed yellowtail damselfish, these quick swimmers are a constant source of delight.

The deep reef

Beyond a buttress zone of rock and rubble at about 15ft, the **deep reef** begins, in water some 20-35ft in depth. The framework of the buttress zone is the same as that of the patch reef, with stars and dome corals supported by pillars and valleys of smaller corals like the lace or lettuce coral. As the water deepens, everything becomes larger and more developed; systems grow in fantastic shapes, encrusting corals of huge dimensions, sponges, and swarms of reef fish, along with pelagic species.

At almost all depths, one kind of reef fish or another lives, from the common parrotfish, giant rainbow parrotfish, which can weigh up to 5lb and comes in many hues, all with green throats, and queen triggerfish, to wrasse, gobies, and angelfish. The deep reef is also the realm of the **spiny lobster**, a favourite with diners in Nassau.

Also roaming the deep reef are numerous kinds of grouper, jewfish (some of which can be well over 6ft in length and attain a weight of 135lb) and the lovely fairy basslet, with its distinctive blue head and yellow tail.

At a depth of 50ft, the cliff walls become jagged, corals begin to disappear, and you enter the world of the sponge. Even hunters like shark, jack, tuna and rays treat these depths with caution. At the heads of cliffs, one often sees huge grouper and jewfish, while cardinalfish, squirrelfish and barracuda hug the cliff wall. Still, many divers go over the edge in search of sharks, which can include hammerheads, tigers, white-tips, silkys, and the occasional great white. As light diminishes, ahermatypic corals have the upper hand, fragile branch-like corals that do not shelter algae. Sponges at depth come in many shapes and sizes, most huge, and colour at depth is important, with fragile glass sponges sometimes turning bright red and the Venus fly-basket a pale yellow or white. At the bottom, where no diver goes, is the abyssal plain, its muddy bottom inhabited only by deep-water invertebrates such as crustaceans, worms, and burrowing anemones.

Books

A substantial amount of printed matter, scientific as well as popular, is available to those interested in the Bahamas – though some of it can be hard to find. One of the best sources for books on the Bahamas is Macmillan Caribbean Publishers (Between Towns Road, Oxford, England OX4 3PP; ☎1865/405700, ⓦwww.macmillan-caribbean.com), who produce a solid list of books on history, natural studies, geography cooking and more, many of which are available at bookstores in both the UK and Nassau. They will send a catalogue on request, and you can order from them direct as well. Below, we've starred any books that are highly recommended.

History

Paul Albury *The Story of the Bahamas*. Written by a member of the old school of Bahamian society, this slightly dated book remains, despite its stilted style, a rather charming introduction to the history of the islands.

David Allen *The Cocaine Crisis*. Written during the 1980s when the Bahamas were undergoing a crisis of mismanagement, corruption and smuggling, this is one reporter's take on the cocaine problems that so staggered Bahamian society.

Wayne Alleyne *Caribbean Pirates*. With contemporary and historical illustrations in black and white, and a faithful rendering of the historical circumstances of the Spanish Main, this relatively short book on pirates is a good introduction to the tactics, politics and reality of pirating. Though mainly focusing on Hispaniola and Cuba, the book sheds light on the Bahamian connections as well.

P.J.H Barratt *Grand Bahama*. A comprehensive account of the history and economic development of Grand Bahama, written by a former town planner in charge of creating Freeport. Dense, with plenty of photos and maps.

Philip Cash *Sources of Bahamian History*. An up-to-date analysis of many social and political trends in Bahamian history that continue to have an impact. Not overly technical, the book hits all the high points and draws some fearless conclusions as well.

⭐ **Michael Craton and Gail Saunders** *Islanders in the Stream, A History of the Bahamian Peoples: Vol I* and *Vol II*. This definitive study of Bahamian history by two respected scholars comes in two volumes, the first running from aboriginal times to slavery, the second completing the story through the twentieth century. Both scholarly and accessible, it is the most detailed and exhaustive history of the Bahamas to date.

William F. Keegan *The People who Discovered Columbus: The Prehistory of the Bahamas*. This volume in a monograph series is both technical and expensive ($55), but it is one of the few complete paleo-historical analyses of the Lucayan Indians and their cultural and social practices.

Gail Saunders *Bahamian Loyalists and Their Slaves*. A slim volume written by one of the Bahamas' pre-eminent historians, detailing the sudden influx of American Loyalists and their African slaves in the dying days of the American Revolution. Enlivened by lots of interesting and evocative historical photographs and by descriptions of the lives and fortunes of particular Loyalist families and estates.

Everild Young *Eleuthera, the Island Called Freedom.* Although the style is rather florid in places, this island history contains some interesting glimpses of Bahamian and expatriate lifestyles on the Eleuthera in the 1950s and 1960s.

Culture and society

Harry G. Dahl *Literature in the Bahamas 1724-1992: The March Towards National Identity.* Best for serious students, this somewhat dry dissertation-like tome is the only exhaustive study of Bahamian literature for those seeking an in-depth disquisition.

Robert and Dalia Fleming *Design Guide for Building a House on a Tropical Island.* If you decide you just don't want to go home, this is a practical, self-published guide (Ⓦwww.tropichouse.com) to building your dream getaway. Based on firsthand experience – the authors built their own home on Long Island – tips include everything from siting your house to take advantage of trade winds to getting the contractor to finish the job in less than five years.

Patricia Glinton-Meicholas *How to be a True True Bahamian* and *More Talkin' Bahamian.* Humorous pocket guides to Bahamian culture and language, reviewing such topics as the art of "liming" and why dogs are called "potcakes" (because they were traditionally fed the leftover peas 'n' rice congealed at the bottom of the pot).

Leslie Higgs *Bush Medicine in the Bahamas.* Descriptions of native plants and their traditional uses accompanied by illustrations.

Karen Knowles *Straw! A Short Account of the Straw Industry in the Bahamas.* Plaited straw baskets, hats and bags are big business in the Bahamas and this little book, aimed primarily at schoolchildren, provides the low-down on the craft and the development of the industry for export and sale to visiting tourists.

Travellers' tales

Evans Cottman *Out Island Doctor.* A dated but mildly engaging memoir of a retired American school teacher who set up shop as a self-taught physician on Crooked and Acklins islands in the 1940s.

⭐ **Gilbert Klingel** *Inagua, Which is the Name of a Very Lonely and Nearly Forgotten Island.* As a young man on his first scientific expedition in 1930, Klingel was shipwrecked on Great Inagua, and this magical and often poetic book is his account of

the voyage and the months that followed. The human inhabitants of Inagua are not as sympathetically treated in his recounting of events as the myriad of other creatures he meets. However, you may never look at the ocean surf in the same way again after reading his dramatic description of the battles for survival fought daily at the water's edge. Reprinted by Lyons and Burford (US) in a new edition as part of the *Wilder Places* series, with an introduction by naturalist Stephen J. Bodio.

L.D. Powles *The Land of the Pink Pearl: Recollections of Life in the Bahamas.* A colourful memoir of an English magistrate's two tours of duty through the Out Islands as a Circuit Court judge in 1887, after which he was recalled to London for sentencing a white man to one month hard labour for assaulting his African maid. Particularly interesting

are Powles' disillusioned impressions of Nassau society and of the colonial government.

Aileen Vincent-Barwood *This Sweet Place: Island Living and Other Adventures.* A slightly self-satisfied but readable account of a retired couple's relocation from the northern US to Great Exuma, filled with local characters, local history and lore, and descriptions of many of the island's settlements and landmarks.

Fiction

Marion Bethel *Guanahane, My Love.* Probably the best-known poet in the Bahamas, Bethel's work has appeared in many American journals. She won the Casas de las Americas Prize in 1994 for this volume.

Jimmy Buffett *Tales from Margaritaville: Fictional Facts and Factual Fictions.* Better known for a string of mellow hits in the 1970s, Buffett also spins a fine rollicking tale with a cast of cowboys, sailors and no-nonsense women in roadside diners, cozy beach bars and boats. The Bahamas are a favourite locale of his, and this collection of sunny, whimsical short stories evokes an image of laid-back island living.

College of the Bahamas *Bahamian Anthology.* Home-grown fiction is still in a nascent stage in the Bahamas, but this collection of short stories, poetry and drama by contemporary writers offers a glimpse of what is on the minds of emerging authors. Recurring themes include the legacy of slavery and colonialism and the authors' relationship with the landscape and the sea that surround them.

Barry Estabrook *Bahama Heat.* An amusing drug-deal-gone-wrong

thriller that is tailor-made for lazy beach reading.

Amos Ferguson and Elaine Greenfield *Under the Sunday Tree.* Along with a pleasing story by Greenfield, the book features beautiful illustrations by the visual artist Ferguson; this is a children's book for everybody.

Ernest Hemingway *Islands in the Stream.* Hemingway's novel, published posthumously, concerns the adventurers of an artist-fisherman, which, as usual, is a metaphor for the author's own internal contradictions and boasts. Though it isn't a particularly good novel, it nevertheless accurately reflects Bimini and Gulf Stream life.

Gregor Robinson *Hotel Paradiso.* Almost to the exclusion of all other subject matter, the Bahamas are the chosen setting for a plethora of novels about drug smuggling and rum-soaked expatriates on the run from something or other, most of it dross. This book is about best of the lot, with rough-drawn vignettes of a dissipated life in an island outpost in the Abacos peopled by wealthy American retirees, Haitian refugees and drifters in limbo, as seen through the eyes of a burnt-out banker from Montreal.

Herman Wouk *Don't Stop the Carnival*. First published in the 1960s, this entertaining cautionary tale concerns a dyed-in-the-wool New Yorker who buys a resort hotel on an idyllic Caribbean island. He spends the next three hundred-odd pages of the novel fixing burst water mains, wrestling with the local bureaucracy and ferrying disgruntled guests to and from the airport, while pursuing a torrid affair with a faded movie star, downing copious quantities of rum and disposing of corpses. Still popular and widely available throughout the Bahamas, it was also made into a musical by Jimmy Buffett in the 1990s.

Nature and the environment

David G. Campbell *The Ephemeral Islands: A Natural History of the Bahamas*. One of the best overall studies of Bahamian natural history, complete with a generous scattering of colour plates and detailed line drawings of various plants and sea creatures. Chapters tell the tale of paleo-Bahamian structure, and progress through clear-eyed descriptions of every Bahamian habitat. It is thorough in its treatment of marine life as well, though it focuses on terrestrial habitats.

Osha Gray Davidson *Fire in the Turtle House*. A naturalist, Davidson reports on the habitat of the green turtle, and in particular on the neoplasms (growths) which have been attacking and killing large numbers of green turtles around the world. It's a compelling story which ought to act as a wake-up call to environmentalists and citizens everywhere. Along the way, he delineates everything you might want to know about turtles and their astonishing lives.

Paul Humann and Ned DeLoach *Reef Fish, Reef Coral, Reef Creatures* and *Snorkelling Guide to Marine Life: Florida, Caribbean, Bahamas*. The first three are beautiful full-colour books that will help you identify every living thing in the waters of the Bahamas, Florida and the Caribbean; available separately or in a boxed set. *Reef Fish in a Pocket* and *Reef Creatures in a Pocket* are drastically abridged waterproof editions for divers and snorkellers. The snorkelling guide contains plentiful locale descriptions along with colour photos of 260 species.

Erika Moultrie *Natives of the Bahamas: A Guide to Vegetation and Birds of Grand Bahama*. A pocket-size spiral-bound booklet that provides an overview of the six different terrestrial ecosystems found on Grand Bahama, colour photographs of native plants and detailed illustrations of the varied birdlife on the island.

Rob Palmer *Baha Mar: The Shallow Seas*. A complete analysis of the structure and dynamics of every underwater habitat found in the Bahamas. Filled with good photographs and scientific descriptions, this book is a must for serious divers and naturalists alike. Moreover, it contains an excellent bibliography for anyone who wishes to pursue studies of sharks, invertebrates, and other marine life in Bahamian waters.

Peterson Field Guides *Coral Reefs: Caribbean and Florida*. Standard high-quality and comprehensive Peterson field guide. Loaded with clear colour and black and white photographs and line drawings, as well as extensive listings and factual information, including descriptions of 33 different species of sea stars, the nine kinds of sharks that are found in the Bahamas and a section on the sex life of coral.

Neil E. Sealey *Bahamian Landscapes: An Introduction to the Geography of the Bahamas.* A textbook chock-full of charts, graphs and illustrations, it is great for beginning students of geography and climate, but also good for anyone who wants to discover the hows and whys of Bahamian geology, geography and natural resources.

★ **Anthony White** *A Birder's Guide to the Bahama Islands (including Turks and Caicos).* This expensive volume, published by the American Birding Association (ⓦ www.americanbirding.org), is the ultimate bird book, and should be considered only by serious bird-watchers. It contains a wealth of information on behaviour, habitat and seasonal variation, and has detailed maps and practical advice, as well as travel and weather information. The book comes with a complete bibliography on technical birding information, articles and serious scientific studies, along with a glossary and bird checklist.

Lawson Wood *The Dive Sites of the Bahamas.* An expensive book for committed divers, *Dive Sites* is worth it for the exquisite colour photography alone. It provides advice on diving sites, equipment, lodging and prices, safety and underwater photography.

Nautical guides

Monty and Sara Lewis *Explorer Chartbooks* for *Exuma and the Exuma Cays*; *Far Bahamas* (from Eleuthera south to Inagua); *Near Bahamas* (the northern islands). Each spiral-bound 12 x 18-inch book contains seventy detailed nautical charts of Bahamian waters accompanied by photographs, text and tide tables. Available from ⓦ www.explorercharts.com.

Maptech *Chart Kit: The Bahamas.* The only full set of nautical charts for the Bahamas, in a larger 22 x 18-inch format, spiral-bound in a vinyl case. See ⓦ www.maptech.com for more information.

Stephen J. Pavlidis *The Exuma Guide: A Cruising Guide to the Exuma Cays.* A comprehensive guide aimed primarily at boaters, but also recommended for sea kayakers and others planning a visit to the Exuma Land and Sea Park. With detailed information on approaches, routes, anchorages, dive sites, flora and fauna and the history and lore of the Exuma Cays.

Index

and small print

Index

Map entries are in **colour**.

Twenty Years of Rough Guides

In the summer of 1981, Mark Ellingham, Rough Guides' founder, knocked out the first guide on a typewriter, with a group of friends. Mark had been travelling in Greece after university, and couldn't find a guidebook that really answered his needs. There were heavyweight cultural guides on the one hand – good on museums and classical sites but not on beaches and tavernas – and on the other hand student manuals that were so caught up with how to save money that they lost sight of the country's significance beyond its role as a place for a cool vacation. None of the guides began to address Greece as a country, with its natural and human environment, its politics and its contemporary life.

Having no urgent reason to return home, Mark decided to write his own guide. It was a guide to Greece that tried to combine some erudition and insight with a thoroughly practical approach to travellers' needs. Scrupulously researched listings of places to stay, eat and drink were matched by careful attention to detail on everything from Homer to Greek music, from classical sites to national parks and from nude beaches to monasteries. Back in London, Mark and his friends got their Rough Guide accepted by a farsighted commissioning editor at the publisher Routledge and it came out in 1982.

The Rough Guide to Greece was a student scheme that became a publishing phenomenon. The immediate success of the book – shortlisted for the Thomas Cook award – spawned a series that rapidly covered dozens of countries. The Rough Guides found a ready market among backpackers and budget travellers, but soon acquired a much broader readership that included older and less impecunious visitors. Readers relished the guides' wit and inquisitiveness as much as the enthusiastic, critical approach that acknowledges everyone wants value for money – but not at any price.

Rough Guides soon began supplementing the "rougher" information – the hostel and low-budget listings – with the kind of detail that independent-minded travellers on any budget might expect. These days, the guides – distributed worldwide by the Penguin group – include recommendations spanning the range from shoestring to luxury, and cover more than 200 destinations around the globe. Our growing team of authors, many of whom come to Rough Guides initially as outstandingly good letter-writers telling us about their travels, are spread all over the world, particularly in Europe, the USA and Australia. As well as the travel guides, Rough Guides publishes a series of dictionary phrasebooks covering two dozen major languages, an acclaimed series of music guides running the gamut from Classical to World Music, a series of music CDs in association with World Music Network, and a range of reference books on topics as diverse as the Internet, Pregnancy and Unexplained Phenomena. Visit **www.roughguides.com** to see what's cooking.

Rough Guide credits

Text editor: Richard Koss
Series editor: Mark Ellingham
Editorial: Martin Dunford, Jonathan Buckley, Kate Berens, Ann-Marie Shaw, Helena Smith, Judith Bamber, Olivia Swift, Ruth Blackmore, Geoff Howard, Claire Saunders, Gavin Thomas, Alexander Mark Rogers, Polly Thomas, Joe Staines, Richard Lim, Duncan Clark, Peter Buckley, Lucy Ratcliffe, Clifton Wilkinson, Alison Murchie, Matthew Teller, Andrew Dickson, Fran Sandham (UK); Andrew Rosenberg, Stephen Timblin, Yuki Takagaki, Hunter Slaton, Julie Feiner (US)
Production: Susanne Hillen, Andy Hilliard, Link Hall, Helen Prior, Julia Bovis, Michelle Draycott, Katie Pringle, Zoë Nobes, Rachel Holmes, Andy Turner

Cartography: Melissa Baker, Maxine Repath, Ed Wright, Katie Lloyd-Jones
Cover art direction: Louise Boulton
Picture research: Sharon Martins, Mark Thomas
Online: Kelly Cross, Anja Mutic-Blessing, Jennifer Gold, Audra Epstein, Suzanne Welles, Cree Lawson (US)
Finance: John Fisher, Gary Singh, Edward Downey, Mark Hall, Tim Bill
Marketing & Publicity: Richard Trillo, Niki Smith, David Wearn, Chloë Roberts, Demelza Dallow, Claire Southern (UK); Simon Carloss, David Wechsler, Megan Kennedy (US)
Administration: Tania Hummel, Julie Sanderson, Karoline Densley

Publishing information

This first edition published January 2003 by **Rough Guides Ltd**,
80 Strand, London WC2R 0RL.
375 Hudson Street, 4th Floor,
New York, NY 10014, USA.
Distributed by the Penguin Group
Penguin Books Ltd,
80 Strand, London WC2R 0RL
Penguin Putnam, Inc.
375 Hudson Street, NY 10014, USA
Penguin Books Australia Ltd,
487 Maroondah Highway, PO Box 257,
Ringwood, Victoria 3134, Australia
Penguin Books Canada Ltd,
10 Alcorn Avenue, Toronto, Ontario,
Canada M4V 1E4
Penguin Books (NZ) Ltd,
182–190 Wairau Road, Auckland 10,
New Zealand
Typeset in Bembo and Helvetica to an original design by Henry Iles.

Printed in Italy by LegoPrint S.p.A

400pp includes index
A catalogue record for this book is available from the British Library

ISBN 1-85828-828-2

The publishers and authors have done their best to ensure the accuracy and currency of all the information in **The Rough Guide to the Bahamas**, however, they can accept no responsibility for any loss, injury, or inconvenience sustained by any traveller as a result of information or advice contained in the guide.

SMALL PRINT

Help us update

We've gone to a lot of effort to ensure that the first edition of **The Rough Guide to the Bahamas** is accurate and up to date. However, things change – places get "discovered", opening hours are notoriously fickle, restaurants and rooms raise prices or lower standards. If you feel we've got it wrong or left something out, we'd like to know, and if you can remember the address, the price, the time, the phone number, so much the better.

We'll credit all contributions, and send a copy of the next edition (or any other Rough Guide if you prefer) for the best letters. Everyone who writes to us and isn't already a subscriber will receive a copy of our full-colour thrice-yearly newsletter. Please mark letters: "**Rough Guide Bahamas Update**" and send to: Rough Guides, 80 Strand, London WC2R 0RL, or Rough Guides, 4th Floor, 345 Hudson Street, New York, NY 10014. Or send an email to **mail@roughguides.com**

Have your questions answered and tell others about your trip at **www.roughguides.atinfopop.com**

Acknowledgements

Gaylord Dold would like to acknowledge the many kindnesses shown him by the staff of the Bahamas Ministry of Tourism, especially Craig Woods.

Natalie Folster thanks Charity Armbrister at the Bahamas Ministry of Tourism; Carmeta Miller and the Grand Bahama Tourism Board; Warden Ray and Evelyn Darville at the Exuma Land and Sea Park; David 'Blue' Brown; Mike and Valerie Dudash; Peter and Betty Oxley; Peterina Hannah and her colleagues at the Exuma Ministry of Tourism; the Goede family; Tommy Sands; Charlie Moore; Eurene Nottage; Peter Kuska; and Andrew Rosenberg, Richard Koss and Stephen Timblin at Rough Guides.

Adam Vaitilingam would like to thank Sarah, Alex, Hilary and Jesse for fantastic recent visits and great conch fritters. Particular thanks, too, on Grand Turk, go to Herbert and Peggy; on Provo to Lynn and Rolf; and in New York to Richard Koss for patient and consummate editing.

Heartfelt thanks go to Katie Pringle for her fathomless patience and dexterous production work, Maxine Repath for her mapmaking ingenuity, Derek Wilde for his diligent proofreading, Melissa Krupanski for her photo-researching skills, Hunter Slaton for the judiciously compiled index and to Stephen "Boomer" Timblin for his exuberant guidance.

SMALL PRINT

Photo credits

SMALL PRINT

● TRAVEL ● MUSIC ● REFERENCE ● PHRASEBOOKS ●

Music

Acoustic Guitar
Blues: 100 Essential CDs
Cello
Clarinet
Classical Music
Classical Music: 100 Essential CDs
Country Music
Country: 100 Essential CDs
Cuban Music
Drum'n'bass
Drums
Electric Guitar & Bass Guitar
Flute
Hip-Hop
House
Irish Music
Jazz
Jazz: 100 Essential CDs
Keyboards & Digital Piano
Latin: 100 Essential CDs
Music USA: a Coast-To-Coast Tour
Opera
Opera: 100 Essential CDs
Piano
Reading Music
Reggae
Reggae: 100 Essential CDs
Rock
Rock: 100 Essential CDs
Saxophone
Soul: 100 Essential CDs
Techno
Trumpet & Trombone
Violin & Viola
World Music: 100 Essential CDs

World Music Vol1
World Music Vol2

Reference

Children's Books, 0–5
Children's Books, 5–11
China Chronicle
Cult Movies
Cult TV
Elvis
England Chronicle
France Chronicle
India Chronicle
The Internet
Internet Radio
James Bond
Liverpool FC
Man Utd
Money Online
Personal Computers
Pregnancy & Birth
Shopping Online
Travel Health
Travel Online
Unexplained Phenomena
Videogaming
Weather
Website Directory
Women Travel

Music CDs

Africa
Afrocuba
Afro-Peru
Ali Hussan Kuban
The Alps
Americana
The Andes
The Appalachians
Arabesque
Asian Underground
Australian Aboriginal Music
Bellydance
Bhangra
Bluegrass

Bollywood
Boogaloo
Brazil
Cajun
Cajun and Zydeco
Calypso and Soca
Cape Verde
Central America
Classic Jazz
Congolese Soukous
Cuba
Cuban Music Story
Cuban Son
Cumbia
Delta Blues
Eastern Europe
English Roots Music
Flamenco
Franco
Gospel
Global Dance
Greece
The Gypsies
Haiti
Hawaii
The Himalayas
Hip Hop
Hungary
India
India and Pakistan
Indian Ocean
Indonesia
Irish Folk
Irish Music
Italy
Jamaica
Japan
Kenya and Tanzania
Klezmer
Louisiana
Lucky Dube
Mali and Guinea
Marrabenta Mozambique
Merengue & Bachata
Mexico
Native American Music
Nigeria and Ghana
North Africa

Nusrat Fateh Ali Khan
Okinawa
Paris Café Music
Portugal
Rai
Reggae
Salsa
Salsa Dance
Samba
Scandinavia
Scottish Folk
Scottish Music
Senegal & The Gambia
Ska
Soul Brothers
South Africa
South African Gospel
South African Jazz
Spain
Sufi Music
Tango
Thailand
Tex-Mex
Wales
West African Music
World Music Vol 1: Africa, Europe and the Middle East
World Music Vol 2: Latin & North America, Caribbean, India, Asia and Pacific
World Roots
Youssou N'Dour & Etoile de Dakar
Zimbabwe

Rough Guides music, reference & CDs

Rough Guide Reference

THE ROUGH GUIDE TO
cult**movies**
THE GOOD, THE BAD AND THE VERY WEIRD INDEED

THE ROUGH GUIDE TO
Man Utd
2001–02 SEASON
An UNOFFICIAL GUIDE in association with UNITED WE STAND

THE ROUGH GUIDE TO
Videogaming

the soundest,
sanest, wittiest
advice you'll
ever get

THE ROUGH GUIDE TO
Pregnancy
and birth
KAZ COOKE

Unexplained *Phenomena*
A ROUGH GUIDE SPECIAL
Mysteries and Curiosities of Science, Folklore and Superstition
Bob Rickard and John Michell

THE ROUGH GUIDE TO
Children's Books 0–5 years

THE ROUGH GUIDE TO
Children's Books 6–11 years

THE ROUGH GUIDE TO
Elvis
THE MAN • THE MUSIC • THE MOVIES • THE MYTH

Pocket History Series

The Rough Guide Chronicle
England

The Rough Guide Chronicle
China

The Rough Guide Chronicle
India

The Rough Guide Chronicle
France

"Solidly written, immaculately researched, Rough Guides
are as near as modern guides get to essential"
Sunday Times, London

www.roughguides.com

Music Reference Guides

Rough Guide Music Guides

CD Guides

Mini Guides

"The Rough Guides are near-perfect
reference works"
Philadelphia Inquirer

Essential Tipbook Series

Rough Guide Instrument Guides

THE ROUGH GUIDE TO
Acoustic Guitar
THE ESSENTIAL TIPBOOK

THE ROUGH GUIDE TO
Clarinet
THE ESSENTIAL TIPBOOK

THE ROUGH GUIDE TO
Electric Guitar
THE ESSENTIAL TIPBOOK

THE ROUGH GUIDE TO
Flute
THE ESSENTIAL TIPBOOK

THE ROUGH GUIDE TO
Keyboards & Digital Piano
THE ESSENTIAL TIPBOOK

THE ROUGH GUIDE
Piano
THE ESSENTIAL TIPBOOK

THE ROUGH GUIDE TO
Reading Music & Basic Theory
THE ESSENTIAL TIPBOOK

THE ROUGH GUIDE TO
Saxophone
THE ESSENTIAL TIPBOOK

THE ROUGH GUIDE TO
Trumpet & Trombone
THE ESSENTIAL TIPBOOK

THE ROUGH GUIDE TO
Cello
THE ESSENTIAL TIPBOOK

THE ROUGH GUIDE TO
Drums
THE ESSENTIAL TIPBOOK

THE ROUGH GUIDE TO
Violin & Viola
THE ESSENTIAL TIPBOOK

"These Rough Guides are admirably informative. They are ideal
for anyone wanting to learn or discover an instrument"
Julian Lloyd Webber

www.roughguides.com

NOTES

The ideas expressed in this code were developed by and for independent travellers.

Learn About The Country You're Visiting

Start enjoying your travels before you leave by tapping into as many sources of information as you can.

The Cost Of Your Holiday

Think about where your money goes - be fair and realistic about how cheaply you travel. Try and put money into local peoples' hands; drink local beer or fruit juice rather than imported brands and stay in locally owned accommodation. Haggle with humour and not aggressively. Pay what something is worth to you and remember how wealthy you are compared to local people.

Embrace The Local Culture

Open your mind to new cultures and traditions - it will transform your experience. Think carefully about what's appropriate in terms of your clothes and the way you behave. You'll earn respect and be more readily welcomed by local people. Respect local laws and attitudes towards drugs and alcohol that vary in different countries and communities. Think about the impact you could have on them.

Exploring The World – The Travellers' Code

Being sensitive to these ideas means getting more out of your travels - and giving more back to the people you meet and the places you visit.

Minimise Your Environmental Impact

Think about what happens to your rubbish - take biodegradable products and a water filter bottle. Be sensitive to limited resources like water, fuel and electricity. Help preserve local wildlife and habitats by respecting local rules and regulations, such as sticking to footpaths and not standing on coral.

Don't Rely On Guidebooks

Use your guidebook as a starting point, not the only source of information. Talk to local people, then discover your own adventure!

Be Discreet With Photography

Don't treat people as part of the landscape, they may not want their picture taken. Ask first and respect their wishes.

We work with people the world over to promote tourism that benefits their communities, but we can only carry on our work with the support of people like you. For membership details or to find out how to make your travels work for local people and the environment, visit our website.

www.tourismconcern.org.uk

TourismConcern
Campaigning for Ethical and Fairly Traded Tourism